D1500226

# INTERACTION AND CONNECTIVITY IN THE GREATER SOUTHWEST

## PROCEEDINGS OF THE SOUTHWEST SYMPOSIUM

# INTERACTION AND CONNECTIVITY IN THE GREATER SOUTHWEST

EDITED BY
**KAREN G. HARRY AND BARBARA J. ROTH**

UNIVERSITY PRESS OF COLORADO
*Louisville*

© 2019 by University Press of Colorado
Published by University Press of Colorado
204 Century Circle, Suite 202
Louisville, Colorado 80027

The University Press of Colorado is a proud member of
the Association of American University Presses.

 The University Press of Colorado is a proud member of
the Association of University Presses.

The University Press of Colorado is a cooperative publishing enterprise supported, in part,
by Adams State University, Colorado State University, Fort Lewis College, Metropolitan State
University of Denver, University of Colorado, University of Northern Colorado, Utah State
University, and Western State Colorado University.

∞ This paper meets the requirements of the ANSI/NISO Z39.48-1992 (Permanence of Paper).

ISBN: 978-1-60732-734-9 (cloth)
ISBN: 978-1-60732-735-6 (ebook)
DOI: https://doi.org/10.5876/9781607327356

Library of Congress Cataloging-in-Publication Data

Names: Southwest Symposium (1988– ) (14th : 2014 : Las Vegas, Nev.), author. | Harry, Karen G.
(Karen Gayle), editor. | Roth, Barbara J., 1958– editor.
Title: Interaction and connectivity in the Greater Southwest / edited by Karen G. Harry and
Barbara J. Roth.
Description: Boulder : University Press of Colorado, [2018] | Includes bibliographical references
and index.
Identifiers: LCCN 2017042884 | ISBN 9781607327349 (cloth) | ISBN 9781607327356 (ebook)
Subjects: LCSH: Indians of North America—Southwest, New—Antiquities—Congresses. |
Indians of North America—Southwest, New—Social conditions—Congresses. | Social
interaction—Southwest, New—Congresses. | Group identity—Southwest, New—Congresses.
| Social archaeology—Southwest, New—Congresses. | Excavations (Archaeology)—Southwest,
New—Congresses. | Southwest, New—Antiquities—Congresses. | LCGFT: Conference papers
and proceedings.
Classification: LCC E78.S7 S576 2014 | DDC 979.004/97—dc23
LC record available at https://lccn.loc.gov/2017042884

The University Press of Colorado gratefully acknowledges the generous support of the
Southwest Symposium toward the publication of this book.

Cover illustration of MimPIDD 3641 by Will G. Russell.

# Contents

## Part II: Social Units and Social Interaction

## Part III: Northern Periphery

# INTERACTION AND CONNECTIVITY IN THE GREATER SOUTHWEST

# Interaction and Connectivity in the Greater Southwest

*Introduction*

KAREN G. HARRY AND BARBARA ROTH

The chapters in this volume are the outcome of the 14th Southwest Symposium held in Las Vegas, Nevada, in 2014. Inaugurated in 1988, this biennnial conference was established to provide a venue in which Southwestern archaeologists could present new research findings that "contribute to methodological, theoretical, and substantive issues in archaeology" (Nelson and Strawhacker 2011:1). The theme of the 2014 symposium was social interaction. In this volume, authors explore different kinds of social interaction that occurred prehistorically across the Southwest. The authors use diverse and innovative approaches to address how interaction took place and to examine the economic, social, and ideological implications of the different forms of interaction. Social interaction is examined from three perspectives: (1) its role in the diffusion of ideas and material culture, (2) the way that different social units, especially households, interacted within and between communities, and (3) the importance of interaction and interconnectivity in understanding the archaeology of the Southwest's northern periphery. By approaching the topic of interaction using a variety of different data sets, the authors present new ways of examining how social interaction

DOI: 10.5876/9781607327356.c001

3

and connectivity, at a variety of scales, influenced cultural developments in the Southwest. Although hardly a new subject matter, the chapters provide fresh perspectives on this enduring topic. In this introduction, we address the three approaches to social interaction—diffusion, social units, and the northern periphery—that organize the volume's chapters. The discussion in the present essay sets the stage for the more detailed presentations in the chapters that follow.

## PART I: RETHINKING DIFFUSION

The chapters in part I reintroduce the concept of diffusion to Southwestern archaeology. Although once a dominant paradigm in the discipline, diffusion fell out of favor during the rise of processual archaeology in the 1960s and 1970s. Loss of interest in the subject resulted not so much from a lack of belief in diffusion, but from a conviction that such studies were unable to contribute to the types of questions considered important at that time. The diffusion studies that dominated North American archaeology in the early twentieth century had been largely restricted to identifying the origins and distributions of cultural traits; because early scholars considered the spread of behaviors to be an inevitable byproduct of cultural contact, they made no effort to explain *why* individuals might have been motivated to adopt practices with which they came in contact. With its emphasis on systems theory and on identifying the function of objects and behaviors in sustaining the social group, processual archaeology eschewed diffusion as having little to offer the discipline's new anthropological orientation.

More than 50 years have passed since the advent of processualism, and the focus of Southwestern archaeology has long since moved beyond the functionalist approaches of that era. As well, methodological advances (e.g., chemical sourcing techniques and the application of social network analysis) have made it possible to examine the transmission of behaviors in the archaeological record with greater nuance and detail than ever before. Despite these changes, the concept of diffusion has remained largely ignored and theoretically underdeveloped. In chapter 2, Catherine Cameron challenges us to reconsider the utility of this concept and to develop new approaches that investigate not only *whether* diffusion occurred but *how* and *why* it happened.

The case studies presented in part I provide examples of how, when approached through a more comprehensive and contemporary lens, the study of diffusion can stimulate new ways of thinking about the archaeological record. One useful contribution from these studies derives from their focus on the mechanisms by which diffusion occurred. The chapters consider both the nature of the social groups involved in the transmission and the contexts in which the encounters took place. In some instances transmission accompanied the relatively large-scale relocation of people into new areas. In chapter 3, Barbara Mills and Matthew Peeples argue that this was the case for the spread of Salado polychrome ceramics, which they suggest were introduced into the central and southern Southwest by migrants from the Kayenta/Tusayan region. Settling in scattered locations, these migrants maintained broad social connections that contributed to the diffusion and widespread adoption of Salado polychromes.

In other instances practices appear to have been transmitted by specific subsets of people within the societies. Cameron (chapter 2) discusses the role that captives, obtained during raiding and warfare, could have had in the transfer of knowledge, and Kelley Hays-Gilpin and colleagues (chapter 4) propose that ritual specialists were responsible for the transmission of Sikyatki style designs in the Puebloan region. In the latter study, the authors argue that Sikyatki-style imagery, which appears on ceramics and murals at Awatovi (Hopi Mesas) and Pottery Mound (Rio Grande), was associated with a ritual sodality. Transmission of the style, they suggest, occurred when individuals acquired sodality membership and knowledge from one area and introduced it to the other. Ritual specialists are similarly proposed to have been responsible for the transmission of macaws and the Hero Twins saga from Mesoamerica to the Mimbres area. In chapter 5, Patricia Gilman and her colleagues outline a scenario in which the birds and ritual knowledge were acquired by select individuals who, for spiritual purposes, undertook the long trip from the Mimbres area to central Mexico in order to acquire macaws, the knowledge of how to care for macaws, and ideological training.

Finally, Suzanne Eckert (chapter 6) uses three case studies to examine the ways that the diffusion of people and ideas influenced identity formation during different periods in the northern Southwest. She shows how identity was maintained during the thirteenth century in the northern Rio Grande region despite extensive interaction with outside groups, how past aspects of identity were revived in the Zuni region following Spanish missionization efforts, and how a hybrid identity developed in groups at Pottery Mound Village in the Rio Grande region following extensive population movements during the 1400s and 1500s.

The studies presented here contrast with early twentieth-century approaches to diffusion in their consideration of the factors that influence whether a particular trait or practice will be adopted. Most often, as Cameron (chapter 2) points out, people adopt the practices of others whom they admire or consider successful. The transfer of ritual knowledge in the Puebloan and Mimbres regions appears to fall in this category. In some instances, however, diffusion occurs in the direction of the lower- to the higher-status group. Although of low status compared to their subjugators, captives can sometimes successfully introduce practices to their captor community. Cameron discusses several factors that can encourage the adoption of captive practices, including instances in which captives have a set of skills or knowledge desired by the dominant society. Finally, factors other than status can affect whether a practice will be adopted. For example, Mills and Peeples (chapter 3) propose that in the case of Salado polychrome ceramics, the relative lack of complexity of the technology and the high visibility of the vessels were factors that contributed to their adoption.

The chapters in this section demonstrate that the concept of diffusion retains strong explanatory power and has the potential to address the types of questions that archaeologists are asking today. By focusing on the *processes* of diffusion—who is involved and why it occurred—archaeologists can reclaim this concept and reintegrate its study into the discipline in a meaningful way.

## PART II: SOCIAL UNITS AND SOCIAL INTERACTION

The chapters in part II address the varying kinds of social units that existed in prehistoric Southwestern societies and the role that they played in social interaction both within and between communities. As Barbara Roth (chapter 7) notes, for archaeologists interested in reconstructing social units and forming any meaningful understanding of social interaction and culture change, the challenge is to link the static material remains found at archaeological sites to the living, active social beings who lived there. Fortunately, following pioneering work by Rapoport (1969, 1990) and others, we recognize that social units are often visible in the built environment, from domestic architecture to landscapes. Different social units (nuclear families, extended families, immigrants) were linked in different ways into households, communities, and regional social networks. The array of social units present at sites across the Southwest also formed the basis for different kinds of identities, with some households, communities, and regions exhibiting strong identity signatures linked to maintaining social cohesion, status, and power, and others more fluid and changing.

These chapters reveal both the variable nature of social units in different environmental and social settings across the Southwest and the diversity of approaches that can be used to reconstruct them. Most of the chapters rely heavily on architectural features as the basis for reconstructing social units, but draw on other material evidence in inferring the nature of the individuals and groups who occupied and used these features.

Households formed the basic social unit for many Southwestern prehistoric societies and, in fact, for many prehistoric Neolithic societies worldwide (Blanton 1994; Douglass and Gonlin 2012; Hendon 1996; Parker and Foster 2012). Households were configured in multiple ways, and variability in the ways they were organized and interacted had repercussions across all levels of society. Delineating differences between households, be they tied to economic pursuits, social status, ritual practices, and/or identity, can be a powerful tool for examining the nature of social interaction and social change within past societies.

In chapter 7, Roth compares household composition and the nature of social interaction and integration at two sites in the Mimbres region of southwestern

New Mexico: the Harris site, a large pithouse village located along the Mimbres River, and La Gila Encantada, a smaller pithouse settlement located in an upland setting away from the river. She shows that despite the fact that the two sites had similar architectural features (pithouses), they were occupied by different social units, with clusters of pithouses at the Harris site representing the development of extended-family households that played important social and ritual roles in village integration. In contrast, independent, autonomous households occupied La Gila Encantada. Roth documents that these household differences represent contrasting forms of interaction and integration. Tammy Stone (chapter 8) uses the spatial layout of late pithouse and pueblo rooms to examine differences in contemporary households in the Kayenta region of northern Arizona. She views these differences in domestic architecture as reflecting occupation by distinct social units present within a single settlement, illustrating the complex and dynamic nature of social interaction in the Kayenta region. These two chapters illustrate that architectural features can be used as a starting point for addressing social organization and interaction, and more nuanced interpretations can be made when other lines of evidence are used to supplement architectural data.

Social units also form the basis of communities that served to integrate and coordinate individuals and households. Communities formed for a range of reasons, such as for integrated labor, defense, or ritual. They can be observed at the scale of sites, valleys, or larger regions—and the communities themselves interacted on varying scales. The role of ritual in creating and reinforcing community is one of the key similarities observed in the development of communities across the Southwest.

The concept of community and its constituent social units is explored in several of the chapters in part II. In chapter 9, Thomas Rocek compares settlements in highland and lowland settings in the Jornada Mogollon region and explores the development of different kinds of communities in these two settings. He argues that the observed differences between the highlands and lowlands result from a shift in land use. Lowland settlements became larger and more substantial over time as a result of increasing maize dependence, while highland settlements shifted from temporary field sites associated with lowland sites to independent, agriculturally based communities. In chapter 10, Eric Klucas and William Graves show that Hohokam community organization in southern Arizona comprised a series of nested social units from domestic structures to the community. They argue that these nested units formed the basis of Hohokam social identity that appeared early and influenced social relationships and interaction throughout the Hohokam cultural sequence.

John Douglas and colleagues (chapter 11) use data from the Chuska Valley of northern New Mexico to explore the fundamental role of ritual in integrating households into communities. They show that households used ritual performance to "create and maintain relationships between households" (Gilman and Stone 2013:610). This became increasingly formalized over time, as observed in the development of kivas and great kivas to house these rituals. Using a different approach to examine community interaction and integration, Myles Miller (chapter 12) discusses the important role that agave-baking pits played in the Jornada Mogollon region of southern New Mexico. He argues that these features were used to produce fermented beverages for feasts that served to create and enhance social ties across communities and explores the implications that this had for status, power, and ritual integration across the Jornada region.

These chapters illustrate the range of approaches that can be used to address the nature of social units and the importance of including them in reconstructing social interaction. The varying nature of social units across time and space influenced how prehistoric Southwestern societies interacted, coalesced, and formed into communities. Like the chapters in part I, these chapters show the significance of asking new questions of the data—in this case, by looking at how architecture, features, and landscapes, supplemented with other lines of data, can contribute to our understanding of how past societies were organized and interacted.

## PART III: THE SOUTHWEST'S NORTHERN PERIPHERY

The last section of the book presents a series of chapters that deal with the events that unfolded along the far northern edge of the North American Southwest. This area included the Virgin Branch Puebloan (VBP) culture and the Fremont culture, both of which sometimes have been considered a part of the Southwestern culture area and sometimes have been considered external to it (see James Allison, chapter 13 for a discussion of the history of their classification). In short, both of these cultures have received far too little attention by Southwestern archaeologists. As the chapters presented in part III demonstrate, this situation has impacted not only our understanding of these cultures but also of events and trends that occurred in other regions. The chapters consider the role of social interaction in shaping the VBP and Fremont cultures, as well as how this interaction influenced developments in adjacent regions. They demonstrate that these edge areas had vibrant culture histories in their own right, and that their geographic marginality (relative to the Southwestern heartland cultures) does not necessarily equate to other types of marginality (e.g., in terms of their impacts on developments in the heartland, or in terms of their economic, political or social lives; see Harry and Herr 2018).

Several recurrent themes related to this issue emerge from the chapters. First, they illustrate that the cultures of the northern periphery cannot be reduced to simply less populated, socially simpler versions of the core cultures found to the south, as peripheral regions have often been viewed in the past (Lightfoot and Martinez 1995; Rice 1988). In fact, in several instances they do not appear to have been socially simpler at all or any more isolated than contemporaneous social groups living in the core regions. For example, in southern Nevada, the Virgin Branch site of Main Ridge is the largest known settlement in the western Puebloan region during the Pueblo II period. The site has yielded substantial quantities of nonlocal goods, suggesting that its inhabitants participated in thriving trade networks (Karen Harry, chapter 14). Similar evidence of extensive exchange can be found at Virgin Branch sites in Kanab, Utah (Heidi Roberts, chapter 16) and in the Fremont region (Richard Talbot, chapter 17). During the Late Fremont period, Fremont sites were organized in a settlement hierarchy that suggests some level of organizational complexity (Talbot, chapter 17). Katie Richards's design analysis of Fremont and Virgin ceramics (chapter 19) shows that their material cultures were not simply diluted versions of their nearest Puebloan neighbors. Her study indicates that, contrary to what is commonly assumed, Fremont design styles were more similar to those of the eastern Puebloan region than they were to those of the nearer, Virgin region. However, while the Fremont adopted certain aspects of eastern Puebloan designs, they only adopted selected aspects and even those were modified and adapted to make them distinctly Fremont. Thus, while the Fremont appear to have been linking themselves with the eastern Puebloan world, at the same time they actively signaled their uniqueness.

The Virgin and Fremont cultures were clearly influenced by the Ancestral Puebloan cultures, but their trajectories cannot be reduced to those of the latter. Some Fremont sites have yielded oversized pit structures that, as Lindsay Johansson demonstrates in chapter 18, appear to have functioned much like kivas as private spaces for male-oriented activities. However, Fremont sites often also contain central structures that appear to have been used for community-wide activities or gatherings (Johansson, chapter 18), an architectural form that has no precedent in the Ancestral Puebloan heartland. Similarly, although the Virgin Branch culture most closely resembles that of the Kayenta, it differs in significant ways that Harry (chapter 14; see also Harry and Watson 2018) suggests reflects a desire by the VBP people to retain aspects of their ancestral, Great Basin–related, heritage.

A second theme that emerges from the chapters here is that the cultures of the far northern periphery played an active role in events that unfolded in the Ancestral Puebloan region, particularly during the Archaic-to-agriculture transition. Roberts (chapter 16) reports on the recovery of maize dating to more than 3,000 years ago from the Jackson Flat Reservoir in Kanab, Utah. As Roberts notes, this date "is significantly older than the earliest maize in the Kayenta region, which traditionally has been considered the route of cultigen introduction," and raises the possibility that maize was introduced to the western Colorado

Plateaus from the Virgin Branch region rather than the other way around. In Nevada, Richard Ahlstrom (chapter 15) reports that the earliest-known maize comes not from Basketmaker sites in the Moapa Valley, but from sites that pre-date the Basketmaker period in the Las Vegas Valley. These data, he suggests, raise the possibility that agriculture entered southern Nevada not from the Kayenta region as traditionally thought, but from the Hohokam region via the Colorado River (a possibility also discussed by Allison and Harry in chapters 13 and 14, respectively).

In chapter 14, Harry argues that southern Nevada likely played an active role, not only in the transmission of agriculture to the Kayenta region, but in the actual formation of the Baskemaker culture. Specifically, she rejects the notion that the lowland Virgin Branch culture was established by Basketmaker immigrants from the Kayenta region, and argues instead that it was an in situ development established by the descendants of local Archaic-period populations. Thus, rather than being mere recipients of practices originating on the Colorado Plateau, she argues these descendants were actively involved in the emergence and creation of the Basketmaker culture.

A final theme suggested by these chapters is that far from being insulated by events that occurred in other regions, the inhabitants of the far northern periphery were often impacted, and sometimes even substantially transformed, by them. Although examples of this can be found in several chapters, the most substantial argument is presented by Allison (chapter 13), who proposes that both the Fremont and the Virgin Branch regions experienced substantial changes triggered by the rise of Chaco in the Pueblo II period. These changes included population increases, the establishment of new settlements in formerly unoccupied areas, and an intensification of intraregional interaction. Allison suggests these changes were triggered by the expansion of Chaco Canyon, which drove people of adjacent areas to resettle into the Fremont and Virgin Branch regions. This, he suggests, created a "shatter zone" in the northern periphery, where people of diverse backgrounds who were fleeing the Chaco expansion came to settle.

Although closely related to the Southwestern cultures, the Virgin and Fremont cultures have traditionally been outside of the mainstream of Southwestern archaeological research. As Talbot (chapter 17) reports, these areas are often considered with other Great Basin cultures, a circumstance that has impacted the types of questions and investigations that have been conducted in the region. By giving careful consideration to the social relationships that the Fremont, Virgin Branch, and other people living in the far northern edge areas had with Southwestern groups and with one another, we will be able to gain a more complete understanding of both these cultures and the cultures of the Southwestern heartland.

## DISCUSSION

This volume highlights innovative approaches used to look at social interaction, connectivity, and social integration across the Southwest. The chapters document diverse ways that these topics can be examined, via a focus on architecture, material culture, iconography, and landscapes. Some underlying themes crosscut these varying approaches. First, the chapters in this volume illustrate the importance of examining social interaction through a focus on cultural processes rather than on cultural traits. This is most clearly exemplified in the nuanced approaches to diffusion presented in part I and to the examination of northern periphery cultures in part III, but it is also manifest in the case studies presented in part II, which explore the variability of social units over time and space and their influence on social interaction and community formation. The chapters in this volume illustrate the insights that can be gained by looking at the *whys* and complex *hows* of social interaction and connectivity versus focusing only on discrete material culture traits that could be configured in a diversity of networks, communities, and identities in the past.

The second crosscutting theme is a movement away from strictly economic-driven models of social connectivity and interaction. The authors in this volume recognize that economics was one of many factors that influenced how and to what degree individuals, social groups, and communities interacted. However, they also demonstrate that by incorporating the role of ritual, households, individuals, immigrants, and captives into the study of the topic, we can build on previous economic-based approaches and expand our understanding of how and why interaction impacted the lived experiences of past peoples.

Finally, the chapters illustrate that new approaches can provide significant insights into long-studied prehistoric groups. Members of these groups lived in dynamic social situations that did not always have clear cut and unwavering social boundaries. Rather, social connectivity and interaction was often fluid and changed over time. The studies in this volume highlight that much remains to be learned from the Southwestern archaeological record.

## REFERENCES

Blanton, Richard E. 1994. *Houses and Households: A Comparative Study.* New York: Plenum Press. https://doi.org/10.1007/978-1-4899-0990-9.

Douglass, John G., and Nancy Gonlin, eds. 2012. *Ancient Households of the Americas.* Boulder: University Press of Colorado.

Gilman, Patricia A., and Tammy Stone. 2013. "The Role of Ritual Variability in Social Negotiations of Early Communities: Great Kiva Homogeneity and Heterogeneity in the Mogollon Region of the North American Southwest." *American Antiquity* 78(4):607–623. https://doi.org/10.7183/0002-7316.78.4.607.

Harry, Karen G., and Sarah Herr, eds. 2018. *Life Beyond the Boundaries: Constructing Identity in Edge Regions of the North American Southwest.* Boulder: University Press of Colorado.

Harry, Karen G., and James T. Watson. 2018. "Shaping Identity in the Prehispanic Southwest." In *Life Beyond the Boundaries: Constructing Identity in Edge Regions of the North American Southwest,* ed. Karen Harry and Sarah Herr, 122–56. Boulder: University Press of Colorado.

Hendon, Julia A. 1996. "Archaeological Approaches to the Organization of Domestic Labor: Household Practice and Domestic Relations." *Annual Review of Anthropology* 25(1):45–61. https://doi.org/10.1146/annurev.anthro.25.1.45.

Lightfoot, Kent G., and Antoinette Martinez. 1995. "Frontiers and Boundaries in Archaeological Perspective." *Annual Review of Anthropology* 24(1):471–492. https://doi.org/10.1146/annurev.an.24.100195.002351.

Nelson, Margaret C., and Colleen Strawhacker. 2011. "Changing Histories, Landscapes, and Perspectives: The 20th Anniversary Southwest Symposium." In *Movement, Connectivity, and Landscape Change in the Ancient Southwest,* ed. Margaret C. Nelson and Colleen A. Strawhacker, 1–13. Boulder: University Press of Colorado.

Parker, Bradley J., and Catherine P. Foster, eds. 2012. *New Perspectives on Household Archaeology.* Indiana: Eisenbrauns Publishing.

Rapoport, Amos. 1969. *House Form and Culture.* California: Prentice Hall.

Rapoport, Amos. 1990. "Systems of Activities and Systems of Settings." In *Domestic Architecture and Use of Space: An Interdisciplinary Cross-Cultural Study,* ed. Susan Kent, 9–20. Cambridge, UK: Cambridge University Press.

Rice, P. 1988. "Contexts of Contact and Change: Peripheries, Frontiers and Boundaries." In *Studies in Culture Contact: Interaction, Culture Change, and Archaeology,* ed. James G. Cusick. Center for Archaeological Investigations Occasional Paper No. 25. Chicago: Southern Illinois University.

# Diffusion

# Beyond Trade and Exchange

*A New Look at Diffusion*

CATHERINE M. CAMERON

*Diffusion* is a word familiar to most archaeologists today, although they seldom use it. It comes from the Latin *diffundere*, which means "to spread out." In particle physics, chemistry, biology, and a number of social sciences, it is a transport phenomenon that results in mixing and mass transport. In anthropology, diffusion has had the same spatial implications. Kroeber defined it as "the process, usually but not necessarily gradual, by which elements or systems of culture are spread; by which an invention or a new institution adopted in one place is adopted in neighboring areas" (Kroeber 1931:139; cited in Lyman 2008:12). Diffusion sounds like a simple and useful concept but in anthropology it has a long and checkered history, including its use in various racist and nationalist theories (Trigger 2006:217–232; Storey and Jones 2011). While we certainly must distance ourselves from the racist and nationalist notions of the nineteenth and early twentieth centuries, diffusion is a conception that archaeology cannot do without. Ideas, styles, technologies, languages—virtually any aspect of culture *does* move from one group of people to another. This chapter represents an effort to reclaim the concept of diffusion and reintroduce it to

DOI: 10.5876/9781607327356.c002

mainstream archaeology (see also Kristiansen and Larsson 2005; Storey and Jones 2011).

Prehistoric archaeology currently lacks a well-developed body of theory for understanding the mechanisms by which diffusion occurs, especially those factors that condition the acceptance or rejection of specific cultural practices when social groups interact (but see Kristiansen and Larsson 2005). This is not a trivial gap in our grasp of prehistoric culture change. No society is an isolate; every social group operates in a context that includes multiple interacting societies. By overlooking the mechanisms through which diffusion occurs, we are unintentionally imagining it as an uncomplicated process, like ink moving across blotter paper. Consideration of the mechanisms of diffusion, and the parameters that affect the adoption or rejection of cultural practices, as illustrated in the following chapters with examples from the Southwest, has the potential to significantly advance our understanding of culture change.

This chapter begins with a consideration of the history of the concept of diffusion and its place within contemporary studies of cultural transmission. I then use a selection of ethnohistoric and ethnoarchaeological examples to suggest factors that encourage or constrain diffusion. Finally, I explore one mechanism for the transmission of cultural practices among societies: the taking of captives.

## A LOOK BACK AT DIFFUSION IN ARCHAEOLOGY

Diffusion and migration were the accepted explanations for culture change through the middle of the twentieth century. In the late nineteenth and first part of the twentieth centuries, diffusion became associated with nationalism and racism, with scholars arguing against the "inventiveness" of Third World or small-scale societies, seeing all culture as diffused from a few important centers of development (Trigger 2006:217–223). This reached an extreme with the "hyperdiffusion" of early twentieth-century scholar Grafton Elliot Smith who posited that all early cultural development began in Egypt (Trigger 2006:220). The idea that most cultural developments had occurred in only one place and spread from there implied superiority of specific peoples (other scholars offered different inventive locales). So conceived, diffusion was seen as a civilizing process: inventions developed by more advanced peoples diffused to the less advanced.

As an aspect of culture-historical archaeology, diffusion played a role in the rise of nationalism in Europe. European archaeologists sought to determine the origin of particular types of artifacts and describe their spread so they could develop (and promote) their own national histories. The uglier sides of nineteenth-century evolutionism did not end with the introduction of diffusion as a model for culture change. In fact, for the hyperdiffusionists of the early twentieth century, the only thing preventing humans from reverting to a natural state of savagery was the firm hand of the ruling classes (Trigger 2006:220). The arrival of processual archaeology in the 1960s focused attention on adaptation to local environments and away from studies of cultural transmission (Trigger 2006:395). For many processual archaeologists, culture change resulted from environmental change, and migration and diffusion were seen as simplistic and outmoded non-explanations (Binford 1962, 1965; see also Hays-Gilpin et al., chapter 4, this volume, Cabana 2011:19–21; Trigger 2006:401).

Interaction among social groups did not completely fall off the radar of processual archaeologists, however. Instead, it was directed toward the study of exchange and trade using a number of then-new techniques for determining the source of prehistoric objects, such as X-ray fluorescence and neutron activation analysis (e.g., Ericson and Earle 1982). Complementing the processual focus on environment and subsistence, studies of exchange and trade focused on the role of these activities in prehistoric economies and were especially aimed at explaining the development of complex societies (e.g., Schortman and Urban 1992). However, as Agbe-Davies and Bauer (2010) have recently pointed out, these studies largely ignored the social implications of material exchange stressed by early anthropologists, such as Marcel Mauss (1990) and Claude Lévi-Strauss (1969). As archaeologists of the 1990s focused increasingly on social and ideological issues raised by post-processual archaeology, studies of exchange and trade decreased markedly (Agbe-Davies and Bauer 2010:14). Meanwhile, what we might call diffusion has taken on a variety of additional labels, including *culture contact* (Cusick 1998a), *interregional interaction* (Stein 2002, 2005), and *intergroup transmission* (Mills 2008:246).

In archaeology today, diffusion (although the word is not often used) is part of the broader study of cultural transmission (see Mills and Peeples, chapter 3, this volume). Cultural transmission is a focus of three quite different fields of study: ethnoarchaeology, historical archaeology, and several of the evolutionary approaches to archaeology (Collard and Shennan 2008; Mills 2008). However, ethnoarchaeologists and archaeologists using evolutionary approaches tend to focus on teaching and learning *within* social groups, rather than transmission between groups. For example, four recent edited volumes on cultural transmission include few or no chapters on intergroup transmission (O'Brien 2008; O'Brien and Shennan 2010; Shennan 2009; Stark et al. 2008). In fact, evolutionary scholars, using the term *horizontal transmission*, believe that this form of cultural transmission is rare (Jordan and Shennan 2003; Tehrani and Collard 2002; Shennan 2002:49; Shennan and Steele 1999:376; Van Pool et al. 2008:77; see also Gosselain 2008:151; Cavalli-Sforza and Feldman 1981; for some scholars using evolutionary approaches to archaeology, horizontal transmission can also refer to transmission among generational peers within a society). While most ethnoarchaeologists who study cultural transmission focus on within-group transmission, a few have explored the spread of cultural practices among groups (see examples discussed below).

For historical archaeologists, "culture contact" studies have long been a major focus because of their disciplinary emphasis on encounters between Europeans and indigenous societies. In early studies of colonial interactions historical archaeologists operating under the acculturation model assumed that "cultural traits" were passed from an active, dominant Western culture to passive subordinate, indigenous cultures. The acculturation model has been heavily critiqued as a "top down" view of transmission (Stein 2002:904–905; see also Cusick 1998b who reviews critiques of acculturation and argues that aspects of the model are still useful) and a variety of new models of interaction were introduced: transculturation (Deagan 1998), creolization (Dawdy 2000; Ferguson 1992), ethnogenesis (Sidbury and Cañizares-Esguerra 2011; Voss 2008a), and hybridity (Bhabha 1990, 1994). In contrast to the acculturation model as originally formulated (Redfield et al. 1936), each of these models recognizes that subordinate peoples are actively involved in the process of intercultural transmission. More than simply recognizing the agency of those involved in cultural interactions, these models also require consideration of gender, race, class, sexuality, and labor regimes, among other factors that affect the ways social groups interact and change (Deagan 1974, 1983; Voss 2008a, 2008b).

Developments in prehistoric archaeology are also building knowledge that will further our understanding of processes of diffusion. Archaeologists have, in the past two decades, returned to the study of migration, a concept traditionally linked with diffusion as an explanation for culture change. Migration was the movement of people, diffusion the movement of ideas or innovations. Various aspects of the migration process have been recently considered: migration causes, how people move, the consequences of migration, and how to identify migration in the archaeological record, and more (Clark 2001; Cabana and Clark 2011; Kohler et al. 2010; Ortman and Cameron 2011; Mills 2011). Contact among people is essential for diffusion to occur ("diffusion means transmission by contact"; Rouse 1986:6) so our progress in understanding migration serves as a good starting point for a consideration of diffusion. Especially important are Southwestern studies of how migrants interacted with populations on the receiving end of a migration (Anschuetz and Wilshusen 2011; Bernardini 2005; Bernardini and Fowles 2011; Clark 2011; Clark and Laumbach 2011; Mills 2011; Ortman and Cameron 2011; Stone 2003; Stone and Lipe 2011). It is here that we can begin to study what migrants contributed to indigenous culture and whether or not that culture was changed in the process; these are concerns integral to understanding diffusion. (See also Hays-Gilpin et al., chapter 4, this volume, and Gilman et al., chapter 5, this volume for diffusion resulting from the movement of people).

Social network analysis, currently being applied by a number of archaeologists, especially in the Southwest, also has much to contribute to understanding the diffusion of cultural practices. A broad field of study initially developed in sociology, archaeological studies have used material culture distributions to examine networks of social relationships and their influence on cultural developments (Borck et al. 2015; Crabtree 2015; Mills and Peeples, chapter 3, this volume). Social network analysis uses data that are similar to those used in studies of trade and exchange, but within a theoretical framework that considers many aspects of the nature of connections among actors in the network, such as strength of ties between and among "nodes," the prestige of innovators, and how innovators are related to one another (through direct ties or structurally similar social positions). Mills and Peeples (chapter 3, this volume) provide an illustration of the power of network analysis for understanding how cultural practices were transmitted.

## DISSECTING DIFFUSION

Intergroup transmission processes similar to diffusion have been studied in other fields such as biology (exploring gene flow), linguistics ("contact-induced language change"; Thomason and Kaufman 1988:47), sociology (Rogers 2003; Mills and Peeples, this volume), and geography. The basic linking concept is the flow of genes, language, or cultural practices through contact among interacting groups of people (a similar concept in epidemiology involves the spread of disease [Fass 2003; see also Jones 2014]). Each of these fields has recognized barriers to transmission or conditions that encourage transmission. In the social sciences and linguistics, barriers often consist of attitudes toward the donor group or toward the introduced practice. Transmission can be accelerated when practices are introduced by people of higher status or when they are seen as particularly advantageous. Linguists have examined social factors that condition language change and identified a number of factors that affect the diffusion of culture traits: the intensity of contact between groups, group size, the role of prestige (languages with higher prestige predominate over those of lower prestige), the influence of colloquial usage, and positive or negative attitudes among speakers about potential donor languages and culture (Kroskrity 1993; Thomason and Kaufman 1988). Sociology has developed a somewhat different set of factors that include how easy the practice is to observe and experiment with (Mills and Peeples, chapter 3, this volume).

In archaeology, interacting groups have generally been conceived as "cultures" (people with a common social identity), a concept that extends back to the nineteenth century (Trigger 2006:232–233). Although we assume that technologies (agricultural practices, pottery production, architectural styles, etc.) are transmitted from group to group, we have few well-developed models for how this transmission occurs. Especially for small-scale societies like those that characterize much of Southwestern prehistory, our understanding of diffusion is hindered by our tendency to envision boundaries between archaeological cultures as rigid, even though recent theoretical developments and cross-cultural research have largely overturned this notion (Cameron 2013; Schachner 2010; Stahl 1991). Since the study of migration reentered archaeology more than 25 years ago, we have been increasingly willing to examine long-distance migration and the transmission of exotic technological practices (Stanford and Bradley 2012 for transatlantic contact; Jones et al. 2011 for transpacific contact; Lekson 2009 for transcontinental interaction), a topic once relegated to the fringe of the field. Southwestern archaeology has had a long-standing interest in contacts with Mesoamerica, although arguments often represent attempts to verify that contact actually happened. In general, archaeologists have assumed that the social actors involved in Southwest–Mesoamerican interactions were either Mesoamerican traders or political operatives (see Gilman et al., chapter 5, this volume for a different argument; see Lekson 2009 for the Southwest as part of Mesoamerica).

Studies of diffusion in geography, linguistics, and especially historical archaeology show it to be a complex process, but one with definable parameters. The goal for prehistoric archaeologists will be to comprehend more precisely how cultural practices moved across the landscape, factors that encourage or impede their transmission, and how introduced practices were incorporated in a new social context. Perhaps most difficult will be going beyond the observed distribution of "traits" to identify factors behind their distribution. The following examples highlight factors to consider, developed by archaeologists, ethnoarchaeologists, and others.

### Copying?

In the process of diffusion as originally conceived (and as often unconsciously assumed today) the transfer of technological knowledge happened readily, often through "trade" or "exchange." In other words, simply visiting a foreign market or acquiring foreign goods would allow an individual to reproduce an object, technology, or even ideology. But as Frank has noted with regard to her ethnographic study of potting in the Kadiolo region of southern Mali: "it is not a craft that someone could simply take up upon seeing a skilled potter work, much less upon being presented with the finished product (Frank 1993:387–388)." In other words, simply buying a pot at a market does not give the purchaser the ability to reproduce it. Potting is a complex technology requiring considerable skill and knowledge and therefore is a conservative practice; potters might develop new vessel forms, but rarely changed the technology with which they were made. Significantly for this chapter, Frank (1993), in explaining the differences in the pottery produced by Kadiolo potters and Mande potters to the north, argues that the potters she observed were the daughters of slave women, brought into the Kadiolo region: "it is possible that somewhere along the line, a group of women forced by circumstance to lose their social identity, chose to keep their skills as potters and to continue making pottery in the distinctive way their mothers had taught them" (1993:396).

Even decoration may be difficult to reproduce without cultural familiarity and training that would allow a novice to develop the technological and cultural knowledge, motor skills, and semiotic knowledge necessary to reproduce the design (Hardin 1970; Hardin and Mills 2000). In an experimental study, Washburn (2001) asked college art students to reproduce a variety of images with which they were more or less familiar: images from their cultural heritage that they had seen all of their lives, an image from another culture shown once in class, and an image from another culture whose cultural meanings were explained in detail. The results showed that the structure of a design was most often retained, while details were more commonly lost. Significantly, knowledge of the cultural meaning of a design was an exceptionally important factor in a subject's ability to reproduce it. However, "merely being visually exposed to an image does not insure that something is remembered, even if it is from the individual's own culture. The individual must also have had active personal involvement with the image or object, and/or the object or image must have some meaning for them" (Washburn 2001:82). In other words, in modeling how cultural transmission happens, archaeologists should be aware that even a seemingly simple act such as copying involves a multitude of factors that condition the resulting "copy" (Hardin 1970).

## What Gets Transmitted

In studies of migration, archaeologists have found that "low visibility" technological methods (such as twist direction for cordage, McBrinn and Smith 2006; Minar 2001) are most resistant to change and therefore tend to be the best way to identify migrant producers in their new homes (Clark 2001; Carr 1995; but see Ortman and Cameron 2011:238–240). Ethnoarchaeological studies have emphasized, however, that different aspects of technical production sequences, or *chaînes opératoires*, are more amenable to change, and thus diffusion, than others. In a panregional study of African pottery-production methods, Gosselain (2000) found differences in how particular aspects of the production process reflected ethnic or linguistic boundaries. Methods used to decorate pots, accomplished with *roulettes* (carved wood or knotted fiber), were widespread and reflected only superficial and temporary aspects of identity. Pottery-forming techniques (coiling, forming over a mold, drawing up a lump of clay), in contrast, were more stable over time and space, quite resistant to change, and mapped well onto language and caste divisions. How a pot is formed is not easy to determine from the finished product; it is a more difficult skill to acquire than decorating and therefore is less subject to borrowing or change (Gosselain 2000:209–210;

see also Frank 1993). Several aspects of Gosselain's approach are important for understanding diffusion. Significantly, he looks at the distribution of tools and techniques, not objects (Gosselain 2000:194). Furthermore he contexturalizes these traits by looking at how obvious they might be to a viewer, how easy it might be to change techniques (technical malleability), and the context in which learning about the techniques takes place. His approach shows the importance of understanding the factors behind the distribution of traits we observe in the archaeological record.

## The Power of Prestige

It is a commonplace notion that people tend to adopt the behavior of others who appear successful or whom they admire. For some evolutionary scholars, *prestige-biased transmission* (in the terms of Boyd and Richerson 1985) "takes place when an individual adopts the cultural attribute of someone who appears to be more successful in terms of some locally accepted criterion, even if the attribute concerned is not actually the reason for their success" (Bentley and Shennan 2003:460). For prestige-biased transmission to take place, the adopter would need to be aware of the success of the person whose behavior he or she was adopting. As with technology, we might expect that more than brief contact would be necessary for such awareness to take place. An example of language shift from Africa shows the operation of this mode of transmission. In the seventeenth century, the Luo language was introduced into southern Sudan by chiefly groups who arrived with symbols of ritual power, including stools that they displayed (Anthony 1997). They took a number of steps to insinuate themselves into the local population. They married into local lineages (who spoke a number of different languages), gave lavish gifts to local lineage heads, and provided military assistance. The Luo speakers assumed control of the trade in iron objects that were used for bride price and this allowed them to encourage (through prestige enhancement) or threaten local leaders to join the introduced chiefly system. Locals became subchiefs who were required to use the Luo language. "The Luo language became the language of privilege and power, and was widely adopted" (Anthony 1997:29).

Prestige-biased transmission as defined by evolutionary scholars and the Luo language-shift example makes the impact of prestige on cultural transmission seem fairly straightforward. But historical archaeologists studying culture contact situations have revealed a great deal of complexity in the acceptance or rejection of cultural practices, even when such practices are associated with powerful others. Individuals and groups in subordinate and dominant relationships use material culture to maximize or reinforce their social position. They must often negotiate complex situations in which access to material culture may be restricted or contested. Archaeologists should explore such complexity in order to provide accurate reconstructions of prehistoric cultural transmission in situations with an imbalance of power. Such situations may be more common than we think. Examples based on historical archaeology and ethnohistory highlight these issues.

When Hernán Cortés conquered the Aztecs, they were a stratified society. In the confusion of the early decades after the conquest, some people attempted to move up the social hierarchy, at times incorporating Spanish material culture into precontact practices involving the display of status through costume and ornamentation (Rodríguez-Alegría 2010:53). Indigenous men who claimed elite status petitioned the Spanish for permission to wear Spanish clothing, carry Spanish weapons, and ride horses. Yet at times they also wore the feathered headdresses and other ritual garments that denoted status in precontact times, depending on who would be observing them. In Spanish contexts, "elites marked their bodies as those of people fit to rule" (Rodríguez-Alegría 2010:64). When appearing to their native followers they legitimized their power using garb that had meaning in an indigenous context. Archaeological evidence from the site of Xaltocan in central Mexico shows that at this same time commoners were incorporating Spanish majolica pottery into their feasts. Feasts were important political activities and Rodríguez-Alegría (2010:65) argues that commoners used Spanish pottery in an effort to enhance their status, secure followers, and build a sense of community among the people of Xaltocan, many of whom were newcomers forced by the Spanish to migrate there. Clearly the people of colonial central Mexico, whether elite or commoner, were thinking strategically about their adoption of Spanish material culture.

After the conquest, indigenous leaders in Mesoamerican also adapted aspects of European heraldry in order to protect their lands and promote their personal goals, and as a strategy for both accepting and resisting colonial power (Gutiérrez 2015). Prior to colonization, indigenous polities had used military insignia in various ways similar to European coats of arms, including to commemorate praiseworthy actions on the battlefield or to create institutional hierarchies. Indigenous communities and their leaders were, therefore, not unfamiliar with the purpose of European coats of arms and during the decades after the conquest, a number of them acquired such emblems as part of their negotiation of alliance with the Spanish. Indigenous coats of arms often included both Spanish and native elements. Gutiérrez (2015) shows how the pueblo of Chiepetlan in eastern Guerrero was threatened by its neighbors during the seventeenth century and was at risk of losing its communal lands. Chiepetlan leaders appealed to the colonial authorities who attempted to resolve the land disputes. At the end of the negotiations, a set of heraldic banners were produced with Chiepetlan land rights produced as pictorial narratives. Gutiérrez (2015) explains the appropriation and blending of imagery in New World heraldry:

I argue that these coats of arms exhibit a practical and goal-oriented use of the image of the Spanish monarch to promote native agency, as well as to protect communal lands from the Spanish bureaucracy and individual colonists. I further propose that although ambivalent narratives of pro- and anti-Spanish sentiment can be found in indigenous heraldic practices (Haskett 1996; Wood 2003), one faces a continuum of strategies that changed according to particular historical circumstances confronting each community in the formation of New Spain. (Gutiérrez 2015:53)

Asymmetries in power among interacting groups can result in cultural entanglements that transform material culture but do not result in the wholesale adoption of "superior" goods of a dominant group. During the seventeenth and eighteenth centuries, the Seneca (an Iroquois people) traded for European fabric and notions, but then adapted them to Iroquoian cultural patterns (Kane 2014). *Stroud*, a woolen fabric, was produced in several European countries and brought to North America for sale. Variations in the stroud found in Seneca burials suggest that indigenous demand and preferences actually drove the European production of these goods (Kane 2014:14). The woolen material was then used in the creation of uniquely Iroquoian fabrics. Yarn unraveled from blankets was dyed in distinctive colors and often ornamented with beads. "While European materials replaced plant materials, this merely shifted the labor burden of the production of raw materials to European workers, allowing the Seneca producer to spend more time on decorative work" (Kane 2014:15). The Seneca example highlights the fact that we must relinquish top-down assumptions about the effects of dominant cultures on subordinate ones. Rather than accepting dominant cultural practices wholesale, people at every social level manipulate the material available in their world in ways that seem culturally appropriate and personally beneficial.

### Impediments to Diffusion

Diffusion as originally conceptualized assumed that useful practices would naturally spread among groups who recognized the utility of a new practice. Similarly, evolutionary scholars argue that natural selection operates to select for the most useful cultural traits. But even evolutionary scholars recognize social impediments to transmission and a number of ethnoarchaeological and other studies demonstrate that simply knowing about a cultural practice does not ensure it will be adopted; the attitudes toward innovations, not just knowledge of them, affects their adoption. (See Mills and Peeples, chapter 3, this volume, for discussion of Rogers's [2003] "Knowledge-Attitude-Practice Gap.")

In contemporary India, Hindu and Muslim potters living in the same villages both produce a range of vessels but use different methods (Roux 2013).

Hindu potters use the flywheel and fire their pots in open fires; Muslim potters use the foot wheel and fire in a vertical updraft kiln. The Muslim forming and firing methods are clearly superior to those of the Hindu potters in terms of efficiency, quality of finished products, and risk. Yet, with the exception of one individual and his descendants, Hindu potters have not adopted Muslim potting methods. Hindus offer a variety of explanations for why they feel their own system is more efficient and why it would make no sense to change (Roux 2013:316). Roux's study discredits "the hypothesis that contacts between people are necessary and sufficient for social learning to occur" (2013:313). Clearly, social group membership and social learning provide powerful incentives that restrict technology transfer.

Social and ideological conditions that restrict adoption of a particular cultural practice at one point in time can change as the practice itself changes meaning. Wheat bread was initially rejected at Zuni Pueblo because of its association with Spanish domination (Mills 2008). Instead, Zuni people continued to make the more labor-intensive corn-based bread, called *hewe*. In the late nineteenth century, however, Zuni families were able to gain wealth by growing wheat and selling it to American migrants moving west. This new source of wealth allowed them to fund feasts and give gifts of food that were vitally important ceremonial obligations at Zuni. Because of this new association between wheat and ceremonial obligation, wheat bread became an important food at Zuni (Mills 2008:260). Additional aspects of wheat bread production, such as visible outdoor ovens and the large size of a wheat bread loaf when carried to places of ritual consumption, also played into its importance in comparison to *hewe*. The old acculturation model would have assumed that the easier-to-make wheat bread would have been immediately adopted in the Pueblo world. But in fact wheat bread was not adopted until it offered a clear social and ideological benefit to Zuni people. Perhaps equally important, wheat bread had different meanings for Zuni people than it did for the Europeans from whom they borrowed it. This example makes especially clear the complexities that condition when and how novel cultural practices were incorporated into a new cultural setting.

The examples presented in this section have highlighted some of the parameters that affect the transmission of cultural practices between social groups. Ethnoarchaeological, ethnohistoric, and archaeological examples reveal some of the parameters involved. Copying is not a straightforward process but is restricted by levels of social learning and cultural understanding. In complex technologies like pottery, the simplest and most easily observable production steps may be most easily transmitted and widely distributed. Powerful groups have the advantage in introducing novel cultural practices to their subordinates, but dominant practices are not automatically adopted wholesale. Instead, receptor groups may pick and choose which practices they will accept. They may use rejection as an act of resistance to dominant culture. Even when accepting foreign cultural practices, they may integrate aspects of dominant practices in ways that are beneficial to them and that maximize their social position. These are only some of the parameters that affect the transmission of cultural practices among social groups and knowing them is not enough. Archaeologists need detailed models of the process of diffusion. The next section describes some early steps in developing such models.

## ARCHAEOLOGISTS EXPLORE DIFFUSION

The distribution of archaeological material is the basis on which archaeological cultures are defined and through which diffusion is discovered. The challenge for archaeologists is to identify the behavior that created the distributions we see. Kristian Kristiansen and Thomas Larsson have already begun the process of creating an archaeological model of diffusion. Their book, *The Rise of Bronze Age Society: Travels, Transmissions and Transformations* (Kristiansen and Larsson 2005), calls for a redefinition of the concept of diffusion and spells out how it should be studied by prehistorians. They borrow from Mary Helms (1988, 1993, 1998), who maintained that people can use long-distance travel to create power for themselves. Kristiansen and Larsson argue that traveling European Bronze Age "chiefs" returned with special knowledge, particularly of craft skills such as metal working, and were able to transform knowledge of distant societies and craft skills into power. Chiefs used their knowledge of distant places to gain status and power and then used that status to influence people to accept the new cultural practices they brought back with them. Most important, Kristiansen and Larsson emphasize the connectedness and multidimensionality of diffusion. They argue that we should study institutions, not cultural traits. As all societies are organized around social, political, and religious institutions, by studying the "structured material evidence of social institutions through time and space," we gain a more holistic and integrated understanding of the transmission of cultural practices among social groups. Archaeologists can recover these institutions and their meaning by tracing their symbols in different cultural contexts. In spite of the power of their new approach, Kristiansen and Larsson's focus on the role of elite groups in the diffusion of social institutions highlights our tendency to see the process of diffusion as "top-down," (not unlike the heavily critiqued acculturation and world systems models; Cusick 1998b; Stein 2002).

Taking a more bottom-up approach, Warren DeBoer (2011) made a detailed study of the material culture of over 40 groups occupying western Amazonia along the Ucayali River. He compared male- and female-linked material culture along parameters of geography and language. Not unexpectedly, the material culture of adjacent groups tends to be more similar and fell off in a normal distance-decay manner. Perhaps even more important for the present discussion, female-linked material culture in the western Amazon was more widely distributed than male-linked traits (DeBoer 2011:80–91). Patrilocality, with women moving into the community of their husbands, might explain this pattern, but the groups in the material culture sample were overwhelmingly matrilocal. Instead, the prevalence of raiding in this region and the frequent capture of alien women (see also DeBoer 1986, 2008) is a better explanation of this pattern. Complicating this explanation, however, are ethnographic and ethnohistoric accounts suggesting that captive women were readily incorporated into the community of their captors and at least in some cases made assiduous attempts to copy captor culture exactly (DeBoer 1990; 2008; 2011:91). As DeBoer notes, we have much to learn about the parameters that surround cultural transmission:

> For example, knowledge of the developmental schedule by which various sorts of cultural knowledge are acquired is limited. Likewise, the effects of trauma, both at demographic and personal levels, on cultural transmission and acquisition are poorly understood, as is the human capacity to "unlearn" old and learn new cultural information at various life stages. (DeBoer 2011:95)

Building models that we can use to study diffusion prehistorically will require, in addition to archaeological studies, the use of analyses from ethnoarchaeology, ethnohistory, historical archaeology, and related social sciences where factors that affect the adoption of material culture practices can be observed. In addition to DeBoer's (2011) call to study personal aspects of cultural learning, we should also consider (1) the contexts and ways in which people from different groups encounter one another, including differences in status among social actors; (2) the opportunities, impediments, and imperatives that influence the adoption or rejection of new practices (see Schiffer's [2010] *differential adoption*, or evolutionary scholars' *biased transmission*); (Mills 2008:249); and (3) the ways novel cultural practices are incorporated and transformed in a new cultural setting. Of course, these are not separate lines of research. Diffusion is not only spatial and historical, it is also multidimensional. There are always multiple considerations and conditions that surround any change in cultural practices. While we are at a disadvantage without the rich textual record available to historical archaeologists, model-building in other fields can be applicable to prehistory.

Chapters in this volume contribute to the process of model-building that can be used to understand diffusion. Hays-Gilpin and her colleagues (chapter 4) point to the diffusion of ritual knowledge through the migration of social groups and emphasize that intentionality may have been involved in this process. Mills and Peebles (chapter 3) bring important concepts from the field of social network theory to examine diffusion, pointing out, for example, that the structure of social networks will affect the spread of ideas. Gilman and colleagues (chapter 5) look at long-distance movement of material culture linked to ideology and, like Hays-Gilpin and colleagues, see the diffusion of this material as intentional. They point to the travels of small groups as the means of diffusion.

## Diffusion and Captives

Like DeBoer (2008, 2011), I have argued that one way in which cultural practices could move between social groups is by taking captives. This discussion is part of my larger study of the impact of the practice of captive-taking on small-scale societies in prehistory. Captives are a common product of raiding and warfare worldwide and they can be found in considerable numbers in small-scale societies, ranging between 5 and 25 percent of the population (Cameron 2008b, 2011, 2016). Captives were most frequently women and children, as men were difficult to transport and incorporate. Captives could be adopted into captor culture, they could be enslaved, or they could occupy a variety of intermediate positions as concubines, drudge wives, or other marginal social positions. While children, especially the youngest, might readily adopt the culture of their captors and adult captives might undergo intense reprogramming (DeBoer 2011), captives (at least those past childhood) did arrive with knowledge of different technological, social, and ritual practices. In this section, I explore captives' role in technology transfer. I consider how they might fit into captor communities of practice and I use case studies to describe situations in which captives might be able to contribute to captor culture in spite of their low social position. In contrast to Kristiansen and Larsson's diffusion through the actions of an empowered elite, captives provide a "bottom-up" route for this process, with many impediments to transmission.

The communities-of-practice concept situates learning within a social group. Instead of the unilinear transmission of knowledge from teacher to student, learning is accomplished by members of a social group who range from beginners to accomplished practitioners. Newcomers are initially marginal but with time and socialization can become full members of the group (Lave and Wenger 1991; Wenger 1998:100–101). The community-of-practice concept assumes that these early learners are motivated by a desire to acquire competency so they can become full group members and that communities of practice have developmental cycles in which "the younger cohort gain competency, widen their participation . . . move into a position of full participation, and begin to displace other core members" (Bowser and Patton 2008:108). This process has an inherent dynamic tension that learners create as they establish their own identities through practice and supplant senior practitioners. Wenger notes that communities of practice are not necessarily peaceful, but can involve generational and other differences: "the working out of these [different] perspectives involves a dynamics of continuity and discontinuity that propels the practice forward" (1998:101). In an observation especially important for understanding the contribution of captives, Bowser and Patton (2008:108) note that it is here, where newcomers are establishing their own identity through practice, that change resides.

The community-of-practice concept conjures images of compatible groups of producers working, learning, and growing together. The introduction of captives into this image requires some rethinking about how practices are transmitted. If captives were forced, say, to make pottery, textiles, or basketry, or to build houses, they may have been instantly immersed in a field of social activities with which they had little or no familiarity. Their survival often depended on becoming active and rapid learners of captor cultural practices, yet the process of social learning for the captive could be coercive and it could involve verbal or physical abuse. Captives may be especially peripheral and they may always have been limited in their ability to become full group members. They may have been older when they joined captor communities of practice and had a steeper learning curve than other beginners. Their mistakes, rather than serving as teaching moments, may have served only to stress their alien origin.

How would captives accomplish the tasks they were assigned? Would they have been motivated or forced to mimic exactly the cultural practices of their captors in order to "fit in"? Or might they have more latitude for social expression and contribution to the communities of practice they joined? As outsiders they may have created an exceptionally potent dynamic tension as the native members of the group observed their different ways of doing with interest, approval, or distain. Captives generally entered captor society at the lowest rung of the social ladder and the anger and violence of recent warfare could be directed at them. One might assume that captors had little desire to learn from their captives, yet in my cross-cultural study of captives in small-scale societies I have found examples of captors who actively mined their captives for useful knowledge, including technological, medical, and religious (Cameron 2016).

I suggest that there are at least three situations that might allow captives more latitude in introducing novel cultural practices into the culture of their captors: (1) where captives form a large proportion of the population; (2) where captives introduce cultural practices that are considered somewhat useful by their captors; and (3) where captives have been specifically selected for their skills. Each of these situations is illustrated with an example taken from the edited volume *Invisible Citizens: Captives and Their Consequences* (Cameron 2008a), which explores captive-taking and cultural transmission around the world

Where captives make up a large proportion of the population, they may be able to form their own communities of practice and would be less constrained by "indigenous" ways of doing. In the Philippines from the eleventh to the sixteenth centuries, extensive maritime raiding was undertaken by chiefly polities that represented a variety of different ethnic and linguistic groups operating out of large coastal settlements (Junker 2008). Raids were frequently made on smaller, upland groups who lived along river corridors. Raiders captured women to be used as labor and as marriage partners, in addition to other booty. Some captive wives were set to agricultural tasks, but others made pottery and textiles, allowing their masters to gain wealth through trade. Documentary sources indicate that more than half of the women in some coastal settlements were captives and, as Junker notes, the tendency to integrate captive women into chiefly communities means that their impact would be significant (Junker 2008:119). In fact, Junker's excavations at chiefly settlements have revealed that many of the designs used on pottery originated in smaller settlements from which captives were taken. In spite of our assumption that material culture innovations tend to develop in larger and more populous centers, large numbers of captive women apparently formed their own communities of practice, which gave them freedom to use designs that they brought from their original homes.

Captives might be able to introduce new cultural practices into captor society if those practices were perceived by captors as useful and they did not intrude on or interrupt existing and valued activities. During the protohistoric period (AD 1500–1700), the southern High Plains of North America were occupied by nomadic bison hunters (Habicht-Mauche 2008). Women in these groups were the primary producers of hides, a labor-intensive undertaking, and processed hides were a key element in the establishment of male wealth and prestige. The larger number of women a man controlled, the more processed hides he could amass, and the greater his prestige grew. Archaeological and documentary evidence has established that the mobile groups on the southern High Plains interacted frequently with the adjacent Pueblo people of the Rio Grande valley in ways "both friendly and violent" (Habicht-Mauche 2008:183). One indicator of this interaction is pottery on archaeological sites along the frontier between the Puebloan and Plains regions that dates to the protohistoric period. These sites were clearly occupied by bison hunters, but the locally made pottery resembles Pueblo pottery. Habicht-Mauche (2008) argues that in order to increase the number of women who could produce hides, bison hunters raided Pueblo settlements and captured women who became lower-ranking secondary wives. She suggests that it was captive Pueblo women who introduced pottery-making techniques to these bison-hunting communities. The pots were probably useful and pottery technology did not compete with hide preparation. In other words, the main focus of these communities was not challenged—pottery making was likely an occasional activity that bison hunters permitted.

Captors not only extracted knowledge and skills from the captives they acquired, they sometimes targeted specific people whose talents they desired. In Europe, prior to the fifth century, there is archaeological evidence indicating that skilled Roman captives were present in Germanic settlements a considerable distance north of the Roman Empire (Lenski 2008). Both metal objects and ceramics were made locally in these Germanic settlements, but by using Roman techniques and designs. Some of these objects are found as far north as Denmark and they suggest that Roman metalworkers and potters were captured and taken far to the north. Germanic peoples were not alone in targeting specific Roman craftspeople for capture; it appears to have been a common practice (Cameron, 2016). For example, seventeenth-century accounts of the Atlantic slave trade document the consistent demand for captive slaves from Senegambia where cattle herding was the primary livelihood and captive people brought this knowledge with them (Carney and Rosomoff 2009:172–173). Many European colonizers came from urban areas and had no understanding of agricultural practices. Those who were trying to get livestock businesses started in the Americas needed slaves who had skills in livestock management; they were desperate for the sort of pastoral knowledge that Africans had. Some African livestock management techniques are still evident in the Americas today (Holloway 2005:55–56).

These are some very obvious examples of the kinds of contributions captives have made to the societies they joined. But I believe they contributed in more subtle ways, too. In communities of practice, newcomers are assumed to be child learners or apprentices. Captives must have been very different kinds of learners. With the knowledge they brought and through daily interaction they almost certainly contributed to and changed aspects of the societies they joined.

## CONCLUSIONS

This chapter argues that archaeologists need to refocus on the concept of diffusion and develop a body of theory for how cultural practices are transmitted between social groups. As Rouse (1986) pointed out more than three decades ago, in order for diffusion to occur, people need to be in contact with one another. Beyond this evident fact, there are many questions we must ask. Who are the people that interact: traveling chiefs? trained ritual specialists? traders? captives? What are the parameters that affect the types of cultural practices they introduce: their status, influence, knowledge, or numbers? What are the factors that condition the acceptance or rejection of cultural practices by the receiving group? How are practices modified, shaped, or changed when they are performed in a new cultural context?

This chapter is an initial attempt to address such questions. Although I do not emphasize diffusion in the Southwest, the chapters that follow do use Southwestern examples to explore diffusion at both large and small scales. In the process, they offer models that can be applied to other places and time. Whether we reinvigorate the term *diffusion* or substitute some of the many new terms used in other disciplines, we believe that this concept must be addressed if we are to develop nuanced models of ancient culture change.

# REFERENCES

Agbe-Davies, Anna S., and Alexander A. Bauer. 2010. "Rethinking Trade as a Social Activity: An Introduction." In *Social Archaeologies of Trade and Exchange: Exploring Relationships among People, Places, and Things*, ed. Alexander A. Bauer and Anna S. Agbe-Davies, 13–28. Walnut Creek, CA: Left Coast Press.

Anschuetz, Kurt F., and Richard H. Wilshusen. 2011. "Ensouled Places: Ethnogenesis and the Making of the Dinétah and Tewa Basin Landscapes." In *Movement, Connectivity, and Landscape Change in the Ancient Southwest*, ed. Margaret C. Nelson and Colleen Strawhacker, 321–344. Boulder: University Press of Colorado.

Anthony, David W. 1997. "Prehistoric Migration as Social Process." In *Migrations and Invasions in Archaeological Explanation*, ed. John Chapman and Helena Hamerow, 21–32. BAR International Series. Oxford: Archaeopress.

Bentley, R. A., and S. J. Shennan. 2003. "Cultural Transmission and Stochastic Network Growth." *American Antiquity* 68(03):459–485. https://doi.org/10.2307/3557104.

Bernardini, Wes. 2005. "Reconsidering Spatial and Temporal Aspects of Prehistoric Cultural Identity: A Case Study from the American Southwest." *American Antiquity* 70(1):31–54. https://doi.org/10.2307/40035267.

Bernardini, Wes, and Severin Fowles. 2011. "Becoming Hopi, Becoming Tewa: Two Pueblo Histories of Movement." In *Movement, Connectivity, and Landscape Change in the Ancient Southwest*, ed. Margaret C. Nelson and Colleen Strawhacker, 253–274. Boulder: University Press of Colorado.

Bhabha, Homi K. 1990. "The Third Space." In *Identity: Community, Culture, Difference*, ed. Jonathan Rutherford, 207–221. London: Lawrence and Wishart.

Bhabha, Homi K. 1994. *The Location of Culture*. London: Routledge.

Binford, Lewis. 1962. "Archaeology as Anthropology." *American Antiquity* 28(02):217–225. https://doi.org/10.2307/278380.

Binford, Lewis. 1965. "Archaeological Systematics and the Study of Culture Process." *American Antiquity* 31(02):203–210. https://doi.org/10.2307/2693985.

Borck, Lewis, Barbara J. Mills, Matthew A. Peeples, and Jeffery J. Clark. 2015. "Are Social Networks Survival Networks? An Example from the Late Prehispanic U.S. Southwest." *Journal of Archaeological Method and Theory* 22(1):33–57. https://doi.org/10.1007/s10816-014-9236-5.

Bowser, Brenda J., and John Q. Patton. 2008. "Learning and Transmission of Pottery Style: Women's Life Histories and Communities of Practice in the Ecuadorian Amazon." In *Cultural Transmission and Material Culture: Breaking Down Boundaries*, ed. Miriam T. Stark, Brenda J. Bowser, and Lee Horne, 105–129. Tucson: University of Arizona Press.

Boyd, R., and P. J. Richerson. 1985. *Culture and the Evolutionary Process*. Chicago: University of Chicago Press.

Cabana, Graciela S. 2011. "The Problematic Relationship between Migration and Culture Change." In *Rethinking Anthropological Perspectives on Migration*, ed. Graciela S. Cabana and Jeffery J. Clark, 16–28. Gainesville: University Press of Florida. https://doi.org/10.5744/florida/9780813036076.003.0002.

Cabana, Graciela S., and Jeffery J. Clark, eds. 2011. *Rethinking Anthropological Perspectives on Migration*. Gainesville: University Press of Florida. https://doi.org/10.5744/florida/9780813036076.001.0001.

Cameron, Catherine M., ed. 2008a. *Invisible Citizens: Captives and Their Consequences*. Salt Lake City: University of Utah Press.

Cameron, Catherine M. 2008b. "Captives in Prehistory: Agents of Social Change." In *Invisible Citizens: Captives and Their Consequences*, ed. Catherine M. Cameron, 1–24. Salt Lake City: University of Utah Press.

Cameron, Catherine M. 2011. "Captives and Culture Change: Implications for Archaeology." *Current Anthropology* 52(2):169–209. https://doi.org/10.1086/659102.

Cameron, Catherine M. 2013. "How People Moved among Ancient Societies: Broadening the View." *American Anthropologist* 115(2):218–231. https://doi.org/10.1111/aman.12005.

Cameron, Catherine M. 2016. *Captives: How Stolen People Changed the World*. Lincoln: University of Nebraska Press. https://doi.org/10.2307/j.ctt1fzhg08.

Carney, J., and R. N. Rosomoff. 2009. *In the Shadow of Slavery: Africa's Botanical Legacy in the Atlantic World*. Berkeley: University of California Press.

Carr, Christopher. 1995. "Building a Unified Middle-Range Theory of Artifact Design." In *Style, Society, and Person: Archaeological and Ethnological Perspectives*, ed. C. Carr and J. Neitzel, 151–170. New York: Plenum Press. https://doi.org/10.1007/978-1-4899-1097-4_6.

Cavalli-Sforza, L. L., and M. W. Feldman. 1981. *Cultural Transmission and Evolution: A Quantitative Approach*. Monographs in Population Biology 16. Princeton, NJ: Princeton University Press.

Clark, Jeffery J. 2001. *Tracking Prehistoric Migrations: Pueblo Settlers among the Tonto Basin Hohokam*. Anthropological Papers of the University of Arizona 65. Tucson: University of Arizona Press.

Clark, Jeffery J. 2011. "Disappearance and Diaspora: Contrasting Two Migrations in the Southern Southwest." In *Rethinking Anthropological Perspectives on Migration*, ed. Graciela Cabana and Jeffery Clark, 84–107. Gainesville: University Press of Florida. https://doi.org/10.5744/florida/9780813036076.003.0006.

Clark, Jeffery J., and K. W. Laumbach. 2011. "Ancestral Pueblo Migrations in the Southern Southwest: Perspectives from Arizona and New Mexico." In *Movement, Connectivity, and Landscape Change in the Ancient Southwest*, ed. Margaret Nelson and Colleen Strawhacker, 297–320. Boulder: University Press of Colorado.

Collard, Mark, and Stephen J. Shennan. 2008. "Patterns, Processes, and Parsimony: Studying Cultural Evolution with Analytical Techniques from Evolutionary Biology." In *Cultural Transmission and Material Culture: Breaking Down Boundaries*, ed. Miriam T. Stark, Brenda J. Bowser, and Lee Horne, 17–33. Tucson: University of Arizona Press.

Crabtree, Stefani A. 2015. "Inferring Ancestral Pueblo Social Networks from Simulation in the Central Mesa Verde." *Journal of Archaeological Method and Theory* 22(1):144–181. https://doi.org/10.1007/s10816-014-9233-8.

Cusick, James G., ed. 1998a. *Studies in Culture Contact: Interaction, Culture Change, and Archaeology*. Center for Archaeological Investigations Occasional Paper No. 25. Carbondale: Southern Illinois University.

Cusick, James G. 1998b. "Introduction." In *Studies in Culture Contact: Interaction, Culture Change, and Archaeology*, ed. James G. Cusick, 1–22. Center for Archaeological Investigations Occasional Paper No. 25. Carbondale, IL: Southern Illinois University.

Dawdy, Shannon Lee. 2000. "Evidence of Creolization in the Consumer Goods of an Enslaved Bahamian Family." *Historical Archaeology* 34(3):1–4. https://doi.org/10.1007/BF03373636.

Deagan, Kathleen. 1974. *Sex, Status, and Role in the Mestizaje of Spanish Colonial Florida*. PhD dissertation, Department of Anthropology, University of Florida, Gainesville Ann Arbor, MI: University Microfilms International.

Deagan, Kathleen. 1983. *Spanish St. Augustine: The Archaeology of a Colonial Creole Community*. New York: Academic Press.

Deagan, Kathleen. 1998. "Transculturation and Spanish American Ethnogenesis: The Archaeological Legacy of the Quicentenary." In *Studies in Culture Contact: Integration, Culture Change, and Archaeology*, ed. James G. Cusick, 23–43. Carbondale, IL: Center for Archaeological Investigations.

DeBoer, Warren. 1986. "Pillage and Production in the Amazon: A View through the Conibo of the Ucayali Basin, Eastern Peru." *World Archaeology* 18(2):231–246.

DeBoer, Warren R. 1990. "Interaction, Imitation, and Communication as Expressed in Style: The Ucayali Experience." In *The Uses of Style in Archaeology*, ed. Margaret W. Conkey and Christine A. Hastorf, pp. 82–104. Cambridge: Cambridge University Press.

DeBoer, Warren R. 2008. "Wrenched Bodies." In *Invisible Citizens: Captives and Their Consequences*, ed. Catherine M. Cameron, 233–261. Salt Lake City: University of Utah Press.

DeBoer, Warren. 2011. "Deep Time, Big Space: An Archaeologist Skirts the Topic at Hand." In *Ethnicity in Ancient Amazonia: Reconstructing Past Identities from Archaeology, Linguistics, and Ethnohistory*, ed. Alf Hornborg and Jonathan D. Hill, 75–98. Boulder: University Press of Colorado.

Ericson, Jonathan E., and Timothy K. Earle. 1982. *Contexts for Prehistoric Exchange*. New York: Academic Press.

Fass, Marion Field. 2003. *Epidemiology: Understanding Disease Spread.* The BioQUEST Curriculum Consortium.

Ferguson, Leland G. 1992. *Uncommon Ground: Archaeology and Colonial African America, 1650–1800.* Washington, DC: Smithsonian Institution Press.

Frank, Barbara E. 1993. "Reconstructing the History of an African Ceramic Tradition: Technology, Slavery and Agency in the Region of Kadiolo (Mali)." *Cahiers d'Études Africaines* 33(131):381–401. https://doi.org/10.3406/cea.1993.1505.

Gosselain, Olivier P. 2000. "Materializing Identities: An African Perspective." *Journal of Archaeological Method and Theory* 7(3):187–217. https://doi.org/10.1023/A:1026558503986.

Gosselain, Olivier P. 2008. "Mother Bella Was Not a Bella: Inherited and Transformed Traditions in Southwestern Niger." In *Cultural Transmission and Material Culture: Breaking Down Boundaries*, ed. Miriam T. Stark, Brenda J. Bowser, and Lee Horne, 150–177. Tucson: University of Arizona Press.

Gutiérrez, Gerardo. 2015. "Indigenous Coats of Arms in Títulos Primordiales and Techialoyan Códices: Nahua Corporate Heraldry in the Lienzos de Chiepetlan, Guerrero, Mexico." *Ancient Mesoamerica* 26(01):51–68. https://doi.org/10.1017/S09565 36115000127.

Habicht-Mauche, Judith. 2008. "Captive Wives? The Role and Status of Non-local Women on the Protohistoric Southern High Plains." In *Invisible Citizens: Captives and Their Consequences*, ed. Catherine M. Cameron, 181–204. Salt Lake City: University of Utah Press.

Hardin Friedrich, Margaret A. 1970. "Design Structure and Social Interaction: Archaeological Implications of an Ethnographic Analysis." *American Antiquity* 35(03):332–343. https://doi.org/10.2307/278343.

Hardin, Margaret A., and Barbara J. Mills. 2000. "The Social and Historical Context of Short-Term Stylistic Replacement: A Zuni Case Study." *Journal of Archaeological Method and Theory* 7(3):139–163. https://doi.org/10.1023/A:1026554403077.

Haskett, Robert. 1996. "Paper Shields: The Ideology of Coats of Arms in Colonial Mexican Primordial Titles." *Ethnohistory* 43:99–126.

Helms, Mary W. 1988. *Ulysses' Sail: An Ethnographic Odyssey of Power, Knowledge, and Geographical Distance.* Princeton, NJ: Princeton University Press. https://doi.org/10.1515/9781400859542.

Helms, Mary W. 1993. *Craft and the Kingly Ideal: Art, Trade, and Power.* Austin: University of Texas Press.

Helms, Mary W. 1998. *Access to Origins: Affines, Ancestors, and Aristocrats.* Austin: University of Texas Press.

Holloway, Joseph E. 2005. "'What Africa Has Given America': African Continuities in the North American Diaspora." In *Africanisms in American Culture*, ed. Joseph E. Holloway, 82–110. Bloomington: Indiana University Press.

Jones, Eric E. 2014. "Spatiotemporal Analysis of Old World Diseases in North America, AD 1519–1807." *American Antiquity* 79(3):487–506. https://doi.org/10.7183/0002-7316.79.3.487.

Jones, Terry L., Alice C. Storey, Elizabeth A. Matisoo-Smith, and José Miguel Ramírez-Aliaga. 2011. *Polynesians in America: Pre-Columbian Contacts with the New World*. New York: Altamira Press.

Jordan, Peter, and Stephen Shennan. 2003. "Cutural Transmission, Language, and Basketry Traditions amongst the California Indians." *Journal of Anthropological Archaeology* 22(1):42–74. https://doi.org/10.1016/S0278-4165(03)00004-7.

Junker, Laura L. 2008. "The Impact of Captured Women on Cultural Transmission in Contact Period Philippine Slave-Raiding Chiefdoms." In *Invisible Citizens: Captives and Their Consequences*, ed. Catherine M. Cameron, 110–137. Salt Lake City: University of Utah Press.

Kane, Maeve. 2014. "Covered with Such a Cappe: The Archaeology of Seneca Clothing, 1615–1820." *Ethnohistory* 61(1):1–25.

Kohler, Timothy A., Mark D. Varien, and Aaron M. Wright, eds. 2010. *Leaving Mesa Verde: Peril and Change in the Thirteenth-Century Southwest*. Tucson: University of Arizona Press.

Kristiansen, Kristian, and Thomas B. Larsson. 2005. *The Rise of Bronze Age Society: Travels, Transmissions and Transformations*. Cambridge, UK: Cambridge University Press.

Kroeber, Alfred L. 1931. "Diffusionism." *Encyclopedia of the Social Sciences* 5:139–142.

Kroskrity, Paul V. 1993. *Language, History, and Identity: Ethnolinguistic Studies of the Arizona Tewa*. Tucson: The University of Arizona Press.

Lave, Jean, and Etienne Wenger. 1991. *Situated Learning: Legitimate Peripheral Participation*. Cambridge, UK: University of Cambridge Press. https://doi.org/10.1017/CBO9780511815355.

Lekson, Stephen H. 2009. *A History of the Ancient Southwest*. Santa Fe, NM: School for Advanced Research.

Lenski, Noel. 2008. "Captivity, Slavery, and Cultural Exchange between Rome and the Germans from the First to the Seventh Century CE." In *Invisible Citizens: Captives and their Consequences*, ed. Catherine M. Cameron, 80–109. Salt Lake City: University of Utah Press.

Lévi-Strauss, Claude. 1969 [1947]. *The Elementary Structures of Kinship*. Trans. James Harle Bell, John Richard vonSturmer, and Rodney Needham. Boston, MA: Beacon Press.

Lyman, R. Lee. 2008. "Cultural Transmission in North American Anthropology and Archaeology, ca. 1895–1965." In *Cultural Transmission and Archaeology: Issues and Case Studies*, ed. Michael J. O'Brien, 10–20. Washington, DC: Society for American Archaeology.

Mauss, Marcel. 1990 [1928]. *The Gift: The Form and Reason for Exchange in Archaic Societies.* Trans. W. D. Halls. New York: W. W. Norton.

McBrinn, Maxine, and Christina Peterson Smith. 2006. "A New Spin on Cordage: The Effects of Material and Culture." *Kiva* 71(3):265–273. https://doi.org/10.1179/kiv.2006.71.3.003.

Mills, Barbara J. 2008. "Colonialism and Cuisine: Cultural Transmission, Agency, and History at Zuni Pueblo." In *Cultural Transmission and Material Culture: Breaking Down Boundaries,* ed. Miriam T. Stark, Brenda J. Bowser, and Lee Horne, 245–262. Tucson: University of Arizona Press.

Mills, Barbara J. 2011. "Themes and Models for Understanding Migration in the Southwest." In *Movement, Connectivity, and Landscape Change in the Ancient Southwest,* ed. Margaret C. Nelson and Colleen Strawhacker, 345–362. Boulder: University Press of Colorado.

Minar, C. Jill. 2001. "Motor Skills and the Learning Process: The Conservation of Cordage Final Twist Direction in Communities of Practice." *Journal of Anthropological Research* 57(4):381–405. https://doi.org/10.1086/jar.57.4.3631352.

O'Brien, Michael J., ed. 2008. *Cultural Transmission and Archaeology: Issues and Case Studies.* Washington, DC: The Society for American Archaeology Press.

O'Brien, Michael J., and Stephen J. Shennan, eds. 2010. *Innovation in Cultural Systems: Contributions from Evolutionary Anthropology.* Cambridge, MA: MIT Press.

Ortman, Scott G., and Catherine M. Cameron. 2011. "A Framework for Controlled Comparisons of Ancient Southwestern Movement." In *Movement, Connectivity, and Landscape Change in the American Southwest,* ed. Margaret Nelson and Coleen Strawhacker, 233–252. Boulder: University Press of Colorado.

Redfield, Robert, Ralph Linton, and Melville J. Herskovits. 1936. "Memorandum for the Study of Acculturation." *American Anthropologist* 38(1):149–152. https://doi.org/10.1525/aa.1936.38.1.02a00330.

Rodríguez-Alegría, Enrique. 2010. "Incumbents and Challengers: Indigenous Politics and the Adoption of Spanish Material Culture in Colonial Xaltocan, Mexico." *Historical Archaeology* 44(2):51–71.

Rogers, Everett M. 2003. *Diffusion of Innovations.* 5th ed. New York: The Free Press.

Rouse, Irving. 1986. *Migrations in Prehistory: Inferring Population Movement from Cultural Remains.* New Haven, CT: Yale University Press.

Roux, Valentine. 2013. "Spreading of Innovative Technical Traits and Cumulative Technical Evolution: Continuity or Discontinuity?" *Journal of Archaeological Method and Theory* 20(2):312–330. https://doi.org/10.1007/s10816-012-9153-4.

Schachner, Gregson. 2010. *Population Circulation and the Transformation of Ancient Zuni Communities.* Tucson: The University of Arizona Press.

Schiffer, Michael Brian. 2010. *Behavioral Archaeology Principals and Practice.* Equinox Handbooks in Anthropological Archaeology. Sheffield, UK: Equinox Publishing.

Schortman, Edward M., and Patricia A. Urban, eds. 1992. *Resources, Power, and Interregional Interaction*. New York: Plenum Press. https://doi.org/10.1007/978-1-4757-6416-1.

Shennan, Stephen J. 2002. "Learning." In *Darwin and Archaeology: A Handbook of Key Concepts*, ed. J. P. Hart and J. E. Terrell, 183–200. Westport, CT: Bergin and Garvey.

Shennan, Stephen J., ed. 2009. *Pattern and Process in Cultural Evolution*. Berkeley: University of California Press.

Shennan, Stephan J., and J. Steele. 1999. "Cultural Learning in Hominids: A Behavioral Ecological Approach." In *Mammalian Social Learning: Comparative and Ecological Perspectives*, ed. H. O. Box and K. R. Gibson, 367–388. Cambridge, UK: Cambridge University Press.

Sidbury, James, and Jorge Cañizares-Esguerra. 2011. "Mapping Ethnogenesis in the Early Modern Atlantic." *William and Mary Quarterly* 68(2):181–208. https://doi.org/10.5309/willmaryquar.68.2.0181.

Stahl, Ann B. 1991. "Ethnic Style and Ethnic Boundaries: A Diachronic Case Study from West-Central Ghana." *Ethnohistory* 38(3):250–275. https://doi.org/10.2307/482355.

Stanford, Dennis J., and Bruce A. Bradley. 2012. *Across Atlantic Ice: The Origin of America's Clovis Culture*. Berkeley: University of California Press.

Stark, Miriam, Brenda J. Bowser, and Lee Horne, eds. 2008. *Cultural Transmission and Material Culture: Breaking Down Boundaries*. Tucson: University of Arizona Press.

Stein, Gil J. 2002. "From Passive Periphery to Active Agents: Emerging Perspectives in the Archaeology of Interregional Interaction." *American Anthropologist* 104(3):903–916. https://doi.org/10.1525/aa.2002.104.3.903.

Stein, Gil J., ed. 2005. *The Archaeology of Colonial Encounters: Comparative Perspectives*. Santa Fe, NM: School of American Research Press.

Stone, Tammy. 2003. "Social Identity and Ethnic Interaction in the Western Pueblos of the American Southwest." *Journal of Archaeological Method and Theory* 10(1):31–67. https://doi.org/10.1023/A:1022808529265.

Stone, Tammy, and William D. Lipe. 2011. "Standing Out versus Blending In: Pueblo Migrations and Ethnic Marking." In *Movement, Connectivity, and Landscape Change in the Ancient Southwest*, ed. Margaret C. Nelson and Colleen Strawhacker, 275–296. Boulder: University Press of Colorado.

Storey, Alica A., and Terry L. Jones. 2011. "Diffusionism in Archaeological Theory: The Good, the Bad, and the Ugly." In *Polynesians in America: Pre-Columbian Contacts with the New World*, ed. Terry L. Jones, Alice C. Storey, Elizabeth A. Matisoo-Smith, and José Miguel Ramírez-Aliaga, 7–24. New York: Altamira Press.

Tehrani, Jamshid, and Mark Collard. 2002. "Investigating Cultural Evolution through Biological Phylogenetic Analyses of Turkmen Textiles." *Journal of Anthropological Archaeology* 21(4):443–463. https://doi.org/10.1016/S0278-4165(02)00002-8.

Thomason, Sarah Grey, and Terrence Kaufman. 1988. *Language Contact, Creolization, and Genetic Linguistics*. Berkeley: University of California Press.

Trigger, Bruce G. 2006. *A History of Archaeological Thought*. 2nd ed. Cambridge, UK: Cambridge University Press. https://doi.org/10.1017/CBO9780511813016.

VanPool, Todd L., Craig T. Palmer, and Christine S. VanPool. 2008. "Horned Serpents, Traditions, and the Tapestry of Culture: Culture Transmission in the American Southwest." In *Cultural Transmission and Archaeology: Some Fundamental Issues*, ed. M. J. O'Brien, 77–90. Washington, DC: Society for American Archaeology.

Voss, Barbara L. 2008a. *The Archaeology of Ethnogenesis: Race and Sexuality in Colonial San Francisco*. Berkeley: University of California Press.

Voss, Barbara L. 2008b. "Gender, Race, and Labor in the Archaeology of the Spanish Colonial Americas." *Current Anthropology* 49(5):861–893. https://doi.org/10.1086/591275.

Washburn, Dorothy K. 2001. "Remembering Things Seen: Experimental Approaches to the Process of Information Transmittal." *Journal of Archaeological Method and Theory* 8(1):67–99. https://doi.org/10.1023/A:1009573932096.

Wenger, Etienne. 1998. *Communities of Practice: Learning, Meaning, and Identity*. Cambridge, UK: Cambridge University Press. https://doi.org/10.1017/CBO9780511803932.

Wood, Stephanie. 2003. *Transcending Conquest: Nahua Views of Spanish Colonial Mexico*. Norman: University of Oklahoma Press.

# Reframing Diffusion through Social Network Theory

BARBARA J. MILLS AND MATTHEW A. PEEPLES

Diffusion is a fundamental part of social life, referring to the processes through which ideas about materials, technologies, and other cultural practices flow among individuals. It is often discussed in terms of novel ideas such as technological innovation and adoption. Diffusion can be contrasted with two other processes, the flow of goods through exchange and the flow of people, whether through marriage, migration, or forced movement and captivity. In reality, the flow of ideas rarely occurs without the flow of people or things and so materials, ideas, and people are all involved in diffusion. But it is the emphasis on ideas and the spread of innovations that makes diffusion of particular interest. Archaeologists have gotten quite good at identifying exchange of materials and the movement of people, especially through migration. But as Catherine Cameron (chapter 2, this volume) points out, diffusion and the flow of ideas are equally important for understanding social relationships and their change over time.

Processual archaeologists saw diffusion embedded within the culture historical paradigm, and considered it "unscientific," while other explanations for

DOI: 10.5876/9781607327356.c003

culture change—such as climate change and demography—were given priority (Hegmon 2003; Storey and Jones 2011:14). Although a number of archaeologists have recently called for the need to rethink how diffusion happened in the past (e.g., Chami 2007; Storey and Jones 2011), diffusion never really left archaeology. Diffusion has instead been "recast" within two highly distinct approaches in archaeology. One approach is neo-Darwinian, in which diffusion is viewed as an example of horizontal transmission, usually by tracking stylistic variables that are considered to be "neutral" traits (see for example the chapters in O'Brien 2008). By contrast, approaches infused with more agency look at learning frameworks and communities of practice (e.g., Stark et al. 2008).

An important part of diffusion is the process of innovation. Approaches to this topic include those that draw on information theory and experimentation (e.g., Stone 2008; Van der Leeuw and Torrence 1989) as well as a host of studies that focus on specific innovations such as metallurgy (e.g., Killick 2015). Thus, while many archaeologists have abandoned the term *diffusion*, the process by which innovations are spread is still an important topic. However, the gap between the neo-Darwinian approaches and the more agent-centered and practice-based approaches is a very real one not just in terms of their epistemic bases but also in the temporal and spatial scales at which they are applied.

We think that one way to bridge the micro- and the macroscales, as well as to think more relationally about diffusion, is to draw on social network theory. As Cameron (chapter 2, this volume) also points out, diffusion did not undergo widespread rejection in other disciplines as it has in archaeology. Social network theory also addresses diffusion and takes a relationist, structural approach that emphasizes how ideas and practices are transmitted through social interactions within different kinds of networks. Different network structures and the position of agents within the network promote alternative outcomes and are therefore useful for understanding how ideas and practices are adopted.

In this chapter, we bring out important work that has been, and continues to be done, on diffusion in other fields, especially network science. These studies emphasize several aspects of diffusion that we think are useful for reframing diffusion within archaeology: (1) how diffusion processes are modeled over time, (2) the importance of different network structures in promoting or limiting the spread of ideas, and (3) how sudden phase transitions or cascades occur within social networks. We apply these ideas to the archaeology of the late prehispanic Southwest to better understand the widespread adoption of decorated ceramics over large portions of the region as well as to bring a more agent-centered approach to large-scale social changes. We especially focus on the innovation and diffusion of Roosevelt Red Ware, and place this within the context of the movement of people, ideas, and goods in the late thirteenth through fifteenth centuries.

## SOCIOLOGY'S CONTRIBUTIONS TO DIFFUSION

Sociologists attribute the earliest contribution to diffusion theory to Gabriel Tarde and his 1903 book, *The Laws of Imitation* (Tarde 1903). His book is comparative and wide ranging and was translated into English by Elsie Clews Parsons.[1] It contains a chapter titled "What Is History? Archaeology and Statistics" in which Tarde acknowledges how archaeology contributes to understanding where ancient technologies originated and how they were adopted over time. But the part of his book that is most frequently cited is his discussion of how diffusion typically adheres to a predictable trajectory marked by innovation, followed by a period of geometric growth, and then a plateau. With this work, Tarde was one of the first researchers to recognize the predictable cumulative curve (the logistic or S-shaped curve[2]) marking the spread of innovations—a concept that launched several different lines of inquiry over the following decades.

The "invisible college"[3] (Rogers 2003) of rural sociologists took up diffusion research in the 1930s and 1940s to understand why some farmers adopted new technologies while others did not. One of the most widely cited papers produced by scholars within this group looked at the success of the introduction of hybrid varieties of corn among rural Iowa farmers (Ryan and Gross 1943)—an interesting process that can be compared to the adoption of maize in the Southwest (e.g., Vint and Mills 2016). They reconfirmed the logistic or S-shaped curve (in terms of cumulative adoption) and pointed out the importance of farmer-to-farmer communication in the decision to adopt. They concluded that "diffusion is a fundamentally social process" (Rogers 2003:35) and that knowledge alone was not enough to convince others to adopt. It depended on who the early adopters were and what their social positions were within the network. Ryan and Gross were also the first to differentiate among (1) early adopters, (2) early majority, (3) late majority, and (4) laggards, depending on their position in the curve.

Probably the most definitive sociological work on diffusion is Everett Rogers's *The Diffusion of Innovations*, first published in 1962 and now in its fifth (2003) edition. His work is comparative and treats diffusion as a process with a similar structure around the world. Although Rogers drew on the work of rural sociologists, his work explored many cases of diffusion, including how rap music became popular among white middle-class high school students; Nintendo's rise and fall; and even barriers to diffusion, such as the introduction and rejection of new rice varieties in Bali. Like his predecessors he found that diffusion generally conformed to a logistic or S-shaped curve over time (figure 3.1), but that it had different rates of adoption, depending on a number of factors. This produced some curves with steep slopes and others with smoother slopes, although he noted that there is a place in the curve at 10–25 percent adoption where the curve generally takes off, producing its characteristic S-shape.

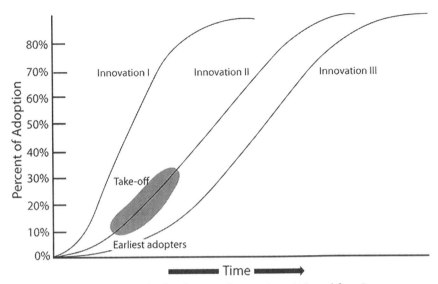

**FIGURE 3.1.** *Different curves for the adoption of innovations. (Adapted from Rogers 2003:figure 1.2.)*

Rogers (2003:222, figure 6.1) summarizes several salient variables in diffusion (table 3.1). Of the many variables he identities, he suggests that 49–87 percent of the variance in rates of adoption can be explained by (1) perceived advantage of the innovation; (2) compatibility with other practices and ideas within knowledge systems; (3) complexity of use and understanding; (4) trialability, or degree to which the practice can be experimented with; and (5) observability or the social field of performance. Other significant variables in the rate of adoption include whether the decision to adopt is individual and optional, collective, or imposed; how innovations are communicated; and the kind of social system. He treated the social system as "a kind of collective learning system in which the experiences of the early adopters of an innovation, transmitted through inter-personal networks, determines the rate of adoption of their followers" (Rogers 2003:67). As others have noted, this approach fits well with the communities-of-practice theory, in which learning is transmitted among networks of practitioners (e.g., Borgatti and Foster 2003:1005). But one important aspect of this is that the "social system" is more explicitly treated as a network.

The perceived relative advantage of an innovation led Rogers and later researchers to what is known as the knowledge-attitude-practice (KAP) gap. It is not enough to know about an innovation for it to be adopted—strongly positive or strongly negative attitudes toward a practice could accelerate or inhibit its adoption. But having a positive attitude did not necessarily result in the immediate adoption of an innovation. Shown graphically, over time, knowledge comes

**TABLE 3.1.** Factors contributing to the adoption of innovations (after Rogers 2003:222, figure 6.1)

| Factor |
| --- |
| I. Perceived Attributes of Innovations |
|     a. Relative advantage |
|     b. Compatability |
|     c. Complexity |
|     d. Trialability |
|     e. Observability |
| II. Type of Innovation-Decision |
|     a. Optional |
|     b. Collective |
|     c. Authority |
| III. Communication Channels |
|     a. Mass media |
|     b. Interpersonal |
| IV. Nature of the Social System |
|     a. Norms |
|     b. Degree of network interconnectedness |
| V. Extent of Change Agents' Promotion Efforts |

first, followed by a positive or negative attitude toward the innovation, and then adoption of a practice (figure 3.2). The horizontal distance between knowledge and practice is the gap, which can be of different sizes at different times in the diffusion process. The importance of the KAP-gap is twofold. First, it points out that the process of adoption includes the key element of attitude, which can be shaped in a number of ways, including the variables Rogers identified above (namely, perceived advantage, compatibility, complexity of use, trialability, and the social field of performance). He especially noted that attitude could be strongly affected when individuals with higher status are the earliest adopters. Second, the KAP-gap also suggests that strongly *negative* attitudes may be responsible for creating boundaries to adoption—the kinds of boundaries that may show up in the spatial as well as social distribution of different practices (see also Borck and Mills 2017).

Another important strand of research on diffusion was promoted in geography by Hägerstrand (1967). He showed that spatial propinquity was an important way in which ideas and technologies were transmitted. His analyses preceded the more widespread use of geographic information systems (GIS) analyses but spatial and social analytic approaches now allow archaeologists to use both in tandem (e.g., Östborn and Gerding 2015).

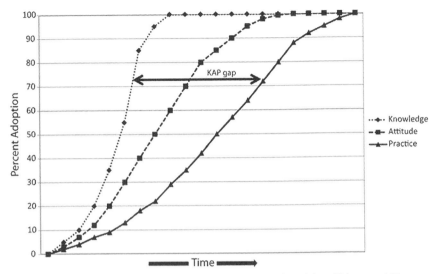

**FIGURE 3.2.** *The knowledge-attitude-practice (KAP) gap. (Adapted from Valente and Myers 2010:figure 1.)*

## DIFFUSION THROUGH SOCIAL NETWORKS

Rogers and others who considered the process of diffusion recognized that it was strongly influenced by the structure of social networks. For those unfamiliar with formal social network analyses (SNA) we introduce here a few key terms (see also Collar et al. 2015 for an extensive glossary). First, networks are composed of *nodes* (also called *vertices*), whether these are individuals, households, or, as we will discuss soon for our Southwest data, villages and towns. Second, nodes are connected to each other through ties or edges that represent a relationship whether through kinship, friendship, sodality, residence, ideology, or religion, for example. For the analyses that we discuss here, relationships are based on shared consumption of decorated ceramics (Mills 2016), which are assessed using a version of the Brainerd–Robinson similarity coefficient (Mills, Clark, et al. 2013; Mills, Peeples, et al. 2013). Briefly, we calculate the similarities in the proportions of decorated ceramic wares among sites and use this measure of similarity as a proxy for the presence and strength of social connections among those sites.

The most common form of network is called a *one-mode network*, which consists of a set of actors (nodes) and the connections among them. Such one-mode networks may be directed (meaning that flows through a network happen only in prescribed directions, as in citation or communication networks) or undirected (meaning that flows happen simultaneously in both directions as in networks among individuals who share a belief system). Figure 3.3 (left) shows an example

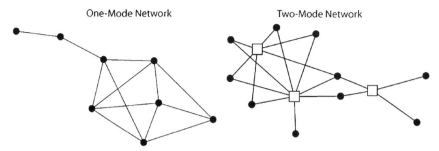

One-Mode Network          Two-Mode Network

**FIGURE 3.3.** *Examples of one-mode and two-mode networks with undirected ties.*

of a one-mode network with undirected connections or ties. Another way of looking at networks is through a two-mode network (figure 3.3, right), where connections among one set of actors are mediated though their mutual connection to another kind of node, such as sodality membership or all actors in a movie (the latter has resulted in the famous calculation of the degrees of separation of any actor from Kevin Bacon). An archaeological example of this is the shared use of a specific source material, such as obsidian, or all archaeologists who have a link by virtue of their participation in the same field project even if they were not in the field during the same season. Although the visual displays resemble spatial clusters, it is important to point out that the clusters in these diagrams are based only on the structure of social ties. The degree to which social ties are predicted by spatial ties has been addressed elsewhere but we note that for most time periods that we discuss in this chapter, spatial propinquity is a poor predictor of strong social relationships, as measured by shared decorated ceramic assemblages (Mills, Clark, et al. 2013). Thus, social relationships must also be brought into consideration.

There are several different ways in which social network theory has been used to understand how diffusion flows through networks and how this process is affected by network structure (see especially Borgatti and Foster 2003:1003–1005). A classic contrast has been made between structural versus relational embeddedness (Granovetter 1992) or equivalence versus cohesion (Burt 1987) (table 3.2). In network terms, structural equivalence, where nodes are located in similar kinds of network positions, can help promote the acceptance of new innovations. For example, if two nodes are connected through someone else—for example, they shared the same dissertation advisor but were not in the same graduate student cohort—they are more likely to adopt a new practice even though they are not directly tied to each other. The alternative view is that actors only adopt practices when they are directly tied to someone who has already adopted that practice. The distinction can also be summarized as *how* you know them (positional) versus *who* you know (relational). In practice, it is quite likely that both of these will

**TABLE 3.2.** Structural versus relational embeddedness in networks (summarized from Borgatti and Foster 2003)

| Structural | Relational |
|---|---|
| Structural equivalence of nodes (attitudes similar because of shared affiliations even if nodes don't know each other) | Connections between nodes (attitudes flow through friendship, kinship and other ties; more ties indicate greater influence) |
| Positional/Topological | Interactionist/Cohesion |
| How one knows someone | Who one knows |
| Structure | Agency |
| Weak or bridging ties | Strong ties |

result in the spread of ideas—that is, through both structural equivalence, also called convergence, as well as through critical thresholds of interpersonal ties with others who have adopted.

An important network concept is that of structural holes (Burt 1987). Different social clusters or subgroups within the network may be present and a node that connects these subgroups acts as a bridge thereby linking actors in these subgroups that are separated by the structural hole. Nodes in certain kinds of bridging positions are also known as *brokers* (Peeples and Haas 2013) and are usually weakly linked to sets of actors that would otherwise not be connected (often referred to as *cliques*). Bridging or weak ties do a number of things but one of the most important is their potential to provide a conduit for the spread of new knowledge, beliefs, and technological innovations in heterogeneous populations.

Granovetter's (1973, 1983) classic work demonstrated "the strength of weak ties" not only for providing bridges between distinct communities but also in creating "small worlds." Weak ties decrease the path length from one node to other nodes in the network even if they are spatially distant, and decreasing path length increases rates of diffusion (Cowan 2006). Globalization is an example of how our own world has become small; archaeologically, however, small worlds were created through a number of different social processes and by a number of different actors. Migrants, especially those in diaspora who keep contact with each other, are often in structurally bridging positions (Peeples and Mills 2018). Religious specialists are also in potential brokerage positions through transmission of ritual practices between groups and through procurement and pilgrimages (see also Hays-Gilpin et al. and Gilman et al., chapters 4 and 5, respectively, this volume). Researchers have made important distinctions among the kinds of information and technologies being transferred. For example, "while strong ties may be better suited for an exchange of complex knowledge, weak ties could be more beneficial for searching for information" (Fritsch and Kauffeld-Monz 2008).

The path length from one node to another is one way of measuring relational embeddedness in a network (see especially summaries in Freeman 1978; Wasserman and Faust 1994). Another measure is degree centrality, which is the number of ties (or the total weight of ties) each node has to all other nodes. In terms of diffusion, having more or stronger ties doesn't necessarily mean that there is a higher probability of adoption (Watts and Dodds 2007). But the more ties that have already adopted a practice as a proportion of the total number of ties does make a difference in terms of theories of thresholds and cascades (Valente 1998; 2005:103, figure 6.1.2; Watts 2003:234–235, figure 8.4). There is a threshold or "tipping point" that leads to a *cascade* effect. Each person or node can be regarded as having a different threshold and the number of direct ties that individuals require before they will adopt an innovation will be different. If those early adopters are key social figures in the network, then they may have more influence than others and affect others' thresholds of acceptance.

Duncan Watts's (2002, 2003) work shows that different individuals or nodes in social networks have different thresholds in terms of the number of their neighbors it takes for them to alter their behavior. This is conditioned by temporal position on the curve but also by the personal attributes and even statuses of both early adopters and their ties. If an early adopter is in a position of high status or influence, then others will be influenced positively to adopt. Group size matters as well, since "the larger the connected cluster of early adopters in which the innovation lands, the farther it will spread" (Watts 2003:235). In a similar vein, Hegmon and Kulow (2005) explore innovation in the designs painted on Mimbres black-on-white ceramics in terms of agency and structure, again suggesting that the status (and perhaps skill) of a particular artist likely has an impact on whether or not a new stylistic practice spreads or remains anomalous. Thus, multiple early adopters of higher statuses, especially within larger networks, will cause cascades. Cascades take many forms—including social and religious movements. They are identified by higher rates of adoption and especially those that crosscut many subgroups.

An important observation in network studies is that people are more likely to have network ties with people like themselves. This characteristic is called *homophily* or, more colloquially, "birds of a feather" (Lazarsfeld and Merton 1954; McPherson et al. 2001), and has been strongly associated with the diffusion of innovations, whether those similarities were based on gender, language, skill, or status. Homophily will enhance internal diffusion at the risk of group isolation. But at the same time it has been recognized that diffusion must also involve some degree of transmission between people who were not like themselves (also called *heterophily*) (Rogers 2003; Rogers and Bhowmik 1970). This is especially the case for innovations that are made in one geographic area and then are diffused to other areas no matter what the specific social processes of diffusion are. This crosscutting of groups is why weak ties can be important as bridges from one group to another. Nonetheless, Centola and Macy (2007) showed that the strength of weak ties (as originally defined by Granovetter 1973), may be overstated. They point out that for "complex contagions"—or those requiring multiple sources of affirmation, such as unproven technologies—strong ties may be more effective in transmitting information. Strong ties are usually those associated with close family members.

As Valente (2005:104) has noted, the difficulty of collecting time-series data on networks long enough for diffusion to have occurred has prohibited assessments of how the process unfolds in real or empirical networks over substantial periods. Network data are usually used retroactively and/or simulations are conducted to look at how diffusion might have happened. The latter are often compared to diffusion models using random networks of the same size and density. What these analyses generally show is that diffusion through random networks is slower than diffusion through more centralized networks (Valente 2005:figure 6.1.3). In Valente's analyses of two Cameroon networks, he also showed that there are "fits and starts" in the diffusion process as innovations spread rapidly when hitting pockets of highly interconnected nodes and then slow between groups (Valente 2005:104), producing inflection points in the adoption curve.

More recently, Kandler and Caccioli (2016) use simulated networks to look at the relationships of network topology or structure, social status (measured by centrality), and different degrees of homophily within the network on different rates of adoption. Their work reinforces the work of Valente, Watts, and others by showing that in networks with different social statuses, if the early adopt-ers were higher-status/more-central nodes, then the innovation spread more quickly and to the entire population than if lower-status/less-central nodes were the early adopters. This was true whether or not the parameter of homophily was present, that is the probability of individuals to interact more often with people like them (in this case with others of similar status). But, interestingly, when the innovation was introduced by a lower-status individual in homophilous subgroups—the high-status subpopulation did not adopt unless a high percent-age of the low-status population did. Status in the Kandler and Caccioli study is purely based on network centrality or position in the network, and assumes that status is correlated with number of ties (or who one knows as opposed to how one knows them in the classic structural vs. relational embeddedness contrast).

These studies parallel and expand upon the work of Watts and others and further underscore the importance of different network structures, homophily, network size, strong and weak ties, and social status in the diffusion process. Whether sociologist or computer scientist, however, those engaging in the simulation of diffusion through networks have pointed to the need to look at diffusion within empirical networks. This makes historical networks, including those contributed by archaeology, significant for looking at how network diffusion occurs. In the remainder of this chapter we summarize the social and network characteristics of the adoption of decorated Roosevelt Red Ware in the Southwest as an example of how archaeological case studies may contribute to network studies of diffusion and consider several variables, including relational versus structural embeddedness, prestige, homophily, and cascades.

## THE DIFFUSION OF SALADO POLYCHROMES

We apply the concept of diffusion through social networks to the case of Roosevelt Red Ware, which includes the Salado polychromes. Patricia Crown's (1994) work on Salado polychromes was instrumental in bringing to the forefront the widespread adoption of this distinctive ware throughout a large area of the Southwest. Crown set up a number of oppositional explanations for the distribution of Salado polychromes, including (1) elite exchange, (2) symbols of economic alliance, (3) evidence for religious ideology, and (4) the products of migrant producers. Her compositional analyses showed that it was made in most areas that it is found, was produced by migrants and nonmigrants, and that the widespread distribution is not based on a regional political alliance. Because of the active content in its painted decoration, she argued that Salado represented the spread of a cult or ideology. McGuire (2011:45) has pointed out that Crown's alternative hypotheses opposed religion and politics, and that researchers should instead look at how all of her hypotheses might be interrelated.

Since Crown's work a number of researchers have focused renewed attention on Roosevelt Red Ware, providing further evidence for how the movement of people, pots, and ideas were responsible for its widespread distribution (Clark and Lyons 2012; Lyons et al. 2011; Mills 2007; Mills et al. 1999; VanPool and Savage 2010; Zedeño 1994). The data compiled for the Southwest Social Networks Project allows us to look more closely at the relationship of formal social networks over time and how these networks enhanced or inhibited the diffusion of Salado polychromes, as well as the relationship of different stages in its adoption to other social factors.

To consider the spread of Roosevelt Red Ware within our study area, we first used methods described by Roberts and others (2012) to apportion ceramic assemblages into 25-year intervals based on the occupation spans of sites and the production dates of specific types. Using these data, we then calculated the cumulative proportion of settlements with Roosevelt Red Ware through time. The cumulative adoption curve for Roosevelt Red Ware generally follows the expected distribution, with a short period of low adoption followed by rapid growth and a plateau toward the end (figure 3.4). What is interesting about this is the relatively quick "take off"—relative to the 10–25 percent documented cross-culturally by Rogers (2003), Roosevelt Red Ware takes off after only 5 percent

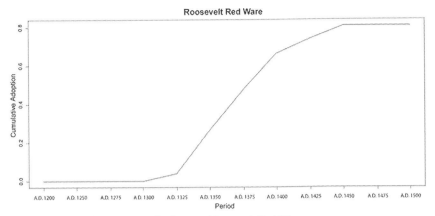

**FIGURE 3.4.** *The adoption curve for decorated Roosevelt Red Ware.*

adoption, at ca. AD 1325. A second feature is the relatively steep growth. And a third is the point of inflection, ca. AD 1400, when the rate of adoption slows but does not yet plateau.

Among the questions to ask about the networks through which Roosevelt Red Ware diffused are these: Who were the innovators or early adopters? What were the structural and relational aspects of their networks? There is general consensus among researchers that the earliest Salado polychromes were produced in the late AD 1200s by migrants from the Kayenta/Tusayan region. This conclusion is based on the design layouts of the ceramics and their association with perforated plates, whether in migrant enclaves, or as in the Mogollon Rim area, at sites where migrants and local populations lived in the same settlements (Clark and Lyons 2012; Lyons and Lindsay 2006; Mills et al. 1999). The earliest tree-ring dates for Pinto Polychrome, the first of the Salado polychromes, are from the Mogollon Rim region (Crown 1994:15, 205), including those from Chodistaas Pueblo and Bryant Ranch Pueblo. Tree-ring dates from Chodistaas Pueblo, where both locally made and exchanged Pinto Polychrome were recovered, are in the AD 1263 to 1300 range (Crown 1994:178; Montgomery and Reid 1990). Petrography (summarized in Mills et al. 1999) and tree-ring dates from Bryant Ranch Pueblo in the AD 1280s (see Fenn et al. 2006) show that Pinto Polychrome was also made above the Mogollon Rim in the late thirteenth century. Pinto Polychrome was associated with the 1280s room block at Point of Pines, farther to the southeast (Crown 1994), and is also associated with migrant enclaves in the San Pedro and Safford areas. Compositional analyses show that some of these were locally made in each area, but not all, indicating that the production was through the spread of ideas as well as through shared technologies. In recent years the diaspora model for the migration out of northeastern

Arizona has been suggested as an explanation for how these disparate pockets of migrants maintained social networks across a large area of the central and southern Southwest (Lyons and Clark 2012).

Thus, the innovators and earliest adopters of Roosevelt Red Ware were migrants who maintained connections over a relatively large area. As predicted by the structural theory of diffusion, weak or bridging ties were the most important in the early consumption of this ware, whether through exchange or expanding areas of production. Recent analyses using the Southwest Social Networks Database showed that brokers characterized by bridging ties after about AD 1300 are most prevalent in the Transition Zone, the area between the Colorado Plateau and the Basin and Range provinces, a major area that migrants moved into during the late thirteenth and early fourteenth centuries (Peeples and Haas 2013; Peeples and Mills 2018). After AD 1300, settlements characterized by brokerage and a high proportion of bridging ties were marked both by high frequencies of Roosevelt Red Ware ceramics and connections spanning both the northern and southern Southwest. This suggests that the initial adoption and diffusion of Roosevelt Red Ware ceramics may have been facilitated by the inter-mediate network positions of early adopters at the macroregional network level.

It is also instructive to examine patterns of strong ties (as distinct from bridg-ing ties) through time. The following network diagrams are based on decorated ceramics, including information on over 800,000 decorated ceramic artifacts from 520 sites dating to AD 1200–1500 west of the Continental Divide in New Mexico and Arizona (figure 3.5). Networks were constructed by 50-year intervals as discussed by Roberts et al. (2012; see also Mills, Clark, et al. 2013; Mills, Peeples, et al. 2013; Mills et al. 2015). In the period AD 1250–1300, the southern Southwest (shown generally at the bottom of these figures) was characterized by several distinct subgraphs or connected components, largely representing strong con-nections within major valleys, with few strong connections between these groups. The size of each node indicates its (eigenvector) centrality within the network. These connections are based on shared proportions of all decorated ceramics, using the Brainerd–Robinson similarity index, so they represent com-munities of practice in consumption (see Mills 2016 for an expansion). During this interval the largest component is in the northern Southwest—especially representing the widespread distribution of Cibola White Ware. After AD 1300, following the major migration out of northeastern Arizona into central and southern Arizona and southwest New Mexico, the center of gravity for the regional network shifted to the southern Southwest.

The 50-year period between AD 1300 and 1350 straddles the "take-off" por-tion of the Roosevelt Red Ware adoption curve and shows the emergence of a major network component or subgroup that includes the San Pedro, Safford, Tonto Basin, and Upper Gila areas. The strong connections among settlements

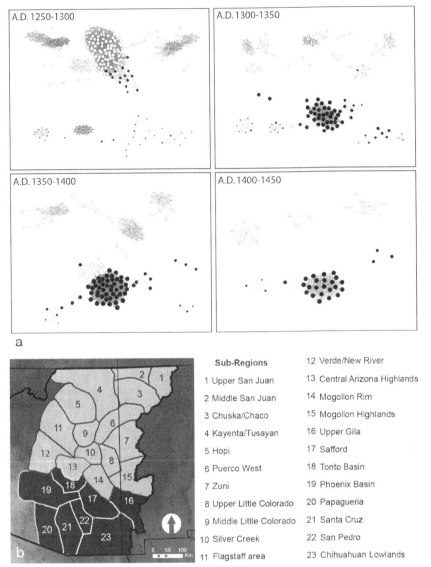

**FIGURE 3.5.** *Top: One-mode networks of the western Southwest in 50-year intervals. (Based on data in Mills, Clark, et al. 2013). Bottom: Lightest shading of nodes represents regions in the northern Southwest, darkest in the southern Southwest.*

in this large southern component are largely driven by shared consumption of Roosevelt Red Ware ceramics. By the end of this period both migrants and their hosts were consuming, and many of the latter were also producing, Roosevelt Red Ware. Within each valley or basin, then, similarities in the proportions of decorated wares were not just based on structural equivalence but also by direct relational ties as migrants intermarried into local groups and shared in communities of practice in both production and consumption. These within-settlement strong ties would have facilitated the diffusion of information about how to make Salado ceramics at the intrasite level.

The large southern component continued to increase in size in the AD 1350–1400 interval as Phoenix and Tucson Basin settlements became strongly connected to the others. This subnetwork also pulled in settlements from the central Southwest including the "Verde" area. The southern component remained the largest in the following AD 1400–1450 interval, although by this time the number of sites, and population size as well, had started to decline.

If we look at areas with the highest eigenvector centralities (a recursive measure of how connected a site is to other highly connected sites) in the full project area, by period, we can see how high levels of centrality clearly shift over time from the northern to the southern Southwest (table 3.3). The Safford Valley, along the Middle Gila, ranks highest for the later time periods—an area where migrant enclaves like Goat Hill were replaced by coresidences of the descendants of migrants and nonmigrants alike (Neuzil 2008). Each of the areas has a diversity of architecture and almost certainly included people with very different backgrounds and histories despite their strong network connections. In fact, we might characterize these as socially heterogeneous (or heterophilous, in network terminology). Based on both the visual representations of the social networks and their eigenvector centralities, it is clear that the southern Southwest became more connected over time until the end of the Classic period. Driving these strong connections in the southern Southwest are the shared consumption and discard of Roosevelt Red Ware, including Salado polychromes.

To recap thus far, the adoption and diffusion of Roosevelt Red Ware followed a model in which structural over relational embeddedness was more important for innovators and early adopters, who were linked over a large area through weak ties. This was followed by a cascade effect in which strong, relational ties characterized the network of the southern Southwest. After AD 1325, or about two generations after migration, Roosevelt Red Ware was consumed by more than migrant households in most areas of the southern Southwest. Decorated Roosevelt Red Ware increased dramatically in popularity after this time as entire valley subnetworks joined in the production and especially consumption of the ware. Some of this was likely because of intermarriage between migrants and nonmigrants, but it was also because of the widespread acceptance of the ware among diverse populations within central and southern Arizona.

So how did Salado polychromes become so widely accepted? We think that there were multiple, mutually reinforcing reasons for what turned knowledge into a positive attitude, and then into practice, for so many in the southern

**TABLE 3.3.** The Most Highly Connected Regions in the Southwest by Period, Based on Eigenvector Centralities[1]

| Time Period (AD) | Regions |
|---|---|
| 1200–1250 | Zuni, Mogollon Highlands |
| 1250–1300 | Zuni, Mogollon Highlands |
| 1300–1350 | Tonto Basin, San Pedro, Safford |
| 1350–1400 | San Pedro, Safford, Tonto Basin, Upper Gila, Santa Cruz, Phoenix Basin |
| 1400–1450 | Safford, San Pedro, Phoenix Basin, Santa Cruz, Tonto Basin |

1. Based on the highest 20 centralities of individual settlements within each region and 50-year interval.

Southwest. Recalling the results of Rogers and others, one of the most important is the prestige of early adopters. We think that migrants initially held positions of high status in their respective communities because of their high skill (Mills, Roberts, et al. 2013; Mills et al. 2016). northern Arizona potters, most likely women, were highly proficient and often specialized producers accustomed to working with a variety of clays, pigments, and firing regimes in their homeland, who brought those skills with them to their new homes. This was one way that migrants overcame some of the structural inequalities that are often created between "first comers" and "late comers" in an area and that we think promoted the adoption of Roosevelt Red Ware.

Second is the complexity of the innovation. The early innovators of Roosevelt Red Ware worked with some high-quality raw materials, especially above the Mogollon Rim, but they were also able to work with poor raw materials that characterize the Transition Zone and the southern Southwest's basin and range environment. The ware itself is very "forgiving"—the usually brown paste is covered with slips that are widely available and the temper is most often sand. In fact, it has many characteristics of an earlier ware that was made in the area, Puerco Valley Red Ware—an important point since many technological and social innovations are rarely de novo. Unlike the limonite and kaolinite of White Mountain Red Ware, the slips are derived from hematite and a variety of white sources that are rarely pure kaolinite (including a salmon variety that replaces white with a buff). The paint is carbon based in most cases (Crown 1994) and can be replicated with a number of materials. And finally, it was fired at relatively low temperatures. Two more complex aspects of the technology are that the atmosphere needed to be controlled to prevent oxidation that would burn off the carbon paint and the majority of examples were constructed with coil-and-scrape technology, which was not part of the existing ceramic repertoire in many areas where Roosevelt Red Ware was ultimately made[4] (Crown 1994). Overall, however, Roosevelt Red Ware had more advantages than disadvantages. Such relative lack of technological complexity in the innovation (Rogers 2003) helped to promote its more widespread practice once the decision had been made that making Roosevelt Red Ware was a good thing to do.

Late varieties of Roosevelt Red Ware, in particular those produced after AD 1350, appear to have taken on certain characteristics of local pottery traditions that predate the arrival of this ware in some areas. For example, Dinwiddie Polychrome is a smudged variety of Roosevelt Red Ware most common in the eastern half of the study area in the Upper Gila and Safford areas where smudging was a common practice. This similarity relates to how well the new innovation fits with existing practices. The acceptance and perhaps freedom of experimentation and innovation is what initiated the rapid growth after AD 1325 in Roosevelt's diffusion curve. In the KAP-gap terms, there was increasing acceptance that led to practice.

A final factor that Rogers mentioned as promoting the rate of adoption of new innovations includes the performativity of the practice, or how visible the practice is to potential adopters. The production of Roosevelt Red Ware was probably not highly visible to nonproducers, but the context of its use was more public. The earliest bowls of the Salado polychromes, Pinto Polychrome, were, on average, larger than those of contemporaneous whitewares, although not as large as bowls of the contemporaneous Late White Mountain Red Ware. It rarely had decoration on the exterior, but after AD 1325, corresponding with the "take off" phase in the diffusion curve, exterior designs were much more common. There is nothing subtle about Roosevelt Red Ware painted designs. Its visual and content accessibility must have been important parts of its diffusion, especially after AD 1325 when the exterior of bowls became an important design field for many wares (Mills 2007). In fact, their boldness is almost cartoon-like, particularly when compared to contemporaneous Late White Mountain Red Ware and Jeddito Yellow Ware.

The lack of centralization in Roosevelt Red Ware production is also important—it was a technology accessible to many. As Collar (2007) has pointed out, the lack of centralization is one of the features of widespread social movements. Easily understood symbols allow heterogeneous populations to participate, which in network terms resulted in the giant connected component that linked most sites in the southern Southwest in the fourteenth and early fifteenth centuries.

## CONCLUSION

In conclusion we think that there are many insights to be drawn from network analysis and theory for understanding the process of innovation and diffusion. In our case we explored the adoption of Roosevelt Red Ware in the southern Southwest, emphasizing the embeddedness of the practice in structural and relational characteristics of networks, especially weak and strong ties. As predicted by social network theories of diffusion, the prestige or skill of early adopters led to a relatively swift positive attitude, followed by practice. This acceptance spread through spatially disconnected and heterogeneous populations of the southern Southwest based on the high performativity of the use of Salado vessels, fit with previous practices, and its relative simplicity in acquisition of materials and production. The production and consumption of Roosevelt Red Ware created a "small world" in the southern Southwest, one that was built on shared practices with all the hallmarks of a social movement. Roosevelt Red Ware also offers some lessons for network theories of diffusion, especially the need to balance micro- and macro-approaches, such as the role and prestige of migrants.

*Acknowledgments.* We appreciate the invitation of Cathy Cameron and Steve Lekson to participate in the session that led to the writing of this chapter. Our work could not have been accomplished without the support of our collaborators on the first phase of the Southwest Social Networks Project (especially Jeff Clark, Lewis Borck, Ron Breiger, Aaron Clauset, Wm. Randall Haas Jr., Deb Huntley, John Roberts, Susan Ryan, Steve Shackley, and Meaghan Trowbridge) and the support of the National Science Foundation (Awards 0827007 to Mills and 0827011 to co-PI Jeffery Clark). We also thank the many individuals and institutions contributing data to our project, including the Arizona State Museum, Arizona State University, Museum of New Mexico, Museum of Northern Arizona, US Forest Service, National Park Service, and our colleagues at Archaeology Southwest and the University of Arizona.

## NOTES

1. The Southwest ethnologist Elsie Clews Parsons was better-known as a sociologist early in her career and was influenced by the sociologist Franklin Giddings (Heib 1993:63–64), who wrote the preface to Parsons's translation of Tarde.

2. Although many subsequent references suggest that he came up with the well-known logistic curve, Tarde did not graph this curve but instead described it verbally based on a number of historical examples.

3. Rogers called it an "invisible college" because these researchers represented a group of scholars working on similar issues and drawing similar conclusions but largely conducting research in isolation from one another, thus never representing a true paradigm.

4. Coil-and-scrape technology was part of the technological repertoire of potters in the Silver Creek and other Mogollon communities in which Pinto Polychrome first appears, but was not used to finish pottery in many of the other areas it was adopted in, such as the San Pedro valley.

## REFERENCES

Borck, Lewis, and Barbara J. Mills. 2017. "Approaching an Archaeology of Choice: Consumption, Resistance, and Religion in the Prehispanic Southwest." In *Foreign Objects: Rethinking Indigenous Consumption in American Archaeology*, ed. Craig N. Cipolla, 29–43. Tucson: University of Arizona Press.

Borgatti, Stephen P., and P. C. Foster. 2003. "The Network Paradigm in Organizational Research: A Review and Typology." *Journal of Management* 29(6):991–1013. https://doi .org/10.1016/S0149-2063(03)00087-4.

Burt, Ronald S. 1987. "Social Contagion and Innovation: Cohesion vs. Structural Equivalence." *American Journal of Sociology* 92(6):1287–1335. https://doi.org/10 .1086/228667.

Centola, Damon, and Michael Macy. 2007. "Complex Contagions and the Weakness of Long Ties." *American Journal of Sociology* 113(3):702–734. https://doi.org/10.1086 /521848.

Chami, Felix. 2007. "Diffusion in the Studies of the African Past: Reflections from New Archaeological Findings." *African Archaeological Review* 24(1–2):1–14. https://doi .org/10.1007/s10437-007-9012-y.

Clark, Jeffery J., and Patrick D. Lyons, eds. 2012. *Mounds and Migrants: Late Prehistoric Archaeology of the Lower San Pedro River Valley*. Arizona. Anthropological Papers No. 45. Tucson, AZ: Center for Desert Archaeology.

Collar, Anna. 2007. "Network Theory and Religious Innovation." *Mediterranean Historical Review* 22(1):149–162. https://doi.org/10.1080/09518960701539372.

Collar, Anna, Fiona Coward, Tom Brughmans, and Barbara J. Mills. 2015. "Networks in Archaeology: Phenomena, Abstraction, Representation." *Journal of Archaeological Method and Theory* 22(1):1–32. https://doi.org/10.1007/s10816-014-9235-6.

Cowan, Robin. 2006. "Network Models of Innovation and Knowledge Diffusion." In *Clusters, Networks, and Innovation*, ed. Stefano Breschi and Franco Malerba, 29–53. Oxford, UK: Oxford University Press.

Crown, Patricia L. 1994. *Ceramics and Ideology: Salado Polychrome Pottery*. Albuquerque: University of New Mexico Press.

Fenn, Thomas R., Barbara J. Mills, and Maren Hopkins. 2006. "The Social Contexts of Glaze Paint Ceramic Production and Consumption in the Silver Creek Area." In *The Social Life of Pots: Glaze Wares and Cultural Dynamics in the Southwest, AD 1250–1680*, ed. Judith A. Habicht-Mauche, Suzanne L. Eckert, and Deborah L. Huntley, 60–85. Tucson: University of Arizona Press.

Freeman, Leslie. 1978. "Centrality in Social Networks Conceptual Clarification." *Social Networks* 1(3):215–239. https://doi.org/10.1016/0378-8733(78)90021-7.

Fritsch, Michael, and Martina Kauffeld-Monz. 2008. "The Impact of Network Structure on Knowledge Transfer: An Application of Social Network Analysis in the Context of Regional Innovation Networks." *Jena Economic Research Papers* No. 2008 36:3.

Granovetter, Mark S. 1973. "The Strength of Weak Ties." *American Journal of Sociology* 78(6):1360–1380. https://doi.org/10.1086/225469.

Granovetter, Mark S. 1983. "The Strength of Weak Ties: A Network Theory Revisited." *Sociological Theory* 1:201–233. https://doi.org/10.2307/202051.

Granovetter, Mark S. 1992. "Problems of Explanation in Economic Sociology." In *Networks and Organizations: Structure, Form, and Action*, ed. N. Nohria and R. G. Eccles, 25–56. Cambridge, MA: Harvard Business School Press.

Hägerstrand, Thor. 1967. *Innovation Diffusion as a Spatial Process*. Chicago: University of Chicago Press.

Hegmon, Michelle. 2003. "Setting Theoretical Egos Aside: Issues and Theory in North American Archaeology." *American Antiquity* 68(2):213–243. https://doi.org/10.2307/3557078.

Hegmon, Michelle, and Stephanie Kulow. 2005. "Painting as Agency, Style as Structure: Innovations in Mimbres Pottery Designs from Southwest New Mexico." *Journal of Archaeological Method and Theory* 12(4):313–334. https://doi.org/10.1007/s10816-005-8451-5.

Heib, Louis. 1993. "Elsie Clews Parsons in the Southwest." In *Hidden Scholars: Women Anthropologists and the Native American Southwest*, ed. Nancy J. Parezo, 63–75. Albuquerque: University of New Mexico Press.

Kandler, Anne, and Fabio Caccioli. 2016. "Networks, Homophily, and the Diffusion of Innovations." In *The Connected Past: Challenges to Network Studies of the Past*, ed. Tom Brughmans, Anna Collar, and Fiona Coward, 175–198. Oxford, UK: Oxford University Press.

Killick, David. 2015. "Invention and Innovation in African Iron Smelting Technologies." *Cambridge Archaeological Journal* 25(1):307–319. https://doi.org/10.1017/S0959774314001176.

Lazarsfeld, P. F., and Robert K. Merton. 1954. "Friendship as Social Process." In *Freedom and Control in Modern Society*, ed. M. Berger, T. Abel, and C. Page, 18–66. New York: Van Nostrand.

Lyons, Patrick D., and Jeffery J. Clark. 2012. "A Community of Practice in Diaspora: The Rise and Demise of Roosevelt Red Ware." In *Potters and Communities of Practice: Glaze Paint and Polychrome Pottery in the American Southwest AD 1200–1700*, ed. L. S. Cordell and J. A. Habicht-Mauche, 19–33. Anthropological Papers of the University of Arizona No. 75. Tucson: University of Arizona Press.

Lyons, Patrick D., J. Brett Hill, and Jeffery J. Clark. 2011. "Irrigation Communities and Communities in Diaspora." In *Movement, Connectivity, and Landscape Change in the Ancient Southwest*, ed. Margaret C. Nelson and Colleen Strawhacker, 375–402. Boulder: University Press of Colorado.

Lyons, Patrick D., and Alexander J. Lindsay. 2006. "Perforated Plates and the Salado Phenomenon." *Kiva* 72(1):5–54. https://doi.org/10.1179/kiv.2006.72.1.001.

McGuire, Randall H. 2011. "Pueblo Religion and the Mesoamerican Connection." In *Religious Transformation in the Late Pre-Hispanic Pueblo World*, ed. Donna M. Glowacki and Scott Van Keuren, 23–49. Tucson: University of Arizona Press.

McPherson, J. M., L. Smith-Lovin, and J. Cook. 2001. "Birds of a Feather: Homophily in Social Networks." *Annual Review of Sociology* 27(1):415–444. https://doi.org/10.1146/annurev.soc.27.1.415.

Mills, Barbara J. 2007. "Performing the Feast: Visual Display and Suprahousehold Commensalism in the Puebloan Southwest." *American Antiquity* 72(2):210–239. https://doi.org/10.2307/40035812.

Mills, Barbara J. 2016. "Communities of Consumption: Cuisines as Networks of Situated Practice." In *Knowledge in Motion: Constellations of Learning across Time and Place*, ed. Andrew P. Roddick and Ann B. Stahl, 248–270. Tucson: University of Arizona Press.

Mills, Barbara J., Jeffery J. Clark, and Matthew Peeples. 2016. "Migration, Skill, and the Transformation of Social Networks in the Pre-Hispanic Southwest." *Economic Anthropology* 3:203–215.

Mills, Barbara J., Jeffery J. Clark, Matthew Peeples, W. Randall Haas Jr., John M. Roberts Jr., Brett Hill, Deborah L. Huntley, Lewis Borck, Ronald L. Breiger, Aaron Clauset, and M. Steven Shackley. 2013. "The Transformation of Social Networks in the Late Prehispanic U.S. Southwest." *Proceedings of the National Academy of Sciences* 110(15):5785–5790.

Mills, Barbara J., Sarah A. Herr, Susan L. Stinson, and Daniela Triadan. 1999. "Ceramic Production and Distribution." In *Living on the Edge of the Rim: Excavations and Analysis of the Silver Creek Archaeological Research Project 1993–1998*. Arizona State Museum Archaeological Series 192. Tucson: University of Arizona.

Mills, Barbara J., Matthew Peeples, Jeffery Clark, and John M. Roberts, Jr. 2013. "How Migrants in Diaspora Overcame Inequality in the Late Prehispanic Southwest: A Social Network Approach." Paper presented at the 112th American Anthropological Association Annual Meeting, Chicago.

Mills, Barbara J., Matthew A. Peeples, W. Randall Haas, Lewis Borck, Jeffery J. Clark, and John M. Roberts Jr. 2015. "Multiscalar Perspectives on Social Networks in the Prehispanic Southwest." *American Antiquity* 80(1):3–24. https://doi.org/10.7183/0002-7316.79.4.3.

Mills, Barbara J., John M. Roberts, Jr., Jeffery J. Clark, William R. Haas, Jr., Deborah Huntley, Matthew A. Peeples, Lewis Borck, Susan C. Ryan, Meaghan Trowbridge, and Ronald L. Breiger. 2013. "The Dynamics of Social Networks in the Late Prehispanic US Southwest." In *Network Analysis in Archaeology: New Approaches to Regional Interaction*, ed. Carl Knappett, 181–202. Oxford, UK: Oxford University Press. https://doi.org/10.1093/acprof:oso/9780199697090.003.0008.

Montgomery, Barbara K., and J. Jefferson Reid. 1990. "An Instance of Rapid Ceramic Change in the American Southwest." *American Antiquity* 55(01):88–97. https://doi .org/10.2307/281494.

Neuzil, Anna A. 2008. *In the Aftermath of Migration: Renegotiating Ancient Identity in Southeastern Arizona.* Anthropological Papers of the University of Arizona No. 73. Tucson: University of Arizona Press.

O'Brien, Michael J., ed. 2008. *Cultural Transmission and Archaeology: Issues and Case Studies.* Washington, DC: SAA Press.

Östborn, Per, and Henrick Gerding. 2015. "The Diffusion of Fired Bricks in Hellenistic Europe: A Similarity Network Analysis." *Journal of Archaeological Method and Theory* 22(1):306–344. https://doi.org/10.1007/s10816-014-9229-4.

Peeples, Matthew A., and W. Randall Haas Jr. 2013. "Brokerage and Social Capital in the Prehispanic U.S. Southwest." *American Anthropologist* 115(2):232–247. https://doi .org/10.1111/aman.12006.

Peeples, Matthew A., and Barbara J. Mills. 2018. "Frontiers of Marginality and Mediation in the U.S. Southwest: A Social Networks Perspective." In *Life beyond Boundaries: Constructing Identity in Edge Regions of the North American Southwest,* ed. Karen G. Harry and Sarah A. Herr, 25–56. Boulder: University Press of Colorado.

Roberts, John M., Jr., Barbara J. Mills, Jeffery J. Clark, W. Randall Haas, Jr., Deborah L. Huntley, and Meaghan A. Trowbridge. 2012. "A Method for Chronological Apportioning of Ceramic Assemblages." *Journal of Archaeological Science* 39(5):1513–1520. https://doi.org/10.1016/j.jas.2011.12.022.

Rogers, Everett M. 2003. *Diffusion of Innovations.* 5th ed. New York: The Free Press.

Rogers, Everett M., and Dilip K. Bhowmik. 1970. "Homophily-Heterophily: Relational Concepts for Communication Research." *Public Opinion Quarterly* 34(4):523–538. https://doi.org/10.1086/267838.

Ryan, Bryce, and Neal C. Gross. 1943. "The Diffusion of Hybrid Seed Corn in Two Iowa Communities." *Rural Sociology* 8(March):15–24.

Stark, Miriam T., Brenda J. Bowser, and Lee Horne, eds. 2008. *Cultural Transmission and Material Culture: Breaking Down Boundaries.* Tucson: University of Arizona Press.

Stone, Tammy. 2008. "Social Innovation and Transformation during the Process of Aggregation." In *Cultural Transmission and Archaeology: Issues and Case Studies,* ed. Michael J. O'Brien, 158–163. Washington, DC: SAA Press.

Storey, Alice A., and Terry L. Jones. 2011. "Diffusionism in Archaeological Theory: The Good, the Bad, and the Ugly." In *Polynesians in the Americas: Pre-Columbian Contacts with the New World,* ed. Terry L. Jones, Alice A. Storey, Elizabeth A. Matisoo-Smith, and José Miguel Ramírez-Aliaga, 7–24. Walnut Creek, CA: AltaMira Press.

Tarde, Gabriel. 1903. *The Laws of Imitation.* Translated from the French, Second Edition, by Elsie Clews Parsons. New York, NY: Henry Holt and Company.

Valente, Thomas W. 1998. "Social Network Thresholds in the Diffusion of Innovations." *Social Networks* 19:60–89.

Valente, Thomas W. 2005. "Network Models and Methods for Studying the Diffusion of Innovations." In *Models and Methods in Social Network Analysis*, ed. Peter J. Carrington, John Scott, and Stanley Wasserman, 98–116. Cambridge, UK: Cambridge University Press. https://doi.org/10.1017/CBO9780511811395.006.

Valente, Thomas, and Raquel Myers. 2010. "The Messenger is the Medium: Communication and Diffusion Principles in the Process of Behavior Change." Mexico: Universidad de Colima. *Estudios sobre las Culturas Contemporaneas* 16 31):249–276.

Van der Leeuw, Sander, and Robin Torrence, eds. 1989. *What's New? A Closer Look at the Process of Innovation*. London: Unwin, Hyman.

VanPool, Todd L., and Chet Savage. 2010. "War, Women, and Religion: The Spread of Salado Polychrome in the American Southwest." In *Innovation in Cultural Systems: Contributions from Evolutionary Anthropology*, ed. Michael J. O'Brien and Stephen J. Shennan, 251–266. Cambridge, MA: MIT Press.

Vint, James, and Barbara J. Mills. 2016. "Niches, Networks, and the Pathways to the Forager to Farmer Transition in the U.S. Southwest/Northwest Mexico." In *The Origins of Food Production,* Los Orígenes de la Producción de Alimentos, ed. Nuria Sanz, 264–281. Mexico City: UNESCO.

Wasserman, Stanley, and Katherine Faust. 1997 [1994]. *Social Network Analysis: Methods and Applications*. Reprint with corrections. Cambridge, UK: Cambridge University Press. https://doi.org/10.1017/CBO9780511815478.

Watts, Duncan J. 2002. "A Simple Model of Global Cascades on Random Networks." *Proceedings of the National Academy of Sciences of the United States of America* 99(9):5766–5771. https://doi.org/10.1073/pnas.082090499.

Watts, Duncan J. 2003. *Six Degrees: The Science of a Connected Age*. New York: Norton.

Watts, Duncan J., and P. S. Dodds. 2007. "Influentials, Networks, and Public Opinion Formation." *Journal of Consumer Research* 34(4):441–458. https://doi.org/10.1086/518527.

Zedeño, Maria Nieves. 1994. *Sourcing Prehistoric Ceramics at Chodistaas Pueblo, Arizona*. Anthropological Papers of the University of Arizona No. 58. Tucson: University of Arizona Press.

# 4

# There and Back Again

KELLEY A. HAYS-GILPIN, DENNIS A. GILPIN,
SUZANNE L. ECKERT, JOHN A. WARE, DAVID A. PHILLIPS JR.,
HAYWARD H. FRANKLIN, AND JEAN H. BALLAGH

This chapter explores the possibility that sodalities, largely voluntary organizations whose membership crosscuts kin groups, could have played influential roles in migration and diffusion. It examines how corporate-group migration versus sodality "diffusion" interpretations might affect our reconstruction of a proposed example of migration in the Puebloan Southwest, the "Hopis" at Pottery Mound.

Based largely on (1) similarities in kiva architecture and murals, (2) a higher concentration of imported Hopi yellow ware pottery at Pottery Mound than at other Rio Grande pueblo sites, and (3) a lack of Rio Grande Glaze Ware pottery in sites on the Hopi Mesas, Hibben (1975), Crotty (1995, 2007), Eckert (2007; chapter 6, this volume), and others have hypothesized that a Hopi population migrated to Pottery Mound. In this scenario, a coherent corporate group moved from Hopi to Pottery Mound in much the same manner as a group of migrants from the Kayenta region moved south to establish an enclave in Point of Pines Pueblo in the Mogollon highlands of southeastern Arizona in Emil Haury's (1958) migration model. Research in the lower Rio Puerco of east-central New

Mexico—including Eckert's (2007, 2008) and Franklin's (2007) independent analyses of pottery from a stratigraphic test unit at Pottery Mound (see also Cordell, Eckert, and Franklin 2008), Ballagh and Phillips's (2014) study of ceremonial rooms, and David Phillips, Hayward Franklin, and Jean Ballagh's (Phillips, Franklin, and Ballagh n.d.; Franklin 2014) study of Hopi yellow ware distribution at Pottery Mound—contribute to understanding this possible Hopi migration. Eckert's work suggests that this migration occurred during the early 1400s, and Phillips et al.'s work suggests the migrants formed an enclave within the community. Several of the lines of evidence (kivas, kiva murals, pottery, and the Sikyatki style—a distinctive complicated, asymmetrical style dominated by bird and feather imagery) for a Hopi migration to Pottery Mound have ritual connotations. We examine the possible role of ritual sodalities in the hypothesized Hopi migration. We look at ethnographic accounts of how sodalities and ritual practices have spread among Pueblos as recorded in recent times. We critique the idea that the Sikyatki style developed at Hopi and spread by migration to Pottery Mound, and present a hypothetical alternative scenario in which ritual specialists could have influenced the spread of the Sikyatki style (Watson Smith's 1952 mural layout group III), and a related but distinct figurative style (Smith's 1952 mural layout groups I and II) with probable origins in the Rio Grande, in murals and pottery between the Hopi Mesas and Pottery Mound.

We discuss the nature of interaction and migration in the Pueblo world during the era in which Pottery Mound was occupied (AD 1375–1475), and critique the idea that Hopi identity had crystallized at this time. By *identity* we mean overtly expressed but potentially fluid social roles that include but are not limited to "ethnicity" (see Eckert, chapter 6, this volume). Identities include expressions of belonging to a kin group, a community, a place, or a region, and to one or more ritual organizations such as sodalities that crosscut kinship and community. These may be widespread and discontinuously distributed. When people cross ethnic boundaries, they may change their identity in doing so, and may express more than one identity in different social contexts.

We consider the evidence for interaction between Pottery Mound and villages on the Hopi Mesas. We focus on kiva murals, textiles, and pottery. Evidence suggests that the Sikyatki style did not originate on the Hopi Mesas and diffuse to Pottery Mound. Instead, we explore two additional possibilities. First, the Sikyatki style in murals may have originated at Pottery Mound and diffused to the Hopi Mesas, where migrants (or returning migrants) painted it on the walls of kivas at Awat'ovi. The Sikyatki style in pottery may well have originated on the Hopi Mesas (Hays-Gilpin and LeBlanc 2007:113–115), perhaps derived in part from Fourmile Polychrome, which was produced from the Upper Little Colorado River valley to Silver Creek, and in part from mural and painted textile styles originating at Pottery Mound. Sikyatki style (design schemata) appears on pottery, textiles, and murals (different media). The contemporaneous, but more naturalistic and figurative, Rio Grande mural and petroglyph style probably originated in the Rio Grande (Schaafsma 2007b) and diffused west to the Hopi Mesas, possibly carried by traveling sodality initiates, as immigrants or returning migrants. Alternatively, the Sikyatki and Rio Grande styles might have developed simultaneously in both areas, as a result of frequent interaction that produced shared, but not homogeneous, ritual practices.

## ETHNOGRAPHY

Historic accounts describe Pueblos recruiting ritual specialists from other communities to enhance their leader's (or faction's) own prestige, as well as to aid the entire community with promoting crop growth and bringing rain, good health, success in hunting and war, and so forth. For example, a Zuni migrant brought the Tsakwayna (formerly spelled "Chakwena") katsina to Laguna Pueblo "under the sponsorship of a local faction" (Ellis 1979:445, 447). In the Laguna Break of the late nineteenth century, Laguna traditionalists, including the leaders of most of the important medicine societies and of the Katsina society (including the Tsakwayna katsina), left Old Laguna in a factional dispute and headed toward Sandia Pueblo. Isleta seized the chance to augment its own ritual program, and promised the Lagunas land in exchange for pledging that the Katsina paraphernalia would never leave Isleta. The Lagunas agreed. Even though some Laguna practitioners eventually returned to Mesita, near Laguna, the head of the Katsina society had to stay at Isleta to care for the katsinas. Many Lagunas intermarried with Isletas. Isleta still has a council called the Laguna Fathers, representing the society leaders from Laguna (Ellis 1979:448; Parsons 1932:348–357). In this case, high-status leaders traveled to reside elsewhere, some temporarily and some permanently. Ethnographers also have recorded numerous accounts of community members traveling to another village to be initiated into a sodality that had died out at home, in order to bring it back home and "replant" the ceremony. Following the ceremonial vacuum left in Laguna after the "break," a Laguna Antelope clansman went to Acoma for installation rituals so he could serve as Katsina Father at Laguna (Ellis 1979:448). These transfers of ritual knowledge, authority, personnel, and paraphernalia are not just recent phenomena in the Pueblo world. When Awat'ovi was destroyed during the winter of 1700–1701, some ritual specialists were spared in order to transfer their ceremonies to neighboring Hopi villages (Whiteley 2002). Other examples include the diffusion of bear medicine societies from the Rio Grande Keresans to the Tewa and beyond; the spread of Keresan clowns along similar lines; and the spread of Tanoan moieties to the Rio Grande Keresans and then to the Towa (see Fox 1967; Hill 1982; Lange 1959; Ortiz 1969; Parsons 1939; Ware 2014:64–66; Ware and Blinman 2000; White 1930, 1932, 1942).

**FIGURE 4.1.** *Sikyatki-style pottery. A: Sikyatki Polychrome jar, Hopi Mesas. (Courtesy of the Museum of Northern Arizona. © 2017. Catalog number A–5900. Photo by Gene Balzer.) B: Pottery Mound Polychrome bowl from Pottery Mound. (After Eckert 2007:figure 4.3b. Courtesy of Suzanne Eckert.)*

In considering the how and why of diffusion, with or without small-scale or short-term migration, we explore how ritual practices, information, and technologies move from one place to another. In our brief examples, *individuals* traveled to obtain ritual training in ceremonies, and *groups* traveled for a variety of reasons, but in the process would have given or received ritual knowledge and initiation. In *most* historic Pueblo examples, individuals went to a sodality's original community to be trained and initiated, and then went back home to either establish or join an existing chapter of the sodality there. Historic Pueblo sodalities are collectives, and training is not a master–apprentice relationship the way Navajo rituals are transmitted, for example. Individuals, not groups, usually went to other Pueblos for training.

## SIKYATKI AND FIGURATIVE MURAL AND POTTERY STYLES

To develop our hypothetical example of archaeological evidence for diffusion of patterns of practice in the archaeological record via sodalities, we focus on two mural and pottery styles that appeared suddenly and perhaps simultaneously in the 1400s in several large Pueblo communities in the Hopi, Zuni, and Rio Grande regions. Flamboyant, asymmetric Sikyatki-style imagery seems to refer to a sky-world of abstract birds, particularly macaws and eagles, as well as flowers, spattered paint, and—sometimes—katsinas (Hays-Gilpin 2013; Hays-Gilpin and LeBlanc 2007) (figure 4.1). The figurative style, which we call the *Rio Grande style*, due to its resemblance to Rio Grande–style rock art, emphasizes depictions of ritual practitioners or personages dressed in elaborate textiles, with shields, weapons, ritual paraphernalia, and animals (Schaafsma 2007b) (figure 4.2). Although both styles include depictions of birds, katsinas, and flowers, the styles of rendering and composition and the ranges of colors used differ. We

**FIGURE 4.2.** *Rio Grande–style figures in Awat'ovi and Pottery Mound murals. A: Reproduction of figurative painting, Awat'ovi, Room 788. (© President and Fellows of Harvard University, Peabody Museum of Archaeology and Ethnology, PM#39–97–10/23108C.) B: Reproduction of figurative mural, Pottery Mound, Kiva 2 layer 4, west wall. (Courtesy of the Maxwell Museum of Anthropology, University of New Mexico.)*

propose that each style represents membership in ritual sodalities that crosscut kin and community membership, and that had responsibility for particular artistic techniques, styles, and ritual practices.

## THE POST-1300 PUEBLO WORLD

Settlement-pattern maps generated by Hill and others (2004:figure 3; Wilcox et al. 2007) show that prior to about AD 1300, settlement was fairly continuous across the Southwest. After 1300, discontinuous settlement clusters began to form, and by 1450 the clusters of pueblos observed by Spanish explorers in 1540 had formed. Even as settlement clusters were beginning to differentiate into areas that later became the Hopi, Zuni, Acoma, and Rio Grande pueblos, regional interaction and multiethnic communities persisted, as exemplified by the pueblos on Antelope Mesa, the easternmost of the Hopi Mesas. There, Kawàyka'a may have begun as a Keresan-speaking pueblo in what we think of now as Hopi territory, and according to oral tradition Awat'ovi was a place where many languages were spoken. Prior to the arrival of the Spaniards, then, at least some settlement clusters (e.g., Antelope Mesa) and even individual pueblos (e.g., Point of Pines, Hawikku, and Pottery Mound) comprised multi-ethnic populations. Throughout the Spanish colonial period, migrations across ethnic boundaries continued, with Rio Grande peoples moving to the Hopi Mesas and some then moving back to the Rio Grande; people from the Hopi Mesas moving to Zuni in times of famine; Rio Grande peoples joining the Navajos; and so forth. Laguna is the classic multiethnic pueblo. The original founding population, according to Ellis and others, consisted of Rio Grande Keresans and "some disgruntled Acomas" (Ellis 1979:438).

## HOPI, AWAT'OVI, AND ANTELOPE MESA

Fewkes (1898, 1919) originally defined the Sikyatki style based on his excavations at the site of Sikyatki, at the foot of First Mesa near present-day Polacca village. Since then, the style has been considered "Hopi," one of the assumptions we examine here.

The most extensive excavations in the Hopi area were conducted by the 1935–1939 Awatovi Expedition of the Harvard Peabody Museum (Montgomery et al. 1949; Smith 1952). The Awatovi Expedition worked on Antelope Mesa, east of First Mesa (and therefore closer to Zuni, Acoma, Pottery Mound, and the Rio Grande pueblos than the other Hopi Mesas). The Awatovi Expedition conducted most of its excavations at the site of Awat'ovi, which was founded about AD 1200 and destroyed by warriors from some of the other Hopi villages in the winter of 1700–1701. The Awatovi Expedition excavated about 750 rooms, including 22 kivas, out of the estimated 5,000 rooms at the site. The Awatovi Expedition also excavated 12 kivas at the nearby site of Kawàyka'a, occupied from about AD 1250 to 1500 (Smith 1972). Excavations at these sites indicated that manufacture of yellowware began about AD 1325, and manufacture of early Sikyatki Polychrome (relatively simple red-and-black designs on a yellow ground) began about AD 1375, but manufacture of Sikyatki-style (flamboyant asymmetrical designs dominated by bird and feather imagery) late Sikyatki Polychrome began between about AD 1400 and 1450 (Hays-Gilpin 2013). Throughout the time Sikyatki Polychrome was manufactured, Jeddito Black-on-yellow pottery remained more common than

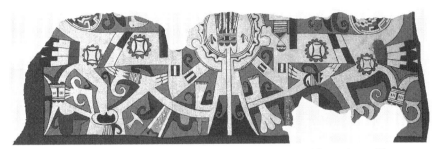

**FIGURE 4.3.** *Sikyatki-style mural, Test 14 Room 3, Awat'ovi. (For additional mural layers in this room see Hays-Gilpin and LeBlanc 2017:118.) (© President and Fellows of Harvard University, Peabody Museum of Archaeology and Ethnology, PM#39–97–10/23061C.)*

Sikyatki Polychrome, and Sikyatki Polychrome never constituted more than about 20 percent of the pottery in any ceramic assemblage.

The kivas excavated at Awat'ovi ranged in date from about AD 1275 to 1700, and most had walls painted with murals ranging from simple geometric designs to the elaborate Sikyatki-style design layout and figurative Rio Grande–style compositions. The Sikyatki-style murals, though, were found in only one kiva (Test 14 Room 3), which was probably constructed about AD 1415 and used until AD 1500 (figure 4.3). As discussed below, the Sikyatki-style murals in this kiva were probably created early in the use of this kiva, before about AD 1450.

## POTTERY MOUND

Pottery Mound is on the lower Rio Puerco of the East, southwest of Albuquerque. Eckert and Cordell (2004 :38–39, 168) date Pottery Mound to AD 1350–1475, though some evidence indicates that a few people may have lived there or visited as late as the early 1500s. The site consisted of about 300 rooms organized around two to four plazas. Frank Hibben excavated two large so-called moiety kivas (one rectangular and one circular, possibly not contemporaneous) and 11 of the 14 rectangular kivas, many with mural paintings. Linda Cordell conducted additional work, including a stratigraphic test, at the site in 1979 (Cordell et al. 2008). In more recent research Crotty (1995, 2007), Eckert (2007, 2008), Franklin (2007, 2014) Schaafsma (2007a), and Ballagh and Phillips (Ballagh 2011; Ballagh and Phillips 2006, 2008, 2014) have reported data from previous excavations and presented new analyses and interpretations. For example, analysis of Pottery Mound non-kiva architecture strongly suggests the presence of rooms like those used by historical Pueblo sodalities for storage of ceremonial paraphernalia and for ritual practices in non-kiva contexts (Ballagh and Phillips 2014).

Many researchers have interpreted Sikyatki-style kiva murals and Hopi yellow ware pottery (Jeddito Yellow Ware and Awatovi Yellow Ware) at Pottery Mound as evidence for resident migrants from the Hopi Mesas. Helen Crotty's dissertation (1995) detailed parallels in mural paintings between Pottery Mound and sites on Antelope Mesa, just east of the present-day Hopi villages; she suggests a "Hopi" enclave at Pottery Mound. More recently, Eckert (2007, 2008) examined the only available stratigraphic pottery sequence at Pueblo Mound and proposed that a generation or two after the initial founding of the village, migrants from the Zuni area and then migrants from the Hopi area took up residence. Of the stylistic similarities between Hopi and Pottery Mound ceramic and mural paintings, Eckert (2008:53) wrote: "Although pottery designs can be copied, it seems unlikely that Hopi designs would be heavily incorporated into ceremonial paintings without their associated ritual knowledge. Ritual specialists living at Pottery Mound could have learned aspects of the Hopi ritual system in a variety of ways: they may have traveled to the Hopi region to learn ceremonies or they may have been immigrants who originally learned their knowledge on the Hopi Mesas or they may have been taught ritual practice by an immigrant from the Hopi area." Evidence for these scenarios is the key idea we want to explore—and invert.

## MURALS AND TEXTILES

In arguing that Hopi people were present at Pottery Mound, Crotty (2007) and others have focused on similarities in imagery, layout, and color schemes in kiva murals at Pottery Mound and Antelope Mesa villages. Our chronologies are not fine-grained enough to discern which set of murals is earliest. Some kivas at Pottery Mound, Awat'ovi, and Kawàyka'a were contemporaneous in the early to mid-1400s. Distribution of the Sikyatki style in murals and pottery is not similar, however. Most of the excavated painted kivas at Pottery Mound have Sikyatki-style murals. Many Pottery Mound murals clearly depict textiles painted in Sikyatki-style designs—these appear as blankets hung on walls, and as kilts worn by dancers and ritual personages (Hays-Gilpin and LeBlanc 2007; Webster 2007) (figure 4.4). Oddly, Sikyatki-style murals are in fact very rare on the Hopi Mesas—one kiva at Awat'ovi has two Sikyatki-style mural layers. Possibly the most elaborate and portable expression of this style was textiles, which did not survive in the archaeological record. Textiles are one of the most powerful indicators of social identities. Although many Pueblo textile traditions are complex and many techniques are difficult to replicate without hands-on instruction, here we probably see depictions of painted designs on plainweave kilts and blankets, a technique that might easily be emulated. Webster (2007) notes that Pottery Mound and Antelope Mesa murals depict textiles derived from two different technological traditions: a northern tradition emphasizing elaborately painted plainweave textiles, and a southern tradition emphasizing weft-wrapped openwork. The latter are not techniques that could be emulated simply by looking at a complete textile or a picture of one in a mural.

**FIGURE 4.4.** *Textiles depicted in a mural from Pottery Mound, Kiva 16, Layer 11, west wall. (Courtesy of the Maxwell Museum of Anthropology, University of New Mexico.)*

The techniques and decorative patterns are complicated, and would have been learned by apprenticeship. Loom holes in kiva floors suggest men wove textiles in kivas, and depiction of textiles in painted murals shows how they were displayed and danced in ritual contexts.

The most frequent mural style at Pottery Mound, Awat'ovi, and Kawàyka'a comprises figurative depictions of ritual practitioners wearing elaborate and diverse textiles (see figure 4.2). The figures' shapes and facial features resemble Rio Grande–style rock art (Schaafsma 2007b). This style appears relatively late in the Hopi pottery and mural sequence, and the Awat'ovi and Kawàyka'a murals in this style could postdate the founding of Pottery Mound. Contemporary Hopi consultants identify the hair and clothing styles depicted in the murals as characteristic of "New Mexico Pueblos," not Hopi (Hays-Gilpin and LeBlanc 2007:124–125). They further identify the residents of Kawàyka'a as "Laguna people" and those of Awat'ovi as coming from many places and speaking many languages, including "Laguna." Published Hopi oral histories suggest that residents of these and other Antelope Mesa sites might have spoken Keresan, Towa (Jemez), or both (Courlander 1971:268; Ellis 1967:40; Hargrave 1935:23; Hays-Gilpin and LeBlanc 2007:124, 126–127; Stephen 1936:578, 714; Whiteley 2002; Yava 1978). And they might not have identified themselves as kin groups or residential groups, so much as members of sodalities drawn from many kin groups (see especially Bernardini 2005; Ware 2014). We therefore propose several alternative scenarios to a migration from the Hopi Mesas to Pottery Mound. First, the movement might have gone the other way. Second, if people did come from the Hopi Mesas to Pottery Mound, they were not necessarily "Hopi" in the sense we use that term today, as a distinct identity associated with the Hopi Mesas, or as people who speak primarily the Hopi language. Third, simultaneous interactions in both directions might have cross-fertilized a diverse ritual, stylistic, and linguistic repertoire that was broadly shared yet not homogeneously distributed.

Whichever directions the mural styles spread, those who painted them understood the intricacies of obtaining, preparing, and applying a wide variety of paints to plaster surfaces as well as the elaborate iconographies and styles appropriate to ritual sodalities. The possible connection between craft specialization and ritual specialization, or access to specialized ritual knowledge, fits with both ethnographic and archaeological evidence for earlier traditions of painted wood and basketry (Lewis 2002; Odegaard and Hays-Gilpin 2002).

## POTTERY

The asymmetric Sikyatki-style bird/feather designs appear on a small amount of locally produced Pottery Mound Polychrome at Pottery Mound (Eckert 2007) as well as on a larger proportion of late Sikyatki Polychrome pottery on the Hopi Mesas. Sikyatki style appears after 1400 on the Hopi Mesas and is not the only or dominant pottery style of the 1400s and later. The frequencies and contexts of uses of Sikyatki style in the two areas are reversed: more Sikyatki-style murals at Pottery Mound, more Sikyatki-style pottery at Hopi sites (Hays-Gilpin and LeBlanc 2007). And we have no Sikyatki-*style* Sikyatki Polychrome at Pottery Mound, only earlier styles, such as the late-1300s Jeddito style (see Hays-Gilpin 2013:figure 2 for style sequence of Sikyatki Polychrome). The possible gendering of this distribution—if pottery was painted by women and murals by men—would be worth exploring in the contexts of family-level migrations and individual male travel for ritual sodality training.

Based on her examination of pottery from Cordell's 1979 test excavation at Pottery Mound, Eckert (2007:66; 2008) hypothesizes that a fairly substantial group from the Western Pueblos, probably the Acoma-Zuni area, entered Pottery Mound about a generation after the village was founded in the early or mid-1300s. This has now been verified through an analysis of surface-collected pottery, which demonstrated that the most numerous ceramic imports at Pottery Mound derive from the Acoma-Zuni tradition (Kwakina Polychrome and Pinnawa Glaze-on-white) (Franklin 2014). Immigrant potters from the Acoma-Zuni area made local copies of their own glaze-paint types, using local red clay and basalt temper, while decorating with the contrasting white and red slips characteristic of their tradition. A population from the Hopi area may have arrived a decade or two later, and resided there in the late 1300s to early 1400s. Immigrant potters apparently tried making pottery without temper, then switched to local igneous rock temper. Eckert (2007) proposes that immigrant potters from both areas adopted red-slipped bowl exteriors to emulate local conventions, but decorated bowl interiors with styles common in their home communities, thus signaling community incorporation on the "public" surface, and segmentation or distinct migration histories and identities on the "private" surface. These ceramic expressions of incorporation and segmentation persist another 70–80 years, until the end of the site's occupation peak in the mid-1400s.

In the Rio Grande region, almost all of the yellowware pottery imported from the Hopi Mesas occurs within one site, Pottery Mound (Phillips et al. n.d.). Moreover, the surface distribution of yellowware sherds at Pottery Mound is nonrandom. Hopi painted pottery (Jeddito Yellow Ware) and Hopi utility pottery (Awatovi Yellow Ware) were most highly concentrated in the southwest quadrant of the site, including on the South Midden (Franklin 2014; Phillips et al. n.d.). Phillips and his colleagues tentatively interpret this distribution as evidence for a small enclave of immigrants from the Hopi area in the southwest part of the site. If the immigrants were there to obtain ritual information to take home after temporary residence (or less likely, to plant a sodality from Hopi), this residential pattern might suggest that sodalities imported to or from Antelope Mesa were tied to a kin-linked unit, as is the case for Hopi and Zuni sodalities today. Alternatively, this pattern could represent people from Pottery Mound who traveled to Hopi and returned with a preference for yellowware utility vessels as well as new knowledge and ritual practices.

Either way, what we know from ethnography is that multiethnic communities are important in Southwest history, especially after 1300, and that ritual knowledge and practices were exchanged widely within and among multiethnic communities. In the *ethnographic* record we rarely see residential groups going to other pueblos to obtain ritual training, but rather individuals. Yet in the 1400s, we do have evidence for more mobility than we see in the post-contact period. We wonder whether ritual exchange might have been a reason for some residential mobility in the past; certainly, ritual diffusion was greatly enhanced by mobility.

## AWAT'OVI AND POTTERY MOUND

The six kivas excavated in Test 14 at Awat'ovi are at the eastern base of the Western Mound, the earliest part of the site, which was occupied from about AD 1200 to 1375. The earliest kiva excavated in Test 14 (Room 10) was probably constructed about AD 1325 and used until about 1400. The later five kivas were built above the early kiva after about AD 1400. One of these kivas was vacated after about 1430, three were in use until about 1500, and one was in use until about 1525. Throughout the Sikyatki period at Awat'ovi (1375–1629), most construction was to the east and north of the Western Mound, so these kivas would have been at the southwestern edge of the occupied village (thus not in the expected position to house men serving as guardians of the village).

Smith (1952:144) wrote, "whether the paintings of this style were done in imitation of pottery decoration and were therefore primarily of only aesthetic

**TABLE 4.1.** Estimates of the dates of Sikyatki-style murals in Awat'ovi Test 14 Room 3

| Wall and Mural Design Number | Total Murals on Wall | Approximate Date of Mural (AD) |
|---|---|---|
| Front A Design 4 | 4 | 1415–1435 |
| Front B Design 9 | 15 | 1450 |
| Front B Design 11 | 15 | 1445 |
| Front B Design 11x | 15 | 1445 |
| Right Design 12 | 19 | 1450 |
| Right Design 16 | 19 | 1435 |
| Right Design 18 | 19 | 1420 |

Note: for distribution of Sikyatki-style murals at Pottery Mound, see Crotty (2007:91) and Hays-Gilpin and LeBlanc (2007:121).

significance, or whether the pottery was inspired by a mural art that was inherently ceremonial and ritualistic in symbolism can hardly be determined. Probably it is of no significance, since the two things are correlative expressions of the same artistic and cultural inspiration." Smith thus thought the two developed at approximately the same time.

It appears to us that the Sikyatki-style murals at Awat'ovi were painted in the first half of the fifteenth century. The earliest kiva in Test 14 (Room 10) was built in the 1300s and remained in use perhaps into the early 1400s. Gilpin estimates that the Test 14 Room 10 kiva was built after AD 1325 and was used until about 1400. The other five kivas in Test 14 were built after 1400. Beams in the fill of Kiva 2 dated from 1372 to 1429, so that kiva fell into disuse and was filled after 1429, suggesting that it was in use from about 1400 to 1430. Construction of Kiva 3 involved remodeling of Kiva 2, so Kiva 3 must have been built between 1400 and 1430 (so ca. 1415), and Kiva 3 continued in use until about 1500. The number of painted plaster layers in Kiva 3 ranged from four to 19. The murals were numbered in the order in which they were exposed by the archaeologists, so the higher numbers are earlier than the lower numbers. The Sikyatki-style murals were among the earliest half of those murals (see table 4.1), and probably dated between about 1415 and 1450.

At Awat'ovi, the painting of Sikyatki-style murals was restricted to one kiva (and thus likely to one sodality and one controlling clan). This kiva's members evidently stopped painting Sikyatki-style murals after AD 1450, and the sodality must have died out or moved on by about AD 1500. The "Hopi" migrants to Pottery Mound circa 1405–1435 migrated about the time that the Sikyatki style became common in pottery made on the Hopi Mesas, and about the time that the earliest Sikyatki-style murals were painted at Awat'ovi (see table 4.2). These migrants may have included one or more members of the sodality that was starting to paint Sikyatki-style murals on the wall of their kiva. The Sikyatki

**TABLE 4.2.** Comparative chronologies of Awat'ovi and Pottery Mound.

| Awat'ovi (inferences from architecture and ceramics) | Pottery Mound (inferences from ceramics*) |
|---|---|
| 1200 Awat'ovi founded | |
| 1275 Orangeware | |
| 1325 Yellowware | |
| 1375 Sikyatki Polychrome (but not in Sikyatki style) | 1350 Pottery Mound founded 1375 or later: Pottery Mound Polychrome (1375–1450+) with Sikyatki-style designs may begin |
| 1400–1450 Sikyatki style on pottery | 1395–1415 Zuni-Acoma migration to Pottery Mound |
| 1415–1450 Estimated date of Sikyatki-style murals in Test 14 Room 3 | 1405–1435 Hopi migration to Pottery Mound |
| 1500–1630 Late Sikyatki style on pottery | 1475–1500? Pottery Mound vacated |
| 1629 Mission established | |

*Note that the Pottery Mound kiva murals cannot (yet) be correlated with the ceramic chronology.

style in murals was expressed more broadly at Pottery Mound than at Awat'ovi. By the time Pottery Mound was depopulated by or soon after AD 1500, the kiva users at Awat'ovi were no longer painting Sikyatki-style kiva murals, but Sikyatki-style polychrome pottery was widely produced and sometimes traded. Late Sikyatki Polychrome moved from the Hopi Mesas to Zuni and Rio Grande sites in small amounts; Matsaki Polychrome made at Zuni was rarely traded far. Rio Grande Glaze Ware, interestingly, appears rarely at Zuni and never on the Hopi Mesas. The alternative scenario, which seems more likely to us now, is that the Sikyatki style in murals developed at Pottery Mound circa AD 1375–1425 and was transplanted to Hopi, where it remained restricted to a single sodality or clan, which stopped painting Sikyatki-style murals circa AD 1450 and closed its kiva by 1500. The Sikyatki style in pottery, though, flourished at Hopi (and also at Zuni). The group that traveled from Pottery Mound to Hopi to introduce the Sikyatki style in mural and pottery painting (and the sodality and ceremony) could have returned to Pottery Mound as the "Hopi" migrants of 1405–1435. The key is dating the Sikyatki-style murals at Pottery Mound—a task that may be impossible without new excavations at the site. On the other hand, while archaeologists want to trace the movement of styles, ideas, and people from east to west or west to east, the reality might have been a constant cross-fertilization, a pervasive and simultaneous cosmopolitanism.

In addition, any explanation of the modes and media of style transmission should take into account that in the two Sikyatki-style murals at Awat'ovi the design radiates out from a center, like on a pot, suggesting that it derives from pottery (although Smith [1952] seems to think of mural and pottery designs as developing more or less simultaneously). And as Hays-Gilpin and LeBlanc (2007) suggest, painted textiles could have been the primary mode of transmission of the Sikyatki style, and they are depicted *as textiles* at Pottery Mound but not at Awat'ovi.

## CONCLUSIONS

Pottery Mound and Antelope Mesa villages may have housed sodalities with mural styles and techniques, textiles, and ritual paraphernalia that we see unevenly distributed throughout the late Pueblo IV world. One or more of these proposed sodalities codified some of the design elements and ritual practices that we eventually see expressed in the greater Pueblo area in a few mural paintings and a fairly high proportion of painted pottery at Hopi, in many murals and a small proportion of pottery at Pottery Mound, and likely in painted textiles throughout the Pueblo world. This Sikyatki-style imagery also appears at Zuni in the late 1400s in the form of Matsaki Polychrome. Because murals at Pottery Mound depict Sikyatki-style textiles, it is probable that textiles were one medium of transmission, while distinctive ritual dress—worn in ritual performance and depicted in ritual spaces and signaling membership in a sodality—might have been one mode of transmission. The presence of this imagery in various media may reflect the presence of peoples from the Hopi Mesas, although not necessarily Hopi speakers, at Pottery Mound and Zuni.

When we consider patterns in Pueblo ethnography, one scenario seems most likely: one or more residential groups from some Western Pueblos took up residence in Pottery Mound for at least a generation, during which time some of its members were initiated into local sodalities. These immigrants might have been low-status families without land or ceremonies. While residing at Pottery Mound, these migrants or their descendants learned local ceremonies. Some descendants moved back home, bringing along their newly acquired ritual and technological knowledge, transplanting it to their Western Pueblo home communities—where they might have been welcomed back in part because they had a new ritual to contribute.

These scenarios are difficult to sort out archaeologically, but we suggest that multiple working hypotheses be examined with multiple lines of evidence—including not just style and iconography but details of technical practice; utility ware as well as decorated pottery; textiles and other fiber perishables (or at least pictures of them); rock art; architecture; and oral traditions. We advocate a more complicated view of the diffusion-migration spectrum, including (1) scales and types of social groups involved in social interaction (household, kin group, village, sodality, region—and communities of technological practice); (2) the objectives of both the migrants and their host communities; (3) intentional acts of negotiation, conflict, and cooperation by social groups; and (4) a multivalent, relational approach to social identities, which were and are complex and chang-ing. All of these combined in the forging of the Sikyatki style—and other distinct but related styles and ritual complexes—and their development and roles in cre-ating internally diverse community identities at Pottery Mound and villages of the Hopi Mesas.

What does this chapter contribute to the understanding of diffusion? It examines a situation in which assumptions about diffusion, migration, ethnic identity, and cultural contact and change have been implicit and unexamined. It demonstrates the importance of dated events. It incorporates historical contin-gency and agency in which cultural changes are accomplished by people who have multivalent identities and objectives (even if archaeologists do not know their names or specific objectives). It is nonutilitarian in that symbols, ideology, and styles of visual expression are at least as important as economic and politi-cal relationships.

In summary, various types of social groups and social arrangements are involved in migration and diffusion. Almost all the donor and host communities involved in Haury's Kayenta migration were smaller and less complicated than the later communities involved in exchanging people, ceremonies, and technolo-gies that resulted in in the development of the Sikyatki style and the formation of Hopi identity—and other Pueblo identities. Identities evolve; Hopi identity specifically was forming and changing during the time Pottery Mound was occu-pied, and could have incorporated migrants, sodality initiates, or ceremonies or any combination of the three that came from Pottery Mound as well as those that were "home grown."

## REFERENCES

Ballagh, Jean H. 2011. *Pottery Mound: The 1957 Field Season*. Maxwell Museum Technical Series No. 10. Albuquerque: Maxwell Museum of Anthropology, University of New Mexico.

Ballagh, Jean H., and David A. Phillips, Jr. 2006. *Pottery Mound: The 1954 Field Season*. Maxwell Museum Technical Series No. 2. Albuquerque: Maxwell Museum of Anthropology, University of New Mexico.

Ballagh, Jean J., and David A. Phillips, Jr. 2008. *Pottery Mound: The 1955 Field Season*. Maxwell Museum Technical Series No. 8. Albuquerque: Maxwell Museum of Anthropology.

Ballagh, Jean J., and David A. Phillips, Jr. 2014. "'Ceremonial Rooms' at Pottery Mound, New Mexico." *Kiva* 79(4):405–427. https://doi.org/10.1179/0023194014Z.00000000032.

Bernardini, Wesley. 2005. *Hopi Oral Tradition and the Archaeology of Identity*. Tucson: University of Arizona Press.

Cordell, Linda S., Suzanne L. Eckert, and Hayward H. Franklin. 2008. "Profiles at Pottery Mound: The 1979 UNM Test Units." In *Chasing Chaco and the Southwest: Papers in Honor of Frances Joan Mathien*, ed. Regge N. Wiseman, Thomas C. O'Laughlin, Cordelia T. Snow, and Cathy Travis, 67–82. Papers of the Archaeological Society of New Mexico No. 34. Albuquerque: Archaeological Society of New Mexico.

Courlander, Harold. 1971. *The Fourth World of the Hopis*. New York: Crown Publishers.

Crotty, Helen. 1995. *Anasazi Mural Art of the Pueblo IV Period, A.D. 1300–1600: Influences, Selective Adaptation, and Cultural Diversity in the Prehistoric Southwest*. Ann Arbor: University Microfilms.

Crotty, Helen. 2007. "Western Pueblo Influences and Integration in the Pottery Mound Painted Kivas." In *New Perspectives on Pottery Mound Pueblo*, ed. Polly Schaafsma, 85–107. Albuquerque: University of New Mexico Press.

Eckert, Suzanne. 2007. "Understanding the Dynamics of Segregation and Incorporation at Pottery Mound through Analysis of Glaze-Decorated Bowls." In *New Perspectives on Pottery Mound Pueblo*, ed. Polly Schaafsma, 55–73. Albuquerque: University of New Mexico Press.

Eckert, Suzanne. 2008. *Pottery and Practice: The Expression of Identity at Pottery Mound and Hummingbird Pueblo*. Albuquerque: University of New Mexico Press.

Eckert, Suzanne L., and Linda S. Cordell. 2004. "Pueblo IV Community Formation in the Central Rio Grande Valley: The Albuquerque, Cochiti, and Lower Rio Puerco Districts." In *The Protohistoric Pueblo World, A.D. 1275–1600*, ed. E. C. Adams and A. I. Duff, 35–42. Tucson: University of Arizona Press.

Ellis, Florence Hawley. 1967. "Where Did the Pueblo People Come from?" *El Palacio* 74(3):35–43.

Ellis, Florence Hawley. 1979. "Laguna Pueblo." In *Handbook of North American Indians*, Volume 9, *Southwest*, ed. Alphonso Ortiz, 438–449. Washington, DC: Smithsonian Institution.

Fewkes, Jesse Walter. 1898. "Archaeological Expedition to Northern Arizona in 1895." In *17th Annual Report of the Bureau of American Ethnology 1897–1898*, Part 2, 519–742. Washington, DC: US Government Printing Office.

Fewkes, Jesse Walter. 1919. "Designs on Prehistoric Hopi Pottery." In *33rd Annual Report of the Bureau of American Ethnology*, 207–284. Washington, DC: US Government Printing Office.

Fox, Robin. 1967. *The Keresan Bridge: A Problem in Pueblo Ethnology*. London: Althone.

Franklin, Hayward H. 2007. *The Pottery of Pottery Mound: A Study of the 1979 UNM Field School Collection, Part 1, Typology and Chronology*. Maxwell Museum Technical Series No. 5. Albuquerque: Maxwell Museum of Anthropology, University of New Mexico.

Franklin, Hayward H. 2014. *The Pottery of Pottery Mound: Ceramic Surface Sampling, External Trade, and Internal Diversity*. Maxwell Museum Technical Series No. 22. Albuquerque: Maxwell Museum of Anthropology, University of New Mexico.

Hargrave, Lyndon Lane. 1935. "The Jeddito Valley and the First Pueblo Towns in Arizona Visited by Europeans." *Museum Notes* 8(4):17–23.

Haury, Emil. 1958. "Evidence at Point of Pines for a Prehistoric Migration from Northern Arizona." In *Migrations in New World Culture History*, ed. Raymond H. Thompson, 1–8. University of Arizona Bulletin 29(2). Social Science Bulletin 27. Tucson: University of Arizona.

Hays-Gilpin, Kelley. 2013. "Sikyatki Polychrome: Style, Iconography, Cross-Media Comparisons, and Organization of Production." *Kiva* 79(2):175–204. https://doi.org/10.1179/0023194014Z.00000000019.

Hays-Gilpin, Kelley, and Steven A. LeBlanc. 2007. "Sikyatki Style in Regional Context." In *New Perspectives on Pottery Mound Pueblo*, ed. Polly Schaafsma, 109–135. Albuquerque: University of New Mexico Press.

Hibben, Frank. 1975. *Kiva Art of the Anasazi at Pottery Mound*. Las Vegas, NV: KC Publications.

Hill, J. Brett, Jeffery J. Clark, William H. Doelle, and Patrick D. Lyons. 2004. "Prehistoric Demography in the Southwest: Migration, Coalescence, and Hohokam Population Decline." *American Antiquity* 69(4):689–716. https://doi.org/10.2307/4128444.

Hill, W. W. 1982. *An Ethnography of Santa Clara Pueblo, New Mexico*. Edited and annotated by C. H. Lange. Albuquerque: University of New Mexico Press.

Lange, Charles H. 1959. *Cochiti: A New Mexico Pueblo, Past and Present*. Albuquerque: University of New Mexico Press.

Lewis, Candace K. 2002. "Knowledge is Power: Pigments, Painted Artifacts, and Chacoan Ritual Leaders." Unpublished MA thesis, Department of Anthropology, Northern Arizona University, Flagstaff.

Montgomery, Ross Gordon, Watson Smith, and John Otis Brew. 1949. *Franciscan Awatovi: The Excavation and Conjectural Reconstruction of a 17th-Century Spanish Mission Establishment at a Hopi Indian Town in Northeastern Arizona*. Report of the Awatovi Expedition No. 3, Papers of the Peabody Museum of American Archaeology and Ethnology. Vol. 36. Cambridge, MA: Harvard University.

Odegaard, Nancy, and Kelley Hays-Gilpin. 2002. "Technology of the Sacred: Painted Basketry in the Southwest." In *Traditions, Transitions, and Technologies: Themes in Southwestern Archaeology*, ed. Sarah H. Schlanger, 307–331. Boulder: University Press of Colorado.

Ortiz, Alfonso. 1969. *The Tewa World: Space, Time, Being, and Becoming in a Pueblo Society*. Chicago: University of Chicago Press.

Parsons, Elsie Clews. 1932. *Isleta, New Mexico*. 47th Annual Report of the Bureau of American Ethnology, 1929–1930, 193–466. Washington, DC: United States Government Printing Office.

Parsons, Elsie Clews. 1939. *Pueblo Indian Religion*. 2 vols. Chicago: University of Chicago Press.

Phillips, David, HaywardFranklin, and JeanBallagh. n.d. "Deciphering the Hopi Presence at Pottery Mound." Manuscript on file at the Maxwell Museum of Anthropology, University of New Mexico, Albuquerque.

Phillips, David A., Jr., Hayward H. Franklin, Jean Ballagh, Kelley Hays-Gilpin, and Dennis Gilpin. n.d. "Examining the Hopi presence at Pottery Mound, New Mexico." Ms. on file at the Maxwell Museum of Anthropology, University of New Mexico, Albuquerque.

Schaafsma, Polly, ed. 2007a. *New Perspectives on Pottery Mound Pueblo*. Albuquerque: University of New Mexico Press.

Schaafsma, Polly. 2007b. "The Pottery Mound Murals and Rock Art." In *New Perspectives on Pottery Mound Pueblo*, ed. Polly Schaafsma, 137–166. Albuquerque: University of New Mexico Press.

Smith, Watson. 1952. *Kiva Mural Decorations at Awatovi and Kawaika-a, with a Survey of Other Wall Paintings in the Pueblo Southwest*. Reports of the Awatovi Expedition No. 5. Papers of the Peabody Museum of Archaeology and Ethnology. Cambridge, MA: Harvard University.

Smith, Watson. 1972. *Prehistoric Kivas of Antelope Mesa, Northeastern Arizona:* Reports of the Awatovi Expedition No. 9. Papers of the Peabody Museum of Archaeology and Ethnology 39(1). Cambridge, MA: Peabody Museum, Harvard University.

Stephen, Alexander M. 1936. *Hopi Journal of Alexander M. Stephen*, ed. Elsie C. Parsons. 2 vols. New York: Columbia University Contributions to Anthropology No. 23.

Ware, John A. 2014. *A Pueblo Social History: Kinship, Sodality, and Community in the Northern Southwest*. Santa Fe, NM: School for Advanced Research Press.

Ware, John A., and Eric Blinman. 2000. "Cultural Collapse and Reorganization: Origin and Spread of Pueblo Ritual Sodalities." In *The Archaeology of Regional Interaction, Religion, Warfare, and Exchange across the American Southwest and Beyond*, ed. Michelle Hegmon, 381–409. Proceedings of the 1996 Southwest Symposium. Boulder: University Press of Colorado.

Webster, Laurie D. 2007. "Ritual Costuming at Pottery Mound: The Pottery Mound Textiles in Regional Perspective." In *New Perspectives on Pottery Mound Pueblo*, ed. Polly Schaafsma, 167–206. Albuquerque: University of New Mexico Press.

White, Leslie. 1930. "A Comparative Study of Pueblo Medicine Societies." In *Proceedings of the 23rd International Congress of Americanists*, 604–619. New York.

White, Leslie. 1932. *The Pueblo of San Felipe*. Memoirs No. 38. Menasha, WI: American Anthropological Association.

White, Leslie. 1942. *The Pueblo of Santa Ana, New Mexico*. Memoirs No. 60. Menasha, WI: American Anthropological Association.

Whiteley, Peter. 2002. "Re-imagining Awat'ovi." In *Archaeology of the Pueblo Revolt*, ed. Robert W. Preucel, 147–166. Albuquerque: University of New Mexico Press.

Wilcox, David R., David A. Gregory, and J. Brett Hill. 2007. "Zuni in the Puebloan and Southwestern Worlds." In *Zuni Origins: Toward a New Synthesis of Southwestern Archaeology*, ed. David A. Gregory and David R. Wilcox, 165–209. Tucson: University of Arizona Press.

Yava, Albert. 1978. *Big Falling Snow: A Tewa-Hopi Indian's Life and Times and the History and Traditions of His People*. Edited and Annotated by Harold Courlander. New York: Crown Publishers.

# 5

# The Diffusion of Scarlet Macaws and Mesoamerican Motifs into the Mimbres Region

PATRICIA A. GILMAN, MARC THOMPSON,
AND KRISTINA C. WYCKOFF

How did scarlet macaws from at least 1,300 km away and Mesoamerican Hero Twins mythology reach people living in the Mimbres region of southwestern New Mexico during the Classic period (AD 1000–1130)? Why did those people accept the macaws and the Hero Twins saga as useful and meaningful? Did they diffuse, with people passing the macaws and knowledge about the saga to their neighbors to the north? Did this kind of movement continue until the macaws and the saga reached the Mimbres region? Perhaps traders brought the birds and the ideas north with them—as in Di Peso's (1974) pochteca model. Or, as we will propose, did people who were not traders for economic goods go south to acquire macaws and ritual knowledge for spiritual purposes and for personal or family power? The initial movement of people could also have started in Mesoamerica. We suggest that the latter model accounts for more of the facts, and that the diffusion of ideas and goods occurred through purposeful long-distance acquisition (Gilman et al. 2014). That is, those with the macaws and the knowledge of the Hero Twins saga actively taught willing students how to care for the macaws physically and ritually and simultaneously imparted the Hero

DOI: 10.5876/9781607327356.c005

Twins saga. As we note below, this is a rather specific kind of diffusion, and most Southwestern archaeologists have rarely considered it.

Southwestern archaeologists have examined the movement of goods over long distances and have commonly used economic exchange models to explain these behaviors (Di Peso 1974; Reyman 1995; Riley 2005). Such models generally involve traders from hierarchical societies to the south bringing goods and ideas north. Less well documented or understood are additional means of obtaining exotic materials, including diffusion and long-distance acquisition for other than economic reasons.

Most archaeologists working in the Mimbres region have not addressed the question of how people obtained scarlet macaws, but Creel and McKusick (1994:517) briefly posited down-the-line trade, in which goods passed from one group to the next, who in turn traded them to the next group. Di Peso (1974) presented his pochteca model to explain Mesoamerican items and influence at the later site of Paquimé (AD 1150/1200–1450/1475), and that model also could be applied to the Mimbres macaws. Both of these explanations are economic, and neither accounts for the contemporary presence of Hero Twin iconography on Mimbres Classic Black-on-white pottery. We suggest a more complete answer. This includes direct, long-distance acquisition by people from the Mimbres region. Alternatively, people from Mexico's Gulf Coast, the closest source of scarlet macaws in the tropical forests of Mexico, could have brought the birds and ideology surrounding their use to the Mimbres region. Both would have involved long-distance journeys in which the same individuals traveled the entire round-trip distance across many social, political, and linguistic boundaries, and between hierarchical and nonhierarchical groups.

We (Gilman et al. 2014) have suggested that Mimbres direct, long-distance acquisition rather than down-the-line trade of scarlet macaws and Hero Twins mythology brought them north from Mexico to the Mimbres Valley. This occurred during the Classic period when people had moved from pit structures to pueblos and after they were no longer using great kivas. Following Helms (1991) and Carr (2005), we proposed that people were making these trips for specific purposes that did not necessarily include trade. Rather, the expeditions may have involved individuals or small groups of people traveling to a center of learning to obtain spiritual/religious knowledge and prestige (Carr 2005:581). Acquisition of scarlet macaws and knowledge of Hero Twins mythology would likely require extensive training because both are equated with powerful mythic and magical prowess. Since macaws that are raised in captivity bond to a single person, the person who would carry a macaw north might need to be present at its birth to raise it to an age for travel, an argument against down-the-line trade. Helms (1991) indicates that people make journeys to and from mythic and dangerous realms, that is, those beyond their everyday experience, for religious skills and understandings that they can bring back to their group, simultaneously enhancing their own power in this realm. In this regard, a Hopi epic recounts the travels of Tiyo into Mesoamerica and perhaps South America (Hopkins 2012). When Tiyo returned to Hopi, he had obtained the knowledge of the snake dance and a Snake Maiden wife. Given that acquisition of macaws and ideology may have been the objects of religious quests, it seems unlikely that down-the-line trade was involved or that economic exchange was the primary reason to procure scarlet macaws or the Hero Twins ideology. Whalen (2013) has recently suggested a similar argument for the acquisition and use of marine shell at Paquimé, a much larger site south of the Mimbres in Chihuahua. He posits that shell was not gathered or stored for trade, and that the economic value of the shell was minimal.

Here, we build on our previous argument (Gilman et al. 2014) and provide new research investigating how much of the Hero Twins saga is represented on Mimbres Classic Black-on-white bowls to consider the kind of diffusion that might have occurred. Our results show that the vast majority of the saga is portrayed. The completeness of the Hero Twins saga represented on Classic Black-on-white pottery hints that people with a full understanding of the story taught it to those living in the Mimbres region. That is, people in the Mimbres had more than isolated elements of the saga, as one might expect had it been passed from one person to the next over a long distance. Both this and the peculiarities of transporting scarlet macaws suggest that direct long-distance acquisition of macaws and the Hero Twins mythology was most likely.

Trigger (1968:27–29) defines *diffusion* as the process by which an invention gains social acceptance, and he says that diffusion occurs when an idea or an item is transmitted from person to person. Successful diffusion is the result of evaluation, during which individuals and groups come to appreciate and accept an idea or item. People make that evaluation in terms of their needs and beliefs. Since one group's needs and values are different from those in other cultures, Trigger suggests that diffusion is less likely between cultures. However, this is precisely what we argue occurred with the transfer of macaws and the Hero Twins saga into the Mimbres region. Trigger notes that it is rare that all attributes move together, and so our case study is one of the rare examples of this, given that the scarlet macaws and the Hero Twins saga appear apparently simultaneously in the Mimbres region during the Classic period. Our example suggests that there are many different ways an idea or item can be transmitted from person to person, and that some of those do not fit parts of Trigger's definition. Although our example is of diffusion through long-distance acquisition, we indeed have an item (scarlet macaws) and a set of ideas (the Hero Twins saga) that are transmitted from person to person, with each person evaluating these in terms of his or her needs and beliefs.

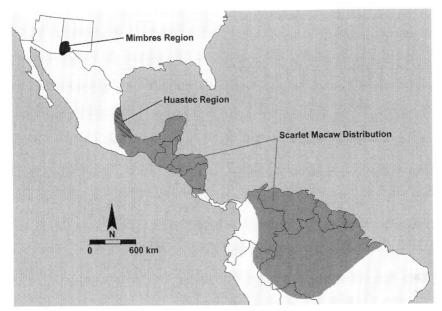

**FIGURE 5.1.** *The Mimbres and Huastec regions and the distribution of scarlet macaws. (Map by Will G. Russell.)*

In this chapter, we first discuss that which diffused into the Mimbres: scarlet macaws and the Hero Twins narrative as represented by motifs on Mimbres Classic Black-on-white pottery. In terms of the latter, we are particularly interested in whether the entire saga is depicted on the pottery. We next consider the contexts (why) and the mechanisms (how) of diffusion and the reasons that Mimbres people might have sought and accepted these items. We end by discussing the continuation of scarlet macaws and Hero Twins mythology in later Southwestern groups.

## WHAT DIFFUSED?

By their physical presence in Mimbres sites, we know that scarlet macaws were moved north from their homelands in the tropical forests of southern Mexico (figure 5.1), an indication of connectivity between the two areas and of interactions among various people at either end and along the way. Some investigators (Brody 2004:174–175; Carr 1979; Hegmon and Nelson 2007; Moulard 1984: 113, 115, 124; Schaafsma 1999; Shafer 1995; 2003:212) have previously suggested that Mimbres painters represented the Hero Twins on Mimbres black-on-white pottery, but beyond that of Thompson (1994, 1999), there has been little in-depth analysis of this possibility. Here we provide the background for considering these diffusions into regions far to the north of their original locales, and why scarlet macaws and the Hero Twins saga might have been chosen among all the things that people could have brought north or collected along the way.

## Scarlet Macaws

Scarlet macaws are magnificent in stature (approximately 85 cm in length), brilliantly colored, and, like many other parrots, capable of replicating human speech, all of which may have made them appealing creatures to be brought north. As its name suggests, the scarlet macaw has bright red feathers with light blue, dark blue, yellow, and sometimes green feathers along the rump and wing coverts. Scarlet macaws seem to be the largest, reddest birds available in Mesoamerica and Central America (Forshaw 2010). We know that the color red has important symbolic value for Southwestern Native American groups, and that the color had symbolic value for protohistoric groups in the region. Red is associated with the south and with the sun whose home is in the south (Di Peso 1974:555; Hays-Gilpin et al. 2010:129; Livesay 2013:88–89; Thompson and Brown 2006). It is likely that the symbolic value of the color red also existed prehistorically for people residing in this region. Although whether scarlet macaws speak or not depends on several factors, including personality and temperament, the fact that some of them do speak must have augmented their supernatural properties.

Of the 20 exotic macaws and parrots recovered from Mimbres archaeological contexts, seven are definitely scarlet macaws, and eight others, currently identified only to the macaw genus (*Ara*), could be. The very presence of scarlet macaw skeletal remains in Mimbres archaeological sites indicates long-distance interaction between people in the Mimbres region and groups to the south. The context of these remains is more important still. Although people in the Hohokam region to the west obtained macaws, or at least portions of macaws, as early as AD 200–600, these remains were minimal and fragmented (Haury 1976:376; Lekson 2008:138; Woosley and McIntyre 1996:284). In Mimbres archaeological sites (Creel and McKusick 1994), macaw and parrot skeletal remains were relatively complete, with the consistent exception of the left wing. Most these birds were also approximately one year old, having just grown their long, prominent, red tail feathers, which are half the length of the bird. The consistency in the age at death, a regularity that becomes even clearer when one considers the southwestern United States and northwestern Mexico as a whole, points to their use as sacrificial victims, perhaps at the vernal (spring) equinox (McKusick 2001:72). Thus, the use of macaws in ritual rather than for economic purposes is likely.

Except for the scarlet macaw at the Wind Mountain site west of the Mimbres Valley, macaws and thick-billed parrots were buried intramurally at Mimbres sites (Gilman et al. 2014:table 2). They were virtually the only avian species to receive such distinction. Even turkeys, hawks, and eagles, which were also afforded special funerary treatment by people in the Mimbres region, were

**FIGURE 5.2.** *This painting shows the left-handed Twin in his feminine guise and the right-handed masculine Twin with three immature macaws (with short tail feathers), staffs, a ring, and a basket. (MimPIDD 3641 from the Mattocks site [Brody 2004:plate 2; Nesbitt 1931:plate 23B]. Illustration by Will G. Russell.)*

interred extramurally. An exception is one turkey burial at the Lake Roberts site in a deposit placed above the floor of a Classic-period kiva when it was filled (Roth 2007). Macaws and parrots from other Mimbres sites were included in at least five human interments (Gilman et al. 2014:table 2), including adults of both sexes and children of various ages, and in ceremonial spaces (Room 73 at Galaz; Anyon and LeBlanc 1984:130). At the Galaz site, all macaws and parrots were recovered from the north room cluster. Two newly fledged scarlet macaws, two thick-billed parrots, and an elaborate newly fledged military macaw burial, which included 82 turquoise beads near the skull and 500 shell beads around the legs, were all recovered from Room 73, the "Kiva of the Parrot." Again, the distinction of these birds from other local, large birds, and their burial with people and in ceremonial contexts suggests noneconomic purposes.

Macaws were important enough to people living in the Mimbres region to paint them on Classic Black-on-white pottery (Gilman et al. 2014). For example, on MimPIDD 3641 (figure 5.2; appendix 5.1) from the Mattocks site, we see the Hero Twins using staffs, a ring, and a basket with three immature (denoted by their short tail feathers) macaws. It may be important that images of the Hero Twins saga and scarlet macaws came together to the Mimbres Valley, at least temporally. The motif of macaws does not appear in the written version of the Hero Twins saga that is part of the Mesoamerican creation story recounted in the *Popol Vuh* (Tedlock 1985:105–160), and people in the Mimbres seem to have added that to their version of the saga.

The remains of scarlet macaws found in Mimbres sites are generally between 10 and 13 months, and this consistency in their age at death, combined with the special burial treatments they were afforded, suggests that they were sacrificial victims and would have been transported alive into the Mimbres region. Specialized knowledge would have been necessary to acquire and then care for a young macaw on such a journey. Modern macaw breeders and research regarding these birds indicate that macaws would have required frequent hand feeding and that their food needs to be heated to match the temperature of their bodies (Gilman et al. 2014:102). The special care required would have made diffusion of these birds via down-the-line trade challenging. This is especially so because macaws that are raised in captivity bond to a single individual and are notoriously difficult to handle by any other person (Greiser 1995:501).

### The Hero Twins Saga and Mimbres Iconography

We (Gilman et al. 2014) have previously argued that the iconography on Mimbres Classic Black-on-white pottery includes images from the Hero Twins saga. Further, we suggested that people from the Mimbres region obtained this story at the same time and place that they obtained scarlet macaws—in the Huastec region on the east coast of Mexico (figure 5.1), the farthest north that scarlet macaws occur naturally (Forshaw 2010:178). The Huastec people spoke and speak Mayan, making our use of the *Popol Vuh*, which was translated from K'iche' Mayan, particularly relevant. Although we suggest that the Hero Twins saga diffused to the Mimbres region during the Classic period (AD 1000–1130), the painting style is clearly not that of the Huasteca or any other region of Mexico.

The *Popol Vuh* (literally "Council Book") manifests a broad mythological pattern and widely shared cosmology describing ideological concepts, such as duality, found throughout the indigenous Americas. Written in K'iche' Mayan using Spanish characters, it was completed between 1550 and 1555 in Santa Cruz del Quiché, Guatemala, by an unknown Maya scribe. The original manuscript, now lost, was discovered between 1701 and 1704 by Dominican friar Francisco Ximénez in Chichicastenango, Guatemala. Ximénez transcribed the K'iche' text and produced a Spanish translation. A copy of the Ximénez manuscript is preserved in the Newberry Library, Chicago. The Hero Twins saga in parts 2 and 3 of the alphabetic *Popol Vuh* (Tedlock 1985:89–160) provides a large and intact portion of the precepts and context necessary for consistent cross-cultural interpretation of cognate myths, motifs, elements, and related iconographic depictions. This tale is at once metaphorical, allegorical, and metonymical with simultaneous and multiple levels of fused symbolism. Graphic images of the Hero Twins and other *dramatis personae* are depicted in Mesoamerican media as early as AD 1 on Late Preclassic sculpture, as well as on Late Classic (AD 600–900) Maya ceramics, and in Late Postclassic (AD 1200–1519) Maya and Central Mexican codices.

For our analysis here, we focused on images from the Hero Twins saga that came north. We examined a sample of Mimbres Classic Black-on-white bowls for evidence of the completeness or incompleteness of the Hero Twins saga representation. Specifically, we looked for images of the birth, adventures, death, and apotheosis of the Hero Twins as the sun and the moon. For our analysis of Mimbres Classic Black-on-white bowls, we used the images archived in the Mimbres Pottery Image Digital Database (MimPIDD), which includes digital pictures of more than 10,000 whole or partial Mimbres vessels. Darrell Creel also sent us pictures of Classic representations from the Old Town and Pruitt sites that are not yet in MimPIDD. We used only bowls with site-specific pro-veniences (appendix 5.1) to address the issue of potential modern overpainting of the designs. The 13 sites we used are in or near the Mimbres River Valley, and they have the largest collections of Classic Black-on-white pottery, although some of the collections are quite small.

There are 100 representational vessels in our sample from 13 sites that could reference the Hero Twins. We chose to be conservative in our analysis and selected images that are clearly from the saga, including the Twins, the mon-ster Seven Macaw, his first son Zipakna, bats, macaws/parrots, twin fish, and fishmen (appendix 5.1). Although macaws and parrots are not prominent in the *Popol Vuh*, we counted vessels with those images, because at least some of them likely represent exotic scarlet macaws. Other motifs, especially paired figures in general along with fish, deer, and pronghorn, could refer to the Hero Twins less obviously. Even such a conservative approach presents little doubt that the saga is embedded in Mimbres iconography. People did modify the Hero Twins saga to fit their cosmological understandings, since the imagery is in the unique Mimbres style and not clearly related to anything in Mesoamerica.

In terms of all representational paintings on Classic Black-on-white bowls from our sample of 13 sites, they compose between 27 and 38 percent (average is 34%) of all Classic painted bowls from the sites in the MimPIDD (table 5.1). In an earlier analysis using only about half the current vessels from all sites then in the Mimbres Archive, Thompson (1999:94) calculated that representationals are about 28 percent of all Classic painted bowls. The two figures correspond well, suggesting that our sample from the 13 sites is an accurate representation of all such bowls. Thompson calculated that the proportion of painted bowls with motifs definitely attributable to the Hero Twins saga is 12 percent of all

**TABLE 5.1.** Numbers and percentages of Classic representational and Hero Twins bowls

| Site | Total Classic Bowls | Number of Classic Representational Bowls | Percentage of Classic Representationals to All Classic Bowls | Number of Hero Twins Bowls | Percentage of Hero Twins Bowls to All Classic Representationals |
|---|---|---|---|---|---|
| Swarts | 592 | 221 | 37 | 19 | 9 |
| Galaz | 578 | 207 | 36 | 25 | 12 |
| Cameron Creek | 306 | 88 | 29 | 10 | 11 |
| Mattocks | 238 | 85 | 36 | 7 | 8 |
| NAN Ranch | 178 | 66 | 37 | 12 | 18 |
| Eby | 151 | 53 | 35 | 5 | 9 |
| Old Town | 146 | 52 | 36 | 3 | 6 |
| Pruitt | 113 | 33 | 29 | 5 | 15 |
| Baca | 104 | 40 | 38 | 6 | 15 |
| Treasure Hill | 49 | 13 | 27 | 1 | 8 |
| McSherry | 46 | 15 | 33 | 2 | 13 |
| Mitchell | 36 | 11 | 31 | 2 | 18 |
| Osborn | 25 | 17 | 68* | 3 | 18 |
| Total | 2,562 | 901 | average = 34 | 100 | average = 12 |

* Purchased by Fewkes, and so representationals are probably overrepresented

representational bowls. Our sample of 13 sites provides a range of six to 18 percent (table 5.1), varying by site, with an average of 12 percent, again implying concordance between the two samples. In these conservative analyses, iconography from the Hero Twins saga is not a major percentage of all representational paintings, but images from the saga are definitely present. We do not yet know whether Hero Twins vessels have different contexts (more or less often in burials, associated with women versus men versus children, for example) or use wear than other painted bowls.

Mimbres Classic Black-on-white bowls contain the most prominent and many of the minor characters and episodes from parts 2 and 3 (Tedlock 1985:105–160) of the *Popol Vuh*. The births and deaths of the Hero Twins are in part 3 of the *Popol Vuh*, while some of their adventures are in part 2. Individual paintings follow the sequence of the main events from the Twins' birth to their apotheosis as the sun and moon. We demonstrate the presence of the characters and episodes on Mimbres pottery in the following sections, using examples from our sample of 100 bowls and following that with exemplative bowls from the MimPIDD as a whole. While the paintings on particular bowls may not be convincing in terms of representing episodes from the Hero Twins saga, the entire corpus of such paintings makes our case much stronger. As well, the contexts of the

**FIGURE 5.3.** *Birth of the younger, left-handed Twin. The baby is in the unusual position of facing forward to show that he is left-handed. (MimPIDD 9552 from the Swarts site [Brody 2004:figure 66; Cosgrove and Cosgrove 1932:plate 225F]. Illustration by Kristina C. Wyckoff.)*

items presented together on some of the narrative paintings match well with episodes in the saga. We suggest that this correspondence of some Mimbres paintings to the Hero Twins saga negates a more naturalistic explanation that the scenes and creatures in them simply depict everyday activities and animals in the Mimbres environment.

*Mimbres Depictions of the Hero Twins Saga in Part 3 of the Popol Vuh*

Xquik (Blood Woman), daughter of Blood Gatherer (one of the Lords of Death in the Underworld), is the mother of the Twins. She appears to be represented in our sample by MimPIDD 9552 (figure 5.3; appendix 5.1) from the Swarts site, which depicts the miraculous birth of the left-handed Younger Twin. This interpretation accounts for the oddity of a face-forward birth (Hegmon and Trevathan 1996), which was painted this way to show that the baby / Twin is left-handed.

We also examined representational bowls in the MimPIDD that were not from our sample for other characters and episodes from the Hero Twins saga, again to see how completely the story is painted on Classic vessels. Starting with the Twins' predecessors, Xpiyacoc and Xmucane are the grandmother and grandfather of the Twins and the mother and father of One Hunahpu and Seven Hunahpu (father and uncle of the Twins, respectively). MimPIDD 3844 (Fewkes 1923:figure 6; Thompson et al. 2014:40) seems to show the Twins and Xpiyacoc, their grandmother. MimPIDD 178 (Thompson et al. 2014:39) and MimPIDD 7967 (Thompson 2006:173; Townsend 2005:plate 14) may represent One Hunahpu and Seven Hunahpu in Mimbres pottery. One Hunahpu (Twins' father) becomes Venus as evening star, and Seven Hunahpu (Twins' uncle) becomes Venus as the morning star (Tedlock 1985:353) after their defeat by the Lords of Death. MimPIDD 178 and MimPIDD 7967 each exhibit two Venus glyphs, which are crosses with equal arms (Thompson 1994, 1999; Thompson et al. 2014). The superior Venus glyph and the figure on MimPIDD 178 represent the father of the Twins, and the left (west) Venus glyph and the figure on MimPIDD 7967 also represent the father. The lower and right Venus glyphs on each bowl represent the Twins' uncle. Both figures are in birthing positions with fish elements behind them indicating they are dead, but, like the Twins, they have been reincarnated as twin celestial bodies—the evening and morning stars.

The Twins must endure a series of tortuous tests in five underground chambers that the Lords of Death devised and that defeated their father and uncle. The first test in the House of Gloom is likely represented in our sample on MimPIDD 3496 (figure 5.4; appendix 5.1) from the Osborn site. Here, the Twins pretend to smoke with cloud blowers (tubular clay pipes). In the *Popol Vuh*, the father and uncle of the Twins smoked proffered cigars and burned torches (Tedlock 1985:112–113) and failed the test. When the Twins are offered cigars and torches, they entice fireflies to the ends of the cigars and attach macaw tail feathers to the wood torches. Thus, they appear to be smoking the cigars and burning the torches. In the morning, they return the intact cigars and torches as instructed and pass the test in the House of Gloom through trickery (Tedlock 1985:147).

The final trial is in the House of Bats, occupied by killer bats (Tedlock 1985:143). The Twins hide from the bats, but the Elder Twin becomes impatient for the dawn and with their torment. He exposes his head and is decapitated by a bat. Later, the Younger Twin retrieves his head (Tedlock 1985:147). The Bat House test of the Twins may be represented by 14 depictions of bats (appendix 5.1) in our sample. Some, like MimPIDD 4284 (figure 5.5; appendix 5.1) from the Mattocks site, have a Venus glyph on each wing, hinting at the relationship of these bats to the Hero Twins saga. *Kama zotz* (killer bat) figures prominently in both the Hero Twins saga and Classic Maya pottery. Mesoamerican images depict icons such as crossed bones on outstretched bat wings (Coe 1973:14). These depictions, like those in Mimbres bowls, typically represent the ventrum of a bat with the head turned to one side. The graphic and stylistic similarities between Maya and Mimbres bats is considerable. Depictions of bat icons on other prehistoric southwestern pottery are rare to nonexistent. There is no evidence that bats were a

FIGURE 5.4. *Twins smoking. (MimPIDD 3496 from the Osborn site [Fewkes 1914:27]. Illustration by Kristina C. Wyckoff.)*

FIGURE 5.5. *Bat with Venus symbols on wings. (MimPIDD 4284 from the Mattocks site [Gilman and LeBlanc 2017]. Illustration by Will G. Russell.)*

food source, nor is there another naturalistic explanation for their appearance in Mimbres bowls.

The episode of immolation, or trial by fire, follows the Twins' survival in the five houses and the retrieval of the Elder Twin's head during a ballgame with

**FIGURE 5.6.** *Twin on fire. (MimPIDD 2758 from the Galaz site [Anyon and LeBlanc 1984:plate 46D]. Illustration by Will G. Russell.)*

the Underworld Lords. The Twins are asked to jump over a wide stone oven. Knowing that the Lords intend to kill them, they jump into the pit, are consumed by flames, and perish. In our sample, MimPIDD 2758 (figure 5.6; appendix 5.1) from the Galaz site could represent one of the Twins jumping into the oven / fire pit prepared by the Lords of Death.

The Twins leave behind instructions that their bones are to be ground and thrown into a stygian stream. This is done, and later they reappear as "channel catfish." Fish and fishmen (combinations of humans and fish) are present on Classic Black-on-white pottery. Bowls with twin but not identical fish may represent the Twins (Tedlock 1985:149), and fishmen may show the transition the Twins make from fish to men. In our sample (appendix 5.1), there are many twin fish (e.g., MimPIDD 1149 from Cameron Creek; figure 5.7; appendix 5.1) and some fishmen (MimPIDD 2764 from Galaz; figure 5.8; appendix 5.1) and humans with fish (MimPIDD 2827 from Galaz; figure 5.9; appendix 5.1). MimPIDD 2764 may represent the transition from fish to men, especially regarding the catfish "whiskers" on the chin.

According to Powell (2000; Powell-Martí and James 2006), fish, along with birds, are the two most common figures on Classic Black-on-white pottery. About 25 percent of the fish motifs are paired, and most are depicted with leg-like appendages rather than dorsal or ventral fins. Paintings of paired fish appear to emphasize duality and, ostensibly, the Twins as fish and fishmen, through slight differences in body size, distinctive decorative elements, and color differentiation.

**FIGURE 5.7.** *Twin fish that are not identical. (MimPIDD 1149 from the Cameron Creek site [Bradfield 1931:plate 72 #38]. Illustration by Will G. Russell.)*

**FIGURE 5.8.** *Fishman. (MimPIDD 2764 from the Galaz site [Anyon and LeBlanc 1984:plate 98D; Brody 2004:figure 24]. Illlustration by Will G. Russell.)*

In other cases, paired fish initially appear to be identical, but closer examination reveals that one is larger than the other, suggesting the individual identities of the larger and smaller Twins. These depictions are not mirror images, but rather fish are depicted head to tail. These and other images of humans with fish elements, or fish behind human heads, refer to souls of the dead in the watery

**FIGURE 5.9.** *Man and fish. (MimPIDD 2827 from the Galaz site [Anyon and LeBlanc 1984:plate 87F]. Illustration by Will G. Russell.)*

Underworld. Similar images of paired fish are found on Classic Maya pottery and other Mesoamerican media (Christenson 2007:figure 50).

The Twins next appear as "vagabonds" who entertain the Lords with dances and miracles. One of the most dramatic episodes in the Hero Twins saga is the decapitation of the Elder Twin by the Younger (Tedlock 1985:153). The Younger Twin then brings the Elder Twin back to life. In our sample, MimPIDD 1604 (figure 5.10; appendix 5.1) from the Eby site shows the decapitation of the right-handed older by left-handed Younger Twin. The right arm of the prostrate brother is larger (wider) than his left arm, suggesting right-handedness. The Younger Twin holds what appears to be a rabbit stick at the end of his left arm, also implying left-handedness. A lifeline extends between the Elder Twin's body and his head, signifying that he is not really dead. Fewkes (1916:figure 68, 1923:29 and figure 13) depicts another decapitation bowl from the Mimbres region, which he described as "found in a ruin near the NAN ranch" (Fewkes 1916:538).

The Lords of Death beg to be put to death and brought back to life in the same way. The Twins obligingly kill them but fail to revive them. This is followed by the apotheosis of the Elder and Younger Twins, respectively, as the sun, for which a deer is the avatar, and the moon, for which a rabbit is the avatar. The Elder Twin appears to be represented iconically, and associated with the sun, by the image of a deer. For example, the deer avatar is shown in the central Mexican Borgia Codex (Díaz and Rodgers 1993:45; Thompson 1999:figure 5) where a deer bears a solar symbol, and a rabbit carries a lunar symbol, common

FIGURE 5.10. *Left-handed Younger Twin decapitating right-handed Elder Twin. The figure on the back of the Younger Twin may be a horned serpent, which appears very rarely on Mimbres painted pottery (MimPIDD 1604 from the Eby site [Brody 2004:figure 31]. Illustration by Kristina C. Wyckoff.)*

FIGURE 5.11. *Elder Twin apotheosizing into a deer. (MimPIDD 6186 from the Cameron Creek site [Bradfield 1931:plate 76 #380]. Illustration by Kristina C. Wyckoff.)*

motifs in Mesoamerican iconography. As with the deer and the sun, the association of rabbits with the moon is well established in both Mesoamerican and Southwestern lore (Thompson 1994:97–98).

In our sample, MimPIDD 6186 (figure 5.11; appendix 5.1) from the Cameron Creek site shows the Elder Twin becoming a deer, suggesting his apotheosis as the sun. MimPIDD 1342 (Brody 2004:figure:4; Thompson et al. 2014:43) depicts the Younger Twin with rabbit elements as an avatar for the moon. He is lateralized to the left, like the rabbit icon visible in a full moon, with a lunate body, rabbit ears and tail, and bearing a burden basket symbolic of his lunar burden. The moon is nearly always considered feminine in Mesoamerican and Southwestern mythology, and baskets are almost exclusively associated with females. Numerous other deer and rabbits on Classic Black-on-white pottery may be related to this theme, including MimPIDD 7974 (Gilman et al. 2014:100; Townsend 2005:plate 20), which shows both Twins and their individual and combined associations with the rabbit, deer, Bird of Doom, pronghorn and rabbit heads, and left and right hands.

*Mimbres Depictions of the Hero Twins Saga in Part 2*
*of the* Popol Vuh

Part 2 of the *Popol Vuh* describes other adventures and episodes of the Hero Twins saga. There are encounters with and the subsequent deaths of the monsters Seven Macaw and Zipakna (Tedlock 1985:89–101). These include references to the Twins, Seven Macaw, Chimalmat (wife of Seven Macaw and mother of both Zipakna and second son Earthquake) as well as two "grandparents." These characters and this episode appear to be represented in 20 Classic bowl motifs in our sample (appendix 5.1). The story begins with the confrontation of the Twins (MimPIDD 2702), in this case, the right-handed Twin (Gilman et al. 2014:99), with Seven Macaw, during which Seven Macaw tears off the arm of the right-handed Twin. MimPIDD 811 (Gilman et al. 2014:99) from the Baca site shows Seven Macaw depicted as a bear and the arm of right-handed Twin. MimPIDD 1199 (Gilman et al. 2014:99) and MimPIDD 3653 (figure 5.12; appendix 5.1) are both from the Mattocks site and depict the younger, left-handed Twin on the back of Seven Macaw shown as a huge bird. In the painting on MimPIDD 1199, the right-handed Twin's arm is in front of the bird's beak. On MimPIDD 3552 (Fewkes 1923:28), probably from the Old Town or Osborn site, the Twins blind Seven Macaw by poking their fingers in his eyes.

Zipakna is shown (MimPIDD 2459 from the Swarts site; Cosgrove and Cosgrove 1932:plate 230a; Gilman et al. 2014:100) carrying a mountain range— "lifting up mountains by night" (Tedlock 1985:97)—and in the bottom of a hole during a failed attempt to kill him (MimPIDD 1488 from the McSherry site; Gilman et al. 2014:100). Earthquake, second son of Seven Macaw, may be depicted in MimPIDD 2902 (figure 5.13; appendix 5.1) from the Galaz site that shows the elder, right-handed Twin shooting arrows into Seven Macaw and his two sons, all depicted as bears. This motif could summarize the demise of Seven Macaw, Zipakna, and Earthquake where the Elder Twin shoots arrows into them, "shot by Hunahpu," (Tedlock 1985:91). The Mimbres painter of this scene substituted a bow and arrows for the blowgun mentioned in the *Popol Vuh*.

**FIGURE 5.12.** *Younger Twin on back of Seven Macaw. The fish on the back of the Younger Twin may signify the death of Seven Macaw (MimPIDD 3653 from the Mattocks site [Gilman and LeBlanc 2017]. Illustration by Will G. Russell.)*

**FIGURE 5.13.** *Elder Twin killing Seven Macaw and his two sons, Zipakna and Earthquake, all represented as bears. (MimPIDD 2902 from the Galaz site [Anyon and LeBlanc 1984:plate 83E; Brody 2004:plate 1]. Illustration by Will G. Russell.)*

Although it is possible that the MimPIDD 2902 bowl simply depicts a man with a bow and arrows hunting a mother bear and two cubs, this seems unlikely considering other bowls depicting human and bearlike figures in active postures. There are at least 22 figures that appear to be bears in Mimbres bowls. Of these, several, including the bowls discussed above, retain images suggestive of episodes in the Hero Twins saga. These form a narrative sequence described in the *Popol Vuh*. This is not to say that every bearlike figure is a representation of Seven Macaw, but those with human figures conform to the story line of the Hero Twins saga and motifs described in the *Popol Vuh* and Southwestern folktales. A naturalistic paradigm does not explain the relationship among these bowls.

Seven Macaw and Zipakna are well represented in Mimbres bowls in our sample, and even Earthquake may be present. Seven Macaw is also well represented in Mesoamerican media, but Zipakna and Earthquake are not common icons there (Cortéz 1986).

## Summary

The main characters and episodes from the Hero Twins saga of the *Popol Vuh* are painted on Mimbres Classic Black-on-white bowls. The presence of the relatively complete saga on Mimbres paintings supports the idea that people, either from the Mimbres or from Mesoamerica, learned or knew the characters, episodes, and details of the story well enough to transmit it to those who painted the bowls. Further, exotic macaws are found in the Mimbres region contemporaneous with Mimbres illustrations of the Hero Twins saga. Considering the relative completeness of the saga in Mimbres illustrations combined with the evidence that exotic scarlet macaws would have been transported directly into the Mimbres region, we suggest that Mimbres individuals learned the Hero Twins saga directly and not through down-the-line transmission.

## DIFFUSION CONTEXTS AND MECHANISMS: WHY AND HOW SCARLET MACAWS AND THE HERO TWINS SAGA DIFFUSED

Travel imbued with physical and spiritual danger suggests that only a few individuals, families, or small groups were appropriate for the training required before the journey and after the goal was reached. Acquisition of powerful ideology and scarlet macaws also implies that only specific individuals would be eligible for such training, travel, and acquisition. We do not envision these individuals as traders or merchants. One of the unsolved questions with the model of trade between the Southwest and Mesoamerica is what the Mesoamericans received in exchange for their goods. So far, archaeologists have found little that is clearly from the southwestern United States or northwestern Mexico farther south in Mexico. Religious stories and items instead moved north, and we suggest that people willingly accepted the Hero Twins saga and the scarlet macaws and may in fact have purposely set out to obtain such things. That they painted both characters and episodes from the saga along with macaws on their pottery hints at willing acceptance. We also do not recognize this travel as an example of inter-elite exchange, because there is no evidence of elites in the Mimbres region during the Classic period (Gilman 1990, 2006) and because so many of the Classic Black-on-white bowls have pictures of the Hero Twins saga.

Physically and spiritually, how did people in the past, particularly people moving between the ancient Southwest and Mesoamerica, make long-distance trips that allowed for the diffusion of scarlet macaws and Hero Twins mythology? They would have walked between the Mimbres Valley and the Huastec region, the closest place with scarlet macaws, or vice versa. Such travel is hardly unique now or in the distant past. For example, Reynolds and Langlands (2011) discuss long-distance travel in England in the second half of the first millennium. They note that major linear routes in England were understood on a national scale. They also suggest that people employed large-scale mental mapping for such journeys, using the landscape as a document to be read. This mental map was a series of panoramas with way points, markers, and topography, and movement was funneled over ground amenable for travelers. Before the advent of maps, Reynolds and Langlands posit that people on journeys gained an understanding of places by communicating with land occupants and owners who spoke of the landscape in both pragmatic and symbolic terms. The use of physical mnemonics suggests to us that travelers would have been trained before the journey with respect to mental maps and to places with friendly and helpful occupants. People traveling between the Mimbres Valley and Mesoamerica or vice versa would have had similar mental maps in place before they began such dangerous trips.

Paralleling Helms's (1991) ideas about long-distance trips to liminal places that are dangerous both physically and spiritually, Reynolds and Langlands (2011) note that travelers make connections between their known landscapes and those through which they travel with respect to myths and folklore. That is, travelers read familiar cues in new landscapes, and we suggest that such cues would have been important to the essence of such journeys. These cues could have provided some comfort for familiar and spiritual safety of being surrounded by ones' own deities. Ideological cues from the homeland also became part of the mental map for the trip.

Reynolds and Langlands (2011) suggest that movement focused on landscapes amenable to travel allows for the creation of places that express power, belief, and identity that would have had meaning for all travelers, regardless of origin. Such places likely existed along the routes to, from, and through Mesoamerica and may have been elements in mental maps. Further, they observe that the long-term survival of names, including pre-Roman and Roman for rivers, hills, and distinctive landforms in England, facilitated travel. They note that rivers often have the same names along their entire courses, even though they cross cultural and political divisions. Universal names may have been a key to mental maps for long-distance travel through terrestrial and mythical landscapes.

In sum, individuals, families, or small groups who wanted, earned, or were entitled to religious and sacred experiences in exotic and dangerous places traveled to and from Mesoamerica to obtain such experiences and the powerful material items that demonstrated their new ritual knowledge. They did this for their group back home, as in the example of Tiyo, but they also gained personally from it. The "why" of such acquisition and diffusion of ideas and things is thus in the ritual rather than the economic realm. Reynolds and Langlands (2011) have discussed some of the mechanisms that might have encouraged the kinds of long-distance trips suggested here—the "how" of acquisition and diffusion.

## POST–MIMBRES CLASSIC IMPORTANCE OF SCARLET MACAWS AND HERO TWINS ICONOGRAPHY

The Mimbres Classic period and the production of Mimbres black-on-white pottery ended by AD 1130–1140 in the Mimbres Valley. Thompson (1994; Thompson and Brown 2006) has previously presented data on scarlet macaws and Hero Twins imagery suggesting post-Mimbres continuity in symbolism and the longevity of the iconography through the prehistoric, historic, and modern periods. Here we present a brief discussion of post–Mimbres Classic scarlet macaws, Hero Twins ideology, and their continuing importance.

### Scarlet Macaws

The largest concentration of scarlet macaws in the United States Southwest and the Mexican Northwest is in the Casas Grandes region of Chihuahua, specifically at the site of Paquimé (Di Peso et al. 1974; Hargrave 1970). Paquimé was at its height between AD 1150/1200 and 1450/1475, shortly after the Mimbres Classic period. There is apparent consensus that scarlet macaws were bred at Casas Grandes sites (Di Peso et al. 1974; Minnis et al. 1993; Rizo 1998), and the remains of many macaws suggest that they were sacrificed at about the time of the vernal equinox, as at sites in the United States Southwest (Hargrave 1970; McKusick 2001). Although it was once thought that people at Casas Grandes sites bred macaws for live trade or feather export, this remains an untested assumption requiring verification. Considering Whalen's (2013) study of marine shell at Paquimé, showing that people used it internally and not for trade, it is possible that macaw breeding there was also for internal use. Macaws are also depicted on Casas Grandes polychrome ceramics, including effigy vessels (VanPool and VanPool 2007). Clearly, the importance of scarlet macaws continued later in time for this Mimbres neighbor.

Between AD 1200 and 1500, scarlet macaw remains are also found at pueblos to the north (Hargrave 1970; McKusick 2001) and appear in kiva murals, such as those at Awat'ovi (Smith 1952), Pottery Mound (Hibben 1975), and Kawàyka'a (Hays-Gilpin et al. 2010). During this same period, petroglyphs representing macaws similar to those in Mimbres rock art are found at Petroglyph National Monument in Albuquerque and at Arroyo de los Monos near Paquimé. Sikyatki Polychrome and other contemporary painted types often have macaw images (Hays-Gilpin et al. 2010:figure 6.3). The desire for scarlet macaw feathers continues among modern pueblos, and the demand is met through the cooperative efforts of zoos, breeders, and others (Reyman 1995).

### Hero Twins Saga Motifs

Like scarlet macaw ideology and depictions, graphic Hero Twins saga motifs are represented after the Mimbres Classic period continuing from AD 1200 to 1500. Two bowls painted on their interiors depict paired fish in the Classic Mimbres tradition—that is, the fish are neither identical nor mirror images (Thompson 1999:figures 41 and 42). The former is an El Paso Polychrome, provenience unknown, at the Centennial Museum and Chihuahuan Desert Gardens, University of Texas at El Paso, and the latter, a Biscuit Ware Black-on-white, from Kuaua, now at the Maxwell Museum of Anthropology, University of New Mexico. In addition, a kiva mural fragment from Kuaua is on display at Coronado State Monument, New Mexico (Dutton 1963:plate XXV; Thompson 1999:figure 37). Here the Twins are presented as fishmen on either side of a niche. On the right is the right-handed, light-colored Twin associated with the sun; on the left is the left-handed, dark-colored Twin associated with the moon.

Likewise, Pueblo and Athabaskan folklore is rife with Warrior Twin mythology corresponding to Hero Twins saga episodes and characters described in the *Popol Vuh*, including the Twins killing monsters, the five houses (kivas) where the Twins are tested, a grandmother figure, a reference to the Twins and bears/giants, and the father and uncle of the Twins (Thompson 1994, 1999). For example, Stirling (1942:96) recounts a folk tale from Acoma describing how the "Little War Twins" were tested in five kivas, with the tests being nearly equal in number and purpose to the denizens and tortures described in the Maya legend (Tedlock 1985:140–143). At Zuni, Stevenson (1904:57–58) recorded a tale in which the "Little War Gods" killed each other only to revive the slain Twin unharmed and then vanquish their tormentors as the Hero Twins tricked and then slew the Lords of Death (Tedlock 1985:153). Finally, the adventures and birth of the War Twins are commemorated in their Navajo names "Monster Slayer" and "Born from Water." These epithets recapitulate and commemorate the adventures of the Twins, the defeat of the monsters Seven Macaw and Zipakna, and their miraculous conception from their father's spittle (Tedlock 1985:89–101, 14).

## SUMMARY AND CONCLUSIONS

In this chapter, we have examined the diffusion of scarlet macaws and the Hero Twins saga from Mesoamerica into the Mimbres region of the southwestern

United States during the Mimbres Classic period. Building on our previous arguments (Gilman et al. 2014; Thompson et al. 2014), we suggest that these became part of things Mimbres for ritual and not economic reasons, and that their presence in the Mimbres region was the result of long-distance acquisition rather than trade in any form. Here, we have supported this contention further with data showing that the entire Hero Twins saga is painted on Mimbres Classic Black-on-white bowls, and we have suggested that this could not have occurred with the scattered knowledge that down-the-line trade or Mesoamerican traders with limited stays in the Mimbres region would produce. Instead, our interpretation of the data is that people went directly to the Huasteca on the east coast of Mexico to obtain both the scarlet macaws and the Hero Twins saga, although of course the movement could have been in the other direction with people from there spending much time in the Mimbres region.

Either way, this movement was diffusion, according to Trigger (1968), in that it involved person-to-person transmission of the Hero Twins saga and information about caring for scarlet macaws. It also involved the evaluation of the utility of the items diffusing and then their acceptance. However, the scarlet macaws and the Hero Twins saga do not fit with Trigger's idea that diffusion is less likely between cultures and that all parts of the thing diffusing rarely move together. The diffusion in our case study occurred over a long distance within which were many cultures with people speaking many languages, and it occurred between people in a state and those in a non-state with vastly different social, political, and religious organizations. Because of their contemporaneity in the Mimbres region and the likelihood that the scarlet macaws and the Hero Twins saga came from the same area of Mexico, they may well have moved together as a package. Perhaps this kind of travel for goods and ideas is better described as the purposeful long-distance acquisition of exotic goods and knowledge. Such procurement was for ritual and not economic purposes, and it may have elevated the standing of those who successfully made such trips. While this may be diffusion, it is a specific kind of diffusion, and it behooves us to begin to define such specificities.

*Acknowledgments.* We thank Paul Minnis for suggesting this next step in our research and Stephen Lekson and Catherine Cameron for inviting us to present our work at the Southwest Symposium. Darrell Creel provided information and photos of Old Town and Pruitt site vessels that are not in MimPIDD. The University of Oklahoma College of Arts and Sciences Travel Assistance Program supported Gilman's attendance at the conference. Will Russell and Kristina Wyckoff have spent much time and effort producing the figures.

*Appendix 5.1*

## Hero Twins Imagery on Classic Black-on-White Pottery from Mimbres-Region Sites

**TABLE 5.2**

| MimPIDD No.* | Site | Description | Temporal Style | Reference |
|---|---|---|---|---|
| 779 | Baca | twin fish | Middle Classic | Evans et al. 1985:284 #106 |
| 782 | Baca | twin fish | Transitional/Classic | Evans et al. 1985:284 #108 |
| 798 | Baca | scarlet macaw | Middle Classic | Creel and McKusick 1994:figure 2A; Evans et al. 1985:284: #100 |
| 802 | Baca | parrots | Middle Classic | Evans et al. 1985:285 #115 |
| 809 | Baca | twin fish | Middle Classic | Evans et al. 1985:285 #116 |
| 811 | Baca | Seven Macaw and arm | Middle Classic | Evans et al. 1985:285 #117 |
| 1149 | Cameron Creek | twin fish | Middle Classic | Bradfield 1931:Plate 72 #38 |
| 1152 | Cameron Creek | twin fish | Middle Classic | Bradfield 1931:Plate 77 #40 |
| 1188 | Cameron Creek | fish human | Middle Classic | Bradfield 1931:Plate 79 #222 |
| 1201 | Cameron Creek | twin fish | Middle Classic | Laboratory of Anthropology |
| 2906 | Cameron Creek | bat | Middle Classic polychrome | University of Minnesota |
| 6083 | Cameron Creek | twin fish | Middle Classic | Bradfield 1931:Plate 72 #67 |
| 6097 | Cameron Creek | twin fish | Middle Classic | Bradfield 1931:Plate 72 #221 |
| 6177 | Cameron Creek | twin fish | Middle Classic | Bradfield 1931:Plate 73 #196 |
| 6186 | Cameron Creek | Elder Twin apotheosizing as deer | Middle Classic | Bradfield 1931:Plate 76 #380 |
| 6188 | Cameron Creek | bat | Middle Classic | Bradfield 1931:Plate 69 #311 |
| 1163 | Eby | Zipakna | Middle Classic | Laboratory of Anthropology |
| 1193 | Eby | twin fish | Middle Classic | Laboratory of Anthropology |

*continued on next page*

TABLE 5.2—*continued*

| MimPIDD No.* | Site | Description | Temporal Style | Reference |
|---|---|---|---|---|
| 1604 | Eby | Younger Twin decapitates Elder | Middle Classic | Brody 2004:figure 31 |
| 4586 | Eby | twin fish | Middle Classic | University of Arkansas |
| 7861 | Eby | bat | Early Classic | St. Louis Art Museum |
| 521 | Galaz? | twin fish | Transitional | Western New Mexico University Museum |
| 2758 | Galaz | Twin on fire (jumping into fire pit) | Middle Classic | Anyon and LeBlanc 1984:Plate 46D |
| 2763 | Galaz | Zipakna | Middle Classic | Anyon and LeBlanc 1984:Plate 115F |
| 2764 | Galaz | fishman | Middle Classic | Anyon and LeBlanc 1984:Plate 98D; Brody 2004:figure 24 |
| 2775 | Galaz | Zipakna | Middle Classic | Anyon and LeBlanc 1984:Plate 32F |
| 2779 | Galaz | twin fish | Middle Classic | Anyon and LeBlanc 1984:Plate 34E |
| 2783 | Galaz | twin fish | Middle Classic | Anyon and LeBlanc 1984:Plate 34A |
| 2789 | Galaz | twin fish | Middle Classic | Anyon and LeBlanc 1984:Plate 34D |
| 2792 | Galaz | twin fish | Middle Classic | Anyon and LeBlanc 1984:Plate 36F |
| 2807 | Galaz | bat | Middle Classic | Anyon and LeBlanc 1984:Plate 73F |
| 2823 | Galaz | twin fish | Middle Classic | Anyon and LeBlanc 1984:Plate 81A |
| 2826 | Galaz | parrot | Middle Classic | Anyon and LeBlanc 1984:Plate 67B |
| 2827 | Galaz | fish and man | Middle Classic | Anyon and LeBlanc 1984:Plate 87F |
| 2845 | Galaz | parrot and woman | Middle Classic | Anyon and LeBlanc 1984:Plate 76F |
| 2860 | Galaz | bat | Late Classic | Anyon and LeBlanc 1984:Plate 103F |
| 2878 | Galaz | parrots and human | Middle Classic | Anyon and LeBlanc 1984:Plate 58C |
| 2887 | Galaz | twin fish | Transitional | Anyon and LeBlanc 1984:Plate 46E |

*continued on next page*

**TABLE 5.2**—*continued*

| MimPIDD No.* | Site | Description | Temporal Style | Reference |
|---|---|---|---|---|
| 2901 | Galaz | twin fish | Transitional | Anyon and LeBlanc 1984:Plate 63E |
| 2902 | Galaz | Twin, Zipakna and his two sons | Middle Classic | Anyon and LeBlanc 1984:Plate 83E; Brody 2004:Plate 1 |
| 2910 | Galaz | bat | Middle Classic | Anyon and LeBlanc 1984:Plate 53E |
| 2983 | Galaz | twin fish | Middle Classic | Anyon and LeBlanc 1984:Plate 5B |
| 6253 | Galaz | Seven Macaw | Middle Classic | Anyon and LeBlanc 1984:Plate 7F |
| 6261 | Galaz | twin fish | Early Classic | Anyon and LeBlanc 1984:Plate 25D |
| 6262 | Galaz | twin fish | Middle Classic | Anyon and LeBlanc 1984:Plate 37D |
| 6265 | Galaz | twin fish | Middle or Late Classic | Anyon and LeBlanc 1984:Plate 10E |
| 1199 | Mattocks | Younger Twin and Seven Macaw | Middle Classic | Gilman and LeBlanc 2017 |
| 1213 | Mattocks | bat | Middle Classic | Gilman and LeBlanc 2017 |
| 3641 | Mattocks | right-handed masculine Twin, left-handed feminine Twin, three immature macaws, ring, basket | Middle Classic polychrome | Brody 2004:Plate 2; Nesbitt 1931:Plate 23B |
| 3653 | Mattocks | Younger Twin, Seven Macaw, fish (see MimPIDD 1199) | Middle Classic | Gilman and LeBlanc 2017 |
| 3672 | Mattocks | Twins | Middle Classic | Nesbitt 1931:Plate 25A |
| 3674 | Mattocks | twin fish | Middle Classic | Gilman and LeBlanc 2017 |
| 4284 | Mattocks | bat | Middle Classic | Gilman and LeBlanc 2017 |
| 1488 | McSherry | Zipakna | Middle Classic | University of Colorado Museum |

*continued on next page*

TABLE 5.2—*continued*

| MimPIDD No.* | Site | Description | Temporal Style | Reference |
|---|---|---|---|---|
| 1608 | McSherry | two macaws and human with macaw tail | Middle Classic | Creel and McKusick 1994:figure 2C |
| 470 | Mitchell | bat | Middle Classic | Anyon and LeBlanc n.d. |
| 907 | Mitchell | bat | Middle Classic | Anyon and LeBlanc n.d. |
| 2100 | NAN Ranch | twin fish | Middle Classic | Peabody Museum of Archaeology and Ethnology 96020 |
| 7560 | NAN Ranch | Zipakna | Early Classic | Shafer 2003:A.7H |
| 7563 | NAN Ranch | Zipakna | Early Classic | Shafer 2003:A.8B |
| 7578 | NAN Ranch | twin fish | Early Classic | Shafer 2003:A.9I |
| 7595 | NAN Ranch | twin fish | Middle Classic | Shafer 2003:A.11H |
| 7617 | NAN Ranch | twin fish | Middle Classic | Shafer 2003:A.14C |
| 7619 | NAN Ranch | twin fish with front legs | Middle Classic | Shafer 2003:A.14E |
| 7624 | NAN Ranch | twin fish | Middle Classic | Shafer 2003:A.15A |
| 7628 | NAN Ranch | twin fish | Middle Classic | Shafer 2003:A.15E |
| 7641 | NAN Ranch | bat | Middle Classic | Shafer 2003:A.16I |
| 7876 | NAN Ranch | twin fish | Middle Classic | Sweden Museum #1950.45.0032 |
| None | NAN Ranch | decapitation of Elder Twin by Younger Twin | Middle Classic | Brody 2004:figure 33; Fewkes 1916:figure 68, 1923:29, figure 13 |
| 3560 | Old Town | twin fish | Middle Classic | Fewkes 1914:45 |
| 10138 | Old Town | twinned macaw heads | Middle Classic polychrome | Fewkes 1914:38, 41 |
| None - F401 | Old Town | Seven Macaw | Middle Classic | Fewkes 1914:30 |
| 1117 | Osborn | twin fish | Early Classic | Davis 1995:139 |
| 3496 | Osborn | Twins smoking | Late Classic | Fewkes 1914:27 |
| 3573 | Osborn | twin fish | Middle Classic | Smithsonian Institution |
| 537 | Pruitt | bat | Middle Classic | Western New Mexico University Museum |
| 842 | Pruitt | Zipakna | Middle Classic | Maxwell Museum of Anthropology |
| 1015 | Pruitt | twin fish | Middle Classic | Maxwell Museum of Anthropology |

*continued on next page*

**TABLE 5.2**—*continued*

| MimPIDD No.* | Site | Description | Temporal Style | Reference |
|---|---|---|---|---|
| 4771 | Pruitt | bat | Middle Classic | Private collection |
| None-ASM 20321 | Pruitt | fishman | Middle Classic | Arizona State Museum |
| 2104 | Swarts | Twins, twin fish tails | Late Classic | Cosgrove and Cosgrove 1932:Plate 227F |
| 2180 | Swarts | fish with arms and legs | Middle Classic | Cosgrove and Cosgrove 1932:Plate 231D |
| 2224 | Swarts | fish and man | Middle Classic | Cosgrove and Cosgrove 1932:Plate229E |
| 2272 | Swarts | twin fish | Middle Classic | Cosgrove and Cosgrove 1932:Plate 205F |
| 2459 | Swarts | Zipakna | Middle Classic | Cosgrove and Cosgrove 1932:Plate 230A |
| 2474 | Swarts | twin fish | Middle Classic | Cosgrove and Cosgrove 1932:Plate 207C |
| 2502 | Swarts | bat | Middle Classic polychrome | Peabody Museum of Archaeology and Ethnology 95967 |
| 2573 | Swarts | Zipakna | Middle Classic | Cosgrove and Cosgrove 1932:Plate 194F |
| 2659 | Swarts | twin fish | Transitional | Cosgrove and Cosgrove 1932 Plate 120B: |
| 2664 | Swarts | twin fish | Transitional | Cosgrove and Cosgrove 1932:Plate 120F |
| 2672 | Swarts | Twins | Middle Classic | Cosgrove and Cosgrove 1932:Plate 225E |
| 2698 | Swarts | Twins and Bird of Doom | Middle Classic | Cosgrove and Cosgrove 1932:Plate 228F |
| 2702 | Swarts | Younger Twin and Seven Macaw | Middle Classic | Cosgrove and Cosgrove 1932:Plate 225D |
| 2708 | Swarts | Zipakna | Middle Classic | Cosgrove and Cosgrove 1932:Plate 195B |
| 9165 | Swarts | Zipakna | Early Classic | Peabody Museum of Archaeology and Ethnology 94473 |
| 9552 | Swarts | birth of younger left-handed Twin and mother | Early Classic | Brody 2004:figure 66; Cosgrove and Cosgrove 1932:Plate 225F |

*continued on next page*

**TABLE 5.2**—*continued*

| MimPIDD No.* | Site | Description | Temporal Style | Reference |
|---|---|---|---|---|
| 9553 | Swarts | Zipakna | Indeterminate | Peabody Museum of Archaeology and Ethnology 95982 |
| 9557 | Swarts | Zipakna | Middle Classic | Cosgrove and Cosgrove 1932:Plate 195A |
| 9568 | Swarts | Elder Twin with quiver and sunflower symbol | Transitional/Classic | Cosgrove and Cosgrove 1932:Plate 227A |
| 198 | Treasure Hill | Twins | Early Classic | Brody 2004:figure 30 |

* Mimbres Pottery Image Digital Database Number.

## REFERENCES

Anyon, Roger, and Steven A. LeBlanc. 1984. *The Galaz Ruin: A Prehistoric Mimbres Village in Southwestern New Mexico.* Albuquerque: University of New Mexico Press.

Anyon, Roger, and Steven A. LeBlanc. n.d. "The Mitchell Site: A Small Mimbres Classic Site in the Mimbres Valley, Southwestern New Mexico." Manuscript on file with authors.

Bradfield, Wesley. 1931. *Cameron Creek Village: A Site in the Mimbres Area in Grant County, New Mexico.* Santa Fe, NM: School of American Research.

Brody, J. J. 2004. *Mimbres Painted Pottery.* 2nd ed. Santa Fe, NM: School of American Research Press.

Carr, Christopher. 2005. "Rethinking Interregional Hopewellian 'Interaction.'" In *Gathering Hopewell: Society, Ritual, and Ritual Interaction,* ed. Christopher Carr and D. Troy Case, 575–623. New York: Springer. https://doi.org/10.1007/0-387-27327-1_16.

Carr, Pat. 1979. *Mimbres Mythology.* Southwestern Studies Monograph No. 56. El Paso: University of Texas, Texas Western Press.

Christenson, Allen J. 2007. *Popol Vuh: The Sacred Book of the Maya.* Norman: University of Oklahoma.

Coe, Michael D. 1973. *The Maya Scribe and His World.* New York: Grolier Club.

Cortéz, Constance. 1986. "The Principal Bird Deity in Preclassic and Early Classic Maya Art." Unpublished Master's thesis, Department of Anthropology, University of Texas, Austin.

Cosgrove, H. S., and C. B. Cosgrove. 1932. *The Swarts Ruin: A Typical Mimbres Site in Southwestern New Mexico.* Report of the Peabody Museum of Archaeology and Ethnology, Harvard University. vol. 15. Cambridge, MA: Peabody Museum Press.

Creel, Darrell, and Charmion McKusick. 1994. "Prehistoric Macaws and Parrots in the Mimbres Area, New Mexico." *American Antiquity* 59(03):510–524. https://doi.org/10.2307/282463.

Davis, Carolyn O'Bagy. 1995. *Treasured Earth: Hattie Cosgrove's Mimbres Archaeology in the American Southwest.* Tucson, AZ: Sanpete Publications and Old Pueblo Archaeology Center.

Díaz, Gisele, and Alan Rodgers. 1993. *The Codex Borgia: A Full-Color Restoration of the Ancient Mexican Manuscript.* New York: Dover.

Di Peso, Charles C. 1974. *Casas Grandes: A Fallen Trading Center of the Gran Chichimeca.* Amerind Foundation Series No. 9. Vol. 1–3. Dragoon, AZ: Northland Press.

Di Peso, Charles C., John B. Rinaldo, and Gloria J. Fenner. 1974. *Casas Grandes: A Fallen Trading Center of the Gran Chichimeca. Amerind Foundation Series No. 9.* vol. 8. Dragoon, AZ: Northland Press.

Dutton, Bertha P. 1963. *Sun Father's Way: The Kiva Murals of Kuaua.* Albuquerque: University of New Mexico Press.

Evans, Roy H., Evelyn R. Ross, and Lyle Ross. 1985. *Mimbres Indian Treasure in the Land of Baca: Excavating an Ancient Pueblo Ruin.* Kansas City, MO: Lowell Press.

Fewkes, J. Walter. 1914. *Archaeology of the Lower Mimbres Valley, New Mexico.* Smithsonian Miscellaneous Collections 63(10). Washington, DC: Smithsonian.

Fewkes, J. Walter. 1916. "Animal Figures on Prehistoric Pottery from Mimbres Valley, New Mexico." *American Anthropologist* 18(4):535–545. https://doi.org/10.1525/aa.1916.18.4.02a00080.

Fewkes, J. Walter. 1923. *Designs on Prehistoric Pottery from the Mimbres Valley, New Mexico.* Smithsonian Miscellaneous Collections 74(6). Washington, DC: Smithsonian.

Forshaw, Joseph M. 2010. *Parrots of the World.* Princeton, NJ: Princeton University Press. https://doi.org/10.1515/9781400836208.

Gilman, Patricia A. 1990. "Social Organization and Classic Mimbres Period Burials in the SW United States." *Journal of Field Archaeology* 17:457–169.

Gilman, Patricia A. 2006. "Social Differences at the Classic Period Mattocks Site in the Mimbres Valley." In *Mimbres Society,* ed. Valli S. Powell-Martí and Patricia A. Gilman, 66–81. Tucson: University of Arizona Press.

Gilman, Patricia A., and Steven A. LeBlanc. 2017. *Mimbres Life and Society: The Mattocks Site of Southwestern New Mexico.* Tucson: University of Arizona Press.

Gilman, Patricia A., Marc Thompson, and Kristina C. Wyckoff. 2014. "Ritual Change and the Distant: Mesoamerican Iconography, Scarlet Macaws, and Great Kivas in the Mimbres Region of Southwestern New Mexico." *American Antiquity* 79(01):90–107. https://doi.org/10.7183/0002-7316.79.1.90.

Greiser, Sally Thompson. 1995. "The Sacred Bird: The Scarlet Macaw among Puebloan Peoples." In *The Large Macaws: Their Care, Breeding, and Conservation,* ed. Joanne

Abramson, Brian L. Speer, and Jorgen B. Thomsen, 497–510. Fort Bragg, CA: Raintree Publications.

Hargrave, Lyndon. 1970. *Mexican Macaws: Comparative Osteology and Survey of Remains from the Southwest*. Tucson: University of Arizona Press.

Haury, Emil. 1976. *The Hohokam Desert Farmers and Craftsmen: Excavations at Snaketown, 1964–1965*. Tucson: University of Arizona Press.

Hays-Gilpin, Kelley, Emory Sekaquaptewa, and Elizabeth Newsome. 2010. "Sìitálpuva 'Through the Land Brightened with Flowers': Ecology and Pottery Painting, Hopi and Beyond." In *Painting the Cosmos: Metaphor and Worldview in Images from the Southwest Pueblos and Mexico*, ed.Kelley Hays-Gilpin and Polly Schaafsma, 121–138. Flagstaff: Museum of Northern Arizona Bulletin 67.

Hegmon, Michelle, and Margaret C. Nelson. 2007. "In Sync, but Barely in Touch: Relations between the Mimbres Region and the Hohokam Regional System." In *Hinterlands and Regional Dynamics in the Ancient Southwest*, ed. Alan P. Sullivan III and James M. Bayman, 70–96. Tucson: University of Arizona Press.

Hegmon, Michelle, and Wenda R. Trevathan. 1996. "Gender, Anatomical Knowledge, and Pottery Production: Implications of an Anatomically Unusual Birth Depicted on Mimbres Pottery from Southwestern New Mexico." *American Antiquity* 61(04):747–754. https://doi.org/10.2307/282015.

Helms, Mary W. 1991. "Esoteric Knowledge, Geographical Distance, and the Elaboration of Leadership Status: Dynamics of Resource Control." In *Profiles in Cultural Evolution*, ed. Robert D. Drennan, 333–350. Anthropological Papers No. 85. Ann Arbor: Museum of Anthropology, University of Michigan.

Hibben, Frank. 1975. *Kiva Art of the Anasazi at Pottery Mound*. Las Vegas, NV: KC Publications.

Hopkins, Marin P. 2012. "A Storied Land: Tiyo and the Epic Journey down the Colorado River." Unpublished Master's thesis, School of Anthropology, University of Arizona, Tucson.

Lekson, Stephen H. 2008. *A History of the Ancient Southwest*. Santa Fe, NM: School for Advanced Research Press.

Livesay, Alison K. 2013. "Oxidized Mimbres Bowls: An Example of Technological Style." Unpublished Master's thesis, Department of Anthropology, University of Oklahoma, Norman.

McKusick, Charmion R. 2001. *Southwest Birds of Sacrifice*. The Arizona Archaeologist No. 31. Tucson: Arizona Archaeological Society.

Minnis, Paul E., Michael E. Whalen, Jane H. Kelley, and Joe D. Stewart. 1993. "Prehistoric Macaw Breeding in the North American Southwest." *American Antiquity* 58(2):270–276. https://doi.org/10.2307/281969.

Moulard, Barbara. 1984. *Within the Underworld Sky: Mimbres Ceramic Art in Context*. Pasadena, CA: Twelvetrees Press.

Nesbitt, Paul H. 1931. *The Ancient Mimbreños: Based on Investigations at the Mattocks Ruin, Mimbres Valley, New Mexico.* Logan Museum of Anthropology Bulletin 4. Beloit, WI: Beloit College.

Powell, Valli S. 2000. *Iconography and Group Formation during the Late Pithouse and Classic Periods of the Mimbres Society, A.D. 970–1140.* PhD dissertation, Department of Anthropology, University of Oklahoma, Norman. Ann Arbor, MI: University Microfilms International.

Powell-Martí, Valli S., and William D. James. 2006. "Ceramic Iconography and Social Asymmetry in the Classic Mimbres Heartland, A.D. 970–1140." In *Mimbres Society,* ed. Valli S. Powell-Martí and Patricia A. Gilman, 151–173. Tucson: University of Arizona Press.

Reyman, Jonathan E. 1995. "Value in Mesoamerican-Southwestern Trade." In *The Gran Chichimeca: Essays on the Archaeology and Ethnohistory of Northern Mesoamerica,* ed. Jonathan E. Reyman, 271–279. Brookfield, VT: Avebury Press.

Reynolds, Andrew, and Alexander Langlands. 2011. "Travel *as* Communication: A Consideration of Overland Journeys in Anglo-Saxon England." *World Archaeology* 43(3):410–427. https://doi.org/10.1080/00438243.2011.615158.

Riley, Carroll L. 2005. *Becoming Aztlan: Mesoamerican Influence in the Greater Southwest, A.D. 1200–1500.* Salt Lake City: University of Utah Press.

Rizo, Michael J. 1998. "Scarlet Macaw Production and Trade at Paquimé, Chihuahua." Unpublished Master's thesis, Department of Anthropology, Arizona State University, Tempe.

Roth, Barbara. 2007. "The Pithouse Period Occupation of the Lake Roberts Vista Site." In *Exploring Variability in Mogollon Pithouses,* ed. Barbara J. Roth and Robert Stokes. Anthropological Research Papers No. 58. Tempe: Arizona State University.

Schaafsma, Polly. 1999. "Tlalocs, Kachinas, Sacred Bundles, and Related Symbolism in the Southwest and Mesoamerica." In *The Casas Grandes World,* ed. Curtis F. Schaafsma and Carroll L. Riley, 164–192. Salt Lake City: University of Utah Press.

Shafer, Harry J. 1995. "Architecture and Symbolism in Transitional Pueblo Development in the Mimbres Valley, SW New Mexico." *Journal of Field Archaeology* 22:23–47.

Shafer, Harry J. 2003. *Mimbres Archaeology at the NAN Ranch Ruin.* Albuquerque: University of New Mexico Press.

Smith, Watson. 1952. *Kiva Mural Decorations at Awatovi and Kawaika-a with a Survey of Other Wall Paintings in the Pueblo Southwest.* Papers of the Peabody Museum of American Archaeology and Ethnology 37. Cambridge, MA: Harvard University.

Stevenson, Matilda Cox. 1904. *The Zuni Indians.* Twenty-third Annual Report of the Bureau of American Ethnology, 1901–1902. Washington, DC: Smithsonian Institution.

Stirling, Matthew W. 1942. *Origin Myth of the Acoma and Other Records.* Bureau of American Ethnology Bulletin 35. Washington, DC: Smithsonian Institution.

Tedlock, Dennis. 1985. *Popol Vuh: The Definitive Edition of the Mayan Book of the Dawn of Life and the Glories of Gods and Kings*. New York: Simon and Schuster.

Thompson, Marc. 1994. "The Evolution and Dissemination of Mimbres Iconography." In *Kachinas in the Pueblo World*, ed. Polly Schaafsma, 93–105. Albuquerque: University of New Mexico Press.

Thompson, Marc. 1999. "Mimbres Iconology: Analysis and Interpretation of Figurative Motifs." PhD dissertation. Department of Archaeology, University of Calgary, Alberta. Ann Arbor, MI: University Microfilms International.

Thompson, Marc. 2006. "Pre-Columbian Venus: Celestial Twin and Icon of Duality." In *Religion in the Prehispanic Southwest*, ed. Christine S. VanPool, Todd VanPool, and David A. Phillips Jr., 165–183. New York: Altamira Press.

Thompson, Marc, and R. B. Brown. 2006. "Scarlet Macaws: Sunbirds of the Southwest." In *Mostly Mimbres: A Collection of Papers from the 12th Biennial Mogollon Conference*, ed. Marc Thompson, Jason Jurgena, and Lora Jackson, 93–98. El Paso: El Paso Museum of Archaeology.

Thompson, Marc, Patricia A. Gilman, and Kristina C. Wyckoff. 2014. "The Hero Twins in the Mimbres Region: Representations of the Mesoamerican Creation Saga Are Seen on Mimbres Pottery." *American Archaeology* 18(2):38–43.

Townsend, Richard F., ed. 2005. *Casas Grandes and the Ceramic Art of the Ancient Southwest*. New Haven, CT: Yale University Press.

Trigger, Bruce. 1968. *Beyond History: Methods of Prehistory*. New York: Holt, Rinehart and Winston.

VanPool, Christine S., and Todd VanPool. 2007. *Signs of the Casas Grandes Shamans*. Salt Lake City: University of Utah Press.

Whalen, Michael E. 2013. "Wealth, Status, Ritual, and Marine Shell at Casas Grandes, Chihuahua, Mexico." *American Antiquity* 78(4):624–639. https://doi.org/10.7183/0002-7316.78.4.624.

Woosley, Anne I., and Allan J. McIntyre. 1996. *Mimbres Mogollon Archaeology: Charles C. Di Peso's Excavations at Wind Mountain*. Albuquerque: University of New Mexico Press.

# 6

# Maintenance, Revival, or Hybridization?

*Distinguishing between Types of Identity*
*Reconstruction in the American Southwest*

SUZANNE L. ECKERT

Archaeologists in the Southwest United States have spent a great deal of effort attempting to reconstruct identities such as ethnicity, gender, class or culture group. However, one of the difficulties that we face is that the people we study were involved in reconstructing their own identities in light of new social situations brought on by the migrations of peoples and the diffusion of ideas. Cameron (chapter 2, this volume) points out that archaeologists lack well-developed theories focused on understanding the mechanisms by which diffusion occurs and argues that to truly understand past social contexts we need to develop more sophisticated models of diffusion.

While Cameron focuses on the taking of captives as one mechanism by which diffusion of ideas occurs, other authors in this volume consider the influential role of sodalities (Hays-Gilpin et al., chapter 4, this volume), social networks (Mills and Peeples, chapter 3, this volume), and long-distance acquisition (Gilman et al., chaoter 5, this volume). In this chapter, I examine yet another mechanism—the construction and reconstruction of identity in the context of culture contact. Specifically, I consider three concepts of identity reconstruction

DOI: 10.5876/9781607327356.c006

commonly used by anthropologists and historic archaeologists—continuity/maintenance, revivalism, and creolization/hybridization—to describe the different ways people reconstruct their own identities. Within the framework of understanding the process of diffusion, the concepts of identity reconstruction can be considered separate factors "that condition the acceptance or rejection of specific cultural practices when social groups interact" (Cameron, chapter 2, this volume). Drawing upon three specific case studies, I argue that these (and probably other) types of identity reconstruction can be distinguished in the archaeological record.

## IDENTITY RECONSTRUCTION

The concept of identity can be, and has been, debated to great extent. For my purposes here, the term *identity* incorporates the concept of maintaining a social group "despite changes in membership and practice over time" (Sampeck 2011:38). Identity is useful for disentangling the changing categories by which people participate in their community at various scales and organizational levels (Cameron 2013:221). More specifically, identity is a set of possibilities from which diverse elements—ethnicity, class, age, gender, captivity—are variously mobilized in different contexts and scales of social performance (Sunseri 2017). It is a set of relations that are historically constituted, fluid, and constantly changing (Wurst 1999). In other words, identity (like diffusion) is a complex behavior.

I recognize that identity is fluid and situational and relational for individuals participating in their community, but what I am specifically interested in here is group identity that is reconstructed and performed in the specific frameworks of migration and diffusion—that of culture contact. In Southwest archaeology and anthropology, this type of group identity has been referred to as *ethnicity*, *tribe*, *sociolinguistic group*, and maybe even *lineage*, *clan*, or *sodality* (see Hays-Gilpin et al., chapter 4, this volume). Whatever its name, I am interested in identities developed around a common geographic history within a specific context of sustained culture contact. Understanding and recognizing such behavior can help "to comprehend more precisely how cultural practices moved across the landscape . . . and how introduced practices were incorporated in a new social context" (Cameron, chapter 2, this volume) and thus help archaeologists develop more meaningful models of migration and diffusion.

All contexts of culture contact are a potential arena for the diffusion of ideas. Further, contexts of culture contact are especially promising for "seeing" identity in the archaeological record, as these contexts can be transformative (Heinz and Linke 2012:185–186). The mere presence of new people with new material culture and social practices changes a group's perceptions of social space and movement (Stockhammer 2012:90). Further, culture contact includes a variety of cultural interactions with a diverse range of participants—such encounters have potential for considerable influence on the social, political, cultural, and religious life of actors who have been exposed to "the other" (Heinz and Linke 2012) as they live together within a village or region. In such contexts, people are likely to consciously reconstruct their identities as they mull over what it means to be "us" versus "them," or what it means to create a new "us" that incorporates various peoples (Heinz and Linke 2012:185).

Much method and theory concerning identity in culture contact situations have been developed in historical archaeology and ethnographic studies, and it is from here that I borrow the three fruitful concepts of continuity/maintenance, revivalism, and creolization/hybridization when considering identity reconstruction in the Southwest United States. These concepts do not cover every possibility and other researchers have developed alternative means of exploring identity that are also important to consider (e.g., see Hill et al. 2004 for a discussion of the creation of new identity against a background of change and discontinuity). One could view these three concepts as finite options; however, these options should be viewed as a range of possibilities that could have been pursued simultaneously by the same individual in different contexts, or by different individuals within the same context. Further, identity reconstruction is an ongoing performance with the selection of possibilities potentially changing as generations change.

## Concepts of Identity

Identity continuity or maintenance is an active continuation of a group identity while having regular interactions with a group (or groups) that holds a different identity. Emphasis is placed on the importance of maintaining the "old" or "traditional" ways despite the introduction of new ideas that results from interaction with others (Yasur-Landau 2012:193). Such continuity or maintenance can be a denial of change (González-Ruibal 2013:16), a clinging to the repetition of activities that are sanctioned by tradition and may (or at least be believed to) be extremely old. While the Amish provide an obvious modern example of identity continuity, other ethnographic examples include the Mao of western Ethiopia (González-Ruibal 2013) and the Rarámuri (Tarahumara) of northwestern Mexico (Levi 1998).

Revivalism does accept change; it demands change, but of a particular kind, the idea being to transform the present in order to make it look like the past (González-Ruibal 2013:16; Liebmann 2012). Indigenous groups have often engaged in revivalist activities to reenact an idealized moment before colonialism (González-Ruibal 2013:16). It can involve the rejecting of foreign technologies and beliefs while sanctioning a return to traditional practices, but it can also incorporate the emergence of new ideas of spiritual purity or community. Ethnohistorical examples of revivalism include the religious movements seen to develop among the Western Toba of Argentina (Mendoza 2004) and the members of the Native American Church of North America (Maroukis 2010). The line that divides continuity/maintenance from revivalism can be thin and it is important to realize that, from an *emic* perspective, people who consciously engage in maintenance activities do not perceive that they are *returning* to any specific past while people who engage in revivalism perceive themselves as doing exactly that (González-Ruibal 2013:16).

Hybridization or creolization is perhaps the most problematic concept presented in this chapter, and yet possibly the most common. This process involves a blending of identities, or an attempt to combine traits from two or more cultures into one shared identity (Liebmann 2013). But the idea of one "identity" coming into contact with another "identity" is overly simplistic (Maran 2012:121) in that it assumes clear-cut divisions between the traits that define each group. Further, Dietler (2009) cautions that these terms should only be used to describe specific colonial contexts, otherwise they will come to be used to describe every culture contact situation and therefore become meaningless. It is no doubt difficult to disentangle elements of different origins that are combined to create a new identity (Jung 2012:104), as the values and meanings negotiated between groups with different origins will differ significantly from group to group. But difficult is not impossible, and the commonality of this identity reconstruction warrants attempts at distinguishing it in the past.

## Archaeological Correlates

Ultimately, identity is about belonging. However, identities are also constructed so as to define "us" versus "them." In culture contact situations, there must be some marker that identifies one as "belonging," in other words, some way to perform the identity. But can we see these markers in the past? Archaeologists have considered identity primarily as suites of shared strategies and as sets of rules for when and where those strategies are employed to signify inclusion (Sunseri 2017). The underlying assumption is that identity affects one's ideas, self-view, worldview, and values and that these are all expressed through material culture (Heinz and Linke 2012:185). More specifically, identity is expressed through style (Feldman 2012).

*Style* is tricky to define (Bowser 2000; Crown 1994; Hegmon 1995) but for the purposes of this chapter, it is considered to be the characteristic patterns of embellishment that result in a unique set of visually represented design attributes (Rice 1987). This definition explains *what* style is, not *how* it is. By viewing style through a materialist framework, I assume that cultural practice intersects with style and identity. Specifically, style can be understood as part of the practice of identity through performance with material objects (Feldman 2012: 204). This performance can take the form of production, display, or use of

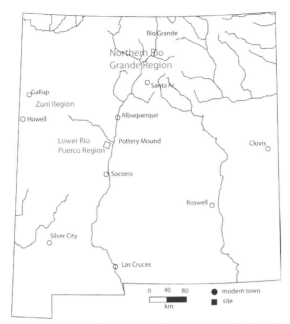

**FIGURE 6.1.** *Map of the American Southwest showing location of regions and sites discussed in this chapter.*

such objects. Style need not be intentional, as people's aesthetics are internalized and become part of their identity (Feldman 2012). As identities transform, so will styles.

Although the intersection of identity and style can be considered through a variety of forms of material culture, I focus this discussion on ceramic style. I am aware that I am conflating at least two contexts here: pottery production and pottery use (Jung 2012). I assume that the potters decorating the vessels are performing their identity and that these vessels were then being used by people who shared that same identity. There have been many exceptional essays in recent years exploring identity in the Southwest United States (Clark et al. 2013; Gilpin and Hays-Gilpin 2012; Hill et al. 2004; Mills 2007; Nelson and Habicht-Mauche 2006 among others) and it is my goal to complement and expand the discussion by considering three case studies of sustained culture contact in light of these three concepts of identity (figure 6.1, 6.2).

## THREE CASE STUDIES FROM THE SOUTHWEST UNITED STATES

### Identity Maintenance in the Thirteenth-Century Northern Rio Grande Region

The first case study considers identity maintenance—continued identity while having regular interactions with other groups—during the twelfth and thirteenth

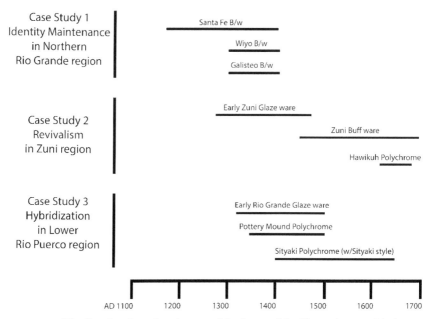

**FIGURE 6.2.** *Timeline showing cultural events of the Ancestral Pueblo pertinent to this chapter.*

centuries in the northern Rio Grande region (figure 6.1). The transition between these centuries (figure 6.2) witnessed a change in settlement patterns from dispersed to nucleated settlements (Ruscavage-Barz 1999) as well as an increase in population brought on by both immigration (Ortman 2010) and local population increase (Wilson 2008). During this time, Santa Fe Black-on-white (figure 6.3) was produced at the household level in numerous villages across the region (Eckert et al. 2015; Habicht-Mauche 1993; Lang 1989; Schmader 1988). The type is characterized by white slip, black carbon paint, blue-gray paste, and a wide range of surface finishes (Habicht-Mauche 1993; Kidder 1931:23–24; Mera 1935:11–14; Shepard 1936:461–464; Stubbs and Stallings 1953; Honea 1968a, 1968b; Lang 1982, 1992). Despite over 200 years of production at multiple provenances, this ceramic type was decorated in a very consistent manner.

What is of interest to the understanding of identity maintenance is that, prior to AD 1300, Santa Fe Black-on-white was *the* major decorated type being produced in the region. After AD 1300, it was one of numerous Black-on-white types being produced (Habicht-Mauche 1993, 1995). Habicht-Mauche (1993, 1995) has argued that this was a moment of tribilization, where social and territorial boundaries emerged as identifiable archaeological districts within the region. These different ceramic traditions reflect these different tribal identities; for example, Galisteo Black-on-white is reminiscent of the Mesa Verde style and may have reflected the presence of immigrants from that area. I argue further that the

**FIGURE 6.3.** *Santa Fe Black-on-white from Paa'ko. (Photographed by Karen E. Price, catalog No. 60.24.3, courtesy of the Maxwell Museum of Anthropology, University of New Mexico.)*

continued production of Santa Fe Black-on-white may reflect a *lack* of immigrants at certain villages, or at least represent a village-wide identity focused on a long-standing history in the region. In other words, the producers of Santa Fe Black-on-white were maintaining their identity while interacting with a diverse range of newly consolidated social groups (Eckert et al. 2015).

But how was Santa Fe Black-on-white used to perform identity? This type and other contemporary decorated types occur primarily as small bowls and are assumed to have been the primary service ware of the period (Eckert et al. 2015; Habicht-Mauche 1993:41). The performance of identity would have occurred in the context of production, as women from the same community prepared and decorated their vessels and taught the next generation the craft. But identity would also have been performed as vessels were distributed to kith and kin for use in food preparation and service. The designs were painted almost exclusively on the interior of bowls and would have been viewed only by those in the immediate vicinity of the vessels. As such, these designs and their method of execution would have served as a reminder to viewers of their identity as residents with a long history in the region—a reminder that would have helped enforce the rejection of new ideas and practices being adopted by individuals sharing that identity.

**FIGURE 6.4.** *Hawikuh Polychrome from the Zuni region. (Photographed by Barbara Mills, catalog No. 10–1519, courtesy of the National Museum of the American Indian.)*

## Revivalism in the Seventeenth-Century Zuni Region

The second case study considers revivalism—transformation of aspects of identity in order to make it look like the past—during the 1600s in the Zuni region (figure 6.1). Starting at approximately AD 1630 (figure 6.2), Zuni potters began to make Hawikuh Polychrome (figure 6.4), a late Zuni Glaze Ware type (Eckert 2006). Schachner (2006) has argued that potters in the Zuni region discontinued their early glazeware tradition at around AD 1450 in response to a large demographic reorganization that included migration of groups both into and out of the area. At this time, a new mineral-painted pottery type associated with a newly formed (hybridized?) identity was produced called Zuni Buff Ware, which continued to be produced after Spanish contact up until the Pueblo Revolt of 1680. But at some point in the 1600s, Zuni potters also began to produce late Zuni Glaze Ware after almost 200 years of not producing glaze-painted pottery. Why?

Mills (1995, 2002) argues that Hawikuh Polychrome is reminiscent of contemporary Rio Grande Glaze Ware types. However, in terms of aesthetics, Hawikuh Polychrome has glaze paint and red and white slip colors similar to early Zuni Glaze Ware types (Eckert 2006). In other words, Hawikuh Polychrome is reminiscent of early Zuni Glaze Ware (although, to be clear, some late Zuni Glaze Ware vessels have a buff slip and the designs are reminiscent of the contemporary Zuni Buff Ware). Why go back to making glaze-painted pottery with red and white slips? It is assumed that glaze-paint technology was reintroduced from Rio Grande pueblos when the Spanish established two missions at Zuni. Although it is possible that immigrants from Rio Grande villages were making the vessels, there is no record of such immigrants. Archaeologists working in the region are confident that Zuni potters were making Hawikuh Polychrome (Mills 1995, 2002). The Zuni did not wholeheartedly adopt Spanish missionization; as a matter of fact, they killed the priests soon after missions were built, suggesting active resistance (Mills 2002).

I argue that the adoption of Hawikuh Polychrome—with its glaze paint and bright red and white slips—was a revival of an older identity, a harkening back to the past before the Spanish were known, a statement of continuity in the region. Unlike Santa Fe Black-on-white discussed above, Hawikuh Polychrome was produced in a variety of vessel forms including bowls, jars, and Spanish forms. This suggests that this glaze-painted type was used in a variety of Pueblo and Spanish cultural contexts. Mills (2002) has argued that the feather designs on Hawikuh Polychrome and contemporary Zuni Buff Ware were a reflection of a shared Pueblo ritual system that was being suppressed by the Spanish missionaries. The presence of feather designs combined with glaze paint and bright colors on numerous vessel forms would have allowed a subtle performance of a revived Zuni identity. Every time a woman carried a Hawikuh Polychrome water jar on her head through the village, or a child ate from a Hawikuh Polychrome bowl, or a servant served dinner to a missionary in a Hawikuh Polychrome platter, the Zuni within viewing distance of these vessels would have been reminded of their long-standing cultural heritage.

## Hybridization at the Fifteenth-Century Village of Pottery Mound

The third case study explores hybridization—the combining of two or more identities into one identity—at the village of Pottery Mound along the Lower Rio Puerco (figure 6.1). This site has 200+ pueblo rooms, at least four plazas, and 16 kivas, and dates from AD 1300 to the late 1400s/early 1500s (figure 6.2). Throughout its occupation, potters at the site made various Rio Grande Glaze Ware types that combined different slip and paint color combinations. I have argued elsewhere (Eckert 2008) that these various combinations reflect different potter communities reaffirming their identity in terms of both village residency and immigration history. Of interest in this chapter is Pottery Mound Polychrome (figure 6.5), a Rio Grande Glaze Ware type produced almost exclusively at Pottery Mound and not widely distributed outside of the Lower Rio Puerco area.

Pottery Mound Polychrome is a hybridization of Early Rio Grande Glaze Ware types and Hopi Yellow Ware types: potters combined the red slip of the former on bowl exteriors with the yellow-buff slip of the latter on bowl interiors. Further, although the designs were executed in glaze paint identical to contemporary Rio Grande Glaze Ware types, potters incorporated the elements and layouts of the Hopi-area Sikyatki design style (Eckert 2006, 2008; see also Hays-Gilpin et al., chapter 4, this volume). It is my contention that the hybridization

**FIGURE 6.5.** *Pottery Mound Polychrome from Pottery Mound Pueblo. (Photographed by Karen E. Price, catalog no. 87.50.18, courtesy of the Maxwell Museum.)*

of this pottery type reflects the hybridization of the potters' identity, a reconstruction based on connections to two different cultural groups. On the one hand, potters were using their vessels to signal their unique connection to the Hopi Mesas; on the other hand, the same vessels were being used to signal potters' connection to Rio Grande social dynamics.[1]

However, the performance of this hybridized identity was complex. The exterior of Pottery Mound Polychrome bowls was indistinguishable from the exterior of most other decorated bowls made in the Lower Rio Puerco region during this period (Eckert 2006, 2008). Individuals viewing Pottery Mound Polychrome bowls from a distance—across a plaza or a kiva—would view the bowls (and therefore the identity of the individuals using them) as no different from other bowls and individuals in the same performance space. But bowl interiors have a hybridized decoration—combining design and paint technology from both the Hopi and Rio Grande regions. These interiors would have been viewed only by those in close proximity to the bowls—the producers and users of the vessels. These bowls were being used in a complex social performance in which both a public identity and a private identity were being expressed at the same time in the same space but to different individuals.

## CONCLUSION

I have presented a variety of means by which Ancestral Pueblo potters may have constructed and reconstructed their identity within the context of sustained culture contact. I am not arguing that my case studies are thoroughly convincing; indeed, they each need to be examined further through other types of material classes. My goal is to show that identity is a factor of people's daily life, it is complex and flexible, and yet it is a social performance and therefore probably often detectable in the archaeological record.

How does this help our understanding of diffusion? Historical archaeologists have long recognized that culture contact provides the scenarios in which new cultural practices can be introduced and evaluated (Deagan 1998). Maran (2012:120) points out that archaeologists, when considering contexts of culture contact, often think in two extremes: one group was completely subsumed by the other or the two groups remained completely segregated. But these are two extremes along a continuum, with many possible trajectories in between. Ideas and practices can be wholly adopted, partially adopted, reworked and adopted, or rejected as people struggle with their identities in light of new culture contacts. With this in mind, by considering the various types of identity reconstructions available in any given social setting and trying to detect those reconstructions, and understanding how the adoption of new ideas and practices can be accepted or rejected as part of that process, we develop a richer understanding of the daily lives of past peoples.

## NOTE

1. It should be noted that my interpretation of Sikyatki design style as presented in this chapter is very different than the interpretation presented in chapter 4 by Hays-Gilpin and colleagues—a chapter of which I am a coauthor. I assume in this chapter that Sikyatki design style occurs first in the Hopi region; Hays-Gilpin and colleagues assume Sikyatki design style occurs first at Pottery Mound. Until absolute dates are determined for Sikyatki design style in both regions, the "correct" interpretation in the Pottery Mound case study cannot be determined. However, I contend that both interpretations are reflective of the greater range of behaviors practiced by social groups throughout time and space in the Ancestral Pueblo world, regardless of which is ultimately shown to be the case at Pottery Mound.

## REFERENCES

Bowser, Brenda J. 2000. "From Pottery to Politics: An Ethnoarchaeological Case Study of Political Factionalism, Ethnicity, and Pottery Style in the Ecuadorian Amazon." *Journal of Archaeological Method and Theory* 7(3):219–248. https://doi.org/10.102 3/A:1026510620824.

Cameron, Catherine M. 2013. "How People Moved among Ancient Societies: Broadening the View." *American Anthropologist* 115(2):218–231. https://doi.org/10.1111/aman.12005.

Clark, Jeffery J., Deborah L. Huntley, J. Brett Hill, and Patrick D. Lyons. 2013. "The Kayenta Diaspora and Salado Meta-identity in the Late Precontact U. S. Southwest." In *The Archaeology of Hybrid Material Culture*, ed. Jeb J. Card, 399–424. Center for Archaeological Investigations Occasional Paper No. 39. Carbondale: Southern Illinois University Press.

Crown, Patricia L. 1994. *Ceramics and Ideology: Salado Polychrome Pottery*. Albuquerque: University of New Mexico Press.

Deagan, Kathleen. 1998. "Transculturation and Spanish American Ethnogenesis: The Archaeological Legacy of the Quincentenary." In *Studies in Culture Contact: Integration, Culture Change, and Archaeology*, ed. J. G. Cusick, 23–43. Carbonedale: Center for Archaeological Investigations.

Dietler, M. 2009. "Colonial Encounters in Iberia and the Western Mediterranean: An Exploratory Framework." In *Colonial Encounters in Ancient Iberia: Phoenician, Greek, and Indigenous Relations*, ed. M. Dietler and C. López-Ruiz, 3–48. Chicago: Chicago University Press. https://doi.org/10.7208/chicago/9780226148489.003.0001.

Eckert, Suzanne L. 2006. "The Production and Distributed of Glaze-Painted Pottery in the Pueblo Southwest: A Synthesis." In *The Social Life of Pots: Glaze Wares and Cultural Dynamics in the Southwest, AD 1250–1680*, ed. J. A. Habicht-Mauche, S. L. Eckert, and D. L. Huntley, 34–59. Tucson: University of Arizona Press.

Eckert, Suzanne L. 2008. *Pottery and Practice: The Expression of Identity at Pottery Mound and Hummingbird Pueblo*. Albuquerque: University of New Mexico Press.

Eckert, Suzanne L., Kari L. Schleher, and William D. James. 2015. "Communities of Identity, Communities of Practice: Understanding Santa Fe Black-on-white pottery in the Española Basin of New Mexico." *Journal of Archaeological Science* 63:1–12. https://doi.org/10.1016/j.jas.2015.07.001.

Feldman, Marian H. 2012. "The Practical Logic of Style and Memory in Early First Millennium Levantine Ivories." In *Materiality and Social Practice: Transformative Capacities of Intercultural Encounters*, ed. J. Maran and P. W. Stockhammer, 198–212. Oxford, UK: Oxbow Press.

Gilpin, Dennis, and Kelley Hays-Gilpin. 2012. "Polychrome Pottery of the Hopi Mesas." In *Potters and Communities of Practice: Glaze Paint and Polychrome Pottery in the American Southwest, AD 1250–1700*. Tucson: The University of Arizona Press.

González-Ruibal, Alfredo. 2013. "Houses of Resistance: Time and Materiality among the Mao of Ethiopia." In *Mobility, Meaning and Transformations of Things: Shifting Contexts of Material Culture through Time and Space*, ed. H. P. Hahn and H. Weiss, 15–26. Oxford, UK: Oxbow Press.

Habicht-Mauche, Judith A. 1993. *The Pottery from Arroyo Hondo Pueblo, New Mexico: Tribalization and Trade in the Northern Rio Grande*. Arroyo Hondo Archaeological Series 8. Santa Fe: School of American Research Press.

Habicht-Mauche, Judith A. 1995. "Changing Patterns of Pottery Manufacture and Trade in the Northern Rio Grande Region." In *Ceramic Production in the American Southwest*, ed. B. J. Mills and P. L. Crown, 167–199. Tucson: University of Arizona Press.

Hegmon, Michelle. 1995. *The Social Dynamics of Pottery Style in the Early Puebloan Southwest*. Occasional Paper No. 5. Cortez, CO: Crow Canyon Archaeological Center.

Heinz, Marlies, and Julia Linke. 2012. "Hyperculture, Tradition and Identity: How to Communicate with Seals in Times of Global Action. A Middle Bronze Age Seal Impression from Kamid el-Loz." In *Materiality and Social Practice: Transformative Capacities of Intercultural Encounters*, ed. J. Maran and P. W. Stockhammer, 185–190. Oxford, UK: Oxbow Press.

Hill, J. Brett, Jeffery J. Clark, William H. Doelle, and Patrick D. Lyons. 2004. "Prehistoric Demography in the Southwest: Migration, Coalescence, and Hohokam Population Decline." *American Antiquity* 69(04) 689–716. https://doi.org/10.2307/4128444.

Honea, Kenneth H. 1968a. "Material Culture: Ceramics." In *The Cochiti Dam Archaeological Salvage Project,* Part 1, *Report on the 1963 Field Season*, assembled by Charles H. Lange, 111–169. Museum of New Mexico Research Records No. 6. Santa Fe: Museum of New Mexico Press.

Honea, Kenneth H. 1968b. "Appendix C: Newly Described and Redefined Pottery Types." In *The Cochiti Dam Archaeological Salvage Project,* Part 1, *Report on the 1963 Field Season*, assembled by Charles H. Lange, 323. Museum of New Mexico Research Records No. 6. Santa Fe: Museum of New Mexico Press.

Jung, Reinhard. 2012. "Can We Say, What's Behind All those Sherds? Ceramic Innovations in the Eastern Mediterranean at the End of the Second Millennium." In *Materiality and Social Practice: Transformative Capacities of Intercultural Encounters*, ed. J. Maran and P. W. Stockhammer, 104–120. Oxford, UK: Oxbow Press.

Kidder, Alfred V. 1931. *The Dull Paint Wares. With a Section on the Black-and-white wares by Charles A. Amsden*. Papers of the Phillips Academy Southwestern Expedition No. 5. vol. 1. The Pottery of Pecos. New Haven: Yale University Press.

Lang, Richard W. 1982. "Transformations in White Ware Pottery of the Northern Rio Grande." In *Southwestern Ceramics: A Comparative Review*, ed. Albert H. Schroeder, 152–199. Arizona Archaeologist 15. Phoenix: Arizona Archaeological Society.

Lang, Richard W. 1989. "Pottery from LA 2, the Agua Fria Schoolhouse Site: Chronology, Change and Exchange: Circa A.D. 1300–1957." In *Limited Excavations at LA 2, the Agua Fria Schoolhouse Site, Agua Fria Village, Santa Fe County, New Mexico*, ed. Cherie L. Scheick and Richard W. Lang, 57–97. Research Series 216. Santa Fe: Southwest Archaeological Consultants.

Lang, Richard W. 1992. *Archaeological Excavations at Dos Griegos, Upper Canada de Los Alamos, Santa Fe County, New Mexico: Archaic through Pueblo V.* Research Series 283. Santa Fe, NM: Southwest Archaeological Consultants.

Levi, Jerome M. 1998. "The Bow and the Blanket: Religion, Identity, and Resistance in Rarámuri Material Culture." *Journal of Anthropological Research* 54(3):299–324. https://doi.org/10.1086/jar.54.3.3630650.

Liebmann, Matthew J. 2012. *Revolt: An Archaeological History of Pueblo Resistance and Revitalization in 17th Century New Mexico.* Tucson: The University of Arizona Press.

Liebmann, Matthew J. 2013. "Parsing Hybridity: Archaeologies of Amalgamation in Seventeenth-Century New Mexico." In *The Archaeology of Hybrid Material Culture*, ed. Jeb J. Card, 25–49. Center for Archaeological Investigations Occasional Paper No. 39. Carbondale: Southern Illinois University Press.

Maran, Joseph. 2012. "Ceremonial Feasting Equipment, Social Space, and Interculturality in Post-Palatial Tiryns." In *Materiality and Social Practice: Transformative Capacities of Intercultural Encounters*, ed. J. Maran and P. W. Stockhammer, 121–136. Oxford, UK: Oxbow Press.

Maroukis, Thomas C. 2010. *The Peyote Road: Religious Freedom and the Native American Church.* Norman: University of Oklahoma Press.

Mendoza, M. 2004. "Western Toba Messianism and Resistance to Colonization, 1915–1918." *Ethnohistory* 51(2):293–316. https://doi.org/10.1215/00141801-51-2-293.

Mera, Harold P. 1935. *Ceramic Clues to the Prehistory of North Central New Mexico.* Laboratory of Anthropology Technical Series Bulletin 8. Santa Fe: Museum of New Mexico.

Mills, Barbara J. 1995. "Gender and the Reorganization of Historic Zuni Craft Production: Implications for Archaeological Interpretation." *Journal of Anthropological Research* 51(2):149–172. https://doi.org/10.1086/jar.51.2.3630252.

Mills, Barbara J. 2002. "Acts of Resistance: Zuni Ceramics, Social Identity, and the Pueblo Revolt." In *Archaeologies of the Pueblo Revolt: Identity, Meaning, and Renewal in the Pueblo World*, ed. R. W. Preucel, 85–98. Albuquerque: University of New Mexico Press.

Mills, Barbara J. 2007. "Performing the Feast: Visual Display and Suprahousehold Commensalism in the Puebloan Southwest." *American Antiquity* 72(2):210–239. https://doi.org/10.2307/40035812.

Nelson, Kit, and Judith A. Habicht-Mauche. 2006. "Lead, Paint, and Pots: Rio Grande Intercommunity Dynamics from a Glaze Ware Perspective." In *The Social Life of Pots: Glaze Wares and Cultural Dynamics in the Southwest, A.D. 1250–1680*, ed. J. A. Habicht-Mauche, S. L. Eckert, and D. L. Huntley, 197–215. Tucson: University of Arizona Press.

Ortman, Scott G. 2010. "Evidence of a Mesa Verde Homeland for the Tewa Pueblos." In *Leaving Mesa Verde: Peril and Change in the 13th Century Southwest*, ed. Timothy A. Kohler, Mark D. Varien, and Aaron Wright, 222–261. Tucson: The University of Arizona Press.

Rice, Prudence M. 1987. *Pottery Analysis: A Sourcebook*. Chicago: University of Chicago Press.

Ruscavage-Barz, Samantha M. 1999. *Knowing Your Neighbor: Coalition Period Community Dynamics on the Pajarito Plateau, New Mexico*. PhD dissertation, Department of Anthropology, Washington State University, Pullman. Ann Arbor, MI: University Microfilms International.

Sampeck, Kathryn E. 2011. "Understanding Identity: Archaeological Insights from Colonial and Post Colonial North America and the Caribbean." *SAA Archaeological Record* 11(4):38–42.

Schachner, Gregson. 2006. "The Decline of Zuni Glaze Ware Production in the Tumultuous Fifteenth Century." In *The Social Life of Pots: Glaze Wares and Cultural Dynamics in the Southwest, AD 1250–1680*, ed. J. A. Habicht-Mauche, S. L. Eckert, and D. L. Huntley, 124–141. Tucson: The University of Arizona Press.

Schmader, Matthew F. 1988. *Excavation of the Santo Niño Site (LA64677): An Early Coalition Period Pithouse in North Santa Fe*. Albuquerque, NM: Rio Grande Consultants.

Shepard, Anna O. 1936. "Technology of Pecos Pottery." In *The Pottery of Pecos*, Vol. II, Part II, compiled by Alfred V. Kidder and Anna O. Shepard, 389–587. Papers of the Philips Academy Southwest Expedition No. 7. New Haven: Yale University Press.

Stockhammer, Philipp W. 2012. "Entangled Pottery: Phenomena of Appropriation in the Late Bronze Age Eastern Mediterranean." In *Materiality and Social Practice: Transformative Capacities of Intercultural Encounters*, ed. J. Maran and P. W. Stockhammer, 89–103. Oxford, UK: Oxbow Press.

Stubbs, Stanley A., and William S. Stallings, Jr. 1953. *The Excavation of Pindi Pueblo, New Mexico*. Monographs of the School of American Research and the Laboratory of Anthropology 18. Santa Fe: School of American Research, Santa Fe / Laboratory of Anthropology, Museum of New Mexico.

Sunseri, Jun. 2017. "Grazing to Gravy: Faunal Remains and Indications of Genízaro Foodways on the Spanish Colonial Frontier of New Mexico." *International Journal of Historical Archaeology* 21:577–597.

Wilson, C. Dean. 2008. "Pottery Analysis." In *Living on the Northern Rio Grande Frontier*, ed. J. Moore, Vol. 2: 39–52. Archaeology Notes 315. Sana Fe: Office of Archaeological Studies, Museum of New Mexico.

Wurst, Louann. 1999. "Internalizing Class in Historical Archaeology." *Historical Archaeology* 33(1):7–21.

Yasur-Landau, Assaf. 2012. "The Role of the Canaanite Population in the Aegean Migration to the Southern Levant in the Late Second Millennium BCE." In *Materiality and Social Practice: Transformative Capacities of Intercultural Encounters*, ed. J. Maran and P. W. Stockhammer, 191–197. Oxford, UK: Oxbow Press.

# Social Units and Social Interaction

# 7

# Identifying Social Units and Social Interaction during the Pithouse Period in the Mimbres Region, Southwestern New Mexico

BARBARA J. ROTH

Archaeologists have long battled with the issue of linking living, active social beings with the static remains they left behind. With the advent of household archaeology, ceramic sociology, and "actualistic studies" in the 1970s and 1980s, attempts were made to bridge the archaeological record, especially architecture and artifacts, with the people who lived in and used them (e.g., Longacre 1970; Wilk and Rathje 1982). In the decades since these landmark attempts, archaeologists have used a variety of new techniques and new theoretical approaches to develop these linkages (Bandy and Fox 2010; Douglass and Gonlin 2012; Varien and Potter 2008).

The chapters in this section represent some of the most recent attempts to define, delineate, and understand various kinds of social groupings that were present at prehistoric sites and the role of social interaction in shaping them. The "social units" that these chapters address range from family groups to households to lineages to communities. In each case, the authors use a variety of tactics to reconstruct these social units and address the role that social interaction played in their development and maintenance. The insights derived from

DOI: 10.5876/9781607327356.c007

their work have important and far-reaching implications for our knowledge of social organization, social relations, and social change.

In this chapter, I examine the linkages between pithouse architecture and associated features and the people who occupied and used them using data from two sites, the Harris site and La Gila Encantada, occupied during the Late Pithouse (AD 550–1000) period in the Mimbres region of southwestern New Mexico (figure 7.1). The two sites represent distinct occupations in terms of population size, subsistence practices, social organizational complexity, and the nature of the social units who occupied them. Data from these sites show that different kinds of social units can use the same basic suite of architectural features. By focusing on the context and characteristics associated with the social units that lived within these features, it is possible to expand our understanding of the reasons for the development of different social configurations.

The primary social unit at both sites and at others occupied during the Pithouse period in the Mimbres region was the household (Hegmon et al. 2000; Roth 2010a). Cross-cultural studies have established that households were the basic social and economic unit in middle-range societies and were the means for maintaining and transmitting land rights and resource access (Blanton 1994; Douglass and Gonlin 2012; Hendon 1996). Social relations within and between households across much of the prehistoric Southwest were structured primarily along kinship lines (Ensor 2013; Peregrine 2001). For this study, the basic premise for reconstructing "social units," in this case the kin groups who occupied the houses, has followed Tringham (2000) in viewing pithouses and associated extramural features as material manifestations of the social group. Data from these sites indicate that they were occupied by different kinds of households and this affected social relations between households and within the overall community. Differences in the nature of these social units appear to be tied to agricultural intensification, population size, and the overall extent of the social network, with groups living at the Harris site in the Mimbres River Valley part of a dynamic, interacting community both within the site and within the valley, and those at the La Gila Encantada site representing a more rural, insular occupation. The fact that both of these sites were occupied during the same time period and that their constituent households occupied similar architectural features indicates that differences between social units must be examined using multiple lines of evidence. In the remainder of this chapter, I address some of the insights that have been gleaned on the nature of the social units at the two sites and then discuss how and why these different kinds of household configurations developed.

## SOCIAL UNITS AND SOCIAL INTERACTION AT THE HARRIS SITE

The Harris site is a large pithouse village located in the north-central portion of the Mimbres River Valley (figure 7.1) and is best known for Haury's seminal work

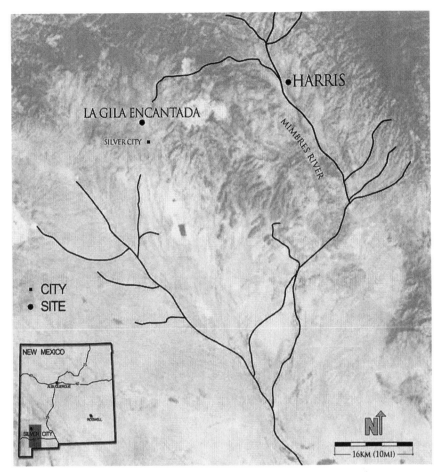

**FIGURE 7.1.** *Locations of the Harris and La Gila Encantada sites, southwestern New Mexico*

there in the early 1930s, which contributed to his development of the Mogollon concept (Haury 1936). Haury worked in the southern portion of the site, where he documented 34 houses, including three sequentially used communal structures (kivas) surrounding a central plaza. Investigations by archaeologists from the University of Nevada, Las Vegas, directed by the author, focused on the northern portion of the site (figure 7.2), with the goal of examining household organization at a large riverine pithouse village and the attendant changes in sedentism and subsistence practices that occurred over time (Roth 2015).

A total of 20 houses (five sets of which are superimposed), 34 extramural features, 20 burials, and portions of a large Three Circle–phase communal structure were excavated during UNLV's investigations at the Harris site, along with the center posthole of a large Three Circle–phase kiva (Pithouse 10) excavated by Haury

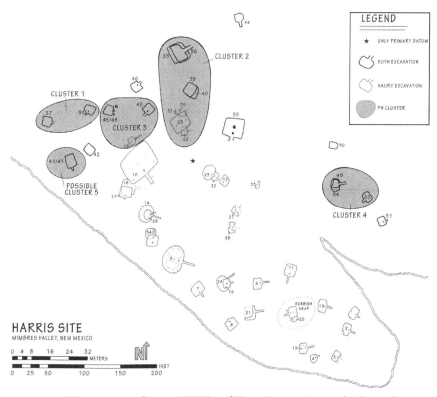

**FIGURE 7.2.** *Harris site map showing UNLV's and Haury's excavations and pithouse clusters.*

(Roth 2015; Roth and Baustian 2015). As a result of this fieldwork, three levels of community organization were identified and evidence for changes in household organization over time were documented. The three levels include (1) clusters of pithouses that are interpreted as the remains of extended-family corporate groups, similar to what has been proposed for other large Late Pithouse–period sites in the Mimbres River Valley (Creel 2006a; Shafer 2003, 2006) and in the Hohokam region to the west (Howard 1985; Doyel 1991); (2) autonomous households akin to what has been observed at other nonriverine sites (Roth 2010b); and (3) community-level integration, which was accomplished via the communal structures and central plaza. These data and those from NAN Ranch (Shafer 2003, 2006) and Old Town (Creel 2006a, 2006b) indicate that the development of extended-family corporate groups in the Mimbres region was tied to an increased commitment to irrigation agriculture and the labor requirements, land-tenure issues, and other social changes associated with it. These extended families are first observed during the San Francisco phase (AD 650–750), with the number expanding significantly during the Three Circle phase.

The clusters of pithouses were first identified based on a magnetometer survey. These clusters were spatially discrete and separated from one another by open areas, one of which was clearly identified on the ground as a small open plaza area north of the central plaza (figure 7.2). Excavations of houses within the clusters revealed that different clusters shared architectural traits that were not shared with other clusters, enabling the delineation of relationships between them (table 7.1). The clusters often did not face each other but opened onto shared extramural areas containing ramadas, storage pits, and processing areas. Burial data have been especially crucial in reconstructing the nature of these clusters and in illustrating the important role that they played in the community (Roth and Baustian 2015).

The presence of extended-family households had been inferred by previous researchers in the Mimbres region because of the presence of clustered houses observed at other sites (Shafer 2003; Creel 2006b), but most of the large pithouse villages in the Mimbres River Valley were beneath large pueblos, making them difficult to interpret and discern. The Harris site does not have a pueblo component and this made it possible to document the presence of extended-family households. The fact that these clusters were spatially distinct and shared unique traits was critical to establishing that they were distinct social units but it did not necessarily establish how they maintained this distinction, how they were integrated into the overall community, or the nature of intrahousehold social relations. Those data were gleaned via an examination of the shared traits, architectural features, and burial characteristics.

Cluster 1, dating to the early Three Circle phase, was perhaps the easiest to interpret as an interacting social unit because it consists of two houses (Pithouses 37 and 38) that opened onto a common area that contained a ramada, processing features, and a large storage pit (figure 7.2). They were identified as an interacting social group because the houses face each other, share an extramural work space, and have the shared trait of ceramic vessels plastered into the floor behind the hearth (figure 7.3). The assemblages recovered from them suggest that they were not one of the clusters inhabited by individuals holding significant levels of social power, however (Roth and Baustian 2015). The houses lack the evidence for craft production and socially important individuals that has been found in the other clusters, and this cluster does not have a superimposed "anchor household" (see below).

Cluster 3, the earliest extended-family household on the site (dating to the San Francisco phase) is interpreted as an extended-family household whose members played an important social role in the community and perhaps in the overall development of the community (Roth and Baustian 2015; Roth n.d.). The houses in this cluster (Pithouses 43, 48/45, and Haury's Pithouse 28) shared the trait of vessels plastered in the floor behind the hearth and surrounded a common

**TABLE 7.1.** Pithouse clusters and autonomous households at the Harris site, UNLV excavations.

| Pithouse # | Cluster # or Autonomous | Phase Assignment | Shared Traits (for clusters) |
|---|---|---|---|
| 35 | 2 | Three Circle | Same architectural footprint as PH 36—upper house; superimposed hearths |
| 36 | 2 | Three Circle | Same architectural footprint as PH 35—lower house; superimposed hearths; child burial in floor pit |
| 37 | 1 | Three Circle | Pot plastered in floor behind hearth; faces shared communal work area |
| 38 | 1 | Three Circle | Pot plastered in floor behind hearth; faces shared communal work area |
| 39 | 2 | Three Circle | Upper house above PH 40—superimposed hearth |
| 40 | 2 | Georgetown? | Lower house below PH 39—superimposed hearth |
| 41 | 5 | Three Circle | Same architectural footprint as PH 47—upper house; burial through house floor and seated on floor of PH 47 |
| 42 | Autonomous | Three Circle | |
| 43 | 3 | San Francisco | Pot plastered in floor behind hearth; shared extramural work and burial area |
| 44 | Autonomous | Three Circle | |
| 45 | 3 | San Francisco | Beneath PH 48; shared extramural work area; child burial in floor pit |
| 46 | Autonomous | Three Circle | |
| 47 | 5 | Three Circle | Same architectural footprint as PH 41—lower house; burial seated on floor |
| 48 | 3 | Three Circle (early) | Above PH 45; pot plastered in floor behind hearth; shared extramural work area |
| 49 | 4 | Three Circle (late) | Same architectural footprint as PH 54—upper house; tabular knives |
| 51 | Autonomous | Three Circle | |
| 52 | Autonomous | Transitional | |
| 53 | 4 | Three Circle | Tabular knife |
| 54 | 4 | Three Circle | Same architectural footprint as PH 49—lower house; tabular knives |

**FIGURE 7.3.** *Ceramic vessel plastered into floor of Pithouse 38, Cluster 1.*

area with three burials—two adult males and an older adult female—which contained many grave goods and represent some of the wealthier burials on the site
(Roth and Baustian 2015). Social standing for Cluster 3 was further inferred from
the presence of a superimposed structure (Pithouse 48/45) with a child buried
in a floor pit in the bottom structure with multiple ceramic vessels, two shell
bracelets, and two turquoise pendants. Roth and Baustian (2015) linked the presence of this child burial and a similar one in a superimposed house (PH 35/36) in
Cluster 2 (see below) to both household social power and to the maintenance of
social memory associated with land tenure.

Cluster 2, located north of the central plaza and consisting of superimposed
Pithouses 35/36, 39/40, and Haury's 23/22/31/30 (figure 7.2), was occupied
throughout much of the Three Circle phase and represents another cluster interpreted as having significant social standing. The houses excavated by UNLV had
the shared trait of having the hearths of the upper house touching the hearths
of the lower house, which Roth and Baustian (2015) tie to the maintenance of
social memory, an interpretation further supported by the presence of a child
burial in a floor pit with multiple grave goods noted above.

Cluster 4 was found to the east of the central plaza (figure 7.2) and appears to
have been another important extended family who played a key role in community

integration during the Three Circle phase (Roth n.d.). The houses in this cluster (Pithouses 49/54 and 53) have the majority of the tabular knives (5 of 8; 62.5%) found at the site, indicating fiber production and perhaps fermentation activities. The recovery of ceramic vessels from the superimposed house associated with this cluster (Pithouse 49/54) with heavy pitting and wear characteristic of fermentation (Miller and Graves 2012; Miller, chapter 12, this volume) has led Roth (2015) to argue that this extended-family household was sponsoring ritual activities. This is further supported by the recovery of a palette on the floor of PH 53, which is one of only five occurrences of palettes on the site. Two of the other palettes were found in a feasting pit in the central plaza outside the entryway of Three Circle–phase kiva Pithouse 55 and the other two were associated with a burial in a superimposed house (Pithouse 41/47) in Cluster 5 on the opposite end of the plaza.

The occupants of the superimposed structures thus appear to have played important social roles both within the household clusters, perhaps as heads of households, and within the community at large (Roth and Baustian 2015; Roth n.d.). Roth and Baustian (2015) use architectural, artifact, and burial data to argue that these served as "anchor" households because of their association with the central plaza and the presence of wealthy burials in them. The restricted location of these structures near the central plaza and the artifact assemblages recovered from several of them suggest that they were participating in and probably sponsoring community-level rituals.

The autonomous houses identified during investigations at the Harris site were spatially distinct, do not share any artifact or architectural traits with the clustered houses, and do not contain socially important burials, yet they appear to have been integrated into the larger community (Roth n.d.). Reconstructing the role of these autonomous households within the community has helped clarify both the nature of social organization and differences in social relations through time at the site.

Data from excavated autonomous pithouses indicate that they were integrating into the community using a number of different strategies. Pithouse 42 contained evidence in both the architecture and the ceramic assemblage of interaction with groups to the north of the Mimbres region. The house is a typical Mimbres-style structure with four roof-support posts, a large center post, and an ash-filled hearth with a hearthstone (figure 7.4). However, along the south wall of the house, in front of the hearth, was a large deflector stone, a trait atypical of the Mimbres region but common in sites to the north. Deflector stones in northern pithouses are usually associated with ventilators, but no ventilator was present in Pithouse 42. Cibola whiteware was recovered from the structure along with Mimbres Style I Black-on-white ceramics, again indicating some degree of contact with groups to the north. The house contained a large storage pit with evidence of ceramic production activities, including a lap stone with evidence

**FIGURE 7.4.** *Hearth with deflector stone, Pithouse 42.*

of pigment processing and two loafs of unfired clay. I interpret this household as reflecting occupation by a nonlocal person who married into the community, based on the presence of the deflector stone and nonlocal whitewares. This person was likely male, given the evidence of household production of local-style ceramic vessels and the abundant ethnographic data that women were the potters in Southwestern societies (e.g., Bunzel 1929). This house serves as a reminder that the occupants of Harris participated in an even larger social community, since intermarriage likely explains the diverse characteristics present in this structure.

The dynamics of social interaction at the Harris site are also visible in a second autonomous household, Pithouse 46. Two metates were found on the floor of Pithouse 46 and represent two different metate styles, one a vesicular-basalt open trough and the second a volcanic three-quarter-trough metate. The open-trough design is characteristic of the Hohokam region to the west, leading Falvey (2015) to argue that either a nonlocal person lived in the house or that the metate was gifted to someone in the household. If this was a nonlocal person, then it was most likely a male, as the wear management strategies observed on the metate (which represent women's use based on cross-cultural ethnographic data) were identical to those observed on other metates at the site but dissimilar to those observed in the Hohokam region (Falvey 2015:300). This again illustrates that the Harris site participated in a larger regional social network.

Finally, autonomous Pithouse 44 contained evidence of activities that potentially served to integrate its residents into the community. The house was abandoned after flooding collapsed the eastern wall, leaving numerous artifacts that were stored against the wall buried under a layer of mud. Four Three Circle neck-corrugated jars were found in this area and these jars exhibit evidence of heavy pitting, like those observed in Cluster 4. It is thus possible that members of this household were fermenting liquids to participate in community-wide gatherings and rituals.

## SOCIAL UNITS AND SOCIAL INTERACTION AT LA GILA ENCANTADA

La Gila Encantada (LGE) is located on an isolated ridge top above Little Walnut Canyon north of Silver City, New Mexico, in an upland setting away from the Mimbres River Valley (figure 7.1). The site contained a dense ceramic and chipped- and ground-stone scatter with numerous pithouse depressions but lacked a pueblo component. It is estimated that there were perhaps 20–25 pithouses at the site, but these represent occupations dating to all phases of the Late Pithouse period, so the overall site size, even during the peak of the occupation during the Three Circle phase, remained relatively small, especially in comparison to the Harris site and other large riverine villages such as Galaz (Anyon and LeBlanc 1984), Swarts (Cosgrove and Cosgrove 1932), NAN Ranch (Shafer 2003), and Old Town (Creel 2006b).

The goal of excavations at LGE was to obtain data on Late Pithouse–period occupations in upland settings away from the Mimbres River Valley and to explore the relationship between sedentism, agricultural dependence, and household organization at these upland sites (Roth 2010b). These topics were addressed with excavations focused on pithouses and their associated extramural

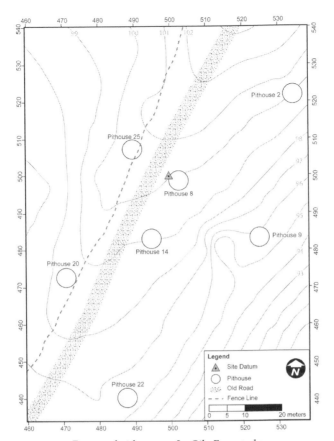

**FIGURE 7.5.** *Excavated pithouses at La Gila Encantada.*

features. A cesium magnetometer survey was done in the northwest portion of the site prior to beginning excavations (Rogers et al. 2010) and confirmed the presence of numerous pithouses on the site. Three pithouses were excavated in their entirety (PH 2, 14, and 22), excavations of one house (PH 8) encompassed most of the interior of the house, three houses (PH 9, 20 and 25) were tested, and data from one previously excavated pithouse (PH 23) were available (figure 7.5; table 7.2). Data from these excavated pithouses indicate that the site was occupied throughout all phases of the Pithouse period by households whose members practiced some level of mobility until the Three Circle phase, in part because of delayed agricultural intensification in these upland settings.

Data from LGE indicate that the site was occupied by autonomous households throughout its occupation, despite some evidence for increased sedentism over time (Roth 2010b). No evidence of pithouse clusters or communal structures was found in the magnetometer survey or during the excavations, despite

**TABLE 7.2.** Excavated pithouses at La Gila Encantada

| Pithouse | Phase of Occupation | Excavation Extent | Date |
|---|---|---|---|
| 2 | Three Circle | Fully excavated | 735–865[†] (wall) |
| | | | 660–710 (I = 680)** |
| | | | 790–900 (I = 880)** |
| 8 | Three Circle | Three-quarters excavated | 690–810 (I = 770)** |
| 9 | Three Circle | Tested—1 × 3 m unit | 835–1015[†] (hearth) |
| | | | 810–840; 860–910, 920–960 (I = 890)** |
| 14 | Georgetown | Fully excavated | 600–660 (I = 640)** |
| | | | 380–530 (I = 420)** |
| 20 | Three Circle | Tested—4 × 2 m unit | |
| 22 | San Francisco | Fully excavated | 670–690 (I = 660)** |
| | | | 679v[††] |
| 23 | San Francisco* | Previously excavated | |
| 25 | Three Circle | Tested—4 × 2 m unit | 770–900 (I = 810, 840, 860)** |

\* Previously excavated by Raymond Mauldin.
[†] Archaeomagnetic dates determined using Sternberg's (1982) statistical dating method.
** One sigma, calibrated date; all radiocarbon dates were calibrated using INTCAL 98 (Stuiver et al. 1998).
[††] Dendrochronology date.
I = intercept point

the fact that it is estimated that approximately 40 percent of the houses present at the site were excavated or tested.

LGE appears to represent small family groups who moved seasonally to the uplands, starting in the Georgetown phase (AD 550–650), to farm, hunt, and gather, and who probably initially overwintered there. The excavated Georgetown-phase structure was ritually retired and a number of offertory items, including an Early Archaic projectile point, a shell-bracelet fragment, and a stone bowl with corn pollen, were placed on the floor before it was burned (Roth and Schriever 2015). This kind of behavior is usually associated with some form of maintenance of social memory (cf. Hodder 2006; Hodder and Cessford 2004). It is possible that by the Georgetown phase this particular spot on the landscape had become important to the families who initially lived there and the ritual retirement of the house was a commemorative behavior that linked the occupants to the land, which is in one of the most productive portions of the Little Walnut Creek valley. This suggests that groups were marking the site and access to the land and resources associated with it for their return.

Evidence from the San Francisco–phase structures indicates that some level of seasonal mobility continued into the AD 700s, followed by increased sedentism during the early Three Circle phase (ca. AD 800). Architectural data illustrate this shift, especially in Pithouse 2, which is rectangular with well-plastered floors, walls, and entryway. Three Circle–phase Pithouse 25 also had a well-plastered floor and north wall (the other walls and entryway were not found). Perhaps the best evidence indicating that sedentism increased during the Three Circle phase comes from the abundance of Three Circle–phase trash found in the abandoned pithouses. As Schlanger (1991) has noted, the presence of artifacts with varying use lives in trash deposits is a key characteristic associated with longer-occupied sites.

This increase in sedentism was likely tied to an increasing emphasis on agriculture, as the location of the site above an expanse of arable land above Little Walnut Creek would have enabled floodplain farming, but paleobotanical and faunal data point to the continued use of a wide range of wild resources, including walnuts, cattails, and piñon, along with the hunting of deer and rabbits. Diehl (1996) has used paleobotanical data to argue that the introduction of a new strain of eight-rowed maize around AD 700 led to increased agricultural dependence in the broader Mogollon region, providing larger yields that were easier to grind than earlier varieties. The new maize variety was apparently correlated with an increase in the use of trough metates, which Adams (1999) has shown are more efficient for grinding maize. The ground-stone data from LGE reflect this changing technology. It is important to note, however, that despite an increased focus on agricultural production, wild resources remained an important part of the diet during the Three Circle phase and little change in the diet composition was noted from the earliest occupation during the Georgetown phase (Roth 2010b).

With the exception of Pithouse 22, a San Francisco–phase house with an internal storage pit that is thought to be associated with overwintering at the site, no storage pits were found at LGE. While this could be due to the limited amount of extramural excavation, no storage pits were visible in the magnetometer survey. Portions of numerous large jars were found in extramural, roof fall/wall fall, and trash fill contexts, and these may have been used for storage. In contrast, the Harris site had a number of large storage pits (usually 1 m deep) in extramural contexts, often in extramural work areas and ramadas shared by the pithouse clusters. This apparently represents communal storage at the Harris site by the extended-family households, with small interior storage pits representing individual household storage. The presence of these communal storage facilities further illustrates the distinction between the social units that occupied these two sites.

No burials were found at LGE and this is not typical of Pithouse-period habitation sites. Given the ritual retirement of structures at the site, it is surprising that no burials were found. It is possible that burials were present in unexcavated portions of the site or in houses that were not excavated; however, even if this were the case, the overall lack of burials provides further contrast with the large riverine villages.

## COMPARING SOCIAL UNITS AT THE HARRIS
## AND LA GILA ENCANTADA SITES

Data from the Harris site and LGE indicate that the nature of social units present during the Late Pithouse period in the Mimbres region changed over time and also varied spatially, with more complex social groupings (and consequently site structure) present at large riverine sites. At Harris, clusters of households that share characteristics that indicate that they are the remains of extended families have been identified. This has been an important step in the reconstruction of the social dynamics that occurred during the latter portion of the Pithouse period in the Mimbres River Valley, a process that is seen as associated with irrigation, land tenure, and the rise to social prominence of some households. By combining architecture, artifact, and burial data, it is possible to discern that some Three Circle–phase households were socially distinct and that they marked this via their houses and their activities. These extended-family households, all but one of which had superimposed houses as a key component of the household, represent a different kind of social unit than that observed in the other houses at the Harris site, and evidence from them indicates that these differences were tied to social power that likely derived from economic sources, probably agricultural intensification associated with irrigation, and perhaps ritual sponsorship. Other households that did not share these social distinctions were still involved in the community. The fact that the site is organized so that most activities took place in the open—in extramural areas and on rooftops—indicates that we may be making more of these social distinctions than they did, however. The role of the communal structures and central plaza appears to have been a critical component of community integration (Roth n.d.). Artifact data (shell, turquoise, obsidian, ceramics) and evidence of possible intermarriage indicate that the occupants of the Harris site participated in a social network that extended outside the Mimbres Valley.

The agricultural intensification, population growth, and organizational differences observed at the Harris site are not present at LGE. In fact, the families who lived at this site followed a very different trajectory than that seen at the large pithouse villages in the Mimbres River Valley. Data from LGE indicate that the site was occupied by independent households during all phases of the Late Pithouse period. The houses are distributed across the site, no clusters of houses or patterning to house orientations were observed, and no superimposed houses, which represent such significant social units at the Harris site, were present. The distribution of houses indicates that they were discrete households and the material remains recovered from them point to household-level production. This apparently did not change over time, despite some evidence for increased sedentism and agricultural dependence, as household layout and activities remained similar from the Georgetown phase on. It is likely that cooperation occurred during farming, hunting, and gathering forays, but the data from LGE do not indicate that households participated regularly in a wider social network. Non-Mimbres pottery and shell are rare at the site and the bulk of lithic procurement appears to have been done locally.

## CONCLUSION

*Social units* really means "people"—and peopling sites has always been a challenge for archaeologists (Tringham 1991). It is easy to talk about "households"—configurations of architecture and artifacts—but much harder to talk about the men, women, children, and families who lived in them. So in the end what can we say about the "social units" that occupied the Harris and La Gila Encantada sites? First, the reconstruction of these "units" highlights the difficulties involved in using the archaeological record to get at social systems and the importance of using multiple lines of evidence in this process. This is especially true for the two sites described here, as distinct social units lived in similar architectural features. By integrating excavated data from all contexts at the sites and using a range of techniques (like those highlighted in the other chapters in this section), it was possible to move from pithouses to independent and extended families and to examine the different causes and consequences of these differences in social unit configurations. As a result, we are beginning to get a picture of the true dynamics of what life was like in pithouse villages in the Mimbres region and how it differed temporally and spatially.

*Acknowledgments:* Funding for work at the Harris site was provided by the National Science Foundation (Grant #1049434). Permission to work at La Gila Encantada was granted by the Archaeological Conservancy. Thanks are due to the many students and volunteers who worked on the project, especially to Leon Lorentzen and to Grant County Society volunteers Marilyn Markel, Kyle Meredith, Josh Reeves, and Judy and Carroll Welch. Thanks to Justin DeMaio, Christina Dykstra, Lauren Falvey, Thomas Gruber, Ashley Lauzon, Danielle Romero, Denise Ruzicka, and Robert Stokes for their analysis of the artifacts from the sites. Finally, thanks to Roger Anyon, Darrell Creel, Robert Stokes, and Aaron Woods for their input on many of the ideas discussed in this chapter.

## REFERENCES

Adams, Jenny L. 1999. "Refocusing the Role of Food-Grinding Tools as Correlates for Subsistence Strategies in the U.S. Southwest." *American Antiquity* 64(03):475–498. https://doi.org/10.2307/2694147.

Anyon, Roger, and Steven A. LeBlanc. 1984. *The Galaz Ruin: A Prehistoric Mimbres Village in Southwestern New Mexico.* Maxwell Museum of Anthropology Publication Series. Albuquerque: University of New Mexico Press.

Bandy, Matthew S., and Jake R. Fox, eds. 2010. *Becoming Villagers: Comparing Early Village Societies*. Amerind Studies in Archaeology. Tucson: University of Arizona Press.

Blanton, Richard E. 1994. *Houses and Households: A Comparative Study*. New York: Plenum Press. https://doi.org/10.1007/978-1-4899-0990-9.

Bunzel, Ruth. 1929. *The Pueblo Potter*. New York: Columbia University Press.

Cosgrove, H. S., and C. B. Cosgrove. 1932. *The Swarts Ruin: A Typical Mimbres Site in Southwestern New Mexico*. Papers of the Peabody Museum of Archaeology and Ethnology. Vol. 15. Cambridge, MA: Harvard University.

Creel, Darrell. 2006a. "Evidence for Mimbres Social Differentiation at the Old Town Site." In *Mimbres Society*, ed. Valli S. Powell-Marti and Patricia A. Gilman, 32–44. Tucson: University of Arizona Press.

Creel, Darrell. 2006b. *Excavations at the Old Town Ruin, Luna County, New Mexico, 1989–2003*. Santa Fe: US Bureau of Land Management, New Mexico State Office.

Diehl, Michael. 1996. "The Intensity of Maize Processing and Production in Upland Mogollon Pithouse Villages, A.D. 200–1000." *American Antiquity* 61(01) 102–115. https://doi.org/10.2307/282305.

Douglass, John G., and Nancy Gonlin, eds. 2012. *Ancient Households of the Americas*. Boulder: University Press of Colorado.

Doyel, David E. 1991. "Hohokam Cultural Evolution in the Phoenix Basin." In *Exploring the Hohokam: Prehistoric Desert Peoples of the American Southwest*, ed. George J. Gumerman, 231–278. Albuquerque: University of New Mexico Press.

Ensor, Bradley E. 2013. *The Archaeology of Kinship: Advancing Interpretation and Contributions to Theory*. Tucson: University of Arizona Press.

Falvey, Lauren W. 2015. "Ground Stone from the Harris Site." In *Archaeological Investigations at the Harris Site (LA 1867), Grant County, New Mexico*, ed. Barbara J. Roth, 225–299. Report on file, Department of Anthropology, UNLV.

Haury, Emil W. 1936. *The Mogollon Culture of Southwestern New Mexico*. Medallion Papers 20. Globe, AZ: Globe.

Hegmon, Michelle, Scott G. Ortman, and Jeannette L. Mobley-Tanaka. 2000. "Women, Men, and the Organization of Space." In *Women and Men in the Prehispanic Southwest*, ed. Patricia L. Crown, 43–90. Santa Fe: School of American Research Press.

Hendon, Julia A. 1996. "Archaeological Approaches to the Organization of Domestic Labor: Household Practice and Domestic Relations." *Annual Review of Anthropology* 25(1):45–61. https://doi.org/10.1146/annurev.anthro.25.1.45.

Hodder, Ian. 2006. *The Leopard's Tale: Revealing the Mysteries of Çatalhöyük*. London: Thames and Hudson.

Hodder, Ian, and Craig Cessford. 2004. "Daily Practice and Social Memory at Çatalhöyük." *American Antiquity* 69(01):17–40. https://doi.org/10.2307/4128346.

Howard, Jerry. 1985. "Courtyard Groups and Domestic Cycling: A Hypothetical Model of Growth." In *Proceedings of the 1983 Hohokam Symposium*, Part 1, ed. A. E. Dittert Jr.

and D. Dove, 311–326. Occasional Paper No. 2. Phoenix: Arizona Archaeological
Society.

Longacre, William A. 1970. *Archaeology as Anthropology: A Case Study.* University of
Arizona Anthropological Papers No. 17. Tucson: University of Arizona.

Miller, Myles R., and Tim B. Graves. 2012. *Sacramento Pueblo: An El Paso and Late Glencoe
Phase Pueblo in the Southern Sacramento Mountains.* Fort Bliss Cultural Resources
Report No. 10–22. Fort Bliss, Texas: Environmental Division.

Peregrine, Peter N. 2001. "Matrilocality, Corporate Strategy, and the Organization of
Production in the Chacoan World." *American Antiquity* 66(01):36–46. https://doi.org
/10.2307/2694316.

Rogers, Michael, Kevin Faehndrich, Barbara Roth, and Greg Shear. 2010. "Cesium
Magnetometer Surveys of a Pithouse Site near Silver City, New Mexico." *Journal of
Archaeological Science* 37(5):1102–1109. https://doi.org/10.1016/j.jas.2009.12.010.

Roth, Barbara J. 2010a. "Engendering Mimbres Mogollon Pithouses." In *Engendering
Households in the Prehistoric Southwest*, ed. Barbara J. Roth, 136–152. Tucson: University
of Arizona Press.

Roth, Barbara J. 2010b. *Archaeological Investigations at La Gila Encantada (LA 113467), Grant
County, New Mexico.* Albuquerque, NM: Report submitted to the Archaeological
Conservancy.

Roth, Barbara J. 2015. *Archaeological Investigations at the Harris Site (LA 1867), Grant County,
New Mexico.* UNLV: Report on file, Department of Anthropology.

Roth, Barbara J. n.d. "Pithouse Community Development at the Harris Site,
Southwestern New Mexico." In *Communities and Households in the Greater Southwest*,
ed. Robert J. Stokes. Boulder: University Press of Colorado.

Roth, Barbara J., and Kathryn M. Baustian. 2015. "Kin Groups and Social Power at the
Harris Site, Southwestern New Mexico." *American Antiquity* 80(03):451–471. https://
doi.org/10.7183/0002-7316.80.3.451.

Roth, Barbara J., and Bernard Schriever. 2015. "Ritual Dedication and Retirement at
Mimbres Valley Pithouse Sites." *Kiva* 81:179–200.

Schlanger, Sarah. 1991. "On Manos, Metates, and the History of Site Occupations."
*American Antiquity* 56(3):460–474. https://doi.org/10.2307/280895.

Shafer, Harry J. 2003. *Mimbres Archaeology at the NAN Ranch Ruin.* Albuquerque:
University of New Mexico Press.

Shafer, Harry J. 2006. "Extended Families to Corporate Groups: Pithouse to Pueblo
Transformation of Mimbres Society." In *Mimbres Society*, ed. Valli S Powell-Marti and
Patricia A. Gilman, 15–31. Tucson: University of Arizona Press.

Sternberg, R. S. 1982. *Archaeomagnetic Secular Variation of Direction and Paleointensity in
the American Southwest.* Ph.D. dissertation, University of Arizona. Ann Arbor, MI:
University Microfilms International.

Stuiver, M., P. J. Reimer, and T. F. Braziunas. 1998. "High-Precision Radiocarbon Age Calibration for Terrestrial and Marine Samples." *Radiocarbon* 40:1127–1151.

Tringham, Ruth E. 1991. "Households with Faces: The Challenge of Gender in Prehistoric Architectural Remains." In *Engendering Archaeology: Women and Prehistory*, ed. Joan M. Gero and Margaret W. Conkey, 93–131. Oxford, UK: Blackwell.

Tringham, Ruth E. 2000. "The Continuous House: A View from the Deep Past." In *Beyond Kinship: Social and Material Reproduction in House Societies*, ed. Rosemary A. Joyce and Susan D. Gillespie, 115–134. Philadelphia: University of Pennsylvania Press.

Varien, Mark D., and James M. Potter, eds. 2008. *The Social Construction of Communities: Agency, Structure, and Identity in the Prehispanic Southwest*. Lanham, MD: Altamira Press.

Wilk, Richard, and William L. Rathje. 1982. "Towards an Archaeology of the Household." *American Behavioral Scientist* 25(6):617–639. https://doi.org/10.1177/000276482 025006003.

# 8

# House Variability during the Pueblo III Period in the Kayenta Region of the American Southwest

TAMMY STONE

There has long been an interest in domestic architecture among archaeologists concerned with issues of household structure, mobility, economic organization, and status differentiation (Amerlinck 2001; Blanton 1994; Dawson 2001; Gilman 1987; Jewett and Lightfoot 1986; Kamp 1993; Lightfoot and Feinman 1982; McGuire and Schiffer 1983; Rapoport 1990; Rocek 1995; Steadman 1996; Wilk 1990; Wills 2001). Architecture provides shelter from the elements as well as a way to delineate social space and activity areas. As with other chapters in this section of the volume, I assume that clustering of houses within villages and differences between houses are material manifestations of social constructs that both structure interactions and are the stage upon which social structures are challenged. Domestic architecture, in particular, houses social action at the most basic level: it serves as a locus of enculturation of the next generation as well as providing a setting for social interaction between socially close individuals. Its external appearance provides a physical manifestation of the inhabitant's identity and concepts of their place in society in terms of social status. At the same time, the house's internal organization structures daily life in a physical way. As such, it is "not only the physical stage on which the dramas of social interaction are enacted but also an integral component of the drama itself, structuring culture while being structured by it" (Kamp 1993:293; see also Rapoport 1990; Wilk 1990).

In state-level societies, differentiation in the external appearance of the house, as well as its size and construction, is often interpreted in terms of status differentiation (Blanton 1994; Wilk 1990). Similarly, differences in house size in middle-range societies, including the Southwest, have been interpreted as evidence of the emergence of powerful leaders (Lightfoot and Feinman 1982; Wallace 2003). In both cases, however, similarity in basic styles of domestic architectural layout and construction exists and differences are restricted to size, quality of construction, and external embellishments.

Differences in domestic structures that go beyond size, quality of construction, and external embellishments in middle-range societies are more complicated, especially when variability in the internal organization of space and placement of mnemonic markers are evident. In situations where two different types of domestic structures are used simultaneously, such as semisubterranean pithouses with brush superstructures and aboveground masonry pueblos, issues other than status may be represented. For example, in the American Southwest, a period of transition in domestic architecture from the use of semisubterranean pithouses to aboveground masonry pueblos occurs concomitant with increasing sedentism and reliance on corn agriculture (Gilman 1987; McGuire and Schiffer 1983; Rocek 1995). Once the pithouse-to-pueblo transition is complete, relative homogeneity in the type of domestic structure used is again present, with a few notable exceptions. Substantial use of pithouses after the pithouse-to-pueblo transition in the Kayenta region of northern Arizona is one of these exceptions. In the Kayenta area during Pueblo III (PIII) times (AD 1150–1300), pithouses are found in both isolated locations, possibly serving as field houses (Ambler 1994), integrated into villages that also contain masonry architecture (Hobler 1964, 1974), and in pithouse villages (Bliss 1960; Dean 1996, 2002; Geib 2011). This study concentrates on this late use of pithouses and compares house size, construction method, and the use of space and mnemonic markers in contemporaneous PIII pithouse and masonry pueblos to better understand this variability in domestic architecture and its implications for social and political life in the Kayenta region.

## THE DUAL NATURE OF ARCHITECTURE

When examining architectural diversity and its relationship to the cultural constructs in which it is created and used, archaeologists make use of theoretical constructs in which issues of agency figure prominently (Archer 2000; Giddens 1984, 1991). From this perspective, architectural structures are the outcome of ongoing conscious social choices and actions that occur within the constraints of a historical and cultural context. At the same time, the manner in which space is bounded by architectural structures dictates movement through space and contact with and interpretation of mnemonic codes that may be present. As such, architecture affects the inhabitants' perceptions of the world in which they live their everyday lives and their place in it, frequently on a subconscious level (Bailey 1990; Kamp 1993; Parker Pearson and Richards 1994; Rapoport 1990; Scott 1994; Steadman 1996). To better understand this theoretical stance, an examination of the dual nature of the architecture is helpful, in terms of both its intentionally built and its subconsciously experienced aspects.

## Houses as Intentional Constructs

In middle-range societies, where houses are built by those who live in them with the aid of their relatives and close social allies, there should be similarity at the most general level due to similar availability of material, learning frameworks, and cultural concepts of what constitutes an appropriate design for domestic structures (Kamp 1993; Locock 1994). Variability around this broad level exists as the builders make conscious choices beyond the broad cultural template in terms of size and the appearance of the exterior facade. Decisions made in these arenas send messages not only to the inhabitants of the house but to the community as a whole in terms of the social and cosmic order and the household's place in it (Blanton 1994; Fisher 2009; Rapoport 1990; Romankiewicz 2009; Sanders 1990; Wilk 1990). As Wilk states "the house . . . faces both inward and outward, to the household and to the rest of society" (Wilk 1990:40). The house, therefore, can be viewed as the result of an ongoing negotiation between its inhabitants and other members of the community. House inhabitants make statements about themselves through house design and placement, thus reifying their household's position in the community or, conversely, project a new, desired position within the community. The remainder of the community does not passively stand by while this occurs. Rather, it signifies its acceptance of the statements the inhabitants of the house make through their house construction or it can contest them by stopping further construction and/or dismantling buildings (Locock 1994).

Beyond their role in the negotiation of social order, the construction of houses also transforms space to place and provides meaning (Amerlinck 2001; Creese 2012; Scattolin et al. 2009; Tilley 1994). Architecture transforms the meaning of the landscape by increasing the permanence of a locus of social action that is anchored in time and place. As pointed out in chapters 7 by Roth and 10 by Klucas and Graves in this volume, continuity in architecture and its location within a community through time reinforces structure and the place of certain segments of the community within villages. Conversely, variation in architecture through time and/or across space is part and parcel of ongoing dialogues transforming structure and meaning. The conscious decisions made by the builders during dialogues of social negotiations have far-reaching impacts because of the transformative nature of architecture in terms of how the landscape is perceived and experienced on both a conscious and a subconscious level.

## Houses as Subconscious Experience

In addition to conscious choice, variability in domestic architecture is the result of and can reinforce heterogeneity within communities at a subconscious level. Specifically, because vernacular architecture is built by its inhabitants, differences in building methods can indicate differences in learning frameworks of the inhabitants (Riggs 2001, 2013). As individuals from different areas coalesce into larger, more geographically aggregated settlements, they can be expected to bring differing frameworks with them. These differences, however, can have far-reaching consequences. Because individuals, families, and communities live their everyday lives within, between, and around architectural structures, these structures become a part of how daily life is experienced (Creese 2012; Gamble 2007; Johnson 2012; Pauketat and Alt 2003, 2005; Scattolin et al. 2009; Tilley 1994; Thomas 1996). Architecture not only contains interaction but directs physical movement through domiciles, communities, and the larger landscapes by creating physical barriers that must be negotiated in daily routines as individuals move from house to community to surrounding areas and back again. Architecture, and the way it defines place, becomes an integral part of the events and interactions that occur, the tasks that are performed in and around them, and how these events, interactions, and tasks are experienced and perceived. This relationship between architecture and experience is particularly powerful in houses, where initial enculturation occurs as do mundane daily routines of sleeping and waking, storing and preparing food, and interaction with individuals with the closest kin and social relationships (Creese 2012; Pauketat and Alt 2005).

## The Meaning of Variability in Houses

Given the strong ties between houses and the individuals who inhabit them, what does it mean to have radically different types of architectural structures serving as houses that go beyond size and exterior decoration in middle-range societies in terms of social identity, status, and the way space and place is experienced and perceived? If differences exist in houses that affect the movement through space as part of daily routines within the same communities, differing perceptions of the community experience may arise. The differences in community experience produce differences in the view of the existing social orders and future direction of both families and the community. The result is tension between households.

If these differences in house structure are temporary or activity specific (e.g., field houses or ritual structures), these tensions may be minimized. If, on the other hand, differences are more permanent, it is an indication of heterogeneity in experience and perception in a variety of realms, including the learning frameworks of construction and concepts of the organization of domestic life, self, and place. It also is an indication of heterogeneity within the community in terms of what the house means in the daily lives of its inhabitants. These tensions may escalate, resulting in either the factional splitting of the community or the negotiation of new concepts of domestic and community place. This view of domestic architecture complements a growing literature on the heterogeneous and dynamic nature of aggregated communities in middle-range societies in general (Bandy and Fox 2010; Canto and Yaeger 2000; Knapp 2003) and in the Southwest in particular (Rautman 2013; Stone 2015, 2016; Varien and Potter 2008; Wilshusen and Ortman 1999). This study examines differences and similarities in contemporaneous semisubterranean pithouses and aboveground masonry pueblos used as houses in the Kayenta region of the northern Southwest during PIII times to better understand this issue.

## HOUSE DIVERSITY IN THE KAYENTA REGION DURING PIII

The domestic structures of the PIII period were inhabited during a period of considerable change within a longer historical context. Summaries of Kayenta culture history by Dean (1996, 2002), Geib (2011), and Haas (1986, 1989) indicate considerable movement of peoples across the landscape through time and considerable variability in village layout and room function. The greatest geographic extent of Kayenta settlement occurred during the PII period (AD 1000–1150), when Kayenta communities can be found in the interior of Black Mesa north to Navajo Mountain and along the tributaries of the Colorado River in northwestern Arizona and southeastern Utah (figure 8.1). Domestic structures during PII times include pithouses, surface masonry (or masonry and jacal) rooms, and ramadas. Functionally specific milling rooms in a variety of structure types (pit structures, masonry rooms, ramadas) and small kivas are common (Dean 1996; Haas 1986). Villages are widely spread across the landscape and are generally fairly small (fewer than 10 rooms/structures), representing one or at most a few families, although occasionally larger sites (30 rooms) are present during the PII period and represent a limited number of families. These small settlements appear to be loosely affiliated into large, overlapping, dispersed communities linked through ritual and kin ties (Stone 2013). Where present, masonry roomblocks were organized in classic "unit pueblo" organization with a trash mound and kiva in front of a row of masonry and jacal rooms used for storage and generalized living activities.

The PIII period (AD 1150–1300) is divided into two phases in the Kayenta area. The Transition phase, from AD 1150–1250, is a socially dynamic period in which the settlement pattern changes from highly dispersed, small settlements linked

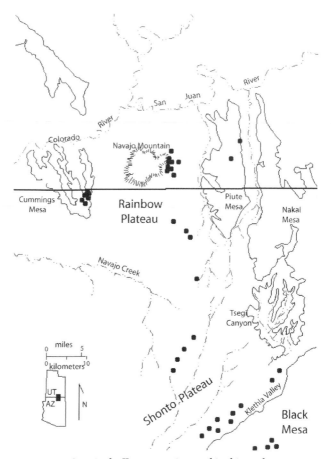

**FIGURE 8.1.** *Sites in the Kayenta region used in this study.*

by kin and ritual ties of the PII period to the dense concentrations of settlements integrated into community clusters in the Kayenta, Klethla, and Long House Valleys, in Tsegi Canyon, on the Shonto Plateau, in the areas of the Segazlin, Paiute, and Cummings Mesas, and at the base of Navajo Mountain during the subsequent Tsegi phase (AD 1250–1300). Environmental reconstructions indicate a decrease in annual precipitation and periodic droughts of varying severity after AD 1150 (Dean 2002; Haas 1989), which probably contributed to the abandonment of the outlying areas during the Transition phase. Concomitant with the movement of peoples from outlying areas like Black Mesa, Monument Valley, and possibly the Virgin River into better-watered areas during the Transition phase is the appearance of larger settlements containing multiple families (Geib 2011). Pithouses and masonry rooms are found by themselves and in combination in settlements that start to conform to definite patterns of site layout. Four habitation site types are generally recognized (Dean 1996). Pithouse villages and unit pueblos are joined by plaza pueblos that consist of masonry roomblocks, and sometimes rows of pit structures, and enclosing walls that contain defined plazas and one or more kivas. Finally, Dean (1996) notes the presence of "ad hoc" sites in which community structure is in some way constrained by topographic features on the landscape, most frequently rockshelters. The size of sites increases during the Transition phase, although they are still generally smaller than 25 rooms, frequently by quite a bit. In addition, throughout this phase, sites tend to cluster in fewer areas with empty space between the clusters leading to the formal community clusters of the next phase.

By the beginning of the Tsegi phase (AD 1250–1300), outlying areas are completely abandoned and community clusters are found in the core area of the Kayenta region. Within large cliff dwellings of the period (like Betatakin and Kiet Siel), as many as 10 different functionally specific room types may be present (Dean 1996) including generalized living rooms, two types of storage facilities, milling rooms, three types of extramural spaces, and three types of ceremonial spaces. Cliff dwellings, pithouse villages, and plaza pueblos similar to the previous period continue to be used. In addition, courtyard pueblos are found. At these sites, rooms are organized around courtyards, and sometimes in long linear galleries or roomblocks and plazas are absent. All of these site types can be of varying size with some of the plaza and courtyard pueblos and cliff dwellings having up to 160 rooms with multiple small kivas in open-air sites. Many sites, however, remain very small in size with fewer than 25 rooms.

Subsistence stress is evident throughout the Tsegi phase and water-control features (most commonly reservoirs used to collect and store water) appear in some settlements (Haas 1989) and storage increases dramatically by number of features (more than 60% at Kiet Siel) in others (Dean 2006) as strategies for mitigating the impacts of decreased precipitation. The region is abandoned completely by AD 1300.

Despite changes in settlement pattern and community organization during the PIII period, pithouses continue to be used. During the PIII period, masonry structures and pithouses alike are found both in isolation and in larger settlement types, sometimes in the same community. A variety of different models can be tested to better understand the simultaneous use of pithouses and aboveground masonry structures in the Kayenta region during the PIII period. The first group of models conceives of PIII-period pithouses as temporary housing used concomitantly with masonry rooms, which served as more permanent housing. Three models have been proposed within this larger grouping to understand the persistence of pithouse use in the Kayenta region and elsewhere.

An alternative view is proposed and tested here: specifically, that PIII pithouses may represent permanent domestic structures used alongside masonry structures within a socially complex and dynamic cultural landscape. The use of very different types of houses by the inhabitants of the Kayenta region for an extended period, sometimes within the same community, suggests considerable variability in the learning frameworks of house construction, mnemonic cues deemed appropriate for the exterior and interior of houses, and the way in which space and community life are perceived and experienced spatially. Each of the models proposed to account for the persistence of pithouses has test implications that allow them to be evaluated against the archaeological record (table 8.1).

## Pithouses as Temporary-Use Structures

The first group of models suggests that late-period pithouses, because of their low initial construction cost, were occupied as temporary housing in contrast to permanent masonry structures. Within this larger theme, three specific models of pithouse use have been advanced. The first suggests pithouses were used as temporary housing when people moved to a new location, while more substantial and permanent masonry structures were being built. This model was first suggested by Fred Wendorf in 1950 to explain the presence of pithouses at the late PIII site of Point of Pines Pueblo in the Mogollon Highlands and expanded to the Southwest more generally by McGuire and Schiffer (1983). Ethnographically, the use of pithouses as temporary housing while more permanent pueblos were constructed was implemented by migrants to the modern Hopi village of Bacavi after the factional split of Orayvi in 1906 (Whiteley 1988). If the PIII Kayenta pithouses functioned in this way, then they should be found in close proximity to the pueblos that were constructed while the pithouses were occupied (McGuire and Schiffer 1983) but not in other locations (i.e., they should not be found by themselves or in pithouse villages). Since construction of new pueblo structures occurred throughout the PIII period, pithouses adjacent to pueblos should be evident in both the Transition and Tsegi phases. In addition, because they were constructed with an anticipated short length of use (Kent 1992), the pithouses should be relatively shallow, have small floor areas relative to pueblo houses, and have packed earthen walls and floors that lack plaster or other modification. As with pithouses used as temporary housing in the Mogollon Highlands (Stone 2005; Wendorf 1950), there should be little or no investment in internal features beyond hearths. Specifically, if pithouses served only as temporary housing, they should lack evidence of formal segregated activity areas (mealing bins, storage bins), architectural elaboration (masonry line walls, flagstone floors, elaborate entrances), or remodeling (multiple coats of plaster on the floor and walls) (Stone 2005).

The second model considers pithouses as temporary structures that served as field houses in outlying agricultural areas that lacked sufficient stone for masonry field houses (Ambler 1994). If this is the case, then the landscape should contain

**TABLE 8.1.** Overview of models of pithouse use and their test implications.

| Model | Pithouse Location | Pithouse Structure |
|---|---|---|
| Temporary structures used while constructing masonry rooms. | Pithouses should be found only in sites that also contain masonry rooms | Pithouses should be relatively small, lacking internal features (beyond a hearth) or evidence of elaboration (masonry-lined walls, flagstone floors, wall or floor plaster) or maintenance (multiple floors). |
| Temporary structures used as field houses. | Pithouses should be found only in isolated contexts. | Pithouses should be relatively small, lacking internal features (beyond a hearth) or evidence of elaboration (masonry-lined walls, flagstone floors, wall or floor plaster) or maintenance (multiple floors). |
| Temporary structures used as guest houses in pueblo villages. | Pithouses should be found only in sites that also contain masonry rooms | Pithouses should be smaller than masonry rooms but have similar levels of elaboration (wall or floor plaster, elaborate entrances) and hearths. They should lack evidence of food storage. |
| Permanent structures used by groups with different views of house construction and space. | Pithouses should be found both on their own and in sites that contain masonry rooms. | Pithouses should be of similar size as masonry rooms and show similar investment in internal features (hearths, pits, storage, food preparation) and maintenance (multiple floors), though variability in mnemonic codes may be present. |

isolated field houses of both pithouse and masonry construction, depending on the availability of stone throughout the PIII period. Alternatively, we should not find pithouse villages or villages that contain masonry rooms and pithouses. These field houses should be located near agricultural fields, some distance from the pueblos that served as the permanent home base for the populace. In addition, because the field houses served as temporary housing used only during the warm growing season, the principles of efficiency of work effort in the design-decision process suggests the thermal properties of deeply excavated pithouses is not needed, especially if extramural space or ramada structures are present; pithouses used as field houses, therefore, should be relatively shallow. Finally, given the short anticipated length of use, both pithouse and masonry field houses should be relatively small in terms of floor area (compared to house size in larger pueblos) and have a limited number of internal features beyond hearths.

The third model, proposed by Geib (2011), is based on ethnographic data from the Raramuuri (Tarahumara) of northern Mexico. In particular, given the dispersed nature of the settlement pattern, families from outlying areas would come to existing pueblos periodically to participate in "social and ceremonial activities, communal work efforts . . . , defensive alliances, economic alliances" (Geib 2011:348). While visiting, the families from outlying areas would use pithouses as temporary guest houses for time periods ranging from a day to a few weeks. If this model is correct, then the pithouses should be found at sites with pueblo construction throughout the PIII period but not in isolated locations or in pithouse villages. As in the previous two models, they served as temporary housing and so should be relatively shallow and small in floor area relative to pueblo houses. Unlike the previous two models, however, if pithouses served as guest houses to families who came from outlying areas to participate in ritual affirmation of social alliances, then there should be some investment in internal features beyond the hearth to serve as mnemonic codes that reinforce shared concepts of the cosmic and social order. This should be particularly evident in the internal arrangement of space and entrances (Rapoport 1990; Sanders 1990). Conversely, formal segregated activity areas concerned with food storage (storage bins) and preparation (mealing bins) should be limited. In addition, there should be some evidence of continued maintenance in the form of multiple plaster floors, as alliances are cemented with frequent return visits.

## Pithouses as Permanent Structures

An alternative model is proposed here. This model views both pueblo and pithouse structures as used for similar lengths of time by families with different learning frameworks in terms of construction and views of the nature of what constitutes appropriate domestic space. As noted above, the Transition phase of the PIII period is a dynamic one, as outlying areas are abandoned and populations from far-flung regions concentrate in a limited number of environmentally favorable locations, resulting in large Tsegi-phase villages. As part of this transition, relationships between families change as settlement patterns shift from widely dispersed settlements of a single or at most a few families loosely linked through kin and ritual ties to a settlement pattern of villages containing multiple families living side-by-side and in close proximity to other villages, forming integrated community clusters (Dean 1996, 2002; Haas 1986, 1989; Stone 2013). These community clusters were not, however, homogeneous. Rather, they were made up of peoples with varying histories and concepts of self, place, and relationships with others. This model has similarities to that proposed by Pauketat and Alt (2003; Alt 2006) during periods of aggregation in the Cahokia region of the American Bottoms, by Rautman (2013) for early aggregated communities in the Salinas area of the Rio Grande, and by Stone (2015) for aggregated communities in the Mogollon Highlands. In all of these areas, as well as in the Kayenta region (Stone 2016), there is a transitional phase when individuals and families move from outlying areas into more geographically constrained locations. These transitional periods are dynamic not only in terms of movement across the landscape but in terms of social relationships and concepts of self and others as individuals and families forged new ways of interacting and living with others. Although the resulting communities in the Kayenta region are considerably smaller than those of the American Bottoms, the Salinas region, and the Mogollon Highlands, similar heterogeneity would be present. Alt (2006) refers to this process as *hybridity*, resulting in communities that are heterogeneous mosaics of previous conceptions, histories, and interpretations of place. "Hybridity would imply that the mix of immigrants and local people and the encounters with differences created third spaces, in which the creation of new cultural forms became possible . . . People with different traditions met and such meetings resulted in changed sensibilities for those engaged in the encounters" (Alt 2006:300), given sufficient time (see Stone 2015 for a similar argument from the Mogollon Highlands).

Given this view of the impact of movement across the landscape and the aggregation into increasingly restricted locations, the presence of differing cultural concepts of domestic space is to be expected in the Kayenta region during the PIII period. Heterogeneous mosaics of people are created and new cultural concepts are negotiated and reified within this social dynamic as individuals and families who consciously conceive of and subconsciously experience and perceive domestic place differently are brought together in new ways during the Transition phase. Through time, these heterogeneous mosaics coalesce into shared cultural hybrids in which both conscious choice and subconscious experience shift through daily practice to form new concepts of domestic place.

If this model is correct, then we should find pithouses in multiple situations (isolated field houses, pithouse villages, and settlements with both pithouses and pueblos) during the Transition phase and see decreasing differences in house construction methods during the Tsegi phase. In addition, since the pithouses were constructed as primary residences rather than temporary shelters, considerable investment should be evident in their initial construction. In other words, pithouses are likely to be deep, have floor areas of similar size to pueblo houses, and have plaster- or stone-lined floors and walls in about the same proportion as masonry rooms. They should contain a full complement of internal features. The arrangement of internal space and the nature of the entrance into the houses would serve as mnemonic cues of cosmic and social order and may demonstrate considerable variability in both pithouse and masonry structures due to the heterogeneous views of space by the inhabitants of the region. Finally, because the pithouses are occupied year round, activity areas dedicated to food storage and preparation should be present and similar to those found in masonry rooms.

## DATA SET AND ANALYSIS

Data from pithouse and masonry rooms dated to the PIII period recorded in published reports, theses, dissertations, and articles, and in the archived files of the Northern Arizona Museum, are used in this analysis (table 8.2). Rooms

**TABLE 8.2.** Sites used in this analysis.

| Site | Pithouses (n) | Masonry Rooms (n) | Domestic Structures* (n) | Reference |
|---|---|---|---|---|
| AZ:D:10:16 | 1 | — | 1 | Ambler 1994 |
| AZ:D:10:17 | 4 | | 25 | Callahan 1985 |
| AZ:J:2:3 | — | 3 | 3 | Geib 2011 |
| AZ:J:2:6 | 10 | 1 | 11 | Geib 2011 |
| AZ:J:2:58 | — | 4 | 4 | Geib 2011 |
| AZ:J:14:21 | 3 | — | 5 | Geib 2011 |
| AZ:J:18:5 | 1 | — | 1 | Schroedl 1989 |
| AZ:J:31:2 | 7 | 4 | 11 | Schroedl 1989 |
| AZ:J:31:5 | 2 | 5 | 8 | Schroedl 1989 |
| AZ:J:31:8 | 1 | — | 1 | Schroedl 1989 |
| AZ:J:54:3 | 1 | — | 1 | Linford 1982 |
| AZ:J:55:2 | 2 | — | 2 | Linford 1982 |
| AZ:J:58:4 | 4 | — | 4 | Linford 1982 |
| AZ:J:58:9 | — | 3 | 7 | Linford 1982 |
| LHV72 | — | 2 | 2 | Haas and Creamer 1993 |
| LHV73 | — | 8 | 8 | Haas and Creamer 1993 |
| NA5815 | — | 18 | 24 | Lindsay, Ambler, Stein, and Hobler 1968 |
| NA7455 | 1 | 3 | 4 | Ambler, Lindsay and Stein 1964 |
| NA7456 | — | 7 | 7 | Ambler, Lindsay and Stein 1964 |
| NA7472 | — | 2 | 2 | Ambler, Lindsay and Stein 1964 |
| NA7485 | — | 5 | 5 | Ambler, Lindsay and Stein 1964 |
| NA7486 | — | 7 | 7 | Ambler, Lindsay and Stein 1964 |
| NA7498 | 2 | 7 | 12 | Ambler, Lindsay and Stein 1964 |
| NA7544 | — | 10 | 10 | Lindsay, Ambler, Stein, and Hobler 1968 |
| NA7548 | 2 | 1 | 3 | Lindsay, Ambler, Stein, and Hobler 1968 |
| NA7713 (Pottery Pueblo) | 1 | 78 | 160 | Stein 1984; Museum of Northern Arizona archives |
| NA7719 | 16 | 6 | 24 | Hobbler1964 |

*continued on next page*

**TABLE 8.2.**—*continued*

| Site | Pithouses (n) | Masonry Rooms (n) | Domestic Structures* (n) | Reference |
|------|---------------|-------------------|--------------------------|-----------|
| NA7827 | I | — | I | Lindsay, Ambler, Stein, and Hobler 1968 |
| NA7828 | 2 | — | 2 | Lindsay, Ambler, Stein, and Hobler 1968 |
| NA7841 | — | 2 | 2 | Lindsay, Ambler, Stein, and Hobler 1968 |
| NA7902 | I | — | I | Ambler, Lindsay and Stein 1964 |
| NA8163 | 8 | — | 8 | Ambler and Olson 1960 |
| NA11,032 | 5 | — | 5 | Swarthout et al. 1986 |
| NA11,034 | I | — | I | Swarthout et al. 1986 |
| NA11,047 | 3 | — | 3 | Swarthout et al. 1986 |
| NA11,095 | — | 2 | 2 | Swarthout et al. 1986 |
| NA11,103 | 2 | — | 2 | Swarthout et al. 1986 |
| Segazlin Mesa[+] | 2 | 54 | 61 | Lindsay, Ambler, Stein, and Hobler 1968; Museum of Northern Arizona archives |
| UT:B:63:14 | 4 | — | 4 | Geib 2011 |
| UT:B:53:39a | 3 | 0 | 3 | Geib 2011 |
| UT:B:53:39b | I | 6 | 7 | Geib 2011 |
| Total | 87 | 238 | | |

* Count includes all domestic structures (including those not excavated) but excludes kivas, milling rooms, and jacal/ramada structures.
[+] Segazlin Mesa contains a number of roomblocks in close proximity that are considered a single site here but that were given individual site numbers in the field. Included here are NA4075, NA7519A, NA7519B, NA7520B, and NA7520C

located in cliff dwellings (including Kiet Siel and Betatakin) are not included here because of the possible constraints placed on room size, depth, and other features by the topography of the caves in which they are located. In addition, emphasis is placed on pithouse and masonry domestic rooms; kivas, grinding rooms, ramadas, and structures made exclusively of jacal construction are not included. Data from 329 rooms located in 41 different sites dated to the two phases of PIII are used (table 8.3). Although pithouse and masonry rooms are present in both the Transition and Tsegi phases, a chi-square analysis of the distribution of room type to specific phase (eliminating those assigned to the general PIII period with no phase designation) indicates that pithouses are more common during the Transition phase while masonry rooms are more common during the Tsegi phase ($\chi^2$ = 46.929; $p$-value = .000) although the association is moderately

**TABLE 8.3.** Room-type distribution by phase with the PIII period used in this study.

| Phase | Pithouse | Masonry Room | Total |
|---|---|---|---|
| Transition phase | 52 | 54 | 106 |
| Tsegi phase | 29 | 184 | 213 |
| General PIII with no phase distinction | 10 | 0 | 10 |
| Total | 91 | 238 | 329 |

weak (Cramer's $V$ = .384). The 41 sites investigated in this study range in size from one to 160 domestic rooms, although most ($n$ = 39, 95.1%) contain 25 or fewer domestic rooms, and the majority ($n$ = 33, 80.5%) contain 10 domestic rooms or fewer. Finally, 18 of the sites contain only pithouse domestic structures (43.9%), 13 contain only masonry domestic rooms (31.7%), and 10 contain both pithouse and masonry rooms (24.4%). Sites with all three structure combinations are found throughout the PIII period and there is no association between site type and phase within the PIII period ($\chi^2$ = .078, $p$ = .962). There is, however, a difference in site size for these three site types ($F$ = 5.800, $p$ = .006), with sites containing both pithouses and masonry rooms being significantly larger than sites with only pithouses (mean difference 26 rooms, $p$ = .010) or only masonry rooms (mean difference 23 rooms, $p$ = .026). This large difference is due to the presence of a small number of pithouses at the two largest sites (one with 160 rooms and one with 61 rooms). When these two sites are removed and only sites with 25 or fewer rooms are considered, sites with only pithouses are significantly ($F$ = 2.857, $p$ = .071) smaller than sites with both pithouses and masonry rooms (mean difference 6 rooms, $p$ = .023) but there is no difference between sites with only masonry rooms and the other two site types. In other words, pithouse are found throughout the PIII period, both by themselves and in sites with masonry structures. Sites with only pithouses average 3.889 domestic structures, while sites with only masonry structures average 6.38 rooms and sites with both pithouses and masonry domestic rooms average 9.875 domestic rooms (when the two largest sites are removed).

There appears to be considerable stability in how both pithouses and masonry rooms are constructed through time, and similarities between the two structure types in terms of size. For example, there is no difference in floor area for either masonry rooms or pithouses between the Transition and Tsegi phases (table 8.4). Further there is no difference in the depth of the pithouse structures through time. Finally, masonry rooms and pithouses are roughly the same size. In addition, basic construction methods for pithouses are consistent through the two phases. Pithouse walls are either earthen ($n$ = 59, 64.8%) or have at least one wall that is lined with masonry ($n$ = 32, 35.2%). However, both methods are found in both the Transition and Tsegi phases and there is no relationship between

**TABLE 8.4.** Comparison of structure site through time

| Variable | t-score | p-value | Mean time 1 | Mean time 2 |
|---|---|---|---|---|
| PITHOUSES ONLY (N = 91) | | | | |
| Floor area (m²) | .786 | .434 | 5.7767 | 5.3172 |
| Depth (m) | .610 | .544 | .6409 | .5878 |
| MASONRY ROOMS ONLY (N = 202) | | | | |
| Floor area (m²) | .375 | .708 | 5.9331 | 6.234 |
| PITHOUSES VS. MASONRY REGARDLESS OF TIME | | | | |
| Floor area (m²) | 1.244 | .214 | Pithouses = 5.4379 | Masonry = 6.1560 |

wall type and phase ($\chi^2$ = .365, $p$ = .546). There is no difference in the depth of pithouses with these two wall styles ($t$ = 1.07; $p$-value = .284) but pithouses with at least one masonry-lined wall are larger ($t$ = 2.699; $p$-value = .008; mean difference = 1.4595 m²).

When asking if pithouses are temporary structures used by the same individuals who built the masonry rooms, it is also relevant to ask if equivalent effort is put into the original manufacture and maintenance of the structures. If pithouses served as temporary housing, they should lack many of the internal features found in masonry rooms and lack evidence of maintenance (Kent 1992; McGuire and Schiffer 1983; Stone 2005). However, chi-square analysis of the presence/absence of internal features while controlling for structure type (pithouse vs. masonry room) indicates there is either no relationship between structure type and the presence of the feature or the relationship is very weak, as indicated by the Cramer's $V$ (table 8.5). The strongest relationship exists for the presence of storage pits, suggesting differences in the way food is stored. This interpretation is supported when the presence of doors into adjacent rooms is examined. Related to this is a difference in the distribution of hearths. Combined, these three variables probably are related to the use of functionally different rooms (living vs. storage) for the masonry-room houses compared to pithouse rooms. However, even in these cases the association is weak. Further, there is no difference in the number of floors present in the structure (an indication of long-term structure maintenance) and structure type. In addition, both pithouses and masonry rooms contain entry boxes in approximately equal numbers. Finally, loom holes are more common in pithouses than in masonry rooms, but in both cases they are extremely rare. In sum, the chi-square analysis indicates very little difference between the types of internal features that are present and the structure type. This parallels the findings that the structures types are roughly the same size. Combined, these findings suggest that pithouses are not different from masonry rooms in initial construction and maintenance and thus are not anticipated to be used for different lengths of time by their inhabitants.

**TABLE 8.5.** Comparison of structure type (pithouse vs. masonry room) to the presence/absence of internal features.

| Variable | Present in Pithouses | Present in Masonry Rooms | $\chi^2$ | p-value | Cramer's V |
|---|---|---|---|---|---|
| Doors to other rooms | 4 (4.7%) | 47 (20.1%) | 10.980 | .001 | .186 |
| Wall plaster | 23 (25.3%) | 41 (18.1%) | 2.102 | .147 | n/a |
| Floor plaster | 32 (37.8%) | 60 (26.1%) | 4.262 | .039 | .115 |
| Entry box | 27 (32.5%) | 57 (24.2%) | 2.222 | .136 | n/a |
| Hearth | 72 (83.7%) | 129 (54.9%) | 22.351 | .000 | .264 |
| Metate bin | 5 (6.0%) | 41 (17.4%) | 6.625 | .010 | .144 |
| Storage bin | 2 (2.3%) | 5 (2.1%) | .109 | .925 | n/a |
| Wall bench | 3 (3.4%) | 11 (4.7%) | .250 | .617 | n/a |
| Flagstone floor | 3 (3.3%) | 25 (10.6%) | 4.411 | .036 | .116 |
| Storage pits | 35 (37.4%) | 18 (7.6%) | 43.929 | .000 | .365 |
| Loom holes | 9 (9.9%) | 2 (0.9%) | 16.439 | .000 | .225 |
| Multiple plaster floors | 8 (9.0%) | 21 (8.9%) | .000 | .988 | n/a |

## CONTEMPORANEOUS USE OF VARIABLE HOUSE STRUCTURES

When the models presented above (table 8.1) are evaluated, it is clear that pithouses are found in a variety of locations, both on their own and in settlements that also contain masonry rooms. In addition, pithouses and masonry rooms are of similar size and do not differ significantly in the features found within them, nor is there evidence of different levels of maintenance as indicated by multiple plaster floors. Conversely, within the categories of masonry and pithouse structures, there is considerable variability in the features present. This variability indicates consistent mnemonic cues are absent, or at least extremely limited. The most common feature present is a hearth, which is present in 62.7 percent of the structures examined. The other features examined are present in fewer than 30 percent of the structures, and most features are present in fewer than 20 percent of the structures. Even the most common feature, hearths, demonstrates considerable variability, with five different hearth types present. In other words, the alternative model arguing for heterogeneous mosaics of people in which both pithouses and masonry rooms were permanent structures used by groups with differing views of house construction is supported. These differences were maintained even as families moved from very small household-centric settlements that were linked into dispersed communities through marriage and ritual to larger, multihousehold settlements during the PIII period. The use of pithouses does appear to decrease slightly during the Tsegi phase, but the area is

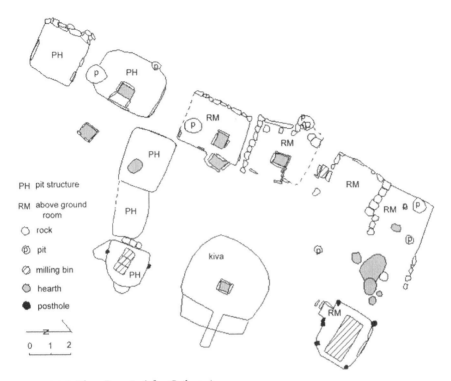

PH  pit structure

RM  above ground
    room

◯  rock

◉  pit

⊘  milling bin

◖  hearth

●  posthole

0   1   2

**FIGURE 8.2.** *Three Dog site (after Geib 2011).*

abandoned before the two different house types are completely replaced with hybrid forms.

To better understand the nature of these communities, an in-depth examination of three Transition-phase settlements containing both pithouse and masonry domestic structures is useful. The case studies represent the two most common settlement types (Dean 1996): courtyard pueblos and plaza pueblos. These three sites are chosen for further examination because they are the most completely excavated sites in the sample with both structures types. The Three Dog site (UT = B–63–39) is a courtyard pueblo located at the base of Navajo Mountain (Geib 2011). The second component of the site consists of two courtyard groups (figure 8.2), one of masonry rooms and one of pithouses, along with a single kiva. Neskahi Village (NA7719; Hobler 1964, 1974) is a D-shaped plaza pueblo with a central plaza containing a kiva (figure 8.3) located on Paiute Mesa. The back spine of the plaza is a series of masonry rooms. Pithouses are integrated into the double masonry wall surrounding the plaza on the north and south sides. The entrances to the pithouses on the south side of the site occur at breaks in the outer wall. Conversely, the pithouses on the north side of the

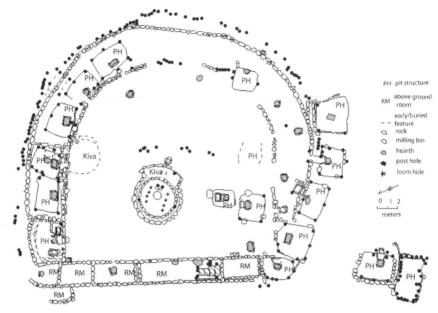

PH  pit structure
RM  above ground room
early/buried feature
rock
milling bin
hearth
post hole
loom hole

0  1  2
meters

**FIGURE 8.3.** *NA7719 (after Hobler 1964, 1974).*

site are fully contained inside the outer wall and the entrances exist at breaks in the interior wall. This pattern can be contrasted with Surprise Pueblo (NA 7498; Ambler, Lindsay, and Stein 1964), located on Cummings Mesa. Surprise Pueblo also has a wall surrounding a central plaza and kiva with a double wall in the location of the pithouses, but is square in shape (figure 8.4). A row of masonry rooms is found along the north side and pithouses, whose entrances are found at breaks in the outer wall, are lined up along the east wall. Comparison between the pithouse and masonry components of these three sites is restricted to an examination of architecture and floor features because of the difficulty of identifying artifacts tied directly to their use. In the case of the Three Dog site (Geib 2011), there is clear evidence that the rooms were cleaned out and partially dismantled prior to abandonment, so there are no artifacts in primary context. Discussions of abandonment processes are not included in the site reports for the other two sites but at Surprise Pueblo the mealing bins were dismantled prior to abandonment and storage pits contained construction debris and no artifacts, suggesting similar abandonment processes (Ambler, Lindsay, and Stein 1964). Similarly, at Neskahi Village, metates were removed from the mealing bins, though other features were not dismantled. Ceramics and chipped-stone artifacts reported from the fill and floors of both structure types are the same at Neskahi Village and Hobler (1974:13) notes the high likelihood of mixing of material from different levels at the site. As a result, artifacts near or on the floor

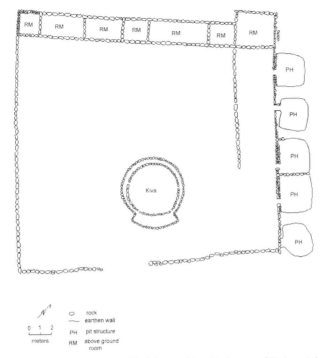

rock
earthen wall
PH pit structure
RM above ground room

**FIGURE 8.4.** *Surprise Pueblo (after Ambler, Lindsay, and Stein 1964).*

appear to represent the initial process of post-abandonment deposition rather than location of their use. Therefore, the most useable data source in examining the difference in structure types are the architecture and floor features.

In all three cases, there is a clear segregation of space at the sites, with pithouses clustered in one area and masonry rooms in another. For example, at the Three Dog site (figure 8.2), pithouses are arranged into one courtyard cluster and masonry rooms into another. Each cluster has its own milling room and external hearth as part of its courtyard cluster. At Neskahi Village (figure 8.3), masonry rooms are clustered together in the west side of the pueblo while pithouses are found along the north and south walls. In addition, milling rooms exist within both masonry and pithouse rooms, and extramural hearths are evident outside both structure types. The pithouses and masonry rooms are also segregated into different areas at Surprise Pueblo (figure 8.4). However, separate extramural space is not as evident, but the pithouses and extramural space were not as extensively tested (Ambler, Lindsay, and Stein 1964). Internal milling bins are included inside individual rooms instead of in separate designated milling rooms in the masonry rooms.

At all three sites, a single kiva is present: for the Three Dog site, it is located in the courtyard of the masonry rooms, and for Surprise Pueblo and Neskahi Village, it is located in the center of the site. If pithouses and masonry rooms represent different groups with different learning frameworks and perceptions of space, coming together in multifamily settlements, then the presence of only a single kiva is interesting. Previous studies of kivas in the Kayenta region (Stone 2013) indicate that kivas are likely used by men living in their wife's village who return to their natal village to participate in matriclan ceremonies and in the transmission of clan history and esoteric knowledge to the children of their sisters. The presence of a single kiva at the sites examined here may suggest a change in the social unit using kivas. Stone (2013), however, notes Kayenta kivas are of consistent size through time, indicating consistency in the size of the group using the structure. Further, large late (Tsegi phase) sites in the region have multiple kivas, each associated with different village segments (Stone 2016), indicating a continuity in their clan function. An alternative possibility is the use of the partially enclosed courtyards associated with pithouses at sites like Three Dog, and walls enclosing extramural space within the plaza near the pithouses at Surprise Pueblo and Neskahi Village, for ceremonial activities. This would indicate ceremonies/ activities may have occurred in very different contexts for different segments of the society, a difference that would have been reinforced with the continued use of different house types. The investigation of these two possibilities is beyond the scope of this chapter and needs to be further investigated in the future.

## CONCLUSIONS

The distribution, size, and internal features of pithouses and masonry rooms indicate that they are two different forms of domestic architecture that were used for approximately the same length of time by individuals with different learning frameworks who experienced community space in very different ways. Alt's (2006; Pauketat and Alt 2003) study of the process of aggregation at Cahokia, Rautman's (2013) study of early aggregated communities in the Salinas area, and Stone's (2015) study of aggregated communities in the Mogollon Highlands suggest that as families move from highly dispersed settlements into situations where populations are aggregated into large settlements they bring together different concepts of self, resulting in settlements that are heterogeneous mosaics of individual family histories, interpretations of place, and relationships. I argue that this heterogeneity is apparent any time families coalesce into larger settlements, even relatively small settlements like we find in the Kayenta region. Differences in concepts of place and the organization of space are not only a reflection of design choices made in different traditions of vernacular architecture (in this case pithouses and masonry rooms) but also are maintained and reinforced by these differences; houses simultaneously structure and are structured by concepts of place, self, and meaning (Creese 2012; Parker Pearson and Richards 1994; Pauketat and Alt 2005; Pluckhahn 2010; Scattolin et al. 2009; see also chapters 7 by Roth and 10 by Klucas and Graves in this volume) through daily reminders of spatial order and the movement through, into, and out of the house. The difference in house construction in PIII Kayenta settlements fits well into a pattern of community structure we see in a number of places in the world (Alt 2006; Bandy and Fox 2010; Canto and Yaeger 2000; Knapp 2003; Varien and Potter 2008) that is characterized more by heterogeneity than homogeneity and in which negotiation of place and relationships are constant.

In terms of the Kayenta region specifically, we have long known of considerable variability in the nature of settlement layout and room function within masonry rooms (Dean 1996). In addition, it has been suggested that prior to AD 1300, the inhabitants of the Kayenta area lacked a strong sense of regional identity (Stone and Lipe 2011) and that kinship ties, particularly the matrilineage and matriclan, were the overriding organizing principles (Bernardini 2008, 2011; Stone 2013). Matriclans kept their own histories, ceremonies, and esoteric knowledge and these differed from clan to clan. From this perspective, this study is further support of an emerging picture of heterogeneity within the Kayenta region on multiple scales and in which house and kin may be the most important organizing principles.

## REFERENCES

Alt, Susan M. 2006. "The Power of Diversity: The Roles of Migration and Hybridity in Culture Change." In *Leadership and Polity in Mississippian Society*, ed. Brian M. Butler and Paul D. Welch, 289–308. Center for Archaeological Investigations, Occasional Paper No. 33. Carbondale: Southern Illinois University.

Ambler, J. Richard. 1994. "The Shonto Junction Doghouse: A Weaver's Field House in Klethla Valley." *Kiva* 59(4):455–473. https://doi.org/10.1080/00231940.1994.11758250.

Ambler, J. Richard, Alexander J. Lindsay Jr., Mary Anne Stein. 1964. *Survey and Excavations on Cummings Mesa, Arizona and Utah, 1960–1961*. Bulletin No. 39, Glen Canyon Series No. 5. Flagstaff: Museum of Northern Arizona.

Ambler, J. Richard, and Alan P. Olson. 1960. *Salvage Archaeology in the Cow Springs Area*. Technical Series No. 15. Flagstaff: Museum of Northern Arizona.

Amerlinck, Mari-Jose. 2001. "The Meaning and Scope of Architectural Anthropology." In *Architectural Anthropology*, ed. M.-J. Amerlinck, 1–26. Westport, CT: Bergin and Grave.

Archer, Margaret. 2000. *Being Human: The Problem of Agency*. Cambridge, UK: Cambridge University. https://doi.org/10.1017/CBO9780511488733.

Bailey, Douglass W. 1990. "The Living House: Signifying Continuity." In *The Social Archaeology of Houses*, ed. Ross Samson, 19–48. Edinburgh: Edinburgh University.

Bandy, Matthew S., and Jake R. Fox. 2010. *Becoming Villagers: Comparing Early Village Societies*. Tucson: University of Arizona.

Bernardini, Wesley. 2008. "Identity as History: Hopi Clans and the Curation of Oral Traditions." *Journal of Anthropological Research* 64(4):483–509. https://doi.org/10.3998 /jar.0521004.0064.403.

Bernardini, Wesley. 2011. "North, South, and Center: An Outline of Hopi Ethnogenesis." In *Religious Transformation in the Late Pre-Hispanic Pueblo World*, ed. Donna M. Glowacki and Scott Van Keuren, 196–220. Tucson: University of Arizona.

Blanton, Richard E. 1994. *Houses and Households, a Comparative Study*. New York: Plenum Press. https://doi.org/10.1007/978-1-4899-0990-9.

Bliss, Wesley. 1960. "Impact of Pipeline Archaeology on Indian Prehistory." *Plateau* 33(1):10–13.

Callahan, Martha M. 1985. "Excavations at Dogtown: A Pueblo III Pithouse Village in the Klethla Valle." Unpublished MA thesis, Department of Anthropology, Northern Arizona University, Flagstaff.

Canto, Marcello A., and Jason Yaeger. 2000. *The Archaeology of Communities: A New World Perspective*. London: Routledge.

Creese, John L. 2012. "The Domestication of Personhood: A View from the Northern Iroquoian Longhouse." *Cambridge Archaeological Journal* 22(03):365–386. https://doi .org/10.1017/S0959774312000455.

Dawson, Peter C. 2001. "Interpreting Variability in Thule Inuit Architecture: A Case Study from the Canadian High Arctic." *American Antiquity* 66(03):453–470. https://doi .org/10.2307/2694244.

Dean, Jeffrey S. 1996. "Kayenta Anasazi Settlement Transformations in Northeastern Arizona, AD 1150–1350." In *The Prehistoric Pueblo World, AD 1150–1350*, ed. Michael A. Adler, 29–47. Tucson: University of Arizona.

Dean, Jeffrey S. 2002. "Prehistoric Culture Change on the Colorado Plateau." In *Ten Thousand Years on Black Mesa*, ed. Shirley Powell and Francis Smiley, 121–157. Tucson: University of Arizona.

Dean, Jeffrey S. 2006. "Subsistence Stress and Food Storage at Kiet Siel, Northeastern Arizona." In *Environmental Change and Human Adaptation in the Ancient American Southwest*, ed. David E. Doyel and Jeffrey S. Dean, 160–179. Salt Lake City: University of Utah Press.

Fisher, Kevin D. 2009. "Placing Social Interaction: An Integrative Approach to Analyzing Past Built Environments." *Journal of Anthropological Archaeology* 28(4):439–457. https://doi.org/10.1016/j.jaa.2009.09.001.

Gamble, Clive. 2007. *Origins and Revolutions: Human Identity in Earliest Prehistory*. Cambridge, UK: Cambridge University. https://doi.org/10.1017/CBO9780511618598.

Geib, Phil R. 2011. *Foragers and Farmers of the Northern Kayenta Region*. Salt Lake City: University of Utah.

Giddens, Anthony. 1984. *The Constitution of Society: Outline of the Theory of Structuration*. Cambridge, UK: Polity Press.

Giddens, Anthony. 1991. "Structuration Theory: Past, Present, and Future." In *Giddens' Theory of Structuration: A Critical Appreciation*, ed. C. G. Bryant and D. Jary, 201–21. New York: Routledge.

Gilman, Patricia A. 1987. "Architecture as Artifact: Pit Structures and Pueblos in the American Southwest." *American Antiquity* 52(03):538–564. https://doi.org/10.2307/281598.

Haas, Jonathan. 1986. "The Evolution of the Kayenta Anasazi." In *Tse Yaa Kin: Houses beneath the Rock*, ed. David Grant Noble, 14–23. Santa Fe, NM: School of American Research.

Haas, Jonathan. 1989. "The Evolution of the Kayenta Regional System." In *The Sociopolitical Structure of Prehistoric Southwestern Societies*, ed. Steadman Upham, Kent G. Lightfoot, and Roberta Jewett, 491–508. Boulder, CO: Westview.

Haas, Jonathan, and Winifred Creamer. 1993. *Stress and Warfare among the Kayenta Anasazi of the Thirteenth Century A.D.* Fieldiana Anthropology, New Series No. 21. Chicago, IL: Field Museum of Natural History.

Hobler, Philip M. 1964. "The Late Survival of Pithouse Architecture in the Kayenta Anasazi Area." Unpublished MA thesis, Department of Anthropology, University of Arizona, Tucson.

Hobler, Philip M. 1974. "The Late Survival of Pithouse Architecture in the Kayent Anasazi Area." *Southwestern Lore* 40(2):1–44.

Jewett, Roberta, and Kent G. Lightfoot. 1986. "The Intra-Site Spatial Structure of Early Pithouse Villages." In *Mogollon Variability*, ed. Charlotte Benson and Steadman Upham, 9–44. Las Cruces: New Mexico State University.

Johnson, Matthew H. 2012. "Phenomenological Approaches in Landscape Archaeology." *Annual Review of Anthropology* 41(1):269–284. https://doi.org/10.1146/annurev-anthro-092611-145840.

Kamp, Kathryn A. 1993. "Towards an Archaeology of Architecture: Clues from a Modern Syrian Village." *Journal of Anthropological Research* 49(4):293–317. https://doi.org/10.1086/jar.49.4.3630152.

Kent, Susan. 1992. "Studying Variability in the Archaeological Record: An Ethnoarchaeological Model for Distinguishing Mobility Patterns." *American Antiquity* 57(4):635–660. https://doi.org/10.2307/280827.

Knapp, A. Bernard. 2003. "The Archaeology of Community on Bronze Age Cyprus: Politicko Phorades in Context." *American Journal of Archaeology* 107(4):559–580. https://doi.org/10.3764/aja.107.4.559.

Lightfoot, Kent G., and Gary M. Feinman. 1982. "Social Differentiation and Leadership Development in Early Pithouse Villages in the Mogollon Region of the American Southwest." *American Antiquity* 47(01):64–86. https://doi.org/10.2307/280053.

Lindsay, Alexander J., Jr., J. Richard Ambler, Mary Anne Stein, Philip M. Hobler. 1968. *Survey and Excavations North and East of Navajo Mountain, Utah, 1959–1962.* Bulletin No. 45, Glen Canyon Series No. 8. Flagstaff: Museum of Northern Arizona.

Linford, Laurance D. 1982. *Kayenta Anasazi Archaeology on Central Black Mesa, Northeastern Arizona: The Pinon Project.* Navajo Nation Papers in Anthropology No. 10. Window Rock, AZ: Navajo National Cultural Resource Management Program.

Locock, Martin. 1994. "Meaningful Architecture." In *Meaningful Architecture: Social Interpretations of Buildings,* ed. Martin Locock, 1–13. Brookfield, VT: Asgate.

McGuire, Randall H., and Michael B. Schiffer. 1983. "A Theory of Architectural Design." *Journal of Anthropological Archaeology* 2(3):277–303. https://doi.org/10.1016/0278-4165 (83)90002-8.

Parker Pearson, Michael, and Colin Richards. 1994. "Ordering the World: Perceptions of Architecture, Space and Time." In *Architecture and Order: Approaches to Social Space,* ed. Michael Parker Pearson and Colin Richards, 1–37. London: Routledge. https://doi .org/10.4324/9780203401484_chapter_1.

Pauketat, Timothy R., and Susan M. Alt. 2003. "Mounds, Memory and Contested Mississippian History." In *Archaeologies of Memory,* ed. Ruth M. Van Dyke and Susan E. Alcock, 151–179. Malden, MA: Blackwell. https://doi.org/10.1002/9780470774304.ch8.

Pauketat, Timothy R., and Susan M. Alt. 2005. "Agency in a Postmold? Physicality and the Archaeology of Culture-Making." *Journal of Archaeological Method and Theory* 12(3):213–237. https://doi.org/10.1007/s10816-005-6929-9.

Pluckhahn, Thomas J. 2010. "Household Archaeology in the Southeastern United States: History, Trends, and Challenges." *Journal of Archaeological Research* 18(4):331–385. https://doi.org/10.1007/s10814-010-9040-z.

Rapoport, Amos. 1990. "Systems of Activities and Systems of Settings." In *Domestic Architecture and Use of Space: An Interdisciplinary Cross-Cultural Study,* ed. Susan Kent, 9–20. Cambridge, UK: Cambridge University.

Rautman, Alison. 2013. "Social Interaction and the Built Environment of Aggregated Communities in North American Puebloan Southwest." In *From Prehistoric Villages to Cities: Settlement Aggregation and Community Transformation,* ed. Jennifer Birch, 111–133. New York: Routledge.

Riggs, Charles R. 2001. *The Architecture of Grasshopper Pueblo.* Salt Lake City: University of Utah Press.

Riggs, Charles R. 2013. "A Grasshopper Architectural Perspective on Kinishba." In *Kinishba Lost and Found: Mid-Century Excavations and Conteporary Perspectives,* ed. John R. Welch, 123–145. Arizona State Museum Archaeological Series 206. Tucson: University of Arizona.

Rocek, Thomas. 1995. "Sedentarization and Agricultural Dependence: Perspectives from the Pithouse-to-Pueblo Transition in the American Southwest." *American Antiquity* 60(02):218–239. https://doi.org/10.2307/282138.

Romankiewicz, Tanja. 2009. "Simple Stones but Complex Constructions: Analysis of Architectural Developments in the Scottish Iron Age." *World Archaeology* 41(3):379–395. https://doi.org/10.1080/00438240903112278.

Sanders, Donald. 1990. "Behavioral Conventions and Archaeology: Methods for the Analysis of Ancient Architecture." In *Domestic Architecture and Use of Space: An Interdisciplinary Cross-Cultural Study*, ed. Susan Kent, 43–72. Cambridge, UK: Cambridge University.

Scattolin, María Cristina, Leticia Inés Cortés, María Fabiana Bugliani, C. Marilin Calo, Lucas Pereyra Domingorena, Andrés D. Izeta, and Marisa Lazzari. 2009. "Built Landscapes of Everyday Life: A House in an Early Agricultural Village of North-Western Argentina." *World Archaeology* 41(3):396–414. https://doi.org/10.1080/00438240903112310.

Schroedl, Alan R. 1989. *Kayenta Anasazi Archaeology and Navajo Ethnohistory on the Northwestern Shoto Plateau: The N-16 Project*. Salt Lake City: P-III Associates.

Scott, Barbara. 1994. "The Viking Move West: House and Continuity in the Northern Isles." In *Meaningful Architecture: Social Interpretations of Buildings*, ed. Martin Locock, 132–146. Brookfield, VT: Asgate.

Steadman, Sharon R. 1996. "Recent Research in the Archaeology of Architecture: Beyond the Foundations." *Journal of Archaeological Research* 4(1):51–93. https://doi.org/10.1007/BF02228838.

Stein, Mary Anne. 1984. *Pottery Pueblo: A Tsegi Phase Village on Paiute Mesa, Utah*. PhD dissertation, Department of Anthropology, Southern Methodist University, Dallas. Ann Arbor, MI: University Microfilms International.

Stone, Tammy. 2005. "Late Period Pithouses in the Point of Pines Region of Arizona." *Kiva* 70(3):273–292. https://doi.org/10.1179/kiv.2005.70.3.004.

Stone, Tammy. 2013. "Kayenta Ritual Structures from AD 1100–1300." *Kiva* 78(2):177–205. https://doi.org/10.1179/kiv.2013.78.2.004.

Stone, Tammy. 2015. *Migration and Ethnicity in Middle-Range Societies: A View from the Southwest*. Salt Lake City: University of Utah.

Stone, Tammy. 2016. "Organizational Variability in Early Aggregated Communities in Middle-Range Societies: An Example from the Kayenta Region of the American Southwest." *American Antiquity* 81(01):58–73. https://doi.org/10.7183/0002-7316.81.1.58.

Stone, Tammy, and William D. Lipe. 2011. "Standing Out versus Blending In: Pueblo Migrations and Ethnic Marking." In *Movement, Connectivity, and Landscape Change in the Ancient Southwest*, ed. Margaret C. Nelson and Colleen Strawhacker, 275–296. Niwot: University of Colorado.

Swarthout, Jeanne, Sara Stebbins, Pat Stein, Bruce Harrill, and Peter J. Pilles, Jr. 1986. *The Kayenta Anasazi: Archaeological Investigation along the Black Mesa Railroad Corridor*. MNA Research Paper 30, Vol. 2. Flagstaff: Museum of Northern Arizona.

Thomas, Julian. 1996. *Time, Culture and Identity*. London: Routledge.

Tilley, Christopher. 1994. *A Phenomenology of Landscape, Places, Paths and Monuments*. Oxford, UK: Berg.

Varien, Mark D., and James M. Potter. 2008. *The Social Construction of Communities: Agency, Structure, and Identity in the Prehistoric Southwest.* Lanham, MD: Altamira.

Wallace, Henry. 2003. *Roots of Sedentism: Archaeological Excavations at Valencia Viejo, a Founding Village in the Tucson Basin of Southern Arizona.* Anthropological Papers No. 20. Tucson, AZ: Center for Desert Archaeology.

Wendorf, Fred. 1950. *A Report on the Excavation of a Small Ruin Near Point of Pines, East Central Arizona.* University of Arizona Bulletin 21(3). Social Science Bulletin 19. Tucson: University of Arizona.

Whiteley, Peter M. 1988. *Bacavi: Journey to Reed Spring.* Flagstaff, AZ: Northland Press.

Wilk, Richard R. 1990. "The Built Environment and Consumer Decisions." In *Domestic Architecture and Use of Space: An Interdisciplinary Cross-Cultural Study,* ed. Susan Kent, 34–42. Cambridge, UK: Cambridge University.

Wills, W. H. 2001. "Pithouse Architecture and the Economics of Household Formation in the Prehistoric American Southwest." *Human Ecology* 29(4):477–500. https://doi.org/10.1023/A:1013198022095.

Wilshusen, Richard H., and Scott G. Ortman. 1999. "Rethinking the Pueblo I Period in the San Juan Drainage: Aggregation, Migration, and Cultural Diversity." *Kiva* 64(3):369–399. https://doi.org/10.1080/00231940.1999.11758389.

# 9

# Jornada Formative Settlements in the Highlands and Lowlands

*Contrasting Paths to Pueblo Villages*

THOMAS R. ROCEK

The adoption of agriculture and the transition to village life are critical transformations that share striking parallels worldwide. Despite these similarities, however, comparisons of Mesolithic to Neolithic and Late Archaic to Formative transitions also reveal important differences among the regional manifestations of these processes. Within the US Southwest, the Jornada Mogollon region in particular offers a valuable and underutilized laboratory for examining variation *within* a limited region in the pattern and speed of economic and settlement shifts associated with the Formative transition. This chapter summarizes several aspects of this intraregional diversity, and considers the social implications of the variation. I focus particularly on the Capitan / Sierra Blanca highlands of south-central New Mexico in contrast to the better-studied Jornada lowlands to the south and west in southern New Mexico and extreme western Trans-Pecos Texas. The highlands show several punctuated changes in economic and social development that differ from the more gradual sequence in the lowlands, and I propose that the contrasting patterns are the result of the split of what was initially a single social group's settlement system into separate highland

and lowland systems with contrasting social groupings and adaptations. In the lowlands, village development seems to take a relatively gradual form of slowly growing farming dependence associated with increasingly more substantial and integrated settlements within a seasonal round. Lowland villages have their roots in the large, winter settlements of that settlement system. By contrast, the pattern in the highlands appears to develop out of a subset of the summer farming portion of that lowland settlement round; occupants of the highland farm sites split off from the lowland groups and rapidly develop scattered agricultural extended-household farmsteads (hence with a summer focus), initially with little indication of inter-farmstead integration or aggregation. Toward the end of the prehistoric sequence, the highland and lowland patterns converge into similar, largely sedentary agricultural villages, but the paths leading to these villages differ considerably between the two areas. These contrasting trajectories may ultimately be traced to economic consequences of the differing environments of these two settings in the Jornada (the more rapid development of reliance on dry farming in the cooler, moister highlands), though similar contrasts may occur in other areas, depending on local circumstances.

The emphasis on variation here does not undercut the observation of broad patterns of similarity within and among regions; early agricultural developments are strikingly similar in many cases worldwide. However, both V. Gordon Childe (1936:63–64) and Willey and Phillips (1958:144–146) in their classic definitions of the Old World "Neolithic Revolution" or roughly analogous American "Formative Stage" emphasized that the Neolithic or Formative package is not a consistent one; nonagricultural societies can exhibit many "Neolithic" features, while agricultural societies sometimes lack typical characteristics of the Neolithic or Formative. Continuing archaeological research such as the discovery of obviously preagricultural 20,000-year-old pottery (Wu et al. 2012) and ethnographic accounts of non-sedentary farmers (e.g., Graham 1993; Hard and Merrill 1992), highlight that there is no simple unitary Neolithic package (cf. Jordan and Zvelebil 2009). The variation *around* the typical pattern encourages exploration away from assumptions of a normative unitary process, while not contradicting the shared underlying economic, technological, and social transformations and the diverse yet often converging paths seen in the development of farming villages.

Within the US Southwest, the pattern of adoption of agriculture varies widely among different areas, and among ecological zones (e.g., Hard et al. 1996; Rocek 1995; Vierra 2008). While researchers have recognized for some time that the contrasting patterns of agricultural adoption are associated with differing social patterns on a broad interregional scale (e.g., Wills 1991), an emphasis on intraregional variation in the speed and pattern of economic and social change has come to receive substantial emphasis only relatively recently (e.g., Mabry and

Doolittle 2008; Wills et al. 2012). Ultimately, the broadly shared patterns across the Southwest as well as worldwide imply shared functional correlates of the social changes associated with the development of agricultural village organization: a narrowing in the locus of control over food resources away from the community-wide to the household level, development of integrative institutions to maintain long-term stability of the village community, and the development of maintainable, modular, often rectilinear residential architecture (e.g., Byrd 1994; Douglass and Gonlin 2012; Flannery 1972, 2002). However, the interplay of these economic and social factors is variable, and within the social realm, the relative development of social units at different scales from household to household-cluster to village to regional community is similarly diverse (see chapters 7 by Roth, 10 by Klucas and Graves, and 11 by Douglass et al., this volume, for examples). The Jornada case shows how, even within a narrow geographic region of the Southwest, these shared economic and social outcomes can represent convergent trends from dissimilar origins rather than strictly parallel developments.

## JORNADA REGIONAL DIVERSITY

The branches of the Mogollon cultural tradition in general and the Jornada branch in particular are markedly diverse in their environmental and cultural patterns. Lehmer's (1948) original definition of the Jornada branch acknowledged this variation by defining separate northern and southern phase sequences within the area, a diversity that was further elaborated in the 1960s by Kelley's (1984) north-south subdivision in the Capitan Highlands portion of the Jornada (figure 9.1; table 9.1; see also Jelinek [1967] for an additional local phase sequence as well as Miller [2005] and Wiseman [2004] for more recent updates on the phase sequences).

This diversity actually reflects at least two confounded or overlapping sources of variation. First, there are geographic differences, including a basic contrast between the core near the Jornada del Muerto valley area in which the branch was originally defined and the outlying surrounding areas; these regional contrasts have raised questions of how far the term *Jornada* can usefully be applied (e.g., Corley 1965; Leslie 1979) and to what extent the term *Jornada Branch*, like the term *Mogollon*, represents a meaningful cultural group or analytical unit (e.g., Kyte 1988; Miller and Graves 2012:277–281; Wilson 2004; Wiseman 2000; 2002:170–174; 2003; cf. Speth 1988).

The second aspect of variation that I focus on here can be tied specifically to environmental contrasts within the region. Broadly speaking, the Jornada includes at least four groups of environmental zones: (1) the lowland basins, such as the Jornada del Muerto and Tularosa, (2) the river valleys of the lower Rio Grande and Pecos, (3) highlands such as the Capitan and Sierra Blanca

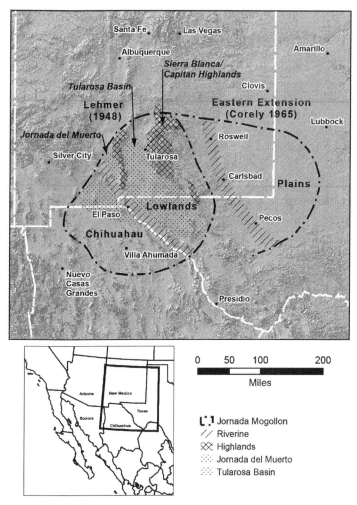

**FIGURE 9.1.** *Jornada region as defined by Lehmer (1948) and extended by Corley (1965) (dot-dash lines) with schematic of environmental sub-regions referred to in text. (Figure by Sandra L. Hannum.)*

Mountains, and, depending on how far east the Jornada is extended, (4) portions of the southern high plains in southeastern New Mexico and western Texas. The riverine zones themselves should probably be further subdivided and thought of as two distinct environments, given the contrast in the basin and range setting of the lower Rio Grande versus the Plains-edge context of the Pecos in southeastern New Mexico. For historical reasons, the lowlands of southern New Mexico and west Texas are much better studied than any of the others—first since they formed the core of Lehmer's definition of the Jornada,

**TABLE 9.1.** Jornada regional diversity as defined in the 1960s.

| Dates AD | Kelley (1984) Capitan/Sierra Blanca Highlands Only | | Lehmer (1948) Entire Jornada Mogollon Region | | Corley (1965) Eastern Extension |
|---|---|---|---|---|---|
| | South | North | South | North | |
| 1400 | Late Glencoe | Lincoln | El Paso | San Andres | Ochoa |
| 1200 | Early Glencoe | Corona | Doña Ana | Three Rivers | Maljamar |
| 1100 | ?? | ?? | Mesilla | Capitan | Querecho |
| ?? | ?? | ?? | Hueco (Archaic) | | |

**TABLE 9.2.** Recent definitions of Formative phase sequences.

| Dates AD | Southern Lowlands (after Miller 2005; cf. Whalen 1981, 1994b; Wiseman 2004) | Capitan Highlands (Campbell and Railey 2008; Wiseman 2004) North | South | |
|---|---|---|---|---|
| 1450 | El Paso | | Late Glencoe | Formative |
| 1300 | | | | |
| 1275/1300 | Late Doña Ana | Lincoln | Middle Glencoe | |
| 1200 | | | | |
| 1150 | | Corona | | |
| 1100 | Early Doña Ana | | | |
| 1000 | Late Mesilla | | Early Glencoe | |
| 650 | | | | |
| 540 | Early Mesilla | | | |
| 200/400 | Archaic | | | |

and then due to large-scale CRM work on military bases around El Paso in the last several decades. Thus, the lowland Formative archaeological sequence of the Mesilla, Doña Ana, and El Paso phases, defined for the area surrounding El Paso, has come to be viewed as the de facto norm of the Jornada region.

## The Southern Lowlands

A broad synthesis of the pattern of development of the Formative in the lowlands is provided by Michael Whalen (1981, 1994a, 1994b); the following description is base primarily on his work combined with some supplementary points from Miller and Kenmotsu (2004) and Miller (2005) (table 9.2). The Formative has its roots in a Late Archaic pattern of seasonally mobile camps dating to the second and first millennia B C and the first few centuries of the current era. Warm-weather sites are concentrated around the bottoms of basins to exploit plants and small game available as a result of spring runoff and summer rainfall. These sites are abundant but small and ephemeral with occasional hearths and, rarely, very small, shallow structures. Larger winter base camps are less common, and occur near alluvial fans at the bases of the slopes of the surrounding mountains or in the Rio Grande valley. These cold-weather sites include more substantial, although still small and ephemeral, pit structures. In general, Archaic shelters show little labor investment, with shallow basin floors 3 m or less in diameter, few or no postholes, and no prepared hearths. During the later portions of the Archaic, the number of sites grows and resource intensification is suggested by an increase in fire-cracked rock middens associated with the processing of succulents such as agave (Miller et al. 2011; Miller and Kenmotsu 2004). This intensification is also indicated by sporadic finds of maize, but these are generally from the highlands or their fringes rather than the lowland basins, a point discussed further below.

The start of the Formative Mesilla phase is defined by the appearance of ceramics around A D 200 to 400 (Miller and Kenmotsu 2004:237; Oakes 1998:97). The transition is gradual, extending the trend in resource intensification of the terminal Late Archaic, with heavy processing of wild resources in burned-rock features (Miller and Kenmotsu 2004:225–226; Miller, chapter 12, this volume). Small warm-season sites continue in the basins although the occasional structures at these sites include some comparable in size to the Archaic cool-weather sites. The structures at cold-weather sites become more substantial than in the preceding period. Round shapes remain the norm, but diameters are typically 3.5 m or more and their floors are deeper than during the Archaic, creating greater insulation for the lower walls and more fill for use in insulating roof-covering as well. These structures often contain hearths, central support postholes, peripheral secondary ones, and small interior pits. Structures show repair and reoccupation and there is more midden accumulation and perhaps longer seasonal duration of site use. The increased duration and intensity of occupation is further reflected by extramural activity areas and features surrounding the houses, including moderately large bell-shaped and cylindrical pits that clearly served storage functions. This increase in storage represents another significant departure from even the more substantial of the Archaic-period sites, and highlights the investment in these cool-weather locations (though see Rocek and Kenmotsu [forthcoming] for a recent find of a terminal Late Archaic site with similar characteristics). Small quantities of maize are found at the cool-weather sites, indicating limited but increasing maize farming in the lowlands.

As in the Archaic, these more substantial winter sites remain rare and are restricted to the moister basin edges and the Rio Grande valley. Whalen (1994a,

1994b) suggests that a half dozen or more contemporary structures occur at some of the cool-weather sites. As a sign of the growing integration of these small but aggregated and increasingly stable communities, atypically large pithouses appear at cool-weather sites around AD 800 or 900. Miller and Graves (2012:250–251; Whalen 1994a:634) have pointed out that in accordance with Johnson's (1982:392–394) argument regarding the growth of information processing and decision-making stress when more than six units interact, communal rooms appear in Jornada pueblo roomblocks when room counts exceed six or seven. Thus it is probably not coincidental that this presumably communal architecture appears at the larger cool-weather sites in the late Mesilla phase, around AD 800 or 900. In addition, during this latter part of the Mesilla phase, increasingly large storage pits are found at some of the cool-weather sites, coupled with a gradual and moderate increase in evidence of agricultural reliance. Furthermore, Miller (chapter 12, this volume) describes a rapid increase and peak in the intensity of use of burned-rock middens in the Mesilla phase; this peak is earlier in the lower-lying areas (the mountain foothills) than in the highlands. Miller's interpretation of these features as indicative of the production of mescal suggests a rise in integrative communal ceremonial or feasting activity. Thus, both the site evidence and the proliferation of burned-rock middens suggest the gradual development of small but increasingly integrated villages, each consisting of a cluster of moderate-sized pit structures and presumably housing a relatively small, household-scale social group interacting daily with its neighbors, and interdependent with them.

This early Formative sequence culminating in clusters of moderate-sized pithouses along basin edges and the Rio Grande valley continues in a smooth development into the subsequent pueblo period. In the transitional Doña Ana phase, communities of square pithouse are concentrated in the basin-edge locations similar to those of the Mesilla-phase winter sites; by the mid-twelfth century they are joined by similarly shaped surface rooms (Miller 2005:69). A drop in the abundance of the small (warm weather) sites in the basin bottoms signals a decrease in seasonal mobility. Some larger settlements, however, cluster around basin bottom playas (Miller and Kenmotsu forthcoming). Some of the surface rooms are aggregated into contiguous pueblo structures by the last part of the Doña Ana phase, and by the late thirteenth century the appearance of these pueblos defines the El Paso phase, the final period of Formative development that persisted until abandonment of the region by settled village populations in the mid-fifteenth century. Pueblos of six rooms or more in this period continue the pattern of integrative communal rooms that has its roots in the communal pit structures of the late Mesilla phase, and larger pueblos have larger (and multiple) communal structures (Miller and Graves 2012:251–252). Evidence of settlement permanence near water sources in river valleys or basin

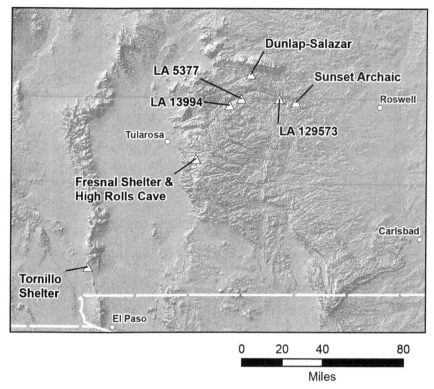

**FIGURE 9.2.** *Highlands and immediately adjacent sites referred to in text. (Figure by Sandra L. Hannum.)*

playas, aggregation, and agricultural reliance all reach a peak during this period. The combination of aggregated pueblo architecture, intensive agricultural reliance, little evidence of seasonal mobility, and ubiquitous appearance of communal architecture all point to the El Paso–phase sites as representing largely sedentary, integrated village communities.

### The Highlands

The Formative sequence from the Capitan Mountain highlands (figure 9.2, table 9.2) culminates in a similar pattern of agriculturally dependent aggregated villages incorporating communal structures. However, the earlier part of the Formative sequence and immediately preceding Late Archaic periods suggest substantial contrasts. Most notable are differences in patterns of the adoption of agriculture, the appearance of pottery, and changes in pre-Pueblo Formative houses. The combined evidence suggests a contrast not only in economic history but in the sequence of Formative changes in settlement and associated social organization.

Despite the much lower level of research in the mountains, evidence of maize agriculture in the Jornada region is earlier and more abundant in the highlands and along the edges of the highlands than in the surrounding lowland areas. The earliest maize date in the region (roughly 1500 cal BC) at Tornillo Rockshelter is somewhat equivocal; the site lies only at about 4,830 feet (1,470 m) but is in the rugged foothills of the Organ mountains east of the Rio Grande valley (MacNeish 1993; Upham et al. 1987). Fresnal Shelter, the next earliest (or possibly chronologically overlapping [Miller and Kenmotsu 2004:227]) site sits higher up the slopes of the Sierra Blanca mountains squarely in the highlands at 6,300 feet (1,920 m) and has more precisely dated maize by 1100 cal BC, evidence of modest-sized storage pits, and beans by around 50 cal BC. Nearby High Rolls Cave also has a storage pit dated around 1100 cal BC (Bohrer 2007; Lentz 2006; Tagg 1996). LA 139944 and LA 5377, two Late Archaic sites that straddle the BC/AD temporal boundary lie near 6,000 feet (ca. 1,830 m) and produced abundant maize remains and multiple large storage features (Campbell and Railey 2008). Finally, the Sunset Archaic site (LA 58971) dates to the first few centuries AD and is again characterized by abundant maize and large storage pits (Wiseman 1996). Like Tornillo Shelter, the site lies more on the edge of the highlands, at 4,920 feet (1,500 m), but it is near the riparian zone leading up into the Sierra Blanca mountains, not in the lowlands.

Farming intensity may be moderate at the three early rockshelters (Tornillo, Fresnal, and High Rolls), but is strongly indicated at the other sites with their abundant maize and large, deep bell-shaped pits by the final centuries BC. Yet despite this evidence of farming, these high-elevation Archaic sites have little indication of architecture; only LA 5377 had possible structures (ca. 2–2.5 m in diameter and 1-m-deep pits) and these may be large storage pits instead (Campbell and Railey 2008).

Given the indications of substantial agricultural investment and few or no dwellings, I suggest that these sites were the warm-season component of a settlement round. Admittedly there is little direct seasonality evidence. Bohrer (2007:132–133) identifies High Rolls as a warm-season site based on its northward orientation and botanical composition, but argues that Fresnal was used most heavily in winter, although also at other times (2007:109–121). On the other hand, the limited faunal data from Fresnal indicate warm-season kills (Bohrer 2007:120) and much of the cool-season botanical evidence at that site *could* result from a fall occupation associated with the maize harvest. Evidence from the other sites is less certain still.[1] Bohrer also documents the incorporation of low-elevation foods such as rice grass and mesquite into the floral assemblage at Fresnal, showing that the highland settlements were in some significant degree tied into either logistical or residential mobility to and from the lowlands.

A plausible scenario is that the Late Archaic highland sites are an extension of the seasonal round of the lowlands: warm-season resources could be collected in both the lowland basin centers *and* highlands, and the higher available moisture due to greater rainfall and reduced evaporation in the highlands encouraged the addition of horticulture into the hunted and collected mix. This interpretation is similar to that suggested by Wills (1988) for the western Mogollon highlands, where Archaic high-elevation agricultural investment was part of the lowland seasonal round, extending the warm-season stay in the mountains. The interesting implication derives from the contrasting trajectories that followed in the lowlands versus the highlands.

## CHANGES IN HIGHLAND–LOWLAND SITE USE

In the lowlands, the start of the Formative around AD 200–400 is marked by the appearance of small storage features, sparse evidence of maize, larger and more substantial houses, and pottery. In the highlands, in the same period, abundant evidence of farming and storage continues from the Late Archaic, while pottery remains absent. The culmination of this early highland pattern is seen at LA 129573, a site dating to roughly AD 370 to 530 with high maize ubiquity and many large bell-shaped pits, but only a total of four sherds, none from feature contexts. As recognized relatively recently (Campbell and Railey 2008:17; cf. Wiseman 1996:188), ceramics came into use in the Capitan / Sierra Blanca highlands only around AD 540–550. Thus, LA 129573 falls right at this transition. Significantly, this site also gives the first indication of the appearance of substantial architecture—a collection of six deep postholes around a clay-lined hearth that is poorly defined but suggests a well-roofed structure at least 6.5 m in diameter (Campbell and Railey 2008). This combination, hinting at the roughly simultaneous start of construction of substantial architecture and pottery in these highland agricultural sites is strongly borne out by subsequent series of sites spanning the mid-sixth through the eleventh centuries AD.

LA 51344, the Dunlap-Salazar site best documents this pattern with a well-dated occupation beginning in the mid-500s and extending into the start of the ninth century AD. The site continues the pattern of agricultural dependence indicated in the sites of the terminal Late Archaic, but adds large, shallow, but well-constructed pit structures and abundant ceramics. Agricultural dependence is borne out by all available evidence; both macrobotanical and pollen maize ubiquity is over 80 percent, and beans are also present. The site has many large bell-shaped storage pits, typically over 1 m in diameter and with minimum depths of 80 cm or often more. Stains of more than 40 of these pits were exposed in a limited area of the site, suggesting that as many as several hundred may be present on the site as a whole (Rocek 2013).

In contrast to the preceding period, however, architecture is also prominent at Dunlap-Salazar, represented by a series of large pithouses, 6–7 m in diameter with small central hearths, large main roof supports, and small peripheral posts.

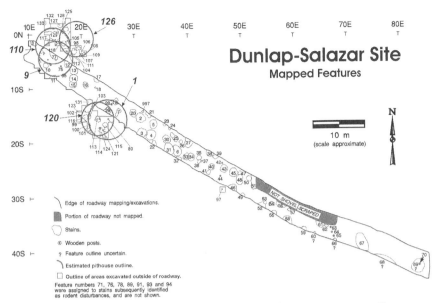

**FIGURE 9.3.** *Dunlap-Salazar site (LA 51344) map of five overlapping pit structures (large circles) and bell-shaped and other pits (smaller circles). Area outlined from upper left to lower right is unpaved roadway within which features were identified; rectangular areas represent excavation units extending beyond roadway.*

Five structures were partially excavated and isolated posts in unexcavated areas suggest more were present (figure 9.3). The architecture is notable in several respects. First, is its size and substantial construction, suggesting much more than short-term use. Second, however, is the relatively shallow depth of construction: the structures are dug a half meter or less into a sloping surface so that their downhill floor was probably at or near the ground surface. This is particularly notable in light of the mountain setting of the sites, raising questions about the seasonality of the site, a point I return to below.

Similar houses are known or implied at other sites dating to this period in the area. A house like those at Dunlap-Salazar is probably what the post and hearth pattern at LA 129573 represents, suggesting that this architecture may have developed just prior to the initial occupation of Dunlap-Salazar. Given their shallow construction, preservation is often poor and many sites lack architecture, but similar large, shallow structures are indicated on at least two other sites—LA 30949 (Del Bene et al. 1986) and LA 116531 (Campbell and Railey 2008:220–223)—extending the pattern to around AD 900. These houses contrast with the pattern of gradual size increase in the lowlands; instead their size *decreases* over time. This reduction is seen more generally among highland sites in the region (Rocek 1998) and has also been documented by Wills (2001) in the western Mogollon Highlands (Rocek 2013).

In addition to houses, the other major contrast with the preceding period is pottery. From their initial appearance, ceramics were large and well made. At Dunlap-Salazar, for instance, a large well-made cooking pot (Howey and Rocek 2008:13, figure 3), which shows heavy internal abrasion and external sooting from use was recovered from a well-dated context at about AD 580 with a two standard-deviation range (based on a Bayesian analysis incorporating stratigraphic relationships) of AD 544–610. The preserved portion of the jar weights 3.94 kg, despite the fact that a significant part of the wall is missing. Thus, the transition in this period involved a rapid heavy investment in non-portable ceramic cooking vessels.

Second, the ceramics from the site, including this vessel, are overwhelmingly Jornada Brown, a type characteristic of this highland area. This observation is confirmed by petrographic and X-ray diffraction analyses, which show not only production in the highlands, but localize the production to the Capitan Mountain region near the site itself (Howey and Rocek 2008).

By the mid-sixth century, then, we see three developments in the highlands that contrast with the lowland Jornada sequence. First is the rapid adoption and continuity in agricultural dependence. Campbell and Railey (2008) find no trend in storage volume or maize ubiquity in a series of sites spanning the first millennium AD and maize ubiquity values are high from the terminal Late Archaic on into even the pueblo period of the fourteenth century (Rocek 1995, 2013). This differs markedly from the gradual increase in evidence of maize from the lowlands which only peaks in the El Paso–phase pueblo period.

The other two contrasts are the abrupt appearance of substantial houses and of pottery in the sixth century AD. The pottery lags the lowlands by several centuries, and the houses postdate the start of the lowland Archaic architectural sequence even more. However, when houses *do* appear at the start of the ceramic period in the highlands, they are larger than any of the domestic structures in the lowlands, and in contrast to the lowland trend of gradual increase in size and elaboration, they decrease in size over time.

I suggest that these contrasts represent a split in the lowland settlement pattern that had characterized the preceramic period. That is, initially the agricultural evidence of the Archaic highlands contrasted with the lowlands because it was a complementary subpart of the lowland settlement round. Winter sites clustered along the lowland basin edges and near the Rio Grande valley; warm-season sites scattered not only in the basin bottoms but also up into the adjacent highlands. As Wills (1988) proposed for the Mogollon highlands, these Archaic highland sites incorporated agriculture as a supplement to the gathering of wild resources in the relatively well-watered hills while planting in the hotter and drier lowlands was more limited or absent. By the first few centuries AD, the lowland winter villages started growing larger and more substantial, maize (either brought from the highlands or grown locally) was important enough to be sparsely represented in the lowland archaeobotanical record, and pottery was added to enhance food processing. The highland sites remained field locations for maize production and storage, thus lacking durable housing, and pottery was not hauled up to these highland field camps. Wild resources were also gathered, but maize was dominant at these sites (figure 9.4, top).

After AD 500, the settlement pattern split (figure 9.4, bottom). Farming slowly continued to increase in the lowlands, and the cool-weather settlements continued to develop into less mobile and more integrated villages, adding communal architecture in the ninth century as their size grew, mobility decreased, and social composition stabilized. Thus, they represent incipient villages integrating a moderate number of aggregated households living in the pithouses on the sites. Meanwhile, the highland sites became the centers of a separate settlement system. They retained heavy agricultural emphasis, but abruptly added large houses and pottery for food processing as they took on full residential roles rather than functioning merely as field camps. Thus, the punctuated nature of the highland pattern results from the shifting role of these sites, first as summer gathering and agricultural field sites of the lowland system, and then as the core of a separate highland settlement round. This sites' function-specific pattern may add yet another element to the range of factors affecting the spread of technologies discussed by Cameron (chapter 2, this volume).

Evidence for a restriction in the mobility of ceramic-period highland groups is implied by the localized ceramic production. In addition, analysis of debitage from the highland sites shows a drop in chert at the transition to the ceramic period, suggesting a restriction in the area over which high-quality lithic materials were collected (Lynch 2009).

The resulting communities that developed in the highlands contrast with their lowland counterparts. The large houses suggest different domestic organization— either larger domestic social units to work the fields or contrasting patterns of indoor storage and labor. On the other hand, despite the concentration of structures and features at Dunlap-Salazar, the pattern of stratigraphically overlapping construction and non-overlapping radiocarbon dating among the five excavated structures and storage pits at the site suggests that they do *not* form an integrated village community such as appears to be developing during this period in the lowlands. In fact, of the five excavated structures at Dunlap-Salazar, no two appear to have been contemporary (Rocek 2013; Rocek and Rautman 2012). Evidence of houses at other highland sites of this period also occurs singly.

Instead of villages, the highland sites appear to represent a scatter of farmsteads along the highland river valleys. In the case of Dunlap-Salazar, these were repeatedly reoccupied, resulting in a palimpsest of structures, as well as storage pits. The large but shallow houses may not have been occupied all winter; I have

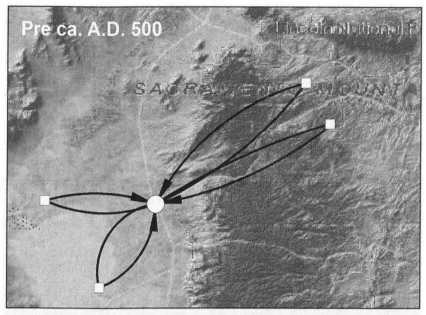

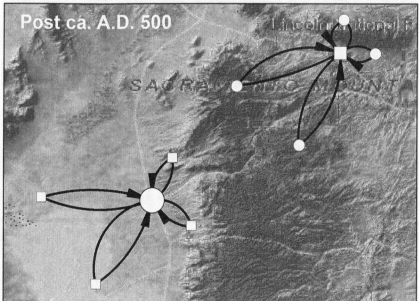

**FIGURE 9.4.** *Schematic of hypothesized shift in settlement patterns ca. AD 500. Top (pre-sixth century AD): highland sites are a part of the warm-season portion of a larger settlement pattern. Bottom (starting in early or mid-sixth century): the highland farmstead sites become central parts of a distinct highland settlement system while the lowland cool-season sites grow into early villages. Round dots (cool season); squares (warm season). (Figure by Sandra L. Hannum.)*

previously argued on several grounds, including the heavy use of extramural pit storage, that the sites were at least briefly seasonally abandoned, most likely during the winter (Rocek 1995, 2013). Rather speculatively this would suggest that sites representing a broader seasonal round should occur in the highlands. The location of associated highland winter sites is not certain; archaeological survey in the highlands (particularly in the wooded hills away from the river valleys where the warm-season agricultural sites are located) is very limited. It is possible that these winter sites were focused on hunting, and might represent only relatively limited-duration occupations (and possibly might not even have ceramics associated with them); they thus may be harder to document. The pattern and degree of mobility of the highland settlements remains uncertain. On the other hand, the farmsteads with their large houses, fields, and storage pits clearly represent the core of heavily tethered settlement systems, and the winter trips may be largely logistical in nature.

Communal architecture and convincing evidence of aggregation into villages is late in the highlands.[2] Each of the early highland Formative houses themselves is comparable in size to one of the contemporary communal structures in the lowlands. Only one extra-large structure in the Capitan Highlands has been identified in the period overlapping with the pithouses I have described. This structure was only partially excavated and yielded a ca. AD 1000 date, based on a single wood radiocarbon date, and is interpreted as a communal structure (Shelley 1992:9; Wilcox 2002). This would place it at the tail end of the large house sequence, but the single wood date is susceptible to old wood and cross-section error, so it may well date substantially later. This suggestion of a later peak in development of integrative architecture in the highlands may also reflect another aspect of Miller's (Miller et al. 2011; chapter 12, this volume) observation of the later (post-Mesilla phase) proliferation of burned-rock middens at higher elevations. An increase in the production of mescal for communal social and ritual consumption is consistent with the development of integrative activities, and may also partially explain the upward shift in burned-rock midden elevations, in addition to the exhaustion of lower-elevation fuel supplies suggested by Miller.

Thus, initially, highland farmsteads may have been relatively autonomous clusters of one or a few extended households. Social integration would have been at this small-scale level, and the integrative functions of religious activities of the few farmstead residents would have been accommodated within the large residential pithouses. Storage appears to have relied heavily on publicly visible extramural pits, so a sharp shift to household-level control of private resources is not suggested. However, the relatively isolated nature of the highland farmsteads limited the scale of the unit potentially sharing food on a regular basis, so a concern with private storage was less urgent than in the more aggregated lowlands.

The transition to unambiguous villages in the highlands corresponds to the shift to aggregated architecture of the fourteenth century. These are the pueblos of the Lincoln phase to the north and the tightly clustered smaller pithouses of the Late Glencoe phase to the south, and they include large communal rooms, heavy agricultural dependence, and every indication of relatively sedentary village organization (Kelley 1984). In both regions, semiautonomous households, presumably controlling at least some of their food stores inside their residences, were tightly bound into a larger village structure, participating in the activities associated with the communal structures. Exchange of ceramics such as Chupadero Black-on-white (made in the highlands) and El Paso Polychrome (made in the lowlands) show regional connections as well (Burgett 2006; Clark 2006).

Thus, by the fourteenth century, the highland communities converge with the lowland pattern—in fact Miller and Graves (2012:277–81) recently proposed that there is no meaningful distinction between the lowland El Paso phase and the Late Glencoe phase of the southern Capitan Highlands. But the path by which these regions arrived at this common pattern is different and counterintuitive. The lowland groups were slow to rely on farming, and yet adopted pottery and integrated into villages early. By contrast, sites in the highlands show early investment in agriculture and storage, and yet the highlanders were late to adopt pottery and build substantial houses. When they made these changes, they did it in a rapid burst. But rather than forming villages, they then lived in dispersed farmsteads that integrated into village aggregates only centuries later.

Interestingly, Roth (chapter 7, this volume) notes a somewhat parallel contrast between relatively autonomous households in the Mimbres highlands, contrasting with stronger development of corporate groups at the Harris site in the Mimbres River valley; she associates the contrast with the development of irrigation in the river valley. I have suggested that in the Jornada case, the divergent highland pattern is the result of these communities having their roots in just a subset of the full lowland Archaic settlement round. Regardless of whether that interpretation is correct, the "package" of Neolithic features, including the degree of agricultural dependence *and* the development of increasingly integrated, multihousehold, aggregated villages disaggregates in two different ways in the two regions, only to recombine by the end of the Formative, a diversity that mirrors in microcosm some of the many paths of the Formative or Neolithic worldwide.

*Acknowledgments* Many thanks to Karen Harry and Barbara Roth for inviting me to the Southwest Symposium and for their help with this publication. Thanks also to two anonymous reviewers for helpful suggestions for revision of this manuscript. Research at the Dunlap-Salazar site was supported by grants from the American Philosophical Society, the National Geographic Society, and National Science Foundation grant 9600581, with an additional REU supplemental grant. Thanks to Sandra L. Hannum for drafting figures 9.1, 9.2, and 9.4.

## NOTES

1. Much of the evidence described by Bohrer (2007) shows spring through fall occupation, as would be expected with a site associated with farm fields, and is consistent with the presence of not merely maize cobs and kernels, but tassels as well. The heavy representation of wild resources such as piñon, cactus, and yucca fruit, which are best gathered in the fall or late fall, are not incompatible with collection timed to coincide with, or follow immediately after, the maize harvest. The most direct evidence of winter gathering that she cites, dried buffalo gourd, seems alternatively consistent with collecting in the spring or transport in dried form. However, it should also be noted that the site clearly has a complex (and stratigraphically mixed) occupation history, so that many scenarios, including shifting seasonality are possibilities. These interpretations also do not preclude likely additional special-purpose sites in the highlands such as late fall or winter hunting camps, probably at higher elevations than the summer field sites.

2. The site of Creekside Village (LA 146443) currently under excavation may complicate this generalization (Greenwald 2016; Kurota et al. 2016). It is located in the valley of Tularosa Creek at 5,300 feet elevation east of the town of Tularosa, and thus may be considered to lie in the highlands, or at least their foothills, although it lies well below the modern tree zone. Creekside is reported to have evidence of considerable agricultural activities, numerous pit structures, and a large, presumably communal structure dating to the late Mesilla phase. Such a find would be of interest, and might link the lowland and highland systems, since the valley serves as a clear travel route from the lowland basin into the highlands. However, so far the site has only been very briefly described and details of dating, subsistence, and architecture remain to be published.

## REFERENCES

Bohrer, Vorsila L. 2007. *Preceramic Subsistence in Two Rock Shelters in Fresnal Canyon, South Central New Mexico*. Arizona State Museum Archaeological Series 199. Tucson: Arizona State Museum, University of Arizona.

Burgett, Jessica Prue. 2006. *El Paso Polychrome in the Casas Grandes Region, Chihuahua, Mexico: Ceramic Exchange Between Paquimé and the Jornada Mogollon*. PhD dissertation, The Pennsylvania State University, State College. Ann Arbor, MI: University Microfilms International.

Byrd, Brian F. 1994. "Public and Private, Domestic and Corporate: The Emergence of the Southwest Asian Village." *American Antiquity* 59(4):639–666. https://doi.org/10.2307/282338.

Campbell, Kirsten, and Jim A. Railey. 2008. *Archaeology of the Hondo Valley, Lincoln County, New Mexico: Archaeological Investigations along US 70 from Ruidoso Downs to Riverside.*

SWCA Cultural Resources Report No. 2008–417. Albuquerque, NM: SWCA; Santa Fe: New Mexico Department of Transportation.

Childe, Vere Gordon. 1936. *Man Makes Himself*. London: Watts & Co.

Clark, Tiffany C. 2006. *Production, Exchange, and Social Identity; A Study of Chupadero Black-on-White Pottery*. PhD dissertation, Department of Anthropology, Arizona State University, Tucson. Ann Arbor, MI: University Microfilms International.

Corley, John. 1965. "Proposed Eastern Extension of the Jornada Branch of the Mogollon Culture." In *Transactions of the First Archeological Symposium for Southeastern New Mexico and Western Texas*, 30–36. Bulletin 1. Hobbs, NM: Lea County Archeology Society.

Del Bene, Terry, Allen Rorex, and Linda Brett. 1986. *Report on Excavations at LA 30949 and LA 30951*. Prepared for the New Mexico State Highway Department. Ed. C. M. Beck and S. C. Schermer. Agency for Conservation Archaeology Report No. MD821. Portales: Eastern New Mexico State University.

Douglass, John G., and Nancy Gonlin, eds. 2012. *Ancient Households of the Americas: Conceptualizing What Households Do*. Boulder: University Press of Colorado.

Flannery, Kent V. 1972. "The Origins of the Village as a Settlement Type in Mesoamerica and the Near East: A Comparative Study." In *Man, Settlement, and Urbanism*, ed. P. J. Ucko, R. Tringham, and G. W. Dimbleby, 23–53. London: Duckworth.

Flannery, Kent V. 2002. "The Origins of the Village Revisited: From Nuclear to Extended Households." *American Antiquity* 67(3):417–433. https://doi.org/10.2307/1593820.

Graham, Martha. 1993. "Settlement Organization and Residential Variability among the Rarámuri." In *Abandonment of Settlements and Regions: Ethnoarchaeological and Archaeological Approaches*, ed. Catherine M. Cameron and Steven A. Tomka, 25–42. Cambridge, UK: Cambridge University Press. https://doi.org/10.1017/CBO9780511735240.003.

Greenwald, David. 2016. "FW: Regge's Abajo de la Cruz Report." Post to NM-ARCH-L listserv group forwarded from David Greenwald by David Atlee Phillips, December 9, 2016. http://www2004.lsoft.se/scripts/wl.exe?SL1=NM-ARCH-L&H=UNM.EDU.

Hard, Robert J., Raymond P. Mauldin, and Gerry R. Raymond. 1996. "Mano Size, Stable Carbon Isotope Ratios, and Macrobotanical Remains as Multiple Lines of Evidence of Maize Dependence in the American Southwest." *Journal of Archaeological Method and Theory* 3(3):253–318. https://doi.org/10.1007/BF02229401.

Hard, Robert J., and William L. Merrill. 1992. "Mobile Agriculturalists and the Emergence of Sedentism: Perspectives from Northern Mexico." *American Anthropologist* 94(3):601–620. https://doi.org/10.1525/aa.1992.94.3.02a00040.

Howey, Meghan, and Thomas R. Rocek. 2008. "Ceramic Variability, Subsistence Economies, and Settlement Patterns in the Jornada Mogollon." *Kiva* 74(1):7–32. https://doi.org/10.1179/kiv.2008.74.1.001.

Jelinek, Arthur J. 1967. *A Prehistoric Sequence in the Middle Pecos Valley, New Mexico*. Anthropological Papers of the Museum of Anthropology No. 31. Ann Arbor: University of Michigan.

Johnson, Gregory A. 1982. "Organizational Structure and Scalar Stress." In *Theory and Explanation in Archaeology: The Southampton Conference*, ed. Colin Renfrew, Michael J. Rowlands, and Barbara A. Segraves-Whallon, 389–421. New York: Academic Press.

Jordan, Peter, and Marek Zvelebil. 2009. "Introduction: *Ex Oriente Lux*: The Prehistory of Hunter-Gatherer Ceramic Dispersals." In *Ceramics before Farming: The Dispersal of Pottery among Prehistoric Eurasian Hunter-Gatherers*, ed. Peter Jordan and Marek Zvelebil, 33–89. Walnut Creek, CA: Left Coast Press. https://doi.org/10.1515/9781400827138.1.

Kelley, Jane H. 1984. *The Archaeology of the Sierra Blanca Region of Southeastern New Mexico*. Museum of Anthropology Anthropological Papers No. 74. Ann Arbor: Museum of Anthropology, University of Michigan.

Kurota, Alexander, Robert Dello-Russo, Evan Sternberg, and Evan Kay. 2016. "The Jarilla Site, LA 37470: A Prehistoric Outpost for Agriculture and Its Possible Role in Regional Trade." *NewsMAC* (Newsletter of the New Mexico Archeological Council) 2016(1):20–43.

Kyte, Michael. 1988. "A Ceramic Sequence from the Chupadera Arroyo Basin, Central New Mexico." Unpublished MA thesis, Department of Anthropology, Eastern New Mexico University, Portales.

Lehmer, Donald J. 1948. "The Jornada Branch of the Mogollon." *Social Science Bulletin* 17. *University of Arizona Bulletin* 19(2). Tucson: University of Arizona.

Lentz, Stephen C. 2006. *High Rolls Cave: Insectos, Burritos, y Frajos; Archaic Subsistence in Southern New Mexico; Excavations at LA 113103, Otero County, New Mexico*. Archaeology Notes 345. New Mexico Department of Transportation Cultural Resource Technical Series 2005–1. Santa Fe: Office of Archaeological Studies, Museum of New Mexico.

Leslie, Robert. 1979. "The Eastern Jornada Mogollon: Extreme Southeastern New Mexico (A Summary)." In *Jornada Mogollon Archaeology*, ed. Patrick H. Beckett and Regge N. Wiseman, 179–199. Las Cruces: Cultural Resource Management Division, New Mexico State University.

Lynch, Shaun M. 2009. "Determining the Mobility of the Inhabitants at Dunlap-Salazar: Through Analysis of Lithic Raw Materials." Unpublished undergraduate honors thesis. Department of Anthropology, University of Delaware, Newark. http://dspace.udel.edu:8080/dspace/handle/19716/4721.

Mabry, Jonathan B., and William E. Doolittle. 2008. "Modeling the Early Agricultural Frontier in the Desert Borderlands." In *Archaeology without Borders; Contact, Commerce, and Change in the U.S. Southwest and Northwestern Mexico*, ed. Maxine E. McBrinn and Laurie D. Webster, 55–70. Boulder: University of Colorado Press.

MacNeish, Richard S., ed. 1993. *Preliminary Investigations of the Archaic in the Region of Las Cruces, New Mexico*. Historic and Natural Resources Report No. 9. Fort Bliss, TX:

Cultural Resources Management Branch, Directorate of Environment, United States Army Air Defense Artillery Center.

Miller, Myles R. 2005. "Revision of the Jornada Mogollon Ceramic Period Sequence and Alignment with the Greater Southwest." In *Archaeology between the Borders: Papers from the 13th Biennial Jornada Mogollon Conference*, ed. Marc Thompson, Jason Jurgena, and Lora Jackson, 59–88. El Paso, TX: El Paso Museum of Archaeology.

Miller, Myles R., and Tim B. Graves. 2012. *Sacramento Pueblo: An El Paso and Late Glencoe Phase Pueblo in the Southern Sacramento Mountains*. Fort Bliss Cultural Resources Report No. 10–22. GMI Report of Investigations No. 800EP. El Paso, TX: Geo-Marine.

Miller, Myles R., Tim B. Graves, Moira Ernst, and Mike Stowe. 2011. *Burned Rock Middens of the Southern Sacramento Mountains*. Fort Bliss Cultural Resources Report No. 09–28. Fort Bliss, TX: Environmental Division.

Miller, Myles R., and Nancy A. Kenmotsu. 2004. "Prehistory of the Jornada Mogollon and Eastern Trans-Pecos Regions of West Texas." In *The Prehistory of Texas*, ed. Timothy K. Perttula, 205–265. College Station: Texas A&M University Press.

Miller, Myles R., and Nancy A. Kenmotsu. Forthcoming. "Measuring Diversity: Land Use and Settlement Intensity in the Western Jornada before and after A.D. 1000." In *Late Prehistoric Hunter-Gatherers and Farmers of the Jornada Mogollon*, ed. by Thomas R. Rocek and Nancy A. Kenmotsu. Boulder: University Press of Colorado.

Oakes, Yvonne R. 1998. *LA 457: An Early Mesilla Phase Occupation along North Florida Avenue, Alamogordo, New Mexico*. Office of Archaeological Studies Archaeology Notes 180. Santa Fe: Museum of New Mexico.

Rocek, Thomas R. 1995. "Sedentarization and Agricultural Dependence: Perspectives from the Pithouse-to-Pueblo Transition in the American Southwest." *American Antiquity* 60(2):218–239. https://doi.org/10.2307/282138.

Rocek, Thomas R. 1998. "Subsistence, Settlement, and Social Variability in the Mogollon: Regional Variation in House Size." Paper presented at the 63rd annual meeting of the Society for American Archaeology, Seattle, WA.

Rocek, Thomas R. 2013. "The Dunlap-Salazar Site (La 51344) and the Context of Village Origins in the Jornada Highlands." In *Papers from the 17th Biennial Jornada Mogollon Conference in 2011*, ed. C. VanPool and E. McCarthy, 137–150. El Paso, TX: El Paso Museum of Archaeology.

Rocek, Thomas R., and Nancy Kenmotsu. Forthcoming. "Introduction: Diversity and Change in a 'Marginal' Region and Environment." In *Late Prehistoric Hunter-Gatherers and Farmers of the Jornada Mogollon*, ed. Thomas R. Rocek and Nancy A. Kenmotsu. Boulder: University Press of Colorado.

Rocek, Thomas R., and Alison E. Rautman. 2012. "First Millennium Pithouse Village Diversity in Southeastern New Mexico." In *Southwestern Pithouse Communities, AD 200–900*, ed. Lisa Young and Sarah Herr, 110–122. Tucson: University of Arizona Press.

Shelley, Phillip H. 1992. "Archaeology and Paleoecology of the Fort Stanton Reservation near Lincoln, New Mexico." In *Interpreting the Past: Research with Public Participation*, ed. LouAnn Jacobson and June-el Piper, 1–19. Cultural Resources Series No. 10. Santa Fe: Bureau of Land Management New Mexico State Office.

Speth, John D. 1988. "Do We Need Concepts Like 'Mogollon,' 'Anasazi,' and 'Hohokam' Today?: A Cultural Anthropological Perspective." *Kiva* 53(2):201–204. https://doi.org /10.1080/00231940.1988.11758093.

Tagg, Martyn D. 1996. "Early Cultigens from Fresnal Shelter, Southeastern New Mexico." *American Antiquity* 61(2):311–324. https://doi.org/10.2307/282428.

Upham, Steadman, Richard S. MacNeish, Walton C. Galinat, and Christopher M. Stevenson. 1987. "Evidence Concerning the Origin of Maiz de Ocho." *American Anthropologist* 89(2):410–419. https://doi.org/10.1525/aa.1987.89.2.02a00090.

Vierra, Bradley J. 2008. "Early Agriculture on the Southeastern Periphery of the Colorado Plateau: Diversity in Tactics." In *Archaeology without Borders: Contact, Commerce, and Change in the U.S. Southwest and Northwestern Mexico*, ed. Maxine E. McBrinn and Laurie D. Webster, 71–88. Boulder: University of Colorado Press.

Whalen, Michael E. 1981. "Cultural-Ecological Aspects of the Pithouse-to-Pueblo Transition in a Portion of the Southwest." *American Antiquity* 46(1):75–92. https://doi .org/10.2307/279988.

Whalen, Michael E. 1994a. "Moving Out of the Archaic Edge of the Southwest." *American Antiquity* 59(4):622–638. https://doi.org/10.2307/282337.

Whalen, Michael E. 1994b. *Turquoise Ridge and Late Prehistoric Residential Mobility in the Desert Mogollon Region.* Anthropological Papers No. 118. Salt Lake City: University of Utah Press.

Wilcox, David. 2002. "A Geoarchaeological Investigation at Upper Bonito I (LA 84319)." In *Archaeological Variation within the Middle Rio Bonito*, ed. Philip H. Shelley and Kristen E. Wenzel, 31–57. Cultural Resources Series No. 14. Santa Fe: Bureau of Land Management New Mexico State Office.

Willey, Gordon R., and Philip Phillips. 1958. *Method and Theory in American Archaeology.* Chicago, IL: University of Chicago Press.

Wills, Wirt H. 1988. "Early Agriculture and Sedentism in the American Southwest: Evidence and Interpretations." *Journal of World Prehistory* 2(4):445–488. https://doi .org/10.1007/BF00976198.

Wills, Wirt H. 1991. "Organizational Strategies and the Emergence of Villages in the American Southwest." In *Between Bands and States*, ed. Susan A. Gregg, 161–180. Carbondale: Southern Illinois University Press.

Wills, Wirt H. 2001. "Pithouse Architecture and the Economics of Household Formation in the Prehistoric American Southwest." *Human Ecology* 29(4):477–500. https://doi.org/10.1023/A:1013198022095.

Wills, W. H., F. Scott Worman, Wetherbee Dorshow, and Heather Richards-Rissetto. 2012. "Shabik'eschee Village in Chaco Canyon: Beyond the Archetype." *American Antiquity* 77(2):326–350. https://doi.org/10.7183/0002-7316.77.2.326.

Wilson, C. Dean. 2004. "Pottery Analysis." In *Fallen Pine Shelter: 3,000 Years of Prehistoric Occupation on the Mescalero Apache Reservation*, by Yvonne R. Oakes, 43–61. Office of Archaeological Studies Archaeology Notes 325. Santa Fe: Museum of New Mexico.

Wiseman, Regge N.1996. *The Land in Between: Archaic and Formative Occupations along the Upper Rio Hondo of Southeastern New Mexico*. Office of Archaeological Studies Archaeology Notes 125. Santa Fe: Museum of New Mexico.

Wiseman, Regge N. 2000. *Bob Crosby Draw and River Camp: Contemplating Prehistoric Social Boundaries in Southeastern New Mexico*. Office of Archaeological Studies Archaeology Notes 235. Santa Fe: Museum of New Mexico.

Wiseman, Regge N. 2002. *The Fox Place: A Late Prehistoric Hunter-Gatherer Pithouse Village near Roswell, New Mexico*. Office of Archaeological Studies Archaeology Notes 234. Santa Fe: Museum of New Mexico.

Wiseman, Regge N. 2003. *The Roswell South Project: Excavations in the Sacramento Plain and the Northern Chihuahuan Desert of Southeastern New Mexico*. Office of Archaeological Studies Archaeology Notes 237. Santa Fe: Museum of New Mexico.

Wiseman, Regge N. 2004. "The Pottery of the Henderson Site (LA-1549): The 1980–1981 Season." In *Life on the Periphery: Economic Change in Late Prehistoric Southeastern New Mexico*, ed. John D. Speth, 67–95. Museum of Anthropology Memoir No. 37. Ann Arbor: University of Michigan.

Wu, Xiaohong, Chi Zhang, Paul Goldberg, David Cohen, Yan Pan, Trina Arpin, and Ofer Bar-Yosef. 2012. "Early Pottery at 20,000 Years Ago in Xianrendong Cave, China." *Science* 336(6089):1696–1700. https://doi.org/10.1126/science.1218643.

# 10

# The Hohokam House

*Identifying Nested Social Groups during the Pioneer Period in the Tucson Basin*

ERIC EUGENE KLUCAS AND WILLIAM M. GRAVES

In most human societies, individuals belong to several, often cooperating, sometimes competing, social groups. The composition, integration, and interaction of these groups vary among different societies, with specific formations reflecting variability in economic, social, and political structures within a specific society. From the perspective of the individual, these groups can be conceptualized as a nested series of entities of increasing size and complexity, beginning with the most intimate personal domestic group and extending to the community and beyond. Between these two extremes lie myriad additional possibilities that reflect a society's unique historical trajectory as well as choices made by individuals throughout their lifetimes.

In this chapter we explore this "nesting" of social identity and group membership as expressed in Hohokam culture of the southern desert region of the American Southwest. Among the Hohokam, these groups begin with the household at the smallest scale and extend to the community at large. We suggest that one of the social groups intermediate between the household and the community was structurally comparable to the "House" as defined by Claude

DOI: 10.5876/9781607327356.c010

Lévi-Strauss (1982, 1987). We believe that this phenomenon was a fundamental aspect of the Hohokam social order—one that, in large part, structured the most basic aspects of Hohokam society. Moreover, we argue that these nested social units were apparent at some of the earliest village sites and may have characterized social identity and social relations from the very beginnings of Hohokam history. Excavations at several of these early village sites have revealed a clear site structure that strongly suggests the existence of nested social units that were founded at the same time as the village, were fundamental characteristics of the overall village or community, and foreshadow the existence of later nested social units described variously as courtyard groups, village segments, or precincts in Colonial-, Sedentary-, and Classic-period Hohokam sites.

In keeping with the theme of this section of the volume, our attention is on the archaeological identification of these nested Hohokam social units, with special attention placed on the nature of an intermediate unit lying between the household (see Roth [chapter 7, this volume] and Douglass et al. [chapter 11, this volume]) and the community. Following a summary of Hohokam culture, we discuss the House-society model as it applies to the Hohokam. We follow this with an examination of the archaeological data that we use to reconstruct early Hohokam social and political organization, focusing on the interpretive power of the built environment. Particular attention is paid to how the distribution of human burials and their spatial relationships to other classes of features can inform on the nature of social relationships at the level of both the individual and the group. This is followed by a case study from the northern Tucson Basin, where we evaluate a set of archaeological data in light of these expectations and assumptions.

## THE HOHOKAM

*Hohokam* is the archaeological-culture term used to refer to the farmers who occupied the Sonoran desert of Arizona from about AD 500 to 1450 (Haury 1976). In the river valleys of the desert, the Hohokam were irrigation farmers who constructed large-scale canal systems and built large villages with communal public architecture. The Preclassic period encompasses most of the Hohokam historical sequence and includes the Pioneer (AD 400 to 750), Colonial (AD 750 to 950), and Sedentary (AD 950 to 1150) periods (Dean 1991). This long span of time includes the beginnings and expansion of the Hohokam archaeological culture, aspects of which are spread throughout southern and central Arizona. In terms of material culture, the Preclassic period is characterized by red-on-buff decorated ceramics (Haury 1976:202–225) and public or communal architecture at large village sites in the form of ballcourts (Wilcox and Sternberg 1983). Houses-in-pits—characterized by a single-room structure constructed in a shallow pit—were the major form of domestic architecture and these were often, but not always, arranged in groups of two or more around shared courtyards (Wilcox et al. 1981; Huntington 1986). Preclassic Hohokam archaeological culture is also characterized by relatively commonly found ritual artifacts such as figurines, palettes, and censers as well as the widespread practice of cremation for mortuary ritual (Rice 2016:58).

## THE HOUSE CONCEPT IN HOHOKAM ARCHAEOLOGY

The existence of an intermediary social formation between the individual household and the community has been proposed by many scholars of the Hohokam. Whether referred to as precincts, village segments, or simply aggregates of individual house clusters, all refer to repeating sets of features and, by extension, activities shared by a collection of individual households. In this section, we explore some ideas about the nature and expression of these intermediate units and their role in the development of Hohokam society in general and House societies in particular.

Most Southwestern archaeologists will attest that the idea of Hohokam villages comprising a hierarchical arrangement of multiple, repeating units is not really ground-shaking news. As Wilcox and his colleagues (1981) and many others (e.g. Ciolek-Torrello et al. 2000; Gregory 1991; Howard 2000; Sires 1987; Whittlesey 2013; Whittlesey and Deaver 2004) have argued, Hohokam site structure can be described as a series of nested elements—houses-in-pits, courtyard groups, village segments, and precincts—that all combine in various ways to form the farmsteads, hamlets, and villages that constitute the generally accepted range of site types of the Hohokam. In this chapter, we offer some suggestions concerning the meaning or sociality behind such patterning in the Hohokam archaeological record. We argue that this "nestedness" of Hohokam social groups or social identity was present at the very beginning of Hohokam culture and remained a fundamental aspect of Hohokam social order for nearly a millennium.

Importantly, it is the House, in the sense of Claude Lévi-Strauss's House-society model (Lévi-Strauss 1982, 1987) that provides a structuring link among these nested units; specifically, between the individual households and larger social formations such as villages and communities. The House was simultaneously a key element in an individual's social identity, a primary structuring principle in determining social relations among members of an individual community or village, and the means by which social links were forged among different Hohokam sites or settlements.

As cogently argued by Douglas Craig (2007, 2010), Lévi-Strauss's concept of the House fits quite well with the material expression of the Preclassic-period Hohokam. Briefly stated, the House represents a social group existing between the individual household and the larger community. In terms of its structure, Gillespie (2000a:1–2) described the House as a "... corporate bod[y], sometimes quite large, organized by its shared residence, subsistence, means of production, origin, ritual actions or metaphysical essence, all of which entails a commitment to a corpus of house property, which in turn can be said to materialize the social group." As such, the shared activities of the member households to maintain their shared resources led to the continual social reproduction of the House as well as to the social reproduction of inequalities among households. Among its many functions, the House acts as a land-controlling entity that affords use rights to its members (Lévi-Strauss 1982:184; 1987:152). The House also provides a ready pool of labor and resources for its individual members. This adds a degree of economic flexibility to the group. Although kin relationships play an important part in determining group membership, shared affinity is not necessarily required. The emergence of social groups that cross-cut kinship is crucial for the formation and continuing cohesion of larger communities.

## HUMAN BEHAVIOR AND INTERACTION AS REFLECTED IN THE BUILT ENVIRONMENT

Having now proposed how the House concept can be applied to the Hohokam culture, we turn our attention to how this idea can be explored using the kinds of data generally available to archaeologists. We focus this part of our discussion on the power of the built environment to act as a window on several aspects of social behavior.

The study of the relationship between the built environment and human behavior has a long tradition in a number of disciplines, including architecture (Bourdier and Alsayyad 1989; Hillier and Hanson 1984), sociology (Durkheim and Mauss 1902), history (Stambaugh 1988), anthropology (Douglas 1972; Wilk 1990), and archaeology (Blanton 1994; Clark 2001; Ferguson 1996; Hegmon 1989; Horne 1994; Klucas 1996, 2009; Klucas and Schwartz 2015; Klucas et al. 1998; Schwartz and Klucas 1998). In very general terms, these studies have approached the relationship between the built environment and human behavior from one of two directions (see also Stone, chapter 8, this volume). In the first, the built environment is seen as operating as the dependent variable, with its form and structure determined by the needs and norms of those who created it. In this view, the built environment has been described as a "sociogram," or the physical expression of a social system (Hillier and Hanson 1984:159). As such, different types of social systems would require a specific, special order created through the conscious manipulation of the built environment, one that would presumably be accessible through archaeological investigations.

In the second perspective, the built environment is seen as taking a more active role in human behavior. The structuring properties of the built environment both direct human behavior (Donley-Reid 1990) and provide concrete cues that communicate the proper behavior for a given setting (Rapoport 1990).

Here, the built environment is seen as both structuring behavior and serving to reinforce and recreate social relationships (Bourdier and Alsayyad 1989:7). These relationships can be expressed at a number of levels, from individual houses to more public spaces existing at the level of the community.

It is most likely, of course, that both aspects of the relationship between human behavior and the built environment are in play at any one time. And from the perspective of the archaeologist interested in reconstructing human interaction from its material correlates, whether the built environment is primarily a passive or an active element may not really matter. It is perhaps more important for our purposes that this relationship simply exists. With this in mind, we turn now to a brief discussion of one aspect of the built environment that we believe possessed the dual purpose of both reflecting and structuring behavior for the early Hohokam. That aspect of the built environment was the cemetery.

## Mortuary Rituals and Cemeteries

Archaeologists have long recognized the information potential of mortuary features and cemeteries, and their description and analysis have held a prominent position in archaeological research for decades (Binford 1971; Saxe 1971). Much early research focused on what burials could tell us about the lives of individuals, such as diseases or injuries that they had suffered or their status within the community—information that could then be used to make assertions about the general health of a population. Data on age at death and sex are also used to reconstruct demographic profiles of populations. Variability in mortuary behavior through time and across space has also been commonly used as a cultural and temporal indicator.

Looking beyond the treatment of the individual to a consideration of the broader social implications of mortuary behavior, several researchers have considered how mortuary activities, especially as reflected in the location and maintenance of cemetery areas can function as a means of fostering and maintaining a shared identity among group members (Ashmore and Geller 2005; Chesson 2001; Hastorf 2003; Kuijt 2001; Potter and Perry 2011). Beyond the more immediate and transitory impact of mortuary ceremony itself, which often centers on reinforcing the shared membership of the participants in a given social group, a cemetery area, whether marked with elaborate monuments or simply within the shared memories of living descendants, can function as a group's claim to a particular place and can serve in part as a physical manifestation of the social rights, responsibilities, and shared history of the participating social group. This declaration and affirmation of group membership is often simultaneously directed at both members and nonmembers of the group.

In a 1980 publication, Lynne Goldstein explored how the mortuary record at two Mississippian-period cemeteries in the lower Illinois River valley could be used to test several hypotheses relating to social organization. The hypotheses that she constructed were grounded in the understanding of Mississippian social organization that was in place at the time. Briefly stated, it was generally believed that large Mississippian centers, such as Cahokia, Spiro, and Etowah, were characterized by a clear-cut status hierarchy. Such hierarchy, it was argued, was reflected in a number of lines of evidence, notably a differential distribution of indicators of wealth and status within and among sites. In terms of the mortuary record, this was manifested in significant differences in mortuary treatment (Goldstein 1980:21). Considerable variability was noted between burials associated with the larger mound sites and those in the smaller, rural villages, with the burials at the mound sites exhibiting significantly greater diversity in burial treatment than their counterparts in the rural areas. High-status burials were far more common at the mound sites.

Beginning with this understanding of the relationship between Mississippian social organization and burial practice, Goldstein (1980) proposed several hypotheses that could be tested with the available mortuary data. In terms of the relationship between the physical manifestation of mortuary behavior and group dynamics, she proposed that "the spatial organization of rural Mississippian cemeteries should be reflective of descent groups or corporate group structure, through which crucial but restricted resources were controlled" (Goldstein 1980:49). She further proposed that "rural Mississippian mortuary sites should exhibit a communal, as opposed to an individualized, emphasis" (Goldstein 1980:49–50).

It is this latter aspect of mortuary ritual that we suggest is applicable to the examination of the Hohokam House. We argue that the Hohokam mortuary ritual possessed a strong communal component and that its audience extended well beyond the deceased individual's immediate household or village. Indeed, it is possible that the Hohokam cemetery served as one of perhaps many totemic representations of the House, reinforcing the reality of the House for both its members and outsiders. We explore this idea in greater depth in the following sections.

## THE HOUSE CONCEPT APPLIED

Having set the stage for the arguments that follow, we will begin with a brief examination of the material expression of the nested social groups that we propose characterized Hohokam society. In our scheme, the first of these nested groups is the household. In Hohokam studies, the household is most often operationalized in one of two ways. Most simply, households are equated with the occupants of a single habitation structure, similar to Peter Laslett's (1972:27) notion of the *houseful*, which he defined as all individuals, regardless of familial ties, that occupy a single structure. Alternately, the household is viewed as a larger social group, encompassing multiple houses-in-pits, some serving as habitation structures and some serving as storage facilities, often arranged to define an exterior space presumably for the exclusive use of the household (Ciolek-Torrello et al. 2000; Whittlesey 2013:12.16–12.28). Within this bounded exterior space or courtyard, occupants of the individual houses engaged in such shared activities as food storage and preparation, reflected in a variety of thermal and non-thermal pits and hearths often found within courtyards. It is likely that both material expressions, the individual habitation structure and the courtyard group, represented coexisting forms of households that differed in their specific composition.

However one defines households in Hohokam sites, it is the habitation structure that is taken to be the primary archaeological expression of the household. Because it is not the purpose of this study to define the precise physical expression of the household, we treat the inhabitants of a single house as the primary social building block of the early Hohokam and, as such, the first and most basic of the nested social groups that we argue constitute Hohokam society.

The second of these nested groups in our scheme is the House. Materially, the House is commonly symbolized by some monument or monuments that provide a physical representation of the abstract concept of the social unit (Beck 2007; Joyce 2007; McKinnon 2000). Such a symbol or monument presumably would be repeated, one for each House present in any given setting. In addition to serving as the physical expression of the group, these monuments symbolize the continuity of the group across multiple generations. One common physical expression of the House well known to archaeologists and anthropologists is the large communally occupied house observed among many cultures along the Northwest Coast of North America (Marshall 2000), the Mayan region of Mesoamerica (Gillespie 2000b), South America (Lea 1995; Rivière 1995), and Southeast Asia (Waterson 1995, 2000). Alternately, the House may be symbolized by an architectural element or embellishment that can be relocated, if necessary. One such example of this can be seen among the Tanimbarese of Indonesia, where the physical manifestation of the House is expressed in the *tavu*, an elaborately carved altar to the ancestors that is placed within the primary structure of the House (McKinnon 2000:163).

In the case of the Preclassic-period Hohokam, we propose that the material expression of the House consists of spatially discrete clusters of houses, extramural features, and, perhaps most important, human burials. As discussed above, the house served residential and storage functions for individual households. Extramural spaces were used by multiple households, some related through lines of kinship and others not, for both individual household activities and communal activities engaged in by several households. In addition to their more mundane domestic functions, we argue that these clusters of houses and

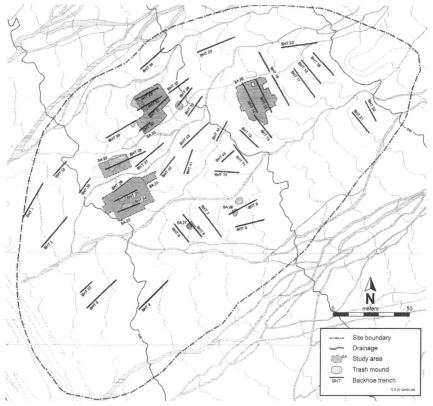

**FIGURE 10.1.** *Richter site (AZ AA:12:242 [ASM]) (after Jones 2010a:figure 2).*

extramural spaces provided a physical manifestation of the more abstract social concept of the House. In the following section we expand on this idea through the examination of the built environment at the Richter site, a large, multi-component habitation site located at the transition of the Tortolita Mountain alluvial fan and the Santa Cruz River floodplain in the northern Tucson Basin (figure 10.1).

## The Richter Site

Excavations at the Richter site were sponsored by Red Point Development, Inc., and were carried out by Tierra Right of Way Services, Ltd., under the supervision of Jeffrey Jones (Jones and Klucas 2010; Klimas and Williams 2010). The eastern portion of the site on the alluvial fan experienced repeated episodes of seasonal aggradation and erosion, resulting in shallowly buried cultural deposits with minimal vertical stratigraphy. The investigated portion of these areas of the site largely dates to the Agua Caliente (AD 50–400) and Tortolita (AD 500–700) phases with a small handful of features, both burials and habitation structures, dating to the Cañada del Oro phase (AD 750–850) of the Colonial period (Dean 1991). The western portion of the site, situated off the terrace on the Santa Cruz River floodplain, contained more deeply buried deposits dating to the Late Archaic period (Thurtle and Levstik 2004; Thurtle and Montgomery 2007). Based on an assessment of surface indicators, which included at least 10 trash mounds, 11 roasting features exposed in shallow drainages, and scattered concentrations of artifacts, the extant portion of the site covers about 40 acres. An unknown portion of the site was impacted by the construction of the Southern Pacific Railroad and Interstate 10, which border the site to the southwest.

Analyses of macrobotanical remains recovered from the Richter site reflect year-round occupation by a population practicing a mixed economy consisting of the cultivation of several domesticated plant species and gathered wild resources (Diehl 2010). The intensity of this occupation, however, is unclear. While numerous examples of the superpositioning of architectural features at the site are consistent with a long-term occupation, it is difficult to ascertain whether such superpositioning of features represents a continuous, unbroken episode of occupation or a pattern of re-occurring, year-round occupation interspersed with periods of temporary site abandonment.

A total of 506 buried cultural features were identified within six spatially discrete mechanically stripped areas at the Richter site, designated as Study Areas 22–28 (figure 10.2). The study areas were selected for excavation based on two criteria. First, information from the testing phase of the project suggested the presence of spatially discrete clusters of features. Second, the testing data suggested that elements from the full temporal range of the site would be included in these six areas. The excavated portion of the site covered approximately 7,300 m², or approximately 2 acres. Documented features within the investigated areas consisted of 110 pit structures, 151 extramural features, and 245 human burials.

In terms of areal exposure, most of the field effort was focused on three spatially discrete occupation areas, which were excavated as Study Areas 22–26 (see figure 10.2). We interpret these three spatially discrete clusters of features as the archaeological remnants of three separate Houses at Richter. The westernmost of the study areas (Study Areas 22–24) included two clusters of features that were separated by a shallow wash between Study Areas 22 and 23 (figure 10.3). Given the presence of the wash, it is unlikely that more than a handful of features may have been left unexcavated between Study Areas 22 and 23. Study Area 25 and Study Area 26 (figures 10.4 and 10.5) revealed two separate, relatively dense clusters of features that were both adjacent to a trash mound that was visible on the site's surface. The areas unexcavated between the study areas, while containing occasional architectural features and pits identified during Phase 1

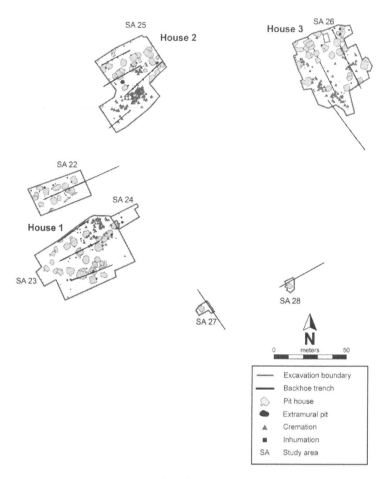

**FIGURE 10.2.** *Relative locations of Study Areas 22–28 at the Richter site.*

test excavations, were not intensively investigated. However, Phase I testing indicated that feature densities dropped off substantially beyond the mechanically stripped study areas, and we assume that the spatial limits of the study areas approximate the actual clustering of features at the site.

When compared, the three clusters of features revealed by the excavation of Study Areas 22–26 exhibit several marked structural similarities. Each was characterized by numerous habitation structures, extramural pits, and cremation burials defined during the excavations. In general terms, the courtyard arrangement of houses typical of later Hohokam periods was not readily apparent in any of the study areas. Rather, architectural features often appear to have been built individually or occur in linear arrangements with many entrances exhibiting a common entry orientation.

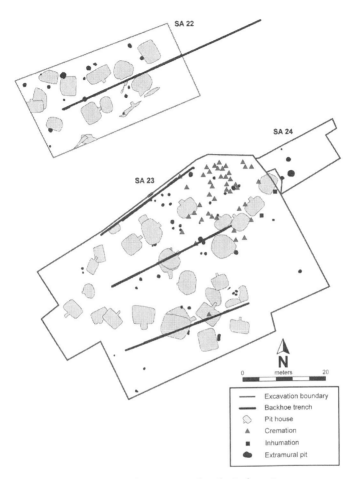

**FIGURE 10.3.** *House 1 (Study Areas 22–24) at the Richter site.*

## Early Hohokam Houses at the Richter Site

It is our contention that Study Areas 22–26 reflect the physical manifestation of three separate Houses as envisioned by Lévi-Strauss and others—House 1 (Study Areas 22, 23, and 24), House 2 (Study Area 25), and House 3 (Study Area 26) (see figure 10.2). We believe that this assertion is supported by two main patterns observed among the features at Richter. The first is the distinct spatial patterning of feature types repeated within each of the Houses, specifically the presence of a grouping of houses and a spatially associated cemetery area. The second is the dating of mortuary and nonmortuary features, which for each House is roughly identical—feature dates range from the late Agua Caliente phase to the early Colonial period, with the majority of features assigned to the Tortolita phase (Jones 2010b).

**FIGURE 10.4.** *House 2 (Study Area 25) at the Richter site.*

Each of the Houses as we define them represents relatively discrete sets of uses, mainly habitation and one aspect of mortuary ritual, that being the secondary interment of portions of the cremated remains of individuals, as well as the long-term control of property or place. Thus, each House area reflects the existence of a persistent place on the social landscape. The distinctiveness of the pairings of cemeteries and house groups and the common superpositioning of structure features suggest that the corporate memory of the location of the cemetery and the general location of the proper habitation area associated with each cemetery persisted through time among House members. However, the common occurrence of superpositioning among individual structures suggests that the memories of the specific locations of houses in the past were not retained or were lost. We suspect this reflects the intermittent use of each of the three feature clusters exposed

FIGURE 10.5. *House 3 (Study Area 26) at the Richter site*

in the study areas as an active habitation locus. The social importance of each feature cluster was as a House cemetery and each feature cluster was not the exclusive locus of habitation by an entire House at all times.

We suspect that the social landscape of each House extended well beyond the confines of the Richter site. In other words, it is possible that a single House may have had members at multiple communities or locations at any given time and that any one House may have had one or more cemetery areas that linked it to specific places on the overall landscape. We believe that this assertion can be examined through a comparison of the number of burial features identified within each of the defined Houses and the presumed population of the House as represented by the number of habitation structures contained within each. If the number of burials associated with an individual House is roughly similar to the estimated population for the House, it could be argued that the Richter site represented that House's lone location on the overall social landscape. Conversely, if the number of identified burials is significantly lower or higher than the assumed total population of a House, it may indicate that the social landscape of individual Houses, including ritual space, extended beyond the settlement documented at the Richter site.

Population estimates for this study were derived from an estimate of total floor area of identified structures associated with each House following Brown's (1987) estimate of 4.7–7.5 m² of interior floor space required per person. Also, because we are concerned here with the total number of individuals residing in Study Areas 22–26 through time, determining which structures may have been occupied contemporaneously was not necessary.

Figure 10.6 graphically indicates that the possibility that the social landscapes of the individual Houses extended well beyond the Richter site best fits the demographic estimates we calculated. Three possible scenarios are represented by the three Houses at the Richter site. The cemetery associated with House 1 contained, at minimum, the remains of 46 individuals, with the estimated population represented by the identified houses ranging from a low of 82 to a high of 212. This relationship is reversed in the case of House 2, where the estimated range of population, falling somewhere between 44 and 114 individuals, is below the estimated 139 individuals represented in the burial population. Finally, the cemetery associated with House 3 comprises a burial population of 76 individuals, which falls within the range of population estimated from the identified architectural features.

When considering the use of the individual cemetery areas through time, several interesting patterns are apparent. Figure 10.7 shows a comparison of confidently dated houses and burials associated with House 1. Although the majority of both burials and architectural features could not be assigned with confidence to an occupational phase, the features that could be dated suggest that the cemetery was most likely in use throughout the long occupation of the area. The data further suggest that by the end of the occupation of the area defined as House 1, more people were being buried at the site than are represented by the architectural features.

This pattern of continued use of a cemetery area through the entire occupational history of a House is also repeated at both House 2 (figure 10.8) and House 3 (figure 10.9). In addition, the securely dated burials associated with House 2 and House 3 suggest an increase in the intensity of use during the Pioneer period. Although the high number of undated features clearly has a negative effect on our ability to evaluate this apparent pattern, these data suggest the continued importance of cemetery spaces through time as totemic representations of the House as a coherent social construct.

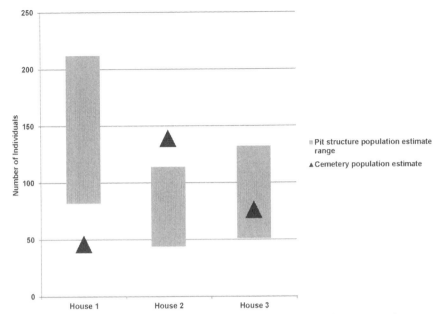

**FIGURE 10.6.** *Comparison of overall population and burial population for Houses at the Richter site.*

## THE PHYSICAL EXPRESSION OF THE EARLY HOHOKAM HOUSE

Our goal in this chapter was to present an exploration of the archaeological signatures of multiple, co-occurring social units that were expressed in the built environment of early Hohokam villages. It is often tempting, in such endeavors, to propose a set of attributes that are applicable to as many specific settings as possible. For example, find attributes *X*, *Y*, and *Z* in the archaeological record and the presence of the phenomenon being investigated is confirmed. Of course, the archaeological reality is rarely, if ever, that tidy. Our brief exploration of the applicability of the Lévi-Strauss–inspired House concept to the Hohokam as first suggested by Craig (2007, 2010) makes this abundantly clear. We close with a brief discussion of these challenges and how different ideas of how the House may have been expressed might provide important insights into the social and economic organization of Hohokam society.

We interpret three discrete clusters of features at the Richter site, and, specifically, their discrete cemetery areas, as totemic representations of individual, multihousehold social groups that we believe reflect many of the defining elements of Lévi-Strauss's (1982, 1987) Houses. We argue that membership in these groups did not require shared kinship, although kinship undoubtedly played a significant role in group membership. Our analysis further suggests that the

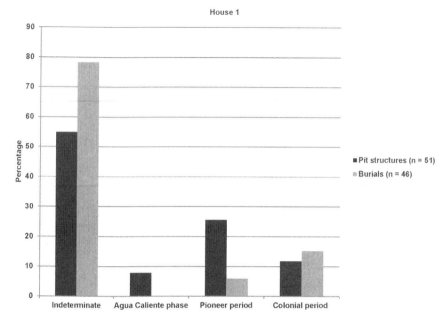

**FIGURE 10.7.** *Comparison of pit-structure and burial counts, House 1.*

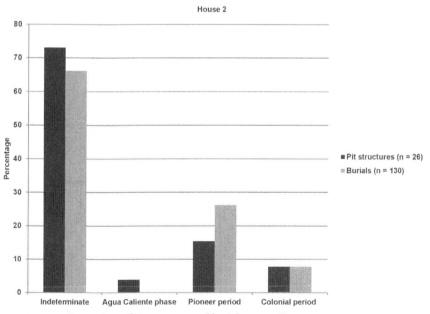

**FIGURE 10.8.** *Comparison of pit-structure and burial counts, House 2.*

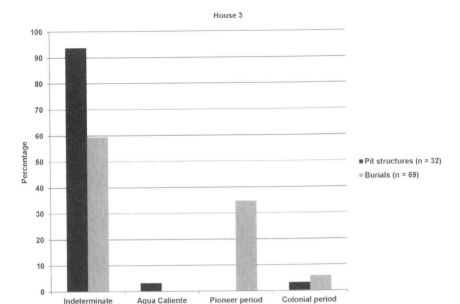

**FIGURE 10.9.** *Comparison of pit-structure and burial counts, House 3.*

archaeological expression of the individual Houses that we identified represented only a part of the total landscape that they controlled. We suspect, for example, that—in addition to agricultural and other resource-procurement areas that were used and possibly controlled by individual Houses—other residence localities existed as well. For the members of the Richter site Houses, for example, individual households may have established and maintained residences at other locations in the northern Tucson Basin, and returned periodically to the main House area for mortuary ceremonies or other activities that reinforced group membership.

In Craig's (2007, 2010) interpretation of the data from the Grewe site, an alternate physical expression of the House was proposed, one that reinterpreted the typical Hohokam courtyard group—that is, several individual habitation structures arranged to create an exterior courtyard space presumably for the corporate use of all the groups' residents—as representing the habitation loci of a House. These courtyard groups are generally accepted as representing continuity of the control of space and resources by a single domestic group over several generations. While Hohokam courtyard groups are often interpreted as comprising a single extended kin group, this may not necessarily have been the case. The possibility that courtyard groups included multiple kin groups pooling resources and labor would be accommodated by the House model.

It is tempting, therefore, to view our interpretation of the archaeological record of the Richter site and Craig's (2007, 2010) notions of the House at the

Grewe site under a single model that views the socioeconomic structure that we are referring to as a House functioning as the linchpin of social structure throughout Hohokam history. While perhaps an overly simplistic interpretation that stretches what can be confidently drawn from the available data, we believe that expressions of the House at both Richter and Grewe may suggest two important trends in Hohokam cultural history. First, the existence of a social unit such as the House that could have effectively encompassed multiple, unrelated kin groups may have had a long history among the Hohokam. Indeed, the House may have been a fundamental aspect of socioeconomic structure from the beginning of the Hohokam sequence. Second, the application of the House concept to explain multiple kinds of archaeological expressions (e.g., courtyard groups or discrete cemetery areas) may reflect a degree of diversity in how Hohokam society and the House itself was organized. As such, any approach seeking a "normative" set of social groups may limit our understanding of Hohokam socioeconomic life and how it may have changed through time.

## CONCLUSION

In closing, we would like to suggest some thoughts about the social function of the early Hohokam House as we describe it here and the possible contribution of Houses to the development of early village life in Hohokam society. First, the existence of an intermediate social unit such as a House between the household and the larger community does not appear to be a phenomenon unique to the Richter site. As Wallace (2003) has argued, similar social units may have existed at other very early Pioneer-period Hohokam village sites such as Valencia Vieja and Los Morteros in the Tucson Basin, and La Ciudad in the Phoenix Basin. These units, variously described as village segments or lineages, suggest that the nested social structure reflected in the spatial patterning of features at Richter had a long and extensive history among the Hohokam. Indeed, one could argue that this nested structure of social groups beyond the individual household existed at the very beginning of what we can refer to with any confidence as Hohokam.

We suggest that beginning in the Agua Caliente phase, and perhaps earlier, people in the southern deserts of Arizona began to experiment with social formations that crosscut kinship. Such social formations that extended beyond kinship, perhaps the Houses we see at Richter, may have been crucial in the development and persistence of communities and settled villages among the Hohokam, providing stability and continuity even if a single kin group comes to an end. The very early existence of sites with a clear structure—that of households arranged into Houses with physical monuments (cemeteries) that mark their claim to land and a role in communal social life—suggest that the Hohokam social order may have been a fundamentally communal one, even at its very earliest inceptions. Thus, the nested social arrangements of households and Houses in the

Lévi-Straussian sense may represent some of the earliest social negotiations and social experimentations that led to the making of community and the persistence of village life that we see throughout the course of Hohokam history.

## ACKNOWLEDGEMENTS

Work at the Richter site was sponsored by Red Point Development, Inc., and carried out by Tierra Right of Way, Ltd. Fieldwork was directed by Jeffrey Jones. We would like to thank Douglas Craig for graciously sharing his thoughts on House societies among the Hohokam. Many of the ideas we include here build on Doug's work at the Grewe site. We would also like to than Jacquelyn Dominguez for her last-minute assistance in improving the quality of the figures. Finally, we want to thank Karen Harry and Barbara Roth, first for the invitation to participate in the symposium, and second for the opportunity to contribute to this volume.

## REFERENCES

Ashmore, Wendy, and Pamela L. Geller. 2005. "Social Dimensions of Mortuary Space." In *Interacting with the Dead: Perspectives on Mortuary Archaeology for the New Millennium*, ed. Gordon F. M. Rakita, Jane E. Buikstra, Lane A. Beck, and Sloan R. Williams, 81–92. Gainesville: University Press of Florida.

Beck, Robin A. 2007. "The Durable House: Material, Metaphor, and Structure." In *The Durable House: House Society Models in Archaeology*, ed. Robin A. Beck Jr., 3–24. Occasional Papers No. 35. Carbondale: Center for Archaeological Investigations, Southern Illinois University.

Binford, Lewis R. 1971. "Mortuary Practices: Their Study and Potential." In *Approaches to the Social Dimensions of Mortuary Practices*, ed. James A. Brown, 6–29. Memoirs of the Society for American Archaeology No. 25. Washington, DC: Society for American Archaeology.

Blanton, Richard E. 1994. *Houses and Households: A Comparative Study*. New York: Plenum Press. https://doi.org/10.1007/978-1-4899-0990-9.

Bourdier, Jean-Paul, and Nezar Alsayyad, eds. 1989. *Dwellings, Settlements and Traditions: Cross Cultural Perspectives*. New York: University Press of America.

Brown, Barton M. 1987. "Population Estimation from Floor Area: A Restudy of Naroll's Constant." *Cross-Cultural Research* 21:1–49.

Chesson, Meredith S. 2001. "Embodied Memories of Place and People: Death and Society in an Early Urban Community." In *Social Memory, Identity, and Death: Anthropological, Perspectives on Mortuary Rituals*, ed. Meredith S. Chesson, 100–113. Archeological Papers of the American Anthropological Association No. 10. Arlington, VA: American Anthropological Association. https://doi.org/10.1525/ap3a.2001.10.1.100.

Ciolek-Torrello, Richard, Eric E. Klucas, and Stephanie M. Whittlesey. 2000. "Hohokam Households, Settlement Structure, and Economy in the Lower Verde Valley." In *The*

*Hohokam Village Revisited*, ed. David E. Doyel, Suzanne K. Fish, and Paul R. Fish, 65–100. Fort Collins, CO: Southwestern and Rocky Mountain Division of the American Association for the Advancement of Science.

Clark, Jeffery J. 2001. *Tracking Prehistoric Migrations: Pueblo Settlers among the Tonto Basin Hohokam*. Anthropological Papers of the University of Arizona No. 65. Tucson: University of Arizona Press.

Craig, Douglas B. 2007. "Courtyard Groups and the Emergence of House Estates in Early Hohokam Society." In *The Durable House: House Society Models in Archaeology*, ed. Robin A. Beck Jr., 446–463. Occasional Papers No. 35. Carbondale: Center for Archaeological Investigations, Southern Illinois University.

Craig, Douglas B. 2010. "Modeling Leadership Strategies in Hohokam Societies." *Journal of Arizona Archaeology* 1(1):71–88.

Dean, Jeffrey S. 1991. "Thoughts on Hohokam Chronology." In *Exploring the Hohokam: Prehistoric Desert Peoples of the American Southwest*, ed. George J. Gumerman, 61–49. Amerind New World Studies No. 1. Albuquerque: University of New Mexico Press.

Diehl, Michael W. 2010. "Charred Plant Macroremains from Flotation Samples from the Richter Site." In *The Cascada Archaeological Project: Changing Land Use and Settlement in the Northern Tucson Basin. Volume 3: Excavations at the Richter Site, AZ AA:12:252(ASM)*, ed. Jeffrey T. Jones and Eric E. Klucas, 387–401. Tierra Archaeological Research Series No. 2, Vol. 3. Tucson, AZ: Tierra Right of Way Services.

Donley-Reid, Linda W. 1990. "A Structuring Structure: The Swahili House." In *Domestic Architecture and the Use of Space*, ed. Susan Kent, 114–126. Cambridge, UK: Cambridge University Press.

Douglas, Mary 1972. "Symbolic Orders in the Use of Domestic Space." In *Man, Settlement, and Urbanism*, ed. Peter J. Ucko, Ruth Tringham, and G. W. Dimbleby, 513–521. Cambridge, MA: Schenkman Publishing Company.

Durkheim, Émile, and Marcel Mauss. 1902. "De Quelques Formes Primitives de Classification." *L'Année Sociologique* 6:1–72.

Ferguson, T. J. 1996. *Historic Zuni Architecture and Society: An Archaeological Application of Space Syntax*. Anthropological Papers of the University of Arizona No. 60. Tucson: University of Arizona Press.

Gillespie, Susan D. 2000a. "Beyond Kinship: An Introduction." In *Beyond Kinship: Social and Material Reproduction in House Societies*, ed. Rosemary A. Joyce and Susan D. Gillespie, 1–21. Philadelphia: University of Pennsylvania Press.

Gillespie, Susan D. 2000b. "Maya 'Nested Houses': The Ritual Construction of Place." In *Beyond Kinship: Social and Material Reproduction in House Societies*, ed. Rosemary A. Joyce and Susan D. Gillespie, 135–160. Philadelphia: University of Pennsylvania Press.

Goldstein, Lynne G. 1980. *Mississippian Mortuary Practices: A Case Study of Two Cemeteries in the Lower Illinois Valley*. Evanston, IL: Northwestern University Archaeological Program.

Gregory, David A. 1991. "Form and Variation in Hohokam Settlement Patterns." In *Chaco and Hohokam: Prehistoric Regional Systems in the American Southwest*, ed. Patricia L. Crown and W. James Judge, 159–193. Santa Fe, NM: School of American Research Press.

Hastorf, Christine A. 2003. "Community with the Ancestors: Ceremonies and Social Memory in the Middle Formative at Chiripa, Bolivia." *Journal of Anthropological Archaeology* 22:305–322. https://doi.org/10.1016/S0278-4165(03)00029-1.

Haury, Emil W. 1976. *The Hohokam: Desert Farmers and Craftsmen*. Tucson: University of Arizona Press.

Hegmon, Michelle. 1989. "Social Integration and Architecture." In *The Architecture of Social Integration in Prehistoric Pueblos*, ed. William D. Lipe and Michelle Hegmon, 15–34. Occasional Papers No. 1. Cortez, CO: Crow Canyon Archaeological Center.

Hillier, Bill, and Julienne Hanson. 1984. *The Social Logic of Space*. Cambridge, UK: Cambridge University Press. https://doi.org/10.1017/CBO9780511597237.

Horne, Lee. 1994. *Village Spaces: Settlement and Society in Northeastern Iran*. Washington, DC: Smithsonian Institution Press.

Howard, Jerry B. 2000. "Quantitative Approaches to Spatial Patterning in the Hohokam Village: Testing the Village Segment Model." In *The Hohokam Village Revisited*, ed. David E. Doyel, Suzanne K. Fish, and Paul R. Fish, 167–195. Fort Collins, CO: Southwestern and Rocky Mountain Division of the American Association for the Advancement of Science.

Huntington, Frederick W. 1986. *Archaeological Investigations at the West Branch Site: Early and Middle Rincon Occupation in the Southern Tucson Basin*. Institute for American Research Anthropological Paper 5. Tucson: Institute for American Research.

Jones, Jeffrey T. 2010a. "Field Methods." In *The Cascada Archaeological Project: Changing Land Use and Settlement in the Northern Tucson Basin*. Volume 3: *Excavations at the Richter Site, AZ AA:12:252(ASM)*, ed. Jeffrey T. Jones and Eric E. Klucas, 11–15. Tierra Archaeological Research Series No. 2, Vol. 3. Tucson, AZ: Tierra Right of Way Services.

Jones, Jeffrey T. 2010b. "Excavations at the Richter Site." In *The Cascada Archaeological Project: Changing Land Use and Settlement in the Northern Tucson Basin*. Volume 3: *Excavations at the Richter Site, AZ AA:12:252(ASM)*, ed. Jeffrey T. Jones and Eric E. Klucas, 403–409. Tierra Archaeological Research Series No. 2, Vol. 3. Tucson, AZ: Tierra Right of Way Services.

Jones, Jeffrey T., and Eric E. Klucas, eds. 2010. *The Cascada Archaeological Project: Changing Land Use and Settlement in the Northern Tucson Basin*. Volume 3: *Excavations at the Richter Site, AZ AA 12:252(ASM)*. Tierra Archaeological Research Series No. 2, Vol. 3. Tucson, AZ: Tierra Right of Way Services.

Joyce, Rosemary A. 2007. "Building Houses: The Materialization of Lasting Identity in Formative Mesoamerica." In *The Durable House: House Society Models in Archaeology*, ed. Robin A. Beck Jr., 53–72. Occasional Papers No. 35. Carbondale: Center for Archaeological Investigations, Southern Illinois University.

Klimas, Tom, and CaraMia Williams. 2010. "Feature Descriptions." In *The Cascada Archaeological Project: Changing Land Use and Settlement in the Northern Tucson Basin.* Volume 3: *Excavations at the Richter Site, AZ AA:12:252(ASM)*, ed. Jeffrey T. Jones and Eric Eugene Klucas, 17–200. Tierra Archaeological Research Series No. 2, Vol. 3. Tucson, AZ: Tierra Right of Way Services.

Klucas, Eric Eugene. 1996. *The Village Larder: Village Level Production and Exchange in an Early State.* PhD dissertation, Department of Anthropology, University of Arizona, Tucson. Ann Arbor: University Microfilms.

Klucas, Eric Eugene. 2009. "Settlement Structure and Domestic Organization in the Sycamore Creek Area." In *From the Desert to the Mountains. Archaeology of the Transition Zone. The State Route 87—Sycamore Creek Project.* Volume 3: *Conclusions and Syntheses*, ed. Richard Ciolek-Torrello, Eric Eugene Klucas, and Rein Vanderpot, 169–200. Technical Series 73. Tucson, AZ: Statistical Research.

Klucas, Eric Eugene, Richard Ciolek-Torrello, and Charles R. Riggs. 1998. "Site Structure and Domestic Organization." In *Overview, Synthesis, and Conclusions*, ed. Stephanie M. Whittlesey, Richard Ciolek-Torrrello, and Jeffrey H. Altschul, 491–530. Vanishing River: Landscapes and Lives of the Lower Verde Valley: The Lower Verde Archaeological Project. Tucson, AZ: SRI Press.

Klucas, Eric Eugene, and Glenn M. Schwartz. 2015. "Spatial and Social Organization of Level 3." In *Rural Archaeology in Early Urban Northern Mesopotamia: Excavations at Tell al-Raqa'i*, ed. Glenn M. Schwartz, 177–191. Monumenta Archaeologica 36. Los Angeles, CA: Cotsen Institute of Archaeology Press.

Kuijt, Ian. 2001. "Place, Death, and the Transmission of Social Memory in Early Agricultural Communities of the Near Eastern Pottery Neolithic." In *Social Memory, Identity, and Death: Anthropological Perspectives on Mortuary Rituals*, ed. Meredith S. Chesson, 80–99. Archeological Papers of the American Anthropological Association No. 10. Arlington, VA: American Anthropological Association. https://doi.org/10.1525/ap3a.2001.10.1.80.

Laslett, Peter. 1972. "Introduction: The History of the Family." In *Household and Family in Past Time*, ed. Peter Laslett with the assistance of Richard Wall, 1–89. Cambridge: Cambridge University Press. https://doi.org/10.1017/CBO9780511561207.003.

Lea, Vanessa. 1995. "The Houses of the Mebengokre (Kayapó) of Central Brazil—A New Door to Their Social Organization." In *About the House: Lévi-Strauss and Beyond*, ed. Janet Carsten and Stephen Hugh-Jones, 206–225. Cambridge, UK: Cambridge University Press. https://doi.org/10.1017/CBO9780511607653.010.

Lévi-Strauss, Claude. 1982. *The Way of the Masks.* Trans. Sylvia Modelski. Seattle: University of Washington Press.

Lévi-Strauss, Claude. 1987. *Anthropology and Myth: Lectures 1951–1982.* Trans. R. Willis. Oxford, UK: Basil Blackwell.

Marshall, Yvonne. 2000. "Transformation of Nuu-chah-nuth Houses." In *Beyond Kinship: Social and Material Reproduction in House Societies,* ed. Rosemary A. Joyce and Susan D. Gillespie, 72–102. Philadelphia: University of Pennsylvania Press.

McKinnon, Susan. 2000. "The Tanimbarese *Tavu*: The Ideology of Growth and the Material Configurations of Houses and Hierarchy in an Indonesian Society." In *Beyond Kinship: Social and Material Reproduction in House Societies,* ed. Rosemary A. Joyce and Susan D. Gillespie, 161–176. Philadelphia: University of Pennsylvania Press.

Potter, James M., and Elizabeth M. Perry. 2011. "Mortuary Features and Identity Construction in an Early Village Community in the American Southwest." *American Antiquity* 76(3):529–546. https://doi.org/10.7183/0002-7316.76.3.529.

Rapoport, Amos. 1990. *The Meaning of the Built Environment: A Nonverbal Communication Approach.* Tucson: University of Arizona Press.

Rice, Glen E. 2016. *Sending the Spirits Home: The Archaeology of Hohokam Mortuary Practice.* Salt Lake City: University of Utah Press.

Rivière, Peter. 1995. "Houses, Places, and People: Community and Continuity in Guiana." In *About the House: Lévi-Strauss and Beyond,* ed. Janet Carsten and Stephen Hugh-Jones, 189–202. Cambridge, UK: Cambridge University Press. https://doi.org/10.1017/CBO9780511607653.009.

Saxe, Arthur A. 1971. "Social Dimensions of Mortuary Practices in a Mesolithic Population in Wadi Halfa, Sudan." In *Approaches to the Social Dimensions of Mortuary Practices,* ed. by James A. Brown, 39–57. Memoirs of the Society for American Archaeology No. 25. Washington, DC: Society for American Archaeology.

Schwartz, Glenn M., and Eric E. Klucas. 1998. "Spatial Analysis and Social Structure at Tell al-Raqa'i." In *Espace Naturel, Espace Habité en Syrie du Nord,* ed. Michel Fortin and Olivier Aurenche, 199–207. Bulletin 33. Quebec: Canadian Society for Mesopotamian Studies.

Sires, Earl W., Jr. 1987. "Hohokam Architectural Variability and Site Structure during the Sedentary-Classic Transition." In *The Hohokam Village: Site Structure and Organization,* ed. David E. Doyel, 171–182. Glenwood Springs, CO: Southwestern and Rocky Mountain Division of the American Association for the Advancement of Science.

Stambaugh, John E. 1988. *The Ancient Roman City.* Baltimore, MD: Johns Hopkins University Press.

Thurtle, Mary Charlotte, and Jennifer Levstik. 2004. *Preliminary Results of Archeological Data Recovery at AZ AA:12:252(ASM), AZ AA:12:256(ASM), and AZ AA:12:486(ASM) within the Right-of-Way of the Outfall Sewer Line for the Oasis Hills Residential Development, Marana, Pima County, AZ.* Archaeological Report No. 2004-94. Tucson, AZ: Tierra Right of Way Services.

Thurtle, Mary Charlotte, and Barbara M. Montgomery, eds. 2007. *Archaeological Investigation of AZ AA:12:252 (ASM), AZ AA:12:256 (ASM), and AZ AA:12:486 (ASM) for the Oasis Hills Outfall Sewer, Marana, Pima County, Arizona.* Archaeological Report No. 2006–143. Tucson, AZ: Tierra Right of Way Services.

Wallace, Henry D. 2003. "The Development and Structure of an Ancient Desert Village." In *Roots of Sedentism: Archaeological Investigations at Valencia Vieja, a Founding Village in the Tucson Basin of Southern Arizona,* ed. Henry D. Wallace, 323–369. Anthropological Papers No. 29. Tucson, AZ: Center for Desert Archaeology.

Waterson, Roxana. 1995. "Houses and Hierarchies in Island Southeast Asia." In *About the House: Lévi-Strauss and Beyond,* ed. Janet Carsten and Stephen Hugh-Jones, 47–68. Cambridge, UK: Cambridge University Press. https://doi.org/10.1017/CBO9780511607653.002.

Waterson, Roxana. 2000. "House, Place, and Memory in Tana, Toraja (Indonesia)." In *Beyond Kinship: Social and Material Reproduction in House Societies,* ed. Rosemary A. Joyce and Susan D. Gillespie, 177–188. Philadelphia: University of Pennsylvania Press.

Whittlesey, Stephanie M. 2013. "Architecture, Site Structure, and Domestic Organization." In *Archaeological Investigations at the Julian Wash Site (AZ BB:13:17 ASM), Pima County, Arizona.* Volume 2: *Analyses and Interpretation of Prehistoric Remains,* ed. William M. Graves and Eric Eugene Klucas, 12.1–12.34. Technical Report 13–38. Tucson, AZ: Statistical Research.

Whittlesey, Stephanie M., and William L. Deaver. 2004. "Domestic Organization." In *Pots, Potters, and Models: Archaeological Investigations at the SRI Locus of the West Branch Site, Tucson, Arizona.* Volume 2: *Synthesis and Interpretations,* ed. Stephanie M. Whittlesey, 231–270. Technical Series 80. Tucson: Statistical Research.

Wilcox, David R., Thomas R. McGuire, and Charles Sternberg. 1981. *Snaketown Revisited: A Partial Cultural Resource Survey, Analysis of Site Structure, and an Ethnohistoric Study of the Proposed Hohokam-Pima National Monument.* Archaeological Series No. 155. Tucson: Arizona State Museum, University of Arizona.

Wilcox, David R., and Charles Sternberg. 1983. *Hohokam Ballcourts and Their Interpretation.* Arizona State Museum Archaeological Series 160. Tucson: Arizona State Museum, University of Arizona.

Wilk, Richard R. 1990. "The Built Environment and Consumer Decisions." In *Domestic Architecture and the Use of Space,* ed. Susan Kent, 34–42. Cambridge, UK: Cambridge University Press.

# 11

# Household Ritual and Communal Ritual

*Kivas and the Making of Community in the Southern Chuska Valley*

JOHN G. DOUGLASS, WILLIAM M. GRAVES, DAVID T. UNRUH,
PHILLIP O. LECKMAN, AND RICHARD CIOLEK-TORELLO

Much attention has been given in recent years to the social creation of communities and the founding of early villages in the northern American Southwest (e.g., Hegmon 2002; Isbell 2000; Kohler and Varien 2012; Kolb and Snead 1997; Varien and Potter 2008a; Wilshusen, Ortman, and Phillips 2012). This section of the volume, dedicated to social units, is an ideal venue in which to explore ideas of how communities were constructed in the early Pueblo periods and what relations may have existed among the constituent groups or "units" of early villages or communities. In this chapter, we focus on how relationships among and between households were formed through ritual performance to create community, as evidenced through architecture.

The concept of "social units" in the prehispanic American Southwest has been an important part of the region's scholarship since the very beginning of archaeological and ethnographic research in the mid-1800s. In the American Southwest, across time and space, it is the household that seems to have consistently been a fundamental unit of social interaction and cooperation. Here, we follow a number of classic and current works (such as Douglass and Gonlin

DOI: 10.5876/9781607327356.c011

2012; Netting and colleagues 1984; and Wilk and Rathje 1982) in defining house-holds as "the most common social component of subsistence, the smallest and most abundant activity group," which is composed of social, material, and behavioral elements (Wilk and Rathje 1982:618). This focus on, and definition of, households is a bit different than some of the other chapters in this section focused on social groups. For example, here we differentiate households from families, which is the focus of Roth's work (chapter 7, this volume) in this section of the volume. Along with everyday subsistence and production activities, households also undertook ritual performance on a regular basis. Anasazi ritual performance, which fluoresced during the Pueblo periods, has its roots in Basketmaker-period pit structures. The topic of our chapter explores some possible relationships among households and how households may have come together to create larger social units—communities—through ritual performance. We focus on excavated household sites in the southern Chuska Valley, in western New Mexico, north of Gallup. Our purpose is not to define the architectural units and all the associated activities that may define households, but, rather, to discuss households more generally in terms of their roles in the performance and function of ritual and in the social construction of community (sensu Varien and Potter 2008b). For detailed information on household units in the project area, see Ciolek-Torello et al. (2014).

Data used in this study were collected as part of data recovery excavations on the Navajo Nation conducted by Statistical Research, Inc. (SRI) at over 20 sites along US 491 (figure 11.1) under contract with the New Mexico Department of Transportation. Although sites in the project area date from the Middle Archaic through the Pueblo IV periods, the households we focus on in this chapter all date between Basketmaker III (ca. AD 500–725) and Pueblo III (ca. AD 1125/1140–1300). This is an ideal time period for examining the rise of communities and the associated architecture among Anasazi groups in the American Southwest, and the data collected from this project are robust. We examine data from 20 excavated pit structures and kivas, including one great kiva, from seven different sites that date within this time span. We focus on the temporal and spatial variability we see in specific architectural aspects of household kivas and pit structures as well as their sizes and overall shapes. By studying the variability among these ritual architectural features, which offers a window into ritual behavior in varied locations and intensities, we can better understand the development and creation of community at different social and historical scales. As has been pointed out recently by Stone (2016:61; see also Stone's chapter 8 in this volume), architecture is "the fundamental physicality of human agency embedded in structures"; that is, how people construct domestic and ritual structures is directly related to both the function and varied interpretations and expressions of social meaning of that space.

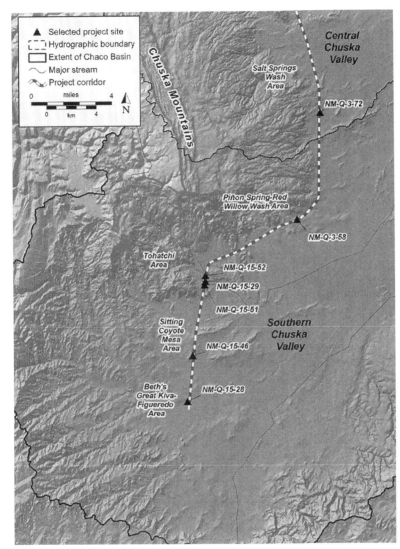

**FIGURE 11.1.** *Map showing the location of the project area, along US 491, north of Gallup, New Mexico, on Navajo Nation. (Map courtesy of Statistical Research, Inc.)*

## HOUSEHOLD RITUAL AND THE CONSTRUCTION OF COMMUNITIES

Ritual performance in any society, including the Anasazi, is important in a variety of ways. First and foremost, among sedentary groups, ritual is a way of creating community among diverse individuals, households, and larger social groups. Ritual brings people together and helps share, formulate, change, reflect, and solidify their identities and the relationships that existed among them. Within any community, there will be tensions and conflicts related to such things as age, gender, perceptions, and other mundane and everyday situations. Ritual may aid in overcoming these conflicts and tensions through ritualized communication that draws people together to larger foci. As Hull (2011:36) argues for southern California, ritual performances "primarily served as vehicles to reinforce community cohesion, identity, and memory, particularly given the absence of strong central authority in . . . these small-scale societies" (see also Hull et al. 2013 for specific examples). Ritualized communication (expressed through architecture, material goods, or performance) can, at times, be more effective in transferring information than other forms of communication and is a resource that helps convey information related to the "daily recreation of identities" (Lucy 2005:103; see also Stone 2013:178). Ritual can express different kinds of information, including both individual belief and identity (indexical information), as well as more consistent and "immutable" information that is independent of the specific performance (canonical information) (see Rappaport 1979:179–180; Van Keuren 2011:191). At the same time, as pointed out by Gilman and Stone (2013), it is important to note that ritual is also a way of presenting one's view of the world and as a result, there may be conflict among participants; ritual behavior may lead to cooperation, but it may also lead to competition.

At both the household level and the suprahousehold or community level, ritual can connect members to one another in ways that may be difficult otherwise. Part of this connection may relate to variable access to specific ritual information or performance. That is, some household members may have access to ritual knowledge not uniformly shared and thus may draw members together (e.g., Bernardini 2011) due to the desire of some members to have access to that ritual insight. Among suprahousehold groups, ritual may be a way of allying diverse members together through time, much like what Isbell (2000; following Anderson 1987) has referred to as *imagined communities*. Imagined suprahousehold communities may have resided apart from one another in the southern Chuska Valley but have come together to interact through ritual performance (see Yaeger and Canuto 2000) for more discussion on this point).

It is certainly accurate to point out, as have Varien and Potter (2008b:3), that the imagined community is hard to pinpoint outside of a conceptual way; Anderson (1987) originally felt that shared identity was the important point, whether community members met face-to-face or not (see Harris 2014:79). That said, following Isbell (2000:248), Varien and Potter (2008b:4) argue that the "imagined community can be understood only through an analysis of the social action and interaction that constitutes community life." Therefore, here, we examine the role that ritual performance, which constitutes an important part of social action and interaction among societies, may have played in the creation of community life in Basketmaker III through Pueblo III settlements in the southern

Chuska Valley, and how ritual performance in these communities may have created a sense of belonging among participating households (e.g., Bell 1997:160). Through analyzing this ritual behavior through time, one is able to gain insight into the size and possible membership of the imagined community.

We argue that, in the southern Chuska Valley, households came to create the constituent parts of communities through ritual practice and performance. From the Archaic period forward, households in the project area used pit structures as a basic building form for performing various and diverse tasks, including the performance or enactment of ritual. By the Basketmaker III period, we begin to see more formal elements of household ritual in pit structures (sipapus, as one example; this is discussed in detail below), although generally these pit structures were still multifunctional. Through time, these pit structures transformed from multiuse to more formal, ritually focused structures with increasingly specific architecture related to ritual performance, likely the result of increasing levels of suprahousehold ritual. By the end of Basketmaker III/early Pueblo I, differential access to ritual knowledge and the ability to perform rituals critical to the continuation of social life, expressed through differences in formal architectural features likely related to ritual, may have led to the creation of relations of autonomy and dependence among households, depending on the degree of access to knowledge of religious rituals. Ritual performance, therefore, from a very early time, was an integral part of Anasazi life, as is likely the case for most cultural groups (Stone 2013; see Triadan 2006 for similar examples among prehistoric Pueblo groups).

Rituals created in pit structures and kivas (both household-related kivas and great kivas) allowed members to participate not in something external and separate from everyday life, but, rather, activities that were "deeply embedded within a wide array of social practices" (Van Keuren and Glowacki 2011:5). These activities allowed for sharing knowledge not only among individual household members and between households, but also were mitigated (and expanded) by their surrounding social setting, experiences, and traditions (Van Keuren and Glowacki 2011:6). As Gilman and Stone (2013:610; see also Stone 2013) have pointed out, "ritual is so important in this process [of creating and maintaining relationships between households] because of both its communicative power and its ability to imbue space with meaning, thus transforming it from mere locale to socially important space with history and memory within emergent communities. The reason for ritual's power in imparting these messages is the packed nature of its performance and symbolism." During early Pueblo periods, kivas functioned as separate sacred space for household and suprahousehold rituals, likely similar in nature to previous household rituals performed in multipurpose, domestic pit structures. At times, of course, kivas were used for domestic activities, but their primary and formal purpose was ritual performance and use. Outside of domestic use, ritual performance in kivas had a transformational power to create sacred space within these multifunctional structures. Pit structures and kivas were not only part of the built environment, they were also parts of a socially constructed ritual landscape.

## HOUSEHOLD RITUAL IN THE SOUTHERN CHUSKA VALLEY

Early on in the settlement history of the southern Chuska Valley, pit structures were fundamental and ubiquitous and served as locations for domestic and ritual activities. As discussed in detail below, through time, pit structures, which were in part foci of ritual activities, became more formalized as household kivas. Household kivas likely served individual or small groups of households (suprahousehold), which did not necessarily coreside (see the discussion above of the imagined community) for ceremony, ritual performance, and other community-building activities, as well as perhaps some domestic use. In the southern Chuska Valley, at one end of the spectrum during the late Basketmaker and Pueblo periods were household kivas (what Wilshusen 1989 has called *corporate kivas*), while at the other end were great kivas (what Wilshusen 1989 has called *community kivas*). Great kivas are different in size, elements, and function than household kivas and served larger communities of at least 20+ households (not necessarily coresiding). While there were architectural elements shared between household-level and great kivas, as we discuss below, the massive size of great kivas in part offers evidence of their function in serving much larger numbers of people. Great kivas have been referred to by some as administrative or ceremonial centers (e.g., Lekson et al. 1988; Lightfoot 1984; Wilshusen 1989), although we believe the settlements, rather than the kivas, were the centers. Below, we discuss the data we have identified related to household pit structures, household kivas, great kivas, and the variability within them through time. While there are many elements that may be a part of household kivas, some of the central ones may include sipapus, altar emplacements, prayer-stick groupings, benches, ventilators, pilasters, and hearths (see Wilshusen 1989).

### Basketmaker III (ca. AD 500–725)

Basketmaker III pit structures are the most numerous and some of the most variable in terms of internal and external architectural details in our sample (see table 11.1; figure 11.2). SRI excavated a total of nine pit structures dating to Basketmaker III within the project area. In addition, SRI excavated a great kiva at site NM-Q-15–28, which was in use from the late Basketmaker III period through the Pueblo I period. Similarities and differences in the external characteristics of these Basketmaker III–period pit structures (table 11.2) suggest that a variety of expression or messaging concerning ritual, household origin, social connectivity, and social identity may have been taking place among households. During

**TABLE 11.1.** Overview of settlement clusters, sites, and structures discussed in this study.

| Settlement Cluster | Site | Basketmaker III Pit Structures | Basketmaker III/Pueblo I Great Kiva | Pueblo I Pit Structures | Pueblo II Kivas | Pueblo II/Pueblo III Kiva | Pueblo III Kivas |
|---|---|---|---|---|---|---|---|
| Salt Springs Wash | NM-Q-3–72 | 2 | | | | | I |
| Piñon Spring-Red Willow Wash | NM-Q-15–58 | 2 | | | | | |
| Tohatchi | NM-Q-15–52 | I | | | | | |
| | NM-Q-15–29 | 3 | | 3 | | | 2 |
| | NM-Q-15–51 | I | | | | | |
| Sitting Coyote Mesa/ Beth's Great Kiva-Figueredo | NM-Q-15–46 | | I | I | 2 | I | |
| | NM-Q-15–28 | | | | | | |
| | Total | 9 | I | 4 | 2 | I | 3 |

Basketmaker III, the domestic and ritual activities of a household were concentrated in pit structures, although small surface storage rooms were associated with some of the bigger pit structures. Thus, as we discuss later in this chapter, variability among these structures can tell us something about the expression of household social identity and political or economic standing as well as ritual or ceremonial performance in emergent communities. Such signaling and messaging through the medium of architecture would have been taking place within the social context of what appears to be the beginnings of community formation in the project area.

With the exception of the Basketmaker III/Pueblo I–period great kiva in the Sitting Coyote Mesa/Beth's Great Kiva–Figueredo cluster in the southern portion of the project area (see figure 11.1, table 11.1), none of the Basketmaker III pit structures had ramped entryways (see table 11.2). In addition, all structures for which orientation could be observed were oriented to the southeast. Such characteristics—similarities in orientation and the general configuration of structures—may indicate the widespread acceptance of basic tenets concerning household form and the placement of dwellings in both local and more esoteric or symbolic landscapes. Similarly, the presence of a ramp in the Basketmaker III/Pueblo I great kiva at Site NM-Q-15–28 would have set this structure apart

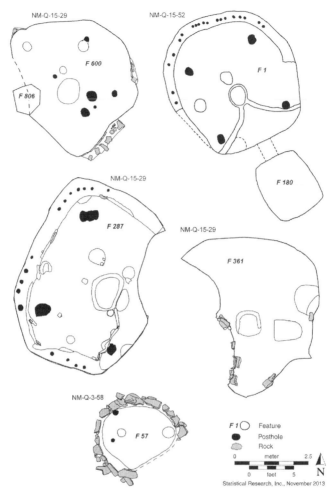

**FIGURE 11.2.** *Plan view drawings of the variability of Basketmaker III–period structures. (From Ciolek-Torello et al. 2014:figure 190; Courtesy of Statistical Research, Inc.)*

in terms of its general form, whereas its orientation to the southeast would have identified it as similar symbolically, or perhaps metaphorically, to household dwellings.

Rather marked differences in both the shape and size of Basketmaker III structures (see table 11.2; figure 11.2) suggest that the households residing in these structures may have used the architecture of the house as a means to express variability in social identity or origin within the context of emerging Basketmaker III communities. These differences in structure shape and size may relate to

**TABLE 11.2.** External and internal characteristics of Basketmaker III pit structures ($n = 10$) (includes great kiva)

| External Characteristics | |
|---|---|
| Similarities | Differences |
| Orientation (to the SE) | Shape |
| | • Subrectangular (n = 3) |
| | • Ovate (n = 3) |
| | Circular (n = 4) (n = 5, with the BMIII/PI great kiva]) |
| No ramp (except for the BMIII/PI great kiva) | Size |
| | • 5 m² to 53 m² (104 m² with the BMIII/PI great kiva) |
| | • Subrectangular average = 40 m² |
| | • Ovate average = 14 m² |
| | • Circular average = 10 m² (without the BMIII/PI great kiva) |

| Internal Characteristics | |
|---|---|
| Similarities | Differences |
| No ventilators | Antechamber |
| | (only in the 2 largest subrectangular structures and the largest circular structure) |
| No subfloor vaults (except for 2 in the BMIII/PI great kiva) | Ash pits |
| | (occur in the 3 subrectangular structures, the largest circular structure, and in the BMIII/PI great kiva) |
| Hearths in 9 of 10 structures | Benches |
| | (occur in the 3 subrectangular structures, 2 of the circular structures, and in the BMIII/PI great kiva) |
| Spatial divisions | (upright slabs in the 3 subrectangular structures and ridges in the largest circular structures) |
| Sipapus | (only one simple sipapu in the largest subrectangular structure and 1 complex sipapu in the BMIII/PI great kiva) |

differences in ritual use of these structures, as well, although interior features are likely more relevant. Besides the great kiva at Site NM-Q-15-28, there were three subrectangular pit structures, three ovate pit structures, and four circular pit structures spread across different settlement clusters (see table 11.2). There does not appear to be a correlation between pit structure shape and settlement cluster, suggesting that emergent communities in the project area may have consisted of migrants from different areas or of groups who varied in origin, either real or imagined (see Potter and Yoder 2008 for a similar discussion in the Ridges Basin area). The great variability in pit-structure size (with a range of 5 m² to 53 m², excluding the great kiva; see table 11.2) indicates variability in household size and structure that could reflect differences among the social units that constituted these early communities.

If we examine the internal characteristics of Basketmaker III structures, we also see differentiation that may reflect variability in household ritual performance (see table 11.2). Here we interpret the presence and absence of certain internal architectural characteristics—including antechambers, ash pits, benches, spatial divisions, and sipapus (see Wilshusen 1989 for additional thoughts on architectural elements of household kivas)—as related to ritual performance. For example, internal walls and ridges in some pit structures represent the partition of domestic space into functionally discrete areas. Some of these areas may have been devoted to ritual activity. Although Gilman and Stone (2013:609) were focused on great kivas in this instance, we believe that, like great kivas, variability in internal features of pit structures may be indications of differentiation in ritual concepts being conveyed by different households. Such variability may reflect both the religious ideals and practices of individual households as well as similarity and heterogeneity in the kinds of religious rituals performed by different household groups.

Internal architectural details clearly differentiate the Basketmaker III/Pueblo I great kiva at Site NM-Q-15-28 from the other excavated Basketmaker III pit-structure dwellings in our sample. The great kiva there contained a complex sipapu and two floor vaults, the only such occurrence of these features in this time period (figure 11.3). The presence of these three internal features suggests that ritual performances requiring such features were restricted to this structure and did not take place within the contemporary pit-structure dwellings excavated at other sites. Wilshusen (1989:102–104) argues that subfloor vaults in the Dolores area were restricted to *community*, as opposed to *corporate* (what we call *household*), kivas. Thus, the size of the great kiva and the presence of a ramped entry, subfloor vaults, and a complex sipapu set it apart from contemporary Basketmaker III pit structures and it appears that the rituals performed within this architectural space differed substantially from those that took place within households.

If we conceive of the use of the great kiva as a reflection of communal ceremony or ritual performance that was shared, then variability in the internal features of pit-structure dwellings may reflect heterogeneity in the performance of ritual that took place in more socially restrictive, household contexts. Internal household pit structure features associated with ritual activities appear to occur only, or more frequently, in subrectangular structures and are absent, or occur less frequently, in the circular or ovate dwellings (see table 11.2). Household size was also a factor, but not entirely. The two largest households contained a great variety of ritual-related features, but these features were also found in

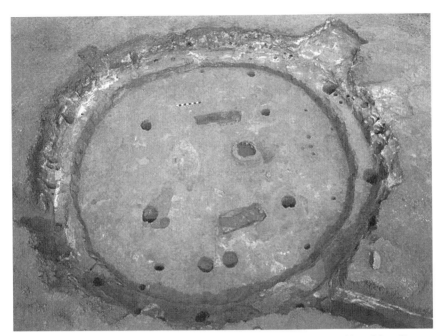

**FIGURE 11.3.** *Plan view photograph of the great kiva at Site NM-Q-15–28. (From Murrell 2014: figure 34; courtesy of Statistical Research, Inc.)*

three smaller households. This variability suggests that households in these early Basketmaker III communities did not all participate equally in the performance of rituals, with the largest households and those residing in subrectangular structures having perhaps a more complete set of rituals they were able to perform than smaller households residing in circular or ovate dwellings. Such variability suggests that at least some households (those associated with subrectangular structures) were more autonomous in terms of their ability to perform religious rituals than groups living in circular or ovate structures. Conversely, those households in circular or ovate structures may have been dependent both on the ritual or ceremonial abilities of families residing in the subrectangular structures. It is interesting to note that circular and ovate shapes of structures generally are associated with groups and people that are more mobile. Were those in circular- or ovate-shaped structures either more recent arrivals to the area or focused on somewhat different subsistence or mobility patterns (Patricia Gilman, personal communication 2016)? We don't know.

### Pueblo I (ca. AD 725–900/920)

Only four Pueblo I pit structures were encountered in the project area (see table 11.1). Aside from the small pit structure associated with the Basketmaker III/

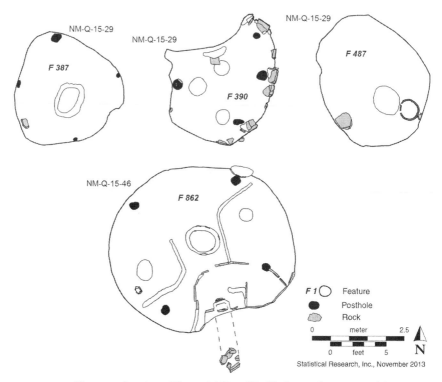

**FIGURE 11.4.** *Plan view drawings of the variability of Pueblo I–period structures. (From Ciolek-Torello et al. 2014: figure 192; courtesy of Statistical Research, Inc.)*

Pueblo I great kiva at Site NM-Q-15–28, three pit structures were encountered at Site NM-Q-15–29 in the Tohatchi cluster and one at Site NM-Q-15–46 in the Sitting Coyote Mesa/Beth's Great Kiva–Figueredo cluster (figure 11.4, see table 11.1). The Pueblo I pit-structure sample is thus smaller than the sample of pit structures dating to the Basketmaker III period from the project area. Despite this small sample size, we suspect that the Basketmaker III/Pueblo I great kiva at Site NM-Q-15–28 and the four other Pueblo I pit-structure habitations reflect some variability in terms of internal architectural features, and thus, in the performance of rituals at the household level, perhaps at a lesser level than what we saw among the Basketmaker III structures.

With the exception of the great kiva, none of the four Pueblo I pit structures had ramped entryways (table 11.3; see figure 11.4). In addition, all structures for which orientation could be observed were oriented to the southeast (see table 11.3). As with the Basketmaker III sample, we suspect that these characteristics—similarities in orientation and the general configuration of structures—indicate the continuing acceptance of basic tenets concerning house form and the

**TABLE 11.3.** External and internal characteristics of Pueblo I pit structures ($n = 5$) (includes great kiva)

| External Characteristics | |
|---|---|
| *Similarities* | *Differences* |
| Orientation (to the SE) | Shape |
| | • Ovate (n = 2) |
| | • Circular (n = 2) (n = 3, with the BMIII/PI great kiva) |
| No ramp (except for the BMIII/PI great kiva) | Size |
| | • 7 m 2 to 18 m² (104 m² with the BMIII/PI great kiva) |
| | • Ovate average = 10 m² |
| | • Circular average = 12 m² (without the BMIII/PI great kiva) |

| Internal Characteristics | |
|---|---|
| *Similarities* | *Differences* |
| No antechambers | Ventilator |
| | (1 present in the largest circular structure) |
| Hearth | Ash pit |
| | (present in 1 ovate structure and the BMIII/PI great kiva) |
| No subfloor vaults | |
| | Spatial divisions |
| (except for 2 in the BM III/P I great kiva) | (upright slabs and ridges only in the largest circular structure) |
| No bench | |
| (except for the BM III/P I great kiva) | |
| No sipapu | |
| (except for the BM III/P I great kiva) | |

placement of households within communities and within a broader cosmological landscape. The presence of a ramp at the great kiva would have continued to set this structure apart from dwellings in terms of its general form (in addition, of course, to things like its massive size), and its southeasterly orientation and subterranean placement continued to make a metaphorical reference to the household.

The external characteristics of the four Pueblo I pit-structure dwellings appear to have only differed in shape; two of the structures are ovate in plan while two were circular (see table 11.3). Despite these differences in shape, they are on average much smaller in size and exhibit much less diversity in size than Basketmaker III pit structures, averaging 11.2 m². During the Pueblo I period, aboveground rooms were constructed and were part of the architectural suite of features that constituted households. Several Pueblo I surface rooms served a habitation function, indicating that these Pueblo I households were also perhaps more complexly organized than their Basketmaker III predecessors and consisted of multiple discrete dwelling units (cf. Lightfoot 1984; Varien and Lightfoot 1989).

How such variability in the external characteristics of dwellings (see table 11.3) expressed social identity or origin in Pueblo I communities of the project area is less clear than it was during the Basketmaker III period. There is not a clear correlation between pit-structure shape and settlement cluster, and perhaps Pueblo I communities in the project area continued to be settled by migrants from different areas or by groups who continued expressing their varied origins and/or ethnicity through time. There is also less diversity in household size, as no large Pueblo I households were identified and none had extensive storage areas. Thus, homogeneity in household size does not suggest the political or economic differences exhibited by Basketmaker III households. However, Pueblo I structures at Site NM-Q-15-52 and Site NM-Q-3-2, were all small surface rooms lacking interior features, suggesting the presence of a distinct type of site, possibly representing seasonal or temporary residence or perhaps storage.

The absence of the complex of ritual features among Pueblo I structures that are found in some Basketmaker III pit structures and later kivas suggests a possible decrease in the frequency of rituals performed within a household context and may represent a lesser degree of social and ritual differentiation among households during this period. The lack of antechambers, benches, sipapus, and subfloor vaults in the Pueblo I pit structures indicates that ritual activities were no longer performed at the household level. A ventilator and internal spatial dividers only appear in the largest circular pit structure (Feature 862 at Site NM-Q-15-46) and the only ash pit among the pit structures occurs in the ovate structure (Feature 487) at Site NM-Q-15-29, although a deflector was present in the surface habitation room associated with Feature 862 at Site NM-Q-15-46. It is possible that religious ritual and ceremony may have become more communal in its performance during Pueblo I and was conducted primarily in communal structures such as the Site NM-Q-15-28 great kiva.

As was the case among the Basketmaker III pit structures, the great kiva at Site NM-Q-15-28 differs significantly from Pueblo I pit-structure dwellings. Pueblo I subfloor vaults, benches, and sipapus were only found within the great kiva. The presence of this ritual complex of features in the great kiva and their absence in Pueblo I dwellings indicate that ritual performances requiring such features were likely restricted to communal structures and did not take place within the individual households.

In sum, then, during Pueblo I there appears to be less external and internal variability among dwellings compared to the Basketmaker III sample. This may reflect an increasing homogeneity, and decreasing frequency, in the performance of household ritual. It is possible that Pueblo I households became increasingly dependent on the community itself for the successful performance of religious ritual and subsequently lost autonomy to an increasingly communal social order that characterized social landscapes at both local and extralocal social scales.

## Pueblo II (ca. AD 900/920–1125/1140)

By the Pueblo II period, we see the virtual disappearance of habitation pit structures and of multipurpose pit structures that served as both dwellings and the loci of household religious ritual. After the Pueblo I period, all but one of the subterranean pit structures are masonry-walled kivas. Although kivas appear to have replaced pit structures in households, their more formal construction and use of unique architectural and interior features suggests they played a much more important role in the performance of religious rituals and ceremonies. Our small sample of three Pueblo II kivas (including a Pueblo II/III kiva) are all examples of relatively small, non-communal kivas that served as the ceremonial architectural spaces (and also, as discussed before, possible domestic space) of three discrete households at Site NM-Q-15-46 in the Sitting Coyote Mesa/Beth's Great Kiva–Figueredo cluster (see table 11.1; figure 11.5). One of these kivas, Feature 190, has a date range that spans the boundary between the Pueblo II and the Pueblo III periods. Undoubtedly, many more Pueblo II households and household kivas as well as communal great kiva and great house structures are located in Pueblo II sites surrounding in the project area.

All three Pueblo II kivas at Site NM-Q-15-46 would have been quite similar in their outward appearance (table 11.4; see figure 11.5). All three were circular with no ramps, were oriented to the southeast, and were quite small. The internal characteristics of these three kivas were also quite similar (table 11.4). Antechambers, as pits, and internal spatial dividers were not present in any structures, but all three had a ventilator, a hearth, and a sipapu. The largest kiva, Feature 190, also had a subfloor vault and a bench, whereas Feature 557 also contained a bench.

The general lack of variability in external and internal characteristics or details of these three kivas suggests that there may have been a general homogeneity among households in terms of the kinds of rituals performed in household kivas as well as the frequency and social scale of such performances. Such apparent homogeneity may indicate a lack of variability among households in terms of ritual performance capabilities and a lack of ritual or ceremonial inequality that we suggest characterized the BM III and Pueblo I periods. Despite our lack of Pueblo II communal ritual architecture such as a great kiva or a Great House, we know that such structures did exist and were used by the Pueblo II communities in and around the project area.

**TABLE 11.4.** External and internal characteristics of Pueblo II kivas ($n = 3$)

| External Characteristics | |
| --- | --- |
| Similarities | Differences |
| Circular | Size |
| | • 5 m² to 15 m² |
| | • Average = 11 m² |
| Orientation (to the SE) | |
| No ramp | |

| Internal Characteristics | |
| --- | --- |
| Similarities | Differences |
| No antechamber | Subfloor vault in the largest structure |
| | (the PII/PIII kiva) |
| Ventilator | |
| | Bench in the largest 2 structures |
| | (including the PI/PII kiva) |
| Hearth | |
| Sipapu | |
| No ash pit | |
| No spatial divisions | |

The presence of household kivas suggests that Pueblo II households once again performed their own rituals and the formal and specialized nature of kivas indicates that such performance became increasingly important at this time. But Pueblo II households were much different than Basketmaker III households. For example, Household 2 at site NM-Q-15–46 was similar in size to the extremely large Basketmaker III household at Site NM-Q-3–72. The Pueblo II household, however, occupied 13 structures comprising a kiva, a small pit structure, an isolated adobe-walled surface structure, and a masonry-walled roomblock with three habitation rooms and seven storage rooms. The three habitation rooms occur in a row, fronting the kiva with three storage rooms aligned behind them in a pattern typical of the Prudden Unit–type pueblo (Prudden 1918). At least one doorway connects the central habitation room to the storage room behind, indicating that the habitation and storage rooms defined three pairs of discrete dwelling units. It is clear that Pueblo II households expand on the pattern of complex households comprising multiple dwelling units established in Pueblo I.

The existence of Pueblo II communal ritual architecture indicates that the dependence of Pueblo I households on the communal performance of religious ritual continued into the Pueblo II period as well and that some loss or absence

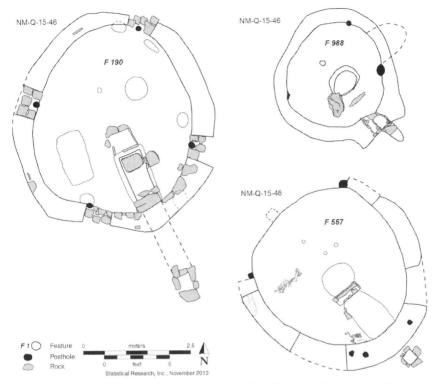

**FIGURE 11.5.** *Plan view drawings of the variability of Pueblo II–period structures. (From Ciolek-Torello et al. 2014: figure 194; courtesy of Statistical Research, Inc.)*

of household autonomy in terms of ceremonial performance also persisted. We see what was apparently a continuation or a strengthening of what was essentially a communal social order that came to structure social landscapes at both local and extralocal scales and determined the course of action or agency available to the inhabitants of the project area.

### Pueblo III (ca. AD 1125/1140–1300)

Pueblo III kivas from the project area illustrate that fundamental changes occurred in the expression of social identity among households, communalism, and the structure of ritual performance during the post-Chacoan era in the southern Chuska Valley. Including the Pueblo II / Pueblo III Feature 190 kiva from Site NM-Q-15–46, four Pueblo III kivas were excavated in the project area (see table 11.1). These include two kivas (Features 58 and 91) from Site NM-Q–15–29 in the Tohatchi cluster and Feature 87 kiva from Site NM-Q-3–72 in the Salt Springs Wash cluster (figure 11.6). All four kivas are relatively small in size and each is associated with large complex households comprising multiple dwelling units.

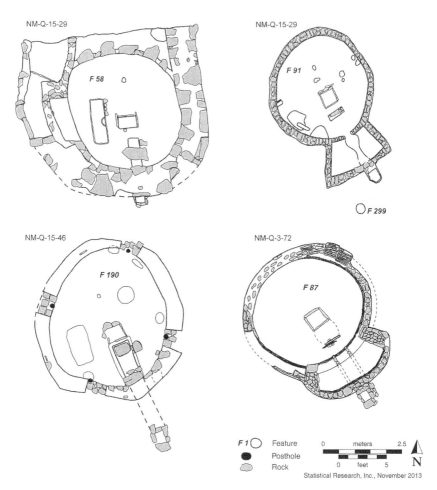

**FIGURE 11.6.** *Plan view drawings of the variability of Pueblo III–period structures. (From Ciolek-Torello et al. 2014:figure 195; courtesy of Statistical Research, Inc.)*

Despite the small sample, both the internal and external characteristics of these kivas suggest greater heterogeneity in the expression of social identity and a possible increase in the variability of household ritual performance when compared to earlier Pueblo I and Pueblo II pit structures and kivas.

In terms of external architectural characteristics, the similarity in orientation (to the southeast) and the lack of ramped entryways convey that aspects of house configuration, the placement of dwellings on the landscape, and the relationships among households remain constant from earlier time periods (table 11.5). Despite these similarities, clear differences in the shapes of Pueblo III kivas exist among the project-area sample that were likely visually distinct

**TABLE 11.5.** External and internal characteristics of Pueblo III kivas ($n = 4$)

| External Characteristics | |
|---|---|
| Similarities | Differences |
| Orientation (to the SE) | Shape |
| | • Circular (n = 2, including the PII/PIII kiva) |
| | • Keyhole (n = 2) |
| | Size |
| No ramps | • Circular ($14 m^2$ and $15 m^2$, including the PII/PIII kiva) |
| | • Keyhole (both $11 m^2$) |

| Internal Characteristics | |
|---|---|
| Similarities | Differences |
| No antechamber | Subfloor vaults in the 2 circular structures |
| | (including the PII/PIII kiva) |
| Ventilator | Ash pit in 1 keyhole structure |
| Hearth | Bench in 3 of 4 structures |
| No spatial divisions | Sipapu in 3 of 4 structures |

when these structures were observed from the outside (see table 11.5; figure 11.6). The two circular kivas (Feature 190 at Site NM-Q-15–46 and Feature 58 at Site NM-Q-15–29) were the largest of the Pueblo III kivas, measuring 15 m² and 14 m² in area, respectively. Two keyhole-shaped kivas were also excavated—Feature 91 at Site NM-Q-15–29 and Feature 87 at Site NM-Q-3–72. These keyhole-shaped kivas were each approximately 11 m² in area.

This variability in Pueblo III kiva shape appears to mark a change in the outward expression of household kiva architecture from what was observed in the Pueblo I or Pueblo II samples and may indicate a change in social meaning and/or logic of expressions or messaging concerning ritual, household origin, social connectivity, and social identity among the households. The two keyhole-shaped kivas suggest that some households may have been expressing social identities that referenced the Mesa Verde/northern San Juan area either directly or historically. At the same time, these expressions of social identity may be local variations, as these keyhole kivas do not contain all aspects of the classic Mesa Verde style. Some of these same sites with keyhole kivas contain ceramics that are generally Mesa Verde style, but petrographic analysis has revealed that they were locally produced (Ownby 2014; Trowbridge 2014). Thus, keyhole kivas may indicate a reimagining or reformulating of household social identities within the context of the collapse of Chaco and the reconfiguration of Pueblo III communities that is evident throughout the San Juan Basin and the adjacent Cibola region (e.g., Kintigh 1994; Schachner 2008). The circular design of the other two kivas, alternatively, is a continuation of a general shape dating back to at least Basketmaker III and is associated with more local traditions.

The internal architectural elements of the Pueblo III kivas in our sample also indicate a level of similarity in kiva function as well as some variability in the kinds of rituals performed in different households (table 11.5). The lack of antechambers and internal spatial dividers as well as the presence of ventilators and hearths all indicate a continuation of shared ideas concerning the layout and functioning of household kivas. At the same time, the presence/absence of certain internal elements—specifically, subfloor vaults, ash pits, benches, and sipapus—indicates probable variability in ritual performance among different households (see table 11.5).

The presence of subfloor vaults in the two circular kivas is interesting in part because these are unique items not recovered in any other household kivas in the sample, but were found in the great kiva, dating to Basketmaker III/Pueblo I. Wilshusen (1989:102–104) has argued that these specific features—also called foot drums or roofed sipapus—in the Dolores area are hallmarks of community structures. These two circular kivas are also approximately 50 percent larger in floor area than the two keyhole kivas. Even if these two circular structures were not communal, but rather simply household-level kivas, the presence of subfloor vaults indicates a specific type of ritual performance, and perhaps a different scale or intensity of ritual use, than other household kivas in the sample, across time and space.

This simultaneous homogeneity and heterogeneity in both the external and internal architectural elements of Pueblo III household kivas may indicate the increasing diversity of household kiva ritual after the collapse of the Chaco Phenomenon as well as an increase in inequality among households in terms of ritual or ceremonial performance capabilities. Although we have no examples of Pueblo III communal ritual architecture in our project area, there are several Pueblo III great kivas located nearby. Thus, communal ritual would appear to retain an important role in the social production and reconfiguration of Pueblo III communities despite what we see as a shift in the variability and importance of household ritual performance during this period.

Overall then, this picture of variability in the ritual-performance capabilities of households and the simultaneous importance of communal ritual is similar to the patterning we see in the Basketmaker III period in the project area. Given the regional social context of the collapse of Chaco at the end of Pueblo II and the beginning of the Pueblo III period, this may not be surprising. Perhaps both periods were a time of the creation of new communities as households came to be bounded together within new sets of social relations. In the case of the Basketmaker III period, perhaps this took place in the context of migrant families settling locales along the southern Chuska Valley from other areas of the

San Juan Basin. During the Pueblo III period, new communities may have been established or old communities may have been reimagined or restructured as the fall of Chaco created social, ceremonial, and political vacuums throughout the San Juan Basin (sensu Kintigh 1994). Such a transformative regional context may have provided the means by which households could vie for autonomy and political dominance or prestige within their local communities since pre-Chacoan times, as shown through time in the data presented in this chapter.

## DISCUSSION AND CONCLUSIONS

In the introduction to this chapter, we stated we would focus on possible relationships among households and how they may have come together to create larger social units—communities—through ritual performance. To do so, we have studied internal and external architectural variation in pit structures and kivas (both household kivas and great kivas) through time to understand some of the ritual homogeneity and heterogeneity that may be related to these structures. Below, we discuss our findings and think about larger implications.

It is clear that there is a great deal of variation in pit structures and kivas within the project area. Certainly, some of this may be due to specific differences between time periods, as particular elements in kivas went into or out of use (see Wilshusen 1989 for a discussion of these trends for the Dolores and Mesa Verde areas). However, while there may be more variation within more fine-grained time allotments than we discuss here, our data suggest that there are similarities and differences both within and between time periods. As Stone (chapter 8, this volume) discusses, these variations in architecture through time represent transformations in the perceptions and expressions of meaning of that space.

During late Basketmaker III and early Pueblo periods, as kivas developed out of earlier pit-structure forms and became widely spread, they were in many ways metaphors for households. Household ritual early on was likely an individualized affair, but as households continued to form and be a part of larger communities, more formalized ritual structures—kivas—were created. The formation of great kivas during the late Basketmaker III and Pueblo I periods reflects the beginnings of the adoption of a communal ethos and the beginning of the creation of distinct Anasazi village communities. During this process, we see that ritual performance and ritual knowledge were transformed and took on greater communal aspects as well. The existence of great kivas tells us that in addition to relations of autonomy and dependence among households, all households were also somehow dependent on the communal social order itself for the performance of key rituals to ensure the completeness of ritual practice of the group. Hence, these social processes related to ritual activities in kivas helped create community.

The external and internal architectural variation we see through time in household kivas within our southern Chuska Valley project area is likely in part the result of varying access to, or different interpretations of, ritual knowledge among and between households. While there were shared ritual identities and understandings of ritual among these households, as seen in similarities in orientation and general overall design of household kivas, the great variation suggests that certain households had greater access to, or different interpretation of, specific ritual knowledge expressed through architectural features and overall design. Individual households likely performed ritual together in suprahousehold events as a way to create "completeness" of ritual knowledge and access.

Potter and Yoder (2008:39) have argued that the variability in pit structures in the Ridges Basin area of southern Colorado was the result of the different expressions of the negotiations of social identity among households. We believe a similar process is occurring in the southern Chuska Valley through the varied expressions of household kiva architecture. It is important to note that Stone's (2013) study of Kayenta kivas suggests that there was little differentiation in size in that area, which may reflect a different ritual organization system than in the southern Chuska Valley.

Architectural evidence from our project area, such as the size of pit structures and kivas, suggest ritual was performed at both the household and community level. Although we don't know exactly what types of performances were created and maintained at each level, they certainly differed in type and scale, based on differential use of architectural features and size of kivas. Wilshusen (1989:102–105) has argued, for example, that the presence of floor vaults in the Dolores area may be indicative of more community-oriented kivas, based on their overall appearance in great kivas and other larger kivas. In our study area, both the great kiva and several household kivas contain these features. For the most part, household kivas likely served to integrate the multiple dwelling units and further-flung, non-coresiding households that comprised the complex households of the Pueblo I to Pueblo III periods (see Ciolek-Torello et al. 2014 for details). The commonality of certain features of household kivas suggest a standardization and formalization of household rituals that was not present in earlier pit structures. Differences in household kiva architecture likely are indications of the variability in access to, and interpretation of, household ritual and connections to the larger imagined communities.

Great kivas, alternatively, were much larger in size and contained some distinct features that convey the idea that they encompassed more specialized activities related to community (rather than more intimate household-level) performance of ritual. The construction of great kivas illustrates that as villages became larger, there was a need for group participation in religious performance. The discovery of the Basketmaker III/Pueblo I great kiva at Site NM-Q–15–28 shows that the need for communal participation occurred much earlier in time than previously suggested. It is possible that great kivas were designed, in part, to create cohesion among and between the larger communities in which they were built. As Allison (2008:45) points out, group solidarity is strengthened by collective activities such as ritual feasting and dancing. Without these collective, integrative activities, he points out, "these social groups are little more than abstractions" (ibid).

Certainly, as Lightfoot (2008) has argued, the labor invested in great kivas was substantial and necessitated a concerted community effort. Household kivas, alternatively, were substantially smaller household-level efforts to construct, even if simple volumetrics are applied. In the Mimbres region, Gilman and Stone (2013:611) have argued that uniformity and homogeneity in great kivas indicates they functioned as a necessity for "social integration of people in dispersed imagined communities, for sharing information and alliance formation at a regional level, and for the creation and negotiation of far flung relationships over rights of access to material and nonmaterial resources, including land tenure, water rights, preferential access to wild resources and raw materials, and status." At the same time, there was also variability in the form of great kivas among three areas of the Mogollon region, indicating that there was variability in ritual interpretation and that there was not a single template (Gilman and Stone 2013:620). Herr (2001:93) in her study of great kivas in the southwestern frontier of the Mogollon Rim, also documented a wide variability in architectural variability both in great kivas and the extensive associated household communities. This variability, Herr argues, may be related to weak central authority. While great kivas in the Mogollon Rim area functioned in part for social integration, through offering a location to perform ritual associated, in part, with regional ideologies and identities, the variability also argues for diversity in the identities and ideologies of the participants.

Rural households—those located away from the larger villages with great kivas—were likely part of the imagined community associated with these great kivas. As has been pointed out by a number of scholars (e.g., Lightfoot 2008; Gilman and Stone 2013), great kivas were generally much larger than what was needed for the village associated with them. Gilman and Stone (2013) have argued that during ritual performance in great kivas, community members from beyond the physical village (what Isbell 2000 has referred to as the imagined community)—including rural households—participated in these rituals and therefore were part of this community. While these larger community members did not coreside with others at villages like Site NM-Q-15–28, they nonetheless were likely frequently copresent (see Gilman and Stone 2013:609; Yaeger and Canuto 2000:6).

In sum, then, overall we see great shifts through time in the variability of household ritual capabilities. Early on, in the emerging communities of Basketmaker III, we see relations of autonomy and dependence characterizing interhousehold relations. Here, we see variability and likely inequality characterize the ritual-performance capabilities of different households. Such autonomy and dependence must have structured somehow the creation of these early communities by those migrating into the southern Chuska Valley from other areas of the San Juan Basin. At the same time, we see the early rise and prominence of communal ritual through the great kiva at Site NM-Q-15-28. During the Pueblo I and Pueblo II periods, the reduction in variability among households in ritual performance and the increasing frequency of communal ritual features in the area suggest a strengthening of communalism and a subsuming of ritual control, from individual households to the community level. Finally, during the Pueblo III period, with the fall of Chaco, we see a possible reconfiguring of communalism, and the structure of communities as an increase in variability in the ritual-performance capabilities of households suggests a return to relations of autonomy and dependence and possibly interhousehold inequalities. The transformative regional context of the post-Chacoan Pueblo III world may have provided the means by which households could vie for autonomy and political dominance or prestige within their local community for the first time since pre-Chacoan times. Much like the variability in great kivas in the Mimbres area studied by Gilman and Stone (2013), some of the differentiation in household kiva architecture seen in the southern Chuska Valley project area may represent experimentation of, differential access to, or differences in the interpretation of, ritual performance related to this decline in larger social networks.

*Acknowledgments.* We would like to thank the Navajo Nation and New Mexico Department of Transportation (NMDOT) for providing this opportunity for SRI to work along the southern Chuska Slope. We also extend our deepest gratitude for the hospitality we experienced from the Naschitti and Tohatchi chapters during our fieldwork efforts. Funding for this project was provided by the Federal Highway Administration and NMDOT. We would like to thank NMDOT Environmental Section Manager Blake Roxlau and NMDOT Environmental Scientist Sharon Brown as well as Navajo Nation Tribal Historic Preservation Officer Ronald Maldonado and the Navajo Nation Historic Preservation Department for all of their support. The fieldwork could not have been accomplished without the efforts of SRI Principal Investigator Bradley Vierra, Project Manager Robert Heckman, Project Director Monica Murrell, Lab Manager Rebecca Kiracofe, and Administrative Research Assistant Lisa Atkinson who accommodated all of our logistical and administrative needs. We would like to extend thanks to former SRI employee Assistant Project Director Meaghan Trowbridge as well as our subcontractor David Greenwald from DMG Four Corners Research, Inc., for providing invaluable support in the field. We also thank all of the US 491 project field staff for their tireless efforts and dedication.

Scott Van Keuren, Patricia Gilman, Kathleen Hull, and several anonymous reviewers were all extremely helpful during the writing and subsequent editing of this chapter, as they shared ideas, feedback, and/or publications with us. Of course, any errors in this chapter are the authors' responsibility and not our colleagues', who tried to get our thinking straight. We also thank Barbara Roth and Karen Harry for inviting us to participate in the Southwest Symposium session and this subsequent edited volume and for offering substantive and constructive feedback on an earlier version of this chapter. A variation of this chapter can be found in a portion of Ciolek-Torello et al. (2014).

## REFERENCES

Allison, James R. 2008. "Exchanging Identities: Early Pueblo I Red Ware Exchange and Identity North of the San Juan River." In *The Social Construction of Communities: Agency, Structure, and Identity in the Prehispanic Southwest*, ed. Mark D. Varien and James M. Potter, 41–68. Lanham, MD: Alta Mira Press.

Anderson, Benedict. 1987. *Imagined Communities: Reflections on the Origins and Spread of Nationalism*. London: Verso.

Bell, Catherine. 1997. *Ritual: Perspectives and Dimensions*. New York: Oxford University Press.

Bernardini, Wes. 2011. "North, South, and Center: An Outline of Hopi Ethnogenesis." In *Religious Transformation in the Late Pre-Hispanic Pueblo World*, ed. Donna M. Glowacki and Scott Van Keuren, 196–220. Tucson: University of Arizona Press.

Ciolek-Torello, Richard, John G. Douglass, William M. Graves, David T. Unruh, and Phillip O. Leckman. 2014. "Households on the Tohatchi Flats, Southern Chuska Valley." In *Bridging the Basin: Land Use and Social History in the Southern Chuska Valley*, Volume 4: *Synthesis*, ed. Monica L. Murrell and Bradley J. Vierra, 399–482. Prepared for New Mexico Department of Transportation, Santa Fe, New Mexico. SRI Technical Report 14–20. Albuquerque: Statistical Research.

Douglass, John G., and Nancy Gonlin. 2012. "The Household as Analytical Unit: Case Studies from the Americas." In *Ancient Households of the Americas: Conceptualizing What Households Do*, ed. John G. Douglass and Nancy Gonlin, 1–44. Boulder: University Press of Colorado.

Gilman, Patricia A., and Tammy Stone. 2013. "The Role of Ritual Variability in Social Negotiations of Early Communities: Great Kiva Homogeneity and Heterogeneity in the Mogollon Region of the North American Southwest." *American Antiquity* 78(4):607–623. https://doi.org/10.7183/0002-7316.78.4.607.

Harris, Oliver J. T. 2014. "(Re)assembling Communities." *Journal of Archaeological Method and Theory* 21(1):76–97. https://doi.org/10.1007/s10816-012-9138-3.

Hegmon, Michelle. 2002. "Concepts of Community in Archaeological Research." In *Seeking the Center Place: Archaeology and Ancient Communities in the Mesa Verde Region,* ed. Mark D. Varien and Richard H. Wilshusen, 263–279. Salt Lake City: University of Utah Press.

Herr, Sarah. 2001. *Beyond Chaco: Great Kiva Communities on the Mogollon Rim Frontier.* Anthropological Papers of the University of Arizona Number 66. Tucson: University of Arizona Press.

Hull, Kathleen L. 2011. "Archaeological Expectations for Communal Mourning in Coastal Southern California." *Journal of California and Great Basin Anthropology* 31:23–36.

Hull, Kathleen L., John G. Douglass, and Andrew L. York. 2013. "Recognizing Ritual Action and Intent in Communal Mourning Features on the Southern California Coast." *American Antiquity* 78(1):24–47. https://doi.org/10.7183/0002-7316.78.1.24.

Isbell, William H. 2000. "What We Should Be Studying: The 'Imagined Community' and the 'Natural Community.'" In *The Archaeology of Communities: A New World Perspective*, ed. Marcello A. Canuto and Jason Yaeger, 243–266. London: Routledge.

Kintigh, Keith W. 1994. "Chaco, Communal Architecture, and Cibolan Aggregation." In *The Ancient Southwestern Community: Models and Methods for the Study of Prehistoric Social Organization*, ed. W. H. Wills and Robert D. Leonard, 131–140. Albuquerque: University of New Mexico Press.

Kohler, Timothy A., and Mark D. Varien, eds. 2012. *Emergence and Collapse of Early Villages: Models of Central Mesa Verde Archaeology.* Berkeley: University of California Press. https://doi.org/10.1525/california/9780520270145.001.0001.

Kolb, Michael J., and James E. Snead. 1997. "It's a Small World after All: Comparative Analysis of Community Organization in Archaeology." *American Antiquity* 62(4):609–628. https://doi.org/10.2307/281881.

Lekson, Steven, T. C. Windes, J. R. Stein, and W. J. Judge. 1988. "The Chaco Canyon Community." *Scientific American* 259(1):100–109. https://doi.org/10.1038/scientificamerican0788-100.

Lightfoot, Kent G. 1984. *Prehistoric Political Dynamics.* DeKalb: Northern Illinois University Press.

Lightfoot, Ricky. 2008. "Roofing an Early Anasazi Great Kiva: Analysis of an Architectural Model." *Kiva* 74(2):227–246. https://doi.org/10.1179/kiv.2008.74.2.009.

Lucy, Sam. 2005. "Ethnic and Cultural Identities." In *The Archaeology of Identity: Approaches to Gender, Age, Status, Ethnicity and Religion*, ed. Margarita Diaz-Andreu, Sam Lucy, Stasa Babic, and David N. Edwards, 86–109. New York: Routledge.

Murrell, Monica L. 2014. "Basketmaker IIII and Pueblo I Period Overview." In *Bridging the Basin: Land Use and Social History in the Southern Chuska Valley, Volume 4: Synthesis*, ed. Monica L. Murrell and Bradley J. Vierra, 23–92. SRI Technical Report 14-20. Albuquerque, NM: Statistical Research.

Netting, Robert McC., Richard Wilk, and Eric J. Arnould. 1984. *Households: Comparative and Historical Studies of the Domestic Group.* Berkeley: University of California Press.

Ownby, Mary F. 2014. "Petrographic Analysis of Gray, White, Brown, and Red Wares from the Chuska Slope, New Mexico." Petrographic Report No. 2013–03. In *Bridging the Basin: Land Use and Social History in the Southern Chuska Valley,* Volume 3: *Analysis,* ed. Monica L. Murrell and Bradley J. Vierra, Appendix E: Petrographic Analysis. Technical Report 14–08. Tucson, AZ: Desert Archaeology; Albuquerque, NM: Statistical Research.

Potter, James M., and Thomas D. Yoder. 2008. "Space, Houses, and Bodies: Identity Construction and Destruction in an Early Pueblo Community." In *The Social Construction of Communities: Agency, Structure, and Identity in the Prehispanic Southwest,* ed. Mark D. Varien and James M. Potter, 21–39. Lanham, MD: Alta Mira Press.

Prudden, T. Michael. 1918. *A Further Study of Prehistoric Small House Ruins in the San Juan Watershed.* Memoirs of the American Anthropological Association, Vol. 5, No. 1. Arlington, VA: American Anthropological Association.

Rappaport, Roy A. 1979. *Ecology, Meaning, and Religion.* Berkeley, CA: North Atlantic Books.

Schachner, Gregson. 2008. "Imagining Communities in the Cibola Past." In *The Social Construction of Communities: Agency, Structure, and Identity in the Prehispanic Southwest,* ed. Mark D. Varien and James M. Potter, 171–190. Lanham, MD: Alta Mira Press.

Stone, Tammy. 2013. "Kayenta Ritual Structures from A.D. 1100–1300." *Kiva* 78(2):177–205. https://doi.org/10.1179/kiv.2013.78.2.004.

Stone, Tammy. 2016. "Organizational Variability in Early Aggregated Communities in Middle-Range Societies: An Example from the Kayenta Region of the American Southwest." *American Antiquity* 81(1):58–73. https://doi.org/10.7183/0002-7316.81.1.58.

Triadan, Daniela. 2006. "Dancing Gods: Ritual, Performance, and Political Organization in the Prehistoric Southwest." In *Archaeology of Performance: Theaters of Power, Community, and Politics,* ed. Takeshi Inomata and Lawrence S. Coben, 159–186. Lanham, MD: Alta Mira Press.

Trowbridge, Meaghan. 2014. "Ceramic Analysis." In *Bridging the Basin: Land Use and Social History in the Southern Chuska Valley,* Volume 3: *Analysis,* ed. Monica L. Murrell and Bradley J. Vierra, 259–342. Technical Report 14–08. Albuquerque, NM: Statistical Research.

Van Keuren, Scott. 2011. "The Materiality of Religious Belief in East-Central Arizona." In *Religious Transformation in the Late Pre-Hispanic Pueblo World,* ed. Donna M. Glowacki and Scott Van Keuren, 175–95. Tucson: University of Arizona Press.

Van Keuren, Scott, and Donna M. Glowacki. 2011. "Studying Ancestral Pueblo Religion." In *Religious Transformation in the Late Pre-Hispanic Pueblo World,* ed. Donna M. Glowacki and Scott Van Keuren, 1–22. Tucson: University of Arizona Press.

Varien, Mark D., and Ricky Lightfoot. 1989. "Ritual and Nonritual Activities in Mesa Verde Region Pit Structures." In *The Architecture of Social Integration in Prehistoric Pueblos,* ed. W.D. Lipe and Michelle Hegmon, 73–88. Cortez, CO: Crow Canyon Archaeological Center.

Varien, Mark D., and James M. Potter. 2008a. *The Social Construction of Communities: Agency, Structure, and Identity in the Prehispanic Southwest.* Lanham, MD: Alta Mira Press.

Varien, Mark D., and James M. Potter. 2008b. "The Social Production of Communities: Structure, Agency, and Identity." In *The Social Construction of Communities: Agency, Structure, and Identity in the Prehispanic Southwest,* ed. Mark D. Varien and James M. Potter, 1–20. Lanham, MD: Alta Mira Press.

Wilk, Richard R., and William J. Rathje. 1982. "Household Archaeology." *American Behavioral Scientist* 25(6):617–639. https://doi.org/10.1177/000276482025006003.

Wilshusen, Richard H. 1989. "Unstuffing the Estufa: Ritual Floor Features in Anasazi Pit Structures and Pueblo Kivas." In *The Architecture of Social Integration in Prehistoric Pueblos,* ed. William D. Lipe and Michelle Hegmon, 89–112. Cortez, CO: Crow Canyon Archaeological Center.

Wilshusen, Richard H., Scott G. Ortman, and Ann Phillips. 2012. "Processions, Leaders, and Gathering Places: Changes in Early Community Organization as Seen in Architecture, Rock Art, and Language." In *Crucible of Pueblos: The Early Pueblo Period in the Northern Southwest,* ed. Richard H. Wilshusen, Gregson Schachner, Jim R. Allison, 198–218. Los Angeles: Cotsen Institute of Archaeology Press, University of California.

Yaeger, Jason, and Marcello A. Canuto. 2000. "Introducing an Archaeology of Communities." In *The Archaeology of Communities: A New World Perspective,* ed. Marcello A. Canuto and Jason Yaeger, 1–15. London: Routledge.

# 12

# The Social Dimensions of Prehistoric Agavaceae Baking Pits

*Feasting and Leadership in the Late Pithouse and*
*Pueblo Periods of South-Central New Mexico*

MYLES R. MILLER

Plant-baking pits and the accumulations of burned rock created during their use have long been thought of as rather mundane and inconsequential features that, in turn, embodied rather mundane and inconsequential aspects of prehistoric subsistence economies. Regrettably, this perspective has obscured and minimized the significant role such features played in political economies, community organization, and social production of prehistoric societies of the American Southwest and northwestern Mexico. Beyond their use for simple food production, plant-baking pits were a crucial component for producing fermented beverages and bulk quantities of food for commensal feasts and to establish and maintain reciprocal social relationships across communities and territories.

Moreover, in emphasizing the role of earth ovens for food production, a century-long history of research on plant baking and fermentation is often overlooked. As early as 1939, Frank M. Setzler, curator of anthropology for the US National Museum of the Smithsonian Institution, contemplated the relationship between plant-baking facilities, fermentation, and social complexity in the northern Chihuahuan Desert. Noting the presence of communities of sotol

DOI: 10.5876/9781607327356.c012

plants (*Dasylirion wheeleri*) growing around Goode Cave, a rockshelter with burned-rock middens in the lower Pecos River region of Trans-Pecos Texas, Setzler suggested that "because of numerous sotol plants in the region, the cave may have served as a ceremonial center where large quantities of sotol stalks were roasted and the liquid, extracted from these roasted plants, permitted to ferment in order to supply a mildly alcoholic beverage" (Setzler 1939:78).

This and other early archaeological impressions were undoubtedly influenced by contemporary ethnographic accounts of the first half of the twentieth century. Bruman (1940), Lumholtz (1902), and Bennett and Zingg (1935) documented practices of alcohol production throughout the Chihuahuan Desert of northern Mexico, often involving baking pits and other forms of earth ovens, sometimes mislabeled as "distilleries." Ethnographers and ethnobotanists working in southern New Mexico and Arizona described the use of earth-oven baking pits for ritual and ceremonies, often involving fermented beverages from agave, yucca, and sotol (Bell and Castetter 1941; Castetter and Opler 1936; Castetter et al. 1938; Crist 1940; Hrdlička 1904; Reagan 1930). Similar accounts mentioned fermentation practices for "wines" and other beverages made from cactus fruits in the Sonoran and Mojave Deserts (Castetter and Underhill 1935; Davis 1920; Hrdlička 1906; La Barre 1938; Russell 1908; Spier 1933).

Taking a longer view of such matters, it is no less significant that numerous archival accounts and ethnohistoric studies mention mescal fermentation and consumption by the Suma, Tarahumara, Toboso, and other indigenous groups encountered by the Spanish from the late sixteenth through the eighteenth centuries across west Texas, southern New Mexico, and northwestern Mexico (Beals 1932). As early as 1582, Diego Pérez de Luxán, chronicler of the Espejo expedition, mentioned the use of *maguey* (agave) by the indigenous tribes (presumably ancestral Suma) encountered to the southeast and southwest of present-day El Paso, Texas (Bolton 1916; Hammond and Rey 1966). Several accounts mention Suma groups participating in ceremonies or communal gatherings involving "drunkenness" (Bandelier 1890; Griffen 1979) that almost certainly involved fermented *mescal* made from liquid extracted from agave hearts baked in earth ovens. Griffen (1979) relates archival accounts of congregations of intoxicated Suma groups in the Bavispe region of northeastern Chihuahua, during which "superstitious dances" were performed and led by a "medicine man." Pennington (1963) lists accounts of Spanish missionaries among the Tarahumara in the mid- and late 1600s that describe "wines" and other fermented drinks made from *maguey* (agave) and Pfefferkorn (1945) and Pérez de Ribas (1999) observed the production of "wines" from *mescal*[1] plants by groups in Sonora and Sinaloa. Several archival sources[2] from the La Junta region of west Texas and northern Chihuahua describe oral testimonies provided by members of the Toboso tribe that mention the act of traveling to distant locations to "make *mescal*" (AHP 1653A, 1655A, 1684A).

In light of this evidence for several centuries of agave fermentation, it requires neither a leap of faith nor inference to assume that such practices extended into prehispanic times. Yet despite the body of literature describing relationships between earth ovens, fermentation, and social production, plant-baking pits are rarely considered in the picture of social organization in the prehispanic Southwest. The few exceptions tend to involve settlements with evidence of large-scale and intensive cultivation of agave (Doolittle and Neely 2004; Fish et al. 2000) or massive plant-baking pits at Paquimé and nearby settlements (Minnis and Whalen 2005; Whalen and Minnis 2001, 2009). But the generic agave-baking pit, so common across the arid lands of the southern Southwest and northern Mexico, continues to be overlooked.

There are many reasons—and probably as many rationales—for this oversight, the most obvious of which is the uninspiring nature and lack of visual appeal of plant-baking pits and burned-rock middens, particularly when compared to the pueblo and pithouse architecture of the Southwest. The influence of Southwestern pueblo ethnographies cannot be ignored, inasmuch as sobriety— or at least public sobriety—was generally encouraged among the historic societies of the eastern and western pueblos and accordingly there is little mention of fermentation methods, facilities, products, or practices among the historic and contemporary ethnographies (Bruman 2000).[3] While the ethnographic record of pueblo societies of the northern Southwest has proven invaluable for modeling and interpreting prehispanic social organization, it also appears that its influence has inhibited awareness of fermentation and social practices in other parts of the Southwest. Perhaps prehispanic and historic societies of the Jornada and other regions of the southern deserts of the southern Southwest followed what might be envisioned as, for lack of a better phrase, a "southern desert model" of fermentation and social production as richly described in the accounts of explorers, missionaries, and ethnographers cited above.

Lastly, considerations of prehispanic subsistence economies tend to focus on maize agriculture, fauna, and occasional wild plant foods. The prevailing view of baking pits, and the agave, yucca, sotol, and cholla baked within, is that they were of secondary importance to prehistoric subsistence economies, serving mainly to supplement or buffer agricultural harvests or to survive periods of famine. This has had a larger influence as archaeologists were predisposed to interpret the exploitation of agave and other succulents within diet-breadth models, risk-reduction models, and other tenets of optimal foraging theory. Such models tend to obscure or minimize the significant roles that plant baking and plant-baking pits played in political economies and social production.

Excavations of 77 plant-baking facilities and associated burned-rock discard middens in the Sacramento Mountains of the Jornada region of south-central New Mexico (figure 12.1) provided what is perhaps the largest and most intensively

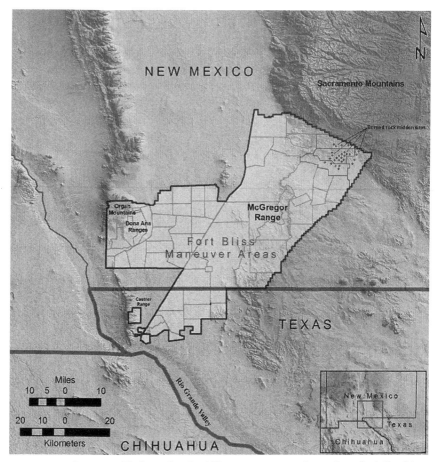

**FIGURE 12.1.** *Location of the burned-rock midden excavations in the southern foothills of the Sacramento Mountains on McGregor Range of Fort Bliss, south-central New Mexico.*

documented sample of such features in the US Southwest (Miller, Graves, and Landreth 2012; Miller, Graves, Frederick, and Landreth 2012; Miller et al. 2011, 2013; Sale et al. 2012). Conducted over a period of four years, the excavations revealed that these facilities had important economic, social, and ritual functions beyond mere subsistence, one of the most significant being the fermentation of liquid extracted from baked Agavaceae[4] plants to produce mescal.

Studies of plant remains recovered from the pits identified over 30 species (Miller et al. 2011, 2013), but the pits were used mainly for long-term baking of the hearts or palms of Agavaceae and Liliaceae family succulents (*Agave neomexicana, Agave lechuguilla, Yucca baccata, Dasylirion wheeleri*) and the fruits, buds, or pads of several genus and species of the Cactaceae family (*Cylindropuntia* [cholla], *Platyopuntia* [prickly pear], *Mammillaria, Echinocereus, Echinocactus*). Of these species, succulents of the Agavaceae family are most commonly represented in macrobotanical samples.

Excavations at nearby pueblo settlements such as Sacramento Pueblo (Miller and Graves 2012) provide additional contexts for interpreting plant-baking pits and Agavaceae use. Archaeological evidence of fermentation and fiber production is rarely recovered from baking facilities because these end products were transported away from the production facilities and taken to settlements for further processing and consumption. An integrated study of plant-baking pits and pueblo settlements where the products of the baking pits were transported and consumed has revealed a much more holistic view of the significance of agave-baking pits. The systematic study of a large sample of such features presents a new approach to understanding how inequality and leadership developed during periods of resource and demographic stress. These interpretations differ from conventional views of cultural complexity based on the interplay of agricultural production, labor, and scheduling. This chapter explores the political economy of intensified Agavaceae exploitation and geographic expansion of plant-baking facilities, developments that led to changes in labor organization, land tenure, and overexploitation of the commons. The implications of feasting, social control of mescal production, and the development of leadership and inequality are explored.

## COMPONENTS OF PLANT-BAKING PITS

Plant-baking pits are often called burned-rock middens. The term *burned-rock midden* is somewhat misleading because it refers to a single component of what was actually a complex of features and refuse-disposal areas that were integral components of plant-baking facilities (figure 12.2). These facilities would more appropriately be called *plant-baking pits* or *earth-oven complexes*, but the term *burned-rock midden* is entrenched in the literature (Black and Thoms 2014). The burned-rock discard midden is the most prominent and visible attribute of plant-baking complexes in the Jornada region and is usually the focus of archaeological excavation. Discard middens consist of accumulations of burned rock, wood charcoal, and soil that were used to cap the centrally located baking pits during the cooking process and were then removed and piled around the perimeter of the pit when it was opened and cleaned out. Discard middens range in size from 2 m to 12 m in diameter, with an average of 8 m, and have depths ranging from a single layer of burned rock to mounded accumulations of a meter or more in height. The second component of the Jornada burned-rock midden is what may be termed the *central pit area*. This is analogous to what Black and Creel (1997) refer to as *center-focused middens* and simply denotes that the main focus of production and processing activities—the actual plant-baking pits or ovens—were

**FIGURE 12.2.** *Components of plant-baking facilities. Upper panel, typical circular burned-rock discard midden on the surface; lower left, central pit area with baking pit and portion of soil borrow pit; lower right, rock-lined baking pits.*

in the center of the burned-rock midden. Each plant-baking complex had a central pit area and, in most instances, one or more rock-lined or unlined baking pits are present in this area. Central pit areas often have other features, the most common being soil borrow pits, from which dirt was excavated to cap the baking pits. Pounding stones and other work areas also are present. The baking pits, also termed *earth ovens* or *roasting pits*, were the primary focus and productive component of plant-baking facilities and the location where the actual baking of plants took place. In other words, the baking pits were the *raison d'être* for the midden. Plant-baking pits include rock-lined and unlined varieties, with the former much more common in the Jornada region. Rock-lined baking pits average around 90 cm in diameter and 20 cm in depth while unlined pits are slightly larger, averaging 1.2 m in diameter and up to 40 cm in depth.

## COOK STONES, FUELWOOD, AND THE LABOR DIMENSION

Archaeological investigations of burned-rock middens in the Sacramento Mountains were designed to place these features in the larger picture of economic, demographic, and social developments of the Jornada Mogollon. From this perspective it is illuminating to take stock of just how many features were constructed and how much burned rock was used in their construction. A striking aspect of these middens involves the massive labor investment they represent. One of the data collection and analysis efforts involved compiling and reviewing quantitative data on the limestone rock used in the construction and operation of prehistoric plant-baking facilities. The excavation techniques and methods of estimating burned-rock counts and weights, along with the quantitative data tables, are reviewed in the technical reports (see Miller et al. 2011; Miller et al. 2013). A summary of the conclusions is presented here.

Based on count and weight data from 66 of the best-preserved and fully documented plant-baking pits and associated burned-rock discard middens excavated at 26 sites, an estimated 292,215 rock cobbles,[5] weighing a total of 179,525 kg, was transported from alluvial and colluvial gravel deposits and used to construct and cap the pits of this sample. Although minimal effort was required to excavate and line the shallow baking pits and sources of rock were usually available within a few hundred yards or less, the collection and transport of such quantities of rock, along with the effort needed to gather, transport, and process cacti and fuelwood, represented a significant expenditure of time and labor.

These data were then extrapolated to larger regional samples. Based on high-resolution survey methods, 532 sites have been recorded in a 16 × 22.5 km (360 km$^2$) area of the southern foothills of the Sacramento Mountains. Burned-rock middens are often considered rather isolated and scattered features, but the reality is that hundreds of such features are present along terraces bordering major drainages, alluvial fans, and valleys of the southern foothills. Several sites, particularly those along the lower floodplains or broad terraces bordering major drainages, are virtual landscapes of 70 or more midden facilities extending for distances of 150 m or more along the terraces. On the basis of several factors, I arrived at a conservative estimate that 7,800 burned-rock middens are present within the 360 km$^2$ area. Using the median rock weights and counts from the excavated sample, it is estimated that 16,380,000 rocks weighing an estimated 9,149,400 kg were gathered and transported to construct plant-baking facilities in this small area of the southern foothills. An estimated 75 percent of the baking facilities were constructed during a 700-year-long interval between AD 600 and 1300. Based on this proportion, approximately 300,000 kg of rock was collected to build 250 baking pits during each generation of settlement within this small geographic segment of the Jornada region.

So just how many numbers and tons of rock cobbles were gathered to bake agave, succulents, cholla, datil, and other foods in the Jornada region? If, for sake of heuristic argument, we assume a conservative estimate of a total of 50,000 middens among mountain ranges and alluvial fans of the Jornada region, the baseline estimate is that 105,000,000 cobbles weighing 58,000,000 kg were collected. Furthermore, these estimates do not take into account the time, energy, organization, and caloric investment to harvest, transport, and prepare the agave and other plants, nor do they consider the time and effort required to gather the fuelwood needed to heat the pits. If Dering's (1999:665) experimental estimate of 224 kg of wood was needed to heat a typical baking pit, the efforts required to harvest fuelwood are indeed staggering. If the conservative estimate of 50,000 middens is used, approximately 11,200,000 kg of wood was needed to heat those baking pits—and this total accounts for only a single use.

## BEYOND BAKING: FIBER PRODUCTION AND FERMENTATION

The cookstone and fuelwood estimates are for expository purposes (the actual totals are probably higher) and clearly underscore the labor investment in plant-baking facilities that took place across the Jornada region. These quantitative estimates of burned-rock weights and counts and fuelwood quantities would have been manifested in labor costs, caloric investments and return rates, and organizational needs in the past. Accordingly, when these values are brought to the forefront, it starts to put things in a much different perspective regarding intensification of plant baking and everything else that it entails, as well as leading to the question as to why such a labor-intensive food preparation technology was adopted.

So what purpose did all of this labor serve? The important subsistence and economic roles of plant-baking pits are reviewed elsewhere (Miller et al. 2011; Miller and Montgomery 2018). These include heat efficiency via the ability to "trap and hold flame heat" (Thoms 2008:445) that, in addition to fuelwood efficiency, allowed for complex carbohydrate and sugars to be broken down and rendered edible and palatable (Wandsnider 1997). The use of Agavaceae and other cacti as a buffering mechanism against crop failure and famine is another possibility (Anderies et al. 2008; Parsons and Parsons 1990; Parsons and Darling 2000; Sauer 1941, 1963). Fiber production was another major function (Miller et al. 2011; Deaver and Prasciunas 2012) and tools such as pounding stones and scraper planes are commonly recovered among plant-baking pits.

Perhaps the most significant, yet most often overlooked, function of pit baking of Agavaceae plants was the extraction of liquid to produce fermented drinks. Given the ubiquity of accounts of agave and cactus-fruit fermentation in the ethnographic and ethnohistoric literature, it is certain that portions of the Agavaceae and other plants baked in the prehistoric burned-rock middens of the Jornada were often, if not regularly, used for the production of fermented drinks. The baked flesh would have been mashed on the pounding stones found in the central pit areas and the liquid collected in ceramic vessels for fermentation in a fashion similar to that documented for the Tarahumara (Bye et al. 1975; Pennington 1963; Zingg 2001) and Mescalero Apache (Basehart 1960; Buskirk 1986; Castetter et al. 1938).

While it is reasonable to propose that agave fermentation was a common practice in the prehispanic southern Southwest, the archaeological substantiation of such claims is a more challenging matter because the tangible material evidence in the form of fermented liquids was either consumed, discarded, or evaporated. The most forthright and universal evidence would be in the form of use alteration and traces of residues left on the ceramic vessels used for fermentation. In fact, fermented saguaro fruit liquid was used by the Hohokam to etch designs on marine shell (Ezell 1937; Haury 1937; Pomeroy 1959), a testament to the strength of the acid content of fermented cacti beverages. Accordingly, ceramic vessels used for fermentation should show evidence of pitting and etching of interior surfaces by such acidic liquids. Pitting and etching are forms of nonabrasive wear that do not result from contact with foods or tools while stirring the contents of a vessel (Skibo 1992). A particular class of ceramic container at the Postclassic center of La Quemada in north-central Mexico often had etched interior surfaces that are thought to have resulted from the use of the vessels to store and serve *pulque* (Anderies et al. 2008). Pitted sherds are present at Paquimé and neighboring settlements, but is unclear if the use alteration resulted from fermentation or boiling corn (Di Peso et al. 1974:6; Whalen and Minnis 2009)

If El Paso Brownware jars produced in the Jornada region were used to ferment liquid extracted from baked Agavaceae, then similar patterns of etched and pitted interiors should be present. It is important to note, however, that such ceramic evidence will seldom be found in direct association with burned-rock middens. Instead, we must search among the remains of vessels recovered from habitation sites where the vessels containing fermenting Agavaceae liquid were transported. Indeed, such evidence exists in the form of several large and thick El Paso Brownware jar sherds with heavily pitted and etched interior surfaces recovered from pithouse and pueblo settlements in the southern Sacramento Mountains (figure 12.3). Several sherds were recovered from Room 1, the communal room of the northern roomblock of Sacramento Pueblo (Miller and Graves 2012) and additional examples were recovered from a house structure adjacent to a plant-baking pit at LA 117092 (Miller et al. 2013). The pattern of semicircular pits and bumpy appearance of the surfaces of these sherds is similar

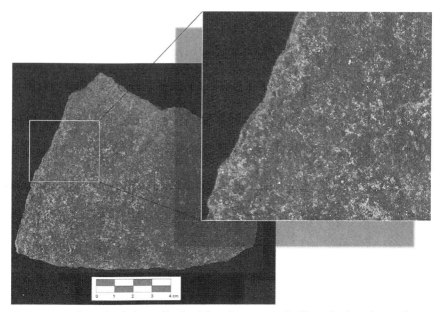

**FIGURE 12.3.** *Example of a large olla sherd from Sacramento Pueblo with a heavily pitted interior surface.*

to use-alteration patterns reported for ceramic containers used to ferment acidic alcoholic beverages in other regions (Arthur 2002, 2003; Merrill 1978; Skibo 1992; Vuković 2011). Although in the absence of residue analysis or some other form of corroborative evidence it cannot be confirmed beyond doubt that the pattern of pitting observed on the jar sherds from Sacramento Pueblo resulted from contact with acidic mescal liquid, it seems unlikely that another form of use could have degraded the interior vessel fabric to such an extent. Such extensively pitted surfaces were not observed on other sooted jar sherds used as cooking vessels.

Another question concerns the nature of vessels used to serve the mescal. While our understanding of fermentation vessels is limited, even less is known of the types of vessels or implements used to serve fermented mescal among several individuals. It is possible that gourds were used; remains of bottle gourd rinds (*Lagenaria siceraria*) have been recovered from several village settlements in the Jornada region. Small ceramic ollas and ladles are commonly found at Jornada pithouse villages and pueblo settlements and may have been used to serve mescal. Another intriguing possibility is that the unique double-chambered El Paso Polychrome jars connected by a cylinder between the bodies and stirrup leading from rim to rim were used to serve mescal in certain social contexts involving different groups or perhaps even moieties. The individual ollas comprising the double-chambered vessels usually have different design layouts and elements.

## THE EXPANSION AND INTENSIFICATION OF PIT BAKING

The evidence for fermentation among Jornada plant-baking pits and habitation sites must be considered within the context of the labor estimates discussed earlier. Why was so much labor invested in the construction of plant-baking facilities, the harvesting of plants and wood, and the time-consuming baking and fermentation processes? A broader historical context regarding temporal patterns and settlement contexts is required to address these questions. Chronological age trends and patterns of use intensity were defined for the recent sample of plant-baking facilities in the Sacramento Mountains as well as others excavated throughout the Jornada region. Examination of several hundred radiocarbon dates determined that the majority of plant-baking facilities were constructed and used during the Mesilla (AD 500–1000), Early Doña Ana (AD 1000–1150), and Late Doña Ana (AD 1150–1300) phases, with the peak of use occurring during the Early Doña Ana and Late Doña Ana phases. Generally around 50 percent (70% in the case of rock-lined baking pits) of the area of the summed radiocarbon probability distributions of radiocarbon dates for these features fall within the 450-year interval between AD 1000 and 1450.

These temporal patterns in midden construction and use are both striking and revealing, particularly when the intensity of use is considered. Several proxy estimates of use intensity were examined (Miller et al. 2011). Rock-fracture rates provide a proxy for use intensity in that the increasingly intensive use and reuse of the facilities results in greater degrees of rock fracturing. Artifact types commonly found in burned-rock discard middens include flake debitage, fragmentary groundstone tools recycled as cookstones, ceramic sherds (in Ceramic-period middens, and often having abraded edges resulting from use as tools to dig and empty the pits), occasional projectile points, and a particular suite of tool forms such as scraper planes, battering stones, denticulate tools, and tabular "agave" knives. Large, flat pounding stones are often found in the central pit area and were used to further process the baked agave hearts and leaves for food, fiber, or liquid to ferment. The densities of these artifacts in the burned-rock discard middens and central pit areas also reflect use intensity of the features and related habitation sites. Examination of these use-intensity variables along a time vector revealed the intriguing finding that—while the construction of plant-baking facilities and formation of midden deposits occurred at increasing rates through time—*the facilities were used less intensively.* Mesilla-phase middens had high rock-fracture rates, indicating intensive use, and had greater artifact densities associated with occupations of longer duration. Middens formed during the subsequent Early Doña Ana phase had significantly less fracturing, indicating lesser degrees of use intensity and less frequent reuse. Fracturing rates and midden use intensity continued to decline during the Late Doña Ana phase and possibly through the El Paso phase (AD 1300–1450). Middens of these periods also had significantly lower artifact densities and other evidence indicating that their use was organized on a logistical basis from residential base camps at pithouse and pueblo settlements.

To frame these conclusions in another manner, analysis of chronometric data and proxy indicators of use intensity establish that during the Early Doña Ana and Late Doña Ana phases of AD 1000 through 1300, the construction and use of cookstone technology and plant-baking pits intensified. Overall, more baking facilities were built, more rock was transported, more wood was collected, more plants were baked, and perhaps more fibers were extracted and liquid fermented. *However, this intensification was manifested by the expansion of facilities, or more middens, across broader swathes of the landscape rather than by more intensive, focused use of fewer individual middens in fewer, select locations.* The tasks were performed at an increasing number of locations across the landscape and were apparently conducted on a logistical basis. This is a critical issue, as this intensification occurred during a period of subsistence, settlement, and demographic change throughout the Jornada region. I return to the possible implications of this below.

### Intensification, Expansion, and the Tragedy of the Commons

It is my impression that a large part of this was tied to limiting factors of the environment. In semiarid regions such as the Jornada, the fuelwood requirements of plant-baking facilities combined with low biomass recovery rates would have resulted in a rapid depletion of fuel sources within the vicinity of earth-oven processing sites. Indeed, these stresses can be isolated in the record of plant-baking pits as analysis of radiocarbon age distributions found that elevations below 1,700 m (5,600 feet) show a marked decrease in the numbers and proportions of plant-baking facilities after AD 1000 (Miller and Montgomery 2018). Thus, at some point, even an efficient technology such as cookstone pit baking will overtax the environment, leading to a situation where ecological constraints required more spatially widespread and less-intensive midden use. Here I propose that these may have contributed to further developments in social organization.

The final musings and speculations deal with the political economy of intensified Agavaceae and cacti exploitation and the social implications of the geographic expansion of plant-baking facilities. The insights gained from the use histories of burned-rock middens serve as illuminating background for studies of landscape use and social organization. The social contexts of burned-rock midden use—including such topics as ownership of the plant-baking facilities, land tenure of the surrounding resource base of plant communities and fuelwood, and the distribution and consumption of the processed plant foods (especially fermented mescal)—merit greater attention.

The spread of plant-baking facilities over the foothills and other landforms had several potential social ramifications. Along with the construction of a greater number of middens across the landscape, there was certainly a greater number of people moving and using various valleys and canyons and the resources located within them. Members of different kin or corporate groups would have encountered each other on an increasingly frequent basis. These encounters may have led to issues of land tenure and overexploitation of the commons (land held to be in communal ownership by multiple social groups and/or settlements). The entangled economic, political, social, and ritual structures would have changed and evolved under such circumstances. The production and distribution of mescal for feasting provided a means of ameliorating social conflicts and provided avenues for exploitation by community leaders and individuals or households of status.

Burwell (1995) offers an insightful case study of what happens when the unregulated commons—communal lands used by several families, lineages, corporate groups, or communities—become overexploited and stressed. Burwell recounts modern developments in the desert lands of eastern Sonora, Mexico, where increasing population growth and expansion of agricultural lands led to an increased demand for income from mescal liquor production. As a result of these demographic and socioeconomic pressures, wild agave plants on communal lands were being overharvested and stressed despite knowledge of sustainable production methods. As noted by Burwell, the belief that no household or village had the right to regulate the manner in which the communal lands surrounding the village were exploited led to overexploitation of agave and severe, unsustainable reduction in agave populations—a tragedy of the commons (after Hardin 1968). The reestablishment of agave populations and design of sustainable harvest practices required structural cultural changes in suprahousehold political organization that necessarily required that the autonomy of individual households be surrendered to some degree.

While a case study involving the modern demographics of northern Mexico and the political economy of commercial mescal production is not directly applicable to the prehistoric Jornada, Burwell's study serves as a useful analogy, providing insights into broad social and political responses to resource stress and conflicts over land tenure arising from increasing demographic and economic pressures on communal landscapes. In a similar manner, the widespread movement of groups and the construction of baking pits across the commons may have created conflicts and ecological stresses. Evidence of such unsustainable practices is manifested in the archaeological record of Agavaceae and cacti exploitation in the Jornada. The pronounced rise in the numbers of baking pits used after at AD 1000 correlates with a shift in the locations of most pits to forested landforms at elevations above 1,700 m (5,600 ft). Baking pits at lower elevations after AD 1000 have poor-quality fuelwood sources such as shrubs, woody plants, and ocotillo and cholla branches. Together, these observations indicate that fuelwood sources were being overutilized (Miller et al. 2013) in the lower-elevation foothills, requiring that baking pits be moved to forested drainages at higher elevations.

One means of integrating the affected social groups and resolving conflicts over land tenure and overexploitation of the commons would have involved feasting, which brings up another path of inquiry. Agave exploitation may have been a contributing factor to increasing social stress and conflict during the late prehistoric period, but in an intriguing turnabout would have also provided one means of ameliorating such conflicts—through the production and distribution of fermented drinks for feasting.

The production and consumption of fermented drinks from corn stalks, corn meal, agave, and cacti among the Tarahumara provides a useful ethnographic analogy for the role of feasting with fermented beverages in social interaction. Consumption of *tesgüino* (mainly corn-based alcohol but also fermented mescal) plays a fundamental role in social production among the Tarahumara and the beer-drinking ceremony—the *tesgüinada*—is an indispensable component of ritual and social action (Kennedy 1963; Merrill 1978; Pennington 1963; Zingg 2001). Almost all social events and ceremonies involve consumption of *tesgüino*. Cooperative endeavors are rewarded with *tesgüinadas*, social gatherings and meetings are initiated or closed with a *tesgüinada*, and all ritual ceremonies involved *tesgüino* consumption. In fact, Kennedy (1963:635) states that "it is no exaggeration to estimate that the average Tarahumara spends at least 100 days per year directly concerned with tesguino and much of this time under its influence or aftereffects." *Tesgüinadas* are a fundamental component of ritual practice. The ceremonies require significant outlays in terms of labor and corn, and thus serve to establish and maintain social status. What little social differentiation exists among the Tarahumara is based on the possession of animals and fields, but primarily on the ability to sponsor *Tesgüinadas*.

One of the more noteworthy aspects of this type of commensal feasting is that the communal labor and ritual feasting serves to integrate disparate social groups residing at some distance from each other, perhaps in a manner somewhat similar to that described by Douglass and others chapter 11, this volume). Kennedy (1963:625) terms this the *tesgüino network*. Each household participates in *tesgüinadas* with other households, who in turn participate in the ceremonies with other households. As noted by Kennedy, this creates a distinctive structural form of relationships:

> The set of people defined by reciprocal tesguino invitation form the meaningful "community" for any particular individual. The important point about this type of structure is its centrifugal character caused by the fact that the meaningful community shifts its locus from household to household. This brings about a general

netlike system of household-centered, overlapping interaction systems, stretching across the region. ([Kennedy 1963:625)

These networks involve reciprocal relationships and obligations. No less significant is that exchange networks follow established social networks, thus allowing for further development of ritually based and socially aggrandizing material exchange systems. Of particular interest in this regard is the recent identification of linear distributions of ceramic artifacts marking prehistoric pathways that have been recorded during high-resolution surveys across the central basins of the Jornada region (Miller et al. 2018). Presently, over 280 km of trails and trail segments marking travel and communication corridors between major pithouse and pueblo settlement areas have been mapped across the Tularosa and Hueco Basins (figure 12.4).

## POLITICAL AND RITUAL ECONOMIES OF AGAVE FERMENTATION

As with most ethnographic analogies, the Tarahumara model may be not be entirely applicable but the importance of fermented Agavaceae and corn beverages in feasting and social production should not be underestimated or understated. Evidence of prehistoric fermentation is known from several settlements in the Jornada and Casas Grandes regions and there is also strong evidence that such production involved communal or suprahousehold organization. Perhaps the most conspicuous evidence for large-scale fermentation is at Paquimé, where exceptionally large and deep rock-lined ovens were present around the margin of the pueblo (Di Peso 1974:2). Such features are also found at peripheral Medio-period Casas Grandes sites (Whalen and Minnis 2001, 2009; Sayles 1936). The typical Medio-period oven is a huge affair: averaging slightly over 4 m in diameter and 2.2 m in depth, lined with large cobbles and boulders, and filled with massive quantities of burned rock. Di Peso (1974:2:405) first proposed that these were baking pits for fermentation of liquid extracted from caramelized hearts, and that the association of four such pits with a small house cluster and mound indicated an association with larger community ceremonies. Minnis and Whalen (2005) suggest that such large features indicate bulk processing of cacti and succulents for feasts or other forms of distribution. The distribution of such features among Medio-period pueblos matches that of other special socially integrative and status features such as ball courts and macaw pens. Based on the ethnographic and ethnohistoric accounts presented in the introduction, I propose that the processing of Agavaceae in these large baking facilities at Paquimé and nearby pueblos was predominantly for the production of mescal liquor, and that these features are a continuation of a long tradition of ritual and social feasting in the northern Chihuahuan Desert using fermented Agavaceae beverages.

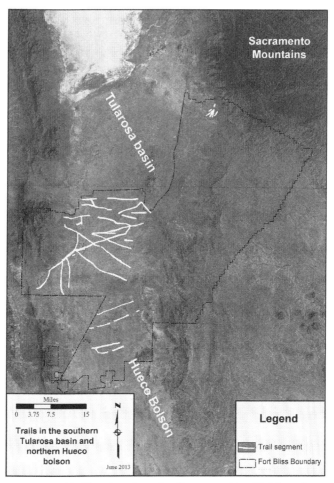

**FIGURE 12.4.** *Prehistoric trails and trail segments identified through high-intensity surveys and analysis of ceramic isolated finds in the Tularosa and Hueco Basins.*

No features of similar size or complexity have been found among Jornada villages, yet it is likely that Agavaceae was baked, and fermented mescal was produced, using the smaller baking pits typical of the region. The evidence for both fermentation and the social context of producing and consuming fermented mescal is subtle, but there are specific instances where material evidence of incipient patterns of feasting and social complexity has been isolated. For example, Speth (2004) describes several large burned-rock roasting facilities in the plaza area of Henderson Pueblo. These features were constructed within the boundaries of the roomblock and were clearly part of the social and economic life of the inhabitants. Several features, such as the 5-m-diameter, 1-m-deep baking pit in Trench K, were of sufficient size to suggest communal use and bulk processing of cacti and succulents.

In a similar manner, a large baking pit was constructed in one of the plaza areas of Sacramento Pueblo. Sacramento Pueblo is located along the Sacramento River, the primary drainage of the southern mountains and is located within the area of plant-baking-pit studies. The pueblo consists of between 50 and 80 rooms, with an unknown number of rooms and plaza area having been washed away by the channel of the Sacramento River (Miller and Graves 2012). The primary excavation focused on the northernmost roomblock. Tree-ring and radiocarbon dates place the occupation of the roomblock between AD 1335 and 1375.

One of the more intriguing findings at Sacramento Pueblo was the multiple lines of evidence for the processing of Agavaceae succulents and, more important, for the use and consumption of the end products of agave baking. Evidence of agave use was recovered in several forms, including a pouch of woven Agavaceae fibers from a room floor, confirming that agave fibers were extracted at plant-baking facilities and subsequently transported to settlements for additional processing and weaving into textiles. As noted earlier, evidence of fermentation was recovered in the form of several large and thick El Paso Brownware jar sherds with heavily pitted interior surfaces, several of which were recovered from the communal room of the northern roomblock.

Of greater significance is the evidence for status, hierarchy, and leadership in the control of the production and consumption of mescal. Agave-processing tools such as tabular knives (agave knives) and fiber-extraction tools such as plane scrapers identified among dozens of plant-baking facilities in the southern Sacramento Mountains were found on floors and in subfloor pits at Sacramento Pueblo. Such informal tools were usually discarded at the plant-processing sites, so their presence on the floors and in subfloor pits of domestic and communal rooms is intriguing and suggests some importance or status may have been ascribed to their possession and use (see Roth, chapter 7, this volume). Supporting this inference is the fact that the distribution of agave tools among the rooms of the northern roomblock is heavily skewed toward the communal room (Room 1) and its adjacent high-status room (Room 4). Nearly 70 percent of the agave tools from floors and subfloor pits were recovered from Rooms 1 and 4, the communal room and adjacent high-status room. Not only is the distribution of the tools important, but so is the context of the tools: an agave knife had been placed as a termination object in the fill of the collared floor hearth of Room 4, a finding that further attests to the status of agave.

Of further relevance is that the expanding ritual and political economy of agave and mescal production after AD 1000 is paralleled by increasingly formal and widespread evidence of ritual behaviors during the construction and use of plant-baking pits. Several forms of ritual behavior are evident in middens dating from this period (Miller et al. 2013), including burned-rock discard piles placed at the intercardinal points around the baking pits, the placement of dedication or termination objects such as turquoise, quartz nodules, and large fossils below baking pits, and perhaps the use of cattail pollen. Articulated turkey skeletons, interpreted as "closure offerings," were found under large slabs situated beneath the largest baking pit at Henderson Pueblo (Speth et al. 2004). Human burials, while rare, are occasionally found in burned-rock discard middens.

## SUMMARY

Carl Lumholtz (1902:I:256–257) observed that the Tarahumara and other indigenous groups of the Sierra Madre of Chihuahua referred to agave in reverent terms as "the first plant God created" and that the fermented liquor was considered indispensable to certain ceremonies. Archival sources from the seventeenth and eighteenth centuries frequently mention the act of "making mescal," including travels to distant locales. The fact that such accounts were often recorded during periods of native revolts and social unrest further attest to the fact that mescal production was a fundamental component of societies and social action of prehispanic and protohistoric groups residing in the Chihuahuan Desert. The preceding discussions establish several trends and new insights into the production and use of plant-baking pits and Agavaceae. The major points of discussion include the labor requirements of plant-baking pits, the intensification and expansion of agave and succulent processing across the landscape, the ecological effects resulting in circumscribed production areas, and the material evidence of the increasing incorporation through time of agave production and consumption in the political economies and social production of the inhabitants of the Jornada region.

What all of this ultimately may have led to in the past is that these factors merged to create a context of increased social interaction and conflict, mediation, and in particular the opening of potential avenues of exploitation for leadership. The tensions arising from conflicts over land tenure and increasing social interaction provided favorable circumstances for the development of leadership and hierarchy (Kantner 2009) and perhaps the early appearance of descent group (or kin based) territories. Feasting, in this case involving fermented mescal, and the resulting social obligations and reciprocal debt formations can provide a means for aggrandizers and ambitious individuals, households, or kin groups to enhance their status, prestige, and authority. Especially in times of environmental and demographic stress when resources or access to resources are distributed unequally, ambitious or high-status individuals or households can provide more food or drink for feasting, thus creating social obligations and debt formations that can be exploited. In other words, certain individuals can give away more food and drink, thus enhancing their status and ultimately promoting the concentration of authority in a smaller number of more-enduring leaders (Adams 2004).

Indeed, it is such processes of incipient inequality that may be reflected in the material record of Sacramento Pueblo. The presence of agave tools in certain high-status contexts indicates that certain households or corporate groups maintained possession of the agave tools and, by extension, control over the products of agave baking, such as mescal. The social implications for the development and maintenance of leadership and hierarchies is quite clear in that certain individuals or households of high status reserved the authority to organize or perform communal feasts and rituals. These findings suggest that agave use—and perhaps control of agave production—carried much more social and ritual significance than has been previously understood and that the movement of mescal reflects the movement of power relations through and among the overlapping and entangled social fields of the Jornada region.

It is suggested here that the such social processes may have, at least in part, originated through changes in land-tenure arrangements, and that the evolution of such land-tenure practices can found in the social and political responses to the demographic pressures leading to intensified and expanded exploitation of the commons beginning after AD 1000 and escalating through the Early Doña Ana and Late Doña Ana phases. The demographic and ecological stresses appear to have led to a rapid progression of land-tenure practices along the continuum from common land rights to kin-group ownership (Kushnick et al. 2014; see also Smith 1988). It appears that the particular set of demographic, ecological, and social conditions created a favorable context through which an incipient form of descent-group territoriality arose. The appearance of ritual behaviors associated with the use of plant-baking pits supports this inference in that the placement of objects below pits and other practices imply the existence of formal relationships between the plant-baking pits, the kin or corporate groups using the pits, and the surrounding landscapes. Once the collective systems of labor associated with the construction of plant-baking pits were mobilized and secured through ritual, they were susceptible to exploitation by individuals or groups.

Whether incipient leadership exploited reciprocal debt obligations through feasting (Hayden 1995) or through ritual and control of ritual knowledge (Blanton 1995) is open to question. There are certainly some hints of ritual performance associated with the use of plant-baking pits during the latter parts of the Jornada pithouse and pueblo periods. Late Prehistoric ritual in the Jornada region was concerned with an ideology and iconography centered on rainmaking, moisture, and maize agriculture. Yet there are echoes, however faint, of more ancient ritual and religious symbolism centered on Agavaceae plants.

Perhaps the focus on the relationship between agriculture and the evolution of social complexity has revealed only part of the picture of Jornada economic, social, political, and ritual developments. The evolution of cultural complexity and inequality in the prehispanic Southwest is conventionally framed in terms of agriculture and its labor-intensive investments leading to a variety of structural changes in economic and social relations. As suggested here, the collection and processing of Agavaceae and all that it entails involved significant labor outlays, too, and required a similar set of social arrangements to mediate conflicts over land, resources, and labor. Perhaps the nondescript burned-rock middens of the Jornada offer another view of another pathway in the evolution of social complexity in the prehispanic Southwest.

*Acknowledgments.* I extend my appreciation to Barb Roth and Jeff Ferguson for the invitation to participate in the 2013 symposium and subsequent invitation to include this essay in the volume. The excavation and study of the plant-baking facilities could not have been possible without the support and funding provided by the Conservation Branch, Environmental Division, of Fort Bliss Military Reservation. Brian Knight, chief, and archaeologists Sue Sitton and Chris Lowry supported and encouraged the field and analytical work. The analyses and interpretations presented in this chapter are built upon the dedicated and detailed fieldwork of the supervisors and crew members and upon Tim Graves's expertise in teasing out the subtleties of burned-rock middens. An intellectual debt is owed to Steve Black, Darrell Creel, Alston Thoms, and to dozens of ethnographers, ethnobotanists, and ethnohistorians cited within the chapter. Nancy Kenmotsu graciously provided archival references for mescal use. Paul Minnis offered critical comments that identified several flaws, errors, and overstatements, and I also wish to thank two anonymous reviewers for their useful comments and critiques. Finally, I thank Karen Harry and Barb Roth for their editorial guidance and support for this chapter.

**NOTES**

1. Pérez de Ribas and other Spanish chroniclers tended to use *mescal* and *maguey* interchangeably, which has resulted in some confusion regarding whether the baked flesh of agave or the fermented beverage was being referred to.

2. Nancy Kenmotsu compiled the references to *mescal* and "making *mescal*" while doing research in Spanish archives and has graciously provided the references for use here.

3. Some accounts do exist that describe fermentation and consumption among the historic pueblos. Stevenson (1915) describes the consumption of corn beer and *mescal* at Zuni. Waddell (1980) provides additional accounts of fermentation and consumption of fermented drinks among the pueblos. Ortiz (1969:100) describes the "bringing the buds

to life" ritual at San Juan Pueblo where a sweet fermented grain beverage is served during the transfer of authority between moieties.

4. The family-level term "Agavaceae" is used here to encompass the genera *Agave* and *Yucca* and the species comprised by these genera. It may also be assumed that the Liliaceae family, specifically sotol, is implied in this discussion.

5. The 66 sampled burned-rock discard middens contain an estimated total of 1,461,075 burned-rock fragments, weighing an average of 0.12 kg. An average of five fragments was equal to the size of the average whole cobble, and thus it is estimated that the discard middens contain approximately 292,215 whole cobbles (one-fifth of the number of fragments), weighing an average of 0.61 kg per cobble.

## REFERENCES

AHP 1653A (Archivo del Hidalgo de Parral). 1653. "Autos de Guerra contra los Indios Tobosos por Diego Guarado Faxado." Microfilm on file, Nettie Lee Benson Latin American Library, The University of Texas at Austin, Frames 595–721.

AHP 1655A (Archivo del Hidalgo de Parral). 1655. "Autos de Guerra con Motivos de los Frequentes Abusos que Cometen los Indios Enemigos de la Real Corona." Microfilm on file, Nettie Lee Benson Latin American Library, The University of Texas at Austin, Frames 231–329.

AHP 1684A (Archivo del Hidalgo de Parral). 1684. "Expediente Formado con Motivo de la Guerra que Hacen los Indios Alzados a la Real Corona." Microfilm on file, Nettie Lee Benson Latin American Library, The University of Texas at Austin, Frames 66–266.

Adams, Ron L. 2004. "An Ethnoarchaeological Study of Feasting in Sulawesi, Indonesia." *Journal of Anthropological Archaeology* 23(1):56–78. https://doi.org/10.1016/j.jaa.2003.10.001.

Anderies, John M., Ben A. Nelson, and Ann B. Kinzig. 2008. "Analyzing the Impact of Agave Cultivation on Famine Risk in Arid Pre-Hispanic Northern Mexico." *Human Ecology* 36(3):409–422. https://doi.org/10.1007/s10745-008-9162-9.

Arthur, John W. 2002. "Pottery Use Alteration as an Indicator of Socioeconomic Status: An Ethnoarchaeological Study of the Gamo of Ethiopia." *Journal of Archaeological Method and Theory* 9(4):331–355. https://doi.org/10.1023/A:1021309616231.

Arthur, John W. 2003. "Brewing Beer: Status, Wealth and Ceramic Use Alteration among the Gamo of Southwestern Ethiopia." *World Archaeology* 34(3):516–528. https://doi.org/10.1080/0043824021000026486.

Bandelier, Adolph F.A. 1890. *Final Report of Investigations among the Indians of the Southwestern U.S. Carried on Mainly in the Years from 1880 to 1885, Part I*. Papers of the Archaeological Institute of America, American Series III. Cambridge, MA: Archaeological Institute of America.

Basehart, Harry W. 1960. *Mescalero Apache Subsistence Patterns and Socio-Political Organization*. The Mescalero-Chiricahua Land Claims Project. United States Indian Claims Commission Reports. New York: Garland Publishing Company.

Beals, Ralph L. 1932. "The Comparative Ethnology of Northern Mexico before 1750." *Iberoamericana (Madrid, Spain)* 2:93–225.

Bell, Willis H., and Edward F.Castetter. 1941. *The Utilization of Yucca, Sotol, and Beargrass by the Aborigines in the American Southwest*. University of New Mexico Bulletin, Ethnobiological Studies in the American Southwest, vol. VII. Albuquerque: University of New Mexico Press.

Bennett, Wendell C., and Robert M. Zingg. 1935. *The Tarahumara: An Indian Tribe of Northern Mexico*. Chicago, IL: University of Chicago Press.

Black, Stephen L., and Darrell G. Creel. 1997. "The Central Texas Burned Rock Midden Reconsidered." In *Hot Rock Cooking on the Greater Edwards Plateau: Four Burned Rock Midden Sites in West Central Texas*, by Stephen L. Black, Linda W. Ellis, Darrell G. Creel, and Glenn T. Goode, 269–305. Studies in Archeology No. 22, Texas Archeological Research Laboratory, The University of Texas at Austin and Report No. 2. Austin: Archaeology Studies Program, Environmental Affairs Division, Texas Department of Transportation.

Black, Stephen L., and Alston V. Thoms. 2014. "Hunter-Gatherer Earth Ovens in the Archaeological Record: Fundamental Concepts." *American Antiquity* 79(02):204–226. https://doi.org/10.7183/0002-7316.79.2.204.

Blanton, Richard E. 1995. "The Cultural Foundations of Inequality in Households." In *Foundations of Social Inequality*, ed. T. D. Price and G. M. Feinman, 105–127. New York: Plenum Press. https://doi.org/10.1007/978-1-4899-1289-3_4.

Bolton, Herbert E. 1916. *Spanish Exploration in the Southwest, 1542–1706*. New York: Charles Scribner's Sons. https://doi.org/10.5479/sil.261021.39088005888821.

Bruman, Henry J. 1940. *Aboriginal Drink Areas in New Spain*. PhD dissertation, University of California, Berkeley. Ann Arbor, MI: University Microfilms International.

Bruman, Henry J. 2000. *Alcohol in Ancient Mexico*. Salt Lake City: University of Utah Press.

Burwell, Trevor. 1995. "Bootlegging on a Desert Mountain: The Political Ecology of Agave (*Agave* spp.) Demographic Change in the Sonora River Valley, Sonora, Mexico." *Human Ecology* 23(3):407–432. https://doi.org/10.1007/BF01190139.

Buskirk, Winfred. 1986. *The Western Apache: Living with the Land before 1950*. Norman: University of Oklahoma Press.

Bye, Robert A, Jr., Don Burgess, and Albino Mares Trias. 1975. "Ethnobotany of the Western Tarahumara of Chihuahua, Mexico. Volume I: Notes on the Genus *Agave*." *Botanical Museum Leaflets* 24(5):5–112. Cambridge, MA: Harvard University Press.

Castetter, Edward F., Willis H.Bell, and Alvin R.Grove. 1938. *The Early Utilization and Distribution of Agave in the American Southwest*. University of New Mexico

Bulletin, Ethnobiological Studies in the American Southwest, vol. VI. Albuquerque: University of New Mexico Press.

Castetter, Edward F., and Morris E.Opler. 1936. *The Ethnobiology of the Chiricahua and Mescalero Apache: The Use of Plants for Foods, Beverages, and Narcotics.* University of New Mexico Bulletin, Ethnobiological Studies in the American Southwest Vol. IIIA. Albuquerque: University of New Mexico Press.

Castetter, Edward F., and Ruth M. Underhill. 1935. *The Ethnobiology of the Papago Indians.* Biological Series 4(3), University of New Mexico Bulletin, Ethnobiological Studies in the American Southwest Vol. II. Albuquerque: University of New Mexico.

Crist, Raymond E. 1940. "Some Geographic Aspects of the Manufacture of Mezcal." *Scientific Monthly* 50:234–236.

Davis, Edward H. 1920. "The Papago Ceremony of Víkita." *Indian Notes and Monographs* 3(4):159–177.

Deaver, William L., and Mary M. Prasciunas. 2012. *Archaeology of an Agave Field: Data Recovery for the Tucson Electric Power Tortolita to North Loop Transmission Line Project, Pinal and Pima Counties, Arizona.* Cultural Resources Report 2012–36. Tucson, AZ: WestLand Resources.

Dering, J. Philip. 1999. "Earth-Oven Plant Processing in Archaic Period Economies: An Example from a Semi-Arid Savannah in South-Central North America." *American Antiquity* 64(4):659–674. https://doi.org/10.2307/2694211.

Di Peso, Charles C. 1974. *Casas Grandes: A Fallen Trading Center of the Gran Chichimeca,* Vol. 2: *Medio Period.* Dragoon, AZ: The Amerind Foundation.

Di Peso, Charles C., John B. Rinaldo, and Gloria J. Fenner. 1974. *Casas Grandes: A Fallen Trading Center of the Gran Chichimeca.* Vol. 6: *Ceramics and Shell..* Dragoon, AZ: The Amerind Foundation.

Doolittle, William E., and James A. Neely. 2004. *The Safford Valley Grids: Prehistoric Cultivation in the Southern Arizona Desert.* Tucson: University of Arizona Press.

Ezell, Paul. 1937. "Shell Work of the Prehistoric Southwest." *Kiva* 3(3):9–12. https://doi.org/10.1080/00231940.1937.11757801.

Fish, Suzanne K., Paul R. Fish, and John H. Madsen. 2000. "Evidence for Large-Scale Agave Cultivation in the Marana Community." In *The Marana Community in the Hohokam World,* ed. S. K. Fish, P. R. Fish, and J. H. Madsen, 73–87. Anthropological Papers of the University of Arizona No. 56. Tucson: University of Arizona Press.

Griffen, William B. 1979. *Indian Assimilation in the Franciscan Area of Nueva Vizcaya.* Anthropological Papers No. 33. Tucson: University of Arizona Press.

Hammond, George P., and Agapito Rey, eds. 1966 [1929]. *Expedition into New Mexico Made by Antonio de Espejo in 1582–1583, as Revealed in the Journal of Diego Perez de Luxan, a Member of the Party.* Los Angeles, CA: Quivera Society Publications, Quivera Society.

Hardin, Garrett. 1968. "The Tragedy of the Commons." *Science* 162(3859):1243–1248. https://doi.org/10.1126/science.162.3859.1243.

Haury, Emil W. 1937. "Shell." In *Excavations at Snaketown: Material Culture*, by H. S. Gladwin, E. W. Haury, E. B. Sayles, and N. Gladwin, 135–153. Medallion Papers No. 25. Globe, AZ: Gila Pueblo.

Hayden, Brian. 1995. "Pathways to Power: Principles for Creating Socioeconomic Inequalities." In *Foundations of Social Inequality*, ed. T. D. Price and G. M. Feinman, 15–86. New York: Plenum Press. https://doi.org/10.1007/978-1-4899-1289-3_2.

Hrdlička, Aleš. 1904. "Method of Preparing Tesvino among the White River Apaches." *American Anthropologist* 6:190–191.

Hrdlička, Aleš. 1906. "Notes on the Pima of Arizona." *American Anthropologist* 8(1):39–46. https://doi.org/10.1525/aa.1906.8.1.02a00080.

Kantner, John. 2009. "Identifying the Pathways to Permanent Leadership." In *The Evolution of Leadership: Transitions in Decision Making from Small-Scale to Middle-Range Societies*, ed. K. J. Vaughn, J. W. Eerkens, and J. Kantner, 249–281. School for Advanced Research Advanced Seminar Series. Santa Fe, NM: School of Advanced Research Press.

Kennedy, John G. 1963. "Tesguino Complex: The Role of Beer in Tarahumara Culture." *American Anthropologist* 65(3):620–640. https://doi.org/10.1525/aa.1963.65.3.02a00080.

Kushnick, Geoff, Russell D. Gray, and Fiona M. Jordan. 2014. "The Sequential Evolution of Land Tenure Norms." *Evolution and Human Behavior* 35(4):309–318. https://doi.org/10.1016/j.evolhumbehav.2014.03.001.

La Barre, Weston. 1938. "Native American Beers." *American Anthropologist* 40(2):224–234. https://doi.org/10.1525/aa.1938.40.2.02a00040.

Lumholtz, Carl. 1902. *Unknown Mexico: A Record of Five Years' Exploration among the Tribes of the Western Sierra Madre, in the Tierra Caliente of Tepic and Jalisco, and among the Tarascos of Michoacan.* 2 vols. New York: Charles Scribner's Sons.

Merrill, William L. 1978. "Thinking and Drinking: A Raramuri Interpretation." In *The Nature and Status of Ethnobotany*, ed. R. I. Ford, 101–117. Ann Arbor: Museum of Anthropology, University of Michigan.

Miller, Myles R., and John Montgomery. 2018. "Plant Baking Facilities and Social Complexity: A Perspective from the Western Jornada and Southeastern New Mexico." In *Late Prehistoric Hunter-Gatherers and Farmers of the Jornada Mogollon*, ed. T. R. Rocek and N. A. Kenmotsu, 000–000. Louisville: University Press of Colorado.

Miller, Myles R., and Tim B. Graves. 2012. *Sacramento Pueblo: An El Paso and Late Glencoe Phase Pueblo in the Southern Sacramento Mountains.* Fort Bliss Cultural Resources Report No. 10–22. Fort Bliss, TX: Environmental Division.

Miller, Myles R., Tim B. Graves, Moira Ernst, and Mike Stowe. 2011. *Burned Rock Middens of the Southern Sacramento Mountains.* Fort Bliss Cultural Resources Report No. 09–28, Fort Bliss, TX: Environmental Division.

Miller, Myles R., Tim Graves, Moira Ernst, and Matt Swanson. 2018. "Deciphering
   Prehistoric Trails and Unraveling Social Networks in the Tularosa and Hueco
   Bolsons." In *Late Prehistoric Hunter-Gatherers and Farmers of the Jornada Mogollon*, ed.
   T. R. Rocek and N. A. Kenmotsu, 000–000. Louisville: University Press of Colorado.

Miller, Myles R., Tim Graves, Charles Frederick, and Melinda Landreth. 2012.
   *Investigations at Four Burned Rock Midden Sites along Wildcat Canyon in the Southern
   Sacramento Mountains*. Fort Bliss Cultural Resources Report No. 11–13. Fort Bliss, TX:
   Environmental Division.

Miller, Myles R., Tim Graves, and Melinda Landreth. 2012. *Further Investigations of
   Burned Rock Middens and Associated Settlements: Mitigation of Three Sites for the IBCT,
   Fort Bliss, Otero County, New Mexico*. Fort Bliss Cultural Resources Report No. 10–21.
   Fort Bliss, TX: Environmental Division.

Miller, Myles R., Tim Graves, Melinda Landreth, Charles Frederick, Brittney Gregory,
   and Tabitha Burgess. J. Phil Dering, Susan J. Smith, Moira Ernst, Michael Stowe, Juan
   Arias, Mark Sale, Matt Swanson, Leonard Kemp, and Lillian Ponce. 2013. *Investigations
   of Burned Rock Middens along the Sacramento Mountains Alluvial Fans: Excavation of 18
   BRMs at Nine Sites and a Summary of 77 BRM Excavations in the Sacramento Mountains
   of Fort Bliss, Otero County, New Mexico*. Historic and Natural Resources Report No.
   12–05. Fort Bliss, TX: Environmental Division.

Minnis, Paul E., and Michael E. Whalen. 2005. "At the Other End of the Pueblo World:
   Feasting at Casas Grandes, Chihuahua, Mexico." In *Engaged Anthropology: Research
   Essays on North American Archaeology, Ethnobotany, and Museology*, ed. by M. Hegmon
   and B. S. Eiselt, 114–128. Anthropological Papers No. 94. Ann Arbor: Museum of
   Anthropology, University of Michigan.

Ortiz, Alfonso. 1969. *The Tewa World: Space, Time, Being, and Becoming in a Pueblo Society*.
   Chicago, IL: University of Chicago Press.

Parsons, Jeffrey R., and J. Andrew Darling. 2000. "Maguey (*Agave* spp.) Utilization
   in Mesoamerican Civilization: A Case for Precolumbian 'Pastoralism.'" *Boletín
   de la Sociedad Botánica de México*, no. 66, 81–91.

Parsons, Jeffrey R., and M. H. Parsons. 1990. *Maguey Utilization in Highland Central
   Mexico: An Archaeological Ethnography*. Anthropological Papers No. 82. Ann Arbor:
   Museum of Anthropology, University of Michigan.

Pennington, Campbell W. 1963. *The Tarahumar of Chihuahua: Their Environment and
   Material Culture*. Salt Lake City: University of Utah Press.

Pérez de Ribas, Andrés. 1999 [1645]. *History of the Triumphs of Our Holy Faith amongst
   the Most Barbarous and Fierce Peoples of the New World*. Translated by Daniel T. Reff,
   Maureen Ahern, and Richard K. Danford. Tucson: University of Arizona Press.

Pfefferkorn, Ignaz S. J. 1945. *Sonora: A Description of the Province*. Translated and
   annotated by Theodore E. Treutlien. Coronado Quatro Centennial Publications

No. 12. Albuquerque: University of New Mexico. (Originally published 1794–1795. *Beschreibung der Landshaft Sonora.* Cologne.)

Pomeroy, J. Anthony. 1959. "Hohokam Etched Shell." *Kiva* 24(4):12–21. https://doi.org/1 0.1080/00231940.1959.11757582.

Reagan, Albert B. 1930. "Notes on the Indians of the Fort Apache Region." *Anthropological Papers of the American Museum of Natural History* 31:281–345.

Russell, Frank. 1908. *The Pima Indians.* Twenty-Sixth Annual Report of the Bureau of American Ethnology, No. 26. [1904–1905], 17–389. Washington, DC: Bureau of American Ethnology.

Sale, Mark, Myles R. Miller, and Amy Silberberg. 2012. *Pits and Pieces: Mitigation of One Site in the IBCT on Fort Bliss Military Reservation, Otero County, New Mexico.* Cultural Resources Report No. 11–26. Fort Bliss, TX: Environmental Division.

Sauer, Carl O. 1941. "The Personality of Mexico." *Geographical Review* 31(3):353–364. https://doi.org/10.2307/210171.

Sauer, Carl O. 1963. *Land and Life: A Selection from the Writing of C. O. Sauer.* Berkeley: University of California Press.

Sayles, Edwin B. 1936. *An Archaeological Survey of Chihuahua, Mexico.* Medallion Papers, No. 22. Globe, AZ: Gila Pueblo.

Setzler, Frank M. 1939. "Exploring a Cave in Southwestern Texas." *Explorations and Fieldwork of the Smithsonian Institution in 1938.* Publication No. 3525, 75–78. Washington, DC: Smithsonian Institution.

Skibo, James M. 1992. *Pottery Function: A Use-Alteration Perspective.* New York: Plenum. https://doi.org/10.1007/978-1-4899-1179-7.

Smith, Eric A. 1988. "Risk and Uncertainty in the 'Original Affluent Society': Evolutionary Ecology of Resource Sharing and Land Tenure." In *Hunters and Gatherers: History, Evolution, and Social Change,* ed. T. Ingold, D. Riches, and J. Woodburn, 222–252. Oxford, UK: Berg Publishers.

Speth, John D. 2004. "The Henderson Site." In *Life on the Periphery: Economic Change in Late Prehistoric Southeastern New Mexico,* ed. J. D. Speth, 4–66. Memoirs No. 37. Ann Arbor: Museum of Anthropology, University of Michigan.

Speth, John D., S. D. Emslie, and S. Olson. 2004. "The Henderson Birds." In *Life on the Periphery: Economic Change in Late Prehistoric Southeastern New Mexico,* ed. John D. Speth, 298–304. Memoirs No. 37. Ann Arbor: Museum of Anthropology, University of Michigan.

Spier, Leslie. 1933. *Yuman Tribes of the Gila River.* Chicago, IL: University of Chicago Press.

Stevenson, Matilda Coxe. 1915. *Ethnobotany of the Zuni Indians.* Thirtieth Annual Report of the Bureau of American Ethnology, 1908–1909, 35–102. Washington, DC: Bureau of American Ethnology.

Thoms, Alston V. 2008. "Ancient Savannah Roots of the Carbohydrate Revolution in Southcentral North America." *Plains Anthropologist* 53(205):121–136. https://doi .org/10.1179/pan.2008.008.

Vuković, Jasna. 2011. "Early Neolithic Pottery from Blagotin, Central Serbia: A Use-Alteration Analysis." In *Beginnings: New Research in the Appearance of the Neolithic between Northwest Anatolia and the Carpathian Basin*, ed. R. Krauß, 205–211. Rahden, Germany: Verlag Marie Leidorf.

Waddell, Jack O. 1980. "The Use of Intoxicating Beverages among the Native Peoples of the Aboriginal Greater Southwest." In *Drinking Behavior among Southwestern Indians*, ed. Jack O. Waddell and Michael W. Everett, 1–32. Tucson: University of Arizona Press.

Wandsnider, LuAnn. 1997. "The Roasted and the Boiled: Food Composition and Heat Treatment with Special Emphasis on Pit-Hearth Cooking." *Journal of Anthropological Archaeology* 16(1):1–48. https://doi.org/10.1006/jaar.1997.0303.

Whalen, Michael E., and Paul E. Minnis. 2001. *Casas Grandes and Its Hinterland: Prehistoric Regional Organization in Northwest Mexico*. Tucson: University of Arizona Press.

Whalen, Michael E., and Paul E. Minnis. 2009. *The Neighbors of Casas Grandes: Excavating Medio Period Communities of Northwest Chihuahua, Mexico*. Tucson: University of Arizona Press.

Zingg, Robert. 2001. *Behind the Mexican Mountains*, ed. H. Campbell, J. Peterson, and D. Carmichael. Austin: University of Texas Press.

# Northern Periphery

# 13

# The Northern Frontier in the History of the Greater Southwest

JAMES R. ALLISON

The northern frontier of the Southwest was occupied prehistorically by people archaeologists lump into two broad groups under the labels of *Fremont* or *Virgin*, or variants of those names. My goal is to provide an introduction to the archaeology of these areas and to put forward some ideas about how those areas, and the people who lived in them, relate to broad trends in the history of the Greater Southwest. In particular, I focus on two main processes: (1) the spread of maize horticulture west to southeastern Nevada and north to the shores of the Great Salt Lake, and (2) changes that occurred in the Fremont and Virgin regions contemporaneous with (and probably in response to) the expansion of the Chaco regional system. These changes included population increases, population movement, and the development of regional trade networks.

Fremont and Virgin peoples occupied a vast area to the north and northwest of the region most Southwestern archaeologists today think of as the Southwest (figure 13.1). The Fremont and Virgin areas straddle the Colorado Plateau and the eastern Great Basin, and include almost all of Utah, the northwest corner of Arizona, and portions of eastern Nevada. This large region is highly diverse

DOI: 10.5876/9781607327356.c013

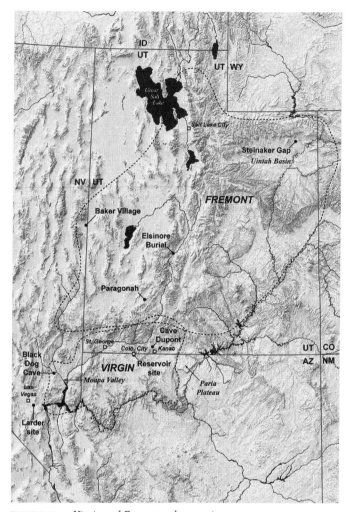

**FIGURE 13.1.** *Virgin and Fremont culture regions.*

geographically, and Fremont and Virgin peoples each had their own complex history. But for many centuries the northern frontier of the Southwest was home to large and stable populations of prehistoric farmers who interacted with other Southwestern peoples and shared a number of traits with them. Settlement types and architecture vary, but most Virgin people lived in small settlements that usually included one or a few habitation rooms, each with a series of attached storage rooms. A few larger sites are known (e.g., Allison 1988:17–27; Lyneis 1992), but even the largest settlements in the Virgin region probably never housed more than a few dozen residents. Virgin people made and painted pottery that shows clear ties to their neighbors in the Kayenta region to the east, and they have generally been seen as the westernmost extension of Anasazi or Ancestral Pueblo populations. Despite the apparent implications of considering the Virgin region part of the Ancestral Pueblo world, Virgin people may also be ancestral to non-Pueblo tribes such as the Southern Paiute. Similarly, links between Fremont people and modern tribes are unclear, and they too may have both Pueblo and non-Pueblo descendants.

Many Fremont settlements are also small, but a few large villages have been excavated; figure 13.2A, for instance shows a portion of the large village at Paragonah excavated by UCLA in the 1950s (Meighan et al. 1956; Ure 2013:97–115). This part of the village has recently been acquired by the Archaeological Conservancy, and still includes some impressive mounds, but not the now-destroyed mound Neil Judd (1919, 1926) called "The Big Mound" (figure 13.2B), which was located about 200 m to the southwest. In contrast to Virgin ceramics, Fremont painted pottery does not closely follow Ancestral Pueblo design traditions. Instead, Fremont designs have their own distinct style (Richards, chapter 19, this volume), but are still clearly within the Southwestern tradition.

Early Southwestern archaeologists had no doubt that the Fremont and Virgin were part of the Greater Southwest. When William Henry Holmes (1886) wrote the first-ever synthesis of prehistoric Southwestern pottery, Virgin pottery from the Saint George Basin in southwestern Utah was an important source of data, and Kidder (1924:141, 163) shows the limits of the "Southwestern culture area" extending west into southeast Nevada and north to the Great Salt Lake, with what we would now call the Fremont and Virgin regions labelled as the *Northern Peripheral* culture area. At least through the 1950s it was common to refer to the Fremont and Virgin areas as the *Northern Periphery* of the Southwest, but some Fremont archaeologists (e.g., Fowler and Jennings 1982:111) objected strongly to what they saw as a derogatory term.

In the latter part of the twentieth century, the combination of increasing specialization, archaeological politics, and distance from the core areas of the Southwest led Fremont archaeology to be aligned with Great Basin archaeology, and most archaeologists ceased to perceive it as part of the Southwest. At the same time, Virgin-region archaeology has had a liminal status—not fully integrated with either Great Basin or Southwestern archaeology, and rarely noticed except by the few archaeologists who work in the region.[1] Fremont archaeology, on the other hand, has come to have its own particular character.

Despite abundant evidence for maize-based horticulture, as Fremont archaeology came to be Great Basin archaeology it came to be dominated by theoretical perspectives that are most often, and most appropriately, applied to hunter-gatherers (Allison 2008a). Some widely read syntheses on Fremont archaeology underestimate the importance of farming in the region (e.g., Madsen 1979; 1982:217) or emphasize subsistence variability in ways that have been read (or misread) as minimizing the extent of farming (e.g., Madsen and Simms 1998). This

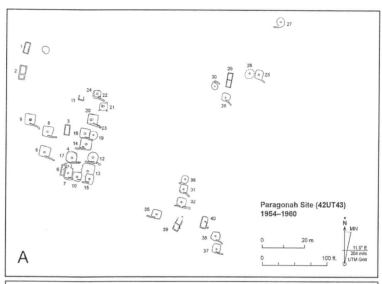

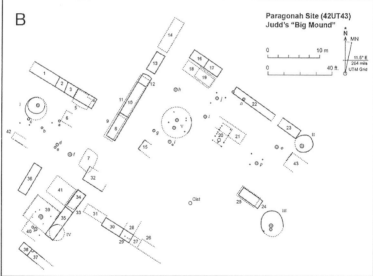

**FIGURE 13.2.** *Map of the Fremont site Paragonah. A: village segment excavated by UCLA in the 1950s; B: segment known as "The Big Mound." The Big Mound was located about 200 m southwest of the UCLA excavations, but uncertainties in the field maps make it difficult to combine the two maps.*

has led some archaeologists to perceive the Fremont as "reluctant" or "sporadic" farmers, essentially hunter-gatherers who grew a little maize on the side. That may accurately describe some Fremont, but many others lived in permanent settlements, including some very large villages, and were as committed to maize farming as most Southwestern people.

Variability in subsistence and settlement is an important aspect of Fremont archaeology, and even sedentary Fremont farmers hunted and used wild plants, as did farmers throughout the Greater Southwest. But it has become common for archaeologists to describe the Fremont by quoting or paraphrasing Madsen and Simms's (1998:323) assertion that "there were full-time sedentary farmers, full-time mobile foragers, sedentary foragers, seasonal farmer/foragers,and people who could have been all of these at one time or another in their lives." I have argued elsewhere (Allison 2008a:71–76) that parts of that statement are undoubtedly true, but other parts are probably wrong, or at best are unproven (the presence of sedentary foragers) or difficult to impossible to test archaeologically (the idea that people switched often and fluidly between full-time farming and full-time foraging). But even if Madsen and Simms's statement could be shown to be true, it fails to get us very far toward understanding where and when, or why, Fremont people practiced these different subsistence strategies.[2] The use of that assertion of extreme variability as a quasi-synthesis of Fremont subsistence practices arguably has caused archaeologists to deemphasize strong patterns in where and when Fremont people farmed.

## THE EXTENT AND DATING OF FARMING IN THE NORTHERN FRONTIER

Figure 13.3 comes from a database that includes 219 radiocarbon dates on maize from the Fremont and Virgin regions, and another 58 dates on human skeletal remains with stable carbon isotope ratios that indicate heavy reliance on C4 plants.[3] The earliest maize dates from the region, from Jackson Flat near Kanab, currently appear to be outliers, although there is no reason to doubt their accuracy. They are discussed by Roberts (chapter 16, this volume).

Maize occurs consistently from about 2100 radiocarbon years BP (roughly 100 BC), but in relatively low amounts for more than 1,000 years, before spiking dramatically between 1050 and 900 radiocarbon years BP. The spike in maize dates, which probably reflects both population growth and increases in maize dependence, occurs contemporaneously with the Pueblo II period in the northern Southwest—the main spike in dates is after about AD 900 and probably mostly after AD 1000—and the decline in maize dates begins about AD 1150. Fremont and Virgin farming probably ends by AD 1300 (Allison 2010a), although figure 13.3 includes two maize dates between 700 and 600 BP that may reflect a later persistence of farming in some areas.

At the peak of maize horticulture, farming villages could be found as far north as the northeastern shore of the Great Salt Lake and the Uintah Basin of northeastern Utah, and maize was grown as far west as the Las Vegas Valley and Baker Village near Great Basin National Park.

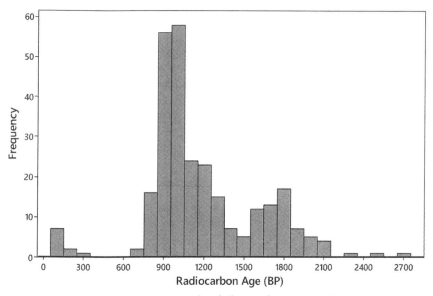

**FIGURE 13.3.** *Radiocarbon dates associated with the use of maize agriculture in the Fremont and Virgin regions.*

It took a long time for maize to spread north to the Great Salt Lake. Figure 13.4 depicts the spread with a series of maps, at intervals of 100 radiocarbon years, cumulatively adding sites from which we have direct dates on maize or on human remains with high-C4 diets indicating maize consumption. Before 2200 radiocarbon years BP (figure 13.4A), or roughly 250 BC, maize is present on the southeast side of the Colorado River (Geib 2011:212–213; Smiley 1997), at the Alvey Site in the Glen Canyon area (Geib 1996), and at Jackson Flat near Kanab (Roberts, chapter 16, this volume). By 2100 radiocarbon years BP (approximately 100 BC) maize is dated from two more sites (figure 13.4B), widely separated from each other and from the core area in southeastern Utah. One of these is the Elsinore Burial (Wilde and Newman 1989; Wilde et al. 1986), near the Sevier River in central Utah; the other is the Larder Site in the Las Vegas Valley (Ahlstrom 2008:96; chapter 15, this volume). This suggests the possibility that maize did not exactly spread across the region, but rather was introduced by small groups of farmers leapfrogging into a few particular locations; it may also be that the first maize farmers came into the Las Vegas Valley from the south rather than the east.

The Elsinore Burial is a clear outlier, although it may not be as old as previously thought. The site is a deeply buried bell-shaped pit discovered during construction of Interstate 70 in the 1980s. The human remains were accompanied by maize cobs that appear to have been accidentally incorporated into the fill. A radiocarbon date of 2140 ± 100 BP (Wilde and Newman 1989) is usually

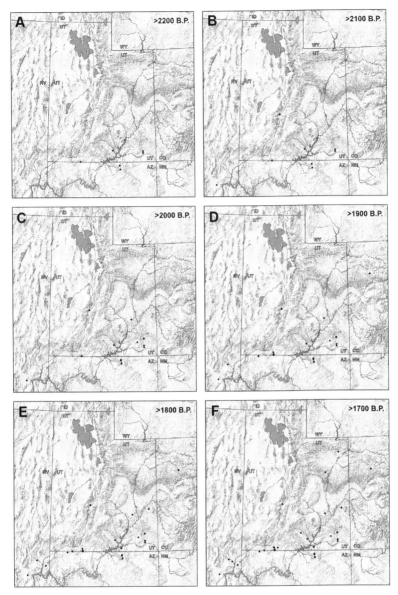

**FIGURE 13.4.** *Sites exhibiting radiocarbon dates on maize or on human remains with high-C4 diets indicating maize consumption, from before 2200 BP to 1700 BP.*

cited as the oldest evidence for maize in the Great Basin; it is, for example, the basis of Grayson's (2011:329) statement that "corn was being grown in . . . central Utah by 200 B.C." But the dated material was "a collection of corn cobs (mixed with less than 10% charcoal)," with a δ13C value of -14.15 (Wilde and Newman

1989:714). The inclusion of charcoal would bias the date to be slightly early, and the reported date also has a large error term. Recent (and not yet published) dating of maize and human remains from the site suggest that the burial more likely dates to the first century A D, about two centuries later than implied by the 2140 B P date. (Using only the new dates and ignoring the original one published by Wilde and Newman would mean the site should first appear in figure 13.4D here, although I have left it on the maps in figures 13.4B and 13.4C.)

Moving forward in time to 1800 radiocarbon years B P (or about A D 225–250; figure 13.4E) fills in some gaps across the southern part of the area without much evidence for a northward spread. The exception is the date of 1940 ± 40 B P from Eagle Point Rock Shelter in northwestern Colorado mentioned by Gardner and Gardner (2016:193) that may represent early experimentation with maize on the margins of the Fremont area. But by 1700 B P (i.e., by about A D 300; figure 13.4F), some people in the Uintah Basin were apparently making a substantial commitment to maize (Talbot and Richins 1996; Talbot 2000). The earliest occupation level at the Steinaker Gap Site comprised numerous bell-shaped pits associated with two small irrigation ditches and is radiocarbon dated to approximately A D 300 or slightly earlier (Talbot and Richins 1996:81–82). Bone chemistry on two sets of human remains (with radiocarbon dates of 1780 ± 39 and 1790 ± 60 B P) indicates both individuals had diets high in C4 plants: δ13C values were -11.2 and -11.9 (Coltrain 1996:118). The lack of unequivocal habitation structures at the site suggests a relatively high degree of mobility, but the labor invested in ditch construction and the level of maize consumption indicated by the bone chemistry shows that farming was not merely a casual activity.

Some of the early farming sites in the Virgin region are worth discussing in more detail, particularly the important clusters of Basketmaker II–aged sites along the Arizona–Utah state line near Kanab and Hildale/Colorado City, and the site of Black Dog Cave, in the Moapa Valley of southeastern Nevada.

Near Kanab there are both open sites and rockshelters that date to this time period. The best-known of the shelters is Cave du Pont (Nusbaum 1922), which is the westernmost site that is generally accepted as being Basketmaker II (Matson 1991:29–31). Like many Basketmaker II shelters farther east, Cave du Pont contained numerous slab-lined cists, and perishable materials from the site are similar to those from classic Basketmaker II sites in the Marsh Pass area. When Kidder and Guernsey (1922) reported the artifacts from Nusbaum's Cave du Pont excavations, they noted a number of similarities to those found in their earlier Marsh Pass work (Guernsey and Kidder 1921; Kidder and Guernsey 1919). Among other things, they specifically noted the crook-handled "digging-sticks" and an S-shaped stick (Kidder and Guernsey 1922:113–115), both of which are good Basketmaker II diagnostics. Square-toed sandals are another similarity that Marsh Pass Basketmaker II sites share with Cave du Pont.

The Basketmaker II–aged sites near the Utah–Arizona state line also include open sites with pithouses. Near the twin cities of Colorado City, Arizona, and Hildale, Utah, several deeply buried sites date from this time period (e.g., Berg et al. 2003; Naylor 1996; Nielson 1998), the largest known of which is the Carling Reservoir site (Walling-Frank 1998), where excavations found 12 aceramic pit houses in an area about 60 m × 60 m. The pit houses varied in size and construction: two of the larger ones had benches, and one had large postholes for a four-post roof support system. Unfortunately, only four of the structures were dated, and those dates are all on charcoal, so it is unclear how many of these structures were in use at the same time.

In contrast to the perishables from the Basketmaker II caves in the Virgin region, the projectile points from the Carling Reservoir Site mostly do not look like typical Basketmaker II points. Instead, a number of them are similar to Gypsum points, typically dated to the Late Archaic period (figure 13.5).

Much farther west, in the Moapa Valley of southeastern Nevada, Black Dog Cave includes a number of slab-lined cists associated with abundant maize remains (Winslow 2003). Radiocarbon dates (including a maize date of 1910 ± 40 BP), indicate that the site is contemporary with the Basketmaker II period (Winslow 2003:521–522). Like Cave DuPont, Black Dog Cave has perishable artifacts, including S-shaped sticks (Winslow 2003:362–370) and square-toed sandals (Winslow 2003:308–315), that appear to be typical Basketmaker II diagnostics. So, based on the perishables, Black Dog Cave appears to be not just Basketmaker II aged, but legitimately Basketmaker II (whatever that actually means in terms of cultural affiliation).

On the other hand, as at the Carling Reservoir site, most of the projectile points do not appear to be typical Basketmaker II dart points. The dart points include some identified as Elko Series points that might fall within the range of Basketmaker II points, but others were leaf-shaped or stemmed (figure 13.5). The contradictory evidence from the perishables and the projectile points might mean that these far-western Basketmaker II populations incorporated a mixture of immigrants and local groups, but that is probably overinterpreting scanty evidence.

From 1700 through 1400 BP, the area from which we have well-dated evidence of maize horticulture increases only slightly (figure 13.6A–C), but between 1400 and 1300 radiocarbon years BP (i.e., probably in the late AD 600s; figure 13.6D) maize is found at several different locations in Utah Valley and the Salt Lake Valley, and essentially reaches its maximum northward distribution.

Based on these radiocarbon dates, it appears that maize horticulture reached the Uintah Basin, its northern limit on the Colorado Plateau, 300 years or more before farming began at comparable latitudes in the eastern Great Basin, although it is not clear why this would have happened. It may be that the apparent late spread of maize into the Utah and Salt Lake Valleys is misleading, and

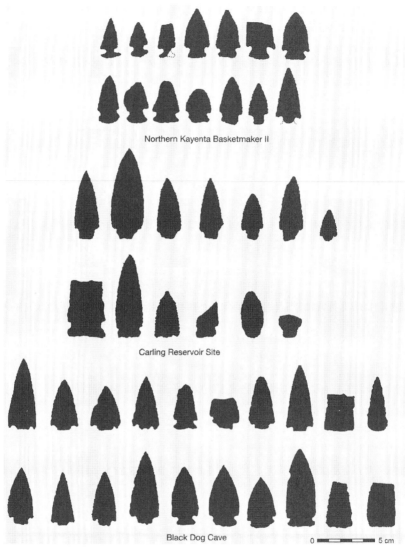

Northern Kayenta Basketmaker II

Carling Reservoir Site

Black Dog Cave

0 ▬▬▬ 5 cm

**FIGURE 13.5.** *A comparison of projectile points from the Northern Kayenta Basketmaker II period (redrawn from photos in figure 5.37 in Geib 2011:272), from the Carling Reservoir Site (redrawn from figures 10.9 and 10.10 in Nielson 1998), and from Black Dog Cave (redrawn from figures 34–36 in Winslow 2003:329–334).*

that archaeologists simply have not yet documented sites with maize that date just as early as the earliest maize in the Uintah Basin.[4]

From the AD 600s until sometime close to AD 1300, maize farming is widespread across both the Virgin and Fremont areas (figure 13.6E), and many

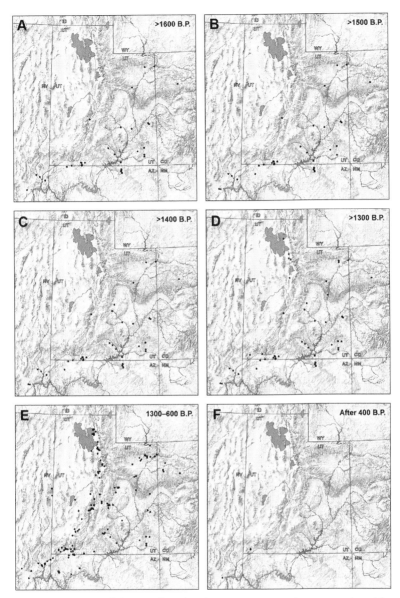

**FIGURE 13.6.** *Sites exhibiting radiocarbon dates on maize or on human remains with high-C4 diets indicating maize consumption, from before 1600 BP to after 400 BP.*

sites have substantial architecture along with abundant and diverse artifact assemblages, indicating a strong commitment to horticulture and a relatively sedentary lifestyle. After AD 1300, sites are fewer and less substantial, and there is no evidence of horticulture except in the southwest corner of the region.

The first European explorers found Southern Paiutes growing maize and other crops in well-watered spots in the Mohave Desert (Allison et al. 2008; Fowler 1995; Fowler and Fowler 1981), and several samples of archaeological maize with dates between 300 and 50 radiocarbon years BP provide additional evidence of Paiute farming both before and after the first European contact in the late eighteenth century (figure 13.6F). It is possible that maize horticulture persisted in the Mohave Desert on a very small scale after its disappearance elsewhere in the region, but there is no direct evidence that maize was grown between about AD 1300 and the protohistoric period, and it is likely that ancestral Paiute farming resulted from a late reintroduction of the practice.

## CONNECTIONS AND DISCONNECTIONS

Once maize horticulture became established across the Northern Frontier, Virgin and Fremont populations remained connected to the Greater Southwest, but the strength and nature of the connections varied. Ceramic styles, trade networks, and changes in population size and distribution provide clues about the changing nature of the relationship, although given the large geographic scales involved, the brief description that follows is necessarily oversimplified and somewhat speculative.

Several authors have recently noted both the dramatic changes that occurred in the Fremont world at about AD 1000 (Lekson 2014; Janetski and Talbot 2014) and the coincidence of these events with the "explosive geopolitics of the eleventh century" (Lekson 2014:116) that accompanied expansion of the Chaco system.

The rise of Chaco influenced events far beyond the distribution of outlying great houses and beyond the political, economic, and ideological connections materialized in Chacoan architecture. Life in the Northern Frontier was transformed by the rise of Chaco, although the effects were indirect. The Fremont and Virgin regions were not incorporated into the Chacoan sphere, but as Chaco's scope increased, some people avoided its clutches by moving away, swelling populations in distant areas, filling previously uninhabited lands, and forging new and transformed connections between the Fremont and Virgin worlds and the Greater Southwest.

### Pueblo I/Early Pueblo II Isolation

To understand the changes that occurred in the tenth and eleventh centuries, it helps to go back to Pueblo I times (approximately AD 750–900). At that time, the Virgin region seems to become disconnected from Puebloan populations to the east, at least judging from ceramic design styles. During Basketmaker III times, painted Virgin bowls have Lino-style designs that resemble contemporary styles in the Kayenta region. But starting sometime around AD 800 or a little before, Virgin painted designs diverge strongly from Kayenta designs. In part this is because Virgin painted designs change more slowly and remain

Lino-like well into the Pueblo I period, long after Kana-a style becomes popular in the Kayenta region. But potters in the Virgin region also develop their own design style, which is most obvious in the use of distinct across-the-bowl layouts (figure 13.7). Fremont ceramics suggest that region was even more loosely connected with the Four Corners region; no Fremont pottery is painted until after AD 900 or 1000. Also, neither Virgin nor Fremont potters adopted the neck-banded grayware styles that were popular during Pueblo I times across the Four Corners region.

These stylistic differences develop at a time when long distances separated Virgin and Fremont populations from their nearest Southwestern neighbors in the Mesa Verde and Kayenta regions. During Pueblo I times, a large area near the Colorado River was largely or entirely uninhabited. In southeastern Utah, Cedar Mesa was heavily populated in Basketmaker III times but was depopulated by the 700s (Matson et al. 1988). A large Pueblo I population spread across the Mesa Verde region to the eastern edge of Cedar Mesa, but no one lived in the triangle formed by the confluence of the Colorado and San Juan Rivers (Allison et al. 2012; Lipe 1970; Matson et al. 1988).

Geib (1996:112–113) argues that a 30–60-km-wide no-man's land separated Fremont and Anasazi populations in the Glen Canyon region, and interprets that as evidence of an ethnic boundary. Similarly, west of the Colorado River, there is little evidence of Pueblo I settlement on the Paria Plateau in the eastern part of the Arizona Strip. Mueller (1974) used ceramics to assign 27 of the sites recorded by the Museum of Northern Arizona's Paria Plateau Survey to the Basketmaker III/Pueblo I time period, but since the collections included exactly one Pueblo I (Kana-a style) painted sherd, this almost certainly represents a Basketmaker III rather than Pueblo I occupation. The vacant Paria Plateau area suggests that the no-man's land extended farther south beyond the Glen Canyon region and also isolated the Virgin region from their closest Puebloan neighbors.

The stylistic differences that differentiate Pueblo I and early Pueblo II Virgin and Kayenta ceramics are probably both a result of this isolation and part of the boundary-reinforcing behavior that caused it.

### Filling In and Connecting

All this changes in the eleventh century. Previously vacant areas rapidly filled with farmers who appear to have come from the east. The hundreds of Pueblo II sites recorded by the Paria Plateau survey all appear to postdate AD 1000 (Mueller 1974), and the collections include almost 5,000 Pueblo II painted sherds (in contrast to the one Pueblo I painted sherd). Similarly, Cedar Mesa, the Red Rock Plateau, and the Glen Canyon region in general are reoccupied in the 1000s (Geib 1996; Lipe 1970; Matson et al. 1988). At the same time, the number of sites increased within the Fremont and Virgin core area, and populations grew

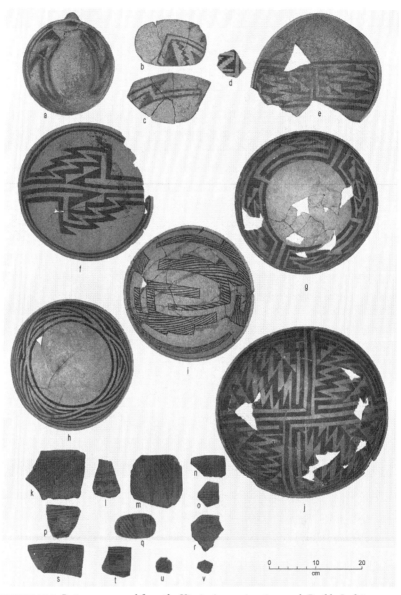

**FIGURE 13.7.** *Pottery recovered from the Virgin Anasazi region: a–d, Pueblo I whiteware designs; e–f examples of across-the-bowl layouts on whiteware bowls; g–j examples of late Pueblo II/Pueblo III whiteware designs; k–o Shinarump Red Ware; p–r Tsegi Orange Ware; s–v San Juan Red Ware. (The bowls designated g and j are included courtesy of the Natural History Museum of Utah: UMNH Nos. 42WS164FS22.1 and 42WS164FS20.1, respectively. All others are courtesy of the Museum of Peoples and Cultures, Brigham Young University.)*

dramatically. The peak in the number of radiocarbon dates after AD 1000 (figure 13.3) reflects this population increase.

As the formerly uninhabited areas filled in, the Virgin region became less isolated. After AD 1050, design styles on painted ceramics strongly resemble the Sosi and Dogoszhi styles that are common in the Kayenta region, and Virgin potters begin corrugating grayware vessels as potters in the Four Corners region had been doing for some time. Ceramic exchange also brings San Juan Red Ware and Tsegi Orange Ware, both made east of the Colorado River, into the Virgin region for the first time. These trade wares are never common, but they consistently represent about one percent of post-1050 ceramic assemblages across the Virgin region as far west as southeastern Nevada (Allison 2008b).

In the Fremont world, painted Black-on-gray or Black-on-white ceramics first occur after AD 900, and possibly not until AD 1000. Fremont designs have their own distinct style, but they usually incorporate the same kinds of design elements (interlocking scrolls, triangles embellished with dots) found on early Pueblo II types in the Four Corners region such as Red Mesa or Cortez Black-on-white (Richards 2014). Small amounts of San Juan Red Ware, Tsegi Orange Ware, and whitewares from the Mesa Verde region found as far north as the Uintah Basin (e.g., at Caldwell Village [Ambler 1966]) also demonstrate increased connectedness with the Four Corners area.

### Immigrant Ceramic Producers

The filling in of the pre-Chaco no-man's land that isolated the Fremont and Virgin regions must have resulted from population movement or expansion, but where did those people come from? Shifts in where redware ceramics were made suggest some of them came from what is now southeastern Utah.

Beginning about AD 750, San Juan Red Ware is widely distributed across the Four Corners area, but it is by far most abundant on Pueblo I sites in southeastern Utah: on some sites more than 25 percent of the pottery is San Juan Red Ware. This distribution along with other evidence, including neutron activation analysis (Allison 2010b; Allison and Ferguson 2015; Hegmon et al. 1997), demonstrates that San Juan Red Ware was produced within a limited area in the western Mesa Verde region. But within this area production appears to have been widespread.

Although suitable clays are found in other areas, redware production remained spatially restricted for almost three centuries. Potters living within the western Mesa Verde production zone made redware vessels for their own use and they supplied them to widely dispersed consumers. But starting around AD 1000 or 1025, San Juan Red Ware production declines, and Tsegi Orange Ware begins to be made in the northern Kayenta area, south of Navajo Mountain. Despite the difference in the color terms, San Juan Red Ware and Tsegi Orange Ware are both made with orange clays and typically have a red slip. The wares are distinguished by differences in where they are made, and by the use of sherd temper in Tsegi Orange Ware rather than the igneous rock temper used in San Juan Red Ware. The fact that one is called *red* and the other *orange* is an artifact of the history of ceramic typology and does not reflect a meaningful distinction.

The earliest Tsegi Orange Ware type, Medicine Black-on-red, is decorated with designs identical to those on the contemporary San Juan Red Ware type, Deadmans Black-on-red. By the late 1100s, Tusayan Black-on-red, a Tsegi Orange Ware type with hachured Dogoszhi-style designs becomes common. Redware production in the western Mesa Verde region had almost ceased by this time, but the latest San Juan Red Ware (still called Deadmans Black-on-red despite stylistic changes similar to the ones that led to the definition of Tusayan Black-on-red as a distinct type within Tsegi Orange Ware), is decorated in the same style as Tusayan Black-on-red. From AD 1000 until San Juan Red Ware production ends at about AD 1100 the two wares are part of the same stylistic tradition, and the only significant technological difference is in the choice of tempering material.

Then, by the late 1000s, Shinarump Red Ware production begins in the eastern part of the Virgin region. Again, stylistically Shinarump Red Ware is like contemporary San Juan Red Ware or Tsegi Orange Ware, although the raw materials used are different.

San Juan Red Ware production appears to have been restricted to a specific social or possibly ethnic group (albeit a group large enough to spread across much of the western Mesa Verde region), and the shift in the location of redware production appears to reflect the movement of this social group out of southeastern Utah.

A similar population movement may be responsible, in part, for the origins of Fremont painted pottery, although this is less clear. While Fremont painted ceramics in general use design elements similar to early Pueblo II types, there are more specific similarities between Ivie Creek Black-on-white, one of the Fremont painted types, and White Mesa Black-on-white. White Mesa Black-on-white is a type made in the western part of the Mesa Verde region, in southeastern Utah, beginning in late Pueblo I times. The type shares some traits with the more widespread Mesa Verde Pueblo I and early Pueblo II types (Piedra Black-on-white and Cortez Black-on-white), but is distinct in several ways, including the fine-line work of its designs, the frequent use of dots as filler (common on Basketmaker III pottery but rare after that, except in White Mesa Black-on-white designs), and the fact that it occurs almost exclusively as bowls. Few White Mesa bowls are complete enough to show the design layout, but those that do tend to have banded designs divided into panels by vertical lines, sometimes with the corners filled by triangles embellished with dots—a layout indistinguishable from the Fremont design style described by Richards (2014; chapter 19, this volume).

White Mesa Black-on-white stops being made sometime close to AD 1000, at about the same time that Ivie Creek Black-on-white starts to be made in the southeastern part of the Fremont world. Like White Mesa, Ivie Creek Black-on-white vessels are always bowls, and Ivie Creek designs frequently use dots as filler. Other similarities between the types are more subjective, and systematic comparison of the two types needs to be done. But the advent of Ivie Creek Black-on-white may result from people moving out of the western Mesa Verde region, bringing a distinctive ceramic tradition with them.

## Focusing In

Paradoxically, as the Fremont and Virgin regions absorbed migrants and became more connected to other Southwestern populations, they also focused inward. Janetski et al. (2011) describe a Fremont interaction sphere "spatially defined by a unique style" (Janetski et al. 2011:47), incorporating similarities in rock art, figurines, ornaments, and ceramic decoration, and distinct from neighboring regions. Within the interaction sphere, goods and raw materials from the Fremont region, including ceramics, lignite beads, and obsidian, circulated widely, along with turquoise and marine-shell beads that entered the Fremont world from the west. Trade in these items predates the eleventh century, but it greatly intensified with the rapid population increases that occurred around AD 1000.

In the Virgin region, ceramic trade intensifies after AD 1050. In particular, Moapa Gray Ware and Shivwits Plain ceramics produced in upland areas north of the Grand Canyon circulate within the Virgin region, especially to settlements in the low deserts of southeastern Nevada (Allison 2000; Harry et al. 2013; Lyneis 1992; Sakai 2014). Other items that circulated within the Virgin region included marine shell, as well as turquoise from mines in southeastern Nevada or the California desert (Allison 2000; Lyneis 1992). Salt was mined in southeastern Nevada (Harrington 1927, 1930) and cotton grown there (Harrington 1937), and these items probably were traded as well.

Marine shell and turquoise may have crossed from the Virgin area into the Fremont region, but other items were rarely traded across the boundary. Several obsidian sources are found in the eastern Great Basin, and obsidian is common on Fremont sites, but it is rare in the Virgin region. And, as figure 13.8 shows, the most widely traded ceramic types in the Virgin and Fremont regions are rare on the other side of the Virgin/Fremont boundary.

## Chaco Wannabes or Chaco Escapees?

So what does all this mean? Major changes occurred across the Northern Frontier within a few decades of AD 1000. Populations increased, former no man's lands were settled, redware potters moved west, apparently en masse, and

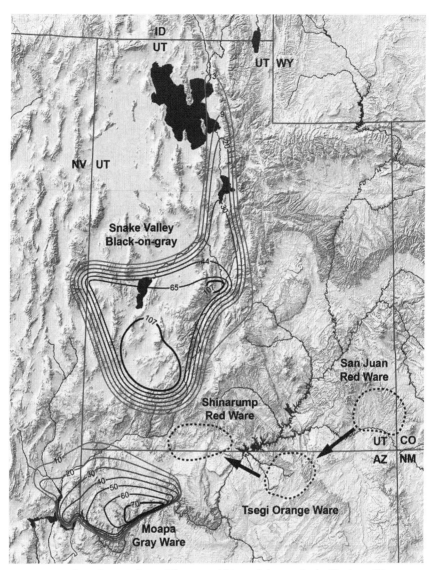

**FIGURE 13.8.** *Distribution of two of the most widely traded wares in the Virgin and Fremont areas. Also shown are the presumed production locations of San Juan Red Ware, Tsegi Orange Ware, and Shinarump Red Ware. (Contour lines for Snake Valley Black-on-gray are based on Janetski et al. 2011; the contour lines represent the number of sherds per residential structure recovered from excavated sites. The data for Moapa Gray Ware are based on Allison 2000; the contour lines represent the percentage of Moapa Gray Ware within total ceramic assemblages from both excavated sites and surface collections.)*

the Fremont and Virgin regions connect to the Four Corners region in new ways while simultaneously turning their back (metaphorically) on the Four Corners by intensifying intraregional interactions. All this happens just as the Chaco system expands north of the San Juan River, into what are now southeastern Utah and southwestern Colorado.

One possibility is that Fremont and Virgin people saw what Chaco had to offer, and wanted to emulate it and participate in it as much as they could given their distance from the center. That might explain why the connections to the Four Corners region become so much stronger in the eleventh century. But I don't think that's what happened.

What Chaco actually represents politically, religiously, and economically is notoriously unclear, but whatever it was, the Chaco system was expanding aggressively, making new converts by force or persuasion. There was much work to be done: great houses to build, roads to clear, ritual landscapes to sculpt, trees and goods to carry to the center, not to mention all the normal tasks required to maintain life as a subsistence-level farmer. People had to be convinced to do this work, again either by force or persuasion. By force might mean making slaves of people living just beyond the boundaries of the system, or it might mean requiring those living within the reach of the system to contribute a certain amount of labor. Persuasion is possible too; people often contribute labor to religious organizations or other causes they believe in.

Whichever it was, some people are likely to have wanted to avoid the expanding system. Even if labor was organized through persuasion or social pressure without overt force, not everyone would have been persuaded. And reasons for wanting to avoid forced labor are obvious. The evidence for population movement out of southeastern Utah coincident with, or just ahead of, the establishment of great houses there suggests that the Chaco expansion north of the San Juan River created something like a shatter zone in areas farther north and west.

Shatter zones are typically ethnically and linguistically diverse regions characterized by heterodox and syncretic religious practices and resistance to political authority. Shatter zones form "wherever the expansion of states, empires, slave-trading, and wars, as well as natural disasters, have driven large numbers of people to seek refuge in out-of-the-way places" (Scott 2009:8). Scott (2009) describes a large shatter zone in the hill country of southeast Asia historically populated largely by people avoiding the taxes and forced labor of city states in the lowland valleys. In that case, some people prefer the security of living within a state system and farming rice, and they willingly acquiesce to the demands of the state, while others are forced into compliance. Still other people escape to the hills, giving up rice farming for a less sedentary life growing maize or foraging.[5]

In suggesting that the Northern Frontier of the Southwest became a shatter zone, I am not suggesting that Chaco was a state (and certainly not an empire) or in the business of enslaving captives (although that is possible). But I do think the Chaco system was something that some people wanted to get out of the way of.

## SUMMARY AND CONCLUSION

The Virgin and Fremont regions are on the northern and northwestern periphery of the Greater Southwest, and for a time they were referred to collectively as "the Northern Periphery." Archaeologists studying the Fremont objected to the implications of marginality and rejected both the Northern Periphery label and the idea that the Fremont were strongly influenced by events in the Greater Southwest. The "Northern Frontier of the Southwest" may not seem much better as a label, but there is no escaping the fact that the Fremont and the Virgin were on the frontier, and many aspects of their archaeology reflect their status as borderlands, where linguistic and social groups mixed and farmers lived side-by-side with hunter-gatherers. But from the introduction of maize to the end of farming, happenings in the Four Corners region affected the lives of Fremont and Virgin peoples.

Maize was introduced from the south and spread north as far as the eastern shore of the Great Salt Lake. The spread of maize farming probably involved both in-migration of farmers and adoption of farming by indigenous hunter-gatherers and their descendants. Some early farming sites in the Virgin region have perishables reminiscent of the classic Kayenta-region Basketmaker II sites but with projectile points that resemble the points used by local late Archaic hunter-gatherers rather than those found on the classic Basketmaker II sites. This mixture of traits might reflect a mixture of local people and immigrants among the residents of those sites, although the evidence is not definitive.

By the Pueblo I period, if not earlier, both the Virgin and Fremont regions became isolated from the Ancestral Pueblo people in the Four Corners region, separated from them by an uninhabited area. But driven by the Chaco expansion, people settled the uninhabited areas and probably moved beyond them to compete for already-occupied places, sometimes displacing the residents. Population grew rapidly in both the Fremont and Virgin regions probably as a result of both immigration and in situ population growth.

As the formerly unoccupied areas filled, the Northern Frontier became less isolated. With input from immigrants arriving from the Four Corners area, painted pottery was made for the first time in the Fremont region, and Virgin ceramic designs became much more like those of the Kayenta region. But the Fremont and Virgin regions remained culturally and economically independent, and distinct from each other, developing broad interaction spheres and exchange networks. The effects of the Chaco expansion on the Northern Frontier were far reaching, but rather than being seduced by Chaco's powerful influence, Fremont and Virgin people reacted against Chaco.

The Northern Frontier was an important part of the history of the Greater Southwest, although thus far I have only discussed influences out from the Four Corners region, and not how the Virgin or Fremont may have influenced other Southwestern peoples. After the changes wrought by the Chaco expansion, life in the Northern Frontier zone was relatively stable for the next 150 years or so. Not entirely uneventful of course, but there are no indications of major influences from the rest of the Southwest. Then in the 1200s, driven by a combination of deteriorating climate and social unrest, people moved out of the Four Corners region. The Virgin and Fremont traditions both ended close to this time (Allison 2010a). Farming ended and populations declined to almost nothing. Small remnant populations may have remained in place as foragers, and some Fremont may have moved north (Ortman 2014). But many people probably moved from the Northern Frontier to the Four Corners region or farther south, contributing to the social unrest that plagued the Mesa Verde region in the 1200s, or helping build new communities in the south.

## ACKNOWLEDGEMENTS

Many of the ideas in this chapter were inspired by, or stolen from, colleagues who usually know the archaeology better than me. Winston Hurst, Margaret Lyneis, Joel Janetski, and all the other authors in the Northern Periphery section of this volume have all been particularly influential. Scott Ure and Daniel King created the figures for this chapter.

## NOTES

1. Lyneis (1995) provides a good summary of Virgin archaeology as of the early 1990s, but more recent work is not well synthesized.

2. It may be useful to imagine defining a "Southwestern Complex," without regard to any culture-historical categories. Parallel to Madsen and Simms's (1998) definition of the "Fremont Complex," this "Southwestern Complex" would include all Southwestern farmers plus all foragers whose behavior was affected by living "within the matrix of farming communities." That viewpoint would probably be useful in some ways, but the existence of variable subsistence strategies within the hypothetical "Southwestern Complex" would be trivially true—a matter of definition rather than a distinguishing feature of Southwestern farmers. Similarly, matters of definition play a large role in perceptions of Fremont subsistence variability.

3. The database relies in part on the earlier compilation of Fremont radiocarbon dates by Berry and Berry (2001) and an unpublished database of Utah radiocarbon dates put together by Richard Talbot with the help of several BYU students. It also includes a large number of not-yet-published dates on maize from my recent fieldwork with BYU archaeological field schools in the Virgin region and at the Fremont site of Wolf Village, as well as from dating maize from previously excavated Fremont sites that has

been curated in museum collections. Also, 35 unpublished dates on human remains with evidence of diets high in C4 plants were provided by Derrina Kopp of the Utah Division of State History, and were added to dates from high-C4 human remains published by Coltrain and Leavitt (2002). The dated skeletal remains included in the database have $\delta13C$ values that range from -5.5 to -13.5.

4. One possible early maize site is excluded from my analysis because no maize from the site has been directly dated. At the Prison Site (Nicoll et al. 2014; Yentsch and Rood 2007; Yentsch et al. 2009), located in the southern part of the Salt Lake Valley, test excavations uncovered a late Archaic housepit and several other features, including one that may be another housepit. These features were associated with radiocarbon dates ranging from 1720 to 2450 BP. Residue analysis of groundstone and fire-cracked rock using Fourier Transform Infrared Spectroscopy (FTIR) found numerous matches consistent with the presence of maize, and several "maize-type rondels" were identified during phytolith analysis (Cummings and Yost 2009). No datable charcoal was preserved on the site, however, so the radiocarbon dates are all on bulk soil samples, and no maize macrofossils or pollen were found.

5. Scott's book length treatment has been criticized as too generalizing and overly simplistic. My one paragraph summary is certainly much worse on both counts, but the concept of a shatter zone seems like a useful way to think about events distant from Chaco but resulting from its expansion.

## REFERENCES

Ahlstrom, Richard V.N., ed. 2008. *Persistent Place: Archaeological Investigations at the Larder and Scorpion Knoll Sites, Clark County Wetlands Park, Nevada.* HRA Papers in Archaeology No. 7. Las Vegas, NV: HRA, Inc., Conservation Archaeology.

Allison, James R. 1988. *The Archaeology of Yellowstone Mesa, Mohave County, Arizona.* Museum of Peoples and Cultures Technical Series No. 88–24. Provo, UT: Brigham Young University.

Allison, James R. 2000. *Craft Specialization and Exchange in Small-Scale Societies: A Virgin Anasazi Case Study.* Unpublished PhD dissertation, Department of Anthropology, Arizona State University, Tempe. Ann Arbor, MI: University Microfilms International.

Allison, James R. 2008a. "Human Ecology and Social Theory in Utah Archaeology." *Utah Archaeology* 21:57–88.

Allison, James R. 2008b. "Shinarump Red Ware and other Red Wares North and West of the Colorado River." *Pottery Southwest* 27(1):21–34.

Allison, James R. 2010a. "The End of Farming in the 'Northern Periphery' of the Southwest." In *Leaving Mesa Verde: Peril and Change in the Thirteenth Century Southwest,* ed. Timothy A. Kohler, Mark D. Varien, and Aaron M. Wright, 128–155. Tucson: University of Arizona Press.

Allison, James R. 2010b. *Animas-La Plata Project*, Volume XIV: *Ceramic Studies*. SWCA Anthropological Research Paper No. 10, Vol. 14. Phoenix, AZ: SWCA Environmental Consultants.

Allison, James R., and Jeffrey R. Ferguson. 2015. "Neutron Activation Analysis of San Juan Red Ware Pottery." Poster presented at the 80th Annual Meeting of the Society for American Archaeology, San Francisco, CA.

Allison, James R., Winston B. Hurst, Jonathan D. Till, and Donald C. Irwin. 2012. "Meanwhile, in the West: Early Pueblo Communities in Southeastern Utah." In *Crucible of Pueblos: The Early Pueblo Period in the Northern Southwest*, ed. Richard H. Wilshusen, Gregson Schachner, and James R. Allison, 35–52. Los Angeles: Cotsen Institute of Archaeology Press, University of California.

Allison, James R., Cathryn M. Meegan, and Shawn S. Murray. 2008. "Archaeology and Archaeobotany of Southern Paiute Horticulture in the Saint George Basin, Southwestern Utah." *Kiva* 73(4):417–449. https://doi.org/10.1179/kiv.2008.73.4.003.

Ambler, J. Richard. 1966. *Caldwell Village. Anthropological Papers No. 84*. Salt Lake City: University of Utah Press.

Berg, Adam M., Stewart Deats, Doug Drake, Joshua S. Edwards, Dennis Gilpin, Jim Hasbargen, Michael O'Hara, and Gordon F. M. Rakita. 2003. *Prehistoric Occupation of the Confluence Valley between the Vermillion Cliffs and Short Creek: Archaeological Investigations of 16 Sites for the Hildale Wastewater Treatment Facility, Hildale, Utah, and Colorado City, Arizona*. SWCA Cultural Resources Report No. 5241-083. Flagstaff, AZ: SWCA Environmental Consultants.

Berry, Michael S., and Claudia F. Berry. 2001. "An Archaeological Analysis of the Prehistoric Fremont Culture for the Purpose of Assessing Cultural Affiliation with Nine Claimant Tribes." Report prepared for the Bureau of Reclamation, Upper Colorado Regional Office, Salt Lake City, UT.

Coltrain, Joan Brenner. 1996. "Stable Carbon and Radioisotope Analysis." In *Steinaker Gap: An Early Fremont Farmstead*, by Richard K. Talbot and Lane D. Richins, 115–122. Museum of Peoples and Cultures Occasional Papers No. 2. Provo, UT: Brigham Young University.

Coltrain, Joan Brenner, and Steven W. Leavitt. 2002. "Climate and Diet in Fremont Prehistory: Economic Variability and Abandonment of Maize Agriculture in the Great Salt Lake Basin." *American Antiquity* 67(3):453–485. https://doi.org/10.2307/1593822.

Cummings, Linda Scott, and Chad Yost. 2009. "Pollen, Starch, Phytolith, and Organic Residue Analysis (FTIR) of Artifacts and Feature Fill From Site 42SL186, Salt Lake Valley, Utah." In *Archaeological Investigations at the Prison Site (42SL186)*, by Andy T. Yentsch, Ronald J. Rood, Kevin T. Jones, and Lindsay A. Fenner, Appendix D. Antiquities Section Selected Papers, No. 17. Salt Lake City: Utah Division of State History.

Fowler, Catherine S. 1995. "Some Notes on Ethnographic Subsistence Systems in Mojavean Environments in the Great Basin." *Journal of Ethnobiology* 15(1):99–117.

Fowler, Catherine S., and Don D. Fowler. 1981. "The Southern Paiute: A.D. 1400–1776." In *The Protohistoric Period in the North American Southwest, AD 1450–1700*, ed. David R. Wilcox and W. Bruce Masse. Anthropological Research Papers No. 24. Tempe: Arizona State University.

Fowler, Don D., and Jesse D. Jennings. 1982. "Great Basin Archaeology: A Historical Overview." In *Man and Environment in the Great Basin*, ed. David B. Madsen and James F. O'Connell, 105–120. Washington, DC: Society for American Archaeology Papers No. 2.

Gardner, A. Dudley, and William R. Gardner. 2016. "Fremont Farming: The Nature of Cultivation in Northwestern Colorado, 2000–500 BP." In *Late Holocene Research on Foragers and Farmers in the Desert West*, ed. Barbara J. Roth and Maxine E. McBrinn, 188–213. Salt Lake City: University of Utah Press.

Geib, Phil R. 1996. *Glen Canyon Revisited. Anthropological Paper No. 119*. Salt Lake City: University of Utah.

Geib, Phil R. 2011. *Foragers and Farmers of the Northern Kayenta Region: Excavations along the Navajo Mountain Road*. Salt Lake City: University of Utah Press.

Grayson, Donald K. 2011. *The Great Basin: A Natural Prehistory*. Berkeley: University of California Press.

Guernsey, Samuel J., and Alfred V. Kidder. 1921. *Basket-Maker Caves of Northeastern Arizona*. Papers of the Peabody Museum of American Archaeology Vol. 8, No. 2. Cambridge, MA: Harvard University.

Harrington, Mark R. 1927. "A Primitive Pueblo City in Nevada." *American Anthropologist* 29:262–277. https://doi.org/10.1525/aa.1927.29.3.02a00050.

Harrington, Mark R. 1930. "Introduction." In *Archaeological Explorations in Southern Nevada*, by Mark Harrington, 4–25. Southwest Museum Papers No. 4. Los Angeles, CA: Southwest Museum.

Harrington, Mark R. 1937. "Ancient Nevada Pueblo Cotton." *Masterkey* 11:5–7.

Harry, Karen, Timothy J. Ferguson, James R. Allison, Brett T. McLaurin, Jeff Ferguson, and Margaret M. Lyneis. 2013. "Examining the Production and Distribution of Shivwits Ware Pottery in the American Southwest." *American Antiquity* 78(2):385–396. https://doi.org/10.7183/0002-7316.78.2.385.

Hegmon, Michelle, James R. Allison, Hector Neff, and Michael Glascock. 1997. "Production of San Juan Red Ware in the Northern Southwest: Insights into Regional Interaction in Early Puebloan Prehistory." *American Antiquity* 62(3):449–463. https://doi.org/10.2307/282165.

Holmes, William H. 1886. *Pottery of the Ancient Pueblos. Fourth Annual Report of the Bureau of Ethnology*. Washington, DC: Smithsonian Institution.

Janetski, Joel C., Cady B. Jardine, and Christopher N. Watkins. 2011. "Interaction and Exchange in Fremont Society." In *Perspectives on Prehistoric Exchange in California and the Great Basin*, ed. Richard E, Hughes, 22–54. Berkeley: University of California Press.

Janetski, Joel C., and Richard K. Talbot. 2014. "Fremont Social Organization: A Southwestern Perspective." In *Archaeology in the Great Basin and Southwest: Papers in Honor of Don D. Fowler*, ed. Nancy J. Parezo and Joel C. Janetski, 118–129. Salt Lake City: University of Utah Press.

Judd, Neil M. 1919. *Archaeological Investigations at Paragonah, Utah*. Miscellaneous Collections 70(3):1–22. Washington, DC: Smithsonian Institution.

Judd, Neil M. 1926. *Archaeological Observations North of the Rio Colorado*. Bulletin 82. Washington, DC: Bureau of American Ethnology.

Kidder, Alfred V. 1924. *An Introduction to the Study of Southwestern Archaeology*. New Haven, CT: Yale University Press.

Kidder, Alfred V., and Samuel J. Guernsey. 1919. *Archaeological Explorations in Northeastern Arizona*. Bulletin 65. Washington, DC: Bureau of American Ethnology.

Kidder, Alfred V., and Samuel J. Guernsey. 1922. "Notes on the Artifacts and on Foods." In *A Basket-Maker Cave in Kane County, Utah*, by Jesse L. Nusbaum, 64–153. Indian Notes and Monographs. New York: Museum of the American Indian.

Lekson, Stephen H. 2014. "Thinking about Fremont: The Later Prehistory of the Great Basin and Southwest." In *Archaeology in the Great Basin and Southwest: Papers in Honor of Don D. Fowler*, ed. Nancy J. Parezo and Joel C. Janetski, 109–117. Salt Lake City: University of Utah Press.

Lipe, William D. 1970. "Anasazi Communities in the Red Rock Plateau, Southeastern Utah." In *Reconstructing Prehistoric Pueblo Societies*, ed. William A. Longacre, 84–139. Albuquerque: University of New Mexico Press.

Lyneis, Margaret M. 1992. *The Main Ridge Community at Lost City: Virgin Anasazi Architecture, Ceramics, and Burials*. Anthropological Paper No. 117. Salt Lake City: University of Utah.

Lyneis, Margaret M. 1995. "The Virgin Anasazi, Far Western Puebloans." *Journal of World Prehistory* 9(2):199–241. https://doi.org/10.1007/BF02221839.

Madsen, David B. 1979. "New Views on the Fremont: The Fremont and the Sevier: Defining Prehistoric Agriculturalists North of the Anasazi." *American Antiquity* 44(4):711–722. https://doi.org/10.2307/279110.

Madsen, David B. 1982. "Get It Where the Gettin's Good: A Variable Model of Great Basin Subsistence and Settlement Based on Data from the Eastern Great Basin." In *Man and Environment in the Great Basin*, ed. David B. Madsen and James F. O'Connell, 207–226. SAA Papers No. 2. Washington, DC: Society for American Archaeology.

Madsen, David B., and Steven R. Simms. 1998. "The Fremont Complex: A Behavioral Perspective." *Journal of World Prehistory* 12(3):255–336. https://doi.org/10.102 3/A:1022322619699.

Matson, R. G. 1991. *The Origins of Southwestern Agriculture.* Tucson: University of Arizona Press.

Matson, R. G., William D. Lipe, and William R. Haase. 1988. "Adaptational Continuities and Discontinuities: The Cedar Mesa Anasazi." *Journal of Field Archaeology* 15(3):245–263.

Meighan, Clement W., Norman E. Coles, Frank D. Davis, Geraldine M. Greenwood, William M. Harrison, and E. Heath MacBain. 1956. *Archeological Excavations in Iron County, Utah. Anthropological Papers No. 25.* Salt Lake City: University of Utah.

Mueller, James W. 1974. *The Use of Sampling in Archaeological Survey. Memoirs No. 28.* Washington, DC: The Society for American Archaeology.

Naylor, Laird P., II. 1996. "A Geoarchaeological Evaluation of Corral Canyon, Mohave County, Arizona." Unpublished MA thesis, Northern Arizona University, Flagstaff.

Nicoll, Kathleen, Andrew T. Yentsch, Kevin T. Jones, and Ronald J. Rood. 2014. "Site Formation and Archaic Geoarchaeology along the Jordan River, Great Salt Lake Valley, Utah USA." *Quaternary International* 342:214–225. https://doi.org/10.1016/j .quaint.2013.08.044.

Nielson, Asa S., compiler. 1998. *Excavation/Mitigation Report: Three Sites near Hildale, Utah: 42WS2195, 42WS2196, AZ B:1:35 (BLM) (Reservoir Site).* Research Report No. 98-8. Orem, UT: Baseline Data.

Nusbaum, Jesse L. 1922. *A Basket-Maker Cave in Kane County, Utah.* Indian Notes and Monographs. New York: Museum of the American Indian. https://doi.org/10.5479 /sil.941359.39088015037575.

Ortman, Scott. 2014. "Evidence of Historical Relationships between Pueblo and Fremont Peoples." Paper presented at the 14th Southwest Symposium, January 10–11, 2014, Las Vegas, NV.

Richards, Katie K. 2014. "Fremont Ceramic Designs and Their Implications." Unpublished MA thesis, Department of Anthropology, Brigham Young University, Provo, UT.

Sakai, Sachiko. 2014. *Explaining Change in Production and Distribution of Olivine-Tempered Ceramics in the Arizona Strip and Adjacent Areas in the American Southwest.* PhD dissertation, Department of Anthropology, University of California, Santa Barbara, CA. Ann Arbor, MI: University Microfilms International.

Scott, James C. 2009. *The Art of Not Being Governed: An Anarchist History of Southeast Asia.* New Haven, CT: Yale University Press.

Smiley, Francis E. 1997. "Toward Chronometric Resolution for Early Agriculture in the Northern Southwest." In *Early Farmers in the Northern Southwest: Papers on Chronometry, Social Dynamics, and Ecology*, ed. Francis E. Smiley and Michael R. Robins, 13–42. Animas-La Plata Archaeological Research Paper No. 7. Flagstaff: Northern Arizona University.

Talbot, Richard K. 2000. "Fremont Farmers: The Search for Context." In *The Archaeology of Regional Interaction: Religion, Warfare, and Exchange across the American Southwest and Beyond*, ed. Michelle Hegmon, 275–293. Boulder: University Press of Colorado.

Talbot, Richard K., and Lane D. Richins. 1996. *Steinaker Gap: An Early Fremont Farmstead.* Museum of Peoples and Cultures Occasional Papers No. 2. Provo, UT: Brigham Young University.

Ure, Scott M. 2013. "Parowan Valley Potting Communities: Examining Technological Style in Fremont Snake Valley Corrugated Pottery." Unpublished MA thesis, Department of Anthropology, Brigham Young University, Provo, UT.

Walling-Frank, Barbara. 1998. "AZ B:1:35 (BLM): The Carling Reservoir Site." In *Excavation/Mitigation Report: Three Sites near Hildale, Utah: 42WS2195, 42WS2196, AZ B:1:35 (BLM) (Reservoir Site),* compiled by Asa S. Nielson, 6.1–6.90. Research Report No. 98-8. Orem, UT: Baseline Data.

Wilde, James D., and Deborah E. Newman. 1989. "Late Archaic Corn in the Eastern Great Basin." *American Anthropologist* 91(3):712–720. https://doi.org/10.1525/aa.1989.91.3.02a00120.

Wilde, James D., Deborah E. Newman, and Andrew E. Godfrey. 1986. *The Late Archaic/Early Formative Transition in Central Utah: Pre-Fremont Corn from the Elsinore Burial, Site 42SV2111, Sevier County, Utah. Museum of Peoples and Cultures Technical Series No. 86-20.* Provo, UT: Brigham Young University.

Winslow, Diane L. 2003. *Black Dog Cave Archaeological Complex (26CK5686/BLM 53-7216),* Volume II: *Black Dog Cave.* HRC Report 5-4-26. Harry Reid Center for Environmental Studies and Marjorie Barrick Museum of Natural History, University of Nevada, Las Vegas.

Yentsch, Andrew T., and Ronald J. Rood. 2007. "The Prison Site: Evidence for Late Archaic Housepits in the Salt Lake Valley." *Utah Archaeology* 20(1):41–56.

Yentsch, Andrew T., Ronald J. Rood, Kevin T. Jones, and Lindsay A. Fenner. 2009. *Archaeological Investigations at the Prison Site (42SL186). Antiquities Section Selected Papers, No. 17.* Salt Lake City: Utah Division of State History.

# 14

# Changing Patterns of Interaction and Identity in the Moapa Valley of Southern Nevada

KAREN G. HARRY

For more than a thousand years, the Moapa Valley—located approximately 80 km (50 miles) northeast of Las Vegas—was home to people participating in what is generally considered the westernmost expression of prehistoric puebloan lifeways. Appearing in the archaeological record at about AD 200, these people were members of what archaeologists refer to as the Virgin Branch Puebloan (VBP) culture. They maintained thriving, albeit fluctuating, trade and interaction networks with people of surrounding areas until about AD 1200 to 1250, when they appear to have abandoned the region. This chapter traces the origin, development, and decline of the Lowland VBP culture in the Moapa Valley and its adjacent areas, with an emphasis on exploring the changes in identity that occurred over time and the shifting patterns of interaction with neighboring people that transpired.

## BACKGROUND

The Moapa Valley is drained by the Muddy River, a tributary of the Virgin River (figure 14.1). Prehistorically, this area was at the interface of several

DOI: 10.5876/9781607327356.c014

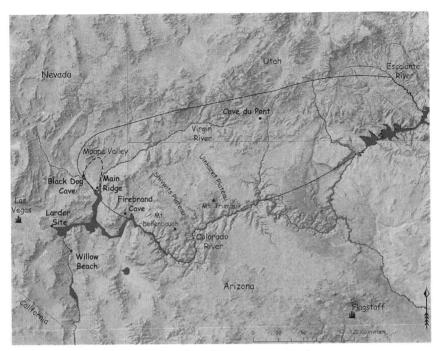

**FIGURE 14.1.** *Map of sites and geographical features discussed in the text.*

environmental and cultural zones. To the north and west lived nomadic hunters and gatherers of the Great Basin; to the northeast were the horticultural
Fremont people; to the south were Ancestral Yuman-speaking farmers who cultivated the Colorado River floodplain; and to the east lived the agriculturally
based Kayenta of the Ancestral Puebloan culture, who farmed the Colorado
Plateau uplands. Archaeological sites are found along the Muddy River's entire
51 km (32 miles) stretch, though the heaviest concentrations occur at the valley's southern end where the two rivers meet. Here, the floodplain stretches
as wide as a mile and a half, providing rich agricultural lands for VBP farmers.
Environmentally, the Moapa Valley is situated at the interface of the Mojave
Desert and the Great Basin ecoregions. At only 360 m (1,180 feet) above sea level,
the valley is characterized by mild winters and hot summers. Rainfall is scarce
with precipitation averaging less than 12 cm (4.7 inches) a year. Away from the
floodplain the landscape is stark, dotted by scattered vegetation consisting of
creosote bush, bursage, and cacti. Along the floodplains, in contrast, the vegetation is lush. There, mesquite, willows, cottonwoods, cattails, and various
grasses can be found. Animals include jackrabbits, cottontails, rodents, desert
tortoises, chuckwallas, migratory water fowl, amphibians, and reptiles. Bighorn
sheep inhabit the red rock formations located about 13 km (8 miles) west of the

floodplain; and higher-elevation resources, including pinyon nuts and deer, can be found in the Virgin Mountains located about 32 km (20 miles) to the east. Other resources that would have been available to the ancient inhabitants of the Moapa Valley include chert nodules, which can be found in the river terrace gravels, and salt, which was mined prehistorically in caves found along the valley edge.

Compared to other areas of the US Southwest, the VBP region has experienced little modern archaeological research. Numerous large-scale surveys and excavations have been carried out in the Moapa Valley, but these were conducted in the early twentieth century, prior to the advent of modern archaeological techniques (for a review of these projects see Harry 2009; Harry et al. 2008; and Shutler 1961). These projects resulted in the excavation of nearly 200 archaeological sites and remain the best source of information we have regarding the VBP culture. Nonetheless, their resulting data have some important limitations. Following the standards of the time, early excavators focused on recovering intact or reconstructible museum-quality pieces. Systematic screening and artifact recovery were lacking, and field notes were of variable quality. Further, nearly all of the identified sites and architectural features were excavated, leaving behind few remains for later study.

Today there exist few intact archaeological remains in the Moapa Valley. Most sites not excavated by early archaeologists have been damaged or destroyed by pothunting, erosion, farming activities, or modern development. Still others lie buried beneath the waters of Lake Mead. Projects conducted in recent decades (for example, Harry 2008; Harry and Watson 2010; Lyneis 1992, 2012; Myhrer and Lyneis 1985) have tended to be small in scale and involved data recovery from sites that otherwise were compromised by earlier excavation or pothunting activities. This archaeological history of the Moapa Valley has resulted in a relatively unique situation for researchers. On the one hand, there exist thousands of artifacts in museum collections; at the same time, however, a paucity of systematic data are available and there exist significant gaps in our knowledge. With this background in mind, the following sections consider what is known regarding the origin, development, and decline of the VBP culture. Because understanding its origin and development requires that we first understand what preceded it, I begin with a review of what is known about the Archaic-period occupation of the region.

## PALEOARCHAIC AND ARCHAIC PERIODS

The recovery of a single fluted point near the northern end of the Moapa Valley indicates that the area was visited, albeit sporadically, during the Paleoarchaic period (Roth 2012:88). Diagnostic artifacts, consisting of Great Basin stemmed dart points, indicate that human use of the region steadily increased over the

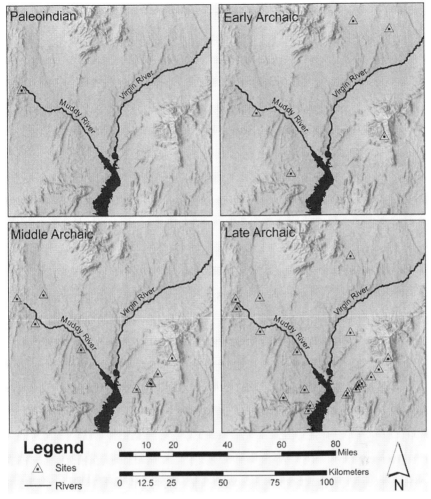

**FIGURE 14.2.** *Distribution of Paleoarchaic and Archaic sites in the region. (Adapted from Roth 2012:figures 5.1, 5.3–5.4 and 5.7.)*

course of the Archaic period (figure 14.2). By the Late Archaic, Lyneis (1995:207) suggests that "a pre-Basketmaker tradition" can be identified that spanned from the California deserts to the eastern Grand Canyon, and which included the VBP region. This tradition is represented by a shared material culture that included split-twig figurines and Gypsum-style dart points.

In southern Nevada the Late Archaic witnessed a substantial growth in population and a shift in settlement patterns (Roth 2012). Whereas in the Middle Archaic period, sites in southern Nevada were clustered around springs in upland locations, by the Late Archaic they were increasingly concentrated in lowland locales. In the Moapa Valley, this meant that site density in the vicinity of the Virgin and Muddy Rivers increased. Population density was higher than it had ever been before, as indicated by the larger number of sites and greater density of deposits. Data from Late Archaic sites that have been excavated in the study region suggest a generalized foraging lifestyle similar to that found elsewhere in the western deserts (Roth 2012). In contrast to Late Archaic sites in the Mojave Desert, however, Roth (2012:114) finds no evidence that Late Archaic populations living in the Moapa Valley participated in extensive exchange systems.

## BASKETMAKER PERIODS

Early researchers assigned several aceramic pithouse sites in the Moapa Valley to the Basketmaker II culture (Harrington 1937, 1953; Schroeder 1973), however, as Lyneis (1995:207–208) has noted, its occurrence this far west has not been universally accepted. Cave du Pont, located some 170 km northeast of the Lowland Virgin region, has been until recently the farthest-west site to be widely accepted as Basketmaker II (Matson 1991:31). This viewpoint has been overturned in the last dozen years with the recovery of new data from the site of Black Dog Cave, located on the Muddy River (see figure 14.1). First excavated in the 1940s, the site was the focus of additional excavations in 2000 and 2001, which included, for the first time, radiocarbon dating of its remains (Winslow and Blair 2003a, 2003b; Winslow 2009), with additional radiocarbon analyses of its remains being conducted in 2011 (Gilreath 2011). These recent projects demonstrated that by at least the end of the first century AD, the inhabitants of Black Dog Cave were growing maize and using material objects similar to those used by Basketmaker II inhabitants of the Colorado Plateau.

Artifacts recovered from Black Dog Cave consistent with those found at other Basketmaker II sites include basketry produced using a close-coiled, two-rod-and-bundle non-interlocking stitch; twined square-toe/square-heel sandals; slab-lined storage cists; two-ply Z-twist cordage; spindle whorls; and S-shaped fending sticks (Winslow and Blair 2003b; Winslow 2009). The abrupt appearance of these remains and their similarity to those recovered from Basketmaker sites to the east have led many archaeologists to accept Shutler's (1961:65) argument that these technologies, along with farming technology and corn itself, were introduced into the valley by founding populations of farmers originating from the western Colorado Plateaus (Gilreath 2011; Lyneis 2008:170–171; Winslow and Blair 2003b:241). According to this viewpoint, the descendants of these Basketmaker immigrants remained in the area and established what would become known to archaeologists as the Lowland Virgin culture.

Several new lines of evidence, though, are now converging to suggest that this scenario may not be correct. First, and perhaps most important, new information from heritable dental traits contradicts the notion that the Lowland Virgin

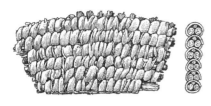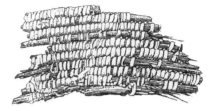

**FIGURE 14.3.** *Two-rod-and-bundle coiled basketry fragments recovered from southern Nevada. A: Basketry from Firebrand Cave, radiocarbon dated to 1890 to 1115 BC. (Reproduced from Winslow 2006:figure 5.) B: Basketry from Black Dog Cave. (Reproduced from Winslow and Blair 2003b:figure 7.)*

people descended from Basketmaker groups from the east. Instead, those data link the Lowland VBP people to an ancestral population that was genetically closer to Great Basin groups than to any group, including Basketmakers, from the Greater Southwest (Harry and Watson 2016). Second, as Ahlstrom (chapter 15, this volume) discusses, early dates obtained from maize recovered from the Larder site raise the possibility that agriculture was introduced into southern Nevada from the south rather than from the east. The Larder site is located on the Las Vegas Wash, a tributary of the Colorado River (see figure 14.1). Maize from that site has been radiocarbon dated to between 350 and 50 BC, or some 100 to 200 years older than the earliest dates for corn in the Moapa Valley (Ahlstrom 2008). The location of the Larder site, 85 km southwest of Black Dog Cave but only 25 km east of the Colorado River, raises the possibility that corn was introduced first into the Las Vegas Valley from the south and from there transmitted to the Moapa Valley.

Finally, an early date obtained on a two-rod-and-bundle coiled basketry (figure 14.3A) fragment from Firebrand Cave (see figure 14.1) calls into question the assumption that this so-called quintessential Basketmaker trait necessarily reflects the presence of Basketmaker populations. When found in early contexts on the Colorado Plateau this type of basketry has long been considered a Basketmaker diagnostic, and it was the presence of several of these remains (i.e., see figure 14.3B) that served as a primary line of evidence that Black Dog Cave had been settled by Basketmaker immigrants (Winslow and Blair 2003b:241). Two-rod-and-bundle coiled basketry is associated with Basketmaker sites across the Colorado Plateau, although it is most dominant in the Kayenta-Tsegi region where "it exists practically to the exclusion of other coiled structures" (Teague and Washburn 2013:32). Despite its prevalence on Basketmaker sites, there is no evidence for two-rod-and-bundle coiled basketry on the Colorado Plateau prior to the advent of agriculture (Teague and Wasburn 2013:32). However, there *is* evidence of such basketry just 40 km southeast of the Moapa Valley, at Firebrand

Cave. There, a radiocarbon date of 1890 to 1115 BC was obtained on a two-rod-and-bundle basketry fragment (Blair and Winslow 2006:25), which is the oldest direct date to be been obtained on any such basketry (Webster 2008:20).

These new data have important implications for our models concerning the origin and spread of the Basketmaker II culture. Specifically, the data contradict the notions that (1) Black Dog Cave was settled by Basketmaker II immigrants from the Colorado Plateau, (2) these immigrants were responsible for introducing agriculture into the valley, and (3) the transmission of Basketmaker II culture was unidirectional, with the flow of material culture and ideas moving only from the east to the west. Instead, I propose that the appearance of the Basketmaker culture in the Moapa Valley was an in situ development that resulted when descendants of local Archaic-period populations, who were culturally and genetically related to Great Basin hunter-gatherer groups, adopted agriculture and new forms of material culture. Their decision to initiate farming would have been encouraged by their increasing use of the Moapa Valley floodplain in the Late Archaic period, and by their presumed interaction with contemporary hunter-gatherer-farmers of the Las Vegas Valley. (See Allison, chapter 13, this volume, for a related but slightly different interpretation of far western Basketmaker II origins.)

Under this model, both the crop seeds and the knowledge of farming technology would have originated from the southern deserts rather than from the eastern plateaus. Although unproven, this idea is consistent with what we know about the farming conditions of the Moapa Valley and other regions. The few inches of annual precipitation that the Moapa Valley receives are insufficient for dry farming. Agriculture would have required the use of irrigation, something that would have been enabled by the reliable flow of the spring-fed Muddy River. During the period that Black Dog Cave was occupied, however, farmers on the Colorado Plateau practiced floodwater farming and therefore are unlikely to have been the source of irrigation knowledge. Irrigation was, however, being practiced in the southern Arizona deserts during this time, making it likely that southern Nevada's agriculture originated in the latter area (see also Ahlstrom and Roberts 2012 for a similar argument regarding a southern origin for agriculture in the Moapa Valley).

Further support for this hypothesis comes from the presence of cotton fibers found on a spindle whorl recovered from Basketmaker contexts of Black Dog Cave (Winslow and Blair 2003b:303). Since cotton was not cultivated in the northern Southwest until after AD 1100 (Ford 1981:354), the presence of these fibers demonstrates the existence of some type of interaction—either direct or indirect—between the Moapa Valley and the Hohokam region during this period. Additional, albeit quite tentative, support is found in attributes of the maize itself. To investigate the origin of corn in the Moapa Valley, Sagmiller

(1998) measured some 55 corncobs and their kernels recovered from Black Dog Cave. His measurements align the corn with Onaveno, a subrace of Pima-Papago maize and a type of corn grown by the Hohokam throughout their sequence. Because Onaveno is statistically indistinguishable from Basketmaker corn, the measurements cannot resolve the question of the maize origins. However, notably the cobs from Black Dog Cave were more similar in size and shape to the cobs from Hohokam sites than to those from other Basketmaker sites, which tended to be larger and more cigar-shaped (Sagmiller 1998).

The data also challenge our assumption that the Moapa Valley was merely a passive recipient of the Basketmaker II culture. The Middle Archaic two-rod-and-bundle basket recovered from Firebrand Cave raises the possibility that this technique was transmitted not from the plateaus into the Moapa Valley, but rather the other way around. As Webster (2008:24) has argued,

> the perishable record suggests a more complicated record for Basketmaker II origins [than previously recognized]. Although some western Basketmaker II material culture traditions may derive from the south, others, such as twined sandals, decorated coiled baskets, and hide industries, suggest strong influences from the Great Basin, the northern plateau, or California . . . [The Firebrand Cave basket] suggests the eastern Great Basin or southern California [as the origin for the two-rod-on-bundle basketry technique], as well as some western Basketmaker II populations. The designs and forms of Basketmaker II two-rod-and-bundle coiled baskets from the Kayenta area also suggest affinities to California.

The perishable data summarized by Webster (2008) suggest that the Basketmaker II culture developed out of a variety of influences from a number of directions, one of which was the eastern Great Basin. The Moapa Valley, located between the eastern Great Basin and the westernmost edge of the Colorado Plateau, would have been ideally situated to both receive and transmit ideas and technologies to and from these areas. With the new information regarding the timing of the introduction of agriculture in southern Nevada, the origin of the two rod-and-bundle basketry technique, and the genetic relationships of the Lowland Virgin people, the role of southern Nevada in the development of the Basketmaker II culture must be reconsidered. Rather than simply being the recipient of a transplanted culture, it appears that the Moapa Valley was an integral part of the landscape in which the Basketmaker II culture emerged.

With the adoption of farming a process of identity renegotiation was initiated by the inhabitants of the Moapa Valley. Changes in material culture suggest that they began increasingly to identify with the emerging Basketmaker world rather than that of their ancestors, though in the earliest farming stages connections with both worlds are apparent. For example, of 15 sandals recovered from Black Dog Cave, eight were in the Basketmaker twined square-toe / square-heel style and five were in the Great Basin plain-weave figure-8 style (Winslow and Blair 2003b). By the Basketmaker III period, however, ties with the Basketmaker region predominate. During this period, production of unpainted Logandale Gray Ware ceramics was initiated in the Moapa Valley using the same construction techniques as those used by contemporary potters on the Colorado Plateaus. These ceramics were supplemented by the acquisition of substantial proportions of plain and painted pottery from Basketmaker sites on the Colorado Plateau.

Elsewhere (Harry and Watson 2018), I have argued that these and other shifts observed in the material culture reflect a change in how the Moapa Valley inhabitants viewed themselves and how they wished to be viewed by others. This shift in identity, I have suggested, was triggered by the substantial transformations that accompanied the transition to a farming lifestyle—transformations that would have encouraged the development of social ties with other farmers. Although the idea (and seeds) for farming may have originated far to the south, the nearest intensive farmers lived on the Colorado Plateau. Thus, it was with the Basketmakers (and, later, the Kayenta) that the Moapa Valley inhabitants intensified their interaction and came to share a general identity. Significantly, however, certain aspects of their ancestral heritage—most notably those related to their chipped-stone technology and hunting practices—were retained, not only throughout the Basketmaker periods but throughout the remainder of the VBP sequence. These ancestral practices included an emphasis on heat treatment and bifacial reduction in their chipped-stone technology, and an importance placed on big-game hunting (see Harry and Watson 2018 for a discussion of these issues).

In contrast to the insular nature of the preceding Archaic-period settlements, during the Basketmaker period thriving trade networks characterized the Moapa Valley. Sites contain abundant shell originating from the California coast and the Gulf of California as well as turquoise that, although unsourced, has often been linked by archaeologists to the Halloran Springs mine located some 260 km to the west of the Moapa Valley, or to the Sullivan mine some 100 km to the east (Roberts and Ahlstrom 2012). Finally, as discussed above, regular interaction and exchange with the Colorado Plateau is suggested by the presence of ceramics from that region. These ceramics consist of Moapa Gray Ware and Moapa White Ware, both of which were produced near Mount Trumbull on the Uinkaret Plateau (see figure 14.1). These nonlocal wares, which comprise as much as 40 percent of the pottery from Moapa Valley Basketmaker III sites (Lyneis 2000:263), mark the beginning of a ceramic production and distribution system that would link the Moapa Valley and the western Colorado Plateaus for the next six hundred years. Why so many nonlocal vessels would have been acquired is unknown, though a scarcity of wood for firing pottery may have played a role (Allison 2000:201; Harry 2005:311), as might have a lack of suitable clays for producing painted pottery. The latter possibility arises from experiments conducted by Margaret Lyneis using the only light-colored clays known to exist in the Moapa Valley. Lyneis found that these clays did not react with organic paint to create good black-on-white designs, a fact that she attributed to their mineralogy (Lyneis 2008:171).

## EARLY AND MIDDLE PUEBLOAN PERIODS

For the remainder of the VBP sequence architectural and ceramic trends generally follow those seen in the Kayenta region, though they often lagged temporally. The Pueblo I period is marked by the appearance of aboveground storage rooms and a new style of painted pottery that echoes the Kana'a designs seen in the Kayenta region. Other than these minor changes, however, the Pueblo I occupation of the lowland region appears to have differed little from that of the Basketmaker III period. Settlements remained small and, as reflected by the infrequency of diagnostic Pueblo I pottery, population remained relatively low.

Population reached its peak during the Pueblo II period and, specifically, during the middle portion of that sequence. Following trends seen elsewhere in the puebloan world, aboveground rooms began to replace subterranean rooms as the primary form of habitation structures, though they never fully replaced underground rooms. During this time settlements were concentrated along a ridge in the southern end of the valley to form what is known archaeologically as the Main Ridge community (Lyneis 1992). Containing some 174 rooms and having an estimated population of more than a hundred people (Lyneis 1992:75), Main Ridge is the largest known settlement of its time in the Virgin and Kayenta regions.

Main Ridge was ideally located to participate in trade networks running both north and south and east and west, and the abundance of nonlocal goods recovered from the site suggest that its inhabitants made use of this advantage. As in the Basketmaker III period, turquoise, shell (including both *Haliotis* shell from the coast of California and *Olivella* and *Spondylus* shell from the Gulf of California), and large quantities of Moapa Ware produced on the Uinkaret Plateau (Sakai 2014) regularly flowed into the valley. During the middle Pueblo II period, additional nonlocal wares made their appearance as well. These include San Juan Redwares and Tsegi Orangewares from the Mesa Verde and Kayenta regions, respectively, and Shivwits Ware from the Mount Dellenbaugh region of the western Colorado Plateau (Harry et al. 2013) (see figure 14.1). Although only small quantities of the San Juan Redwares and Tsegi Orangewares appear to have made their way into the valley (they comprise less than 1% of the ceramic collections), sherds from unpainted Shivwits Ware jars comprise about 14 percent of middle Pueblo II ceramic collections (see Lyneis 1992:table 13). When the proportions of Shivwits Ware and Moapa Ware ceramics are combined, the resulting figure indicates that slightly more than a third of the ceramics discarded in the Moapa Valley during this time originated from the Colorado Plateaus (Harry et. al 2013), a figure approximately comparable to the proportion of ceramics acquired from that area during the Basketmaker III period.

Research conducted by Lyneis (2008) into Tusayan Ware Virgin Series ceramics, however, raises the possibility that an even higher proportion of the ceramics from this time period were produced nonlocally. Tusayan Ware Virgin Series pottery consists of sand-tempered ceramics having either white or gray pastes that are believed to have been produced in multiple locations throughout the Virgin Branch region. Tusayan White Ware (TWW) and Tusayan Gray Ware (TGW) Virgin Series ceramics are the most abundant types at VBP sites in the Moapa Valley, making them plausible candidates for local production. However, this commonsense assumption has been challenged by a study conducted by Margaret Lyneis (2008) of the sands contained in Virgin Series ceramics from the sites of Yamashita-2 and Yamashita-3. Lyneis found that none of the TWW Virgin Series sherds contained sands that matched those available near the sites, and only some of the TGW Virgin Series sherds did. The latter ceramics comprised about half of the TGW Virgin Series ceramics from Yamashita-2 but only 15 percent of the same collection from Yamashita-3. These data suggest that all of the whitewares and from between 50 to 85 percent of the graywares at the Yamashita sites may have been nonlocally produced. Chemical sourcing by Ferguson (2014, 2016) further supports the notion that some Tusayan wares were nonlocally produced.

Because Yamashita-3 was occupied slightly later than Yamashita-2, a comparison of the ceramic collections of the two sites yields clues as to the changing nature of the ceramic production and distribution system in the Moapa Valley. Although both sites date to the middle Pueblo II period, Yamashita-2 contains only small proportions of Shivwits Ware ceramics. However, only a few generations later, Yamashita-2 is characterized by a tenfold increase in Shivwits Ware, which is accompanied by a more than fivefold decrease in the locally produced TGW Virgin Series ceramics. Lyneis (2008) proposes that the drop in locally produced ceramics may have been caused by a depletion in firewood, and that the utilitarian Shivwits Ware vessels may have been acquired to offset this loss.

In addition to the appearance of these nonlocal pottery types, other changes also suggest an increased interaction with the Kayenta region during this time. Corrugated pottery, already in use in other Ancestral Puebloan regions, makes its appearance in the Moapa Valley at about AD 1050 and at about this same time new design styles similar to the Black Mesa and Sosi styles of the Kayenta region are introduced. Finally, small but increasing numbers of Kayenta whiteware bowls are incorporated into middle Pueblo II-period ceramic assemblages (Lyneis 2008).

Despite evidence of growing connections with their Kayenta neighbors, the

Lowland VBP people maintained distinctive practices that kept them from being completely subsumed into the Kayenta culture. For example, although the general design elements on VBP pottery are similar to those found in the Kayenta region, how they were placed on the vessels often differed. In contrast to Kayenta potters, VBP potters seldom painted their jars and often adopted an across-the-bowl layout not found in the Kayenta region when decorating their bowls (figure 14.4).

Further, although like the Kayenta the VBP people eventually moved their habitation rooms from subterranean to aboveground structures, unlike the latter they never adopted separate mealing rooms nor anything resembling the kiva structures that have been identified in other Ancestral Puebloan regions (Douglass et al, chapter 11, this volume; Stone, chapter 8, this volume). Elsewhere, I have suggested that the absence of these structures suggests that the Lowland VBP people opted out of at least some of the changing social and ritual practices that were occurring on the Colorado Plateaus (Harry and Watson 2018) and in an intriguing argument, Allison (chapter 13, this volume) more specifically proposes that the differences between the VBP culture and that of other puebloan groups may reflect an intentional rejection of the Chacoan system.

The abundance and diversity of nonlocal goods found in the Moapa Valley (figure 14.5) have led researchers to suggest that during the middle Pueblo II period the Lowland VBP served as middlemen in a trade network that distributed commodities from the California deserts to the Four Corners region (Lyneis 1995; Rafferty 1990). This hypothesis is supported by recent advances in turquoise sourcing that have demonstrated that some of the turquoise recovered from Chaco Canyon originated from southern Nevada. Further, it was found that some of the turquoise recovered from the Moapa Valley archaeological sites originated from mines located as far away as Colorado and New Mexico (Hull et al. 2014). However, despite evidence of extensive trade networks linking the Lowland VBP region with various adjacent regions, there is no indication of any interaction with the Yuman-speaking people who lived along the Colorado River at this time. Despite a Patayan (or ancestral Yuman) presence as far north as Willow Beach (see figure 14.1) by at least AD 900, few or no Yuman ceramics have been recovered from the middle Pueblo II period or earlier contexts in the Moapa Valley.

## LATE PUEBLOAN PERIOD/ABANDONMENT

By the late Pueblo II period, the Main Ridge community was abandoned and settlement had shifted several miles northward in the valley. Coincident with this shift were several notable changes, the most apparent of which was the collapse of the ceramic exchange network that had linked the Moapa Valley with the western Colorado Plateaus since the Basketmaker III period. The breakdown of this network is reflected by the absence or near absence of any Moapa

**FIGURE 14.4.** *Bowl recovered from House 20 in the Moapa Valley, exhibiting the across-the-bowl design typical of the Lowland Virgin region. (National Museum of the American Indian, Smithsonian Institution, catalog no. 137810.000. Photo by NMAI Photo Services.)*

or Shivwits Ware vessels entering the valley during this time. It was accompanied by a growing conservatism by the Lowland VBP people in relation to the Kayenta world; that is to say, the lowland inhabitants no longer tracked the changes occurring in the Kayenta region as closely as they once had. For example, although the Kayenta by this time had ceased completely to use subterranean rooms for habitation purposes, in the Moapa Valley such rooms continued to be inhabited (albeit infrequently) in addition to aboveground structures. Similarly, while the Kayenta adopted new pottery design styles during this time, potters in the Moapa Valley continued to decorate their pottery in designs that had been popular in preceding decades.

Specifically hachuring, as represented by the Dogoszhi style, came to dominate Kayenta pottery designs during the late Pueblo II period. Hachuring also became popular in the upland Virgin Branch areas; from my research on the Shivwits Plateau I have observed that local variants of the Dogoszhi style represent the most frequent design style at late Pueblo II/early Pueblo III sites in that area (see figure 14.6A). However at House 47, a contemporaneous site in the Moapa Valley, the majority of the painted pottery exhibited variants of the Black Mesa or Sosi styles (see figure 14.6B)—styles popular during the middle Pueblo II period. The House 47 inhabitants were clearly aware of the stylistic shifts occurring elsewhere, since redware pottery from the Kayenta region made its way into the settlement, and this pottery was decorated in the hachuring designs

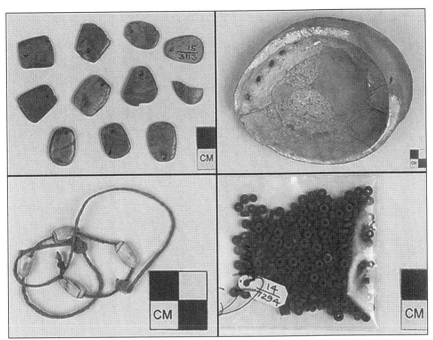

**FIGURE 14.5.** *Nonlocal goods recovered from Moapa Valley Virgin Branch sites. A: turquoise recovered from Mesa House; B: Haliotis shell recovered from Burial Hill; C: cord with Olivella shells recovered from Salt Cave; and D: steatite beads recovered from House 47. (National Museum of the American Indian, Smithsonian Institution, catalog nos. 153113.000, turquoise; 136674.000, shell; 145360.000, cord with Olivella shells; and 147294, steatite beads. Photo by NMAI Photo Services.)*

popular in that area (figure 14.7). The decision not to paint hachured designs, then, must reflect factors other than unfamiliarity with the changing trends of their neighbors.

Although interaction networks with the western Colorado Plateaus were disbanded, other social and exchange ties were unaffected. As discussed above, small proportions of redwares from the Kayenta heartland continued to enter the valley in about the same proportions as before, and acquisition of shell, turquoise, and other exotic objects continued unabated.[1] Further, new trade and interaction networks were apparently forged, as indicated by the appearance of small quantities of buffware pottery in the valley. The presence of this pottery indicates interaction with Patayan people whose homeland was to the south along the Colorado River.

Sometime after these settlement and interaction changes had occurred, the VBP occupation of the Moapa Valley came to an end. The timing, causes, and

**FIGURE 14.6.** *A: Sherd recovered from Coyote site (AZ A:14:82) on the Shivwits Plateau exhibiting local variant of Dogoszhi style; B: sherd recovered from House 47 (26C7592) in the Moapa Valley, exhibiting local variant of the Black Mesa design style.*

consequences of the abandonment are debated, though most archaeologists believe that the Lowland VBP culture ceased to exist sometime between about AD 1200 and 1250. More than two decades ago, Lyneis (1995:232) raised the possibility that the abandonment may have been linked to a mid-twelfth-century drought that disrupted farming on the Shivwits and Uinkaret Plateaus. Although the drought would have had little effect on farming in the Moapa Valley, which was based on the spring-fed waters of the Muddy River, it almost certainly would have impacted upland farming that depended on precipitation. According to this scenario, settlement patterns in the uplands were disrupted by the drought, and this in turn led to the breakdown of the long-standing interaction network with the lowland region. Subsequently this social disruption triggered the abandonment of the latter region. At the time that this scenario was suggested little work had been conducted in the upland regions, and it was reasonable to assume that abandonment of that area coincided with the collapse of the trade networks. Since that time, however, research in the upland regions has demonstrated that occupation there continued (as it did in the lowlands) for at least 50 years after the collapse of the upland-lowland social and exchange networks.

If the drought did not trigger the collapse of upland-lowland exchange networks and ultimately cause the abandonment of the region, then, what did? We are a long ways from being able to answer this question, but recent research in

**FIGURE 14.7.** *Sand-tempered Tusayan redware recovered from House 47, exhibiting hachuring style design. (National Museum of the American Indian, Smithsonian Institution, catalog no. 147218.000. Photo by NMAI Photo Services.)*

the Gold Butte region of southwestern Nevada provides an intriguing possible new twist on an old idea. Decades ago, archaeologists theorized that the demise of the Virgin Branch culture was brought about by conflict accompanying the arrival of the Paiute into the region (Ambler and Sutton 1989; Hayden 1930). Few archaeologists today subscribe to this theory, primarily because our most reliable chronological data (Gilreath 2011) suggest that the Paiute did not arrive in the area until after the VBP people had already left (though see Roberts 2012 for an alternative viewpoint). New information, however, suggests that a different group of people—the Patayan—did overlap with the VBP occupation in southern Nevada, raising the possibility that an influx of newcomers may indeed have contributed to the Puebloan abandonment.

This information comes from the Gold Butte area, located between the Moapa Valley and the Shivwits Plateau (see figure 14.1). An archaeological survey of that area identified a Patayan presence there during the late prehistoric period, with circumstantial evidence further suggesting that the occupation occurred "toward the very end of the Puebloan period" (McGuire et al. 2013:219). One possibility, then, is that the arrival of the Patayan disrupted the longstanding upland-lowland exchange networks. Gold Butte lay within the path of the least-effort travel corridors between the ceramic production centers on the Shivwits and Uinkaret Plateaus and the Moapa Valley; therefore, any direct travel between the two regions would have had to have passed through Gold Butte, and any travelers during the late Puebloan period would likely have encountered Patayan inhabitants or visitors. But if the Patayan presence did disrupt the exchange networks, it does not appear to have done so due to any hostile relations. After observing the high frequency with which Patayan and puebloan sherds co-occur on sites, McGuire et al. (2013:216–217) proposed that there existed between the two groups "a convergence of some combination of subsistence pursuits, settlement practices, social interactions, and/or exchange relationships . . . the overall pattern suggests some level of benign interaction between the two groups as opposed to avoidance or open hostility."

Along the lower stretches of the Colorado River the Patayan people were known for their control of long-distance trade networks. In particular, they played an active role in the exchange of commodities between the Hohokam of southern Arizona and the tribes of California. Likewise, the Yumans, their historical descendants, were known for their dynamic trade relationships that spanned much of the California and Southwestern deserts. Thus, it seems likely that as the Patayans pushed north into Nevada they likewise expanded their trade networks to incorporate the people of this region. If so, they may have opted to forge relations with the Lowland VBP people in order to take advantage of their ongoing trade ties, but the upland VBP inhabitants may have found themselves left out of these newly developing relationships. Support for this assumption is found in the artifact collections of the late Pueblo II/early Pueblo III upland sites, which lack both the Patayan ceramics and the other nonlocal goods such as turquoise and shell that are commonly found at contemporary sites in the Lowland VBP region. Thus, though admittedly speculative at this point, I suggest that the arrival of the Patayan may have triggered a realignment of exchange relationships which severed the long-standing upland-lowland ties that had existed since Basketmaker III times. This realignment of relationships, however, may not have been able to withstand the test of time and may ultimately have contributed to the demise of the Virgin Branch culture.

## CONCLUSION

The Moapa Valley is often considered a far periphery of the North American Southwest culture area. However, the Lowland Virgin Branch was anything but simply a watered-down version of another culture. Rather, the inhabitants of this region played an active role in shaping not only the form that their own culture took but also that of adjacent areas. Once thought to have been the product of Basketmakers from the Colorado Plateau, the evidence presented here suggests that the Lowland Virgin Branch culture was an in situ development that resulted when local Archaic foragers adopted farming and borrowed or developed new technologies. These early farmers were not merely recipients of new lifeways but actively contributed toward the development of the Basketmaker culture that emerged across the North American Southwest. For the next thousand years, their descendants farmed the Moapa Valley and maintained thriving trade and interaction networks with the people of adjacent areas. Although always identifying as Puebloan, the Lowland VBP people retained certain aspects of their ancestral Great Basin heritage throughout the VBP sequence. At the same time, subtle yet important shifts occurred over the course of their millennia of existence.

## NOTE

1. The nature of the data available from the Moapa Valley precludes us from obtaining quantifiable data for comparative purposes. Because there is little data from screened deposits, where all artifacts were systematically collected, it is impossible to compare proportions of nonlocal goods between sites. However, a perusal of the field notes and museum collections from the sites indicates that numerous pieces of turquoise, shell, and burials and abundant quantities of nonlocal goods are present from all time periods.

## REFERENCES

Ahlstrom, Richard V.N. 2008. "Re-Imagining the History of Maize Farming in the Las Vegas Valley." In *Proceedings of the 2007 Three Corners Conference*, ed. Mark C. Slaughter, Steven Daron, Eva Jensen, and Kathleen Sprowl, 1–20. Boulder City: Nevada Archaeological Association.

Ahlstrom, Richard V.N., and Heidi Roberts. 2012. "Puebloan Period (AD 200–1300)." In *A Prehistoric Context for Southern Nevada*, ed. Heidi Roberts and Richard V.N. Ahlstrom, 87–114. Archaeological Report No. 011-05. HRA Inc.

Allison, James. 2000. *Craft Specialization and Exchange in Small-Scale Societies: A Virgin Anasazi Case Study*. PhD dissertation, Department of Anthropology, Arizona State University, Tempe. Ann Arbor, MI: University Microfilms International.

Ambler, J. R., and M. Sutton. 1989. "The Anasazi Abandonment of the San Juan Drainage and the Numic Expansion." *North American Archaeologist* 10:39–53. https://doi.org/10.2190/PD7N-AHB0-VQ59-MKGM.

Blair, Lynda M., and Diane L. Winslow. 2006. *Firebrand Cave: An Archaic Site in Southern Nevada*. Anthropological Series Vol. 1(1). Las Vegas: Harry Reid Center for Environmental Studies, Division of Cultural Resources, University of Nevada.

Ferguson, Timothy J. 2014. "Keeping in Touch: Exchange as an Adaptive Strategy in Southern Nevada." Unpublished MA thesis, University of Nevada, Las Vegas.

Ferguson, Timothy J. 2016. "Behavioral Ecology and Optimality: Seeking Alternative Views." *Journal of Archaeological Science: Reports* 5:632–639. https://doi.org/10.1016/j.jasrep.2015.10.020.

Ford, Richard I. 1981. "Gardening and Farming Before A.D. 1000." In *Prehistoric Food Production in North America*, ed. Richard I. Ford, 341–364. University of Michigan Anthropological Papers No. 75. Ann Arbor: University of Michigan.

Gilreath, Amy J. 2011. *"Improving the Prehistoric Chronology for Southern Nevada."* Report Submitted to the Bureau of Reclamation, Lower Colorado Region, Boulder City, NV.

Harrington, Mark R. 1937. "Some Early Pit-Dwellings in Nevada." *The Masterkey* 11(4):122–124. Los Angeles: Southwest Museum.

Harrington, Mark R. 1953. "Southern Nevada Pit-Dwellings." *The Masterkey* 27(4):136–142. Los Angeles, CA: Southwest Museum.

Harry, Karen G. 2005. "Ceramic Specialization and Agricultural Marginality: Do Ethnographic Models Explain the Development of Specialized Pottery Production in the Prehistoric American Southwest?" *American Antiquity* 70:295–319. https://doi.org/10.2307/40035705.

Harry, Karen G. 2008. "Main Ridge 2006 Research Project: Condition Assessments, Test Excavations, and Data Analysis for the UNLV Fall 2006 Field School." Document submitted to the Lake Mead National Recreation Area by the Department of Anthropology and Ethnic Studies and the Public Lands Institute, University of Nevada, Las Vegas, Great Basin Cooperative Ecosystems Studies Unit, Agreement No. H8R0706001 and Task Agreement J8R0705006.

Harry, Karen G. 2009. "Seven Foot Giants and Silk-Clad Skeletons: A Voyeur's Look Back at the Discovery and Early Fieldwork of Nevada's 'Lost City.'" In *Proceedings of the 2007 Three Corners Conference*, ed. Mark C. Slaughter, Steven Daron, Eva Jensen, and Kathleen A. Sprowl, 111–137. Las Vegas: Nevada Archaeological Association Meetings.

Harry, Karen G., Timothy J. Ferguson, James R. Allison, Brett T. McLaurin, Jeff Ferguson, and Margaret Lyneis. 2013. "Examining the Production and Distribution of Shivwits Ware Pottery in the American Southwest." *American Antiquity* 78(2):385–396.

Harry, Karen G., CherylGregory, and LeilaniEspinda. 2008. "Lost City Archival Project Finder's Guide." Document prepared by Karen G. Harry, Cheryl Gregory, and Leilani Espinda and submitted to the Lake Mead National Recreation Area, Boulder City, NV, by the Department of Anthropology and Ethnic Studies and the Public Lands Institute, University of Nevada Las Vegas, Great Basin Cooperative Ecosystems Studies Unit, Agreement No. H8R0706001 and Task Agreement J8R0705006.

Harry, Karen G., and James T. Watson. 2010. "The Archaeology of Pueblo Grande de Nevada: Past and Current Research within Nevada's 'Lost City.'" *Kiva* 75(4):403–424. https://doi.org/10.1179/kiv.2010.75.4.001.

Harry, Karen G., and James T. Watson. 2018. "Shaping Identity in the Prehispanic Southwest." In *"Life Beyond the Boundaries: Constructing Identity in Edge Regions of the North American Southwest,"* ed. Karen Harry and Sarah Herr, 122–156. Boulder: University Press of Colorado.

Hayden, Irwin. 1930. "Mesa House." In *Archaeological Explorations in Southern Nevada*, 26–92. Paper No. 4. Los Angeles: Southwest Museum.

Hull, Sharon, Mostafa Fayek, F. Joan Mathien, and Heidi Roberts. 2014. "Turquoise Trade of the Ancestral Puebloan: Chaco and Beyond." *Journal of Archaeological Science* 45:187–195. https://doi.org/10.1016/j.jas.2014.02.016.

Lyneis, Margaret M. 1992. *The Main Ridge Community at Lost City: Virgin Anasazi Architecture, Ceramics, and Burials. Anthropological Papers 117.* Salt Lake City: University of Utah.

Lyneis, Margaret M. 1995. "The Virgin Anasazi, Far Western Puebloans." *Journal of World Prehistory* 9(2):199–241. https://doi.org/10.1007/BF02221839.

Lyneis, Margaret M. 2000. "Life at the Edge: Pueblo Settlements in Southern Nevada." In *The Archaeology of Regional Interaction*, ed. Michelle Hegmon, 257–274. Boulder: University Press of Colorado.

Lyneis, Margaret M. 2008. "The Socioeconomic Context of Changing Middle Pueblo II Pottery Frequencies at the Yamashita Sites, Moapa Valley, Southern Nevada." In *Proceedings of the 2007 Three Corners Conference*, ed. Mark C. Slaughter, Steven Daron, Eva Jensen, and Kathleen A. Sprowl, 163–184. Boulder City: Nevada Archaeological Association.

Lyneis, Margaret M. 2012. "Appendix D: A Synopsis of the Yamashita Sites." In *A Prehistoric Context for Southern Nevada*, ed. Heidi Roberts and Richard V.N. Ahlstrom, D-1 through D-20. Archaeological Report No. 011-05. Las Vegas, NV: HRA Inc.

Matson, R.G. 1991. *The Origins of Southwestern Agriculture.* Tucson: University of Arizona Press.

McGuire, Kelly, William Hildrebrandt, Amy Gilreath, Jerome King, and John Berg. 2013. *The Prehistory of Gold Butte: A Virgin River Hinterland, Clark County, Nevada. Anthropological Papers No. 127.* Salt Lake City: University of Utah.

Myhrer, Keith M., and Margaret M. Lyneis. 1985. *The Bovine Bluff Site: An Early Puebloan Site in the Upper Moapa Valley.* Contributions to the Study of Cultural Resources Technical Report 15. Washington, DC: Bureau of Land Management.

Rafferty, Kevin A. 1990. "The Virgin Anasazi and the Pan-Southwestern Trade System, A.D. 900–1150." *Kiva* 56:3–24.

Roberts, Heidi. 2012. "Post-Puebloan Period (A.D. 1300–1776)." In *A Prehistoric Context for Southern Nevada*, ed. Heidi Roberts and V. N. Ahlstrom, 165–208. Archaeological Report No. 0011-05. Las Vegas: HRA Inc.

Roberts, Heidi, and Richard V.N. Ahlstrom. 2012. "Gray, Buff, and Brown: Untangling Chronology, Trade, and Culture in the Las Vegas Valley, Southern Nevada." In *Meetings at the Margins: Prehistoric Cultural Interactions in the Intermountain West*, ed. David Rhode, 211–228. Salt Lake City: University of Utah Press.

Roth, Barbara J. 2012. "Paleoindian and Archaic Periods." In *A Prehistoric Context for Southern Nevada*, ed. Heidi Roberts and Richard V.N. Ahlstrom, 87–114. Archaeological Report No. 011–05. Las Vegas: HRA Inc.

Sagmiller, James J. 1998. "The Maize from Black Dog Cave: Testing the Concept of Races of Maize in the American Southwest." Unpublished MA thesis, Department of Anthropology, University of Nevada, Las Vegas.

Sakai, Sachiko. 2014. *Explaining Change in Production and Distribution of Olivine-Tempered Ceramics in the Arizona Strip and Adjacent Areas in the American Southwest.* PhD dissertation, University of California, Santa Barbara. Ann Arbor, MI: University Microfilms International.

Schroeder, Albert H. 1973. "A Few Sites in Moapa Valley, Nevada." *The Masterkey* 27(1):18–24 and 27(2):62–67. Los Angeles, CA: Southwest Museum.

Shutler, R., Jr. 1961. *Lost City: Pueblo Grande de Nevada. Anthropological Papers 5.* Carson City: Nevada State Museum.

Teague, Lynn S., and Dorothy K. Washburn. 2013. *Sandals of the Basketmaker and Pueblo Peoples: Fabric Structure and Color Symmetry.* Albuquerque: University of New Mexico Press.

Webster, Laurie. 2008. "Technical Styles and Social Boundaries of Pershable Artifacts of the Early Agricultural/Basketmaker II Period." http://www.archaeologysouthwest.org/pdf/pecos2008_webster.pdf.

Winslow, Diane L., and Lynda M. Blair. 2003a. *Mitigation of the Black Dog Mesa Archaeological Complex (26CK5686/BLM 53-7216),* Volume I: *History and Project Overview.* Prepared for the BLM, Las Vegas District Office and Nevada Power Company, Las Vegas, NV.

Winslow, Diane L., and Lynda M. Blair. 2003b. *Mitigation of the Black Dog Mesa Archaeological Complex (26CK5686/BLM 53-7216),* Volume II: *Black Dog Cave.* Prepared for the BLM, Las Vegas District Office and Nevada Power Company, Las Vegas, NV.

Winslow, Diane L. 2009. *Mitigation of the Black Dog Mesa Archaeological Complex (26CK5686/BLM 53-7216). Volume III:Pithouse Excavations, Locus 4 and Volume VI-Conclusions and Research Questions Addressed.* Prepared for the BLM, Las Vegas District Office and Nevada Power Company, Las Vegas.

# 15

# Prehistoric Hunter-Gatherer-Farmer Identities in Las Vegas Valley, Southern Nevada

RICHARD V.N. AHLSTROM

The study of prehistoric cultural identities in Nevada's Las Vegas Valley has been complicated by a scarcity of the ceramic, woven perishable, architectural, and site-layout data that are typically used to distinguish prehistoric cultural complexes in the nearby regions of the American Southwest and eastern Great Basin. Research conducted over the past 15 years has, however, led to a substantial increase in the size and complexity of the data set available for studying prehistoric identities in the valley (Ahlstrom 2011; Roberts and Ahlstrom 2012a). That evidence is less relevant for the traditional study of identity as involving the ways in which the valley's residents might have *identified themselves* than for an alternative approach that focuses on how they might have *identified with their neighbors*, in the sense of recognizing commonalities in their past experiences or their current lifeways. Those connections would have provided context, in the form of explanation or even justification, for ongoing or anticipated interactions with those neighbors. They could, on that basis, have served to encourage the kind of intergroup transmission or diffusion of cultural practices discussed by Catherine Cameron (chapter 2, this volume). This alternative approach to

DOI: 10.5876/9781607327356.c015

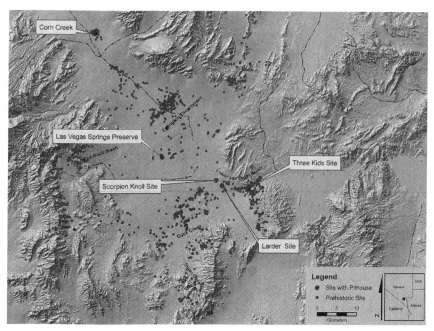

**FIGURE 15.1.** *Map of Las Vegas Valley, showing the locations of sites mentioned in the text. Note that Clark County Wetlands Park extends from just east of the Three Kids site to just north of Scorpion Knoll.*

identity is also relevant to connections of a second kind, involving practices that a group recognized as being held in common with its forebears. Those practices, in turn, are relevant to the broader concept of *culture landscape* that "derives from the notion that the land exists in the mind of a people and that their imagery or knowledge of the land is both shared among them and transferred over generations" (Stoffle et al. 2003:111). Both dimensions of identity considered here, with neighbors on the one hand and ancestors on the other, are relevant to this chapter's primary conclusion, that Las Vegas Valley's long-resident local population was affected over time and to varying degrees by interaction with its neighbors in the American Southwest (figure 15.1). This perspective on identity can also contribute, then, to the study of cultural process in areas like Las Vegas Valley that are marginal to regions with more complex and better-understood culture histories.

The Great Basin volume of the *Handbook of North American Indians* (1986) placed Las Vegas Valley in the Great Basin culture area and, for the prehistoric period, in that region's southwestern subarea. This assignment was based to a considerable degree on the distribution of Native American language groups during the historical period: "the well-defined Southern Paiute bands along the Colorado River constitute *a firm boundary* between speakers of the Southern Numic languages and the Yuman and Hopi-speaking peoples of the Southwest . . . Though there were many influences across the river . . . including the adoption of some horticultural practices, the Southern Paiute maintained an essentially Great Basin pattern of subsistence and general culture" (d'Azevedo 1986:11; emphasis added). The case of the Chemehuevi, a Southern Paiute group that, though it resided in Las Vegas Valley and adjacent desert areas, borrowed a number of material-culture traits and at least some vocabulary from the Yuman-speaking Mohave, casts doubt on the "firmness" of this cultural boundary, even during the historical period (Kelly and Fowler 1986:370; Laird 1976; Roberts 2012:166). The archaeological record makes it clear that any cultural boundary that may have existed between the valley and adjacent portions of the Southwest was substantially porous throughout most if not all of the late prehistoric period (defined here as beginning, ca. 200–300 BC, with the introduction to the valley of maize-farming technology). The relative porosity of this boundary was a function of interaction between the valley's residents and the bearers of two prehistoric southwestern archaeological cultures: the Virgin Branch Puebloan culture, found to the northeast along the Virgin River and its tributaries as well as to the east on the western reaches of the Colorado Plateau, and the Patayan culture, generally identified with ancestral Yuman-speaking peoples and located to the southeast and south along the lower Colorado River.

## WILD PLANT TECHNOLOGICAL COMPLEXES

Though assigned to the Great Basin *culture* area, Las Vegas Valley is not, in fact, part of the Great Basin *geographical* area. It lies instead within the Mojave Desert, which contrasts sharply in elevation, hydrology, temperature, precipitation, and plant communities with the Great Basin proper (Grayson 1993:11–42). Among the most important of these differences, from the perspective of human adaptations, are those relating to plant communities. Catherine Fowler has summarized the technological complexes that were employed by Great Basin peoples to obtain foods from a variety of plant species and that "can be defined in terms of some specific tool types as well as technological procedures" (Fowler 1986:64; also Fowler 2012 and Rhode 2002). Three of the complexes identified by Fowler, those geared to the exploitation of pine nuts, mesquite seed pods, and agave hearts, together with a fourth, an agricultural complex, played important roles in what archaeologist Claude Warren defined as the "double-loop subsistence strategy" of the Las Vegas Paiutes: one loop "based in the valley was dictated by the need to prepare and plant *gardens*, tend them, and harvest the produce, all augmented by the seasonal ripening of *mesquite beans*. [They] would camp at their spring sites during planting season, visiting their gardens to irrigate and control predation by animals and others. The second loop describes the period of movement to the foothills and higher mountain elevations in the warmer months and early fall, to gather, process, and store wild foods, including *agave and pine nut 'crops'"* (Elizabeth Warren 2007:96, citing Claude Warren, emphasis added). Archaeological data indicate that the agricultural, mesquite, agave, and probably piñon complexes were practiced in Las Vegas Valley during the prehistoric period, and they may well have been integrated into something like Warren's double-loop subsistence strategy during that time. The three wild-plant complexes provide evidence for commonalities between the residents of Las Vegas Valley and their neighbors in the Great Basin and the American Southwest.

The piñon complex was held in common with "groups in the central core of the Great Basin" for whom pine nuts "were the focus of intensive activity" (Fowler 1986:65). Pine nuts would have been available from trees growing in the mountains that flank Las Vegas Valley (Charlet 1996:233–267; Fowler 2012; Mayer et al. 2012:figure 2.10). Southern Paiutes consumed some of the pine nuts at or near the collection sites in the mountains, but also transported some to their settlements on the valley floor (Fowler 2012). Archaeological sites investigated in the latter setting have produced only a little evidence for the use of pine nuts. This includes a few fragments of nut hulls recovered from four sites in Clark County Wetlands Park (figure 15.1), located in the valley's southeastern corner, as well as an elevated pine-pollen count from a mano found in a small rockshelter at one of those sites (Ahlstrom 2005a; Holloway 2005). The scarcity of archaeological evidence of pine nuts from valley-floor sites is perhaps to be expected, because the nuts were likely processed in the mountains, with only the archaeologically invisible nut-meal carried to valley settlements.

The mesquite and agave complexes differ from the piñon complex in showing connections to groups living in directions other than to the north. Honey and screwbean mesquite trees as well as agaves are characteristic of the southwestern Mojave Desert portion of the Great Basin culture area, but not of the Great Basin itself (Fowler 1986). Mesquites are found at a number of well-watered locations across Las Vegas Valley (Mayer et al. 2012:figure 2.10), including along washes, near springs, and in dune fields. Recent research along the stretch of Las Vegas Wash that runs through Wetlands Park has, for example, recovered evidence for the presence of mesquites *and* for the exploitation of their seed pods during the late prehistoric period (Ahlstrom et al. 2005; Ahlstrom and Lyon 2008). Mesquite trees also occur in the Sonoran Desert to the south and southeast of the southern Nevada region, both along the Lower Colorado River and in west-central Arizona (Turner et al. 1995:329–333). As exploiters of mesquite pods, residents of Las Vegas Valley might, then, have identified with prehistoric Patayans and their Mohave descendants who lived to the south and, in the case of the Patayans at least, to the east along the Colorado River (Ahlstrom and

Roberts 2012:145–149). Mohaves included mesquite seed pods in their regular diet and depended on this resource when their maize harvests were poor (Stewart 1983:56–59), and there is little reason to doubt that their Patayan ancestors did as well. The idea of a connection between the consumers of mesquite pods in Las Vegas Valley and along the Colorado River has a historical-to-modern period referent: Mohave cultural advisors identified circular clearings in the desert pavement, some ringed with rocks, that have been recorded in Wetlands Park as the kinds of places where their ancestors would have piled the newly collected mesquite pods before processing them. Use of these "fragile pattern" archaeological features (Hayden 1965) may have served in part to mark the ownership of the accumulated pods.

The third wild-plant complex, involving the pit-roasting of the "hearts" of agave plants, was largely restricted to two adjacent portions of the Great Basin culture area, that is, the northeastern Mojave Desert, including Las Vegas Valley, and the Grand Canyon section of the Colorado Plateau (Fowler 1986:67–69). These areas represented but a small component of a shared agave-roasting complex that extended to the southeast and south across the Southwest and into Mexico (Castetter et al 1938:figure 4; Fowler 1986:67; Miller, chapter 12, this volume). The iconic archaeological evidence of this complex consists of annular mounds of ash, charcoal, and burned rocks that were the product of multiple pit-roasting events. These debris mounds and the associated roasting pits are reasonably interpreted as having been used primarily, though perhaps not exclusively, to process agave. This is true in spite of the fact that only *some* features of this kind that have been excavated in southern Nevada (McGuire et al. 2014:74–80) and elsewhere have yielded archaeobotanical samples indicating that they were used for processing this or, in fact, any other plant resource. Of equal importance to the archaeological evidence for defining the agave complex are ethnographic accounts documenting a widely shared body of knowledge concerning the collection, preparation, and cooking of agave hearts, as well as the processing, preservation, and consumption of the resulting foodstuffs and, in the southern Southwest at least, a fermented beverage—though there does not appear to be good evidence for the production of an alcoholic drink from agave in the southern Nevada region nor in adjacent areas of the Southwest (Castetter et al. 1938; Ferg 2003; Miller, chapter 12, this volume; Rhode 2002).

People living in Las Vegas Valley would have found agaves growing on the lower slopes of the nearby mountain ranges (Ahlstrom and Roberts 2012:figure 6.13; Fowler 2012; Mayer et al. 2012:figure 2.10), and large roasting mounds like those just described have been recorded in these areas, both in the vicinity of known stands of agaves and in places where these plants are likely to occur (Ahlstrom and Roberts 2012:figure 6.13). Southern Paiute people are known to have collected agave in several of these locations as well (Fowler 2012). Evidence obtained from excavated roasting mounds indicates that this agave-processing technology was present in and around the valley both early *and* late in the Puebloan period, dating to A D 200–1300 (Ahlstrom and Roberts 2012:152–158; McGuire et al. 2014:74–80; Roberts and Ahlstrom 2012b:Appendix A).

## SOUTHWESTERN FARMING FRONTIER

Las Vegas Valley's prehistoric archaeological record has generally been inter-preted with reference to Julian Steward's (1938) Great Basin model of subsistence based on the exploitation of wild plants and animals. Although at least some Southern Paiute groups in southern Nevada and far southwestern Utah were known to have practiced farming during the historical period (Fowler 1982:126; 1986:94; Kelly and Fowler 1986:371; Steward 1938), the implications of this practice for the prehistoric period were largely ignored. Not agreeing with this interpre-tation was Robert Euler (1966:111–112), who argued that Paiute groups living in this area adopted agriculture from their Puebloan neighbors around A D 1150 *and* that this technology was more important to the lifeways of these groups than Steward, for one, was willing to acknowledge.

One reason for the absence of farming from interpretations of prehistoric settlement-subsistence systems in Las Vegas Valley has been the lack of cor-roborating archaeobotanical evidence. A small but varied body of such data has, however, been unearthed in the valley over the last 15 years (Ahlstrom 2008a; Ahlstrom and Roberts 2012). The telltale evidence comes primarily from two set-tings: the Corn Creek site at the valley's northern end and the Larder–Scorpion Knoll site locality in its southeastern corner (figure 15.1). The best evidence from Corn Creek consists of pollen and several kernels of maize from a habita-tion structure and associated features radiocarbon dated to A D 750–950. Three additional contexts at the site, including a midden deposit and two habitation structures, have produced smaller amounts of maize evidence, including pollen, a phytolith, and a kernel of maize. Radiocarbon dates from samples associated with these contexts suggest that maize was grown at Corn Creek during the A D 400s to 600s, the 1300s to 1500s, and the 1700s or later (Hardin and Roberts 2013; Roberts and Lyon 2012). The Corn Creek data are important because the water used to irrigate the crops would have been obtained from the local springs, a farming technology known to have been practiced by Southern Paiute people, both there and elsewhere in the valley, during the historical period (Fowler 2012).

Las Vegas Valley's most extensive record of maize farming comes from the Larder–Scorpion Knoll site locality on Las Vegas Wash in Clark County Wetlands Park. The relevant evidence from the Larder and Scorpion Knoll sites (figure 15.1), as well as from a third site located a couple miles downstream, includes maize cob fragments, a maize cupule, and maize pollen from 13 archaeologi-cal features (Ahlstrom 2008a, 2008b; Eskenazi and Ahlstrom 2011:Feature 2).

Radiocarbon dates from 12 of the features containing maize remains (one per feature) indicate that maize farming was practiced in the area on many occasions over the 1,900-year interval from 300 BC to AD 1600. The evidence includes a series of overlapping date ranges from 300 BC to AD 200, a lone date at AD 390–550, and two additional runs of overlapping dates from AD 650 to 1000 and from AD 1400 to 1600.

The segment of Las Vegas Wash that passes by the Larder and Scorpion Knoll sites shares characteristics of locations in southeastern Arizona and southwestern New Mexico that were favored by farmers during that region's Early Agricultural period (ca. 2100 BC–AD 200) (Gregory and Nials 2005; Gregory et al. 2008, 2009). Those settings occur at boundaries between reaches of arid-land streams defined by the confluence of a primary drainage and one of its major tributaries, the presence of bedrock or impermeable sediment buried at shallow depth beneath the floodplain of the primary drainage, or both. The associated stream segments would have possessed higher water tables, greater surface flow, and flatter floodplain gradients than elsewhere along the drainage. This combination of factors would have increased the farming potential of the local floodplain, first, by increasing the available soil moisture and, second, by enhancing conditions for the purposeful diversion of surface flow to farm plots.

The reach-boundary relevant in the Larder–Scorpion Knoll case involves the confluence of Las Vegas Wash and one of its major tributaries, Duck Creek, which is located a few hundred meters downstream. Duck Creek would have carried sediment to the Las Vegas Wash floodplain, flattening its gradient in the area of the confluence and, on occasion, contributing to the local soil-moisture levels by way of surface and, probably, subsurface water flow. Duck Creek's potential to provide water to the Las Vegas Wash floodplain was presumably enhanced by discharge from several springs that were located some 5–10 miles upstream along its course (Ahlstrom et al. 2005:figure 2.4; Hogan and Bachhuber 1981; Rafferty 2008:11). The radiocarbon dates cited above suggest that farmers first recognized and took advantage of these favorable floodplain characteristics during the late centuries BC, and that their successors continued to do so for another 1,500+ years. This continuity in practice would have been at least in part a function of the persistence of knowledge across generations.

The evidence for the prehistoric cultivation of maize in Las Vegas Valley fits better with Bruce Smith's (2001) concept of a subsistence strategy involving persistent low-level food production than with an economic model involving a long-term dependence on maize farming. Farming in the valley would, in other words, have been integrated into a predominantly hunter-gatherer lifeway. This inference is based on several observations. First, there is the small size of the "packets" of maize evidence that have been found in the valley, which generally include only minimal counts of maize pollen grains, phytoliths, or macrofossils.

Second, there is the failure of the Three Kids Pithouse—a shallow, fifth-to-sixth-century structure located several miles downstream from the Larder–Scorpion Knoll locality (figure 15.1)—to produce evidence of maize, even though the recovery of such evidence was a major focus of that structure's excavation (Ahlstrom 2005b:part 3). A third factor is the scarcity of maize macrofossils from the several small rockshelters with late-prehistoric-period occupations that have been excavated in Las Vegas Valley (Ahlstrom 2011:48).

This interpretation of low-level food production, if maintained as more data are collected, would set Las Vegas Valley apart from areas to the east and northeast, where Puebloans are thought to have been dependent on maize from the early centuries AD (Matson 31991; Coltrain and Janetski 2013). This is a case, then, in which people in neighboring areas were similar in that both practiced farming, but different in that they integrated this technology into substantially different economies (Jeunesse 2003). Also worth noting is the evidence for continuity in this kind of small-scale farming regimen from the valley's prehistoric to its historical, or Southern Paiute, residents.

The maize-farming technological complex came to Las Vegas Valley from the American Southwest and, thus, reflects commonalities with the residents of that region. Several aspects of that shared farming technology warrant discussion here. The first of these concerns the source or direction from which maize farming was introduced into Las Vegas Valley. Data compiled by Gregory and colleagues (2008:figure 1), together with more recently collected evidence from radiocarbon dates and bone-isotope analysis (Coltrain and Janetski 2013; Roberts, chapter 16, this volume), indicate that farming technology had arrived on the southern Colorado Plateau by the beginning of the first millennium BC and that it had become well established there by the second half of that millennium.

The evidence presented by Gregory and colleagues shows that farming technology initially spread northward into the Four Corners region along a corridor encompassing the present-day border between Arizona and New Mexico and, from there, westward along the Arizona-Utah border. It would logically follow that maize farming came to Las Vegas Valley from Puebloan communities located in the latter area. This is probably how it happened, though the archaeological record from southern Nevada leaves the door open for an alternative history. Las Vegas Valley's evidence of early maize farming can be compared to that from the Moapa and lower Virgin River Valleys, located 40 miles to the northeast, that were home to the lowland Virgin Branch Puebloan archaeological culture. That area has produced a coherent set of nine maize-related radiocarbon dates from preceramic "Basketmaker II" contexts at four archaeological sites that, taken as a group, indicate that farming was being practiced on the floodplains of the Muddy and Virgin Rivers by AD 100–200 (Ahlstrom and Roberts 2012:table 6.3). This is at least a century-and-a-half later than the interval of 350–50 BC indicated by a pair of radiocarbon-dated contexts for the earliest maize farming in Las Vegas Valley (Ahlstrom 2008a). Could this technology have come to the valley at an earlier time and by a more southerly route, one that led westward from southern Arizona down the lower Gila River and then northward up the lower Colorado River? Unfortunately, there are no subsistence-related data from this proposed route that could either support or contradict this idea.

A second noteworthy aspect of Las Vegas Valley's sharing of maize farming with Southwestern neighbors has to do with the inference, discussed earlier, that the valley's farmers were less than fully committed to this mode of subsistence. One can imagine a lower threshold of production *beneath which* an adequate supply of seed corn for future planting could not be guaranteed in every year. There would also be a limit to how many seasons a "sometime" farmer could go without planting, but still maintain a supply of viable seed for future use. Maize seed typically survives for no more than 10 years (Nabhan 1977:145), and there is probably a substantial decrease in the overall viability of a cache of seed corn over a briefer interval than that. This loss in viability would have been exacerbated if the seed were stored in subsurface pits like those at the Larder site, described below (Diehl and Waters 2006:81). Local farmers might, then, be expected to take advantage from time to time of preexisting contacts with trading partners or relatives, either actual or fictive, living in Puebloan communities to the northeast and east or, alternatively, in Patayan communities to the south to obtain the seed necessary for planting. There were times when these Puebloan and Patayan contacts may have actually been living in Las Vegas Valley.

## PUEBLOAN AND PATAYAN VISITORS?

Claude Warren and Robert Crabtree interpreted the presence on archaeological sites in southwestern Nevada of Puebloan materials, primarily grayware potsherds, as evidence that "relatively small parties of Muddy River villagers . . . periodically foraged through parts of this area. The extent of these forays is not as yet determined, but it appears to have been considerable, particularly in well-watered valleys such as Las Vegas Valley and Ash Meadows [located 50 miles west of Las Vegas Valley] and in the [intervening] Spring Mountains" (Warren and Crabtree 1986:191). There are, from a different perspective, several documentary sources indicating that Mojave Indians visited and, in at least one instance, camped in Las Vegas Valley during the mid-nineteenth century (Rafferty 2008:11). The task of confirming the presence of either Puebloans or Patayans in the valley, whether short-term visitors or longer-term settlers, is complicated by the lack of culturally specific traits that was mentioned at the outset of this chapter. Interaction between the valley and neighboring Puebloan and Patayan areas could have involved the movement both of artifacts—including archaeologically visible pottery, but also perishable items with poor archaeological visibility—and of people as well. Ceramic assemblages collected from sites in the valley are typically small, and they often include combinations of Puebloan grayware, Patayan (or Yuman) Lower Colorado Buff Ware, and Southern Paiute Great Basin Brown Ware. The primary concern here is with the first two of these categories, grayware and buffware (Roberts and Ahlstrom 2012a). The Puebloan grayware pottery found in the valley could date anytime from the AD 600s to the 1200s, whereas the buffware pottery probably postdates AD 1000 and could date as late as the AD 1600s or beyond (Ahlstrom and Roberts 2012; Seymour 2005). Spatial patterns in the distribution of these two ceramic wares are reflective of their source areas, with grayware tending to be more abundant on sites in the northern half of the valley and buffware on sites in its southeastern corner (Ahlstrom and Lyon 2004:figure 5.4; Ahlstrom et al. 2005:figure 2.6; Ahlstrom and Roberts 2012: figure 6.5; Rafferty 2008).

A substantial portion of the Puebloan grayware and Patayan buffware pottery found in Las Vegas Valley probably arrived there as trade goods. These pottery assemblages consist almost entirely of potsherds from broken vessels, and it is possible that many of these artifacts were carried to the sites where they were recorded and, even, into the valley itself *not* as whole vessels but as pieces of broken pots that had been curated for use as scrapers, plates, or other kinds of implements or, perhaps, as ornaments. This curation of "sherds as sherds" is at least one explanation for situations, like that observed in Las Vegas Valley, in which archaeological sites are characterized by small assemblages of mostly small, minimally refitable potsherds. The suggestion in these cases is that pottery vessels were not of critical importance to local hunter-gatherer lifeways. An alternative and partial explanation for the presence of Puebloan grayware vessels in the valley is provided by research showing that some pottery of this kind (assignable, that is, to "Puebloan" types) was produced both at the Corn Creek site and, to the west of the valley, at Ash Meadows with local materials, but by individuals, presumably women, schooled in the Puebloan tradition of pottery manufacture (Lyneis 2012a, 2012b).

As discussed earlier, evidence of prehistoric maize farming has been uncovered at Corn Creek, as have the remains of shallow ephemeral habitation structures and of what was probably a half-meter-deep pithouse (Roberts et al. 2007a; Roberts and Lyon 2012; Hardin and Roberts 2013). A dozen potsherds from two or three Puebloan grayware jars were recovered from the bottom 20 cm of pithouse fill, though none from the structure's floor. Charred material from the floor yielded a calibrated two-sigma radiocarbon date range of AD 530–710. Puebloans, including farmers, presumably produced at least some of this archaeological record from Corn Creek.

Other evidence for the presence of Puebloan people in the valley is either less well documented than that from Corn Creek, less convincing than that evidence, or both. Little is known about a five-room, multi-occupation "pueblo" located near the center of the valley at Las Vegas Springs Preserve that was excavated in the 1920s and even less about a possibly similar structure located a short distance away (Seymour 1999:172; Ahlstrom et al. 2005:56). Test excavations conducted at the Scorpion Knoll site in 2005–2006 have, in contrast, been thoroughly reported (Ahlstrom 2008b). In addition to the traces of maize farming described earlier, this work yielded a small ($n = 16$) assemblage of grayware potsherds, as well as a vaguely front-oriented, Puebloan-style site layout that incorporated several ephemeral habitation structures and storage pits along with a low-density trash scatter. A small suite of four radiocarbon dates suggests that Scorpion Knoll was occupied one or probably several times between AD 700 and 1000. The excavators interpreted Scorpion Knoll as a possible field-house site occupied on a seasonal basis for the pursuit of farming on the nearby Las Vegas Wash floodplain. It may have served this function for Puebloans who had settled at Corn Creek or one of the valley's other, poorly documented room-unit sites, or even for farmers who traveled there from Puebloan communities located outside the valley. The site may also have been occupied by members of the valley's resident, non-Puebloan population who obtained a small quantity of grayware pottery through trade.

Evidence of Patayan contacts is relatively abundant in Las Vegas Valley (Rafferty 2008), but identifying the specific mechanisms responsible for its presence is challenging. The relevant evidence consists mostly of buffware potsherds that, unlike grayware ceramics, has produced little convincing evidence of having been produced in the valley (cf. Lyneis 2012b). Gregory Seymour (1997, 2005; Rafferty 2008) has suggested that one buffware type, Las Vegas Buff, was in fact made there, but even if this were the case, the potsherds involved would account for only a fraction of the valley's buffware assemblage. That said, it is important to acknowledge the existence of at least one ethnographic account of Southern Paiutes in the valley making pottery more in keeping with a buffware than a brownware tradition of manufacture. Whether the knowledge involved in this kind of pottery production was brought to the valley by Yuman-language-speaking potters or arrived there by other means is unknown (Lyneis 2012b:I-1 to I-2). This leaves open the question of whether the bulk of the valley's prehistoric buffware assemblage arrived there as a result of exchange or if a significant portion was brought there by members of the communities where it was made and who, on that basis, could be reasonably identified as "Patayans." The best evidence for the presence of the latter individuals comes from the southeastern Las Vegas Valley, particularly the Wetlands Park and Duck Creek areas, where a number of sites have produced ceramic assemblages dominated by buffware types.

Additional, nonceramic evidence for the presence of Patayans in Las Vegas Valley comes from sites in the Wetlands Park area. The possibility has already been mentioned that Yuman ancestors—that is, Patayans—visited this area to collect mesquite pods and, in the process, built some of its desert-pavement features. These visitors may also have been responsible for some of the post- AD 1000 evidence of maize farming recovered from the Larder–Scorpion Knoll locality. Also present in the Wetlands Park area is an example of the kind of intaglio or geoglyph that has been identified with the Patayan/Yuman cultural tradition. This is one of the northernmost of these features that has been recorded and the only one known from Las Vegas Valley (Rafferty 2008). Its presence, together with the spatial distribution of Lower Colorado Buff Ware and, at least as a consistent feature, the observations of Mohave cultural advisors on the function of certain fragile-pattern features, suggests that Patayan forays up Las Vegas Wash mostly extended no farther than the valley's southeastern corner. Whatever their purpose, these visitors may have brought some buffware vessels with them from home.

There may have been other routes by which Patayan ceramics entered the valley. Seymour (2005) has noted a distinction between the buffware potsherds found at sites in the Wetland's Park area and those typically found elsewhere in the valley, with the former belonging primarily to pottery types associated with the lower Colorado River Valley, consistent with the identification of lower Las Vegas Wash as a travel corridor linking Las Vegas Valley to points south. The latter, on the other hand, belong more often to types associated with the Mojave Desert, suggesting contacts with pottery makers living in that nonriverine setting.

Archaeologist Harold Colton provided a demographic context for the presence of prehistoric Patayans and their Yuman-language-speaking descendants in places like Las Vegas Valley. He noted that these groups possessed "a dense . . . population producing a surplus of food [and] a surplus population that radiated out on all the important trails where subsistence was possible" (Colton 1945:118). Gordon Baldwin (1948; Ahlstrom and Roberts 2012:149) recorded Patayan sites along the Colorado River in the western Grand Canyon, well upstream from its confluence with Las Vegas Wash. This would suggest that Patayans were well positioned to, in Colton's terms, "radiate" the relatively short, 15–20-mile distance up Las Vegas Wash to Las Vegas Valley. A similar demographic potential can be assumed for Puebloan communities living in the Moapa and lower Virgin River Valleys, based on the long-term growth that has been inferred for Virgin Branch and other Puebloan populations (Euler 1988:figure 7.1).

## A PERSISTENT PLACE IN LAS VEGAS VALLEY

Systematic backhoe trenching and limited follow-up hand excavation at the Larder site exposed 60 pit features in the walls of the trenches—including 56 storage pits, three hearths, and one small roasting pit—in an area measuring 100 m × 200 m (Ahlstrom 2011:figures 4.4 and 4.5). Based on this sample, the investigators estimated that between 500 and 800 storage pits were present on the site. Comparable testing of the much smaller Scorpion Knoll site located two or three ephemeral habitation structures, a roasting pit, and three storage pits like those at the Larder site. Botanical evidence showed that the sites' inhabitants engaged in maize farming and the exploitation of mesquite seed pods. The interpretation of Scorpion Knoll as a possible field-house site has already been mentioned. The Larder site was named based on the size of its observed and estimated populations of storage pits, the concomitant scarcity of thermal features, and the lack of identified habitation structures—which, taken together, suggested that the site was used primarily for the pit storage of foodstuffs (Ahlstrom 2008b). A recently completed remote-sensing and follow-up testing project has produced evidence of two shallow pithouses and probable signatures of several more associated with a possible outdoor activity area (Rogers 2015). Most of these features are clustered together and may represent a settlement-unit roughly equivalent to that observed at the nearby Scorpion Knoll site. The discovery of the habitation structures indicates that the Larder site was used for more than pit storage alone. The occupation or occupations represented by these features cannot, however, account for the Larder site's recorded and estimated populations of storage pits, so the inference of a specialized storage function remains viable for at least portions of the site's history.

The Larder and Scorpion Knoll sites together produced 16 radiocarbon dates that fall into intervals of 300 BC–AD 200, AD 650–1000, and AD 1400–1600, and it is likely, given the relatively small count of dates, that the Larder site saw use during the intervening periods as well. The evidence suggests that the site was used for pit storage over an interval that was least 1,200 years in length. This count of years greatly exceeds the estimated count of storage pits. The investigated features produced little evidence of having been used more than once, and it is likely that only a handful of years transpired between the loading and unloading of the individual features. Those observations, combined with the possibility, if not likelihood, that two or more features were included in each episode of use supports the conclusion that the site was used intermittently and not continuously for the pit-storage of foodstuffs. The locality's long sequence of radiocarbon dates, together with the size of the Larder site's observed and estimated populations of storage pits, supports the identification of the Larder–Scorpion Knoll locality as a "persistent place" (Schlanger 1992:97) on the prehistoric cultural landscape of Las Vegas Valley.

The characteristics that would have made the confluence of Las Vegas Wash and Duck Creek favorable for farming would likely have been obvious to anyone with experience in aboriginal farming techniques. Mesquite trees also probably grew nearby, though exactly how close to the locality is impossible to say. The presence of farmable soils and a favored wild-plant food resource would have drawn both farmers and collectors to the general area, but not specifically to the two sites themselves. Those particular locations would, however, have held several attractions for those living in the valley, whether on a permanent or a temporary basis. The Larder site in particular occupies a large level area suitable for settlement, though the same can be said of many other spots adjacent to the Las Vegas Wash floodplain. Of greater importance is the fact that the Larder site is underlain by unconsolidated sediments suited to the excavation of storage pits. More important still is the nature of the ground surface itself: it would have been much easier to obscure the locations of storage pits that were dug through the slightly pebbly sand-sheet deposit that covers the surface of the Larder site than through the weakly to moderately well-formed desert pavement surfaces found on the toes of the alluvial fans that more typically overlook the Las Vegas Wash floodplain. Hiding the locations of storage or "cache" pits was probably an important consideration in the use of these features, as has been documented for the Ute and Southern Paiute peoples who inhabited portions of the northern Mojave Desert, southeastern Great Basin, and northwestern Colorado Plateau during the historical period (Fowler and Fowler 1971:49).

A final and seemingly unique attraction of the Larder site stems from the nature of its underlying sediments. The key factor here is the high concentration of gypsum—up to 70 percent of total volume—in the sediment layer into which the site's storage pits were excavated (Ahlstrom 2008b:88–89; Ahlstrom and Lyon 2008:204–207). The storage of foodstuffs in subsurface pits could be risky, as "in-ground spoilage in all varieties of stored wild and domesticated seeds may easily have exceeded 30%" (Diehl and Waters 2006:81). Gypsum is a natural desiccant that would have drawn excess moisture out of the stored foods and into the walls of the Larder site's storage pits. Several of the storage features investigated at the site produced evidence of light burning on their floors or in the immediately overlying feature fill. The small fires that were responsible for this evidence are unlikely to have produced enough heat to harden the walls of the pits in the manner observed in other areas (Wöcherl 2005). These fires would instead have dried the pits in preparation for their use, most importantly by converting the gypsum that was naturally present in the pit walls into anhydrite, "pushing" it toward its anhydrous or "dried-out" phase. This would have significantly enhanced the desiccant properties of the gypsum that was present in the walls of the pits. Whether manipulated in this manner or not, the gypsum found in the subsurface sediment would have resulted in higher than typical success rates for the pit-storage of seeds or other foodstuffs, including maize.

Neither the desiccant properties of the sediments at the Larder site nor the potential to increase their effectiveness in that regard by means of fire would have been immediately obvious to those who built their storage pits at this location. These benefits would, instead, have become apparent only through repeated episodes of use. Once it had been learned, however, this knowledge, together with that concerning the ease of hiding the locations of in-use pits, could have been passed down from generation to generation. Though speculative, this explanation would help to explain the more than 1,500-year range of the Larder site's radiocarbon record, as well as its estimated population of 500 to 800 storage pits. It would also provide a prime example of the commonalities across generations and the underlying concept of a shared cultural landscape that were mentioned at the outset of this chapter (Stoffle et al. 2003:111).

## DISCUSSION

It is clear from the archaeological record that people of Puebloan and Patayan origin spent time in Las Vegas Valley. The small groups involved would have shared direct affinity and, probably, maintained close contact with the home communities from which they or their immediate ancestors had come. They would thus have served as conduits for interaction between those communities and the valley's long-term residents. The existence and survival of this separate resident population is supported, first, by the restriction of strong evidence for the presence of Puebloans to two or three sites in the northeastern and north-central portions of the valley and of Patayans to a handful of sites in its southeastern corner. Second, there is the limitation of that evidence to relatively narrow intervals in what are much longer records of occupation. Ceramic evidence suggests that Puebloans were present at Corn Creek during some portion of the interval from AD 600 to 1200 and perhaps primarily during its final two centuries (Lyneis 2012a). This record can be compared to three sets of evidence—including almost two dozen radiocarbon dates, several score of buried archaeological features identified during testing of the site, and ethnographic accounts—indicating that Corn Creek was occupied during portions at least of the intervals from 6400 to 6200 BC and 4000 to 2200 BC and, then, repeatedly if not continuously from ca. 1000 into the historical period (Roberts et al. 2007b; Roberts and Lyon 2012; Hardin and Roberts 2013). A similar argument applies to Patayans in the valley's southeastern corner: ceramic and associated radiocarbon evidence can support their presence only after AD 1000. There is, by comparison, substantial stratigraphic, radiocarbon, architectural, pit-feature, and projectile-point evidence indicating repeated if not continual use of the valley's southeastern corner from as early as 300 BC (Ahlstrom 2005b, 2008b).

A third argument for the presence of a resident, non-Puebloan and non-Patayan population concerns the long-term use of the Larder site. The survival over many centuries of a cultural memory involving the advantages of this site for the pit storage of foodstuffs is a good explanation for its survival as a "persistent place" on the prehistoric landscape of Las Vegas Valley. A fourth and final reason for identifying a long-resident population is more abstract and involves the level of analytical and interpretive effort expended by archaeologists to tease convincing evidence for the presence of Puebloans and Patayans from the valley-wide archaeological record. There is no basis in that record for reducing the valley's prehistory to the story of the Puebloan or Patayan archaeological cultures, even for periods when bearers of those cultures are most likely to have been present there (Ahlstrom and Roberts 2012:115–16).

The notion that Las Vegas Valley supported a single or unitary "long-term resident population" over the entire late prehistoric period is certainly open to question. The argument presented above concerning the handing down of knowledge about the success rate of pit storage at the Larder site, though consistent with this idea, does not presuppose it. The lesson could have been learned independently more than once and still handed down as traditional knowledge over many generations. There is also evidence of discontinuity in the valley's settlement history that might challenge the idea of a stable resident population. It involves the clustering of radiocarbon dates from a handful of investigated habitation structures in the 600-year interval from AD 400 to 1000 and the related suggestion that this "pithouse period" was characterized by a lesser degree of settlement mobility than the centuries before and after (Ahlstrom and Roberts 2012). Also relevant is the concept of the Numic Spread, or the idea that, beginning around AD 1000, Southern Paiutes and other speakers of Numic languages expanded their range from a homeland in the southwestern Great Basin across the Great Basin region (as summarized by Roberts 2012). That model implies that Numic peoples replaced or possibly absorbed the previous inhabitants of areas falling within the bounds of the demographic expansion, including Las Vegas Valley. This event might explain the post–AD 1000 increase in settlement mobility postulated for the valley and, by the same token, the appearance there of Great Basin Brown Ware, which bears a close, though less than one-to-one, relationship with speakers of Numic languages. The latter event has not, however, been directly dated in the valley and, based on evidence from Moapa valley, may not have occurred there until after AD 1200 (Roberts 2012). Though widely accepted, the concept of the Numic Spread has also been challenged with models that recognize a much earlier spread in the range of Numic-language speakers, greater continuity in the population histories of places like Las Vegas Valley, or both of these alternatives (Lyneis 2012b:I–1 to I–3; Roberts 2012).

With these caveats in mind, we can summarize the evidence for commonalities that Las Vegas Valley's long-term residents might have acknowledged with their Puebloan and Patayan neighbors. To begin with, it would appear that the locals did not adopt ceramic technology from those groups, not at least until late in the prehistoric period. To the extent that they used pottery, the valley's residents mostly obtained the needed vessels through exchange. They may also have considered pottery to be comparably valuable in sherd as in vessel form.

This low level of interest could explain the small counts of potsherds recorded at many sites in the valley. Additional contributions to the valley's ceramic assemblage would have come from vessels broken and discarded there by Puebloans and Patayans during visits to or through the valley. A significant fraction of the grayware found at the Corn Creek site was, however, produced there by resident Puebloan potters, though the rest was presumably brought from production sites in the Moapa and Virgin River Valleys. The notion that the Corn Creek potters did *not* pass their knowledge of ceramic production to their non-Puebloan neighbors does include an element of circularity that should be noted. The observation that the pottery was made in conformity with the Puebloan mode of manufacture *is itself* taken as evidence that the potters were Puebloan in origin. It is nevertheless the case that no other grayware production loci have been identified in the valley, so the inference that ceramic technology did not spread to the valley's non-Puebloan occupants from this source is still the best available.

Also worth discussing further is the parallel claim that the technology for producing buffware pottery did not pass from the Patayans who visited the valley to its long-term residents. It is true that none of the valley's buffware pottery looks like it was made there, or not convincingly so. It also appears that forays by Patayans into the valley were relatively short-term in nature and may, in fact, have consisted largely of seasonal visits for the purpose of collecting mesquite pods. This activity would have provided little opportunity for the sharing of pottery technology. This line of reasoning finds its limitation in the fact that Chemehuevi/Southern Paiute people living in the valley during the historical period are said to have learned pottery making from their Yuman-language-speaking neighbors and to have made pottery using the paddling technique that was characteristic of the pottery made by Yumans and their Patayan ancestors (Lyneis 2012b:I-2 to I-3). Something about the pursuit of pottery manufacture must have changed between the late prehistoric period, represented by the valley's archaeological record, and the historical period, represented by its ethnohistorical record.

Las Vegas Valley's long-term residents would likely have recognized similarities in how they and their Puebloan and Patayan neighbors collected and processed agave hearts and mesquite pods. This sharing of common practices may have helped traders and other travelers feel less foreign when visiting distant communities, including those where unfamiliar languages were spoken. Agaves generally occur as remote resource patches that, while they may have had traditional users, may have engendered little competition for access. The situation may have been different, however, in the case of the mesquite complex. Mesquite pods were an important resource for Yuman-language speakers living along the lower Colorado River during the historical period, and they were probably of comparable importance to their Patayan ancestors. Sharing of the mesquite complex may, then, have fostered competition for access to productive stands of mesquite trees, including those in the southeastern corner of Las Vegas Valley where evidence of Patayan presence has been most clearly demonstrated. The same might have been true for relations between valley residents and Puebloan immigrants who had settled at Corn Creek. Alternatively, the sharing of the mesquite complex between groups might have encouraged cooperation or at least accommodation in the exploitation of this resource.

Competition for access to the most productive stands of mesquite trees might have been most prevalent in areas where a variety of valuable resources, including mesquites, wetland plants, water for domestic consumption, and soil moisture to support crop plants were clustered together. Two such locations with substantial archaeological records are the narrow corridor of Las Vegas Wash in Las Vegas Valley's southeastern corner and the area around Corn Creek springs. Farmer-to-farmer interaction may well have included competition for favored farming sites, but it may also have provided avenues for sharing knowledge about the best farming practices under local conditions and, more specifically, a means for casual farmers to obtain seed corn when their on-hand supply proved inadequate to their needs.

## CONCLUSION

This chapter applies an alternative approach to the study of "identity" in the Las Vegas Valley, one that focuses on the ways in which the area's prehistoric inhabitants may have identified *with* their Puebloan and Patayan neighbors, rather than on how they may have identified *themselves*. This admittedly modest approach to the topic of identity is in keeping with the nature of the valley's archaeological record, which lacks the rich and varied archaeological data sets found in the Puebloan region—the record from the Patayan area being no more and, arguably, even less amenable to this kind of research than that available from the valley.

The Las Vegas Valley section of the Great Basin culture area can be shown to have shared a porous boundary with the neighboring Puebloan and Patayan regions of the American Southwest throughout most if not all of the late prehistoric period (beginning ca. 200–300 bc). Not only artifacts, but important technological practices and at least small numbers of people crossed this boundary—both during the late prehistoric period and before it. The bulk of the relevant archaeological evidence pertains to movement of these entities from the Southwest into Las Vegas Valley, though it is also known or suspected that some trade goods moved in the opposite direction. It is important, in light of these contacts, to emphasize that the valley's prehistory cannot simply be reduced to chapters in Patayan or Puebloan prehistory. The valley appears to have a held a resident population with roots in the Great Basin's southwestern or Mojave Desert subarea that maintained a hunter-gather lifeway, but one that incorporated low-level food production based on maize farming and that also involved the long-term use of specific landscape features within the valley. Members of this population also interacted with their Puebloan and Patayan neighbors, at times through the medium of what were probably small numbers of migrants who came there as temporary visitors or longer-term settlers. This resident population had also obtained the technology of maize farming from a Southwestern source, but exactly from where or by what process remains unresolved. The two processes of persistence and interaction occurred against a backdrop of periodic change in settlement structure not clearly related to either. Determining the proper balance in interpretation between the unfolding of local history and participation in interregional events and historical processes remains a goal for future research in Las Vegas Valley.

## REFERENCES

Ahlstrom, Richard V.N. 2005a. "Site Summaries." In *Desert Oasis: The Prehistory of Clark County Wetlands Park, Henderson, Nevada*, ed. Richard V.N. Ahlstrom, 313–366. HRA Papers in Archaeology No. 4. Las Vegas, NV: HRA, Inc. Conservation Archaeology.

Ahlstrom, Richard V.N., ed. 2005b. *Desert Oasis: The Prehistory of Clark County Wetlands Park, Henderson, Nevada*. HRA Papers in Archaeology No. 4. Las Vegas, NV: HRA, Inc. Conservation Archaeology.

Ahlstrom, Richard V.N. 2008a. "Re-imagining the History of Maize Farming in the Las Vegas Valley." In *Proceedings of the 2007 Three Corners Conference*, ed. Mark C. Slaughter, Steven Daron, Eva Jensen, and Kathleen A. Sprowl, 1–20. Las Vegas: Nevada Archaeological Association.

Ahlstrom, Richard V.N., ed. 2008b. *Persistent Place: Archaeological Investigations at the Larder and Scorpion Knoll Sites, Clark County Wetlands Park, Nevada*. HRA Papers in Archaeology No. 7. Las Vegas, NV: HRA, Inc. Conservation Archaeology.

Ahlstrom, Richard V.N. 2011. "Discovering Significant Subsurface Archaeological Deposits at Open Sites in the Las Vegas Valley." In *Archaeology in 3D: Deciphering Buried Sites in the Western U.S.*, ed. Matthew T. Seddon, Heidi Roberts, and Richard V.N. Ahlstrom, 48–70. Washington, DC: The SAA Press.

Ahlstrom, Richard V. N., and Jerry D. Lyon. 2004. "Las Vegas Valley Site Distribution Analysis." In *An Archaeological Survey for the Las Vegas Valley Disposal Boundary Environmental Impact Statement, Clark County, Nevada*, 261–381. BLM Report No. 5-2467. HRA, Inc. Archaeological Report No. 03-15. Las Vegas, NV: HRA, Inc. Conservation Archaeology.

Ahlstrom, Richard V.N., and Jerry D. Lyon. 2008. "Archaeological Investigations." In *Persistent Place: Archaeological Investigations at the Larder and Scorpion Knoll Sites, Clark County Wetlands Park, Nevada*, ed. Richard V.N. Ahlstrom, 203–224. HRA Papers in Archaeology No. 7. Las Vegas, NV: HRA, Inc. Conservation Archaeology.

Ahlstrom, Richard V.N., and Heidi Roberts. 2012. "Puebloan Period." In *A Prehistoric Context for Southern Nevada*, ed. Heidi Roberts and Richard V.N. Ahlstrom, 115–164. Archaeological Report No. 011-05. Las Vegas, NV: HRA, Inc. Conservation Archaeology, and Carson City, NV: Gnomon, Inc.

Ahlstrom, Richard V. N., Heidi Roberts, and Jerry D. Lyon. 2005. "Environmental and Cultural Setting." In *Desert Oasis: The Prehistory of Clark County Wetlands Park, Henderson, Nevada*, ed. Richard V.N. Ahlstrom, 25–59. HRA Papers in Archaeology No. 4. Las Vegas, NV: HRA, Inc. Conservation Archaeology.

Baldwin, Gordon C. 1948. "Archaeological Surveys and Excavations in the Davis Dam Reservoir Area." Manuscript on file, National Park Service, Region 3, Lake Mead Recreation Area, Boulder City, NV.

Castetter, Edward F., Willis H. Bell, and Alvin R. Grove. 1938. *Ethnobiological Studies in the American Southwest, VI: The Early Utilization and the Distribution of Agave in the American Southwest*. Bulletin No. 335, Biological Series, Vol. 5, No. 4. Albuquerque: University of New Mexico Press.

Charlet, David A. 1996. *Atlas of Nevada Conifers: A Phytogeographic Reference*. Reno: University of Nevada Press.

Colton, Harold S. 1945. "The Patayan Problem in the Colorado River Valley." *Southwestern Journal of Anthropology* 1(1):114–121. https://doi.org/10.1086/soutjanth.1.1.3628785.

Coltrain, Joan B., and Joel C. Janetski. 2013. "The Stable and Radio-isotope Chemistry of Southeastern Utah Basketmaker II Burials: Dietary Analysis Using the Linear Mixing Model SISUS, Age and Sex Patterning, Geolocation and Temporal Patterning." *Journal of Archaeological Science* 40(2013):4711–4730. https://doi.org/10.1016/j.jas.2013.07.012.

d'Azevedo, Warren L. 1986. "Introduction." In *Great Basin*, ed. Warren L. d'Azevedo, 1–14. *Handbook of North American Indians*, Vol. 11, gen. ed. William C. Sturtevant. Washington, DC: Smithsonian Institution.

Diehl, Michael W., and Jennifer A. Waters. 2006. "Aspects of Optimization and Risk During the Early Agricultural Period in Southeastern Arizona." In *Behavioral Ecology and the Transition to Agriculture*, ed. Douglas J. Kennett and Bruce Winterhalder, 63–86. Berkeley: University of California Press.

Eskenazi, Suzanne, and Richard V.N. Ahlstrom. 2011. *Data Recovery at 26CK6139, Clark County Wetlands Park, Clark County, Nevada*. Bureau of Reclamation Report LC-NV-09-17P. Archaeological Report 09-06. Las Vegas, NV: HRA, Inc. Conservation Archaeology.

Euler, Robert C. 1966. *Southern Paiute Ethnohistory*. University of Utah Anthropology Papers No. 78. Salt Lake City: University of Utah.

Euler, Robert C. 1988. "Demography and Cultural Dynamics on the Colorado Plateaus." In *The Anasazi in a Changing Environment*, ed. George J. Gumerman, 192–229. Cambridge, UK: Cambridge University Press.

Ferg, Alan. 2003. "Traditional Western Apache Mescal Gathering as Recorded by Historical Photographs and Museum Collections." *Desert Plants* 19(2):3–51.

Fowler, Catherine S. 1982. "Settlement Patterns and Subsistence Systems in the Great Basin: The Ethnographic Record." In *Man and Environment in the Great Basin*, ed. D. B. Madsen and J. F. O'Connell, 121–138. Society for American Archaeology Papers No. 2. Washington, DC: Society for American Archaeology.

Fowler, Catherine S. 1986. "Subsistence." In *Great Basin*, ed. Warren L. d'Azevedo, 64–97. *Handbook of North American Indians*, Vol. 11, gen. ed. William C. Sturtevant. Washington, DC: Smithsonian Institution.

Fowler, Catherine S. 2012. "Facing Snow Mountain: Las Vegas-Pahrump-Desert Southern Paiute Culture in the Late 19th Century." HRA Inc. Archaeological Report No. 07-28. Las Vegas, NV: HRA, Inc. Conservation Archaeology.

Fowler, Don D., and Catherine S. Fowler, eds. 1971. *Anthropology of the Numa: John Wesley Powell's Manuscripts on the Numic Peoples of Western North America, 1868–1880*. *Smithsonian Contributions to Anthropolgy, No. 14*. Washington, DC: Smithsonian Institution Press.

Grayson, Donald K. 1993. *The Desert's Past: A Natural Prehistory of the Great Basin*. Washington, DC: Smithsonian Institution Press.

Gregory, David A., and Fred L. Nials. 2005. "The Environmental Context of Early Agricultural Period Occupations in the Tucson Basin." In *Subsistence and Resource Use Strategies of Early Agricultural Communities in Southern Arizona*, ed. Michael W. Diehl, 19–64. Anthropological Papers No. 34. Tucson, AZ: Center for Desert Archaeology.

Gregory, David A., Fred L. Nials, and J. Brett Hill. 2008. *Early Agricultural Period Settlement Strategies in the Southern Southwest*. Tucson, AZ: Center for Desert Archaeology http://www.archaeologysouthwest.org/pdf/pecos2008_gregory_et_al.pdf. Accessed on January 14, 2015. http://www. archaeologysouthwest.org/pdf/pecos2008 _gregory_et_al.pdf.

Gregory, David A., Fred L. Nials, and J. Brett Hill. 2009. "Stream Reach Boundaries: Persistent Places on the Landscape of Early Southwestern Farmer." *Archaeology Southwest* 23(1):7–8. Tucson, AZ: Center for Desert Archaeology.

Hardin, Keith, and Heidi Roberts. 2013. *Archaeological Monitoring at the Corn Creek National Register Site, Desert National Wildlife Refuge, Clark County, Nevada*. Prepared for the Desert National Wildlife Refuge Complex, U.S. Fish & Wildlife Service. HRA, Inc. Archaeological Report No. 010-12. Las Vegas, NV: HRA, Inc. Conservation Archaeology.

Hayden, Julian D. 1965. "Fragile-Pattern Areas." *American Antiquity* 31:272–276. https://doi.org/10.2307/2693998.

Hogan, J., and F. W. Bachhuber. 1981. *Las Vegas SE Quadrangle, Vegetation Map*. Scale = 1:24,000. Map 3Ae. Reno: Nevada Bureau of Mines and Geology.

Holloway, Richard. 2005. "Botanical Specimens." In *Desert Oasis: The Prehistory of Clark County Wetlands Park, Henderson, Nevada*, ed. Richard V.N. Ahlstrom, 85–94. HRA Papers in Archaeology No. 4. Las Vegas, NV: HRA, Inc. Conservation Archaeology.

Jeunesse, Christian. 2003. "Néolithique 'Initial,' Néolithique 'Ancien' et Néolithisation dans l'Espace Centre-européen: Une Vision Rénovée." *Revue d'Alsace* 129:97–111.

Kelly, Isabel T., and Catherine S. Fowler. 1986. "Southern Paiute." In *Great Basin*, ed. Warren L. d'Azevedo, 368–397. *Handbook of North American Indians*, Vol. 11, gen. ed. William C. Sturtevant. Washington, DC: Smithsonian Institution.

Laird, Carobeth. 1976. *The Chemehuevis*. Banning, CA: Malki Museum Press.

Lyneis, Margaret. 2012a. "Ceramic Analysis." In *Archaeological Excavations at the Corn Creek National Register Site, Desert National Wildlife Refuge, Clark County, Nevada*, by Heidi Roberts and Jerry Lyon, 137–158. Prepared for the Desert National Wildlife Refuge, U.S. Fish and Wildlife Service. HRA, Inc. Archaeological Report No. 08-22. Las Vegas, NV: HRA, Inc., Conservation Archaeology.

Lyneis, Margaret. 2012b. "The Status of Ceramic Research in Southern Nevada." Appendix I in *A Prehistoric Context for Southern Nevada*, ed. Heidi Roberts and Richard V.N. Ahlstrom, I-1 to I-27. Archaeological Report No. 011-05. Las Vegas, NV: HRA, Inc. Conservation Archaeology, and Carson City, NV: Gnomon, Inc.

Matson, R. G. 1991. *The Origins of Southwestern Agriculture*. Tucson: University of Arizona Press.

Mayer, James, William Eckerle, Sasha Tadie, and Orion Rogers. 2012. "Present and Past Environments of Southern Nevada." In *A Prehistoric Context for Southern Nevada*, ed. Heidi Roberts and Richard V.N. Ahlstrom, 11–60. HRA, Inc. Archaeological Report No. 011-05. Las vegas, NV: HRA, Inc. Conservation Archaeology, and Carson City, NV: Gnomon, Inc.

McGuire, Kelly, William Hildebrandt, Amy Gilreath, Jerome King, and John Berg. 2014. *The Prehistory of Gold Butte: A Virgin River Hinterland, Clark County, Nevada. University of Utah Anthropological Papers, No. 127*. Salt Lake City: The University of Utah Press.

Nabhan, Gary P. 1977. "Viable Seeds from Prehistoric Caches? Archaeobotanical Remains in Southwestern Folklore." *Kiva* 43(2):143–159. https://doi.org/10.1080/0023 1940.1977.11757897.

Rafferty, Kevin. 2008. "The Las Vegas Wash Intaglio and Patayan/Yuman Occupation of the Las Vegas Valley." *Nevada Archaeologist* 23:1–16.

Rhode, David. 2002. *Native Plants of Southern Nevada: An Ethnobotany*. Salt Lake City: The University of Utah Press.

Roberts, Heidi. 2012. "Post-Puebloan Period." In *A Prehistoric Context for Southern Nevada*, ed. Heidi Roberts and Richard V.N. Ahlstrom, 165–207. Archaeological Report No. 011-05. Las Vegas, NV: HRA, Inc. Conservation Archaeology, and Carson City, NV: Gnomon, Inc.

Roberts, Heidi, and Richard V.N. Ahlstrom. 2012a. "Gray, Buff, and Brown: Untangling Chronology, Trade, and Culture in the Las Vegas Valley, Southern Nevada." In *Meetings at the Margins: Prehistoric Cultural Interactions in the Intermountain West*, ed. David Rhode, 211–228. Salt Lake City: The University of Utah Press.

Roberts, Heidi, and Richard V.N. Ahlstrom, eds. 2012b. *A Prehistoric Context for Southern Nevada*. Archaeological Report No. 011-05. Las Vegas, NV: HRA, Inc. Conservation Archaeology, and Carson City, NV: Gnomon, Inc.

Roberts, Heidi, Suzanne Eskenazi, and Christopher Harper. 2007a. "Archaeological Test Excavations." In *Coyote Named This Place Pakonapanti: Corn Creek National Register Archaeological District, Desert National Wildlife Refuge, Clark County, Nevada*, by Heidi Roberts, Elizabeth von Till Warren, and Suzanne Eskenazi, 62–74. Prepared for US Fish and Wildlife Service, Desert National Wildlife Refuge, Las Vegas. Las Vegas, NV: HRA, Inc. Conservation Archaeology.

Roberts, Heidi, and Jerry Lyon. 2012. *Archaeological Excavations at the Corn Creek National Register Site, Desert National Wildlife Refuge, Clark County, Nevada*. Prepared for the Desert National Wildlife Refuge, US Fish and Wildlife Service. Archaeological Report No. 08-22. Las Vegas, NV: HRA, Inc., Conservation Archaeology.

Roberts, Heidi, Elizabeth von Till Warren, and Suzanne Eskenazi. 2007b. *Coyote Named this Place Pakonapanti: Corn Creek National Register Archaeological District, Desert National Wildlife Refuge, Clark County, Nevada, by Heidi Roberts, Elizabeth von Till Warren, and Suzanne Eskenazi*. Prepared for U.S. Fish and Wildlife Service, Desert National Wildlife Refuge, Las Vegas. Las Vegas, NV: HRA, Inc. Conservation Archaeology.

Rogers, Michael. 2015. *Ground-Penetrating Radar and Magnetometry Surveys at the Larder Site, Clark County, Nevada. Report submitted to HRA, Inc. Conservation Archaeology, Las Vegas, NV*.

Schlanger, Sarah H. 1992. "Recognizing Persistent Places in Anasazi Settlement Systems." In *Space, Time, and Archaeological Landscapes*, ed. Jacqueline Rossignol and LuAnn Wandsnider, 91–112. New York: Plenum Press. https://doi.org/10.1007/978-1-4899-2450-6_5.

Seymour, Gregory R. 1997. "A Reevaluation of Lower Colorado Buff Ware Ceramics: Redefining the Patayan in Southern Nevada." Unpublished MA thesis, University of Nevada, Las Vegas.

Seymour, Gregory R. 1999. *Cultural Resource Management Plan for the Las Vegas Springs Preserve, Clark County, Nevada*. Report No. 4-9-4. Las Vegas: Harry Reid Center for Environmental Studies, University of Nevada.

Seymour, Gregory R. 2005. "Ceramic Analysis." In *Desert Oasis: The Prehistory of Clark County Wetlands Park, Henderson, Nevada*, ed. Richard V.N. Ahlstrom, 63–71. HRA Papers in Archaeology No. 4. Las Vegas, NV: HRA, Inc. Conservation Archaeology.

Smith, Bruce D. 2001. "Low-Level Food Production." *Journal of Archaeological Research* 9(1):1–43. https://doi.org/10.1023/A:1009436110049.

Steward, Julian H. 1938. *Basin Plateau Aboriginal Sociopolitical Groups. Bureau of American Ethnology Bulletin 120.* Washington, DC: Smithsonian Institution.

Stewart, Kenneth M. 1983. "Mohave." In *Southwest*, ed. Alfonso Ortiz, 55–70. *Handbook of North American Indians*, Vol. 10, gen. ed. William C. Sturtevant. Washington, DC: Smithsonian Institution.

Stoffle, Richard, Rebecca Toupal, and Maria Nieves Zedeño. 2003. "Landscape, Nature, and Culture: A Diachronic Model of Human-Nature Co-Adaptations." In *Nature across Culture: View of Nature and the Environment in Non-Western Cultures*, ed. by H. Selin, 97–114. New York: Kluwer. https://doi.org/10.1007/978-94-017-0149-5_5.

Turner, Raymond M., Janice E. Bowers, and Tony L. Burgess. 1995. *Sonoran Desert Plants: An Ecological Atlas.* Tucson: The University of Arizona Press.

Warren, Claude N., and Robert H. Crabtree. 1986. "Prehistory of the Southwestern Area." In *Great Basin*, ed. Warren L. d'Azevedo, 183–93. *Handbook of North American Indians*, Vol. 11, gen. ed. William C. Sturtevant. Washington, DC: Smithsonian Institution Press.

Warren, Elizabeth von Till. 2007. "Southern Paiutes in Las Vegas History." In *Coyote Named This Place Pakonapanti: Corn Creek National Register Archaeological District, Desert National Wildlife Refuge, Clark County, Nevada*, by Heidi Roberts, Elizabeth von Till Warren, and Suzanne Eskenazi, 87–99. Prepared for US Fish and Wildlife Service, Desert National Wildlife Refuge, Las Vegas. Las Vegas, NV: HRA, Inc. Conservation Archaeology.

Wöcherl, Helga. 2005. "Pits and the Use of Extramural Space in Early Farming Communities." In *Material Cultures and Lifeways of Early Agricultural Communities in Southern Arizona*, ed. R. Jane Sliva, 19–46. Anthropological Papers No. 35. Tucson, AZ: Center for Desert Archaeology.

# 16

# The Jackson Flat Reservoir Project

*Examples of Culture Change at a Virgin Branch Settlement in Kanab, Utah*

HEIDI ROBERTS

The Virgin Branch Puebloans occupied major tributaries of the Colorado River in southern Nevada, southwestern Utah, and northwestern Arizona between 200 BC and AD 1300 (Roberts and Ahlstrom 2012a; Lyneis 1995). Perhaps because of the culture area's peripheral location on the northwestern edge of the Puebloan region, the Virgin Branch is marginalized and often not included in recent Southwestern syntheses (Gregory and Wilcox 2007; Irwin-Williams 2007:figure 2.7; Lekson 2008:figures 1.2, 1.3; Reed 2000:figure 1.1; Young and Herr 2012:figure 1.1; Wilshusen et al. 2012:figure 1.1). It is typically seen as an outlier that played a minor role in the development of Puebloan society throughout the Greater Southwest (Cordell and McBrinn 2012; Lekson 2008).

Our excavations for the Jackson Flat Reservoir data-recovery project in Kanab, Utah, throw these long-held views into question. Early radiocarbon dates on maize indicate that farming began in the Virgin Region over 3,000 years ago. This date is significantly older than the earliest maize in the Kayenta region, which traditionally has been considered the route of cultigen introduction (see Harry chapter 14, this volume). Furthermore, these early dates came from a component at Jackson Flat's largest site, Eagle's Watch, which included a substantial habitation structure, large storage features, and extramural hearths. The features were associated with a diverse assemblage of ornaments made of a variety of exotic materials.

This is just one example of culture change documented in the Jackson Flat project's archaeological record that can be examined through the lens of this volume's theme, namely diffusion as a mechanism for change. The Jackson Flat project area was occupied fairly continuously between the Middle Archaic period and the Pueblo I period, and the investigated sites contain open habitations with storage features, pithouse structures, and varied artifact assemblages that span the transition to farming and the sedentary lifeway that followed. In this chapter I explore the timing and context of changes in subsistence strategies, food-storage technologies, architecture, and other technological innovations, such as the use of the bow and arrow and pottery. The goal is to examine these data for evidence of culture change and processes like diffusion, migration, or even independent invention.

## THE JACKSON FLAT RESERVOIR ARCHAEOLOGICAL PROJECT

Between 2009 and 2012, HRA Inc. Conservation Archaeology, Brigham Young University's Office of Public Archaeology (OPA), and Bighorn Archaeological Consultants conducted data-recovery investigations at 10 archaeological sites that were impacted by the construction of a new reservoir. The project area was located just south of Kanab, in Kane County, Utah, at the eastern edge of the Virgin Branch area (figure 16.1). Combined, the archaeological sites contained over 60 major features that spanned the last 6,000 years; however, the period of most intensive use, and the focus of this chapter, occurred between the Late Archaic and Pueblo I periods. Because none of the dendrochronology samples produced dates, most of the project's habitation features were radiocarbon dated using cultigens from well-controlled contexts such as pithouse hearths or floors. Table 16.1 summarizes the radiocarbon-dated features that postdate the arrival of cultigens.

The largest habitation site in the project area, Eagle's Watch (42KA6165), was located on a two-lobed ridge sitting between tributaries of Kanab Creek. Until the creek became deeply entrenched late in the last century, the floodplain was likely a fertile marshy wet meadow. Eagle's Watch was occupied during the Early Agricultural (1300–800 BC), Basketmaker II (200 BC–AD 550), Basketmaker III (AD 550–700), and Pueblo I (AD 700–900) periods. The excavated portions of the site, including the eastern half under the footprint of the dam and the western edge along a pipeline corridor, contained 39 habitation structures, including one oversized pithouse that was built toward the end of the Basketmaker II period. The site was divided into three separate loci based on artifact and feature

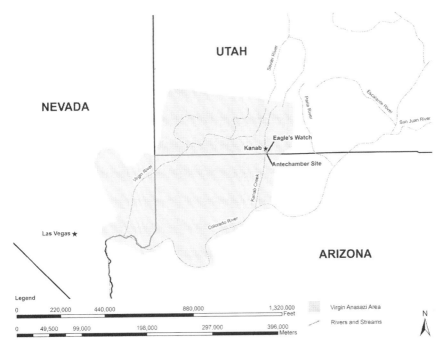

**FIGURE 16.1.** *Location of Eagle's Watch and the Antechamber site.*

distributions. HRA excavated Locus 2 and OPA and Bighorn excavated Loci 1 and 3 together This chapter focuses on Locus 2 at Eagle's Watch (see figure 16.2), and I also briefly discuss portions of smaller habitation sites, including 42KA6163, Loci 2 and 3 (figure 16.3), which was occupied exclusively during the Late Archaic Period and during the Basketmaker II/III transition.

## AN EXAMPLE OF MIGRATION: THE EARLY
## AGRICULTURAL PERIOD (1300–800 BC)

The Late Archaic components in the Jackson Flat project area at Jackrabbit Roast Midden (42KA6163, Loci 2 and 3) represented periodic seasonal use between 3635 and 1525 BC The component contained a thick, heavily bioturbated midden deposit with scattered fire-affected rock, a large roasting pit, and hearths. We inferred from the site's features and artifact assemblage, which included metate fragments, grinding slabs, cores, bifaces, hammerstones, debitage, lanceolate dart points, and a small number of rabbit bones, that the midden represented short-term camping activities that involved processing and cooking activities and perhaps communal jackrabbit hunts using nets. Despite an exhaustive search using backhoe excavation of trenches followed by hand excavation and mechanical

**TABLE 16.1.** Radiocarbon dates from Formative-period features in Locus 2 of Eagle's Watch (42KA6165) and Locus 1 of the Antechamber site (42KA6163).

| Site (42KA) | Feature | Sample: BETA | 14C ± σ Yrs bp | δ13C | Cal Yrs ± 2σ | Dated Material |
|---|---|---|---|---|---|---|
| 6165 | 30.1 | Pithouse hearth | 360452 | 2510 ± 30 | -11.6 o/oo | 920– 810 BC | Maize and Fabaceae |
| 6165 | 30.4 | Bell-shaped pit | 360453 | 2740 ± 30 | -10.4 o/oo | 1310–1120 BC | Maize |
| 6165 | 94 | Bell-shaped pit | 417361 | 2000 ± 30 | -11.2 o/oo | 50 BC–AD 65 | Maize |
| 6165 | 2006.2 | Pithouse floor pit | 360454 | 1580 ± 30 | -10.3 o/oo | AD 410–550 | Maize |
| 6165 | 38.1 | Pithouse hearth | 360443 | 1880 ± 30 | -24.0 o/oo | AD 70–220 | Squash seeds |
| 6165 | 34 | Pithouse floor | 360444 | 1920 ± 30 | -10.6 o/oo | AD 20–130 | Maize |
| 6165 | 2022 | Midden base | 360446 | 1950 ± 30 | -11.2 o/oo | 30–10 BC; AD 0–90, 100–120 | Maize and squash |
| 6165 | 18.1 | Pithouse floor pit | 360447 | 1970 ±3 0 | -10.8 o/oo | 40 BC–AD 80 | Maize |
| 6165 | 92 | Pithouse hearth | 360448 | 2080 ± 30 | -10.2 o/oo | 180–40 BC, 10–0 BC | Maize |
| 6163 | 17.1 | Pithouse hearth | 417357 | 1740 ± 30 | -11 o/oo | AD 235–385 | Maize cupules |
| 6163 | 39.1 | Pithouse hearth | 362329 | 1550 ± 30 | -9.2 o/oo | AD 430–580 | Maize |
| 6163 | 12 | Surface structure | 390947 | 1640 ± 30 | -12.3 o/oo | AD 345–430, 490–530 | Wood charcoal |
| 6163 | 9 | Pithouse floor | 362330 | 1450 ± 30 | -8.7 o/oo | AD 560–650 | Maize kernel |
| 6165 | 2008 | Pithouse floor | 360449 | 1450 ± 30 | -10.2 o/oo | AD 560–650 | Maize |
| 6165 | 45 | Pithouse floor | 360442 | 1320 ± 30 | -10.9 o/oo | AD 650–720, 740–770 | Squash seeds |
| 6165 | 2024 | Hearth in fill | 360445 | 1220 ± 30 | -12.1 o/oo | AD 690–750, 760–890 | Maize cupules |
| 6165 | 50.1 | Pithouse hearth | 368072 | 1150 ± 30 | -10.4 o/oo | AD 780–790, 800–970 | Maize cob |
| 6165 | 69.3 | Pithouse hearth | 360451 | 1250 ± 30 | -10.8 o/oo | AD 680–830, 840–870 | Maize cupules |
| 6165 | 2003 | Activity Surface | 390949 | 1190 ± 30 | -11.0 o/oo | AD 725–740, 770–895, 925-940 | Maize cupules |
| 6165 | 2009.1 | Pithouse hearth | 360450 | 1210 ± 30 | -10.3 o/oo | AD 710–750, 770–890 | Maize cupules |

Dates calibrated by Beta Analytic using INTCAL09 database.

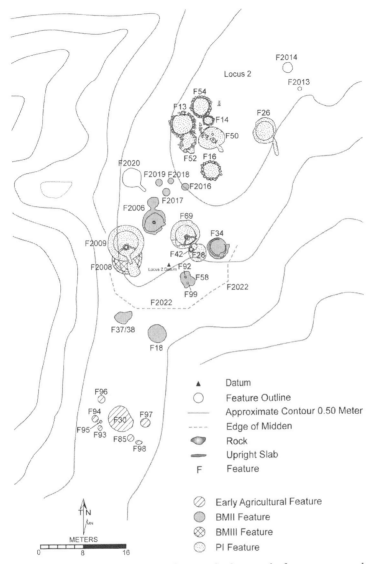

**FIGURE 16.2.** *Map of Locus 2 at Eagle's Watch, showing the features excavated.*

stripping of all cultural deposits to search for human remains, no habitation features were discovered that dated to the Late Archaic period.

A few hundred years after the Archaic component was abandoned, the farming lifeway appeared suddenly in the project area, and it was accompanied by new forms of architecture, storage technology, and artifacts. The Early Agricultural component at Eagle's Watch (42KA6165) was concentrated at the southern end of Locus 2 and consisted of a deep pithouse (Feature 30) surrounded by seven

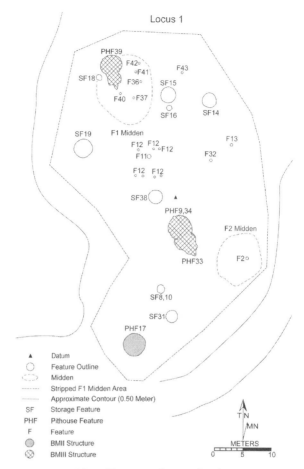

Locus 1

| | |
|---|---|
| ▲ | Datum |
| ◯ | Feature Outline |
| ⬭ | Midden |
| - - - - | Stripped F1 Midden Area |
| ·········· | Approximate Contour (0.50 Meter) |
| SF | Storage Feature |
| PHF | Pithouse Feature |
| F | Feature |
| ◉ | BMII Structure |
| ⊗ | BMIII Structure |

**FIGURE 16.3.** *Map of Locus 1 at the Antechamber site.*

extramural features (Features 85, 93–98) (figure 16.2). The extramural features included two large bell-shaped storage pits (Features 94 and 96), a circular shallow slab-lined pit (Feature 97), a rock-filled pit (Feature 85), two hearths, and a pit of unknown function (Features 93, 95, and 98). Two radiocarbon dates on maize were obtained from the pithouse hearth and from the base of a large bell-shaped pit located in the floor of the pithouse. The 2-sigma calibrated date range from Feature 30's central hearth was 920–810 BC (table 16.1) and the 2-sigma calibrated date range on the sample from the floor of Feature 30's bell-shaped pit was 1310–1120 BC.

These dates do not overlap, and they can be explained in the following way. The bell-shaped pit in the floor of Feature 30 was originally part of Feature 30.7, a smaller and older structure. This older structure was semisubterranean,

**FIGURE 16.4.** *Photograph of pithouse Feature 30 and pithouse Feature 30.7 within Feature 30 at Eagle's Watch.*

it measured just over 2.5 m in diameter, and postholes lined its perimeter. The base of its interior wall was partially lined with slabs and leaning posts that were part of its superstructure. The structure likely lacked a hearth, but contained a large central bell-shaped pit. At some point this smaller pit structure was expanded to a diameter of almost 5 m, the bell-shaped pit in the floor was capped with clay, and a shallow hearth was dug into center of the larger structure, Feature 30 (figure 16.4). Feature 30's expanded floor area doubled the useable floor area of the older structure. Both pit structures had been dug to a depth of 50 cm below the prehistoric surface and were 80–100 cm below the modern ground surface.

A number of flaked-stone tools were found either near the floor (in floor or roof fill) or in contact with the floor of pithouse Features 30 and 30.7 and from extramural pit Feature 85. Artifacts included Elko/San Pedro Corner-notched points, a biface that resembles a Cortaro point, a drill, a graver, a polished chalcedony ornament, a bone flesher, and a stone paint pallet. Tools recovered from the feature's lower fill included the edge of a trough metate fragment, a turquoise object that had been ground on two sides, and a small turquoise cylinder disk bead.

The floor and floor fill of an adjacent shallow slab-lined pit (Feature 97) contained several ornaments and artifacts including a core, two bone awls, a bone

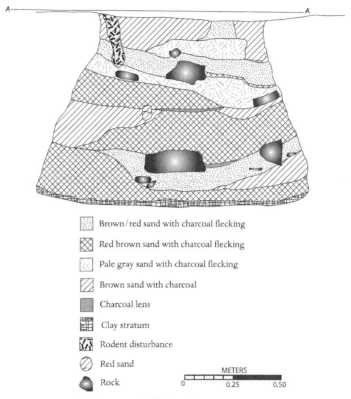

Brown / red sand with charcoal flecking

Red brown sand with charcoal flecking

Pale gray sand with charcoal flecking

Brown sand with charcoal

Charcoal lens

Clay stratum

Rodent disturbance

Red sand

Rock

METERS
0     0.25     0.50

**FIGURE 16.5.** *Profile of eastern half of the fill in Feature 94, one of two bell-shaped pits associated with the Early Agricultural component at Eagle's Watch.*

flesher, two spire-lopped *Olivella* beads, one small end-ground *Olivella* bead, one small ring *Olivella* bead, three bone cylinder beads, two chrysoprase elliptical barrel beads, and debitage.

In addition to the large bell-shaped pit in the floor of the Early Agricultural feature, we identified two large clay-rimmed bell-shaped pits next to the habitation (figure 16.5). One of the pits contained secondary burials in the upper fill that included portions of three individuals and numerous ornaments and other artifacts. A later radiocarbon date on maize from one of these features suggested that the pits were reused during the Basketmaker II period.

The sudden appearance of pithouse architecture, storage technology, and exotic ornaments is in direct contrast with the project area's Late Archaic adaptations. The Jackrabbit Roast Midden's occupation preceded the Early Agricultural component in Eagle's Watch by less than 300 years, yet the contrast between these two components is dramatic. While Jackrabbit Roast consisted of a charcoal-stained and artifact-rich deposit that had accumulated over hearths and a large rock-filled roasting pit, the Early Agricultural component contained a deep pithouse surrounded by extramural features that functioned as storage pits, hearths, and shallow slab-lined pits. Despite an extensive search using backhoe trenches and stripping techniques, no habitation features were found at the Late Archaic site. All of the macrobotanical samples processed from the Early Agricultural component contained maize, yet no cultigens were identified in the samples processed from the features in Jackrabbit Roast Midden. Other differences include projectile-point styles (Elko/San Pedro Corner-notched at Eagle's Watch Early Agricultural component versus lanceolate dart points at Jackrabbit Roast), presence of exotic goods in the Early Agricultural component (shell and turquoise at Eagle's Watch versus no exotic materials in Jackrabbit Roast), and prevalence of ornaments at the Early Agricultural component.

For the following reasons I suggest that the Early Agricultural component represents an intrusion of a small group of farmers from southern Arizona or perhaps even farther south. First, both the older habitation structure (Feature 30.7), with its central bell-shaped pit, and the larger pithouse are architectural forms that are found in southern Arizona's Early Agricultural sites, but not in the Virgin Branch or Kayenta regions until around 200 BC. Second, the pithouses are accompanied by projectile-point changes to styles that resemble those found in southern Arizona. Third, the ubiquity of maize recovered from Early Agricultural samples exceeded the ubiquity rates for the Basketmaker period. This suggests that these first farmers were possibly more reliant on cultigens than were the Basketmaker groups who succeeded them. Last, after this component was abandoned, the entire project area was not reoccupied for at least 400 years, which suggests that resident populations may have discontinued use of the Jackson project area once it was settled by farmers.

## BASKETMAKER II PERIOD (200 BC–AD 550): A CASE FOR THE ADOPTION OF HORTICULTURE

The Basketmaker II component at Locus 2, 42Ka6165 was situated in the center of the locus, between the Basketmaker III and Pueblo I components to the north and the Early Agricultural component to the south (figure 16.2). Radiocarbon dates on maize and squash from the floors, floor pits, or hearths of five pithouses (Features 18, 34, 38, 92, and 2006) indicate that the structures were occupied between 180 BC and AD 550. The base of the 50–70-cm-deep Locus 2 midden (Feature 2022) also dated to the early part of this period and presumably began accumulating at this time.

Pithouse architecture during the Basketmaker II period was variable, yet exhibited increasing complexity through time. Three of the pithouses were shallow (10–20 cm deep) basin-shaped structures that lacked interior postholes. The

**FIGURE 16.6.** *Overview of Feature 2006 with the antechamber in the foreground, view to the south.*

structures were likely ephemeral brush shelters with conical-style roofs. All but one of the Basketmaker II pithouses had a central unlined hearth, and floor pits were present in three of the structures. The sterile clay substrate was used as wall or roof covering on some of the pithouses, and one of the structure's walls was slab-lined. Later in the period, the pithouses contained more floor features, including benches and stepped entries, and one of the structures that dated late in the sequence had a slab-lined antechamber on its northern side (figure 16.6). Only one of the pithouses, Feature 34, had a floor that was excavated more than 50 cm below the prehistoric ground surface. That structure, occupied sometime between AD 20 and 130, had a bench, four or five central posts, a stepped entry, and a hearth that was probably rock-lined.

A cluster of four bell-shaped pits and a grouping of slab-lined hearths were discovered during mechanical stripping to the north and south of the house features. The bell-shaped storage pits were located just to the north of pithouse Feature 2006's antechamber, and they were covered by a thick midden deposit that began accumulating during this period. The features had been excavated into the sterile substrate and they were only partially excavated since they were located just inside the portions of the site preserved by a conservation easement. These features were not radiocarbon dated, yet we have associated them with the Basketmaker II component, rather than the following Basketmaker III component, for three reasons. First, the fill of the features lacked ceramics except in the uppermost levels.

Second, the features were located under the midden deposits generated during the subsequent occupations. Third, the large slab-lined storage cists that were located several meters north of the bell-shaped pits were built during the end of the Basketmaker II period or early in the Basketmaker III period. Since the bell-shaped pits were filled primarily with fine sand deposits without artifacts, it is likely that their use was discontinued after the large slab-lined cists were built.

Because many of the features in the Basketmaker II component were covered with later deposits, it was difficult to determine if ceramic associations were intrusive and due to post-occupational disturbances. Most of the structures lacked pottery associated with the floors and floor fill; however, one of the later pithouses, Feature 2006, located at the north end of the locus, contained plain North Creek Grayware pottery associated with the floor and in the floor pits. Ornaments were rare in the Basketmaker II structures; only one contained a single turquoise pebble in the fill. Bone awls were common, as was evidence of cultigens, and grinding slabs dominated the ground-stone assemblage. The only projectile point associated with a Basketmaker II structure was a single Elko Corner-notched point in the antechambered pithouse, Feature 2006.

There are several reasons to suspect that this Basketmaker occupation represents a local adaptation by Archaic groups who incorporated maize farming into their seasonal round. First, the oldest structures were small, shallow, brush shelters that resembled field houses or Late Archaic brush shelters, rather than the deep, formal pithouses built earlier. The brush shelters were likely seasonal residences and they were associated with small, uniform artifact assemblages that lacked ornaments and formal tools, such as projectile points. The bell-shaped pits that were built during the Early Agricultural period continued to be used at Eagle's Watch, but only one similar bell-shaped pit was built and used at five small Basketmaker II habitation sites (42KA6158, 42KA6160, 42KA6164, 42KA6167, and 42KA6897) investigated elsewhere in the Jackson Flat project area. Between 200 BC and AD 200 Jackson Flat's Basketmaker occupants grew maize and lived in shallow brush shelters at six of Jackson Flat's sites. With one possible exception, they did not construct deep pithouses nor did they build bell-shaped storage features at the other small habitation sites.

## THE ANTECHAMBER SITE: A BASKETMAKER II/III TRANSITIONAL COMPONENT: THE ADDITION OF NEW TECHNOLOGIES AND INCREASING SEDENTISM

One of the smaller habitation sites, the Antechamber site (42KA6163, Locus 1), was occupied toward the end of the Basketmaker II and the beginning of the Basketmaker III periods. During this period the bow and arrow was introduced, pithouse architecture took new forms, and deep slab-lined storage cists replaced unlined pits. Because some of these architectural forms, for example benches, represent gradual incremental additions, it is not clear if Jackson's Basketmaker residents were independently developing these new styles, or borrowing them from adjacent groups.

The Antechamber site was located several hundred meters southeast of Eagle's Watch, and contained a cluster of three pithouses associated with extramural hearths, a surface structure, and several large slab-lined storage cists (figure 16.3). Two of the pithouses (Features 9 and 39) had attached triangular antechambers and benches, while the third pithouse (Feature 17) lacked both of these features. The radiocarbon dates on maize suggests that the antechamber structures were occupied between AD 430 and 650 (see table 16.1) and the pithouse without an antechamber was built slightly earlier, between AD 235 and 385. Although the dates on this component extend into the Basketmaker III period, pottery was not widely used by the site's occupants. No pottery was recovered from the floors, roof fall, or floor fill of the habitation structures, and all told, four pieces of North Creek Grayware were collected from just outside, or from the upper fill, of two of the pithouses. The size of these sherds suggests that this pottery was probably intrusive; however, there is also a possibility that the assemblage represents early use of plain gray pottery by the site's occupants.

Because the Antechamber site was occupied for a briefer time than Eagle's Watch, and underwent minimal reuse after abandonment, it provides temporal resolution on the introduction of new technologies such as the bow and arrow, slab-lined storage structures, and architectural features such as benches, storage bins, and attached antechambers. The radiocarbon dates on maize suggest that the pithouses were occupied sequentially, rather than at the same time.

Feature 17 was the first structure built at the site. It was an earth-lodge-style pithouse that measured 4 m in diameter and the floor was excavated 50–60 cm below the prehistoric surface. The roof was built with four posts placed in each corner, and the structure lacked an antechamber and a bench. It was occupied sometime between AD 235 and 385 (figure 16.7).

Dates on maize indicate that Feature 39, and possibly the deeper floor in Feature 9, were constructed next. Both of these structures had triangular antechambers, which served as entries, and they were appended to the southeastern edge of the main chamber. Floor bins were built into the corners of the antechambers, and the remodeled pithouse, Feature 9, had a hearth in the antechamber rather than in the main chamber. The older antechambered pithouse, Feature 39, probably had a wooden bench lining the western half of the main chamber and both earlier and later floors in pithouse Feature 9 had a wide slab-lined bench. Feature 9's antechamber was likely added when it was remodeled (figure 16.8). The latest date, on maize, came from the upper floor of this structure.

Pithouse Features 9 and 39 each had abundant evidence of maize, and both corn and cheno-ams were also recovered from the extramural features and large storage

**FIGURE 16.7.** *Pithouse Feature 17 after excavation at the Antechamber site, looking north.*

cists. While we see trends in pithouse architecture through time—for example increased depth and the addition of complex floor features—there remained considerable variability throughout the project area, which lends support to our inference that the these culture changes were likely the product of borrowing.

Although the Antechamber site's occupants were not invested in pottery technology, they had embraced bow and arrow technology. Anasazi stemmed, Rosegate, Bull Creek, and two arrow points that could not be typed were collected from the floors and fill of both pithouses and storage features. Two dart points were also recovered, and they included an Elko-series dart point from the older floor of pithouse Feature 9 and an unidentified dart point from Feature 20, a roasting pit. The wide range of point styles recovered from this site lends support to the possibility that this technology was introduced as an idea, via diffusion, and the variation of projectile-point styles represented experimentation to perfect the use of this new technology.

## BASKETMAKER III PERIOD IN EAGLE'S WATCH:
## POPULATION GROWTH AND INCREASED SEDENTISM

A majority of the pithouses occupied during the Basketmaker III (AD 550–700) period at Eagle's Watch were located in Locus 3, excavated by Brigham Young

**FIGURE 16.8.** *Feature 9 at the Antechamber site after excavation, showing the upper and older floors in the main chamber.*

University. Like Locus 2, Locus 3 was occupied between the Basketmaker II and Pueblo I periods, yet the period of most intensive use was likely the Basketmaker III period. Locus 3 also contained an oversized pithouse, which measured 9 m in diameter and was benched. A date on maize from this structure's deep central hearth yielded a two-sigma calibrated date range of AD 420–560 consistent with the late Basketmaker II period. After the oversized structure was abandoned its house pit was reused for two successive structures that were occupied during the Basketmaker III and Pueblo I periods.

The Basketmaker III component in Locus 2 at Eagle's Watch included two pithouses in the central habitation area, two pithouses near Locus 3, five slab-lined storage cists, one hearth, and one activity surface (figure 16.2). Radiocarbon dates on maize and squash from the floors of two of the pithouses (Features 45 and 2008) indicate that they were occupied sometime between AD 550 and 720. We have assigned the other two pithouses—Features 28 and 2007—to this period based on stratigraphic relationships and artifact associations.

All four of the Basketmaker III pithouses in Locus 2 were found in poor condition. In two cases—Features 28 and 2008—Pueblo I pithouses were built directly on top of the burnt Basketmaker III structures. The other two pithouses located

**FIGURE 16.9.** *The southwest quarter of Feature 2008 with the artifact assemblage in situ on the floor, looking south.*

at the northern edge of Locus 2—Features 45 and 2007—were poorly preserved due to extensive rodent activity related to the accumulation of the Locus 3 midden over the structures after their abandonment.

Although the Basketmaker III structures in Locus 2 were incomplete or in poor condition, one of them, Feature 2008, contained a pristine assemblage of floor artifacts on portions of the burnt floor that was left intact when an intrusive pithouse (Feature 2009) was built through its center. We were able to learn about the inhabitants' activities at the time when the structure burned from this floor assemblage (figure 16.9). The artifacts represented a cohesive grouping of functional tools that included several types of ground stone, flaked stone tools, whole pottery vessels, and other artifacts. Macrobotanical samples collected from the base of a Utah-style metate included quantities of wild seeds that were being ground when the feature burnt catastrophically. We do not know if the fire occurred naturally or if it was set intentionally, though we can say that the structure was likely being occupied when it caught on fire.

With the exception of pithouse Feature 2008, pottery assemblages associated with the Basketmaker III structures in Locus 2 were problematic due to the structures' poor conditions and post-occupational disturbances. Only Feature 2008 and a large storage structure, Feature 54, are discussed here in detail. Pottery recovered from pithouse Feature 2008 included North Creek Gray sherds that

**FIGURE 16.10.** *Photograph of a lobed-circle slab-lined storage feature in Locus 2, Eagle's Watch view to the northeast. Feature 54 is to the left and Feature 14 is to the right.*

represented jars, one Shinarump Plain sherd, and one unpainted Tusayan White Ware sherd. Feature 54 was a large slab-lined semisubterranean storage structure that was likely used throughout the Basketmaker III period. A small assemblage of pottery recovered from the floor of this feature was identified by Janet Hagopian (2016) as early brownware. However, a detailed comparison of these sherds to early brownwares recovered elsewhere in the Southwest is needed.

The large cists (Features 13/52 and 54/14) at Eagle's Watch were likely built during the late Basketmaker II/early Basketmaker III periods (figure 16.10). When first built they probably lacked the appended smaller cist and enclosing walls. During the late Basketmaker III period or possibly even the Pueblo I period, smaller cists were appended and a masonry wall was added that encircled the smaller cists. The wall and cist transformed the structure to a distinctive lobed-circle shape (see figure 16.9). This architectural trait has been associated with late Basketmaker III/early Pueblo I rock art images in southeastern Utah known as "procession" panels. Robins and Hays-Gilpin (2000) and more recently Wilshusen et al. (2012) argue that the lobed-circle shapes depicted in these panels are pendants and are associated with fertility or house shapes. Turquoise pendants of this shape were recovered from a child burial near the antechamber of a Pueblo I pithouse (Feature 69) built over a burnt structure.

All but one of the 55 sets of human remains excavated during the project came from Eagle's Watch. Most of the burials were discovered during backhoe stripping that was conducted at all the sites to locate mortuary features. Sixteen burial features, containing 36 individuals, were concentrated in a cemetery area located between Loci 2 and 3. The remaining burials were scattered throughout Locus 2. Since destructive analyses such as radiocarbon dating and carbon isotopes were not allowed by the tribes participating in the federal Section 106 and state NAGPRA processes, sorting the burials chronologically proved challenging. Using shell ornaments, which were common, plus projectile-point and pottery types, we were able to separate most of these individuals into two groups. Thirty-four of the individuals thus dated between the Late Archaic and Basketmaker III periods, between 1800 BC and AD 700, and eight other burials fall between AD 700 and 900, during the Pueblo I period. Twelve individuals had no associated diagnostic artifacts and remain undated.

The Basketmaker-period burials were concentrated in the cemetery area, and the later, Pueblo I, burials were located in and around the habitation features in Locus 2. Perhaps the main difference between the early and late groups is the common practice of multiple burials in the Basketmaker group. Multiple burials included primary and secondary remains in burial features. Spurr and Roberts (2014) have argued that in three multiple burials "human remains," represented by primary and secondary burials, served as grave goods, or "accessory people."

Burial 6 is the best example of this process. In this burial a robust adult male age 30–45 was the first interment, placed supine on the bottom of a shallow, partially lined circular pit. Next, two subadults, aged 6 months and 3–5 years, were primary burials placed on his chest. An adult primary burial, a male aged 25–35 with periosteal lesions on his tibia, was placed along the west wall of the pit, and a third adult primary interment in a flexed position was placed along the north and northeast wall with the head to the south-southeast. The crania from two individuals were disarticulated from their torsos and set down on the slabs lining the pit bottom. In one case, the upper three cervical vertebrae were found directly beneath the cranium. The basilar portion of both crania was too eroded to assess damage due to removal of the cranium from the vertebral column. Remains of a third subadult were identified during the post-excavation inventory, but the position of the individual was not clear during excavation.

The types of grave goods associated with the cemetery burials versus the later Pueblo I burials were also different. The Basketmaker burials contained personal ornaments and "accessory people" that were included in the graves as both primary and secondary interments. Pueblo I burials were furnished with ornaments and household items such as pottery, ground stone, and flaked-stone tools. Shell ornaments were found in a fairly large percentage of all the burials, but turquoise was most prevalent in the Pueblo I infant burials.

Seven burials, which we believe to be associated with the Pueblo period, were interred with turquoise pendants or unworked turquoise, and four of these individuals were between the ages of 1 and 4 years at death. One juvenile burial, aged 3–4 years, contained an unusually large number of grave goods, including 101 shell disk beads, two cut-shell pendants, 56 pieces of partially worked turquoise, and 121 unworked nuggets of turquoise that had been scattered over the body. The fact that juvenile burials are more frequently associated with turquoise pendants and nuggets than are adult burials is an intriguing pattern that needs further study.

## EAGLE'S WATCH PUEBLO I COMPONENT IN LOCUS 2: A CASE FOR A POPULATION INTRUSION

The Pueblo I component at Locus 2 in Eagle's Watch was focused in the center of the locus and in the immediate vicinity of the large storage structures (figure 16.2). The Pueblo I features included five pithouses, five slab-lined storage cists, two hearths, two pits, one midden, and two activity surfaces. Radiocarbon dates on maize or squash from the floors or hearths of two of the pithouses with detached antechambers (Features 69 and 2009) indicate that they were occupied between AD 680 and 890, and a third structure, Feature 50, was likely occupied slightly later, between AD 780 and 970 (see table 16.1). Since cultigens were not recovered from the hearth of pithouse Feature 26, we dated organics recovered from a hearth (Feature 2024) in the structure's lower fill, which indicated the hearth was used between AD 690 and 890. This suggests that the underlying pithouse, Feature 26, was occupied during the earlier range of the Pueblo I period. We have linked a fifth pithouse (Feature 2020), which we did not excavate, to this period based on stratigraphic relationships, architecture, and artifact associations.

The two large slab-lined storage cists continued to be used and an enclosing wall was likely added. Toward the end of the Pueblo I period, the larger slab-lined cist, Feature 13, probably functioned as a temporary habitation or work area (Feature 2003), and the 2-sigma calibrated date range obtained on maize from the hearth indicates it was used for this purpose between AD 725 and 940. Although only this extramural feature was radiocarbon dated, the others were included on the basis of stratigraphic relationships or artifact associations.

Pottery collected from dated Pueblo I contexts included plain grayware and Tallahogan Red. Mesquite and Washington Black-on-gray wares were found in the general fill of Pueblo I structures, but they were not associated with the floor or floor fill contexts. Their presence in the fill suggests that decorated pottery occurs late in the Pueblo I sequence and was rare. One decorated bowl was documented from a burial in the upper fill of Feature 2009. This pithouse had a detached antechamber that had filled with cultural debris and midden deposits before the burial was interred. Unfortunately, the decorations on this bowl could not be classified as a known type. In Locus 2 the only pottery type other

**FIGURE 16.11.** *Pithouse Feature 26 after excavation, looking southeast toward the passage entryway. Note the smoke-hole cover resting on the floor in the center of the structure.*

than plainware that was associated with dated contexts was Tallahogan Red. Projectile points associated with Pueblo I–dated contexts shifted to Parowan Basal-notched arrow points, and the recovery of Parowan points from the floor vault of pithouse Feature 69 indicates that the points were being used in Locus 2 between AD 680 and 870.

The pithouses built during this period represented two different styles of benched earth lodges, including one type with a detached antechamber (figure 16.11) and a second type with a ventilator that may also have functioned as a passageway or entry (figure 16.12). The two pithouses with detached antechambers were adjacent to each other in the center of Locus 2. Both had floor ridges radiating from central hearths, deep floor vaults, slab-lined benches, and slab-lined passageways connecting the antechamber to the main chamber (see figure 16.11). The radiocarbon date ranges for two of the antechamber structures (Features 69 and 2009) and, by inference, the ventilator pithouse (Feature 26), overlap, suggesting they may have been contemporaneous. Unfortunately, the radiocarbon date ranges cover a 200-year period (AD 680–890) and do not provide sufficient precision to determine if the structures were occupied at the same time or sequentially. If pithouses were occupied for 30 years or less, then all three structures could have

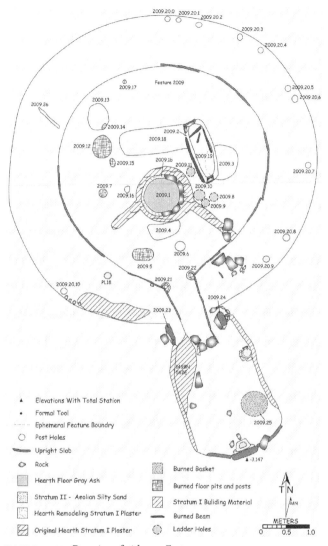

Elevations With Total Station
Formal Tool
Ephemeral Feature Boundry
Post Holes
Upright Slab
Rock
Hearth Floor Gray Ash
Stratum II - Aeolian Silty Sand
Hearth Remodeling Stratum I Plaster
Original Hearth Stratum I Plaster

Burned Basket
Burned floor pits and posts
Stratum I Buliding Material
Burned Beam
Ladder Holes

METERS
0    0.5    1.0

**FIGURE 16.12.** *Drawing of pithouse Feature 2009.*

been occupied sequentially. The fourth pithouse, Feature 50, was a shallow structure that lacked a bench, but contained a ventilator or passageway entry. This
pithouse, and the activity surface (Feature 2003) in the fill of the adjacent slab-lined
cist, Feature 13, may have been the last features occupied in Locus 2. The dates on
both extended 100 years later than the other structures. Features 50 and 26 each
contained ventilators and neither had floor ridges or floor vaults. These structures follow a trend observed elsewhere in the Jackson Flat sites, namely that the
latest Pueblo I structures become more shallow and less architecturally complex.

Three of the pithouses in Locus 2 (Features 26, 69, 2009) were in excellent condition and I argue that they were abandoned in an orderly, perhaps ritual fashion. A ritual abandonment process is argued using three lines of evidence. First, the structures were void of living-floor assemblages, and only a few artifacts were associated with the floor. Second, many of the hearths and floor pits were sealed with clay. Third, certain types of artifacts, such as pigments, pottery vessels, and debitage, appeared intentionally scattered or placed in certain contexts.

Evidence that these three habitation features were occupied by a group of individuals from the south or southeast of the Virgin Branch region is summarized as follows. First, many of the architectural features associated with the detached antechamber pithouses—such as floor vaults and floor ridges—are more typically found in the San Juan and Four Corners region than in the Virgin Puebloan region (Lyneis 1995; McFadden 2000). At Eagle's Watch this suite of floor features appears suddenly and has no antecedent forms; in other words, the architectural changes are abrupt and dramatic.

Second, the detached antechamber structures were associated with new types of artifacts, which included Tallahogan Red pottery and Parowan Basal-notched points. Harry et al. (2016) recently learned that the redware was likely produced in the heartland of the Kayenta region located south and east of the Colorado River. Tallahogan Red has not been widely reported in the Virgin Puebloan region (Lyneis 1995; McFadden 2000), and Parowan points become ubiquitous in the Fremont and Virgin culture areas, but only after AD 900 (Justice 2002:Map 36). Justice (2002) extends the distribution of these points from the western edge of the Virgin Branch region east to Chaco Canyon. Our well-dated contexts demonstrate that this arrow-point style was the dominant type used by the builders of the detached antechamber structures between AD 680 and 870.

Third, the burning of at least one of the Basketmaker III structures (Feature 2008) located underneath the detached antechamber structure, Feature 2009, occurred suddenly and catastrophically while still in use. A large artifact assemblage was left partially undisturbed when the detached antechamber structure was built directly over it. While I could not determine if the fire was set intentionally or accidentally, if it was accidental than why didn't the builders of the new pithouse scavenge the possessions within the burned structure? Is this because the builders of the detached antechamber pithouse viewed these items as not to their liking or perhaps foreign?

Fourth, although obsidian was rare in the flaked-stone assemblages, of the 30 pieces sourced, those associated with Eagle Watch's Pueblo I contexts were dominated by RS Hill and Partridge Creek sources in Arizona. The obsidian associated with Archaic/Basketmaker and post–Pueblo I contexts were more often linked to sources located to the northwest, such as the Panaca Summit/Modena and Wild Horse Canyon sources in southwestern Utah or Nevada.

The final reason to link the Pueblo I occupants to a population intrusion is related to the changes in the mortuary practices. The mortuary practices of the site's new occupants were different in several important ways from the earlier Basketmaker occupants. First, burial location shifted from the cemetery area, located between Loci 2 and 3, to the midden and fill of habitation structures in Locus 2. Second, Pueblo I burials were single primary interments rather than multiple and secondary burials, which dominated the Basketmaker II and III burials in the cemetery area. During the Pueblo I period, utility items, such as pottery and ground stone, become common mortuary furnishings, and turquoise was often included with the juvenile burials. Last, cranial modification was practiced for the first time. Whether this cranial modification is intentional or unintentional is unclear, yet it does represent cultural change, perhaps associated with childcare practices. It is possible that children born to the site's new occupants spent a larger portion of their infancy on cradleboards or that the cradleboard design was altered to intentionally flatten the child's occipital region, or a combination of these factors.

## CONCLUSIONS

Although it is still early to draw conclusions regarding the mechanisms for culture changes observed in the Jackson Flat archaeological record, three major points can be made from the preliminary excavation data. The first is that maize farming was introduced early to the Virgin area, and possibly even before it was adopted in the Kayenta region. New lines of evidence suggest that maize may have followed the same route as European cultigens, namely up the Colorado River from Arizona into southern Nevada and Utah (Fowler and Fowler 1981; Roberts and Ahlstrom 2012b).

Second, the use of turquoise and greenstone for ornaments began in the project area during the Early Agricultural period and increased in intensity during the Pueblo I period. It seems that the site's occupants did not use turquoise to any great extent during the Basketmaker II and III periods; however, during the Pueblo I period ornaments were likely manufactured on site and buried in finished and partially worked forms with child burials. Most archaeologists who have worked in the Virgin Branch area have remarked on the quantities and significance of turquoise and shell trade goods. Margaret Lyneis (1982), Kevin Rafferty (1989, 1990), Richard Ahlstrom and I (Roberts and Ahlstrom 2012b), and recently Sharon Hull et. al. (2014), have suggested that the Virgin Branch played a key role in the long-distance trade of turquoise and shell to Chaco and the Four Corners region. The presence of these minerals early in the archaeological record, and the large quantities of this mineral in infant burials after AD 700, raise new questions.

The third important inference we can make from the Jackson Flat project data is that burial practices and household architecture at Eagle's Watch changed in sudden and dramatic ways after AD 700 (Spurr and Roberts 2014). Pithouses added detached antechambers, floor ridges, and floor vaults, which aren't typically found in the Virgin Puebloan region. Burial location, type, and grave goods also changed significantly. The association of an infant burial with large quantities of exotic goods, both shell and turquoise, offers tantalizing hints that social status may have shifted from attained to inherited status. Since the Tallahogan Redware and the small quantities of obsidian sourced from the Eagle Watch's Pueblo I contexts have been linked to northern Arizona sources, it is possible that the site's Pueblo I occupants were from the Kayenta region. Further comparative research is needed to evaluate the similarities and differences between the Eagle Watch Pueblo I pithouses and those in the Virgin Branch area and in other adjacent culture areas throughout the Southwest. Because the detailed reports of these investigations are still in progress, I would like to caution the reader that these findings are preliminary and our interpretations may change as our analysis continues.

*Acknowledgments.* Many individuals participated in the excavation, analysis, and write-up of these data. I'd particularly like to thank Karen Harry and the reviewers who read and commented on earlier versions of this chapter. I also thank Kenny Wintch of the Utah School and Institutional Trust Land Administration, who served as Project Manager and kept the project moving forward and on track despite numerous administrative and political difficulties. Funding was provided by the Kane County Water Conservancy District and the US Army Corps of Engineers, Sacramento District. I'd also like to offer special thanks the following participants, analysts, and reviewers who made this essay possible, including Chris Harper, Richard Ahlstrom, Keith Hardin, Rich Talbot, Lane Richens (ground stone), Dale Gourley (ornaments), Robert Nash (faunal analyst), Joel Janetski (flaked-stone tools), Kim Spurr (human osteology), Janet Hagopian (ceramics), Stewart Deats (pigments), Amanda Landon, John Jorgenson, Leo Cisneros, Mike Oisfe, Margaret Lyneis, Karen Harry, Don and Kay Fowler, Barb Roth, the Kaibab Band of Paiutes, and crew members and volunteers who are too numerous to list individually.

## REFERENCES

Cordell, Linda S., and Maxine E. McBrinn. 2012. *Archaeology of the Southwest*. Walnut Creek, CA: Left Coast Press.

Fowler, Catherine S., and Don D. Fowler. 1981. "The Southern Paiute, A.D. 1400–1776." In *The Protohistoric Period in the North American Southwest, A.D. 1450–1700*, ed. D. Wilcox and B. Masse, 129–162. Anthropological Paper No. 24. Tempe: Arizona State University.

Gregory, David A., and David R. Wilcox, eds. 2007. *Zuni Origins*. Tucson: University of Arizona Press.

Hagopian, Janet. 2016. "The Ceramics of Jackson Flat." Paper Presented at the 35th Great Basin Anthropological Conference, Reno, NV.

Harry, Karen, Sachiko Sakai, and Janet Hagopian. 2016. "Patterns of Ceramic Production and Distribution at the Jackson Flat Sites." Paper Presented at the 35th Great Basin Anthropological Conference, Reno, NV.

Hull, Sharon, Mostafa Fayek, Francis J. Mathien, and Heidi Roberts. 2014. "Turquoise Trade of the Ancestral Puebloan: Chaco and Beyond." *Journal of Archaeological Science* 45:187–195. https://doi.org/10.1016/j.jas.2014.02.016.

Irwin-Williams, Cynthia. 2007. "Prehistoric Cultural and Linguistic Patterns in the Southwest since 5000 B.C." In *Zuni Origins*, ed. David A. Gregory and David R. Wilcox, 14–21. Tucson: The University of Arizona Press.

Justice, Noel. 2002. *Stone Age Spear and Arrow Points of California and the Great Basin*. Bloomington: Indiana University Press.

Lekson, Stephen H. 2008. *A History of the Ancient Southwest*. Santa Fe, NM: A School for Advanced Research.

Lyneis, Margaret M. 1982. "Prehistory in the Southern Great Basin." In *Man and Environment in the Great Basin*, edited by David B. Madsen and James F. O'Connell, 172–85. SAA Papers No. 2. Washington, DC: Society for American Archaeology.

Lyneis, Margaret M. 1995. "The Virgin Anasazi Far Western Puebloans." *Journal of World Prehistory* 9:199–241. https://doi.org/10.1007/BF02221839.

McFadden, Douglas. 2000. *"Formative Chronology and Site Distribution on the Grand Staircase National Monument (Draft)."* Manuscript on file Grand Staircase National Monument, Kanab, UT.

Rafferty, Kevin. 1989. "Virgin Anasazi Sociopolitical Organization, A.D. 1 to 1150." In *The Sociopolitical Structure of Prehistoric Southwestern Societies*, ed. Steadman Upham, Kent G. Lightfoot, and Roberta A. Jewett, 557–580. Boulder, CO: Westview Press.

Rafferty, Kevin. 1990. "The Virgin Anasazi and the Pan Southwestern Trade System, A.D. 900–1150." *Kiva* 56:3–24. https://doi.org/10.1080/00231940.1990.11758154.

Reed, Paul F., ed. 2000. *Foundations of Anasazi Culture: The Basketmaker–Pueblo Transition*. Salt Lake City: University of Utah Press.

Roberts, Heidi, and Richard V.N. Ahlstrom. 2012a. *A Prehistoric Context for Southern Nevada*. Las Vegas, NV: HRA Inc., Conservation Archaeology. http://nvshpo.org/dmdocuments/SNV_PrehistContext_2012.

Roberts, Heidi, and Richard V.N. Ahlstrom. 2012b. "Gray, Buff, and Brown: Untangling Chronology, Trade, and Culture in the Las Vegas Valley, Southern Nevada." In *Meetings at the Margins: Prehistoric Cultural Interactions in the Intermountain West*, ed. David Rhode, 211–228. Salt Lake City: The University of Utah Press.

Robins, Michael R., and Kelley A. Hays-Gilpin. 2000. "The Bird in the Basket: Gender and Social Change in Basketmaker Iconography." In *Foundations of Anasazi Culture: The Basketmaker–Pueblo Transition*, ed. Paul F. Reed, 231–247. Salt Lake City: University of Utah Press.

Spurr, Kimberly, and Heidi Roberts. 2014. "Mortuary Practices of Fifty-four Individuals Recovered from a Large Virgin Branch Puebloan Habitation in Kanab, Utah." Paper presented at the 79th Annual Meeting of the Society for American Archaeology, Austin, TX.

Wilshusen, Richard A., Gregson Schachner, and James R. Allison, eds. 2012. *Crucible of Pueblos: The Early Pueblo Period in the Northern Southwest*. Los Angeles: Cotsen Institute of Archaeology, University of California.

Young, Lisa C., and Sarah A. Herr, eds. 2012. *Southwestern Pithouse Communities, AD 200–900*. Tucson: The University of Arizona Press.

# 17

# The Late Fremont Regional System

RICHARD K. TALBOT

Regional systems, as applied in the last several decades (e.g., Crown 1991; Doyle 1992; Hegmon and Plog 1996; Kantner 2003; Lekson 1996; McGuire et al. 1994; Neitzel 1994; Upham and Reed 1989; Wilcox 1979, 1980; various in Neitzel 1999 and Hegmon 2000), comprise groups of sites with some degree of social interaction and interrelatedness, as reflected by common material remains, architecture, and symbolism. Commonalities in the Southwest can be variably structured, from the highly complex organization and accoutrements of Chaco, to the more mundane (by comparison) and dispersed settlements of the Hohoham, Rio Grande, Kayenta, or other areas. Regional systems, however, are not prehistoric realities or a replacement for culture area classifications; rather, regional analysis is meant as an analytic and organizational tool in the study of diversity in relationships (Gregory 1991:191–192). As Neitzel (2000:36) notes: "To call some prehistoric pattern a regional system is to say only that the pattern encompasses a broad area and presumably signifies wide-spread interaction. The term implies nothing about the actual extent or boundedness of the area or the nature of the inferred interaction . . . the regional system concept is valuable for future

DOI: 10.5876/9781607327356.c017

research as an impetus for investigating the dimensions of variability encompassed by the term."

Social groups such as those encompassing regional systems operate in an ever-changing and poorly understood web of hierarchical relationships (Barth 1998; Cordell 2008; Creamer 2000; Duff 2002; Nietzel 2000:27; McGuire et al. 1994:244). Archaeological patterns created by the intersection of, and that define, those multiscalar relationships are likely to be as variable as the time and circumstance that created them. Some patterns may be long-lasting and slow to change, while others may develop and diverge rapidly. Regional analysis, to be most useful as an analytical tool, must incorporate both spatiotemporal and scalar perspectives, and the study of those relationships must be as diachronic and far reaching as the data allow.

The issue of defining connectivity within variable patterns has particular relevance to archaeologists studying the Fremont; indeed, if there is a label most commonly ascribed to Fremont, it is *variable*. From the time of Neil Judd's (1926) and Noel Morss's (1931) descriptions of pottery-producing, pithouse-dwelling farmers north of the traditional Southwest, archaeologists have struggled to find a proper context in which to study Fremont variability. For example, the contrasts between what Judd saw in the eastern Great Basin and what Morss saw on the Colorado Plateau seemed to suggest archaeologically distinct traditions. It was not long, however, before these Basin/Plateau groups were combined into a Fremont tradition comparable to other Southwest cultural divisions (i.e., Ancestral Puebloan, Hohokam, Mogollon). Thereafter a number of variant schemes were developed based primarily on ceramic and architectural differences; these were subregional systems, breaking down the variability both between and within the Basin and Plateau regions. Others have felt that economic unevenness relative to degrees of reliance on domesticates explained regional variability; still others have insisted that the traditional trait lists used to define Fremont simply could not encompass such confusing and widespread variability. All of these approaches have faltered, at least in part, because the data base remains weak and/or because they are based in research paradigms inadequate to the task. But more directly they have largely ignored the effects of temporal and scalar variability that would be expected of any archaeological tradition.

In this chapter I discuss the multifaceted nature of Fremont identity, what we do and do not yet know about it, and propose that it is in the context of scale and change through time that variability is best modeled. I suggest that relationships between households and communities in the many river valleys of the eastern Great Basin and northern Colorado Plateau are the appropriate backdrop in which localized variability developed. At least in the Late Fremont period, from where the bulk of Fremont data occurs, and in the context of a combined Basin/

Plateau geographical region, the nature of those relationships and the variability that is exhibited are best studied as a regional system similar to that of contemporary Southwest divisions (e.g., Hegmon et al. 2000:6).

## GREAT BASIN OR SOUTHWEST?

Nearly a century ago A. V. Kidder (1924) referred to the area north of the Ancestral Pueblo as the *Northern Periphery* of the Southwest. The connection with the Southwest was most evident in Puebloan-like architecture, pottery production, and domesticate agriculture. However, the perceived marginality of the "periphery" label was unacceptable to some (e.g., Rudy 1953) and Fremont studies were eventually withdrawn from that Southwest context and instead framed in Jesse Jennings's Great Basin "Desert Culture" model. But because that Desert Archaic model was focused on hunter-gatherers, Fremont farmers were an anomaly. Still, in that context Jennings's students moved forward with trying to define Fremont "variants" that in general were comparable to regionally named Ancestral Puebloan subdivisions. The most commonly referenced of several variant schemes was Marwitt's (1970), which included the Parowan, Sevier, Great Salt Lake, San Rafael, and Uinta areas. In practice each subregion was treated as a homogeneous unit defined primarily on ceramic temper (R. Madsen 1977) and secondarily on often overly extended microdivisions in Fremont architecture (Berry and Berry 2003; Talbot 2000a). Subsequently, many Fremont researchers, especially those trained in Great Basin forager studies, embraced a human behavioral ecology approach that emphasized flexibility in subsistence and settlement behavior while deemphasizing regional commonalities (Barlow 2002; 2006; Madsen 1982, 1989; Madsen and Simms 1998; Simms 1986, 1999a; see Allison 2008:58–59).

The fringe setting of Fremont had essentially left it in a paradigmatic no-man's land between the Great Basin and Southwest. Great Basin archaeologists embraced Fremont as foragers who sometimes farmed (e.g., Barlow 2002; Metcalf et al. 1993; Madsen and Simms 1998; however, see Bettinger 1999) and Upham (2000) included both the Fremont and Virgin Branch Puebloan cultures in a Great Basin macroregion distinct from contemporaneous Southwest Puebloan groups. Southwestern archaeologists, on the other hand, have mostly shown little interest in these northernmost farmers, who generally lack the large villages, social complexity, and rich material culture so common to the south (but see Allison, chapter 13, this volume). They have tended to see the Southwest as ending at the Colorado River (Talbot 2000b), while deferring to the very culture historical and behavioral views that have encouraged a built-up mystique to Fremont (e.g., Cordell 2012; Plog 2008), although Lekson (2014:111) has recently suggested that the later Fremont experienced "one brief shining moment" of Southwest membership. Only recently have Fremont researcher's interests

expanded to include social/community organization, identity, borderland processes, intra- and interregional trade, and other broader issues (see Janetski and
Talbot 2000a, 2014; Simms 2008; and Talbot 2000b for summaries). Fremont commitment to farming has increasingly been demonstrated, particularly in stable
carbon isotope analyses (Coltrain and Leavitt 2002). It is now clear that Fremont
is not an aberration at all, but instead one of many small-scale Southwest agricultural societies that is regionally distinguished by a unique set of material
culture markers, yet an active participant in panregional interaction spheres
(Janetski and Talbot 2014; Simms 2008; Talbot 2000b). If we can look past previous biases and if the Southwest is the periphery of Mesoamerica (McGuire
et al. 1994), then Fremont as the farthest reach of farming with its associated
Puebloan characteristics was indeed (however ironic) the northern periphery of
the northern periphery.

## FREMONT AS A REGIONAL SYSTEM

Farming occurred from ca. AD 1 to AD 1300, between roughly 38 and 41 degrees
north latitude, in the northern Colorado Plateau and eastern Great Basin, and
primarily in a transition zone between the two dominated by a north–south
range of high mountains and plateaus (figure 17.1). The availability and types
of resources vary widely across this large area, but for ancient (and modern)
farmers the primary attractions were the many river valleys and the especially
rich arable lands within them. These river valleys simultaneously allowed most
Fremont farmers easy logistical access to riverine, valley bottom, and upland
resources, a fact demonstrated time and again archaeologically. Beyond this cur-
sory observation, however, Fremont land-use patterns become more difficult to
define and are overtly asymmetric relative to available resources. Large tracts of
land, such as the San Rafael Desert, portions of the Uinta Basin, and the many
desert valleys of western Utah, were not conducive to significant prehistoric
farming or sedentary populations. When and where population concentrations occurred outside of the Basin and Range transition zone, it was always in
smaller but generally similar river valley settings such as along the Snake Range
on the Utah-Nevada border, or on the southern slopes of the Uinta Mountains
in northeastern Utah, or in canyon settings such as those in the Tavaputs Plateau
(Talbot 2000c).

Fremont regional patterns, principally in the later centuries, can be organized relative to networks of communication and interaction (see Janetski
2002; McDonald 1994) that in turn were strongly influenced by the topographic
and geographic context. The eastern rim of the Great Basin—delineated today
by the Interstate 15 and western Interstate 70 corridors—is the most compelling example of a regional Fremont network. The largest Late Fremont
villages occur within the well-watered river valleys in this significant geologic

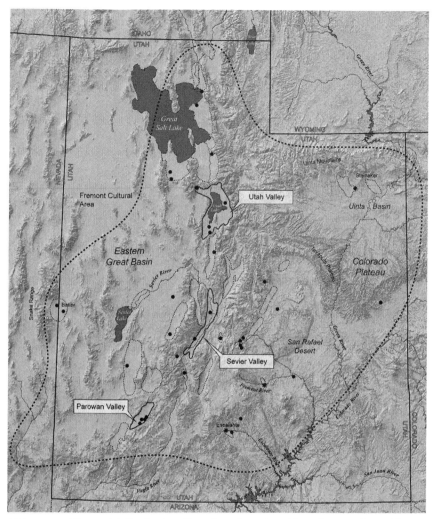

**FIGURE 17.1.** *The spatial distribution of prominent investigated Late Fremont sites, with important river valleys (smaller dotted areas), including three with particularly significant Late Fremont populations (labeled).*

transition zone. Flow of material goods up and down this corridor is best seen in the northward spread of Snake Valley ceramics from the Parowan Valley region to the northernmost reaches of large Fremont settlements around the Great Salt Lake. But the relocation of people, and not just movement of goods, also followed these networks, as suggested by the occasional construction of subregionally specific ceramic or architectural styles at sometimes great distances away from their core production areas (for example, Snake

Valley-like ceramics, or regionally distinct pithouse styles). Similar networks can be posited elsewhere, including along the western and northern rims of the Colorado Plateau. In all cases the potential and opportunities for regional interaction were high.

Frontiers (Parker 2006) and borderland communities in the final few Fremont centuries were particularly active social contexts where participation in panregional networks might combine to influence and give a uniquely local flavor to the archaeological record (Searcy and Talbot 2015). Those borderlands included some areas where hunter-gatherers and Fremont farmers were in very close proximity and where cross-cultural socioeconomic relationships were likely to have been very vibrant. The most compelling example is around the eastern and southern shores of the Great Salt Lake, where Fremont farmers and neighboring forager populations lived in very close proximity, and in particular during the Late Fremont period when populations for both were high (Simms 1999b). A similar situation, although less intense, occurred along the southern Fremont borderland, where Fremont and Ancestral Puebloan groups lived in quite close proximity. Exchange was common, and Ancestral Puebloan influence is strongly manifest in Fremont architecture, and hinting at some possible exogamous relationships (Janetski et al. 2012; Talbot 2006).

On the other hand, trading outposts are evident in these borderlands. The Coombs site (Lister and Lister 1961) and the Lampstand site (Baadsgaard and Janetski 2005), both dating to the AD 1100s, probably functioned in part as Kayenta outposts for trade with the Fremont. Also, the effects of Fremont/Ancestral Puebloan contact and exchange are evident across the region. For example, Mesa Verde and Kayenta wares are found throughout the Fremont area, albeit in relatively low numbers (Lane Richens, personal communication 2015). The various influences on Fremont ceramic style mentioned above are other examples (Richards, chapter 19, this volume). Turquoise brought in from southern sources is found at many Late Fremont sites, although not always in abundance (Jardine 2007). And certain Fremont masonry architecture mirroring Mesa Verdean styles are found as far north as the canyons of the Tavaputs Plateau, most prominently in Nine Mile Canyon and Range Creek Canyon (Talbot 2000a). Despite seemingly different adaptations (McFadden 1997), Fremont architecture in the Escalante region has characteristics of both Kayenta and Virgin styles (Talbot 2006). On the western borderlands, the Baker site (Wilde and Soper 1999) ceramic collection is very diverse, with all but the most distant (Uinta Basin) Fremont ceramic types being present, suggesting that goods were being funneled into the site from the interior. It probably functioned as a Fremont outpost for trade with Great Basin hunter-gatherers and provided a link to trade networks on the Pacific Coast, including the shell trade. In other areas, such as the eastern Uinta Basin and the broad expanses of desert in western and eastern Utah, the interface between Fremont and hunter-gatherers seems less formalized (e.g., Bandy and Baer 2010; Cole 2011; Janetski et al. 2005; Jennings and Sammons-Lohse 1981; Johnson and Loosle 2002; Loosle and Johnson ed. 2000; Searcy and Talbot 2015).

## SPATIOTEMPORAL CHANGE

Early attempts at establishing a timeline for subregional variability were limited to a few named phases, the most common being those summarized by Marwitt (1970). These achieved little, not because they were not useful but because additional work further refining temporal and cultural patterns in the context of those variants was not forthcoming (although it remains a worthwhile goal; see Talbot 2004, 2005; also Talbot et al. 2000). There are markers, however, that establish a general temporal sequence of Early, Middle, and Late Fremont periods (table 17.1). These are, respectively, periods of Early Agriculture, Population Expansion, and Social Integration.

Scant data are available but the Early Fremont (Early Agriculture) period (ca. AD 1–600) is characterized by small-scale farming efforts and low population levels. Farmers utilizing bell-shaped pit storage and ditch irrigation were present in central and northern Utah in the first three centuries AD (Greubel 1996; Talbot and Richens 1996; Wilde and Newman 1989). The transition from dart to arrow points was occurring by AD 200–300 (Talbot and Richens 1996), and Basketmaker-like bone disks are found in northern Utah as early as AD 400 (Janetski 2003). Shortly thereafter the appearance of brown- and gray-ware ceramics ca. AD 500/600 is an appropriate marker for the Middle Fremont (Population Expansion) period (Talbot and Richens 2007). Very limited data on early settlement patterns suggest a general filling in of the landscape at this time with continuing low population levels in small, dispersed farmsteads and hamlets. Unfortunately, many Early and Middle Fremont–period sites were probably in the same locations as later Fremont population centers, most of which have been covered by modern development.

Even less is known of the nature of intra-farmer relationships, and of farmer/forager relations during these two periods. However, a convergence of influences and regional spheres of interaction is expected. Late Archaic hunter-gatherers in the northern Colorado Plateau and eastern Great Basin shared frontiers with other hunter-gatherers in the central Great Basin, Snake River Plain, High Plains, and Rocky Mountains. For example, *Olivella* spp. shell was making its way into Utah at least by the Late Archaic period, but increases dramatically in frequency after the shift to farming, while *Dentalium* spp. shell may only occur after that shift (Bennyhoff and Hughes 1987; Hughes and Bennyhoff 1986; see Richens et al. 1996). The presence of both species at Steinaker Gap suggested to Richens et al. (1996:94) "an expanding network of

**TABLE 17.1.** General Fremont change through time.

| Period | Approx. Time | Characteristics |
|---|---|---|
| Early Fremont (Early Agriculture) | AD 1–600 | • Aceramic |
| | | • Transitional dart to arrow points |
| | | • Large, shallow, circular pithouses |
| | | • Underground storage |
| | | • Farmsteads and hamlets |
| Middle Fremont (Population Expansion) | AD 500–1000 | • Early brown- and graywares, early painted wares and surface manipulation |
| | | • Large, shallow, circular pithouses |
| | | • Underground storage on-site, hidden granaries off-site |
| | | • Some small-village formation |
| Late Fremont (Social Integration) | AD 900–1300 | • Well-developed ceramic designs |
| | | • Corrugation (post– AD 1050) |
| | | • Smaller, deeper quadrilateral pithouses in areas of greater population |
| | | • Medium and large villages appear |
| | | • Community-level facilities (structures and plazas) |
| | | • Aboveground granaries on-site (separate and / or as connected L- or U-shaped roomblocks), hidden granaries off-site |
| | | • Occasional surface houses (possibly late) |

interaction throughout the region shortly after the time of Christ." In this macroregional context, the northward spread and gradual settling in of the farming strategy probably altered existing relationships and encouraged new ones, and most likely resulted in enculturation of some hunter-gatherers into the farming society. Combined, these factors would have had a profound effect on the development of patterns in local and regional variability that would ultimately create a uniquely flavored cultural identity.

The Late Fremont (Social Integration) period (ca. AD 900/1000–1300) is the best-studied and for now the only period for which a regional system can be defined (for example, Janetski et al. 2000). This time period, concurrent (and clearly not-coincidental) with late Pueblo I and early Pueblo II expansionism, marked a significant social shift for these northernmost farmers. As early as AD 900, but certainly by AD 1000, evidence for population aggregation accompanied by significant architectural and material culture changes are manifest in the archaeological record, part of the "Neolithic Demographic Transition" in the American Southwest (Kohler and Glaude 2008). This aggregation was spatially asymmetrical, with the greatest populations occurring in the rich river valleys of the Great Basin/Colorado Plateau transition zone. The causes for Fremont aggregation are tied to a variety of issues (see Flannery 2002), just a few of which include population growth, intensification of farming efforts, the development of larger and more varied storage facilities, reduced sharing and increased privatization of storage, more permanent houses, new strains of maize, probable land tenure, the fostering of more extensive trade alliances and networks, the rise of individuals with apparently acquired influence, and support and safety in numbers from environmental and human threats.

The suite of traits traditionally used to distinguish Fremont from other Southwestern and Great Basin populations, and most clearly evident in the Late Fremont period, includes distinct architectural forms, rock art, and a variety of unique styles in ceramics and potentially in other artifact classes (see Talbot et al. 2005:369 for a summary). The majority of these characteristic traits are as yet not useful in defining patterns in variability, usually because their occurrence is comparatively rare or because they have not been examined in detail for spatiotemporal variability. This is particularly true for Fremont rock art, figurines, footwear, and basketry, while ceramic and architectural traits are more useful.

### Rock Art

Schaafsma (1971, 1980, 1986) has provided the most comprehensive look at Fremont rock art styles, but various authors have contributed regional or local studies as well (especially Baker and Billat 1999; Castleton 1978; Cole 1990; Hurst and Louthan 1979; various in Matheny ed. 2004). The quintessential characteristic of Fremont rock art is "the broad-shouldered human figure in ceremonial regalia. Typically it has a tapering torso and horned or other elaborate headgear" (Schaafsma 1980:166). Although regionally common, the form takes on especially majestic proportions and elaborate style in the Uinta Basin region (Classic Vernal Style) and in the Southern San Rafael region. The heads are often characterized as square or "bucket-shaped," although sometimes round, and with horned or feathered headdresses, earbobs, hairbobs, necklaces, shields, and aprons (Castleton 1978). Various zoomorph and abstract designs also reflect regionally similar general styles but with local variability. Named eastern Fremont (Colorado Plateau) styles include the Uinta Basin, Northern San Rafael, and Southern San Rafael, while western Fremont styles include Great

Basin Abstract, Sevier Styles A and B, and Western Utah Painted. Unfortunately, Fremont rock art lacks a solid chronological foundation. Schaafsma (1971:137–146) sees foundational elements for Fremont rock art in Basketmaker as well as Great Basin and, to a lesser degree, Plains styles. While it is assumed that stylistic variability is well established by the Late Fremont period, it is as yet unclear how far back, and in what manners, those styles developed.

## Figurines

Figurines of various size and form have been described from throughout the northern Colorado Plateau and eastern Great Basin (Green 1964; Gunnerson 1962, 1969; Morss 1931, 1954; Steward 1936). The best-known are anthropomorphic types that are seemingly the embodiment of the two-dimensional trapezoidal-bodied figures in the rock art. These are flattened on the back, and commonly consist of a pinched nose, punched eyes, and leg/foot nubs, and most have breasts. Beyond these well-recognized traits, however, is considerable stylistic variety, ranging from small and plain forms, to larger styles that often contain eye buttons and body decorations, to the most elaborate, which are often painted and exhibit detailed and ornate clothing and jewelry appliqué. Regional variation has been assumed by many archaeologists (see Morss 1954) but never quantified. Many of the most elaborate styles have been recovered from Late Fremont contexts but this also has not been quantified (although a detailed study is currently in progress; David Yoder, personal communication 2015).

## Moccasins

The Fremont are not known to have worn sandals; rather, footwear was apparently three-piece leather moccasins made from the leg skin of a large ungulate, typically deer, antelope, mountain sheep, or bison (Jennings 1978:231). The most unique feature is the incorporation of the dew claws as hobnails on the sole of the moccasin (Morss 1931:63–68). While considered diagnostic of Fremont, surprisingly few have been found, with the best examples coming from the southeastern (Capitol Reef area; Morss 1931) and northwestern (Hogup Cave/ Great Salt Lake Desert area; Aikens 1970) Fremont regions. Other styles have been noted in sparse and widely spaced locations—again, in the frontier regions—and it is unclear if any or all of them are temporally or culturally affiliated with Fremont (e.g., Aikens 1970; Burgh and Scoggin 1948; Gunnerson 1969; Jennings 1957; Madsen 1982). Dating is poor for all of the known examples of Fremont moccasins. Promontory moccasins, which appear to have Athabascan roots, temporally overlap into the Late Fremont period in the Great Salt Lake region (ca. post– AD 1000), but are clearly distinct in general construct (Billinger and Ives 2015; Ives 2014).

## Basketry

Reported Fremont basketry covers the entire region, and is dissimilar from those of surrounding areas. It is dominated by three close-coiled types: half-rod-and-bundle stacked foundation, half-rod-and-welt stacked foundation, and whole-rod-and-bundle foundation. The whole-rod-and-bundle basketry has a deep history in the Great Basin Archaic period but meshes with the half-rod-and-bundle basketry style that also has foundations in the eastern/Durango Basketmaker II period (Adovasio 1979, 1986; Adovasio et al. 2002; Simms 2008; Talbot et al. 2005:371). Additional aspects of construction, including methods of starting, stitch and splice type, work surface and direction, rim finish, and others, are generally regionally consistent (Adovasio 1980:36–37; Talbot et al. 2005:371). Unfortunately, subregional variability still awaits detailed spatiotemporal analysis.

## Ceramics

Marwitt's original five Fremont variant definitions were largely based on differences in ceramic temper, which provided some measure of subregional differentiation (Berry and Berry 2003) related to the geologic variability across the Basin and Plateau, but little more. R. Madsen (1977) described nine pottery types that are still used for basic ceramic field identifications, although Watkins (2009) has recently proposed a more logical reorganization of the types. These include the Snake Valley series in southwestern Utah (named for the Snake Valley along the Utah-Nevada border, but with the primary production zone probably in the Parowan Valley farther east); the Emery series in central Utah (which incorporates R. Madsen's Sevier and Ivie Creek Black-on-white types; the Great Salt Lake series in northern Utah; and the Uinta-series wares in and around the Uinta Basin of northeastern Utah and northwestern Colorado

In addition, recent research has focused on technical and stylistic variability in vessel form, decoration, and coiling techniques (Richards 2014; Richens 2000; Ure 2013). Vessel forms are predominantly bowls, jars, and pitchers. Fremont only rarely constructed mugs, ladles, effigy, or other ceramic forms. Bowls typically have straight rims and not the flattened, flaring rims found to the south. Jars and pitchers commonly exhibit rim-to-shoulder handles, with only rare examples of handles originating below the rim. Horizontal handles are also rare.

Vessel decoration is dominated by painted and surface-manipulated styles. The latter includes primarily punctate (incised), appliqué, and corrugated forms. The use of appliqué, including the well-known "coffee-bean" appliqué style, is fairly widespread, but seems particularly common in northern and central Utah. Snake Valley Corrugated pottery is by far the dominant corrugated Fremont ceramic ware, while Emery Corrugated is much less common, Great Salt Lake Corrugated is very rare, and Uinta wares were never corrugated.

Snake Valley Black-on-gray is the dominant painted style for bowls and (rarely) jars. Stylistic elements including lines, solids, scrolls, spirals, and/or tics are reminiscent of Eastern Ancestral Puebloan Red Mesa style (see Richards, chapter 19, this volume). Emery painted styles are similar although much less common. Rare examples of red-on-gray ceramics, just painted lines, have been found in most of the Fremont region, but only at the Wolf Village site in Utah Valley have they been found in significant numbers. Only one true, locally made, slipped whiteware—Ivie Creek Black-on-white—was constructed, with a production zone in the river valleys along the eastern slopes of the Wasatch Plateau. No local redwares were produced, although Fremont potters often used a red hematite wash on certain utilitarian vessels.

One of the most unusual and passive (or "low visibility"; see Cameron, chapter 2, this volume) characteristics of noncorrugated Fremont pottery may be the construction of vessels with the coils overlapping on the interior rather than the exterior (Geib 1996; Lane Richens, personal communication 2014). The technique is difficult to trace spatially and temporally, since it is only visible on ceramics where the coils were incompletely obliterated. The spatiotemporal extent of this technique has yet to be examined.

## Architecture

Late Fremont is characterized by a hierarchy of site types beginning with the ubiquitous farmsteads and many small hamlets that dot the landscape just about anywhere that water is available for farming (Talbot 2000c). In some favored areas small villages were established, and in the most resource-rich river valleys medium and large village sites developed. Whereas the pithouse was the only significant architectural feature during the Early and Middle Fremont periods and remained the primary residential feature throughout the Fremont era, architectural forms expanded during the Late Fremont period to include individual or multiroom aboveground storage, occasional surface houses, and community/ ritual structures. The storage complexes can be linear but in some of the larger villages they tend to be L- or U-shaped.

Fremont residential architecture reflects many of the generic characteristics found in Basketmaker III and Hohokam sites. The shallow circular pithouse is common in all periods. However, deeper, subrectangular pithouses began to be constructed in the AD 900s, and had replaced the circular forms in much of the Basin/Plateau transition zone by AD 1100. Fremont pithouses, both circular and subrectangular, are characterized by long single or sometimes dual ventilation tunnels. Beginning at least in the AD 1000s, surface houses began to be constructed, although they never replaced pithouse residences. While surface houses are often single room structures, multiroom houses are also common and involve a living room with one or two attached storage rooms; in a few instances, additional small storage rooms have been added on. These (pithouse shape, ventilation facilities, surface structure design) and other characteristics are likely to demonstrate spatiotemporal variability in general form and style (see Talbot 2000a). Of particular interest is the recent recognition of oversized pithouses at many Late Fremont sites suggestive of group leader and/or possible ritually oriented structures (Johansson, chapter 18, this volume; Talbot 2000a).

It is a nonresidential architectural form, however, that may better connect Late Fremont communities while demonstrating variability in form. Fremont Central Structures (Talbot 2000a) are defined as public buildings, probably the locations of community-wide or community subgroup activities such as feasting, ritual, and/or other gatherings. The structure type was first recognized at the Five Finger Ridge site in Clear Creek Canyon (Talbot 2000a) next to a plaza area in the center of the village, and in association with both a probable village leader's house and a singular surface house (in what was otherwise a pithouse village). The Central Structure was rectangular with jacal walls but open on the south. Its size, central location, lack of typical residential features and material remains, and evidence of continual remodeling, suggested that it likely was a public building.

Since that time Central Structures have been definitely or tentatively identified both at village sites and in areas where populations were more dispersed. Central Structures in the southwestern Fremont area at Paragonah, Summit, Beaver, Garrison, and Baker Village are adobe and/or jacal-walled, and most are centrally located to daily village life. All but the Baker Village example have, or may have, open south walls. Examples on the Colorado Plateau (Blue Trail House, Huntington Canyon, and Poplar Knob) are not in villages but instead in remote contexts away from major population centers. They are generally smaller and some are irregular in shape with a mix of adobe/masonry and jacal construction. The Barnson site in the Escalante Valley has a large, subrectangular, semisubterranean structure on a high ridge and associated with a small village. In northern Utah, where good architectural data are wanting, the Wolf Village site in Utah Valley actually contains at least two unusual structures—one a rectangular adobe-surface structure high on a knoll that may be missing a south wall and that contains figurines and other possible ritual paraphernalia, and the other an oversized pithouse-like structure at the base of the knoll that clearly was used for group gatherings and probably ritual. Either or both may be Central Structures, but the latter lacks the open community-use feel that Central Structures have, and seems more restrictive in function; it is as close to a kiva-like structure as has been found in the Fremont region. It is, however, directly associated with a surface house with an attached large storage room and a complex of many smaller rooms added to one side of the house, suggestive of a village leader residence.

## ORGANIZING FREMONT VARIABILITY

To reiterate, researchers have not yet examined Fremont temporal or scalar variability in depth. In fact, the thinness of the empirical record currently available precludes comparative analysis of localized variability and regional interaction during the Early and Middle Fremont periods. The Late Fremont period, on the other hand, has received more attention and exhibits not only a regional tradition of shared traits, but also a blossoming of subregional variability that firmly distinguishes Fremont from all other contemporaneous groups. It is for this reason, at least in part, that some have argued that Fremont was a relatively short-lived experience (e.g., Gunnerson 1960, 1969; see Berry 1980).

The Late Fremont regional system comprises numerous local systems positioned in a network of river valleys (see figure 17.1), as described above. Those local systems in turn contain at least a few and often many settlements, of various spatial size and population levels (Talbot 2000c). Social interactions, like those in other Southwestern regional systems at this time, probably existed in embedded spatial and social hierarchies (Niezel 2000:figure 21), with proximal relationships the most active (Blau 1977). In these contexts the changing scale of relations between individuals and social groups ultimately impacts variability in the archaeological record, and it is in these contexts that variability is best organized.

### Local Systems

As in the neighboring Puebloan population to the south, Fremont population increase and aggregation was regionally asymmetric; the eastern rim of the Great Basin was the focus of the most-intensive population growth. In this as well as most other geographic contexts, socioeconomic relationships and alliance formation would be most pronounced between neighboring communities within the same valley or in proximal valleys (Janetski and Talbot 2000b; Janetski et al. 2011). At least three subregions in this area, where the Great Basin transitions into the Colorado Plateau, exhibit significantly greater population increase and probably eventually became important spheres of regional influence (Janetski and Talbot 2014).

In the southern Fremont area, in a 10-mile stretch at the southern end of the Parowan Valley, there are three large contemporaneous villages situated on the alluvial fans of three separate creeks coming out of the mountains: the Paragonah, Parowan, and Summit communities (figure 17.2). Each probably housed several hundred residents. There is no evidence for the three having been united as a single polity, and they likely functioned as discrete communities. All three participated in constructing the unique and highly sought-after Snake Valley ceramic wares, suggesting close, probably affinal ties. For example, based on Neutron Activation Analysis, Ure (2013:198–199) suggested that similarities

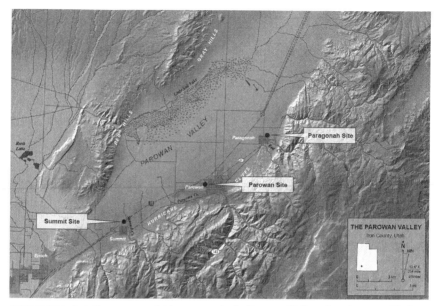

**FIGURE 17.2.** *Late Fremont population centers in the Parowan Valley of southwestern Utah.*

in the technological style of Snake Valley Corrugated pottery in the Parowan Valley "are evidence for an interconnected, valley-wide, community of potters that shared a sense of identity and community larger than the household level" while "variations in technological style . . . may represent expressions of social identity at the village level." The three communities also favored obsidian from the Mineral Mountains, located 35 miles (56 km) to the north, and to a lesser degree the Panaca Summit/Modena source located ca. 60 miles (97 km) to the west (see Haarklau et al. 2005). All three villages, and probably outlier farmsteads and hamlets in the valley, would to some degree have shared the nearby mountain resources and various valley bottom resources, including the rich marshes of the nearby Little Salt Lake. Like next-neighbor farming communities elsewhere in the Southwest, these were potentially socially volatile contexts requiring constant alliance affirmation and dispute mediation.

The Sevier Valley in central Utah probably contained several large villages that were spread along the course of the Sevier River and its side drainages (figure 17.3). Small portions of a very large village below the town of Richfield have been excavated (see Talbot and Richens 1993 for a summary), but most of the other sites are known only through very limited archaeological work or anecdotally. The valley, with its very fertile soils for farming and abundant wetlands and easy access to upland resources, was amenable to large population levels, and numerous neighboring Late Fremont communities. Most important, the valley

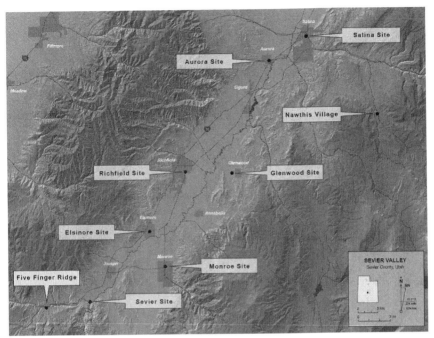

**FIGURE 17.3.** *Late Fremont population centers in the Sevier Valley of central Utah.*

is geographically central to Fremont regional transportation and trade networks. In the northern Utah area, several large villages bordered the freshwater Utah Lake or were along its feeder streams (figure 17.4). In terms of geographical importance, Utah Valley is more or less the gateway to the Fremont settlements farther north, including those in the Salt Lake Valley and along the eastern and southern shores of the Great Salt Lake. Like the Sevier Valley, then, Utah Valley was probably central to Fremont transportation and trade networks.

The socioeconomic relationships between neighboring communities in the Sevier and Utah Valleys were probably as complex as those described for the Parowan Valley. As well, many other intravalley or neighboring valley community networks might be posited, some within and others well away from this core area of Late Fremont population concentration, and each would lend a certain local flavor to patterned variability in the archaeological record. Other valleys along the eastern rim of the Great Basin similarly housed Late Fremont villages, providing important next-neighbor links between the larger population centers, and where localized variability in material culture and architecture should be expected. The same would be true at population centers to the far west in the Snake Valley, along the eastern base of the Wasatch Plateau, and to the northeast along the base of the Uinta Mountains.

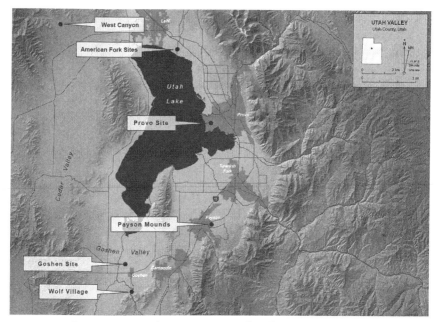

**FIGURE 17.4.** *Late Fremont population centers in Utah Valley of northern Utah.*

Fremont in areas of low, dispersed populations were probably organized and interacted at different scales than those in the population centers. But while local stylistic variability would be expected, they were nevertheless part of the interlocking web of communities across the Fremont region, and periodic gatherings at small villages or other select locations could have served to connect those groups and to familiarize them with events and changing patterns in the larger Fremont world.

### Settlements

All known large villages date to the Late Fremont period, which suggests that most Early- and Middle-period Fremont participated in dispersed communities of neighboring farmsteads and hamlets. The Late-period sites were often occupied or reoccupied for several hundred years, and there is clear diachronicity evidenced in variable architecture, site layout, and material culture. At Five Finger Ridge, a medium-sized village, the community contains distinct pithouse groupings conforming to the landscape itself and with a seemingly prescribed physical distance between households, but with possible sharing of some household storage units, and with a central plaza area and single community structure serving all the site inhabitants (Talbot and Janetski 2000). But at some of the larger sites, where peak populations likely reached several hundred, there are indications of site structure consistent with kinship and / or other groupings. For example, in some larger valley-bottom village sites like those in the Parowan Valley, at Baker Village, or at Nawthis Village, site layout might include dispersed neighborhoods of pithouses, often focused on a central accretional mound. An individual household could have its own associated one-room storage unit, but the neighborhood might also include a central block of storage rooms and perhaps a community Central Structure. Variability in and between these neighborhood groupings is likely to be subtle, reflecting the nuances of shifting intracommunity social relationships.

### Household/Family

The settlement pattern most common throughout the Fremont regional system, and from the Early through Late periods, is that of small farmstead sites consisting of one or two contemporaneous pithouses, and of small hamlets of a few contemporaneous households, likely extended family groups. These tended to be highly mobile populations who would farm along stream terraces for a few years, probably until the soils or other resources were depleted, and then move up or down the stream or to another stream to continue the same pattern (Talbot 2005; Talbot and Richens 2004). A filling in of the landscape by population increase over time was accompanied by the eventual appearance of small villages and, by the Late Fremont period, medium-sized and even several large villages. Still, boom-and-bust cycles were likely common with abandonment and resettlement of village sites (Talbot 2011).

In these contexts, household architectural variability is in large part a function of spatiotemporal variability. Short-lived farmstead pithouses tend to be larger but shallow and overall less labor-intensive, while Late-period village residences are deeper and more durable and evidence greater effort at remodeling, consistent with a reduced household mobility

### SUMMARY

Applying the regional system concept to Fremont provides a promising context for studying long-recognized patterns and localized variability that occurred across the Northern Periphery area during the same time frame that other small-scale farming societies were spread throughout the American Southwest. The framework for organizing Fremont variability described here recognizes differential pattern formation through time and space, nested in different scales. A community is in large part the sum of the history of, and relationships and interaction between, its constituent households. Fremont communities appear socially and politically autonomous, but it is unlikely that they were economically detached from neighboring or more long-distance relationships and alliances. As populations increase, so should also the opportunities for intercommunity relationships, friendly or otherwise, and for the exchange of goods, ideas, and mates. We should expect, therefore, community identity—those local characteristics and ways of doing things—to influence neighboring community identity and relationships. Through time larger-scale contact and interaction between those local communities and subregional neighboring communities would ultimately combine to give the Fremont regional system its unique and locally variable characteristics.

Opportunities for subregional and regional interaction would similarly influence patterns in the archaeological record. Hence, movement up and down the eastern rim of the Great Basin would tend toward more homogenization or spreading of certain general ideas/technologies, as well as increased flow of goods and other contact results. Movement between more distant groups and in particular where populations are lower, will be less homogenizing in general, but more so in prime contact areas, such as along trade routes where centers of influence would tend to be established.

In-depth study of the traits characteristic of Fremont, and the localized variability exhibited in those traits, is the most pressing need for understanding the Fremont Regional System. As a prerequisite, local and regional chronologies need to be developed. Only then can archaeologists hope to explore in greater depth Fremont social behavior both within and away from the Fremont Regional System.

## REFERENCES

Adovasio, James M. 1979. "Comment by Adovasio." *American Antiquity* 44(4):723–731. https://doi.org/10.2307/279111.

Adovasio, James M. 1980. "Fremont: An Artifactual Perspective." In *Fremont Perspectives*, ed. David B. Madsen, 35–40. Antiquities Section Selected Papers Vol. 7, No. 16. Salt Lake City: Utah State Historical Society.

Adovasio, James M. 1986. "Artifacts and Ethnicity: Basketry as an Indicator of Territoriality and Population Movements in the Prehistoric Great Basin." In *Anthropology of the Desert West: Essays in Honor of Jesse D. Jennings*, ed. Carol J. Condie and Don D. Fowler, 43–88. Anthropological Papers No. 110. Salt Lake City: University of Utah.

Adovasio, James M., David R. Pedler, and Jeff S. Illingworth. 2002. "Fremont Basketry." *Utah Archaeology* 15(1):5–26.

Aikens, C. Melvin. 1970. *Hogup Cave*. Anthropological Papers No. 93. Salt Lake City: University of Utah.

Allison, James R. 2008. "Human Ecology and Social Theory in Utah Archaeology." *Utah Archaeology* 21(1):57–88.

Baadsgaard, Aubrey, and Joel C. Janetski. 2005. *Exploring Formative Strategies and Ethnicity in South-Central Utah: Excavations at Lampstand Ruins and the Durfey Site.* Museum of Peoples and Cultures Technical Series No. 00-3. Provo, UT: Brigham Young University.

Baker, Shane A., and Scott E. Billat. 1999. *Rock Art of Clear Creek Canyon in Central Utah.* Museum of Peoples and Cultures Occasional Papers No. 6. Provo, UT: Brigham Young University.

Bandy, Matthew S., and Sarah Baer. 2010. "Fremont on the Fringe of the Great Basin: A Study of the Formative Occupation of the Piceance Basin, Northwestern Colorado." Paper presented at the 32nd Great Basin Anthropological Conference, Layton, UT.

Barlow, K. Renee. 2002. "Predicting Maize Agriculture among the Fremont: An Economic Comparison of Farming and Foraging in the American Southwest." *American Antiquity* 67(1):65–88. https://doi.org/10.2307/2694877.

Barlow, K. Renee. 2006. "A Formal Model for Predicting Agriculture among the Fremont." In *Behavioral Ecology and the Transition to Agriculture*, ed. D. J. Kennett and B. Winterhalder, 87–102. Berkeley: University of California Press.

Barth, Fredrik. 1998. "Introduction." In *Ethnic Groups and Boundaries: The Social Organization of Culture Difference*, ed. Fredrik Barth, 9–38. Prospect Heights, IL: Waveland. (Originally published in 1969: Little, Brown, and Company, Boston).

Bennyhoff, James A., and Richard E. Hughes. 1987. *Shell Bead and Ornament Exchange Networks between California and the Great Basin.* Anthropological Papers Vol. 64, Pt. 2. New York: American Museum of Natural History.

Berry, Michael S. 1980. "Fremont Origins: A Critique." In *Fremont Perspectives*, ed. David B. Madsen, 17–24. Antiquities Section Selected Papers Vol. 7, No. 16. Salt Lake City: Utah Historical Society.

Berry, Michael S., and Claudia F. Berry. 2003. "An Archaeological Analysis of the Prehistoric Fremont Culture for the Purpose of Assessing Cultural Affiliation with Ten Claimant Tribes." Submitted to USDI Bureau of Reclamation. Manuscript on file, Bureau of Reclamation, Upper Colorado Regional Office, Salt Lake City, UT.

Bettinger, Robert L. 1999. "What Happened in the Medithermal." In *Models for the Millennium: Great Basin Anthropology Today*, 62–74, ed. Charlotte Beck. Salt Lake City: University of Utah Press.

Billinger, Michael, and John W. Ives. 2015. "Inferring Demographic Structure with Moccasin Size Data from the Promontory Caves, Utah." *American Journal of Physical Anthropology* 156(1):76–89. https://doi.org/10.1002/ajpa.22629.

Blau, Peter M. 1977. *Inequality and Heterogeneity: A Primitive Theory of Social Structure.* New York: Free Press.

Burgh, Robert F., and Charles R. Scoggin. 1948. *The Archaeology of Castle Park, Dinosaur National Monument. University of Colorado Studies, Series in Anthropology No. 2.* Boulder: University of Colorado Press.

Castleton, Kenneth B. 1978. *Petroglyphs and Pictographs of Utah*. 2 vols. Salt Lake City: Utah Museum of Natural History.

Cole, Clint. 2011. *Prehistoric Archaeology and the Fremont Frontier at North Meadow Valley Wash, Eastern Nevada*. PhD dissertation, Department of Anthropology, University of California, Davis. Ann Arbor, MI: University Microfilms International.

Cole, Sally J. 1990. *Legacy on Stone: Rock Art of the Colorado Plateau and Four Corners Region*. Boulder, CO: Johnson Books.

Coltrain, J. B., and S. W. Leavitt. 2002. "Climate and Diet in Fremont Prehistory: Economic Variability and Abandonment of Maize Agriculture in the Great Salt Lake Basin." *American Antiquity* 67(3):453–485. https://doi.org/10.2307/1593822.

Cordell, Linda S. 2008. "Exploring Social Identities through Archaeological Data from the Southwest: An Introduction." In *Archaeology without Borders: Contact, Commerce, and Change in the U.S. Southwest and Northwestern Mexico*, ed. Laurie D. Webster, Maxine E. McBrinn, and Eduardo Camboa Carrera, 145–154. Boulder: University Press of Colorado.

Cordell, Linda S. 2012. *Archaeology of the Southwest*. 3rd ed. Walnut Creek, CA: Left Coast Press.

Creamer, Winifred. 2000. "Regional Interactions and Regional Systems in the Protohistoric Rio Grande." In *The Archaeology of Regional Interaction: Religion, Warfare, and Exchange across the American Southwest and Beyond*, ed. Michelle Hegmon, 99–118. Boulder: University Press of Colorado.

Crown, Patricia L. 1991. "The Hohokam: Current Views of Prehistory and the Regional System." In *Chacoand Hohokam*, ed. Patricia L. Crown and W. James Judge, 135–157. Santa Fe, NM: School of American Research Press.

Doyle, David E., ed. 1992. *Anasazi Regional Organization and the Chaco System*. Anthropology Papers No. 5. Albuquerque: Maxwell Museum of Anthropology.

Duff, Andrew I. 2002. *Western Pueblo Identities: Regional Interaction, Migration, and Transformation*. Tucson: University of Arizona Press.

Flannery, Kent V. 2002. "The Origins of the Village Revisited: From Nuclear to Extended Households." *American Antiquity* 67(3):417–433. https://doi.org/10.2307/1593820.

Geib, Phil R. 1996. *Glen Canyon Revisited*. Anthropological Papers No. 119. Salt Lake City: University of Utah.

Green, Dee F. 1964. "The Hinckley Figurines as Indicators of the Position of Utah Valley in the Sevier Culture." *American Antiquity* 30(1):74–80. https://doi.org/10.2307/277632.

Gregory, David A. 1991. "Form and Variation in Hohokam Settlement Patterns." In *Chacoand Hohokam*, ed. Patricia L. Crown and W. James Judge, 159–193. Santa Fe, NM: School of American Research Press.

Greubel, Rand A. 1996. *Archaeological Investigations of 11 Sites Along Interstate 70: Castle Valley to Rattlesnake Bench*. Montrose, CO: Alpine Archaeological Consultants.

Gunnerson, James H. 1960. "The Fremont Culture: Internal Dimensions and External Relationships." *American Antiquity* 25:373–380.

Gunnerson, James H. 1962. "Unusual Artifacts from Castle Valley, Central Utah." In *Miscellaneous Collected Papers*, by James H. Gunnerson, David M. Pendergast, and Keith M. Anderson, 67–91. Paper No. 4. Anthropological Papers No. 60. Salt Lake City: University of Utah.

Gunnerson, James H. 1969. *The Fremont Culture: A Study in Culture Dynamics on the Northern Anasazi Frontier*. Papers of the Peabody Museum of Archaeology and Ethnology, Vol. 59, No. 2. Cambridge, MA: Harvard University.

Haarklau, Lynn, Lynn Johnson, and David L. Wagner. 2005. *Fingerprints in the Great Basin: The Nellis Air Force Base Regional Obsidian Sourcing Study*. Nellis Air Force Base, NV: US Air Force.

Hegmon, Michelle, ed. 2000. *The Archaeology of Regional Interaction: Religion, Warfare, and Exchange across the American Southwest and Beyond*. Boulder: University Press of Colorado.

Hegmon, Michelle, Kelly Hays-Gilpin, Randall H. McGuire, Alison E. Rautman, and Sarah H. Schlanger. 2000. "Changing Perceptions of Regional Interaction in the Prehistoric Southwest." In *The Archaeology of Regional Interaction: Religion, Warfare, and Exchange across the American Southwest and Beyond*, ed. Michelle Hegmon, 25–40. Boulder: University Press of Colorado.

Hegmon, Michelle, and Stephen Plog. 1996. "Regional Social Interaction in the Northern Southwest: Evidence and Issues." In *Interpreting Southwestern Diversity: Underlying Principles and Overarching Patterns*, ed. Paul R. Fish and J. Jefferson Reid, 1–21. Anthropological Research Papers No. 48. Tempe: Arizona State University.

Hughes, Richard E., and James A. Bennyhoff. 1986. "Early Trade." In *Great Basin*, ed. Warren L. d'Azevedo, 256–261. Handbook of North American Indians, vol. 11, gen. ed. William C. Sturtevant. Washington, DC: Smithsonian Institution.

Hurst, Winston, and Bruce D. Louthan. 1979. *Survey of Rock Art in the Central Portion of Nine Mile Canyon, Eastern Utah*. Publications in Archaeology, New Series No. 4. Provo, UT: Department of Anthropology, Brigham Young University.

Ives, John W. 2014. "Resolving the Promontory Culture Enigma." In *Archaeology in the Great Basin and Southwest: Papers in Honor of Don D. Fowler*, ed. Nancy J. Parezo and Joel C. Janetski, 149–162. Salt Lake City: The University of Utah Press.

Janetski, Joel C. 2002. "Trade in Fremont Society: Contexts and Contrasts." *Journal of Anthropological Archaeology* 21:344–370. https://doi.org/10.1016/S0278-4165(02)00003-X.

Janetski, Joel C. 2003. "Distinctive Bone Disks from Utah Valley: Evidence of Basketmaker Connections in North Central Utah." *Kiva* 68(4):305–322. https://doi.org/10.1080/00231940.2003.11758480.

Janetski, Joel C., Cady B. Jardine, and Christopher N. Watkins. 2011. "Interaction and Exchange in Fremont Society." In *Perspectives on Prehistoric Trade and Exchange in*

*California and the Great Basin*, ed. Richard E. Hughes, 22–54. Salt Lake City: University of Utah Press.

Janetski, Joel C., Lee Kreutzer, Richard K. Talbot, Lane D. Richens, and Shane A. Baker. 2005. *Life on the Edge: Archaeology in Capitol Reef National Park*. Museum of Peoples and Cultures Occasional Papers No. 11. Provo, UT: Brigham Young University.

Janetski, Joel C., Lane D. Richens, and Richard K. Talbot. 2012. "Fremont-Anasazi Boundary Maintenance and Permeability in the Escalante Drainage." In *Meetings at the Margins: Prehistoric Cultural Interactions in the Intermountain West*, ed. David Rhode, 191–210. Salt Lake City: University of Utah Press.

Janetski, Joel C., and Richard K. Talbot. 2000a. "Project Overview and Context." In *Clear Creek Canyon Archaeological Project: Results and Synthesis*, by J. C. Janetski, R. K. Talbot, D. E. Newman, L. D. Richens, and J. D. Wilde, 1–7. Museum of Peoples and Cultures Occasional Papers No. 7. Provo, UT: Brigham Young University.

Janetski, Joel C., and Richard K. Talbot. 2000b. "Fremont Social and Community Organization." In *Clear Creek Canyon Archaeological Project: Results and Synthesis*, by J. C. Janetski, R. K. Talbot, D. E. Newman, L. D. Richens, and J. D. Wilde, 247–262. Museum of Peoples and Cultures Occasional Papers No. 7. Provo, UT: Brigham Young University.

Janetski, Joel C., and Richard K. Talbot. 2014. "Fremont Social Organization: A Southwestern Perspective." In *Archaeology in the Great Basin and Southwest: Papers in Honor of Don D. Fowler*, ed. Nancy J. Parezo and Joel C. Janetski, 118–129. Salt Lake City: University of Utah Press.

Janetski, Joel C., Richard K. Talbot, Deborah E. Newman, Lane D. Richens, and James D. Wilde. 2000. *Clear Creek Canyon Archaeological Project: Results and Synthesis*. Museum of Peoples and Cultures Occasional Papers No. 7. Provo, UT: Brigham Young University.

Jardine, Cady B. 2007. "Fremont Finery: Exchange and Distribution of Turquoise and *Olivella* Ornaments in the Parowan Valley and Beyond." Unpublished MA thesis, Department of Anthropology, Brigham Young University, Provo.

Jennings, Jesse D. 1957. *Danger Cave*. Anthropological Papers No. 27. Salt Lake City: University of Utah.

Jennings, Jesse D. 1978. *Prehistory of Utah and the Eastern Great Basin: A Review*. Anthropological Papers No. 98. Salt Lake City: University of Utah.

Jennings, Jesse D., and Dorothy Sammons-Lohse. 1981. *Bull Creek*. Anthropological Papers No. 105. Salt Lake City: University of Utah.

Johnson, Clay, and Byron Loosle. 2002. *Prehistoric Uinta Mountain Occupations*. Heritage Report 2-02/2002. Vernal, UT: Ashley National Forest, Intermountain Region, USDA Forest Service.

Judd, Neil M. 1926. *Archaeological Observations North of the Rio Colorado*. Bulletin No. 82. Washington, DC: Bureau of American Ethnology, Smithsonian Institution.

Kantner, John. 2003. "Rethinking Chaco as a System." *Kiva* 69(2):207–227. https://doi .org/10.1080/00231940.2003.11758491.

Kidder, Alfred Vincent. 1924. *An Introduction to the Study of Southwestern Archaeology with a Preliminary Account of the Excavations at Pecos.* New Haven, CT: Yale University Press.

Kohler, Timothy A., and Matt Glaude. 2008. "The Nature and Timing of the Neolithic Demographic Transition in the North American Southwest." In *The Neolithic Demographic Transition and its Consequences*, ed. Jean-Pierre Bocquet-Appel and Ofer Bar-Yosef, 81–106. Dordrecht, Netherlands: Springer Science and Business Media, B.V. https://doi.org/10.1007/978-1-4020-8539-0_5.

Lekson, Stephen H. 1996. "Scale and Process in the Southwest." In *Interpreting Southwestern Diversity: Underlying Principles and Overarching Patterns*, ed. Paul R. Fish and J. Jefferson Reid, 81–86. Anthropological Research Papers No. 48. Tempe: Arizona State University.

Lekson, Stephen H. 2014. "Thinking About Fremont: The Later Prehistory of the Great Basin and the Southwest." In *Archaeology in the Great Basin and Southwest: Papers in Honor of Don D. Fowler*, ed. Nancy J. Parezo and Joel C. Janetski, 109–117. Salt Lake City: University of Utah Press.

Lister, Robert H., and Florence C. Lister. 1961. *The Coombs Site, Part III. Anthropological Papers No. 41.* Salt Lake City: University of Utah.

Loosle, Byron, and Clay Johnson, eds. 2000. *Dutch John Excavations: Seasonal Occupations on the North Slope of the Uinta Mountains.* Heritage Report 1-01/2000. Vernal, UT: Ashley National Forest, Intermountain Region, USDA Forest Service.

Madsen, David B. 1982. "Get It Where the Gettin's Good: A Variable Model of Great Basin Subsistence and Settlement Based on Data from the Eastern Great Basin." In *Man and Environment in the Great Basin*, ed. David B. Madsen and James F. O'Connell, 207–226. SAA Papers No. 2. Washington DC: Society for American Archaeology.

Madsen, David B. 1989. *Exploring the Fremont. Occasional Publication No. 8.* Salt Lake City: Utah Museum of Natural History, University of Utah.

Madsen, David B., and Steven R. Simms. 1998. "The Fremont Complex: A Behavioral Perspective." *Journal of World Prehistory* 12:255–336. https://doi.org/10.1023/A:1022322 619699.

Madsen, Rex. 1977. *Prehistoric Ceramics of the Fremont.* Ceramic Series No. 6. Flagstaff: Museum of Northern Arizona.

Marwitt, John P. 1970. *Median Village and Fremont Culture Regional Variation. Anthropological Papers No. 95.* Salt Lake City: University of Utah.

Matheny, Ray T., ed. 2004. *New Dimensions in Rock Art Studies.* Museum of Peoples and Cultures Occasional Papers No. 9. Provo, UT: Brigham Young University.

McDonald, Elizabeth Kae. 1994. *A Spatial and Temporal Examination of Prehistoric Interaction in the Eastern Great Basin and on the Northern Colorado Plateau.* PhD dissertation, Department of Anthropology, University of Colorado, Boulder. Ann Arbor, MI: University Microfilms International.

McFadden, Douglas A. 1997. "Formative Settlement on the Grand Staircase–Escalante National Monument: A Tale of Two Adaptations." In *Learning from the Land: Grand Staircase–Escalante National Monument Science Symposium Proceedings, Cedar City, Utah*, ed. L. M. Hill, 91–102. Salt Lake City, UT: Bureau of Land Management.

McGuire, Randall H., E. Charles Adams, Ben A. Nelson, and Katherine A. Spielmann. 1994. "Drawing the Southwest to Scale: Perspectives on Macroregional Relations." In *Themes in Southwest Prehistory*, ed. George J. Gumerman, 239–265. Santa Fe, NM: School of American Research Press.

Metcalf, Michael D., Kelly J.Pool, KaeMcDonald, and AnneMcKibbin, eds. 1993. *Hogan Pass: Final Report on Archaeological Investigations along Forest Highway 10 (State Highway 72), Sevier County, Utah*. 3 vols. Eagle, CO: Metcalf Archaeological Consultants. Report prepared for Interagency Archaeological Services, US Department of the Interior, National Park Service, Lakewood, CO. Contract No. CX-1200-6-B052.

Morss, Noel. 1931. *The Ancient Culture of the Fremont River in Utah*. Papers of the Peabody Museum of American Archaeology and Ethnology Vol. 12, *No. 2*. Cambridge, MA: Harvard University.

Morss, Noel. 1954. *Clay Figurines of the American Southwest, with a Description of the New Pillings Find in Northeastern Utah and a Comparison with Certain Other North American Figurines*. Peabody Museum of American Archaeology and Ethnology Papers, Vol. 49, *No. 1*. Cambridge, MA: Harvard University.

Neitzel, Jill E. 1994. "The Chacoan Regional System: Interpreting the Evidence for Sociopolitical Complexity." In *The Sociopolitical Structure of Prehistoric Southwestern Societies*, ed. S. Upham, K. G. Lightfoot, and R. A. Jewett, 509–556. Boulder, CO: Westview Press.

Neitzel, Jill E., ed. 1999. *Great Towns and Regional Polities. The Amerind Foundation New World Studies Series*. Albuquerque: University of New Mexico Press.

Neitzel, Jill E.2000. "What Is a Regional System? Issues of Scale and Interaction in the Prehistoric Southwest." In *The Archaeology of Regional Interaction: Religion, Warfare, and Exchange across the American Southwest and Beyond*, ed. Michelle Hegmon, 25–40. Boulder: University Press of Colorado.

Parker, Bradley J. 2006. "Toward an Understanding of Borderland Processes." *American Antiquity* 71(1):77–100. https://doi.org/10.2307/40035322.

Plog, Stephen. 2008. *Ancient Peoples of the American Southwest*. 2nd ed. London: Thames and Hudson.

Richards, Katie K. 2014. "Fremont Ceramic Designs and Their Implications." MA thesis, Department of Anthropology, Brigham Young University, Provo, UT.

Richens, Lane D. 2000. "Ceramics." In *Clear Creek Canyon Archaeology: Result and Synthesis*, by Joel C. Janetski, Richard K. Talbot, Deborah E. Newman, Lane D.

Richens, James D. Wilde, Shane A. Baker, and Scott E. Billat, 47–65. Museum of Peoples and Cultures Occasional Papers No. 7. Provo, UT: Brigham Young University.

Richens, Lane D., Shane A. Baker, and Joel C. Janetski. 1996. "Material Culture and Faunal Remains." In *Steinaker Gap: An Early Fremont Farmstead*, by Richard K. Talbot and Lane D. Richens, 83–96. Museum of Peoples and Cultures Occasional Papers No. 2. Provo, UT: Brigham Young University.

Rudy, Jack R. 1953. *Archaeological Survey of Western Utah*. Anthropological Papers No. 12. Salt Lake City: University of Utah.

Schaafsma, Polly. 1971. *The Rock Art of Utah*. Papers of the Peabody Museum, vol. 65. Cambridge, MA: Harvard University.

Schaafsma, Polly. 1980. *Indian Rock Art of the Southwest*. Albuquerque: University of New Mexico Press.

Schaafsma, Polly. 1986. "Rock Art." In *Great Basin*, ed. Warren L. d'Azevedo, 215–226. *Handbook of North American Indians*, vol. 11, gen. ed. William C. Sturtevant. Washington, DC: Smithsonian Institution.

Searcy, Michael T., and Richard K. Talbot. 2015. "Late Fremont Cultural Identities and Borderland Processes." In *Late Holocene Research on Foragers and Early Farmers in the Desert West*, ed. Barbara Roth and Maxine McBrinn, 234–264. Salt Lake City: University of Utah Press.

Simms, Steven R. 1986. "New Evidence for Fremont Adaptive Diversity." *Journal of California and Great Basin Anthropology* 8(2):204–216.

Simms, Steven R. 1999a. "Chasing the Will-'o-the-Wisp of Social Order." In *Models for the Millennium: Great Basin Anthropology Today*, ed. Charlotte Beck, 105–110. Salt Lake City: University of Utah Press.

Simms, Steven R. 1999b. "Farmers, Foragers, and Adaptive Diversity: The Great Salt Lake Wetlands Project." In *Prehistoric Lifeways in the Great Basin Wetlands: Bioarchaeological Reconstruction and Interpretation*, ed. B. E. Hemphill and C. S. Larsen, 21–54. Salt Lake City: University of Utah Press.

Simms, Steven R. 2008. *Ancient Peoples of the Great Basin and the Colorado Plateau*. Walnut Creek, CA: Left Coast Press.

Steward, Julian H. 1936. *Pueblo Material Culture in Western Utah*. Bulletin No. 287, Anthropological Series Vol. 1, *No. 3*. Albuquerque: University of New Mexico.

Talbot, Richard K. 2000a. "Fremont Architecture." In *Clear Creek Canyon Archaeological Project: Results and Synthesis*, by J. C. Janetski, R. K. Talbot, D. E. Newman, L. D. Richens, and J. D. Wilde, 131–184. Museum of Peoples and Cultures Occasional Papers No. 7. Provo, UT: Brigham Young University.

Talbot, Richard K. 2000b. "Fremont Farmers: The Search for Context." In *The Archaeology of Regional Interaction: Religion, Warfare, and Exchange across the American Southwest and Beyond*, ed. Michelle Hegmon, 275–293. Boulder: University Press of Colorado.

Talbot, Richard K. 2000c. "Fremont Settlement Patterns and Demography." In *Clear Creek Canyon Archaeological Project: Results and Synthesis*, by J. C. Janetski, R. K. Talbot, D. E. Newman, L. D. Richens, and J. D. Wilde, 201–230. Museum of Peoples and Cultures Occasional Papers No. 7. Provo, UT: Brigham Young University.

Talbot, Richard K. 2004. "Uinta Basin Agricultural Period Dynamics." In *The Steinaker Lake Project: Farming and Mobility on the Far Northern Colorado Plateau*, by Richard K. Talbot and Lane D. Richens, 77–114. Museum of Peoples and Cultures Occasional Papers No. 10. Provo, UT: Brigham Young University.

Talbot, Richard K. 2005. "Discussion of Research Topics—Chronology." In *Life on the Edge: Archaeology in Capitol Reef National Park*, by J. C. Janetski, L. Kreutzer, R. K. Talbot, L. D. Richens, and S. A. Baker, 225–239. Museum of Peoples and Cultures Occasional Papers No. 11. Provo, UT: Brigham Young University.

Talbot, Richard K. 2006. "Architecture and Cultural Identity along the Fremont-Anasazi Interface." In *Learning from the Land: Grand Staircase–Escalante National Monument Science Symposium Proceedings 2006*. Salt Lake City, UT: Bureau of Land Management.

Talbot, Richard K. 2011. "Fremont Farming and Residential Mobility on the Colorado Plateau." In *An Archaeological Legacy: Essays in Honor of Ray T. Matheny*, edited by Deanne G. Mathehy, Joel C. Janctski, and Gloria Nielsen, 125–42. Museum of Peoples and Cultures Occasional Papers. Provo, UT: Brigham Young University.

Talbot, Richard K., Shane A. Baker, and Joel C. Janetski. 2005. "Project Synthesis: Archaeology in Capitol Reef National Park." In *Life on the Edge: Archaeology in Capitol Reef National Park*, by J. C. Janetski, L. Kreutzer, R. K. Talbot, L. D. Richens, and S. A. Baker, 351–407. Museum of Peoples and Cultures Occasional Papers No. 11. Provo, UT: Brigham Young University.

Talbot, Richard K., and Joel C. Janetski. 2000. "Use of Space at Five Finger Ridge." In *Clear Creek Canyon Archaeological Project: Results and Synthesis*, by J. C. Janetski, R. K. Talbot, D. E. Newman, L. D. Richens, and J. D. Wilde, 9–46. Museum of Peoples and Cultures Occasional Papers No. 7. Provo, UT: Brigham Young University.

Talbot, Richard K., and Lane D. Richens. 1993. *Archaeological Investigations at Richfield and Vicinity*. Museum of Peoples and Cultures Technical Series No. 93-15. Provo, UT: Brigham Young University.

Talbot, Richard K., and Lane D. Richens. 1996. *Steinaker Gap: An Early Fremont Farmstead*. Museum of Peoples and Cultures Occasional Papers No. 2. Provo, UT: Brigham Young University.

Talbot, Richard K., and Lane D. Richens. 2004. *Fremont Farming and Mobility on the Far Northern Colorado Plateau*. Museum of Peoples and Cultures Occasional Papers No. 10. Provo, UT: Brigham Young University.

Talbot, Richard K., and Lane D. Richens. 2007. "The Zevon II Site (42PI275) in Piute County, Utah." *Utah Archaeology* 20(1):19–40.

Talbot, Richard K., James D. Wilde, and Lane D. Richens. 2000. "Chronology." In *Clear Creek Canyon Archaeology: Result and Synthesis*, by Joel C. Janetski, Richard K. Talbot, Deborah E. Newman, Lane D. Richens, James D. Wilde, Shane A. Baker, and Scott E. Billat, 125–129. Museum of Peoples and Cultures Occasional Papers No. 7. Provo, UT: Brigham Young University.

Upham, Steadman. 2000. "Scale, Innovation, and Change in the Desert West: A Macroregional Approach." In *The Archaeology of Regional Interaction: Religion, Warfare, and Exchange across the American Southwest and Beyond*, ed. Michelle Hegmon, 235–256. Boulder: University Press of Colorado.

Upham, Steadman, and Lori Stephens Reed. 1989. "Regional Systems in the Central and Northern Southwest: Demography, Economy, and Sociopolitics Preceding Contact." In *Columbian Consequences*, ed. D. H. Thomas, 57–76. Washington, DC: Smithsonian Institutional Press.

Ure, Scott M. 2013. "Parowan Valley Potting Communities: Examining Technological Style in Fremont Snake Valley Corrugated Pottery." MA thesis, Department of Anthropology, Brigham Young University, Provo, UT.

Watkins, Christopher. 2009. "Type, Series, and Ware: Characterizing Variability in Fremont Ceramic Temper." *Journal of California and Great Basin Anthropology* 29:145–161.

Wilcox, David R. 1979. "The Hohokam Regional System." In *An Archaeological Test of Sites in the Gila Butte–Santan Region*, ed. G. E. Rice, D. Wilcox, K. Rafferty, and J. Schoenwetter, 77–116. Anthropological Research Paper No. 18. Tempe: Arizona State University.

Wilcox, David R. 1980. "The Current Status of the Hohokam Concept." In *Current Issues in Hohokam Prehistory: Proceedings of a Symposium*, ed. D. E. Doyel and F. Plog, 236–242. Anthropological Research Paper No. 23. Tempe: Arizona State University.

Wilde, James D., and Deborah E. Newman. 1989. "Late Archaic Corn in the Eastern Great Basin." *American Anthropologist* 91(3):712–720. https://doi.org/10.1525/aa.1989.91.3.02a00120.

Wilde, James D., and Reed A. Soper. 1999. *Baker Village: Report of Excavations, 1990–1994*. Museum of Peoples and Cultures Technical Series No. 99-12. Provo, UT: Brigham Young University.

# 18

# Architecture and Social Organization in the Fremont World

LINDSAY D. JOHANSSON

Fremont people are most commonly cited as living from approximately AD 200 to 1400 in much of modern Utah and parts of Nevada and Colorado (figure 18.1; Watkins 2009; see Allison 2012, 2016 for more details on dating). Regardless of larger questions of cultural and ethnic continuity with both prehistoric and modern groups, as an archaeological culture the Fremont are distinguishable from earlier and later groups of foragers, as well as from other farming cultures such as the Virgin Branch Puebloan culture to the south. Similar to many other Southwestern groups, Fremont were semisedentary horticulturalists who relied on some wild resources (Jennings 1978; Marwitt 1968; Morss 1931). They had a distinctive ceramic tradition (Richards, chapter 19, this volume; Watkins 2009), made basketry and moccasins, and built structures both above and below ground (Talbot 2000a). Diagnostic artifacts, such as ceramics, projectile points, ground stone tools, and architecture are used by archaeologists to recognize a Fremont social identity (see Talbot, chapter 17, this volume), regardless of potential differences in ethnic or linguistic background.

It is this fourth diagnostic artifact type, architecture, on which I focus in this chapter. Architectural studies across both time and space in Southwestern

DOI: 10.5876/9781607327356.c018

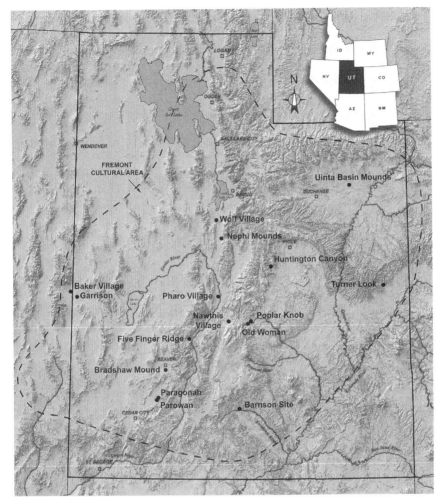

**FIGURE 18.1.** *Fremont cultural area including locations of sites discussed. (Image courtesy of Scott Ure, Department of Anthropology, Brigham Young University.)*

North America have a long and rich history. Since the beginning of archaeological research in the area, architecture has played an important role in defining and distinguishing archaeological cultures (see Clemensen 1992; Elliott 1995; Judd 1922, 1954, 1964; Lekson 2007; and Varien et al. 1996, among others). More recently, architecture has been used to study community and social organization (Longacre 2000:296; Plog 1989:143; Steward 1937). However, while architectural studies are well developed in many areas of the Southwest (e.g., Cameron 2009; Gilman 2010; Wilshusuen et al. 2012), they are much less so in the Fremont area.

This separation between Fremont and the greater Southwest has many causes (see Allison, chapter 13, this volume; Talbot, chapter 17, this volume). While some (see Jennings 1978; Madsen 1979; Madsen and Berry 1975; and Madsen and Simms 1998, among others) argue against Southwestern connections, Richard K. Talbot (2000b:287) believes that "Fremont socioeconomic foundations and history trajectory are distinctly Southwestern," and as a result, connections, relationships, and commonalities with other Southwestern peoples must be investigated. Much of this debate is in the past, but, while more archaeologists are beginning to recognize similarities in subsistence strategies, technological traditions, and interaction of Fremont with the Greater Southwest (in particular, see Geib 1996; Janetski et al. 2000; Janetski et al. 2011; Simms 1986; Upham 1994), architectural theories commonly applied to the Ancestral Puebloan, Hohokam, and Mogollon have not yet been widely applied to analysis of Fremont structures and communities.

The lack of focus on Fremont architecture likely results from the view of the Fremont as a localized outgrowth of the Great Basin Desert Culture (see Jennings and Norbeck 1955 and Wormington 1955, among others). Theoretical differences between archaeologists working in the Great Basin and those working in the Southwest (Allison 2008) have resulted in different questions being asked and different results being reported. Traditionally, Great Basin archaeologists have focused more narrowly on human ecology than have Southwestern archaeologists. Although this focus has resulted in useful information concerning Fremont diet and resource procurement, I, along with others in this volume, believe that Fremont archaeologists need to move beyond these questions. The analysis of architecture offers one mechanism to do so, since architecture not only reflects the people who built it and their views of how the world is organized, but also helps to shape and influence the views of later generations and peoples (Gilman 1987; Lipe and Hegmon 1989; Varien and Potter 2008).

Here I use architecture to illustrate how, due to the interconnected nature of the prehistoric American Southwest, archaeologists working across the Fremont region have much to gain by applying theories used in other areas. Particularly in relation to architecture, by applying theories and analogies developed for understanding structures among the Ancestral Puebloan, Fremont archaeologists will be better equipped to both answer and ask questions of social organization among the Fremont. In this chapter, I explore ways in which Fremont architecture, particularly communal architecture, is similar to the architecture of other Southwestern cultural groups and how these architectural similarities might provide insight concerning functional similarities. Despite these commonalities, however, Fremont architecture is distinct from that built in other areas of the Southwest, and I use artifact information to suggest possible other functions of Fremont communal structures. I conclude with a discussion of how structure function can provide information concerning social organization among the Fremont.

## FREMONT ARCHITECTURAL TYPES

Despite the focus on human ecology, Fremont architecture has been recorded for as long or longer than any other aspect of Fremont material culture. However, it was rarely looked at in any detail, and Talbot (2000a:136–139) was the first to specifically discuss Fremont communal architecture. He created five subcategories of Fremont structures, which were modified by Johansson et al. (2014). At the broadest level, they separate Fremont architecture into categories of residential and communal. These overlap in some areas, as many communal structures were also residences for important individuals and/or families, but in general, pithouses and surface houses are residential architecture, while plazas, central structures, oversized pit structures, and storage structures are communal.

### Residential Architecture

The most common residential structure built among the Fremont is the pithouse, which functioned as the primary habitation units for the household (Talbot 2000a:136). Secondary pit structures are distinguishable from pithouses in that they are much smaller (rarely large enough to hold more than one or two individuals) and were likely used for specific situations, such as seclusion huts. Surface houses are comparable in size and contain all the functional characteristics of a pithouse, such as a central hearth and subfloor features, but were constructed using "freestanding walls of coursed adobe, jacal, or masonry" (Talbot 2000a:138–139; for more details on residential architecture types, see Johansson et al. 2014 and Talbot 2000a).

### Communal Architecture

While pithouses and surface houses were used as residences, they were also built for communal purposes. I follow Michael A. Adler and Richard H. Wilshusen's (1990:133) definition of communal architecture as "structures or prepared spaces that are socially acknowledged as a context for integration of individuals above the household level." Such structures were likely used to help bind the community together and provide mechanisms to alleviate tensions that arise as people aggregate. However, while communal structures served integrative functions, they may also have had some divisive functions. Writing about Fremont communal structures in particular, Johansson et al. (2014:49) argued that "the events hosted in communal structures likely [also] provided opportunities for some individuals to distinguish themselves, and this, combined with the exclusion of some community members from certain events, probably meant that the building and use of 'integrative' structures also contributed to differentiation and factionalism within the community." Among the Fremont and elsewhere, structures identified as communal architecture are those that were created on a scale that would have required community cooperation. The amount of effort needed to make and maintain these structures suggests that they were not used exclusively by one family or kin group, although it is likely that some individuals (possibly socially or ritually important individuals) lived within communal structures and carried out their daily activities there (Talbot 2000a).

Several types of buildings were used to organize public areas within the community, and in many cases two or more forms of communal architecture were associated, creating a structural complex that, although not necessarily in the geographic center of the community, "may represent a center of power within the Fremont village" (Ure and Stauffer 2010:13). These structures contained exotic artifacts such as turquoise, *Olivella* shell, and figurines, but were not used exclusively for communal ritual purposes, and preliminary analysis of structure function indicates that Fremont communal architecture likely served residential and communal roles simultaneously (see also Adler and Wilshusen 1990). Here I focus on four forms of communal architecture that are the most widespread across the Fremont area: plazas, central structures, oversized pit structures, and storage structures.

*Plazas*

Plazas are "a public area in a community or an open space surrounded by or adjacent to buildings" (Kidder 2004:515). Plazas allowed entire communities to participate in public events, and while they served religious functions, they also broadcast to the community who was in charge and who held power within a group (Chamberlin 2011:130, 134). Although plazas are open spaces, necessarily devoid of architecture, because they are integrated into community layouts they are considered part of the planned architectural complex (Kidder 2004:517). In many Ancestral Puebloan sites, plazas incorporate other communal structures such as great kivas. One example of this is Sand Canyon Pueblo located in southwestern Colorado, where the plaza is located next to community buildings, making it an "appropriate place for public rituals" and a place where members of the community could view what was going on in the unroofed great kiva (Ortman and Bradley 2002:64–65).

Several sites in the Fremont area contain plazas (table 18.1). At the Big Mound at Paragonah, the plaza is located next to both oversized pit structures and storage structures (Judd 1919), possibly indicating a function similar to that of the plaza at Sand Canyon Pueblo. The presence of plazas near central structures and oversized pit structures at Beaver, Five Finger Ridge, Turner Look, and the Old Woman site further supports the association between plazas and other types of communal structures in the Fremont area (Judd 1926; Talbot et al. 2000; Taylor 1957; Wormington 1955). In addition, plazas are present at the Snake Rock and Parowan sites (Aikens 1967; Judd 1926).

**TABLE 18.1.** Sites with plazas

| Site | Near Oversized Pit Structure? | Near Central Structure? | Near Communal Storage? | Near Surface Structure with Attached Storeroom? |
|------|------|------|------|------|
| Beaver (Bradshaw Mound) | No | Yes | Yes | No |
| Five Finger Ridge | Yes | Yes | Possibly | Yes |
| Old Woman | Yes | No | Possibly | Yes |
| Paragonah | Yes | Yes | Yes | No |
| Parowan | No | No | No | No |
| Snake Rock | No | No | No | No |
| Turner Look | No | Yes | No | No |

*Central Structures*

Central structures, Talbot's (2000a) only example of Fremont communal architecture, are abnormally large structures built on the ground surface and exhibiting freestanding walls. Central structures exhibit a high degree of variability: construction methods include jacal, coursed adobe, and masonry (table 18.2; Talbot et al. 2000; Taylor 1954, 1957; Wilde and Soper 1999; Worthington 1955). Elements of the environment were often incorporated into these buildings as well: Structure 3 at Huntington Canyon uses a boulder for one of its walls, and the Rock Wall House at Uinta Basin Mounds is built against a cliff face, with masonry on the other three sides (Montgomery and Montgomery 1993; Steward 1933).

To date, central structures have been identified at nine Fremont sites: Baker Village, House 1 at Poplar Knob, Room 15 at Beaver Mounds, Structure 39 at Paragonah, Structure 24 at Five Finger Ridge, Building 8 at the Garrison site, Structure 3 at Huntington Canyon, Structure H at the Turner-Look site, and the Rock Wall House at the Uinta Basin Mounds (see table 18.2 and figure 18.2; Judd 1919, 1926; Montgomery and Montgomery 1993; Steward 1933; Talbot et al. 2000; Taylor 1957; Wilde and Soper 1999; Worthington 1955). While access to central structures would have been more restricted than access to plazas, four and possibly as many as six of these structures have only three walls, with openings found to the south. The lack of a southern wall may have served to increase the number of people who could be involved in the activities taking place within the structure. Because of this, the architecture of central structures suggests that, in general, entire communities were involved in the activities taking place within the structures.

Although considered high-level integrative facilities by Adler (1989:45), unroofed great kivas in the Ancestral Puebloan world may have been constructed for some of the same purposes as central structures, and the open

**TABLE 18.2.** Sites with central structures

| Site | Structure Name | Floor Area (m²) | Construction Method | Source |
|---|---|---|---|---|
| Baker Village | Central Structure | 54.6 | Coursed adobe | Wilde and Soper 1999 |
| Beaver (Bradshaw Mounds) | Room 15 | 22.6 | Adobe | Judd 1926 |
| Five Finger Ridge | Structure 24 | 26.8 | Jacal | Talbot et al. 2000 |
| Garrison | Building 8 | 52.8 | Jacal | Taylor 1954 |
| Huntington Canyon | Structure 3 | 38.5 | Adobe, boulder as one wall | Montgomery and Montgomery 1993 |
| Paragonah | Structure 39 | 33.4 | Jacal | Judd 1919; Judd 1926 |
| Poplar Knob | House 1 | 27.3 | Stone slab and adobe mortar | Taylor 1957 |
| Turner-Look | Structure H | 58.0 | Masonry | Worthington 1955 |
| Uinta Basin Mounds | Rock Wall House | 35.2 | Uncoursed stone with cliff as one wall | Steward 1933 |

architecture of both suggests a desire to include many community members. Scott G. Ortman and Bruce A. Bradley calculate that at Sand Canyon Pueblo (Ortman and Bradley 2002:64), 250 people would have been able to watch and participate in the activities going on in the unroofed great kiva, while only about 100 people would have been able to view the activities inside the kiva if it had been roofed. Due to their aboveground location, central structures would not have been able to involve as many individuals as unroofed great kivas, but the lack of a southern wall may have served to increase involvement beyond simply the number that could comfortably fit inside the structure.

*Oversized Pit Structures*

Like central structures, the effort needed to build and maintain oversized pit structures "would have been much greater than that for most other architectural forms" (Talbot 2000a:139). These buildings are large, semisubterranean, roofed structures with a median size of 37 m², and like the central structures, share certain characteristics (Allison et al. 2012; Johansson et al. 2014; Marwitt 1968; Sharrock and Marwitt 1967; Taylor 1957).

Six oversized pit structures have been identified to date at Fremont sites: Structure 2 at Wolf Village, House 3 at the Old Woman site, Structure 1 at the Barnson site, Dwelling 1 at Pharo Village, Structure 57 at Five Finger Ridge, and

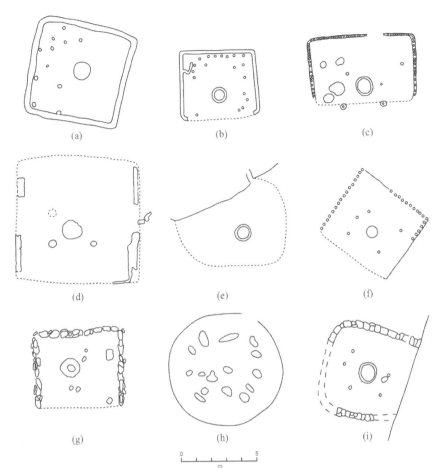

(a)

(b)

(c)

(d)

(e)

(f)

(g)

(h)

(i)

0       5
m

**FIGURE 18.2.** *Plan maps of central structures: (a) the central structure at Baker Village, (b) Room 15 at Beaver (Bradshaw Mounds), (c) Structure 24 at Five Finger Ridge, (d) Building 8 at Garrison, (e) Structure 3 at Huntington Canyon, (f) Structure 39 at Paragonah, (g) House 1 at Poplar Knob, (h) Structure H at Turner-Look, and (i) the Rock Wall House at Uinta Basin Mounds. (Maps redrawn from original publications; images a–g courtesy of Scott Ure, Department of Anthropology, Brigham Young University.)*

Dwelling 1 Mound 5 at Nephi Mounds (table 18.3; figure 18.3; Johansson et al. 2014; Marwitt 1968; Sharrock and Marwitt 1967; Taylor 1957). In contrast to the open nature of central structures and plazas, access to oversized pit structures would have been restricted; their semisubterranean nature would have limited the number of individuals who could be involved in the activities taking place within. Allison et al. (2012) make comparisons between features within the oversized pit

**TABLE 18.3.** Sites with oversized pit structures

| Site | Structure Name | Floor Area (m²) | Source |
|------|----------------|------------------|--------|
| Barnson site | Structure 1 | 56.9 | Office of Public Archaeology 2003 |
| Five Finger Ridge | Structure 57 | 31.6 | Talbot et al. 2000 |
| Nephi Mounds | Dwelling 1, Mound 5 | 36.6 | Sharrock and Marwitt 1967 |
| Old Woman site | House 3 | 26.3 | Taylor 1957 |
| Pharo Village | Dwelling 1 | 32.1 | Marwitt 1968 |
| Wolf Village | Structure 2 | 80.5 | Johansson et al. 2014 |

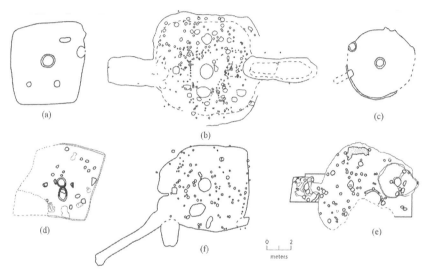

**FIGURE 18.3.** *Plan maps of oversized pit structures: (a) Dwelling 1, Mound 5 at Nephi Mounds, (b) Structure 2 at Wolf Village, (c) House 3 at the Old Woman site, (d) Structure 57 at Five Finger Ridge, (e) Dwelling 1 at Pharo Village, and (f) Structure 1 at the Barnson site. (Maps redrawn from original publications; images a and b courtesy of Katie Richards, Department of Anthropology, Washington State University; image f courtesy of the Office of Public Archaeology, Brigham Young University).*

structure at Wolf Village (Structure 2) and the ritual features typically found in Ancestral Puebloan kivas (e.g., Wilshusen 1989). In particular, they identify possible prayer-stick holes and a sipapu among the floor features. Even without the presence of similar features, the enclosed nature of oversized pit structures makes kivas the most analogous of Southwestern structures. Both types of structures would have been used for community, possibly ritual, activities, and access to both may have been restricted to certain groups or for certain activities.

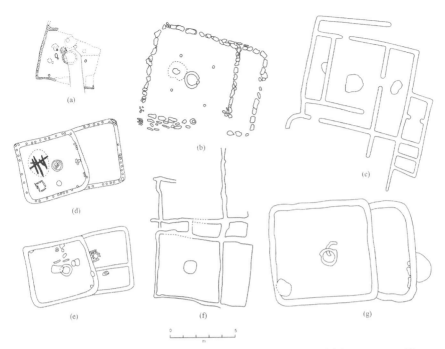

**FIGURE 18.4.** *Plan maps of surface houses with attached storerooms: (a) Structure 25 at Five Finger Ridge, (b) House 2 at Poplar Knob, (c) Heartbreak Hotel at Nawthis Village, (d) House 4 at the Old Woman site, (e) House 5 at the Old Woman site, (f) Structure 1 at Wolf Village, and (g) Dwelling 1, Mound 1 at Nephi Mounds. (Maps redrawn from original publications.)*

*Communal Storage*

In addition to central structures, oversized pithouses, and plazas, some Fremont structures were likely built for communal storage (figure 18.4). One example of this is the Heartbreak Hotel structure at Nawthis Village (Metcalfe and Heath 1990). This structure contains at least nine rooms, with the largest measuring 20 m² and the smallest measuring 1.8 m² (Metcalfe and Heath 1990:784). One or two of the rooms in this structure may have been habitation rooms while the rest were likely used for storage, and it is unlikely that one family or extended family group used the seven storerooms at Heartbreak Hotel at any one time.

Although only one other structure similar to Heartbreak Hotel has been documented at a Fremont site (Structure 1 at Wolf Village), adobe-walled room blocks were identified by Neil M. Judd (1926:27–30) at the Bradshaw Mound near Beaver, Utah. He documented at least four contiguous adobe-walled rooms that lacked hearths and contained a "marked absence of ashes, potsherds, and similar kitchen refuse" (Judd 1926:28). While Judd interpreted them as small dwellings, Meighan et al. (1956) argued that these were instead granaries. At least 40 adobe

**TABLE 18.4.** Sites with surface houses with attached storerooms

| Site | Structure Name | Number of Rooms | Near Other Communal Structures? | Source |
|------|----------------|-----------------|--------------------------------|--------|
| Five Finger Ridge | Structure 25 | 2 | yes | Talbot et al. 2000 |
| Nawthis Village | Heartbreak Hotel | at least 9 | no | Metcalfe and Heath 1990 |
| Nephi Mounds | Dwelling 1, Mound 1 | 2 | yes | Sharrock and Marwitt 1967 |
| Old Woman Site | House 4 | 2 | yes | Taylor 1957 |
| Old Woman Site | House 5 | 3 | yes | Taylor 1957 |
| Poplar Knob | House 2 | 2 | yes | Taylor 1957 |
| Wolf Village | Structure 1 | at least 6 | yes | Johansson et al. 2014 |

structures within the Big Mound at Paragonah, which Judd (1926:9) originally called "court shelters," were also reinterpreted as surface granaries.

Not all Fremont communities contain large storage-room blocks, which are more common in the southern Fremont area. Instead, some sites contain noncontiguous adobe-surface storage structures, freestanding adobe structures containing only one or two small rooms. These smaller storage structures are included by Talbot (2000a) as one of his five architectural forms and are documented farther north than contiguous storage-room blocks. Although the adobe storage structures could have been used by a single family or family group, based on their proximity to public irrigation systems that would have been built and maintained by the entire community, it is more likely that crop surpluses were managed by the group and that these storage structures were used by communities, or at the very least family groups, rather than individuals.

In addition to surface storage structures, aboveground adobe structures with attached storage rooms exist at many sites, particularly those in the northern Fremont area (table 18.4; Johansson 2016). These structures, which are similar to the Heartbreak Hotel structure, though on a much smaller scale, are composed of a residential room with an attached storeroom, or storerooms. These structures have been documented at Five Finger Ridge (Structure 25), Nephi Mounds (Dwelling 1, Mound 1; Dwelling 3, Mound 1), the Old Woman site (House 5), and Poplar Knob (House 2), among others, and are often located near other types of communal architecture (Sharrock and Marwitt 1967; Talbot et al. 2000; Taylor 1957). The proximity between two types of communal structures may indicate that the individuals living in the adobe structures, both two room and larger, not only controlled access to and possibly guarded the materials in the storerooms, but also controlled access and oversaw activities within the public building. This level of control of both resources and activities suggests the presence of leaders or important individuals within Fremont communities.

## FUNCTION OF FREMONT COMMUNAL STRUCTURES

Thus far, this chapter has focused on the fact that the Fremont had structures and architectural forms that were quite large and similar in some aspects to communal architecture found elsewhere in the Southwest, although these structures are distinctly Fremont. While structure use has been explored in these other areas of the American Southwest, few archaeologists have focused on the function of Fremont communal structures. Exploring function can give indications as to why these structures were built and what the organization was of the society that built them. Because of the availability of reliable data, I focus here on only two of the four communal structure types—central structures and oversized pit structures—and on three sites, Wolf Village, Five Finger Ridge, and Baker Village.

Three sites do not make for particularly strong conclusions, especially as only Five Finger Ridge contained both an oversized pit structure and a central structure, but as the overall sample of Fremont communal structures is quite low and much of the data are of poor quality, this problem will likely not be remedied for many years, if ever. However, at these three sites there are obvious distinctions between the artifacts from residential and communal structures. When combined with the distinctive architectural forms discussed previously, the artifacts and quantities found within the communal structures give insights into the roles these structures held in society.

### Methodology

To discuss function, relative quantities of ceramics, lithic debitage, bifaces and projectile points, and ground stone tools from the floor zones were compared between structures at each site. The definition of *floor zone* varied slightly between the three sites and structures at a single site, but was no greater than the 10 cm directly above the structure floor. I chose to include the floor zone as opposed to only floor artifacts because several projects did not differentiate between floor and floor-zone artifacts and because in many cases the floor-zone stratum began directly below a layer of roof fall. The positioning of the floor zone below roof fall indicates that the artifacts within the floor zone were most likely inside the structure when it collapsed and are likely not associated with postdepositional trash fill.

Rather than discussing the fill of structures as a whole, I use only floor-zone artifacts because many Fremont structures were used as trash pits after they fell into disuse and collapsed (Stauffer 2012:67). This was a particularly common practice with communal structures. When communal structures were abandoned, many of them were burned, possibly as part of an abandonment ritual, and several were intentionally buried by a rich midden at or near the time of their abandonment (Allison et al. 2012; King 2012). Valuable information can be gained from these midden deposits but the artifacts within are not necessarily associated with occupation and use of the structure. Analysis and discussion of midden contents is an interesting and worthwhile topic, but unfortunately beyond the scope of this chapter.

Because of the nature of the data from each site, I compare quantities and densities of artifact types rather than the artifacts themselves. To do this, I rely heavily on correspondence analyses, which compare all artifact types and quantities for structures at the sites discussed, and scatterplots, which compare specific artifact types and quantities by mapping artifact density per square meter within each structure. Because the purpose of this chapter is to compare the artifacts from communal structures with the artifact patterning among residential structures at each site, the lines of best fit included on scatterplots were calculated based only on artifact density of the residential structures to mitigate distortion. Because the quantity of residential structures is low at Baker Village and Wolf Village ($n \leq 10$), mean artifact densities were also used because especially high or low quantities of artifacts in a single residential structure could have an undue influence on the regression line when the sample size is low (table 18.5).

### Oversized Pit Structures

Correspondence analysis works best when looking for patterns in the counts or the presence/absence in the data set and then representing those data graphically (Shennan 1997). This analysis cross-tabulates the relationship between variables and represents the data as a set of points along two perpendicular axes. When viewing the plotted data, the angles and distances between variables represent how closely the variables are related to one another, with shorter distances and acute angles indicating greater similarities and longer distances and obtuse angles indicating fewer similarities. Correspondence analysis of the floor-zone artifacts from structures at Five Finger Ridge and Wolf Village suggest that the two oversized pit structures contain similar artifact types. The graphs in figure 18.5 show that both structures are more closely correlated with lithic debitage than with other artifact types. In addition, stone tools (bifaces and projectile points) are also disproportionately associated with the oversized pit structures. Relationships with the other artifact types appear more ambiguous and are not consistent between sites.

*Five Finger Ridge*

Although not strongly correlated, ground stone tools (manos and metates as well as catch basins) were found within the oversized pit structure at Five Finger Ridge, in addition to ceramics and faunal bone. Graphs of artifact density per square meter (figure 18.6) suggest that these artifact types were present on a scale similar to that of residential structures at the site, indicating that food processing at the oversized pit structure was likely being carried out for consumption

**TABLE 18.5.** Artifact densities per square meter

| | Ceramic | Debitage | Stone Tool | Ground Stone Tool | Faunal |
|---|---|---|---|---|---|
| FFR Pithouse Avg: | 10.98 | 20.84 | 0.56 | 0.58 | 5.28 |
| FFR Str. 25 (SH) | 2.26 | 7.83 | 1.13 | 0.00 | 2.17 |
| FFR Str. 24 (CS) | 8.13 | 3.36 | 0.15 | 0.11 | 1.98 |
| FFR Str. 57 (OPS) | 9.21 | 22.25 | 1.42 | 0.47 | 3.77 |
| WV Pithouse Avg: | 35.88 | 65.07 | 2.47 | 1.21 | 28.75 |
| WV Str. 1 (SH) | 21.81 | 41.56 | 1.50 | 0.66 | 81.71 |
| WV Str. 2 (OPS) | 49.96 | 59.92 | 3.07 | 0.41 | 178.08 |
| WV Str. 6 (CS) | 56.39 | 77.17 | 2.93 | 2.20 | 203.66 |
| BV Pithouse Avg | 4.07 | 24.47 | 0.56 | 0.15 | N/A |
| BV CS (CS) | 4.27 | 152.53 | 3.32 | 0.24 | N/A |

* Sites: Baker Village (BV), Five Finger Ridge (FFR), and Wolf Village (WV). Structures: central structures (CS), oversized pit structures (OPS), and surface houses (SH).

by the individuals living within the structure and not for large-scale feasting and community consumption. However, the quantities per square meter of bifaces, projectile points, and lithic debitage indicate that while an average household amount of lithic flaking and stonework was occurring here, an abnormal number of stone tools were brought into the oversized pit structure in comparison to other structures at the site (table 18.5).

*Wolf Village*

Although not as many residential structures from Wolf Village have been excavated, the oversized pit structure follows the trend from Five Finger Ridge: Structure 2 contains a disproportionate number of stone tools in comparison to residential structures (figure 18.7). Correspondence graphs associate both oversized pit structures with lithic debitage, but this is because there are high quantities of lithic debitage at most structures throughout both sites. At Wolf Village, the number of lithic debitage pieces per square meter within the oversized pit structure is actually low in comparison to other structures at the site (table 18.5). Similar to the oversized pit structure at Five Finger Ridge, while artifacts associated with food production and consumption are present within Structure 2, they are on a scale close to that of residential structures at the site.

*Interpretation*

There is some variation between floor-zone artifact counts from the oversized pit structures at Five Finger Ridge and at Wolf Village. Despite this, neither structure is closely associated with food-processing activities, suggesting that communal food production and consumption are not the most likely functions

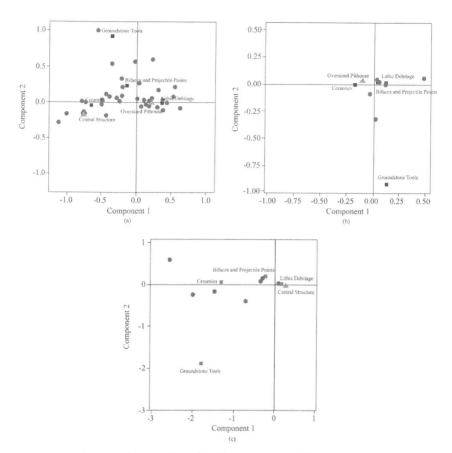

**FIGURE 18.5.** *Correspondence analysis of artifact quantities at (a) Five Finger Ridge, (b) Wolf Village, and (c) Baker Village. Circles indicate residential structures, squares indicate artifact types, and triangles indicate communal structures.*

of these structures. Instead, both appear more strongly associated with stone tools (bifaces and projectile points). While some lithic production (as evidenced by the high quantities of lithic debitage) was occurring within the oversized pit structures, based on the fact that density of lithic debitage was low in comparison or similar to that found within residential structures, it appears that finishing and/or retouching stone tools was occurring more often than earlier stages of production. The disproportionate number of stone tools recovered from the oversized pit structures suggests that at least some of the activities conducted within were male focused: related to hunting and/or priesthood.

As enclosed structures, it would have been easy to restrict access to an oversized pit structure to certain members of the community and/or for certain

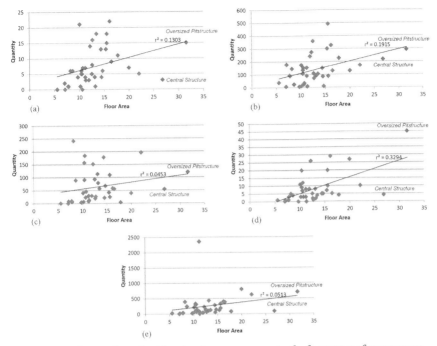

**FIGURE 18.6.** *Scatterplots of artifact density per square meter for floor zones of structures at Five Finger Ridge: (a) ground stone tools (manos and metates), (b) ceramics, (c) faunal bone, (d) stone tools (bifaces and projectile points), and (e) lithic debitage. (Quantities taken from Talbot et al. 2000 and Fisher 2010.)*

events. When viewed in the context of the Greater Southwest, some potential analogues are available. Alfonso Ortiz (1969) used ethnographic discussions of Tewa kiva use to suggest that kivas among the Ancestral Puebloan were considered private spaces "in which secret knowledge was controlled and imparted and that, as such, the kiva and its associated ritual was a center for male ritual power" (Mobley-Tanaka 1997:437). Similarly, artifact information suggests that at least some of the activities within the oversized pit structure were male focused, suggesting that perhaps in addition to the architectural similarities between kivas and oversized pit structures, they may have both served similar functions as male centers for the community.

## Central Structures

The central structures from Five Finger Ridge and Baker Village have comparatively fewer similarities in floor-zone artifact assemblages than the oversized pit structures from Five Finger Ridge and Wolf Village. Correspondence analysis plots the structures quite differently: the central structure from Five Finger

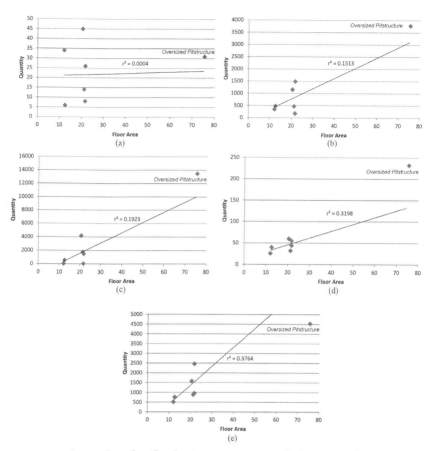

**FIGURE 18.7.** *Scatterplots of artifact density per square meter for floor zones of structures at Wolf Village: (a) ground stone tools (manos and metates), (b) ceramics, (c) faunal bone, (d) stone tools (bifaces and projectile points), and (e) lithic debitage. (Data courtesy of the Brigham Young University Archaeological Field School).*

Ridge is associated with ceramics while that from Baker Village is closely corre-lated with lithic debitage (see figure 18.5). Similar to the oversized pit structures, neither central structure appears to be strongly associated with groundstone tools. The dissimilarities in artifact assemblages that are evident when using cor-respondence analysis are reinforced when artifact density is mapped and when artifact densities are tabulated.

*Five Finger Ridge*

At Five Finger Ridge, scatterplots showing artifact counts in relation to square meters indicate that the artifact density within the central structure is much

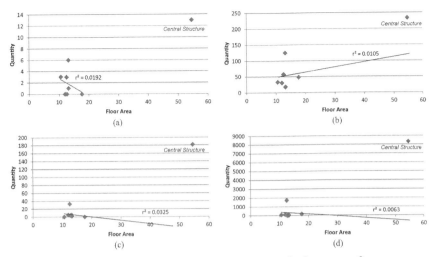

**FIGURE 18.8.** *Scatterplots of artifact density per square meter for floor zones of structures at Baker Village: (a) ground stone tools (manos and metates), (b) ceramics, (c) stone tools (bifaces and projectile points), and (d) lithic debitage. No quantities were available for faunal bone at the time of this publication. (Quantities taken from Wilde and Soper 1999.)*

lower than for other structures at the site (see figure 18.6). Artifact quantities are roughly comparable with those from residential pithouses despite the increased size of the structure, indicating that the majority of refuse was likely produced through typical daily activities of individuals living within the central structure. The only artifact type for which density was comparable to other structures was ceramics (see figure 18.6b). While the oversized pit structure was associated with stone tools and projectile points, the central structure contained particularly low quantities of both, indicating that very different activities are associated with the two types of communal structure at this site.

### Baker Village

Similar to Wolf Village, few structures were excavated at Baker Village. Scatterplots show that there is an inverse relationship between ground stone, lithic debitage, and stone tools and structure size (figure 18.8). Ceramics are the only artifact type in which quantity increases with floor area, but the relationship is only slightly positive ($r^2 = 0.0105$). However, high quantities per square meter of all artifacts were recovered from within the central structure (table 18.5). This change in the relationship between artifact quantity and structure size further emphasizes how differently space within the central structure was being used in comparison to typical residential pithouses at the site. When viewing artifact densities per square meter, the central structure at Baker Village appears to more closely resemble the oversized pit structure at Five Finger Ridge (Structure 57) than the central structure (Structure 24), and contains well over twice the amount of stone tools and pieces of lithic debitage per square meter than was recovered from residential structures at the site.

*Interpretation*

If nothing else, artifact density scatterplots and correspondence analysis demonstrate that artifact counts within central structures are unusual. Structure 24 at Five Finger Ridge had a low artifact density in comparison to other structures at the site, but the density of ceramics was proportionately higher than other artifact types recovered within the structure. In contrast, the central structure at Baker Village has at least double the number of artifacts in comparison to other structures, and a particularly high quantity of lithic debitage. The data might suggest that these structures serve very different functions within the communities, but, while limited, these two structures do give some data regarding the general functions of central structures.

In general, the activities that took place in relation to central structures either were not similar between the two sites or do not appear to have left behind many indicators in the floor refuse of the structure. Ethnographically, communal structures were used for activities such as initiation rites, meetings of religious societies, group-sponsored activities such as feasting or dancing, storage of ritual paraphernalia, daily activities such as cooking or eating, craft production, sleeping, and informal visiting (Adler and Wilshusen 1990), and many of these activities would not necessarily affect the artifact assemblage (Allison et al. 2012). It is likely that central structures served as meeting places for a variety of groups, and possibly also religious and ritual functions. Because central structures and plazas are often associated, activities and rituals that would have produced telltale refuse, such as feasting, may have been conducted outside the structure in order to involve more people. If so, this patterning could explain the lack of artifact indicators of structure function.

## Discussion

Based on the high numbers of bones, particularly those of leporids, within the central structure at Baker Village, Bryan S. Hockett (1998:298) concluded that after the structure was abandoned it was used as a repository for trash following a "final ceremony, or a series of final ceremonies, conducted inside the central structure before the village was abandoned for some length of time." Although I do not necessarily agree with all of Hockett's conclusions (see Johansson 2014), his findings support those presented here and suggest that central structures served as ceremonially important structures among the Fremont. His research confirms the argument put forward by Michael D. Metcalfe (1993:296) that because of dense artifact assemblages and architecture, which "is so much more elaborate than apparently contemporary structures on the site, . . . some speculation must center on implications for ceremonial use of the structure, perhaps even a kiva-like set of domestic and ceremonial functions" (Metcalfe 1993:296).

The artifact information presented here adds to the architectural data and further reinforces that oversized pit structures and central structures were not typical buildings within Fremont villages. In addition to the artifact types discussed above (ground stone, ceramics, lithic debitage, faunal remains, and stone tools), exotic artifacts (turquoise/variscite, marine shell, gaming pieces, ornaments, etc.) and figurines were recovered from almost all of the communal structures discussed in this chapter. The only structures from which exotic artifacts were not recovered are those that were excavated before it was common to collect and record artifact information (i.e., Judd 1919, 1926). On the basis of this information, the argument can be made that Fremont not only built large structures with unusual architecture as a community, but likely used them as a community as well for socially prescribed activities that involved special and exotic items, not unlike other horticultural groups throughout the American Southwest.

## FREMONT SOCIAL ORGANIZATION

This chapter focuses on large Fremont villages, but several other settlement patterns existed among the Fremont, each with a different type of social organization. Within villages, Fremont built structures in a variety of sizes and forms, some of which were built and maintained by the entire community. Similar to other Southwestern groups, these structures were used for a variety of purposes and certain types of structures were reserved for certain types of activities. In comparison to the Ancestral Puebloan to the south, communal structures were built much more infrequently among the Fremont, perhaps as a result of lower population densities and/or differing functions. The presence of architecturally distinct structures and structures that may have served specific functions within the village reflects increasing social and political complexity within Fremont villages. The fact that communal structures are not present in all Fremont villages suggests that these structures may have served to integrate individuals beyond the immediate site as well, drawing on the surrounding community for construction, use, and maintenance. While limited in scope, the data presented here show that although there is some overlap in function between communal structure types, at least one of the activities conducted within oversized pit structures involved completed or very nearly completed stone tools, whereas central structures were typically used for activities that did not leave refuse behind in the structure, such as gathering the community together. These communal structures likely served many other functions, with floor features and exotic artifacts indicating that both structure types were used for ritual purposes as

**FIGURE 18.9.** *Plan map of large Fremont villages organized around communal structures. (Image courtesy of the Office of Public Archaeology, Brigham Young University; redrawn from Allison 2010.)*

well. Although incorporating data from the remaining identified central structures and oversized pit structures will give a more detailed picture of Fremont communal structure function, looking at Fremont use of communal structures through the lens of the Southwest, rather than the Great Basin, provides insight not only into how structures may have been used, but also into Fremont social organization (see also Johansson 2016).

Communal structures were an integral part of the Fremont village and are one of the artifacts that distinguish the Fremont from other Southwestern horticultural groups. While Fremont village sites were organized in a variety of different ways, all appear to have had some planning in regard to the placement of communal structures (figure 18.9). In many cases two or more forms of communal architecture were associated, creating a structural complex that represents a communal and ritual—although not necessarily geographic—center for the village as well as of the wider dispersed community. Spatial analysis of Fremont sites is uncommon, in part because few village sites are fully excavated, but site planning is evident at some. For example, at Five Finger Ridge the central saddle area was left open as a plaza, despite its being arguably the best location for construction. A central structure, oversized pit structure, and surface house with attached storeroom all surround the plaza (Talbot et al. 2000).

At Fremont sites, the presence of communal architecture, site planning, and the control of activities and food surplus by individuals living within the communal structures indicates community cooperation beyond the household level (Johansson 2016; Richards et al. 2013; contrary to Sammons-Lohse 1981). Southwestern architectural theories such as those put forward by William D. Lipe and Michelle Hegmon hold that by planning a village and building communal structures for particular purposes, Fremont people were both defining and recreating the order of their community (Lipe and Hegmon 1989). Community and religious activities must also have been conducted within these structures, and all of these activities would have required community leaders. While communal structures are not identical through time and space in the Fremont region, they are not wholly dissimilar. Although the Fremont style of architecture is similar to other Southwestern culture groups with whom Fremont people had contact, it is also distinct in many ways. Analogues from the Ancestral Pueblo, such as those discussed in this chapter, can provide suggestions for potential uses of Fremont communal structures and point to integrative mechanisms used by other horticultural groups in the region that Fremont people may have adopted or modified as they became increasingly reliant on maize farming. Despite many analogues, as communal structures, oversized pit structures and central structures represent a distinctly Fremont style of architecture and social interaction, and offer important insights into the communities that built them.

*Acknowledgements.* Among those that I must thank are the many scholars who have shared in the development of the ideas included here: in particular Jim Allison, Katie Richards, Rich Talbot, Scott Ure, Lane Richens, and Joel Janetski have been instrumental in developing and solidifying these ideas. Credit for anything I have achieved here should be given to them, although any shortcomings are solely my own. I am also thankful to Barb Roth and Karen Harry for their generous invitations both to speak in the Southwest Symposium and to participate in this volume. In addition, special thanks go to Pascale Meehan, Rachel Egan, Cathy Cameron, Adrien Mooney, and Erin Hughes for comments on various drafts of this chapter as well as to the two anonymous reviewers for their insightful suggestions.

## REFERENCES

Adler, Michael A. 1989. "Ritual Facilities and Social Integration in Nonranked Societies." In *The Architecture of Social Integration in Prehistoric Pueblos,* ed. W. D. Lipe and Michelle Hegmon, 15–34. Occasional Papers of the Crow Canyon Archaeological Center No. 1. Cortez, CO: Crow Canyon Archaeological Center.

Adler, Michael A., and Richard H. Wilshusen. 1990. "Large-Scale Integrative Facilities in Tribal Societies: Cross-Cultural and Southwestern US Examples." *World Archaeology* 22(2):133–146. https://doi.org/10.1080/00438243.1990.9980136.

Aikens, C. Melvin. 1967. "Plains Relationship of the Fremont Culture: A Hypothesis." *American Antiquity* 32(2):198–209. https://doi.org/10.2307/277904.

Allison, James R. 2008. "Human Ecology and Social Theory in Utah Archaeology." *Utah Archaeology* 21(1):57–77.

Allison, James R. 2010. "The End of Farming in the 'Northern Periphery' of the Southwest." In *Leaving Mesa Verde: Peril and Change in the Thirteenth-Century Southwest*, ed. Timothy A. Kohler, Mark D. Varien, and Aaron M. Wright, 128–155. Tucson: University of Arizona Press.

Allison, James R. 2012. "Low-Frequency Temperature Variability and Native American Horticulture in the Northern Southwest and Eastern Great Basin." Paper presented at the 77th Society for American Archaeology Annual Meeting, Memphis, TN.

Allison, James R. 2016. "Rethinking Fremont Chronology, or Why Everything Your Professor Told You about Fremont Chronology is Wrong, or When Were the Fremont Fremont?" Paper presented at the 81st Society for American Archaeology Annual Meeting, Orlando, FL.

Allison, James R., Lindsay D. Johansson, and Scott M. Ure. 2012. "Communal Architecture in the Fremont World." Paper presented at the 33rd Great Basin Anthropological Association Conference, Stateline, NV.

Cameron, Catherine A. 2009. *Chaco and After in the Northern San Juan: Excavations at the Bluff Great House*. Tucson: University of Arizona Press.

Chamberlin, Matthew A. 2011. "Plazas, Performance, and Symbolic Power in Ancestral Puebloan Religion." In *Religious Transformation in the Late Pre-Hispanic Pueblo World*, ed. Donna M. Glowacki and Scott Van Keuren, 130–152. Tucson: The University of Arizona Press.

Clemensen, A. Berle. 1992. *Casa Grande Ruins National Monument, Arizona: A Centennial History of the First Prehistoric Reserve, 1892–1992*. Washington, DC: United States Department of the Interior, National Park Service.

Elliott, Melinda. 1995. *Great Excavations: Tales of Early Southwestern Archaeology, 1888–1939*. Santa Fe, NM: School of American Research Press.

Fisher, Jacob L. 2010. "Costly Signaling and Changing Faunal Abundances at Five Finger Ridge, Utah." PhD diss., Department of Anthropology, University of Washington, Seattle, WA.

Geib, Phil R. 1996. *Glen Canyon Revisited. Anthropological Papers No. 119*. Salt Lake City: University of Utah Press.

Gilman, Patricia A. 1987. "Architecture as Artifact: Pit Structures and Pueblos in the American Southwest." *American Antiquity* 52(3):538–564. https://doi.org/10.2307/281598.

Gilman, Patricia A. 2010. "Substantial Structures, Few People, and the Question of Early Villages in the Mimbres Region of the North American Southwest." In *Becoming Villagers: Comparing Early Village Societies*, ed. Matthew S. Bandy and Jake R. Fox, 119–139. Tucson: University of Arizona Press.

Hockett, Bryan S. 1998. "Sociopolitical Meaning of Faunal Remains from Baker Village." *American Antiquity* 63(2):289–302. https://doi.org/10.2307/2694699.

Janetski, Joel C., Cady B. Jardine, and Christopher N. Watkins. 2011. "Interaction and Exchange in Fremont Society." In *Prehistoric Trade and Exchange in California and the Great Basin*, ed. Richard E. Hughes, 22–54. Salt Lake City: University of Utah Press.

Janetski, Joel C., Richard K. Talbot, Deborah E. Newman, Lane D. Richens, and James D. Wilde. 2000. *Clear Creek Canyon Archaeological Project: Results and Synthesis*. Museum of Peoples and Cultures Occasional Papers No. 7. Provo, UT: Brigham Young University.

Jennings, Jesse D. 1978. *Prehistory of Utah and the Eastern Great Basin: A Review*. Anthropological Papers No. 98. Salt Lake City: University of Utah Press.

Jennings, Jesse D., and Edward Norbeck. 1955. "Great Basin Prehistory: A Review." *American Antiquity* 21(1):1–11. https://doi.org/10.2307/276104.

Johansson, Lindsay D. 2014. "Communal Functions of Fremont Central Structures: Reanalysis of Baker Village Faunal Material." Paper presented at 34th Great Basin Anthropological Association Conference, Boise, ID.

Johansson, Lindsay D. 2016. "The Fremont Experiment: Examining the Evidence of Community Structures, Settlement Clustering, and Leadership among the Fremont." Paper presented at the 35th Great Basin Anthropological Conference, Reno, NV.

Johansson, Lindsay D., Katie K. Richards, and James R. Allison. 2014. "Wolf Village (42UT273): A Case Study in Fremont Architectural Variability." *Utah Archaeology* 27(1):33–56.

Judd, Neil M. 1919. *Archaeological Investigations at Paragonah, Utah*. Miscellaneous Collections 70(3):1–22. Washington, DC: Smithsonian Institution.

Judd, Neil M. 1922. Archaeological Investigations at Pueblo Bonito. *Smithsonian Miscellaneous Collections* 72(15):106–117.

Judd, Neil M. 1926. *Archaeological Observations North of the Rio Colorado*. Bulletin No. 82. Washington, DC: Bureau of American Ethnology, Smithsonian Institution.

Judd, Neil M. 1954. *The Material Culture of Pueblo Bonito*. Miscellaneous Collections 124. Washington, DC: Smithsonian Institution.

Judd, Neil M. 1964. *The Architecture of Pueblo Bonito*. Washington, DC: Bureau of American Ethnology, Smithsonian Institution.

Kidder, Tristram R. 2004. "Plazas as Architecture: An Example from the Raffman Site, Northeast Louisiana." *American Antiquity* 69(3):514–532. https://doi.org/10.2307/4128404.

King, Daniel. 2012. Paper presented at the 34th Great Basin Anthropological Association Conference, Stateline, NV.

Lekson, Stephen H., ed. 2007. *The Architecture of Chaco Canyon, New Mexico.* Salt Lake City: University of Utah Press.

Lipe, William D., and Michelle Hegmon, eds. 1989. *The Architecture of Social Integration in Prehistoric Pueblos.* Occasional Papers of the Crow Canyon Archaeological Center No. 1. Cortez, CO: Crow Canyon Archaeological Center.

Longacre, William A. 2000. "Exploring Prehistoric Social and Political Organization in the American Southwest." *Journal of Anthropological Research* 56(3):287–300. https://doi.org/10.1086/jar.56.3.3631085.

Madsen, David B. 1979. "New Views on the Fremont: The Fremont and the Sevier: Defining Prehistoric Agriculturalists North of the Anasazi." *American Antiquity* 44(4):711–722. https://doi.org/10.2307/279110.

Madsen, David B., and Michael S. Berry. 1975. "A Reassessment of Northeastern Great Basin Prehistory." *American Antiquity* 40(4):391–405. https://doi.org/10.2307/279326.

Madsen, David B., and Steven R. Simms. 1998. "The Fremont Complex: A Behavioral Perspective." *Journal of World Prehistory* 12(3):255–336. https://doi.org/10.1023/A:1022322619699.

Marwitt, John P. 1968. *Pharo Village. Anthropological Papers No. 84.* Salt Lake City: University of Utah.

Meighan, Clement W., Norman E. Coles, Frank D. Davis, Geraldine M. Greenwood, William M. Harrison, and E. Heath MacBain. 1956. *Archaeological Excavations in Iron County, Utah. Anthropological Papers, No. 25.* Salt Lake City: University of Utah.

Metcalfe, Duncan, and Kathleen M. Heath. 1990. "Microrefuse and Site Structure: The Hearths and Floors of the Heartbreak Hotel." *American Antiquity* 55(4):781–796. https://doi.org/10.2307/281250.

Metcalfe, Michael D. 1993. "Round Spring Block and Architectural Descriptions." In *Hogan Pass: Final Report on Archaeological Investigations along Forest Highway 10 (State Highway 72), Sevier County, Utah,* Volume III: *The Round Spring Site, 42SV23,* ed. Michael D. Metcalfe, Kelly J. Pool, Kae McDonald, and Anne McKibbin, 245–340. Submitted to the National Park Service, Lakewood, CO.

Mobley-Tanaka, Jeannette L. 1997. "Gender and Ritual Space during the Pithouse to Pueblo Transition: Subterranean Mealing Rooms in the North American Southwest." *American Antiquity* 62(3):437–448. https://doi.org/10.2307/282164.

Montgomery, Keith R., and Jacki A. Montgomery, eds. 1993. "*Utah Department of Transportation State Route-31 Huntington Canyon Project: Archaeological Excavations at sites 42EM2109 and 42EM2095, Emery County, Utah.*" Prepared for the Utah Department of Transportation and The Federal Highway Administration Utah Division by Abajo Archaeology, Bluff, UT.

Morss, Noel. 1931. *The Ancient Culture of the Fremont River in Utah.* Papers of the Peabody Museum of American Archaeology and Ethnology Vol. 12, *No. 2.* Cambridge, MA: Harvard University.

Office of Public Archaeology. 2003. "Barnson Site Field Notes and Draft Technical Report." Manuscript on file.

Ortiz, Alfonso. 1969. *The Tewa World: Space, Time, Being, and Becoming in a Pueblo Society.* Chicago, IL: University of Chicago Press.

Ortman, Scott G., and Bruce A. Bradley. 2002. "Sand Canyon Pueblo: The Container in the Center." In *Seeking the Center Place: Archaeology and Ancient Communities in the Mesa Verde Region*, ed. Mark D. Varien and Richard H. Wilshusen, 41–78. Salt Lake City: University of Utah Press.

Plog, Stephen. 1989. "Ritual, Exchange, and the Development of Regional Systems." In *The Architecture of Social Integration in Prehistoric Pueblos*, ed. W. D. Lipe and Michelle Hegmon, 143–154. Occasional Papers No. 1. Cortez, CO: Crow Canyon Archaeological Center.

Richards, Katie K., James R. Allison, Richard K. Talbot, Scott M. Ure, and Lindsay D. Johansson. 2013. "Household Variation, Public Architecture, and the Organization of Fremont Communities." Paper presented at the 78th Society for American Archaeology Annual Meeting, Honolulu, HI.

Sammons-Lohse, Dorothy. 1981. "Households and Communities." In *Bull Creek*, by Jessie D. Jennings and Dorothy Sammons-Lohse, 111–135. Anthropological Papers No. 105. Salt Lake City: University of Utah Press.

Sharrock, Floyd W., and John P. Marwitt. 1967. *Excavations at Nephi, Utah, 1965–1966. Anthropological Papers No. 88.* Salt Lake City: University of Utah Press.

Shennan, Stephen. 1997. *Quantifying Archaeology.* 2nd ed. Iowa City: University of Iowa Press.

Simms, Steven R. 1986. "New Evidence for Fremont Adaptive Diversity." *Journal of California and Great Basin Anthropology* 8(2):204–216.

Stauffer, Sara E. 2012. "Parowan Fremont Faunal Exploitation: Resource Depression or Feasting?" Unpublished MA thesis, Department of Anthropology, Brigham Young University, Provo, Utah.

Steward, Julian H. 1933. Early Inhabitants of Western Utah. Bulletin Vol. 23(7): 1–34. Salt Lake City: University of Utah Press.

Steward, Julian H. 1937. *Ancient Caves of the Great Salt Lake Region.* Bulletin No. 116. Washington, DC: Bureau of American Ethnology, Smithsonian Institution.

Talbot, Richard K. 2000a. "Fremont Architecture." In *Clear Creek Canyon Archaeological Project: Results and Synthesis*, by Joel C. Janetski, Richard K. Talbot, Deborah E. Newman, Lane D. Richens, and James D. Wilde. Museum of Peoples and Cultures Occasional Papers No. 7. Provo, UT: Brigham Young University.

Talbot, Richard K. 2000b. "Fremont Farmers: The Search for Context." In *The Archaeology of Regional Interaction: Religion, Warfare, and Exchange across the American Southwest and Beyond*, ed. Michelle Hegmon, 275–293. Boulder: University of Colorado Press.

Talbot, Richard K., Lane D. Richens, James D. Wilde, Joel C. Janetski, and Deborah E. Newman. 2000. *Excavations at Five Finger Ridge, Clear Creek Canyon, Central Utah*. Museum of Peoples and Cultures Occasional Papers No. 5. Provo, UT: Brigham Young University.

Taylor, Dee Calderwood. 1954. *The Garrison Site. Anthropological Papers No. 16*. Salt Lake City: University of Utah.

Taylor, Dee Calderwood. 1957. *Two Fremont Sites and Their Position in Southwestern Prehistory. Anthropological Papers No. 29*. Salt Lake City: University of Utah Press.

Upham, Steadman. 1994. "Nomads of the Desert West: A Shifting Continuum in Prehistory." *Journal of World Prehistory* 8:113–167. https://doi.org/10.1007/BF02220562.

Ure, Scott M., and Sara E. Stauffer. 2010. *The Function of the Central Structure in Fremont Community Organization*. Paper presented at the 32nd Great Basin Anthropological Association Conference, Layton, UT.

Varien, Mark D., William D. Lipe, Michael A. Adler, Ian M. Thompson, and Bruce A. Bradley. 1996. "Southwestern Colorado and Southeastern Utah Settlement Patters: AD 1100–1300." In *The Prehistoric Pueblo World, AD 1150–1350*, ed. Michael A. Adler, 86–113. Tucson: University of Arizona Press.

Varien, Mark D., and James M. Potter, eds. 2008. *The Social Construction of Communities: Agency, Structure, and Identity in the Prehispanic Southwest*. Lanham, MD: AltaMira Press.

Watkins, Christopher N. 2009. "Type, Series, and Ware: Characterizing Variability in Fremont Ceramic Temper." *Journal of California and Great Basin Anthropology* 29(2):145–161.

Wilde, James D., and Reed A. Soper. 1999. *Baker Village: Report of Excavations, 1990–1994. Museum of Peoples and Cultures Technical Series No. 99-12*. Provo, UT: Brigham Young University.

Wilshusen, Richard H. 1989. "Unstuffing the Estufa: Ritual Floor Features in Anasazi Pit Structures and Pueblo Kivas." In *The Architecture of Social Integration in Prehistoric Pueblos*, ed. W. D. Lipe and Michelle Hegmon, 89–112. Occasional Papers No. 1. Cortez, CO: Crow Canyon Archaeological Center.

Wilshusen, Richard H., Scott G. Ortman, and Ann Phillips. 2012. "Processions, Leaders, and Gathering Places: Changes in Early Pueblo Community Organization as Seen in Architecture, Rock Art, and Language." In *Crucible of Pueblos: The Early Pueblo Period in the Northern Southwest*, ed. Richard H. Wilshusen, Gregson Schachner, and James R. Allison, 198–218. Cotsen Institute of Archaeology Monograph 71. Los Angeles: University of California.

Wormington, H. Marie. 1955. *A Reappraisal of the Fremont Culture. Proceedings No. 1*. Denver, CO: Denver Museum of Natural History.

# 19

# Fremont Ceramic Designs and What They Suggest about Fremont–Ancestral Puebloan Relationships

KATIE K. RICHARDS

Fremont archaeologists have traditionally looked to the Virgin and Kayenta regions for comparisons to the distinctive Fremont painted design style found on Snake Valley Black-on-gray and Ivie Creek Black-on-white bowls. Decades of publications have suggested that Fremont designs were born from borrowing and rearranging elements of Sosi, Dogoszhi, and Black Mesa styles; however, no explanation has been provided as to why these are good parallels for Fremont designs. Unfortunately, these assumptions have also never been formally challenged. This chapter uses an analysis of the designs painted on Fremont bowls to demonstrate that the design styles found on Virgin and Kayenta vessels are actually poor correlates for Fremont designs. Design styles from farther east in the Mesa Verde and Chaco-Cibola regions appear to be more appropriate comparisons. Both the way the designs are structured and the design elements used have many similarities to those found on Fremont vessels. When these similarities are placed into the larger context of Fremont archaeology it is not surprising that the painted designs are similar to those of their southeastern neighbors as the southeastern Fremont border appears

DOI: 10.5876/9781607327356.c019

to have been more fluid than the border near the western Virgin Branch Pueblo groups.

## CERAMICS WITHIN THE FREMONT REGION

The Fremont began occupying the area north of the Virgin and Colorado Rivers around A D 300; however, people in the region did not begin producing ceramics until a few centuries later (Geib 1996; Talbot 2000). All Fremont pottery is part of the Fremont Gray Ware tradition, which typically consists of highly polished coil-and-scrape bowls and jars that fire gray (Madsen 1989; Watkins 2009). Ceramics were produced in four or five zones across the Fremont region that are primarily distinguishable from one another by temper (for discussion see Watkins 2009; see also Talbot, chapter 17, this volume); however, the majority of all painted ceramics were produced in only two of those zones: the Snake Valley and Emery production zones (figure 19.1).

Produced in the Snake Valley production zone, Snake Valley Black-on-gray was widely distributed across the Fremont region. These painted vessels are found as far north as the Great Salt Lake and were also recovered from excavations at Baker Village in present-day Nevada (Janetski et al. 2011; Watkins 2009). They were tempered with quartz, feldspar, and biotite mica. In contrast, Ivie Creek Black-on-white was tempered with gray basalt and quartz and was produced farther northeast in the Emery production zone. This type often has a white slip on the interior of the vessel. Ivie Creek bowls have been found at villages outside of the production zone, but were not as widely distributed as Snake Valley Black-on-gray (Janetski et al. 2011:34–38).

Painted designs are almost exclusively reserved for the interior of Fremont bowls. Bowls with painted exteriors are so rare that the author has only encountered one example. Jars with exterior paint or paint on the rim are uncommon but not rare; whereas bilobed and trilobed bowls with painted interiors are rare, but a few examples have been found in the Parowan Valley. Another unusual Fremont painted vessel form is the recurved bowl (Richards 2014a). This form pinches in slightly approximately half way up the bowl and then flares out again (figure 19.2).

Unfortunately, very few Fremont sites have been adequately dated (see Allison, chapter 13, this volume), meaning that researchers do not know exactly when Fremont ceramics were first produced or when painted designs were added to this ceramic tradition. Phil Geib (1996:103) suggests that ceramics were first produced in the Fremont region between A D 400 and 550 and Richard Talbot (2000:278) cites a commonly accepted starting range of between A D 500 and 600; however, painting the surface of ceramics along with a range of other surface decorations such as corrugation and appliquée did not appear until centuries later. Rex Madsen (1977) suggests that the earliest painted ceramics appear

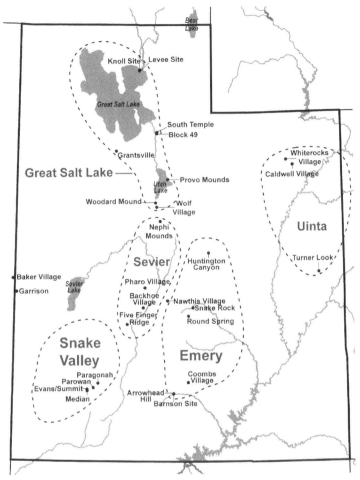

**FIGURE 19.1.** *Map of Fremont ceramic production zones.*

around AD 700, which is generally cited in the literature as the first appearance of Ivie Creek Black-on-white; however, this seems suspiciously early as none of the sites where Ivie Creek Black-on-white is thought to have been produced were occupied until after AD 900 (Allison, chapter 13, this volume; Richards 2014a). This date is also suspicious because R. Madsen does not mention his reasoning for the date. He also suggests a date of AD 900 for Snake Valley Black-on-gray. Based on new dates recently run by James Allison it seems more likely that both types were first produced in the region starting between AD 900 and 1000 but likely closer to 1000 (Allison, chapter 13, this volume). Lane Richens (2000) suggests that the tradition ends around AD 1300.

**FIGURE 19.2.** *Recurved Snake Valley Black-on-gray bowl from the Parowan Valley. (Courtesy of the Museum of People's and Cultures 395.4978.5024.)*

## Past Interpretations of Fremont Painted Bowls

The majority of Fremont research conducted in the last half of the twentieth century focused on detailed studies of regional variation and subsistence strategies (Marwitt 1970; D. Madsen 1979, 1980; Simms 1986; Madsen and Simms 1998). Fremont archaeologists have primarily looked to the archaeology of the Great Basin for theoretical models to help interpret the remains of village sites created by Fremont farmers (Allison 2008, chapter 13, this volume). This focus on subsistence and theoretical models from the Great Basin has had the unfortunate consequence of slighting the complexity and social organization of Fremont villages and mischaracterizing the relationship between Fremont and their Ancestral Puebloan neighbors.

This was not always the case. When archaeologists such as Neil Judd and Noel Morss first started working in the Fremont region they observed a distinct connection with the Greater Southwest. Morss (1931:77–78) made the observation that "the influences which molded the Fremont culture appear to have been Southwestern . . . There is little evidence that they were much affected by Plains culture. Nor . . . can we find any close connection with the primitive, non-agricultural cultures of the Great Basin." However, around the 1950s, Fremont archaeologists pulled away from Southwestern studies and turned to models used to explain Great Basin hunter-and-gatherer groups to the west. This disconnect has done a great disservice to Fremont archaeology. Artifact types that have Southwestern counterparts and parallels have been analyzed independent of the vast knowledge of those items in the literature of the Southwest. Fremont painted ceramics have been one of the casualties of this divide (for a longer discussion of the history of Fremont archaeology see Allison 2008, chapter 13, this volume; Talbot, chapter 17, this volume).

Painted designs on Fremont bowls have been superficially discussed in a number of publications, each generally repeating the ideas of one or two individuals instead of challenging or adding to them. The first archaeologists to identify specific parallels between Fremont painted design style and designs found on other vessels in the Southwest suggested that they were most similar to both wares found in the Kayenta and Northern San Juan regions. They most commonly cite Black Mesa, Sosi, and Dogoszhi styles as the closest Fremont parallels but also mention that similarities exist between Fremont and Mesa Verde, Cortez, and Mancos styles (Lister et al. 1960; D. Madsen 1970). Rex Madsen (1977), in his monograph on Fremont ceramics, repeats observations that originally appeared in publications by David Madsen (1970) and Robert Lister and colleagues (1960). R. Madsen states that Snake Valley Black-on-gray designs are most similar to types found in the Virgin and Kayenta regions, especially Sosi, Dogoszhi, and Black Mesa styles (1977:5–6). He argues that Ivie Creek Black-on-white painted designs are most similar those found in the Kayenta and Mesa Verde regions, primarily Chapin, Piedra, Black Mesa, Sosi and Dogoszhi styles (1977:35–36). After R. Madsen's 1977 publication the few publications that address the issue of Fremont painted designs limit their discussion to a sentence or two that simply repeat what R. Madsen wrote. Unfortunately, none of these archaeologists provided justifications for their choices of similarities. For example, D. Madsen (1970:54–55) once claimed that 90 percent of the design elements on Snake Valley Black-on-gray bowls at Median Village have Black Mesa origins, but provided no discussion of what he considers a Black Mesa design element.

Most archaeologists familiar with Virgin, Kayenta, and Fremont design styles would agree that the similarities between Fremont and the other two are superficial at best. To date the most detailed discussion of this issue is in a paper presented at the Great Basin Anthropological Conference by Charmaine Thompson and James Allison (Thompson and Allison 1988). Thompson and Allison analyzed a few hundred Fremont sherds from the Parowan Valley and Clear Creek Canyon, and Virgin Branch Puebloan sherds from the St. George Basin. They concluded that the design elements used on Fremont painted bowls are in many ways dissimilar to those used on Virgin pottery.

The analyses in this chapter use whole vessels as the primary data set and can therefore go further than Thompson and Allison's paper to look at differences and similarities in design structure as well as elements between Fremont and Virgin and Kayenta styles. The results strengthen Thompson and Allison's conclusions that the Fremont design style, contrary to the majority of the literature, is in fact dissimilar to styles common in the Virgin and Kayenta regions.

## Fremont Design Style

Until recently no detailed study of Fremont design style had ever been completed; however, a few authors have mentioned some general attributes that seem to characterize the designs painted on Fremont bowls, such as the use of banded designs with framing lines and a list of common elements (Aikens 1967; Lister et al. 1960; D. Madsen 1970, 1979, 1986; Rudy 1953). The detailed study discussed here provides us with a more complete understanding of the Fremont design canon (for a more detailed discussion about Fremont design style and the similarities and differences between the designs painted on Snake Valley and Ivie Creek bowls see Richards 2014a). This study shows that although regional variations do exist in the designs painted on Snake Valley and Ivie Creek bowls, they share many design attributes and should be considered part of a broader Fremont painted design style (Richards 2014a). It needs to be mentioned, though, that while Snake Valley Black-on gray and Ivie Creek Black-on-white are by far the most common Fremont painted types, smaller regional painted traditions do exist that follow very different design patterns (Mooney 2014; Richards 2014b).

As mentioned by Allison (chapter 13, this volume) most Fremont sites have been dated using only a few radiocarbon dates on charcoal. Unfortunately, at this time, the chronology at most sites is not refined enough to explore temporal change in Fremont ceramic designs over the 300–400 years that they were produced, although that change inevitably existed.

The results presented here derive from a design analysis of every known whole Fremont painted bowl. Fragmentary bowls where the design structure could still be identified with some degree of confidence were also included. These vessels come from a variety of contexts, some of which are unknown, but many were found in residential contexts and represent the type of painted pottery that was used in Fremont village life. In total 65 Snake Valley and 41 Ivie Creek painted bowls were analyzed. Design structure, including layout and symmetry, design units, and design elements were recorded when possible. Some bowls were too fragmentary or too worn to confidently determine design layout and/or symmetry. These data were supplemented by an element analysis of over 1,800 sherds from the Parowan Valley, the heart of the Snake Valley production zone, and Snake Rock Village in the Emery production zone.

## Design Layout

Design layouts, which refer to the initial division of space on a vessel, are commonly divided into two major categories—banded and non-banded (Amsden 1936; Colton 1953; Crown 1994, among others). Only ten design layouts have been identified on Fremont bowls (figure 19.3), and even though the same number of banded and non-banded design layouts were identified, Fremont painted bowls overwhelmingly have banded designs: 83 percent banded designs versus 17 percent non-banded. Over 88 percent of all banded designs employ one of three major layouts (table 19.1).

The most common banded layout is a paneled band, followed by faux-paneled bands, and undivided bands (figures 19.4 and 19.5). Undivided and paneled bands

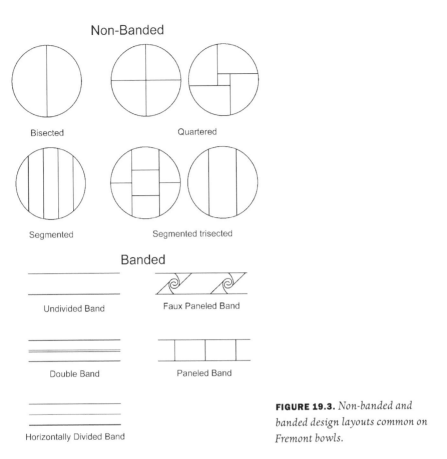

## Non-Banded

Bisected

Quartered

Segmented

Segmented trisected

## Banded

Undivided Band

Faux Paneled Band

Double Band

Paneled Band

Horizontally Divided Band

**FIGURE 19.3.** *Non-banded and banded design layouts common on Fremont bowls.*

are common design layouts elsewhere in the Southwest. The first is a band with no further subdivisions, and the latter is a band that is divided into panels. Faux-paneled bands, however, were created specifically for Fremont pottery. They occur when panel-like divisions are made not with lines perpendicular to the framing lines, but with interlocking scrolls. These bands appear paneled, but have no true structural lines dividing the space.

The most significant non-banded design layouts are segmented and segmented trisected. These layout types have lines that run across the entire interior of the vessel to divide the space into three or five segments. Occasionally these segments are further divided into panels with perpendicular lines (figure 19.6).

All design layouts that were identified on more than two bowls were found on both Snake Valley and Ivie Creek vessels—with the exception of segmented trisected layouts, which were found exclusively on Snake Valley bowls. However, the proportion of the design layouts on each type of bowl was different. For example paneled bands are much more common on Snake Valley

**TABLE 19.1.** Banded and non-banded Fremont layouts

| Layout | Count | % |
|---|---|---|
| BANDED | | |
| Paneled | 28 | 26.4 |
| Undivided | 23 | 21.7 |
| Faux Paneled | 26 | 24.5 |
| Double | 7 | 6.6 |
| Horizontally Divided | 1 | 0.9 |
| Other banded | 1 | 0.9 |
| Unknown banded | 2 | 1.9 |
| Total | 88 | 83.0 |
| NON-BANDED | | |
| Segmented Trisected | 6 | 5.7 |
| Segmented | 4 | 3.8 |
| Quartered | 2 | 1.9 |
| Bisected | 1 | 0.9 |
| Other | 5 | 4.7 |
| Total | 18 | 17.0 |

vessels, whereas faux-paneled bands are more common on Ivie Creek vessels (Richards 2014a).

One of the most prevalent characteristics of Fremont designs is the presence of framing lines. These are listed in even some of the earliest descriptions of Fremont painted designs (Rudy 1953; Lister et al. 1960). Framing lines refer to the most basic structural lines that outline the design field and divide it into either a banded or non-banded layout. At least one framing line is located directly below the rim on 95 percent of all Fremont bowls. Banded designs almost always have a top and bottom framing line, which are often doubled so two parallel lines frame both the upper and the lower limits of most bands.

## Symmetry

Symmetry was another important consideration in this study. Dorothy Washburn and Anna Shepard have both discussed the importance and significance of symmetry studies in multiple publications (e.g. Shepard 1948; Washburn 1999, 2011; Washburn and Crowe 1988). Washburn identifies three basic types of design symmetry that can "move" (or repeat) in one of four basic rigid "motions" within the interior of a bowl, considered as if it were a flat (two-dimensional) plane: *reflection* (in which an object, or design element, is reflected across a line, or axis), *translation* (in which an element is shifted, or repeated, along an

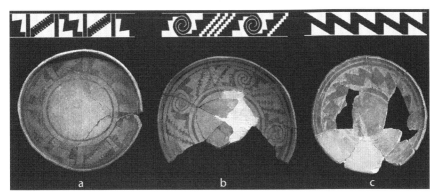

**FIGURE 19.4.** *The three most-common Fremont banded design layouts: (a) paneled band (Snake Valley Black-on-gray bowl, courtesy of the Church of Latter-Day Saints Church History Museum 20–315); (b) faux-paneled band (Snake Valley Black-on-gray bowl, courtesy of the Museum of Peoples and Cultures 1967.43.49); (c) undivided band (Ivie Creek Black-on-white bowl, courtesy of the Anasazi State Park Museum 7963).*

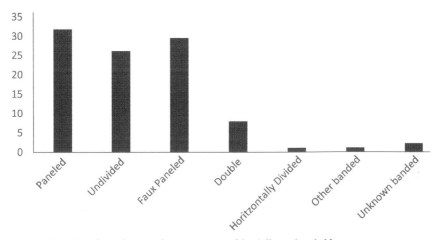

**FIGURE 19.5.** *Bar chart showing the percentages of the different banded layout*

axis), *glide reflection* (in which an element is both shifted along an axis and then reflected across that axis), and *rotation* (in which an element is repeated, not along an axis, but by being rotated around a fixed point, within the plane of the bowl's interior) (figure 19.7). These rigid "motions" are used to make designs that can exhibit three basic types of symmetry: *one-dimensional* (in which the pattern moves, or repeats, continuously along one axis), *two-dimensional* (in which the pattern can move continuously and simultaneously along two per-pendicular axes that define the plane of the bowl's interior), and finite (patterns

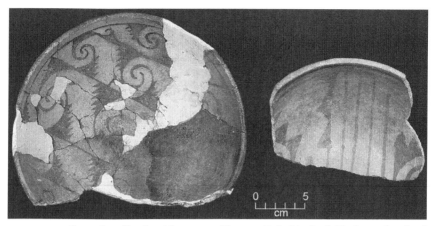

**FIGURE 19.6.** *Examples of bowls with segmented layouts. Left: Ivie Creek Black-on-white bowl (courtesy of the Anasazi State Park Museum, 8253); right: Snake Valley Black-on-gray bowl (courtesy of the Museum of Peoples and Cultures, 125.2063.411).*

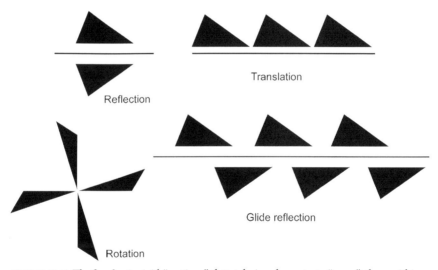

**FIGURE 19.7.** *The four basic rigid "motions" that a design element can "move" along within the plane of a bowl's interior.*

that do not move continuously along any axis but repeat around the surface of the bowl's interior plane). Finite symmetry includes designs that have either rotational symmetry (i.e., symmetry around a fixed point within the plane of the bowl's interior) or dihedral (reflection) symmetry (i.e., symmetry across an axis, which conceivably could also incorporate rotational symmetry as well,

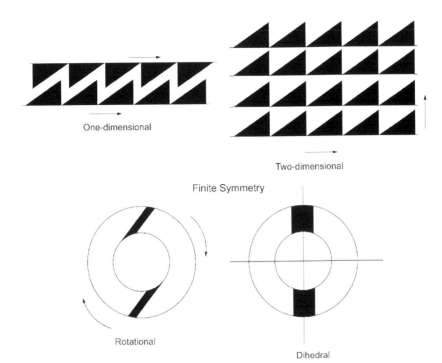

One-dimensional

Two-dimensional

Finite Symmetry

Rotational

Dihedral

**FIGURE 19.8.** *The three basic types of symmetry.*

as is the case for the "dihedral" design element in figure 19.8) (Washburn and Crowe 1988:44–55).

Washburn and Crowe (1988) identify different motions possible in the three types of symmetry and include a coding system, which was used in this analysis. Seven different types of one-dimensional symmetry are possible, four of which are found on Fremont bowls. Washburn also describes 17 types of two-dimensional symmetry. Designs with finite symmetry are patterns that exhibit symmetry, but cannot be perceived as extending infinitely along an axis. These designs exhibit either cyclical (rotational) or dihedral (reflection) symmetry.

Unfortunately, designs are rarely truly symmetrical. Small mistakes are often made that result in what is technically an asymmetrical design; however, it is important to consider if a design is purposefully asymmetrical or asymmetrical due to poor draftsmanship (Anna Shepard 1948). In many cases one row of dots or triangles may have more repetitions than its symmetrical counterparts, but these designs were still considered symmetrical because the overall concept of the design had symmetry.

Designs with all four types of symmetry (including the two types of finite symmetry) are present on Fremont bowls, but rotational symmetry is by far the most common and present on over half of the bowls (table 19.2).

**TABLE 19.2.** Symmetry types of Fremont design layouts

| Design Layout | Count | % |
|---|---|---|
| Dihedral | 10 | 11.9 |
| Rotational | 54 | 64.3 |
| One-dimensional | 12 | 14.3 |
| Two-dimensional | 6 | 7.1 |
| None | 2 | 2.4 |
| Total | 84 | 100.0 |

Over 60 percent of Fremont design layouts have rotational symmetry, the majority of which can be rotated two or four times. The high number of rotational designs is partly due to the connection between rotational symmetry and faux-paneled bands. Since interlocking scrolls on a single band almost always rotate in the same direction, the design can never be reflected. All layouts with rotational symmetry could either be rotated two, three, or four times.

One-dimensional symmetry is the next-most-common type on Fremont bowls. Fremont designs utilized four of the seven possible types of one-dimensional symmetry. Dihedral symmetry was present on ten bowls. The majority of those vessels had two reflection lines. Two-dimensional symmetry is the least common on Fremont vessels and is present on only six bowls. Because it is so rare, the specific type of two-dimensional symmetry was not recorded.

### Design Units

The design unit is based on Allison's (2010) concept of design units used in the Animas–La Plata ceramic analysis and E. Wesley Jernigan's (1986) concept of design schemata. Allison (2010:85) defines *design units* as "a segment of the design containing contiguous or closely spaced elements." Jernigan (1986:9) sees *design schemata* as patterns that were "conceived as a distinct unit by the maker of the style." He identifies them by looking at units of design that repeat on multiple vessels in an assemblage. Design units here were identified as configurations of contiguous or closely spaced elements that are repeated on multiple vessels.

Four design units account for over 40 percent of all design units on Fremont bowls (table 19.3). The first two are similar designs: interlocking scrolls with attached and detached designs (figure 19.9a,b). These design are always present on faux-paneled bands. The next design unit is two rows of offset triangles facing each other (figure 19.9c), and the fourth-most-common is a design in which triangles or stepped elements are present in the opposing corners of a panel (figure 19.9d). These four design units are the four most common designs on both Snake Valley and Ivie Creek bowls, but they naturally appear in different proportions on the two different types of bowls. The most notable difference

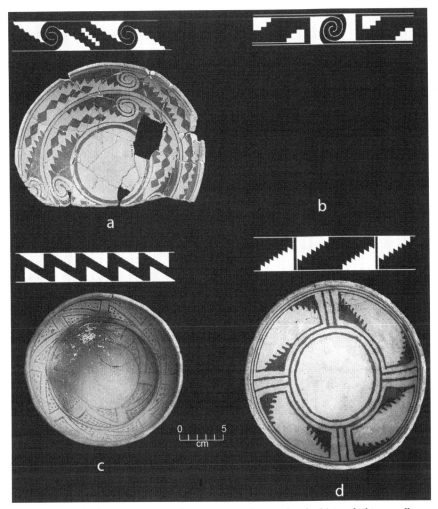

**FIGURE 19.9.** *The four most-common design units on Fremont bowls: (a) interlocking scrolls with unattached designs (Snake Valley Black-on-gray bowl, courtesy of the Museum of People's and Cultures, 395.4978.5024); (b) interlocking scrolls with attached designs (no bowl pictured); (c) two rows of offset triangles facing each other (Ivie Creek Black-on-white bowl, courtesy of the Anasazi State Park Museum, 7937); and (d) triangles or stepped elements in opposing corners of a panel (Ivie Creek Black-on-white bowl, courtesy of the Fremont Indian State Park, 7048.1).*

in design units between the two types of bowls is in interlocking scrolls with attached designs, which account for nearly a fifth of the design units present on Ivie Creek vessels but only 6 percent of design units present on Snake Valley Vessels (Richards 2014a:96).

**TABLE 19.3.** Common design units on Fremont bowls

| Design Unit | Count |
|---|---|
| Interlocking scrolls with an unattached design | 16 |
| Interlocking scrolls with an attached design | 12 |
| Rows of offset triangles facing each other | 11 |
| Element in opposing corners of a panel | 10 |

**TABLE 19.4.** Common design elements on Fremont bowls

| Primary element | Snake Valley | | Ivie Creek | | Total | |
|---|---|---|---|---|---|---|
| | Counts | % | Counts | % | Counts | % |
| Right triangle | 106 | 27.2 | 33 | 20.6 | 139 | 25.3 |
| Non-right triangle | 73 | 18.8 | 31 | 19.4 | 104 | 18.9 |
| Line of dots | 18 | 4.6 | 22 | 13.8 | 40 | 7.3 |
| Terrace/ stepped solid | 28 | 7.2 | 12 | 7.5 | 40 | 7.3 |
| Interlocking scroll- bracket | 23 | 5.9 | 16 | 10.0 | 39 | 7.1 |
| Box/square | 21 | 5.4 | 8 | 5.0 | 29 | 5.3 |
| Interlocking scroll-triangle | 23 | 5.9 | 6 | 3.8 | 29 | 5.3 |
| Diamond | 22 | 5.7 | 1 | 0.6 | 23 | 4.2 |
| Other | 75 | 19.3 | 31 | 19.4 | 106 | 13.1 |
| Totals | 389 | | 160 | | 549 | |

## Design Elements

The analysis and recording of design elements has a long history in the Southwest and has evolved considerably over the past 60 years (Allison 2010; Colton 1953; Hegmon 1995; Hill 1970; Longacre 1970). Design-element analysis is useful because elements can be identified on sherds that are much too small to identify such other aspects of design as layouts or design units.

Eight elements make up 80.7 percent of all non-line design elements on Fremont bowls (figure 19.10; table 19.4). Overwhelmingly, the most common design element is a triangle. Together right and non-right triangles make up over 44 percent of all non-line design elements. Two different types of inter-locking scroll designs are common on Fremont vessels. The first is a bracketed interlocking scroll, where the scroll ends in a rectangle shape that looks like it is bracketing the scroll. The other is a scroll that terminates in a triangle. When combined, these two interlocking scroll designs are the second-most-common

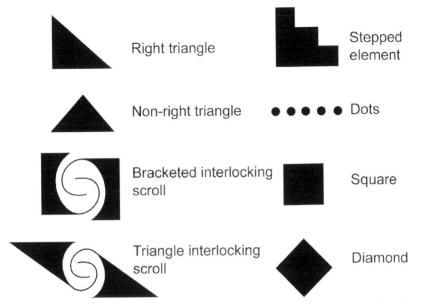

Right triangle

Stepped element

Non-right triangle

Dots

Bracketed interlocking scroll

Square

Triangle interlocking scroll

Diamond

**FIGURE 19.10.** *The eight most-common design elements present on Fremont painted bowls.*

element on Fremont bowls. A variety of other elements are present on Fremont designs, including stepped solids, rows of dots, diamonds, and boxes.

Lines are important elements on Fremont bowls. The average width of lines on Snake Valley Black-on-gray bowls is 3.7 mm, while Ivie Creek Black-on-white lines are slightly narrower at 3.1 mm.

Although this has been a brief summary of the major characteristics of Fremont painted designs, it is difficult to ignore the similarities between Fremont design style and styles found on pottery elsewhere in the Southwest. Unfortunately, due to the development of Fremont archaeology there has been a disconnect between methodologies and theories applied in the Fremont region and those of the greater Southwest. As a result very little attention has been paid to the Southwestern aspects of Fremont designs. This helps put into context why many Fremont archaeologists have often repeated the Puebloan parallels suggested by earlier researchers without questioning the strength of the comparison. As was mentioned above, Fremont ceramic designs are often compared to those found in the Virgin and Kayenta regions. Both R. Madsen (1977) and D. Madsen (1986) have suggested that Fremont design elements were borrowed from Virgin and Kayenta pottery and rearranged in different patterns. Thompson and Allison (1988) have suggested that Virgin pottery is not a good parallel based on an analysis of design elements. An analysis of the design structure of whole vessels provides further support for their argument.

**TABLE 19.5.** Banded and non-banded layouts on Virgin and Fremont vessels

| Layout | Virgin | Fremont |
|---|---|---|
| Banded | 25 | 88 |
| Non-banded | 22 | 18 |

## VIRGIN BRANCH PUEBLOAN DESIGN STYLE

A total of 46 Virgin Branch Puebloan vessels from the Talbot collection were analyzed by James Allison. Those data are used here to compare Fremont and Virgin design styles. The Talbot collection is a collection of whole vessels recovered near Kanab, Utah, and housed at the Museum of Peoples and Cultures at Brigham Young University.

### Design Layout

Just over half of the vessels have either a single- or double-banded layout. The majority of the remaining vessels have either a quartered layout or an "allover" design consisting of elements arranged on the vessels with no structural dividing lines (table 19.5).

Both Fremont and Virgin vessels often utilize banded designs; however, Fremont designs are more commonly banded. Fremont bowls also have more variation in banded designs. Virgin vessels most commonly have continuous banded designs; whereas banded designs on Fremont bowls are split almost evenly among the three main banded layouts: paneled, faux paneled, and continuous.

### Design Symmetry

The design symmetry on Virgin vessels favors one-dimensional designs. Four types of one-dimensional symmetry were identified on the vessels, but only three of the types overlap with one-dimensional symmetries found on Fremont bowls. Rotational symmetry with two rotations and dihedral symmetry with two reflection lines were also favored (table 19.6).

A correspondence analysis emphasizes not only the differences in design symmetry between Fremont and Virgin vessels, but also the similarities between the two Fremont painted types (figure 19.11). The analysis includes data from Fremont painted bowls, collected by the author, vessels in the Talbot collection and at the Lost City Museum in Nevada, collected by Allison, and Chacoan bowls published by Washburn (2011:273). The two Fremont types cluster together and are heavily influenced by rotational symmetries, particularly designs that can be rotated three and four times, as well as one particular type of one-dimensional symmetry. The Talbot collection and Lost City materials correspond more with dihedral symmetries and different one-dimensional designs, while the Chacoan pottery clusters near the two-dimensional symmetries.

**TABLE 19.6.** Symmetry types of Virgin design layouts from the Talbot Collection

| Layout | Counts | % |
|---|---|---|
| Dihedral | 8 | 15.7 |
| Rotational | 11 | 21.6 |
| One-dimensional | 21 | 41.2 |
| Two-dimensional | 5 | 9.8 |
| None | 6 | 11.8 |
| Total | 51 | 100.0 |

## Design Elements

Thompson and Allison (1988) identified triangles as the most common design element on Virgin vessels. This is supported by the Talbot collection data. Triangle elements are also the most common elements in Fremont designs; however, triangles are a common design element on ceramics across the Southwest. The important differences in design elements is in the second-most-common element on both Fremont and Virgin vessels. The second-most-common design element identified in the Talbot collection consists of hachured figures and bands; however, hachured elements have only been identified on six of the over 1,800 Fremont painted sherds. The second-most-common design element on Fremont bowls are interlocking scrolls, which are rare on Virgin vessels.

Significant differences are present in not only the design elements of Fremont and Virgin vessels, but in the design layout and symmetry as well. For these reasons, it seems unlikely that Fremont potters were borrowing and rearranging designs from the Virgin region.

## SOSI, DOGOSZHI, AND BLACK MESA AS FREMONT PARALLELS

Most discussions of Fremont designs include at least three more specific design correlates—Sosi, Dogoszhi, and Black Mesa—all of which are Kayenta styles (Aikens 1967; Lister et al. 1960; D. Madsen 1970, 1979, 1986; R. Madsen 1977; Marwitt 1968). Because these three styles are so commonly cited, they deserve to be addressed individually.

The idea that Fremont bowls are similar to Sosi in that they borrowed and rearranged Sosi design elements is not a very useful conclusion since Sosi designs consist mostly of lines and triangles (Colton and Hargrave 1937), which are common elements in many Southwestern design styles. It is also a weak comparison because Fremont designs commonly consist of a much larger range of elements than are present in Sosi designs. Colton (1955) notes only two Sosi design elements in addition to the two most common mentioned above, stepped elements and interlocking scrolls, but mentions that interlocking scrolls are rare. Interlocking scrolls, however, are one of the most common design elements on

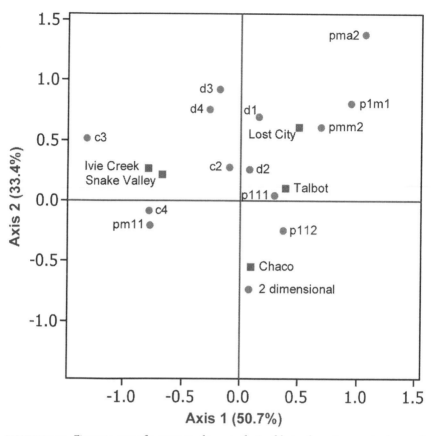

**FIGURE 19.11.** *First two axes of a correspondence analysis of design layout symmetry by type/ site. Symmetry types are marked by their code. Rotational symmetry is designated with a "c" followed by the number of rotations. Dihedral is indicated with a "d" followed by the number of reflection lines. A "p" indicates one-dimensional symmetries, followed by numbers and letters indicating which of the seven types of one-dimensional symmetry it represents*

Fremont painted bowls and are present on 48 of the 106 vessels analyzed. The average line width on Sosi vessels is also around 3 mm (6.7 mm), thicker than lines on either type of Fremont vessel (Colton 1955).

Dogoszhi style is the most puzzling of the three commonly suggested Fremont correlates. It is a distinctive style characterized by hachured designs (Colton 1955). Hachuring is rare on Fremont vessels, and as was mentioned previously, has only been noted on six sherds included in this analysis. The rarity of hachuring on Fremont bowls is a strong indication that Dogoszhi style is a poor comparison for Fremont and that Fremont potters were in no way borrowing and rearranging elements of Dogoszhi style.

Black Mesa style is the best comparison of the three. The style includes banded designs and interlocking scrolls, both of which are important in Fremont designs (Colton 1955; Hays-Gilpin and van Hartesveldt 1998). However, Black Mesa designs typically include wide lines (Colton 1955; Hays-Gilpin and van Hartesveldt 1998), whereas Fremont designs generally do not (Richards 2014a:107). Another difficulty of this comparison is that the style includes a wide range of design elements that overlap with many different design styles and not just Fremont. Without more insight into why many mid-century Fremont archaeologists drew parallels between Fremont and Black Mesa styles, it is safe to assume that it is the banded designs and interlocking scrolls that made it such an appealing candidate. While some aspects of the Black Mesa style may be a good fit for Fremont ceramics, better parallels can be found farther to the east in the Mesa Verde and Chaco-Cibola regions.

## BETTER FREMONT PARALLELS

Contrary to the conclusions of many Fremont archaeologists, the designs painted on Fremont bowls appear to have a different design structure than designs commonly produced in the Virgin and Kayenta regions. Important differences exist not only in the layouts and symmetry but also in the design elements commonly used. Better correlates are present in the Mesa Verde and Chaco-Cibola regions.

At least two of the Mesa Verde whitewares, Cortez Black-on-white and White Mesa Black-on-white, have interesting parallels to Fremont vessels. Cortez Black-on-white incorporates many of the important design elements central to Fremont designs, such as interlocking scrolls, triangles, and stepped elements (Wilson and Blinman 1995:49). The interlocking scrolls are generally attached to either plain triangles or triangles with smaller triangles appended to them, both of which are common forms of Fremont interlocking scrolls (Hays and Lancaster 1975). Many of the Cortez Black-on-white vessels also have a similar design layout. Bands and paneled bands are both common on Cortez vessels (Hays and Lancaster 1975; Wilson and Blinman 1995). One of the most common Fremont design units, triangles in opposing corners of a panel of a band, is also present on Cortez vessels (Hays and Lancaster 1975:figures 125, 126). Ticking and pendent triangles are present on Cortez Black-on-white vessels (Hays and Lancaster 1975), both of which are commonly found in Fremont designs.

Winston Hurst (personal communication 2014) has also suggested that the designs on White Mesa Black-on-white vessels are stylistically similar to those on Fremont vessels, particularly Ivie Creek Black-on-white. Hurst et al. (1985) noted that White Mesa designs are often arranged in bands with framing lines. The layouts include paneled bands, which is the most common Fremont design layout. One of the most interesting similarities is the use of dots. Dots are a common motif used to fill designs on White Mesa pottery (Hurst et al. 1985;

Wilson and Blinman 1995), and while this design is rare on Snake Valley pottery, it is common on Ivie Creek (Richards 2014a). One important discrepancy between the two design styles, however, is the lack of interlocking scroll elements on White Mesa vessels. It is interesting to note, though, that some of the designs found on White Mesa vessels would not seem out of place on a Fremont bowl (figure 19.12). Unfortunately, White Mesa Black-on-white is a fairly rare type, and we do not have many examples of this style.

Thompson and Allison (1988) have suggested that Red Mesa Black-on-white is another good correlate to Fremont design style. Red Mesa Black-on-white is similar to Cortez Black-on-white in many ways, including the use of banded layouts as well as interlocking scrolls and triangle design elements. Some lesser used, but still present, Fremont design elements are also found on this type, such as checkerboards and chevrons (Hays-Gilpin and van Harteveldt 1998).

Even though both Cortez Black-on-white and Red Mesa Black-on-white include interlocking scrolls as an important design element, they are generally only attached to triangles. Finding examples of interlocking scrolls attached to brackets has proved more difficult.

One of the unusual Fremont painted vessel forms, the recurved bowl, also has parallels in the Mesa Verde and Chaco-Cibola traditions. Hays and Lancaster (1975:119; figures 120, 121) make note that both Cortez Black-on-white and Red Mesa Black-on-white "double-flared" vessels—which look very similar to Fremont recurved bowls—are rare but have been found.

Even though design styles found on pottery in the Mesa Verde and Chaco-Cibola regions appear to be more appropriate parallels to Fremont designs, there are obviously significant differences between the design styles discussed above and those found on Fremont vessels. While it seems likely that the Fremont adopted and adapted styles found on pottery farther east than the Virgin and Kayenta regions, they clearly did not adopt every aspect of those styles. It appears that they copied only select aspects that relied heavily on banded layouts and triangles and interlocking-scroll design elements. They also adapted these concepts to make them distinctly Fremont. The design units utilizing interlocking scrolls as well as the bracketed interlocking-scroll elements appear to be adaptations that make these broader eastern Puebloan designs identifiably Fremont.

## DISCUSSION

While more research needs to be done to explore the similarities between design styles found on Fremont bowls and pottery from the eastern Puebloan region, the connection between groups in these two locations is manifest in more than just ceramic designs. Recently Michael Searcy and Richard Talbot have explored Fremont identity at the borderlands (Searcy and Talbot 2016). Their essay includes a discussion of the southern Fremont border, focusing on a series

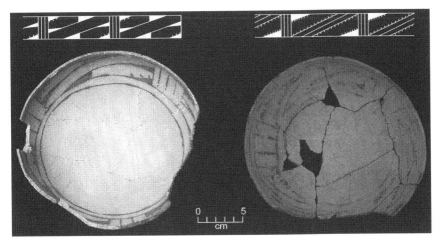

**FIGURE 19.12.** *White Mesa Black-on-white vessels with designs that are not uncommon on Fremont bowls. (Left: courtesy of the Edge of the Cedars State Park Museum, ECPR 601; right: courtesy of the Museum of Peoples and Cultures, 72.197.12.)*

of sites in the Boulder and Escalante Valleys, east of the Parowan Valley sites. Ivie Creek Black-on-white bowls recovered at Coombs Village are difficult to distinguish from Puebloan types also found at the site. Searcy and Talbot (2016) also mention Arrowhead Hill (see also Janetski et al. 2012) in the Escalante Valley, which appears to have been contemporaneously occupied by both Fremont and Puebloan groups.

Searcy and Talbot convincingly argue that the Fremont/Puebloan frontier was permeable, especially in the southeast in the Boulder and Escalante Valleys. Trade and possibly even intermarriage seem to have been common in these regions (Searcy and Talbot 2016). However, there is less evidence for a permeable Fremont/Puebloan border farther west in the Parowan Valley. Even though the St. George Basin is relatively close to the Parowan Valley, very few Virgin ceramics have been recovered from the Parowan Valley sites. Despite the wide distribution of Snake Valley ceramics across the Fremont region (Janetski et al. 2011), only a handful of Puebloan ceramics are present at Fremont sites farther north. The lack of Virgin ceramics at the Parowan Valley sites seems to indicate that this border may have been less permeable than the border farther to the east.

This conclusion is also supported by Fremont painted design style. Despite the close geographic proximity to the Virgin Branch Puebloan groups in the St. George Basin and elsewhere, Fremont design style is quite distinct from Virgin styles. These differences are apparent in design layout, symmetry, and especially in the design elements.

The above discussion has been limited to very visible characteristics of style. Painted designs and vessel forms are attributes of style that can be copied by individuals who have access to the pottery. More passive aspects such of style, such as paste and paint recipes and how the vessels are made, is information about style that is passed on from potter to potter. Incorporating this type of style into our understanding of Fremont/Ancestral Puebloan relationships is a direction for future research.

## CONCLUSIONS

Fremont archaeologists during the last half of the twentieth century suggested that the designs painted on Snake Valley Black-on-gray and Ivie Creek Black-on-white bowls resemble those found on pottery from the Virgin and Kayenta regions. They also suggested that the design elements used on Fremont pottery were borrowed from Sosi, Dogoszhi, and Black Mesa styles. Although succeeding generations of archaeologists often tended to repeat these suggestions without fully reconsidering the appropriateness of the comparisons, Thompson and Allison (1988) argued that the design elements used in Fremont and Virgin types were too different to be considered close parallels.

An analysis of the design structure of Fremont painted bowls only provides further support for Thompson and Allison's conclusions. Fremont design layouts include a greater proportion and variety of banded designs. They also more commonly have rotational than one-dimensional symmetry, which is most common with Virgin layouts. One of the most important differences is the rarity of interlocking scrolls in Virgin designs. One of the most common Fremont design layouts, the two most-common design units, and the second-most-common design element are all centered on this crucial motif.

Additionally, the three Kayenta styles that are most commonly cited as resembling Fremont painted designs—Sosi, Dogoszhi, and Black Mesa—are all poor or unuseful comparisons, despite continuing to be cited as such in the literature. More appropriate and useful design parallels can be drawn from styles farther east. Cortez Black-on-white, White Mesa Black-on-white, and Red Mesa Black-on-white design styles have design structures that resemble those found on Fremont vessels, and the use of interlocking scrolls on Cortez and Red Mesa designs make them a much stronger parallel than Virgin-style designs.

A connection between Fremont and eastern Puebloan design styles is not surprising when considered in the broader archaeological context of the Fremont region. Searcy and Talbot have recently shown that the southeastern Fremont/Puebloan borderlands were permeable. Puebloan settlements, possibly trading outposts, existed along this border, and there is even evidence that Fremont and Puebloan peoples contemporaneously occupied the same village. The Fremont border appears to be more rigid, however, farther to the west at the Parowan

Valley sites. There is less evidence of Fremont/Puebloan interaction despite the closer geographic distance.

The fluidity of the Fremont border to the east may indicate closer ties to those Puebloan groups, which would explain the similarities between Fremont design styles and those found on eastern Puebloan pottery. It may also explain why Fremont style is so dissimilar to that found in the Virgin region.

*Acknowledgments.* I would like to acknowledge the many archaeologists who have helped me develop and refine the ideas presented in this chapter. Most significantly, I would like to thank Jim Allison, Lane Richens, and Winston Hurst for their thoughts and insights into Fremont pottery and the origins of the Fremont ceramic painted design style. I would also like to thank Lindsay Johansson, Rich Talbot, and Andrew Duff for their input on the ideas presented in this chapter.

## REFERENCES

Aikens, Melvin C. 1967. *Excavations at Snake Rock Village and the Bear River No. 2 Site.* Anthropological Paper No. 87. Salt Lake City: University of Utah.

Allison, James R. 2008. "Human Ecology and Social Theory in Utah Archaeology." *Utah Archaeology* 21(1):57–88.

Allison, James R. 2010. "Design Styles." In *Animas–La Plata Project*, Volume XIV: *Ceramic Studies*, 67–110. Anthropological Research Paper No. 10. Phoenix, AZ: SWCA.

Amsden, Charles A. 1936. *An Analysis of Hohokam Pottery Design. Medallion Papers No. XXII.* Globe, AZ: Gila Pueblo.

Colton, Harold. 1953. *Potsherds.* Bulletin No. 25. Flagstaff: Museum of Northern Arizona.

Colton, Harold. 1955. *Pottery Types of the Southwest: Wares 8A, 8B, 9A, 9B, Tusayan Gray and White Ware, Little Colorado Gray and White Ware.* Ceramic Series 3A. Flagstaff: Museum of Northern Arizona.

Colton, Harold S., and Lyndon LaneHargrave. 1937. *Handbook of Northern Arizona Pottery Wares.* Bulletin No. 11. Flagstaff: Museum of Northern Arizona.

Crown, Patricia. 1994. "Salado Polychrome Painted Designs." In *Ceramics and Ideology: Salado Polychrome Pottery*, by Patricia L. Crown, 55–97. Albuquerque: University of New Mexico Press.

Geib, Phil R. 1996. "Sources of Igneous Temper for Fremont Ceramics." In *Glen Canyon Revisited*, ed. Phil R. Geib, 167–180. Anthropological Paper No. 117. Salt Lake City: University of Utah.

Hays, Alden C., and James A. Lancaster. 1975. *Badger House Community, Mesa Verde National Park, Colorado.* Washington, DC: US Department of Interior, National Park Service.

Hays-Gilpin, Kelley, and Eric van Hartesveldt. 1998. *Prehistoric Ceramics of the Puerco Valley: The 1995 Chambers-Sanders Trust. Lands Ceramic Conference.* Museum of Northern Arizona Ceramic Series No. 7. Flagstaff: Museum of Northern Arizona.

Hegmon, Michelle. 1995. *The Social Dynamics of Pottery Style in the Early Puebloan Southwest.* Occasional Paper No. 5. Cortez, CO: Crow Canyon Archaeological Center.

Hill, James N. 1970. *Broken K Pueblo: Prehistoric Social Organization in the American Southwest.* Anthropological Papers No. 18. Tucson: University of Arizona Press.

Hurst, Winston, Mark Bond, and Sloan E. Emery Schwindt. 1985. "Piedra Black-on-white, White Mesa Variety." *Pottery Southwest* 12(3):1–7.

Janetski, Joel, Cady Jardine, and Christopher Watkins. 2011. "Interaction and Exchange in Fremont Society." In *Perspectives on Prehistoric Trade and Exchange in California and the Great Basin,* ed. Richard E. Hughes, 22–54. Salt Lake City: University of Utah Press.

Janetski, Joel C., Lane D. Richens, and Richard K. Talbot. 2012. "Fremont-Anasazi Boundary Maintenance and Permeability in the Escalante Drainage." In *Meeting at the Margins: Prehistoric Cultural Interactions in the Intermountain West,* ed. David Rhode, 191–210. Salt Lake City: University of the Utah Press.

Jernigan, E. W. 1986. "A Non-Hierarchical Approach to Ceramic Decoration Analysis: A Southwestern Example." *American Antiquity* 51(1):3–20. https://doi.org/10.2307/280390

Lister, Robert H., J. Richard Ambler, and Florence C. Lister. 1960. *The Coombs Site,Part II.* Anthropological Paper No. 41. Salt Lake City: University of Utah.

Longacre, William A. 1970. *Archaeology as Anthropology: A Case Study. Anthropological Papers No. 17.* Tucson: University of Arizona Press.

Madsen, David B. 1970. "Ceramics." In *Median Village and Fremont Culture Regional Variation,* by John P. Marwitt. Occasional Publication No. 95. Salt Lake City: Utah Museum of Natural History, University of Utah.

Madsen, David B. 1979. "The Fremont and the Sevier: Defining Prehistoric Agriculturalists North of the Anasazi." *American Antiquity* 44(4):711–722. https://doi.org/10.2307/279110.

Madsen, David B. 1980. "Fremont/Sevier Subsistence." In *Fremont Perspectives,* ed. D. B. Madsen, 13–16. Antiquities Section Selected Papers Vol. 7, No. 16. Salt Lake City: Utah State Historical Society.

Madsen, David B. 1986. "Prehistoric Ceramics." In *Great Basin,* ed. Warren L. D'Azevedo, 161–172. *Handbook of North American Indians,* Vol. 11, gen. ed. William C. Sturtevant. Washington, DC: Smithsonian Institution.

Madsen, David B. 1989. *Exploring the Fremont.* Occasional Papers No. 8. Salt Lake City: University of Utah.

Madsen, David B., and Steven R. Simms. 1998. "The Fremont Complex: A Behavioral Perspective." *Journal of World Prehistory* 12(3):255–336. https://doi.org/10.1023/A:1022322619699.

Madsen, Rex E. 1977. *Prehistoric Ceramics of the Fremont*. Museum of Northern Arizona Ceramics Series No. 6. Flagstaff: Museum of Northern Arizona Ceramics.

Marwitt, John P. 1968. *Pharo Village*. Anthropological Papers No. 91. Salt Lake City: University of Utah.

Marwitt, John P. 1970. *Median Village and Fremont Culture Regional Variation*. *Anthropological Papers No. 95*. Salt Lake City: University of Utah.

Mooney, Adrien. 2014. "An Analysis of the Archaeological Work of the Provo River Delta, Utah." Unpublished MA thesis, Department of Anthropology, Brigham Young University, Provo, UT.

Morss, Noel. 1931. *The Ancient Culture of the Fremont River in Utah*. Papers of the Peabody Museum of American Archaeology and Ethnology Vol. 12, No. 2. Cambridge, MA: Harvard University.

Richards, Katie K. 2014a. "Fremont Ceramic Designs and their Implications." Unpublished MA thesis, Department of Anthropology, Brigham Young University, Provo, UT.

Richards, Katie K. 2014b. "Different Strokes: A Design Comparison of Snake Valley Black-on-Gray and Great Salt Lake Red-on-Gray." Paper presented at the 34th Biennial Great Basin Anthropological Conference, Boise, ID.

Richens, Lane D. 2000. "Ceramics." In *Clear Creek Canyon Archaeological Project: Results and Synthesis*, by Joel C. Janetski, Richard K. Talbot, Deborah E. Newman, Lane D. Richens, James D. Wilde, Shane A. Baker, and Scott E. Billat, 47–66. Museum of Peoples and Cultures Occasional Papers No. 7. Provo, UT: Brigham Young University.

Rudy, Jack R. 1953. *Archaeological Survey of Western Utah*. Anthropological Papers No. 12. Salt Lake City: University of Utah Press.

Searcy, Michael T., and Richard K. Talbot. 2016. "Late Fremont Cultural Identities and Borderland Processes." In *Late Holocene Research on Foragers and Farmers in the Desert West*, ed. Barbara Roth and Maxine McBrinn, 234–264. Salt Lake City: University of Utah Press.

Shepard, Anna O. 1948. *The Symmetry of Abstract Design with Special Reference to Ceramic Decoration*. Contributions to American Anthropology and History No. 47. Washington, DC: Carnegie Institution of Washington.

Simms, Steven. 1986. "New Evidence for Fremont Adaptive Diversity." *Journal of California and Great Basin Anthropology* 8(2):204–206.

Talbot, Richard K. 2000. "Fremont Farmers: The Search for Context." In *The Archeology of Regional Interaction: Religion, Warfare, and Exchange across the American Southwest and Beyond*, ed. Michelle Hegmon, 275–293. Boulder: University Press of Colorado.

Thompson, Charmaine, and James R. Allison. 1988. *Symbolism and Meaning in Fremont Painted Ceramics*. Paper presented at the 21st Great Basin Anthropological Conference, Park City, UT.

Washburn, Dorothy K. 1999. "Perceptual Anthropology: The Cultural Salience of Symmetry." *American Anthropologist* 101(3):547–562. https://doi.org/10.1525/aa.1999.101.3.547.

Washburn, Dorothy K. 2011. "Pattern Symmetries of the Chaco Phenomenon." *American Antiquity* 76(2):252–284. https://doi.org/10.7183/0002-7316.76.2.252.

Washburn, Dorothy K., and Donald W. Crowe. 1988. *Symmetries of Culture: Theory and Practice of Plane Pattern Analysis.* Seattle: University of Washington Press.

Watkins, Christopher N. 2009. "Type, Series, and Ware: Characterizing Variability in Fremont Ceramic Temper." *Journal of California and Great Basin Anthropology* 29(2):145–161.

Wilson, C. Dean, and Eric Blinman. 1995. "Ceramic Types of the Mesa Verde Region." In *Archaeological Pottery of Colorado: Ceramic Clues to the Prehistoric and Protohistoric Lives of the State's Native Peoples*, ed. R. H. Brunswig, B. Bradley, and S. M. Chandler, 33–88. Colorado Council of Archaeologists Occasional Papers 2. Denver, CO: Colorado Council of Archaeologists.

# Contributors

Karen G. Harry

Barbara J. Roth

Richard V.N. Ahlstrom

James R. Allison

Jean H. Ballagh

Catherine M. Cameron

Richard Ciolek-Torello

John G. Douglass

Suzanne L. Eckert

Hayward H. Franklin

Patricia A. Gilman

Dennis A. Gilpin

William M. Graves

Kelley A. Hays-Gilpin

Lindsay D. Johansson

Eric Eugene Klucas

Phillip O. Leckman

Myles R. Miller

Barbara J. Mills

Matthew A. Peeples

David A. Phillips Jr.

Katie K. Richards

Heidi Roberts

Thomas R. Rocek

Tammy Stone

Richard K. Talbot

Marc Thompson

David T. Unruh

John A. Ware

Kristina C. Wyckoff

# Index

in, 152–53; temporary, 158–60; variability in, 153–55, 243–44. *See also by type*
Arroyo de los Monos, 103
Arrowhead Hill, 453
Athabaskans, 103, 387
Awat'ovi, 65, 67, 68; kiva murals at, 69, 70, 71, 102; Sikyatki style designs, 5, 73–74, 75–76
Awatovi Expedition, 68
Awatovi Yellow Ware, 73
Aztecs, social status, 23–24

Baca site, 98
Bacavi, 158
Baker Village, 253, 285, 390, 395, 426, 434; Central Structure at, 411, 413, 417, 421, 423–24
baking pits: Chihuahuan Desert, 251–52, 254–55; excavation of, 253–54; intensified use of, 262–64; ritual evidence in, 269; in Sacramento Mountains, 257–58; structure of, 255–57
Barnson site, 390, 412, 414
Basketmaker tradition/culture, 224, 387; in Moapa Valley, 10, 312–17
Basketmaker II period, 388; on Colorado Plateau, 288–89; at Jackson Flat Reservoir, 354, 355, 361–63; in Southern Nevada, 312–16
Basketmaker II/III transition, at Antechamber site, 363–65
Basketmaker III period: in Chuska Valley, 242–43; at Jackson Flat Reservoir, 354, 355, 362, 363, 365–69, 373; in Moapa Valley, 316–17; pit structures, 228–33
basketry, 98, 388; from southern Nevada, 312, 313–14
bats, Mimbres depictions of, 89, 92–93
bear medicine societies, 65
bears, Mimbres depictions of, 98, 99–100
Beaver (Bradshaw Mounds), Central Structure at, 390, 411, 413, 415
bell-shaped pits, at Eagle's Watch site, 358–59, 360, 362, 363
Betatakin, 157
biased transmission, 27
Bird of Doom, 98
Biscuit Ware Black-on-white, 103
bison hunters, hide processing, 30
Black Dog Cave, 288, 289; Basketmaker II materials, 312, 314–16
Black Mesa, 155, 156, 318
Black Mesa style, 320, 433, 437, 451, 454
Blood Gatherer, 91
Blood Woman, 91

Blue Tail House, 390
borderlands, Fremont, 383–84, 452–53, 454–55
Borgia Codex, 96
Born from Water, 103
boundaries, cultural, 20, 331; Las Vegas Valley as, 346–47
bow and arrow technology, Jackson Flat Reservoir area, 364, 365, 371
Bradshaw Mounds, 413, 415
Brainerd-Robinson similarity coefficient, 45, 52
bride price, Southern Sudan, 22
brokers, in social networks, 47
Bryant Ranch Pueblo, 51
built environment, and human behavior, 202–3
burials: archaeological study of, 203–4; Jackson Flat Reservoir, 368–70, 375; of parrots and macaws, 86, 87; Richter site, 210–15
burned-rock middens, 183, 191, 271(n5); artifacts associated with, 261–62; excavation of, 253–54; formation of, 255–57; in Sacramento Mountains, 257–58

Cactaceae: fermentation, 259; pit baking, 254–55
Cahokia, 160, 170, 204
Caldwell Village, 295
Cameron Creek site, Mimbres vessels from, 94, 95, 97
Cameroon, social networking, 49
campsites, Jornada Mogollon, 181–82
Capitan Highlands, 179; Jornada Mogollon in, 177–78, 179, 184–86, 191
captives, 5, 27; communities of practice, 28–29; maritime raiding, 29–30; skills of, 30–31
Capitol Reef, 387
Carling Reservoir site, 289
Casas Grandes region, macaws in, 102, 103
Cave du Pont, Basketmaker II material, 288, 312
Cedar Mesa, 293
cemetery areas: as communal practice, 203–4; early Hohokam, 209–15
center-focused middens, 255–56
Central Structures, 390, 395, 410, 411–12, 413, 417, 421, 426; artifact densities in, 422–25
ceramics. *See* pottery
Chaco-Cibola styles, 451, 452
Chaco regional system, and Northern Frontier, 10, 281, 297–300
Chapin style, 437
Chemehuevi, 331, 345
chiefs, Bronze Age, 26
Chieptlan heraldry, 23–24

Chihuahuan Desert, earth ovens in, 251–52, 253–55
Chimalmat, 98
Chodistaas Pueblo, 51
cholla (*Cylindropuntia* spp.), 255
Chupadero Black-on-white, 192
Chuska Valley, 7; architectural variation in, 243–44; Basketmaker III pit structures in, 228–33; excavations in, 224, *225*; imagined communities in, 226–27, 245; kivas in, 237–42; pit structures in, 233–37; settlement structure, 242–43
Cibola White Ware, 52
cists: Basketmaker II, 288, 289; slab-lined, 288, 289, 368
Classic Vernal Style rock art, 386
cliff dwellings, Kayenta region, 157
cliques, 47
cloth, Seneca use of, 24
clowns, Keresan, 65
coats of arms, Aztec elite, 23–4
Colorado Plateau, 293; Fremont and Virgin Branch cultures on, 281–82; maize on, 9–10
Colorado Plateau style rock art, 386
commons, overuse of, 263
communication, ritualized, 226
communities, imagined, 226–27
communities of practice, captives and, 28–29, 30
community clusters, 160
complex contagions, 49
conflict, and ritual performance, 226
consumption, ritual, 25
Coombs site, 383, 453
copying, 20–21
Corn Creek site, 334, 338, 339, 343, 345, 346
corrugated pottery, 295, 388
Cortez Black-on-white, 451, 452, 454
cotton, in Black Dog Cave, 314
courtyard groups, Hohokam, 215–216
Coyote Site (AZ A:14:82[ASM]), pottery from, *322*
craft specialization, captives, 30–31
creolization, 18, 118
cultural transmission, 17, 19; captives and, 28–29; and identity, 20–21; prestige-biased, 22–24; process of, 21–22
culture change, at Jackson Flat Reservoir sites, 354, 374–75
culture contact, 18; and identity, 115–17; power balances and, 22–23
Cummings Mesa, 156, 168
*Cylindropuntia*, pit baking, 254–55

dart points, Basketmaker II, 289, *290*
Deadmans Black-on-red, 296
DeBoer, Warren, Amazonian material culture, 26–27
decapitation, in Hero Twins saga, 96, *97*
deer, Mimbres depictions of, 89, 96–97
Dellenbaugh, Mt., pottery from, 317
*Dentalium* spp., at Fremont sites, 384–85
dental traits, in Lowland Virgin populations, 312–13
design elements, 449; Fremont ceramics, 446–47
designs, 21; Fremont ceramics, 437–48, 451–52; Sosi, Dogozshi, and Black Mesa, 449–51; Virgin Branch ceramics, 448–49
design styles, Fremont ceramics, 437–38
design units/schemata, Fremont ceramics, 444–46
direct acquisition, long-distance, 83–84
diffusion, 3, 4, 11, 15, 63, 125; archaeological use of, 16–19; captives and, 28–29; through direct acquisition, 83–84; Hero Twins and scarlet macaws, 82–83, 104; impediments to, 24–26; intergroup transmission, 19–20; migration and, 76–77; to Mimbres area, 85–86; and processual archaeology, 40–41; Salado polychromes, 50–56; social network analysis of, 45–50
*Diffusion of Innovation, The* (Rogers), 42–43
diffusion theory, sociology and, 42–44
Dinwiddie Polychrome, 56
Dogoszhi style, 295, 320; and Fremont ceramic designs, 433, 437, 450, 454
Dolores area, community-oriented kivas, 244
Doña Ana phases, 183, 261–62, 269
dress, and social status, 23
Duck Creek (Las Vegas Valley), 339, 341
Dunlap-Salazar site, 186–88, 189, 191

Eagle Point Rock Shelter, 288
Eagle's Watch site (42KA6165), 354–55, 356(table), 375; Basketmaker component at, 361–69; Early Agricultural component, 357–61; features at, *357, 359*; Pueblo I period, 370–74
Early Agricultural period, 335, 384; at Jackson Flat Reservoir, 354, 357–61
Early Fremont period, 384–85
earth ovens, 251–52, 267; structure of, 255–57
Earthquake (deity), representations of, 98, *99*, 100
Eby site, Mimbres bowls from, 96, *97*

patterns, 180–92; social organization, 262–64, 268–69

journeys, ritual, 83–84, 100–102, 104

Judd, Neil, 283; on Fremont, 379, 415, 416, 436

Kadiolo, pottery making, 20–21

Kama zotz figures, 92

Kanab, 9, 288; early maize dates, 353–54. *See also* Jackson Flat Reservoir

KAP. *See* knowledge-attitude-practice gap

katsinas, Laguna Pueblo, 65

Kawayka'a, 68; kiva murals at, 70, 71, 102

Kayenta region, 5, 7, 9, 171, 373, 447; architectural data, 161–66; domestic structure use, 166–70; and Fremont, 383, 437; and Moapa Valley, 295, 318–19, 320; pithouse use, 152, 157–61, 166–70; Pueblo III period, 155–57; Roosevelt Red Ware and, 51–52, 55

Kayenta Valley, 156

Keresan speakers, 65, 71

keyhole kivas, in Chuska Valley, 241

K'iche' Mayan, *Popol Vuh*, 88

Kidder, A. V., 380

Kiet Siel, 157

kinship, 71, 395; social units and, 134, 216

kivas, 8, 87, 224, 421; Awat'ovi murals, 73–75; Chuska Valley, 237–46; Kayenta region, 169–70; murals, 67, 69, 70–72, 102; ritual performance in, 227–28

Klethla Valley, 156

knowledge, 88; expeditions to gain, 83–84; ritual, 5, 65, 66, 73, 269; technology and imagery, 20–21

knowledge-attitude-practice (KAP) gap, 43–44, 45, 56

knowledge transfer, captives, 5, 29

Kristiansen, Kristian, *The Rise of Bronze Age Society*, 26

Kuaua, 103

Kwakina Polychrome, 72

La Ciudad, 216

LA 5377, 185

LA 117092, 259

LA 129573, 186

LA 139944, 185

*Lagenaria siceraria*, 260

La Gila Encantada, 7, 134; excavation of, 142–43; households at, 143–45, 146

Laguna Break, 65

Laguna Fathers, 65

Laguna Pueblo, 65, 71

La Junta region, 252

Lake Roberts site, 87

Lampstand site, 383

landscapes, 6, 330; and journeys, 101–2; plant-baking complexes, 262–63, 166; social, 211–12

land tenure, overexploitation of, 263

land-use patterns, Fremont, 381–82

language(s), 19, 22; Great Basin, 330–31

La Quemada, 259

Larder Site, 342; maize at, 286, 313, 334–35; storage pits at, 340–41, 342–43

Larsson, Thomas, *The Rise of Bronze Age Society*, 26

Las Vegas Buff, 339

Las Vegas Springs Preserve, 339

Las Vegas Valley: as boundary, 346–47; cultural identity in, 329–30, 343–45; early maize in, 10, 286, 313; and Great Basin, 330–31; maize cultivation in, 285, 314, 334–37; mesquite exploitation, 345–46; Puebloan-Patayan interactions in, 337–40; wild foods in, 331–34

Las Vegas Wash, 313, 340; agriculture on, 335, 341–42; mesquite exploitation in, 332, 333, 346

Late Archaic period, 384; at Jackson Flat Reservoir, 355, 357–61, 369; in Moapa Valley, 311–12, 314

Late Fremont period, 385–86, 387, 389; regional system, 391–95

Late Glencoe phase, 192

*Laws of Imitation, The* (Tarde), 42

learning, cultural, 27

Lévi-Strauss, Claude, 17; on House-society model, 200, 202

Liliaceae family, pit baking, 254

Lincoln phase, 12

linguistics, 19, 20

lithics, in communal Fremont structures, 418, 419, 420, 424

Little Walnut Creek Valley, La Gila Encantada in, 143–45

livestock, African management techniques, 31

Long House Valley, 156

Lords of Death, in Hero Twins saga, 92, 94, 96

Los Morteros, 216

Lost City Museum, 448

Lower Colorado Buff Ware, 340

Lowland Virgin groups. *See* Virgin Branch Puebloans

Lumholtz, Carl, 268

Luo language, 22

Great Salt Lake Corrugated, 388
Great Salt Lake subregion, 380
green stone, Jackson Flat Reservoir, 370, 374
Grewe site, house concept at, 216
Guerrero, post-conquest heraldry, 23–24
guest houses, pithouses as, 159–60
gypsum, and in-ground storage, 342

Hägerstrand, Thor, 44
Halloran Springs mine, turquoise from, 316
Harris site, 7, 134, 146; excavations at, 135–36; pithouse clusters, 136–42
Hawikuh (Hawikku) Polychrome, 68, 121, 122, 123
Heartbreak Hotel (Nephi Mounds), 415
Henderson Pueblo, 266–67, 268
heraldry, Chieptlan, 23–24
Hero Twins saga, 5, 103; on Mimbres Classic Black-on-white, 87, 88, 89–100, 104; and scarlet macaws, 82–83, 84
*hewe*, 25
Hibben, Frank, 69
hide processing, 30
Highlands (Jornada Mogollon), settlement patterns, 184–92
High Rolls Cave, 185
Hindus, pottery making, 24–25
Hogup Cave, Fremont moccasins, 387
Hohokam, 7, 10, 86, 259; house concept, 201–2, 204–7, 209; and Moapa Valley people, 314–15; mortuary ritual, 209–213; Pioneer period houses, 199–200; social units, 215–16
Holmes, William Henry, 283
homophily, 48–49
Hopi, 77, 84
Hopi Mesas, 68; and Pottery Mound, 3–65, 70
Hopi Yellow Ware, 124; at Awat'ovi, 68–69; at Pottery Mound, 63, 64, 69–70, 73
horizontal transmission, 17, 41
horticulture, northern periphery, 285–92
house(s): decisions in construction of, 153–54; in Hohokam archaeology, 201–2, 204–5; Kayenta region, 155–61, 166–70; Pioneer period Hohokam, 207–16; as social unit, 199–200, 215–16; variability in, 154–55
House 47 (Moapa Valley), 320–21
households, 3, 191, 204–5, 395; Basketmaker III, 228–33; in Chuska Valley, 243–46; Mimbres, 6–7, 134, 136, 137–45, 146; Pueblo II communal, 238–39; ritual performance, 7–8, 226, 242–43; as social units, 223–24
House of Bats, 92

House of Gloom, 92
house-society model, 200, 202; at Richter site, 206–16
Huastec region, scarlet macaws in, 88
human behavior, and built environment, 202–3
human remains, Eagle's Watch, 368–70
Hunahpu, 98
hunter-gatherers, Great Basin, 383–84
Huntington Canyon, 390, 411, 413
hybridization, hybridity, 18, 118, 161; at Pottery Mound, 123–25
hyperdiffusion, 16

iconography, Hero Twins, 88–100
identity, identities, 7, 19, 71, 171, 200, 203; through communities of practice, 28–29; continuity and maintenance, 117–18; and culture contact, 115–17; Fremont, 379–80, 452–53; Las Vegas Valley, 329–30, 343–46; Hopi, 64, 77; hybridization, 123–25; maintenance of, 119–20; Moapa Valley people, 315–16; revivalism, 121–23; and style, 118–19
identity formation, 5; culture contact and, 115–16; Sikyatki style and, 76–77
immolation, in Hero Twins saga, 93–94
India, pottery production, 24–25
innovation, 41; adoption of, 42–44; attitudes toward, 24–25; Roosevelt Red Ware as, 55–56
intentionality, 27
invisible college, 42, 57(n4)
iron objects, Luo speakers and, 22
irrigation, Moapa Valley, 314
Isleta, 65
Ivie Creek Black-on-white, 296–97, 388, 433, 434, 435, 453; designs, 438, 439–40, 442, 444–45, 446(table), 447, 451–52, 454

Jackrabbit Roast Midden (42KA6163), 355, 357, 360–61
Jackson Flat Reservoir: archaeology of, 354–55; Basketmaker components, 361–69; culture change, 374–75; Late Archaic–Early Agricultural period in, 355, 357–61; maize from, 9, 285, 286, 353–54; Pueblo I period, 370–74
Jeddito Black-on-yellow, 68–69
Jeddito Yellow Ware, 56, 73
Jennings, Jesse, 380
Jornada Brown, 188
Jornada Mogollon region, 7, 177–78; earth-oven complexes, 8, 253–54, 255–57, 259–61, 265–67; environmental diversity, 179–80; settlement

patterns, 180–92; social organization, 262–64, 268–69

journeys, ritual, 83–84, 100–102, 104

Judd, Neil, 283; on Fremont, 379, 415, 416, 436

Kadiolo, pottery making, 20–21

Kama zotz figures, 92

Kanab, 9, 288; early maize dates, 353–54. *See also* Jackson Flat Reservoir

KAP. *See* knowledge-attitude-practice gap

katsinas, Laguna Pueblo, 65

Kawayka'a, 68; kiva murals at, 70, 71, 102

Kayenta region, 5, 7, 9, 171, 373, 447; architectural data, 161–66; domestic structure use, 166–70; and Fremont, 383, 437; and Moapa Valley, 295, 318–19, 320; pithouse use, 152, 157–61, 166–70; Pueblo III period, 155–57; Roosevelt Red Ware and, 51–52, 55

Kayenta Valley, 156

Keresan speakers, 65, 71

keyhole kivas, in Chuska Valley, 241

K'iche' Mayan, *Popol Vuh*, 88

Kidder, A. V., 380

Kiet Siel, 157

kinship, 71, 395; social units and, 134, 216

kivas, 8, 87, 224, 421; Awat'ovi murals, 73–75; Chuska Valley, 237–46; Kayenta region, 169–70; murals, 67, 69, 70–72, 102; ritual performance in, 227–28

Klethla Valley, 156

knowledge, 88; expeditions to gain, 83–84; ritual, 5, 65, 66, 73, 269; technology and imagery, 20–21

knowledge-attitude-practice (KAP) gap, 43–44, 45, 56

knowledge transfer, captives, 5, 29

Kristiansen, Kristian, *The Rise of Bronze Age Society*, 26

Kuaua, 103

Kwakina Polychrome, 72

La Ciudad, 216

LA 5377, 185

LA 117092, 259

LA 129573, 186

LA 139944, 185

*Lagenaria siceraria*, 260

La Gila Encantada, 7, 134; excavation of, 142–43; households at, 143–45, 146

Laguna Break, 65

Laguna Fathers, 65

Laguna Pueblo, 65, 71

La Junta region, 252

Lake Roberts site, 87

Lampstand site, 383

landscapes, 6, 330; and journeys, 101–2; plant-baking complexes, 262–63, 166; social, 211–12

land tenure, overexploitation of, 263

land-use patterns, Fremont, 381–82

language(s), 19, 22; Great Basin, 330–31

La Quemada, 259

Larder Site, 342; maize at, 286, 313, 334–35; storage pits at, 340–41, 342–43

Larsson, Thomas, *The Rise of Bronze Age Society*, 26

Las Vegas Buff, 339

Las Vegas Springs Preserve, 339

Las Vegas Valley: as boundary, 346–47; cultural identity in, 329–30, 343–45; early maize in, 10, 286, 313; and Great Basin, 330–31; maize cultivation in, 285, 314, 334–37; mesquite exploitation, 345–46; Puebloan-Patayan interactions in, 337–40; wild foods in, 331–34

Las Vegas Wash, 313, 340; agriculture on, 335, 341–42; mesquite exploitation in, 332, 333, 346

Late Archaic period, 384; at Jackson Flat Reservoir, 355, 357–61, 369; in Moapa Valley, 311–12, 314

Late Fremont period, 385–86, 387, 389; regional system, 391–95

Late Glencoe phase, 192

*Laws of Imitation, The* (Tarde), 42

learning, cultural, 27

Lévi-Strauss, Claude, 17; on House-society model, 200, 202

Liliaceae family, pit baking, 254

Lincoln phase, 12

linguistics, 19, 20

lithics, in communal Fremont structures, 418, 419, 420, 424

Little Walnut Creek Valley, La Gila Encantada in, 143–45

livestock, African management techniques, 31

Long House Valley, 156

Lords of Death, in Hero Twins saga, 92, 94, 96

Los Morteros, 216

Lost City Museum, 448

Lower Colorado Buff Ware, 340

Lowland Virgin groups. *See* Virgin Branch Puebloans

Lumholtz, Carl, 268

Luo language, 22

macaws, scarlet, 5, 102–3; and Hero Twins saga, 82–83, 84, 104; at Mimbres sites, 86–88. *See also* Seven macaw

maguey. *See* Agavaceae

Main Ridge site, 9, 317–18, 319

maize, 7; on Colorado Plateau, 9–10; in Kanab area, 364–65; in Las Vegas Valley, 334–37; in Moapa Valley, 313, 314–15; in Northern Periphery, 281, 285–92, 200, 302(n4), 353–54

Mali, pottery making in, 20–21

*Mammillaria* spp., pit baking, 255

Mande, pottery making, 20

Mao, identity continuity, 117

marriage, of Philippine captives, 30

Marsh Pass, Basketmaker II sites, 288

masonry structures, in Kayenta region, 161–66

material culture, 3; gender-linked, 26–27; long-distance movement of, 27–28. *See also* lithics; pottery

Matsaki Polychrome, 75, 76

Mattocks site, pottery from, 87–88, 98, 99

Mauss, Marcel, 17

Maya, 88, 205

McSherry Site, 98

Median Village, 437

Medicine Black-on-red, 296

Medio period, earth-ovens, 265

Mesa Verde, 295, 383; ceramic styles, 437, 451–52

mescal, 262, 270(n1); fermentation and consumption, 252, 258–60

Mescalero Apache, agave fermentation, 259

Mesilla phase, 182, 183, 261

Mesoamerica, 5, 20, 97, 101. *See also* Hero Twins saga; *Popol Vuh*

mesquite, in Las Vegas Valley, 331, 332–33, 340, 341, 345–46

Mesquite Black-on-gray, 370

metal working, power and, 26

middens, burned-rock, 183, 191, 255–56

Middle Fremont, 384

migration, migrants, 18, 20, 63, 68; to Chuska Valley, 242–43; diffusion and, 76–77; Kayenta/ Tusayan, 5, 51–52, 55; knowledge transmission, 21–22; Northern Rio Grande, 119–20; at Pottery Mound, 64, 70, 76; to southeastern Utah, 295–97

Mimbres culture/region, 48, 85; Hero Twins saga and, 83–84, 88–100, 102, 104; Mesoamerican contacts, 5, 82, 101; pithouse villages and households, 6–7, 134–45; scarlet macaws in, 86–88; social units, 146–47

Mimbres Classic Black-on-white: Hero Twins iconography on, 83, 84, 88–100; macaws depicted on, 87–88

Mimbres Pottery Image Digital Database (MimPIDD), 89; vessels from, 91, 105–10(table)

Mineral Mountains obsidian, 392

Mississippian period cemeteries, 203–4

Moapa Gray Ware, 297, 316

Moapa Valley, 308–9, 325, 340, 345; abandonment of, 321–23; Archaic period in, 311–12; Basketmaker period in, 10, 289, 312–16; and Gold Butte, 323–24; maize in, 314–15, 336; Paleoarchaic period in, 310–11; Puebloan periods, 317–19; trade networks, 316–17, 319–20

Moapa Ware, 317, 319

Moapa White Ware, 316

mobility, 73, 233; seasonal, 181–83, 185–86, 188–89

moccasins, Fremont, 387

Mogollon Highlands, 158, 170

moieties, Tanoan, 65

Mojave Desert, 252, 292, 309; Las Vegas Valley and, 331, 340, 346

Mojaves (Mohaves), 331; foodways, 332–33; in Las Vegas Valley, 337, 340

Monster Slayer, 103

Monument Valley, 156

moon, Mimbres iconography, 96–97, 98, 103

Morss, Noel, on Fremont, 379, 436

mortuary features/practices: archaeological study of, 203–4; Eagle's Watch site, 368–70, 374; Hohokam, 209–15

Muddy River, 308, 309, 336

murals, 67, 102; at Pottery Mound and Hopi Mesas, 69–72; Sikyatki style, 64, 73–75

multiethnicity, at pueblos, 68, 71

Muslims, pottery making, 24–25

NAN Ranch site, 136

nationalism, 16

Native American Church, 118

Navajo Mountain, 155, 167

Navajos, War Twins, 103

Nawthis Village, 395, *415*

neo-Darwinism, 41

Neolithic Demographic Transition, 386

Neolithic Revolution, 178

Nephi Mounds, communal architecture at, 413, *414, 415*

Neskahi Village (NA7719), 167–68, 169–70
Nevada: Basketmaker II in, 312–17; early maize
   in, 10, 281; Paleoarchaic and Archaic in,
   310–12
Nine Mile Canyon, 383
NM-Q-3-2, 236
NM-Q-15-28, great kiva at, 228, 229–30, 233, 234,
   235, 236, 244–45, 246
NM-Q-15-29, 234, 236, 239, 241
NM-Q-15-46, 234, 236, 237, 239, 241
NM-Q-15-52, 236
NM-Q-15-72, 239, 241
nodes, social network, 19, 45, 46, 47–48
North Creek Grayware, 363, 364, 367–68
northern periphery/frontier, 301, 380, 453;
   ceramics in, 294–97; Chacoan influence on,
   297–300; cultures of, 8–11, 281–83; horticul-
   ture in, 285–92. *See also* Fremont culture/
   tradition; Virgin Branch Puebloans
Northern San Rafael style rock art, 386
Northwest Coast (North America), communal
   house, 205
Numic Spread, 344

obsidian, 297, 392, 373
Old Town site, 89, 98, 136
Old Woman site, communal architecture at,
   410, 412, 414, 416
*Olivella* spp., at Fremont sites, 384–85
Onaveno maize, 315
one-node network, 45–46
One Hunahpu, 92
Orayvi, 158
Organ Mountains, 185
Osborn site, vessels from, 92, 98
oversized pit structures, 410, 412–14, 417, 426;
   artifact densities in, 418–21

Paiutes, 323. *See also* Southern Paiutes
Paiute Mesa, 156, 167
Paleoarchaic period, in Moapa Valley, 310–11
Panaca Summit/Modena obsidian source, 373
Paquimé, 10, 259; earth-ovens at, 253, 265–66;
   marine shell acquisition, 84, 102
Paragonah, 283, 284, 391, 426; communal archi-
   tecture at, 390, 410, 411, 413, 416
Paria Plateau, 293
Parowan points, 371, 373
Parowan Site, 391, 410
Parowan subregion, 380, 388
Parowan Valley, 453; Fremont villages, 391–92,
   395

parrots, thick-billed, 86, 87
Parsons, Elsie Clews, 42, 57(n1)
Partridge Creek obsidian, 373
Patayan peoples, 331; foodways, 332–33; Gold
   Butte, 323–24; in Las Vegas Valley, 337–38,
   339–40, 343, 344, 345
Pecos River, sotol roasting, 252
Pérez de Luxán, Diego, 252
peripheral cultures, 8–9, 11
Petroglyph National Monument, 103
petroglyphs, macaws on, 102–3
Pharo Village, 412, 414
Philippines, captive taking, 29–30
Phoenix, Roosevelt Red Ware network, 54
Piedra style, 437
pine nuts, in Las Vegas Valley, 331, 332
Pinnawa Glaze-on-white, 72
piñon nuts, in Las Vegas Valley, 331, 332
Pinto Polychrome, 51–52, 56, 57(n4)
Pioneer period, Hohokam, 199–200, 201, 216–17
pithouses, 289; Fremont, 389–90, 409; at Jackson
   Flat Reservoir, 357–58, 359, 360, 361–62, 364–65,
   366–67, 370–73, 375; Jornada Mogollon, 183,
   186–87; Kayenta region, 152, 157–66; in Las
   Vegas Valley, 336, 341; use of, 166–70
pit structures: Basketmaker III, 224, 228–33; in
   Chuska Valley, 243–46; Hohokam, 214–15;
   oversized, 410, 412–14; Pueblo I, 233–37
place names, in journeys, 101
Plains, rock art styles, 387
plant-baking complexes, 266–67; Chihuahuan
   Desert, 251–52, 254–55; excavation of, 253–54;
   Casas Grandes region, 265; intensification
   of, 261–64; Sacramento Mountains, 257–58;
   structure of, 255–57, 261–62
*Platyopuntia* spp., pit baking, 255
plaza pueblos, Kayenta region, 157, 167, 168
plazas, in Fremont sites, 410, 411(table), 426
pochteca model, 82
Point of Pines Pueblo, 51, 68, 158
Poplar Knob, 390, 411, 413, 416
*Popol Vuh*, Hero Twins saga in, 88–89, 90, 91–100
population estimates, Early Hohokam, 212–13
population relocation, 4–5; Fremont area, 382
pottery, 48; Agavaceae use, 259–60; Antelope
   Mesa, 68–69; Fremont, 283, 298, 296–97,
   388–89, 419, 423, 433–49, 454–55; hybridization, 123–25; from Jackson Flat Reservoir, 363,
   364, 367–68, 370–71; Jornada Mogollon, 188,
   192; Las Vegas Valley, 338, 339, 340, 344–45;
   Mimbres Classic Black-on-white, 83, 84,
   87–100, 105–10(table); in Moapa Valley, 316–18,

Salt Cave, *321*
Salt Lake Valley, 393
Salt Springs Wash cluster, 239
sandals, in Black Dog Cave, 315–16
Sand Canyon Pueblo, 410, 412
Sandia Pueblo, 65
San Francisco phase, 136; Harris site, 137–38; La
  Gila Encantada, 144–45
San Juan Red Ware, *294, 298*, 317; production
  of, 295–96
San Pedro Valley, Roosevelt Red Ware in, 52–54
San Rafael subregion, 380, 386
Santa Cruz del Quiché (Guatemala), *Popol
  Vuh*, 88
Santa Fe Black-on-white, *122*; identity mainte-
  nance and, 119–21
Scorpion Knoll site, 339, 341; maize at, 286, 313,
  334–35, 340
seasonal sites, Jornada Mogollon, 181–83,
  185–86, 188–89, 193(n1)
sedentism, Mimbres, 145
Segazlin Mesa, 156
Seneca, European trade goods, 24
Senegambia, slave trade, 31
settlement clusters, post 1300, 68
settlement patterns: Fremont, 381–83, 391–95;
  Jornada Mogollon, 186–92
Setzler, Frank M., 251–52
Seven Hunahpu, 92
Seven Macaw, 89, 98; depictions of, *99–100*
Sevier Black-on-white, 388
Sevier subregion, 380
Sevier Style rock art, 387
Sevier Valley, Fremont settlements in, 392–93
shatter zone, Northern Frontier as, 10, 299–300
shell: at Fremont sites, 383–84; at Paquimé, 84,
  102; in Virgin region, 297, 316, 317, *321*, 374
Shinarump Plain, 368
Shinarump Red Ware, *294, 298*, 296
Shivwits Plain, 297
Shivwits Plateau, *322*; and Gold Butte, 323–24
Shivwits Ware, 317, 318, 320
Shonto Plateau, 156
Sierra Blanca highlands, Jornada Mogollon in,
  177–78, 185
Sikyatki, 68
Sikyatki Polychrome, 68, 69, 72, 75
Sikyatki style design, 5, 65, 125(n1); diffusion
  and migration, 76–77; on kiva murals, 69,
  70–72, 73–75; on pottery, 66, 72–73; at Pottery
  Mound, 64, 124
Sinaloa, mescal fermentation, 252

Sitting Coyote Mesa/Beth's Great Kiva–
  Figueredo cluster, 229, 234, 237
slaves, slavery, 31; social identity, 20–21
Smith, Grafton Elliot, 16
smoking, depictions of, 92, *93*
SNA. *See* social network analysis
Snake dance, 84
Snake Maiden wife, 84
Snake Rock site, 410
Snake Valley, 393
Snake Valley Black-on-gray, *298*, 389, 433, *434,
  435, 436*; designs on, *437, 438, 439–40, 441, 442,
  444–45, 446*(table), 454
Snake Valley ceramics, 388–89; distribution of,
  382–83, 391–92
Snake Valley Corrugated, 388, 392
Snake Valley production zone, 434
social groups, 200; Hohokam House as, 209–15
social interaction, 3–4; household, 6–7;
  Mimbres region, 140–42, 143–45
social landscape, of Hohokam House, 211–13
social network analysis (SNA), 18–19, 41; diffusion through, 45–50, 56–57; long-distance
  movement, 27–28; Roosevelt Red Ware, 50–56
social organization: Fremont, 425–27; and mortuary ritual, 203–4; plant-baking complexes
  and, 261–64
social status, 48, 269; prestige-biased transmission and, 23–24
social units, 3, 6, 8, 133–34; Hohokam House
  as, 200, 209–14, 215–16; household, 223–24;
  integration of, 7–8; Mimbres region, 137–47
sociology, 19, 42
sodalities, 5, 46, 63; in Pueblos, 66, 71; ritual, 64,
  65, 67, 69; Sikyatki-style designs and, 74–75, 76
Sonora, mescal production in, 262
Sonoran Desert, fermentation, 252
Sosi style, 295, 318, 320; and Fremont ceramic
  designs, 433, 437, 449–50, 454
sotol (*Dasylirion wheeleri*), pit baking, 251–52, 254
southern High Plains, captives on, 30
Southern lowlands (Jornada Mogollon), 180,
  184; seasonal camps, 181–83; settlement pat-
  terns, 186–92
Southern Paiute, 283, 292, 339, 342, 344, 345;
  foodways, 331–32, 333–34
Southern San Rafael style rock art, 386
Southwest, and Fremont culture, 380–81
Southwest Social Networks Project and
  Database, 50, 52
Spanish colonial period, 3–4, 5, 68
Spiro Mounds, 204